I0787587

ANTIQUE ROSES

A Catalogue of Roses
introduced before 1900

by

JOHN BAXTER

Copyright ©2017 John Baxter

Copyright @2017 John Baxter
All rights reserved. No part of this book may be used or reproduced by any means, graphic, electronic, or mechanical, including photocopying, recording, taping or by any information storage retrieval system without the written permission of the Publisher except in the case of brief quotations embodied in critical articles and reviews.
Because of the dynamic nature of the internet, any web addresses or links contained in this book may have changed since publication and may no longer be valid. The views expressed in this work are solely those of the author and do not necessarily reflect the views of the Publisher, and the Publisher hereby disclaims any responsibility for them. The author of this book does not dispense medical advice or prescribe the use of any techniques as a form of treatment for physical, emotional, or medical problems without the advice of a physician, either directly or indirectly.
Printed in the United Kingdom

ISBN-13: 978-1976138232
ISBN-10: 197613823X

In memory of
my beloved wife
Elizabeth

INTRODUCTION

Many years ago a friend of mine, sadly now deceased, suggested that I wrote a rose book. He had collaborated on six books about the railway lines out of London, all of which were published. Where could one start?

I had helped to catalogue the Royal National Rose Society's library in the 1980s, so knew what to look for. The modern rose catalogues and the various issues of Modern Roses, published in America, are very helpful, but what about the older roses? We have the books by Peter Beales and David Austin, and before them Graham Stuart Thomas, but there are hundreds more not known about.

I was lucky in seeing the books owned by Dr C.C. Hurst of Cambridge, who introduced Rosa Cantabrigiensis. Among them two stood out. 'Dictionnaire des Roses' by Max Singer published in 1885 and 'Nomenclature des Roses' by Simon and Cochet, published in 1899. A further edition by Simon and Cochet was published in 1906.

These two publications have over 10,000 names in them, so why not start with them? Snag number one, they are in French, so I hope my translation is correct. Singer was a Belgian but the book was published in Berlin and is in two parts. Simon and Cochet went for a slightly larger format but has small typeface so will need a magnifying glass to read it. I was pleased to note some roses from the Paul and Dickson families were also included.

From this I got the title of Antique Roses and all that were introduced prior to 1900. I hope in future to add to this list and include roses from other places. This list is only touching the surface, so time will tell if it has been worthwhile.

Question: How many roses have the title 'Madame' at the front of their name, 40, 50 or more?

Answer: Over nine hundred, so now you know why this record is needed!

With the introduction of modern technology, a computer was necessary. Each time I tried a database it failed so in the end gave it up as a bad job. Having been trained on Microsoft Word, I took the easy way out by using a page setup of landscape and inserting a table. This gives us the current style, which I hope is self-explanatory.

I am grateful to the American Rose Society for the use of Modern Roses 12 and to the Royal National Rose Society for the use of their library.

I hope this will become a 'bible' of rose varieties, as so many have already been lost, or just disappeared, both bush and names. Let us hope that in future we can find them all!

Bibliography

Dictionnaire des Roses	Max Singer	1885
Nomenclature des Roses	L Simon & P Cochet	1899 Edition
List of Geschwind's varieties	Thanks to Peter Harkness	1992
List of cultivars – Sangerhausen Rosarium		1988 Edition
Modern Roses 12	American Rose Society	2007
Les Roses	Jamain & Forney	10th Edition 1873
Prince's Manual of Roses Reproduction by Earl M Coleman, Publisher		1846 1979
The Rose Guide for Amateurs	E Percy Smith	1920
Histoire de la Rose	A Chesnel	1820
The Rose Garden	WM Paul	9th Edition 1898
Le Rosier	J Lachaume	1870
Catalogue des Roses	J-P Vibert	1833
Catalogue du Genre Rosier	Prévost Fils	1829
A Book about Roses	Rev S Reynolds Hole	1896
The Book of the Rose	Rev A Foster-Melliar	2nd Edition 1902
Present Day Gardening – Roses	Edited by H R Darlington	1911
The Graham Stuart Thomas Rose Book	Compilation of his 3 books	1994
Benjamin R Cant	Catalogue	1859
Les Plus Belles Roses de Debut au XXe Siecle Société Nationale Horticulture de France		1912
Paul & Son	Rose Catalogues	1876 – 1898
The Old Rose Adventurer	Brent Dickerson	1999
Antique Roses for the South	William C Welch	1990
Les Roses	Jamain & Ferney	10th Edition 1873

Parentage

À Fleur Pourpre, Panachée Blanc	Sport of L'Ombrée Parfaite
Abel Grant	Jules Margottin x unknown
Abel Carrière (HP- Verdier)	Baron de Bonstetten x seedling
Abbé Berlèze (HP)	Sport of Géant des Batailles
Abbé Bramerel	Géant des Batailles x unknown
Abbé Girardin	Louise Odier x Hermosa
Abbé Giraudier	Géant des Batailles x Victor Verdier
Achille Cesbron	Mme Eugène Frémy x unknown
Achille Gonod	Jules Margottin x unknown
Adam	Possibly Hume's Blush x Rose Edouard
Adélaïde d'Orléans (HSem)	r.sempervirens x Parson's Pink
Adèle Pavié (N)	Lamarque x unknown
Admiral Dewey	Sport of Mme Caroline Testout
Adolphe de Tarlé	Sport of Comtesse Riza du Parc
Aglaia	r.multiflora x Rêve d'Or
Agnes Emily Carman	Possibly r.rugosa x Harison's Yellow
Aimée Vibert	Champneys' Pink Cluster x a double form of r.sempervirens
Alain Blanchard	Probably r.centifolia x r.gallica
Alain Blanchard Panachée	Sport of Alain Blanchard
Alba Odorata (Marioni)	r.bracteata x r.roxburghii
Albert Payé	Victor Verdier x unknown
Albert Stoppard	Général Schablikine x Papa Gontier
Alexander Dupont	Triomphe de l'Exposition x unknown
Alfred Colomb (Lacharme)	Général Jacqueminot x unknown
Alfred de Rougemont	Général Jacqueminot x unknown
Alfred K Williams	Sport of Général Jacqueminot
Alister Stella Gray	William Allen Richardson x Mme Pierre Guillot
Alpenfee	Probably r.setigers x a Hybrid Perpetual
Alphonse Karr	Duchess of Edinburgh x unknown
Alphonse Soupert	Jules Margottin x unknown
Amabilis (T-Touvais)	Moirée x unknown
Amadis	r.chinensis x r.pendulina
A M Amphère	Lion des Combats x unknown
Amazone	Safrano x unknown
Ambrigio Maggi	John Hopper x unknown
Amélie-Suzanne Morin	Clotilde Soupert x Leonie Osterrieth
America (Page)	Solfaterre x Safrano
American Banner	Sport of Bon Silène
American Belle	Sport of American Beauty
Améthyste	Sport of Non Plus Ultra or Non Plus Ultra x r.multiflora
Amoena	Victor Verdier x unknown
Anathalie Chantrier	Duchess of Sutherland x unknown
Ancélin (G)	r.turbinata x unknown –a r.francofurtana variety
André de Garnier des Garets	Luciole x Ophirie
André Fresnoy	Victor Verdier x unknown
Anemone (S)	r.laevigata x r.odorata
Anicet Bourgeois	Sénateur Vaisse x Madame Victor Verdier
Anna Chartron	Kaiserin Auguste Victoria x Luciole
Anna de Diesbach	La Reine x unknown

Comtesse de Casteja   Alfred Colomb x unknown
Comtesse de Frigneuse   Mme Damaizin x unknown
Comtesse de Jaucourt   Triomphe de l'Exposition x unknown
Comtesse de Paris (HP, Verdier)   Victor Verdier x unknown
Comtesse de Serenye   La Reine x unknown
Comtesse d'Oxford   Victor Verdier x unknown
Comtesse Duzy   Innocente Pirola x Anna Olivier
Comtesse Eva Starhemberg   Etendard de Jeanne d'Arc x Sylphide
Comtesse Lily Kinsky   Marie Van Houtte x Victor Pulliat
Comtesse O'Gorman (T)   Baron de St Triviers x unknown
Comtesse Riza du Parc   Comtesse de Labarthe x unknown
Condesa da Foz   Souvenir d'un Ami x unknown
Conrad Ferdinand Meyer   Gloire de Dijon x Duc de Rohan x Rugosa Germanica
Coquette Bordelaise   Sport of Mme Georges Desse
Coquette des Alpes   Mlle Blanche Lafitte x Sappho
Coquette des Blanches   Mlle Blanche Lafitte x Sappho
Cora (Ch)   Madame Laurette Messimy x unknown
Cora (HP)   Général Jacqueminot x unknown
Cora L Barton   Lamarque x unknown
Cornelia Cook   Devoniensis x unknown
Coronet   Paul Neyron x Bon Silène
Corporal Johann Nagy   De la Grifferaie x a Hybrid Perpetual or Bourbon
Countess of Pembroke   Président x Charles Lefebvre
Countess of Roseberry   Victor Verdier x unknown
Coupe d'Hébé   Bourbon x a r.chinensis hybrid
Cramoisi à Fleurs Simples   Seedling by Thos Rivers x seedling by M Laffay
Cramoisi Superieur   Slater's Crimson China x unknown
Cramoisi Superieur, Climbing   Cramoisi Superieur x unknown
Crême   (r.canina x Tea) x (r.canina x Bourbon)
Crested Moss   Probably a seedling of r.centifolia
Crown Prince   Duke of Edinburgh x unknown

Daniel Lacombe   r.multiflora x Margarita or Général Jacqueminot
Danmark   Sport or seedling of La France
Dawn   Mme Caroline Testout x Mme Paul
Dawson   r.multiflora x Général Jacqueminot
De la Grifferaie   Cocchiné x unknown
Décoration de Geschwind   Rosa Rugosa x Multiflora
Deuil de Frédéric Willermoz   Géant des Batailles x unknown
Devoniensis   Probably Parks' Yellow x Smith's Yellow
Devoniensis, Climbing   Sport of Devoniensis
Directeur Constantin Bernard   Abel Grand x Mlle Adèle Jougant
Directeur René Gérard   Mme Falcot x Marquise de Vivens
Distinction   Either Mme de St Joseph x Eugène Verdier
                                        or Mabel Morrison x Devoniensis

Docteur Andry   Victor Verdier x unknown
Docteur Antoine Carlès   Gloire de Dijon x unknown
Docteur Antonin Joly   Baronne Alphonse de Rothschild x unknown
Docteur Bretonneau   Géant des Batailles x unknown
Docteur Grandvilliers   Isabelle Nabonnand x Aureus
Docteur Grill   Ophirie x Souvenir de Victor Hugo
Docteur Hooker   Duke of Edinburgh x unknown
Docteur Pouleur   Lady Zoë Brougham x Alphonse Karr
Docteur Raiment   Général Jacqueminot x unknown

Docteur Tisi	Duplessis Morlay x unknown
Duarte de Oliviera	Ophirie x Rêve d'Or
Duc de Cazes (HP)	Général Jacqueminot x unknown
Duc de Malakoff	Géant des Batailles x unknown
Duc de Rohan	Alfred Colomb x unknown
Duc Engelbert d'Arenberg	Mme Lombard x Belle Siebrecht
Duchesse Antonine d'Ursel	Gustave Coreau x unknown
Duchesse d'Angoulème (G – Miellez)	Probably r.gallica x r.centifolia hybrid
Duchesse d'Auerstädt	Rêve d'Or x unknown
Duchesse de Caylus	Alfred Colomb x unknown
Duchesse de Vallambrosa (HP)	Jules Margottin x unknown
Duchesse d'Orléans	Probably a seedling of La Reine
Duchesse Hedwige d'Arenberg	Belle Siebrecht x Mme Caroline Testout
Duchesse Marie Salviati	Mme Lombard x Mme Maurice Kuppenheim
Duchess of Albany	Sport of La France
Duchess of Bedford	Charles Lefebvre x unknown
Duchess of Connaught (Bennett)	Adam x Duchesse de Vallambrosa
Duchess of Edinburgh	Souvenir de David d'Angers x unknown
Duchess of Fife	Sport of Countess of Roseberry
Duchess of Portland	Possibly Red Quatre Saisons x r.gallica officinalis
Duchess of Westminster	Adam x Marquise de Castellane
Duke of Connaught (HT)	Adam x Louis Van Houtte
Duke of Connaught (HP)	Maurice Bernardin x unknown
Duke of Fife	Sport of Etienne Levet
Duke of Edinburgh	Général Jacqueminot x unknown
Duke of Teck	Duke of Edinburgh x unknown
Duke of Wellington	Lord Macaulay x unknown
Dumnacus	Comtesse d'Oxford x unknown
Dundee Rambler	Possibly r.arvensis x a Noisette
Dunkelrote Hermosa	Reine Marie Henriette x Hermosa
Duplex	r.pomifera x x unknown
Dupontii	Perhaps descended from r.gallica x r.moschata hybrid
Earl of Pembroke	Marquise de Castellane x Maurice Bernardin
Éclair	Général Jacqueminot x unknown
Eclaireur	Duhamel Dumonceau x unknown
Edmond Sablayrolles	Souvenir de Victor Hugo x Mme Cusin
Edouard Dufour	Annie Wood x unknown
Edouard Gautier	Devoniensis x unknown
Edouard Morren	Jules Margottin x unknown
Edouard Pinaert	Antoine Ducher x unknown
Eduard Von Lade	Comte de Sembuy x Socrate
Edward Morren	Jules Margottin x unknown
Egeria	Jules Margottin x unknown
Elisa Beauvillain	Gloire de Dijon x Ophirie
Elisabeth Vigneron	Duchesse de Sutherland x unknown
Elisa Boëlle	Madame Récamier x unknown
Elisa Fugier	Unnamed Tea Rose x Niphetos
Elise Heymann	Mme Lombard x Mont Rosa
Elizabeth Vigneron	La Reine x Duchess of Sutherland
Ella Gordon	Mme Victor Verdier x unknown
Ellen Drew	Sport of Duchesse de Morny

Emile Bardiaux   Mme Isaac Pereire x unknown
Emilie Dupuy   Madame Falcot x Gloire de Dijon
Emily Laxton   Jules Margottin x unknown
Emin Pascha   Gloire de Dijon x Louis Van Houtte
Empereur du Maroc   Géant des Batailles x unknown
Erinerrung an Brod   (r.setigera x unknown) x Génie de Châteaubriand
Ernest Morel   Général Jacqueminot x unknown
Ernest Prince   Antoine Ducher x unknown
Erzherzogin Marie Dorothea   Mme Falcot x Général Jacqueminot
Etendard de Sébastopol   Géant des Batailles x unknown
Etienne Levet   Victor Verdier x unknown
Etoile de Lyon   Mme Charles x unknown
Eugène Appert   Sport of Géant des Batailles
Eugène Fürst   Baron de Bonstetten x unknown
Eugène Verdier (HP)   Victor Verdier x unknown
Eugènie Bourgeois   Mme Bérard x unknown
Eugènie Lamesch   Aglaia x William Allen Richardson
Euphrosyne   r.multiflora x Mignonette
Eurydice (HSet)   r.setigera x Louise Odier
Evergreen Gem   r.wichurana x Maréchal Niel
Exposition de Provins   Triomphe de l'Exposition x unknown
E Y Teas   Alfred Colomb x unknown

Fata Morgana   Niphetos x Mme Lombard
Fatinitga   Complex hybrid of Multiflora and Ayrshire
Félicité-Perpétue   Thought to be r.sempervirens x a Noisette or
                                        maybe Parson's Pink

Ferdinand   Géant des Batailles x unknown
Fiametta Nabonnand   Papa Gontier x Niphetos
Filius Strassheim   Mignonette x Madeleine d'Aoste
Fimbriata (HRg)   r.rugosa x Mme Alfred Carrière
Fisher Holmes   Maurice Bernardin x unknown
F J Segers   Safrano x Adam
Flag of the Union   Sport of Bon Silène
Flore   (r.sempervirens x r.arvensis) x Parson's Pink
Forstmeister's Heim   a Bourbon x a Boursault
Fortunée Besson   Jules Margottin x unknown
Fortuniana   Supposedly r.banksiae x r.laevigata
François Arago   Sport of Géant des Batailles
François Coppée   Victor Verdier x unknown
François Levet   Anna de Diesbach x unknown
François Michelon   La Reine x unknown
François Premier   Géant des Batailles
Franz Degen Junion   Sport of Maréchal Neil
Frau Geheimrat von Boch   Princesse de Monaco x Duchesse Marie Salviati
Frau Syndica Rœloffs   Vallée de Chamonix x Mme Laurette Messimy
Frère Marie-Pierre   Baronne de Rothschild x unknown
Fürst Bismarck   Gloire de Dijon x unknown (probably selfed)
Fürstin Bismarck   Gloire de Dijon x Comtesse d'Oxford
Fürstin Infantin von Hohenzollern   Mlle la Comtesse de Leusse x Marie von Houtte
Fürstin Johanna Auersperg   Victor Verdier x unknown
Gabriel Fournier   Jules Margottin x Victor Verdier
Gallica Macrantha   Said to be r.canina x r.gallica but more probably
                                        r.gallica x r.alba

Gardenia (HT)   Comtesse Dusy x Mlle Hélène Combier
Gardenia (HWich)   r.wichurana x Perle des Jardins
Gaston Chandon   Gloire de Dijon x unknown
Gem of the Prairies   Queen of the Prairies x Mme Laffay
Général Appert   Souvenir de William Wood x unknown
Général Feroy   Triomphe de l'Exposition x unknown
Général Gallieni   Souvenir de Theresa Levet x Reine Emma des Pays-Bas
Général Jacqueminot   Gloire des Rosomanes x unknown
Général von Moltke   Charles Léfèbrve x unknown
Général Washington   Sport of Triomphe de l'Exposition
George Peabody   Joseph Paul x unknown
Georges Moreau   Paul Neyron x unknown
Georges Patinot   Triomphe de l'Exposition x unknown
Georges Pernet   Mignonette x unknown
Georges Schwartz (T)   Kaiserin Auguste Viktoria x Souv de Mme Levet
Georges Schwartz (HMult)   Multiflora x Aimée Vibert
Geschwind's Gilda   De la Grifferaie x a Hybrid Perpetual or Bourbon
Geschwind's Nordlandrose   De la Grifferaie x a Hybrid Perpetual or Bourbon
Geschwind's Orden   r.rugosa x r.multiflora or a r.multiflora cultivar
Gigantesque   Park's Yellow x unknown
Gipsy   Gloire de Dijon x Souvenir de Comte de Cavour
Gloire de Bordeaux   Gloire de Dijon x unknown
Gloire de Bruxelles   Souvenir de William Wood x Lord Macaulay
Gloire de Deventer   Devoniensis x Distinction
Gloire de Guérin   Malton x unknown
Gloire de Libourne   Perle de Lyon x unknown
Gloire de Santenay   Général Jacqueminot x unknown
Gloire des Polyantha   Mignonette x unknown
Gloire de Vitry   La Reine x unknown
Gloire d'Orléans   Triomphe de l'Exposition x unknown
Gloire d'un Enfant d'Hiran   Ulrich Brunner fils x unknown
Gloire Lyonnaise   Baronne Adolphe de Rothschild x Mme Falcot
Glory of Cheshunt   Charles Lefebvre x uinknown
Glory of Waltham   Souvenir de Leveson-Gower x unknown
Golden Gate   Safrano x Cornelia Cook
Goldquelle   KaiserinAuguste Viktoria x Mme Eugène Verdier
Gottfried Keller   (Mme Bérard x r.fortida persiana) x (Pierre Notting x
                                           r.foetida persiana)

Gourdault   Exposition de Londres x unknown
Gracilis (Bslt)   apparently a cross between an early Boursault and
                                           r.arvensis

Graf Fritz Metternich   Sultan of Zanzibar x Thomas Mills
Grand-Duc Adolphe de Luxembourg   Triomphe de la Terre des Roses x Mme Loeben Sels
Grande Duchesse Anastie   Baron de Saint-Triviers x Marie Van Houtte
Griseldis   (r.canina x an HT) x (r.canina x a Bourbon)
Grossherzogin Mathilde von Hessen   Sport of Bougère
Grossherzogin Victoria Melita von Hessen   Safrano x Mme Caroline Testout
Gruss an Teplitz   ((Sir Joseph Paxton x Fellemberg) x Papa Gontier) x
                                           Gloire des Rosomanes
Guillaume Gillemot   Madame Charles Wood x unknown
Gustave Régis   possibly a seedling of Mlle Blanche Durrschmidt
Gustave Révillard   Victor Verdier x unknown

Hardy (Noisette)   Hybrid of r.clymphylla and r.berberifolia
Harison's Yellow   Probably Persian Yellow x r.spinosissima
Harrison Weir   Charles Lefebvre x Xavier Olibo
Hebe's Lip   Thought to be r x damascena x r.rubiginosa hybrid
Heinrich Schultheis   Mabel Morrison x E Y Teas
Hélène (HMult)   HT x (Aglaia x Crimson Rambler)
Hélène Payravaud   Pactole x Regulus
Helen Paul   Victor Verdier x Sombreuil
Henri Bennett (HP)   Charles Lefebvre x unknown
Henri Payravaud   Robusta x Impératrice Eugénie
Henry M Stanley   Mme Lombard x Comtesse Riza du Parc
Her Majesty   Mabel Morrison x Canari
Hermine Madélé   Mignonette x Marquise de Vivens
Hérodiade   Duarte de Oliviera x unknown
Heterophylla   r.rugosa x r.foetida
Hibernica   Probably r.canina x r.spinosissima
Himmelsauge   r.setigera hybrid x r.rugosa rubra plena
Hippolyte Barreau   Comtesse de Labarthe x Louis van Houtte
Hippolyte Jamain   Victor Verdier x unknown
Hippolyte Jamain, Climbing   Sport of Hippolyte Jamain
Hofgartendirektor Graebener   Mme Caroline Testout x Antoinette Duneu
Homère   Believed to be seedling of David Pradel
Honourable Edith Gifford   Mme Falcot x Perle des Jardins
Honourable George Baneroff   Madame de St Joseph x Lord Macauley
Horace Vernet   Général Jacqueminot x unknown
Hovyn de Tronchère   Rgeulus x unknown
Hulthemia Hardii   r.clinophylla x Hulthemia Persica
Hume's Blush Tea-Scented China   Supposedly r.chinensis x r.gigantea

Ida (HMult)   Dawson x r.multiflora
Impératrice Eugénie (HP-Oger)   Madame Récamier x unknown
Indica Alba   Sport of Old Blush
Irene Watts   Mme Laurette Messimy x unknown
Isabella Gray   Chromatella x unknown
Iwara   r.multiflora x r.rugosa

James Bourgault   Sport of Auguste Mie
James Brownlow   Marquise de Castellane x Paul Neyron
James Sprunt   Sport of Cramoisi Supérieur, possibly syn of Cramoisi
                                              Supérieur, Climbing
James Veitch (HP)   La Reine x unknown
Jaune bicolor   Sport of r.foetida bicolor
Jaune Desprez   Blush Noisette x Parks' Yellow Tea-scented China
Jean Liabaud   Baron de Bonstetten x unknown
Jean Lorthois   Gloire de Dijon x unknown
Jean Pernet   Devoniensis x unknown
Jean Rosenkrantz   Victor Verdier x unknown
Jean Sisley   Adam x Emilie Hausbourg
Jean Soupert   Charles Léfèbvre x Souvenir du Baron de Sémur
Jeanne Abel   Comtesse de Labarthe x unknown
Jeanne d'Arc (A)   Elisa x unknown
Jeanne d'Arc (N)   Gloire de Dijon x unknown
Jeanne Mossop   Duchess of Edinburgh x unknown
Jelina   r.rugosa rubra x Perle de Lyon

Jersey Beauty   r.wichurana x Perle des Jardins
Johanna Lebus   P.Notting x Safrano x seedling of Gloire de Dijon
Johannes Wesselhöft   Kaiserin Auguste Viktoria x (Willam Francis Bennett x Comtesse de Frigneuse)

John Hopper   Jules Margottin x Mme Vidot
John Saul   Antoine Ducher x unknown
John Stuart Mill   Beauté de Waltham x unknown
Joseph Tasson   Triomphe de l'Exposition x unknown
Jubilee   Victor Hugo x Prince Camille de Rohan
Jules Bire   Général Jacqueminot x Paul Neyron
Jules Bourquin   Gloire de Dijon x unknown
Jules Finger   Catherine Mermet x Mme de Tartas
Jules Maquinant   Jules Margottin x unknown
Jules Margottin   Probably a La Reine seedling
Jules Margottin, Climbing   Sport of Jules Margottin
Jules Monges   Souvenir de la Reine d'Angleterre x unknown
Jules Roussingihol   Général Jacqueminot x unknown
Jules Seurre   Victor Verdier x unknown
Julius Finger   Victor Verdier x Mlle de Sombreuil or Sombreuil (different roses)

Kaiser Friedrich   Gloire de Dijon x Countess of Oxford
Kaiser Wilheim der Siegreiche   Mme Bérard x Perle des Jardins
Kaiserin Auguste Viktoria   Coquette de Lyon x lady Mary Fitzwilliam also given as Perle des Jardins x Belle Lyonnaise

Kaiserin Auguste Viktoria, Climbing   Sport of Kaiserin Auguste Viktoria
Kaiserin Friedrich   Gloire de Dijon x Perle des Jardins
Kamtchatica   Thought to be r.davurica x r.rugosa. Introducd as r.rugosa kamtchatica c 1770

Katkoff   Charles Léfèbvre x unknown
Ketten Frères   Gloire de Dijon x unknown
Killarney   Mrs W J Grant x Charles J Grahame
König Friedrich II von Danemark, Clg   Sport of König Friedrich II von Danemark
Königin von Danemark   Probably r.alba x a damask hybrid
Krimhilde   Mme Bérard x Perle des Jardins
Kronpronzessin Viktoria von Preussen   Sport of Souvenir de la Malmaison

La France   Mme Victor Verdier x Madame Bravy
La France, Climbing   Sport of La France
La France de 89   Reine Marie Henriette x La France
La Lonquille   Lamarque x unknown
La Madeleine   Golfe Juan x unknown
La Nantaise (HP)   Général Jacqueminot x unknown
La Prosperine   George Schwartz x Duchesse Marie Salviati
La Reine   Possibly a seedling of William Jesse
Lady Alice   Sport of Lady Mary Fitzwilliam
Lady Dorothea   Sport of Sunset
Lady Emily Peel   Mlle Blanche Lafitte x Sapho
Lady Loch   Sport of Aspasia
Lady Mary Fitzwilliam   Devoniensis x Victor Verdier
Lady Penzance   r.rubignosa x r.foetida bicolor
Lady Sheffield   François Michelon x unknown
Lady Zoë Brougham   Isabelle Nabonnand x unknown
Lamarque   Blush Noisette x Parks' Yellow Tea-scented China

L'Ami Maubray	Xavier Olibo x unknown
Laneii	A Moss rose x r.gallica
Le Loiret	Général Jacqueminot x unknown
Le Pactole	Lamarque x Yellow Tea
Léon XIII	Anna Olivier x Earl of Eldon
Léonie Lamesch	Aglaia x Kleiner Alfred or Aglaia x polyantha seedling x Shirley Hibberd
Leonie Osterreith	Sylphide x Mme Bravy
Léopold I	Général Jacqueminot x unknown
L'Etincelante	Bijou de Couasnon x unknown
Letty Coles	Sport of Mélanie Willermoz
Leustern	Daniel Lacombe x Crimson Rambler
Liberty	Mrs W J Grant x Charles J Grahame
Lilian Nordica	Margaret Dickson x Mme Hoste
L'Ingenue	Globe Hip x unknown
L'Innocence	Mme Caroline Testout x unknown
Little White Pet, Climbing	Sport of Little White Pet
Lord Raglan	Géant des Batailles x unknown
L'Orléanaise	Mme de Sancy de Parabère x Blush Boursault
Louis Chaix	Géant des Batailles x unknown
Louis Donadine	Duhamel-Dumonceau x unknown
Louis Gulino	Général Jacqueminot x unknown
Louis Puyravaud	Rêve d'Or x unknown
Louis van Houtte (HP-Lacharme)	Général Jacqueminot x unknown
Louis XIV (HP/Ch)	Général Jacqueminot x unknown
Louise Boyer	Jules Margottin x unknown
Louise d'Arzens	Mlle Blanche Lafitte x Sapho (P)
Louise d'Autriche	Sport of La Reine
Louise Peyronny	Supposedly a seedling of La Reine
Lucie Faure	Mme Léon Février x Niphetos
Luciole	Safrano à fleurs rouges x unknown
Lucy Carnegie	Triomphe du Luxembourg x unknown
Lyonnais	Victor Verdier x unknown
Ma Capucine	Ophirie x r.foetida
Ma Fillette	Mignonette x Luciole
Ma Petite Andrée	Etoile de Mai x unknown
Ma Surprise	Probably r.roxburghii x r.odorata
Ma Surprise (Levet)	Eugène Appert x unknown
Mabel Morrison	Sport of Baronne Adolphe de Rothschild
Madame Abel Chatenay	Dr Grill x Victor Verdier
Madame Adélaïde Cote	Sénateur Vaisse x unknown
Madame Adolphe Loiseau	Merveille de Lyon x Kaiserin Auguste Viktoria
Madame Alégatière	Polyantha Alba Plena x Jules Margottin
Madame Alexandre Bernaix	La France x unknown
Madame Alexandre Julien	Elisabeth Vigneron x unknown
Madame Alfred de Rougement	Mlle Blanche Lafitte x Sapho
Madame Alphonse Seux	Victor Verdier x unknown
Madame Angèle Jacquier (T-Guillot)	Madame Damaizin x unkown
Madame Angélique Veysset	Sport of La France
Madame Arthur Oger	Madame Isaac Pereire x unknown
Madame Anna de Besobrasoff (Gonod)	Charles Lefebvre x unknown
Madame Auguste Rodrigues	Souvenir de Nemours x Max Singer
Madame Azélie Imbert	Madame Falcot x unknown

Madame Barthélemy Levet	Gloire de Dijon x unknown
Madame Bellenden Kerr	Madame Récamier x Madame Falcot
Madame Bérard	Madame Falcot x Gloire de Dijon
Madame Bernard	Madame Falcot x unknown
Madame Berthe Fontaine	Luciole x Claude.Jacquet
Madame Betty Handlé	Madame Victor Verdier x Abel Carrière
Madame Blondel	La France de 89 x unknown
Madame Boll	HP x Belle Fabert or Baronne Prévost x Portlandica
Madame Bonnin	Triomphe de l'Exposition x unknown
Madame Brunner	Sport of Aimée Vibert
Madame Byrne	Lamarque x unknown
Madame C P Strassheim	Mme Adèle Jougant x Mme la Princesse de Bessaraba de Brancovan
Madame Carnot	William Allen Richardson x unknown
Madame Caro	Gloire de Dijon x unknown
Madame Caroline Küster	Le Pactole x unknown
Madame Caroline Schmitt	Solfaterre x unknown
Madame Caroline Testout	Mme de Tartas x Lady Mary Fitzwilliam
Madame Catherine Fontaine	Marie van Houtte x unknown
Madame Charles	Madame Damaizin x unknown
Madame Charles Baltet	Louise Odier x unknown
Madame Chauvry	Mme Bérard x William Allen Richardson
Madame Chavaret	Madame Damaizin x unknown
Madame Chédane-Guinoisseau	Safrano x unknown
Madame Corboeuf	Reine Marie Henriette x Général Jacqueminot
Madame Cornélissen	Sport of Souvenir de la Malmaison
Madame Crozy	Souvenir de la Reine d'Angleterre x unknown
Madame Damaizin	Probably Caroline x Safrano
Madame d'Arblay	r.moschata x r.multiflora
Madame de Selve	Monsieur Fillion x unknown
Madame de Terrouenne	Jules Margottin x unknown
Madame Derepas-Matrat	Madame Hoste x Marie van Houtte
Madame Désir Vincent	Souvenir de Madame Levet x unknown
Madame Desirée Giraud	Sport of Baronne Prévost
Madame Desprez (B)	Rose Edouard x unknown
Madame Docteur Jütté	Ophirie x unknown
Madame Docteur Wettstein	Victor Verdier x unknown
Madame Ducher (T)	Gloire de Dijon x unknown
Madame E Souffrain	Rêve d'Or x Duarte de Oliviera
Madame Elie Lambert	Anna Olivier x Souvenir de Paul Neyron
Madame Emile Metz	Madame de Lochen-Sels x La Tulipe
Madame Emilie Dupuy	madame Falcot x Gloire de Dijon
Madame Ernest Calvat	Sport of Madame Isaac Pereire
Madame Errera	Madame Lombard x Luciole
Madame Etienne Levet	Antoine Verdier x unknown
Madame Eugène Chambeyran	Victor Verdier x unknown
Madame Eugène Résal	Madame Laurette Messimy x unknown
Madame Eugène Verdier (HP-Guillot)	Louise Peyrony x unknown
Madame Eugène Verdier (HP-Verdier)	Gloire de Dijon x poss. Mme Barthélemy Levet
Madame Eugène Verdier (N-Levet)	Mme Barthélemy Levet x Gloire de Dijon
Madame Falcot	Safrano x unknown
Madame Fillion	Madame Domage x unknown
Madame Fortunée Besson	Jules Margottin x unknown
Madame François Bruel	Victor Verdier x Comtesse d'Oxford

Madame François Pittet	Mlle Blanche Lafitte x unknown
Madame Frédéric Dauplas (T)	Charles de Legrady x unknown
Madame Frédéric Dauplas (HT)	Léonie Osterrieth x Belle Siebrecht
Madame Gabriel Luizet	Sport of Jules Margottin
Madame Georges Bruant	r.rugosa alba x Mlle de Sombreuil
Madame Gustave Pierret	Clémentine Duval x unknown
Madame Hardy	Clinophyalla x unknown
Madame Harriet Stowe	La Reine x unknown
Madame Hélène de Lüsemans	Comte Alphonse de Seremye x unknown
Madame Honoré Defresne	Madame Falcot x unknown
Madame Hoste	Victor Pulliat x unknown
Madame Jean Sisley	Ducher x Sombreuil
Madame Jeanne Bouvet	Jules margottin x unknown
Madame John Twombly	Alfred Colomb x unknown
Madame Joseph Bonnaire	Adam x Paul Neyron
Madame Joseph Desbois	Baronne Adolphe de Rothschild x Mme Falcot
Madame Joseph Godier	Souvenir de Marie Détry x unknown
Madame Joseph Schwartz	Sport of Comtesse de Labarthe
Madame Jules Grévy	Triomphe de l'Exposition x Madame Falcot
Madame Jules Grolez	Triomphe de l'Exposition x Madame Falcot
Madame Jules Siegfried	Rêve d'Or x baronne Henriette de Loew
Madame Julie Weidmann	Antoine Verdier x unknown
Madame La Comtesse de Jaucourt	Triomphe de l'Exposition x unknown
Madame La Princesse de Radziwill	Isabelle Nabonnand x unknown
Madame Lacharme (HP)	Jules Margottin x Sombreuil
Madame Laffay	Général Allard x unknown
Madame Laurette Messimy	(Rival de Paestum x Mme Falcot) x Mme Falcot
Madame Lefrançois	Comtesse de Chabrillant x unknown
Madame Léon de St Jean	Madame Falcot x Madame Damaizin
Madame Lépold Moreau	Souvenir de Charles Montault x unknown
Madame Létuvée de Colnet	Madame Dubost x unknown
Madame Levet	Gloire de Dijon x unknown
Madame Lombard	Madame de Tartas x unknown
Madame Louis Donadine	Sport of Comtesse d'Oxford
Madame Louis Gaillard	Madame Bérard x unknown
Madame Louis Lévêque (HP)	Jules Margottin x unknown
Madame Louis Ricard	Possibly a seedling of Baron G B Gonella
Madame Louise Vigneron	Elisabeth Vigneron x unknown
Madame Lucien Chauvré	Baroness de Rothschild x unknown
Madame Lureau-Escalais	Victor Verdier x unknown
Madame Marcel Fauneau	Alexis Lepère x unknown
Madame Marie Bianchi	Victor Verdier x Virginale
Madame Marie Legrange	Sénateur Vaisse x unknown
Madame Marie Röderer	Jules Margottin x unknown
Madame Marthe d'Halloy	Madame Boutin x unknown
Madame Massicault	Baronne de Rothschild x unknown
Madame Maxime de la Rocheterie	Sport of Victor Verdier
Madame Mélanie Vigneron	Elisabeth Vigneron x unknown
Madame Miolan Carvalho	Cloth of Gold (Chromatella) x unknown
Madame Montel	La Reine x unknown
Madame Moreau (HP)	Victor Verdier x unknown
Madame Moreau (T)	Madame Falcot x Madame Bérard
Madame Nachury	La Reine x unknown
Madame Nérard	Rose Edouard x unknown

Madame Nobécourt	Madame Isaac Pereire x unknown
Madame Nomann	Madame Récamier x unknown
Madame Olymphe Téretschenko	Sport of Louise Odier
Madame Oswald de Kerchove	Madame Falcot x (Madame Récamier x unknown)
Madame Paul Marny	Gloire de Dijon x unknown
Madame Pernet-Ducher	Unnamed Tea x Victor Verdier
Madame Philémon Cochet	Sylphide x unknown
Madame Pierre Cochet	Rêve d'Or x unknown
Madame Pierre Margery	Jules Margottin x unknown
Madame Pierre Oger	Sport of Reine Victoria
Madame Plantier	Thought to be r.alba x r.moschata
Madame Prosper Laugier	John Hopper x unknown
Madame Remond	Comtesse de Labarthe x Anna Olivier
Madame Renard	Jules Margottin x unknown
Madame Rocher	Triomphe de l'Exposition xunknown
Madame Rolland (HP)	Victor Verdier x unknown
Madame Rosalie de Wincop	Général Jacqueminot x unknown
Madame Rose Romarin	Papillon x Chromatella
Madame S Mottet	William Allen Richardson x unknown
Madame Sancy de Parabère	A Boursault x a form of r.centifolia
Madame Scipion Cochet (T)	Anna Olivier x Duchesse de Brabant
Madame Sophie Froppet	Victor Verdier x unknown
Madame Trifle	Gloire de Dijon x unknown
Madame Veuve Ménier	Camoëns x unknown
Madame Victor Verdier	Senateur Vaisse x unknown
Madame Viviand-Morel (Ayr)	r.arvensis x Cheshunt Hybrid
Madame Wilson	Elisabeth Vigneron x unknown
Madeleine	Golfe Juan x unknown
Madeleine Guillaumez	Unnamed tea x Mademoiselle de Sombreuil
Mademoiselle Adèle Jougant	Mademoiselle de Sombreuil x unknown
Mademoiselle Alexandrine Bouel	Gloire de Dijon x unknown
Mademoiselle Alice Furon	Lady Mary Fitzwilliam x Mme Chedane-Guinoisseau
Mademoiselle Anna Chartron	Kaiserin Auguste Viktoria x Luciole
Mademoiselle Annette Murat	Gloire de Dijon x unknown
Mademoiselle Augustine Guinoisseau	Sport of La France
Mademoiselle Bertha Ludi	Mignonette x Jules Margottin
Mademoiselle Berthe Clovel	Sport of Souvenir de la Malmaison
Mademoiselle Blanche Durrschmidt	Madame Falcot x unknown
Mademoiselle Brigitte Viollot	Antoine Verdier x unknown
Mademoiselle Cécile Brunner	A climbing Polyantha x Madame de Tartas
Mademoiselle Cécile Brunner, Climbing	Sport of Mademoiselle Cécile Brunner
Mademoiselle Claudine Perreault	Souvenir d'Un Ami x unknown
Mademoiselle Clothilde Soupert	Gloire de Dijon x unknown
Mademoiselle de Sombreuil	Reputed to be a seedling of Parks' Yellow
Mademoiselle Emélie Verdier, Climbing	Sport of Mademoiselle Emélie Verdier
Mademoiselle Emma Hall	Souvenir de la Reine d'Angleterre x unknown
Mlle Eugénie Verdier (HP-Guillot)	Victor Verdier x unknown
Mademoiselle Franziska Krüger	Catherine Mermet x Général Schablikine
Mademoiselle Germaine Caillot	Baronne Adolphe de Rothschild x Mme Falcot
Mademoiselle Germaine Trochon	Victor Verdier x Madame Eugène Verdier
Mademoiselle Hélène Croissandeau	Victor Verdier x unknown
Mademoiselle Jacqueline Bouvet	Avocat Duvivier x unknown
Mademoiselle Jules Grévy	Duhamel du Monceau x unknown
Mademoiselle Julie Péréard	Jules Margottin x unknown

Mademoiselle Juliette Doucet	Gloire de Dijon x unknown
Mademoiselle Louise Boyer	Jules Margottin x unknown
Mademoiselle Lucie Jolicoeur	Comtesse de Caserton x Lady Mary Fitzwilliam
Mademoiselle Marie Chauvet	Baronne Adolphe de Rothschild x unknown
Mademoiselle Marie Digot	Marie Baumann x unknown
Mademoiselle Marie Drivon	Apolline x unknown
Mademoiselle Marie Gonod	Madame Laffay x unknown
Mademoiselle Marie Van Houtte	Madame de Tartas x Madame Falcot
Mademoiselle Marie Verdier	Souvenir de la Reine d'Angleterre x unknown
Mademoiselle Mathilde Lenaerts	Gloire de Dijon x unknown
Mademoiselle Noelie Merle	Gloire de Dijon x unknown
Mademoiselle Thérèse Levet	Jules Margottin x unknown
Maid of Honour	Sport of Catherine Mermet
Malmaison Rouge	Sport of Souvenir de la Malmaison
Maman Cochet	Marie van Houtte x Madame Lombard or Catherine Mermet x unknown
Manda's Triumph	r.wichurana x Pâquerette
Manettii	Probably Blush Noisette x Slater's Crimson China
Marchioness of Exeter	Jules Margottin x unknown
Marchioness of Londonderry	Poss seedling of Baronne Adolphe de Rothschild
Maréchal Niel	Chromatella x unknown (possibly Isabella Gray)
Maréchal Vaillant	Maurice Bernardinx unknown
Margaret Dickson	Lady Mary Fitzwilliam x Merveille de Lyon
Margaret Haywood	Sport of Madame Clémence Joigneaux
Marguerite de St Anand	Jules Margottin x unknown
Marguerite Ketten	Madame Caro x Georges Farber
Maria Graebner	r.palustris x r.virginiana
Maria Leonida	Possibly r.bracteata x r.laevigata or r.laevigata x Tea
Marie Baumann	Alfred Colomb x Général Jacqueminot
Marie Bennett	Baronne de Rothschild x unknown
Marie Berton	Gloire de Dijon x unknown
Marie Dermar	Louise d'Arzens x unknown
Marie Guillot, Climbing	Sport of Madame Guillot
Marie Lambert	Sport of Madame Bravy
Marie Louise Pernet	Baronne de Rothschild x unknown
Marie Louise Puyravaud	Madame Lazarine Poizeau x unknown
Marie Paré	Mistress Bosanquet x unknown
Marie Robert (N)	Isabella Gray x unknown
Marie Soleau	Mademoiselle Suzanne Blanchet x unknown
Marie van Houtte	Madame de Tartas x Madame Falcot
Marie Zahn	Pierre Notting x Safrano
Marion Dingee	(Comtesse de Caserta x Général Jacqueminot) x Maréchal Niel) x (Pierre Notting x Safrano)
Marmorea	Sometimes considered to be a form of r.gallica officinalis
Marquise Adèle de Murinais	Madame Laffay x unknown
Marquise de Castellane	Jules Margottin x unknown
Marquise de Mortmart	Jules Margottin x unknown
Marshall P Wilder	Général Jacqueminot x unknown
Martha Washington	r.roxburghii hybrid
Marthe d'Halloy	Madame Boutin x unknown
Mary Bennett	Baronne Adolphe de Rothschild x unknown
Masterpiece	Beauty of Waltham x unknown
Maurice Bernardin	Général Jacqueminot x unknown
Maxime de La Rocheterie	Victor Verdier x unknown

May Queen (which-Van Fleet)	r.wichurana x Mrs DeGraw
Meg Merrilies	r.rubignosa x Hybrid Perpetual or Bourbon
Mélanie Soupert	Gloire de Dijon x unknown
Menoux (HMult)	Laure Davoust x unknown
Merrie England	Sport of Heinrich Schultheis
Merveille de Lyon	Sport of Baronne Adolphe de Rothschild
Merveille des Blanches	Sport of Baronne Adolphe de Rothschild
Michael Saunders	Adam x Madame Victor Verdier
Mignonette (Guillot)	Double-flowered multiflora x probably China or Tea
Miller-Hayes	Charles Lefèbvre x unknown
Miniature Moss	Rivers' Single Crimson Moss x unknown
Minnie Dawson	Dawson x r.multiflora
Miss Hassard	Marguerite de Saint-Amand x unknown
Miss Lowe's Variety	Possibly a sport of Slater's Crimson China
Miss May Paul	Madame Thérèse Genevay x unknown
Miss Poole	Victor Verdier x unknown
Miss Willmott	L'Ideal x unknown
Mrs Anthony Waterer	r.rugosa x Général Jacqueminot
Mrs Baker	Victor Verdier x unknown
Mrs Caroline Swailes	Mademoiselle Eugénie Verdier x unknown
Mrs Charlotte Guilfoyle	M Berard x unknown
Mrs Cocker	Mrs John Laing x Mabel Morrison
Mrs F W Sandford	Sport of Mrs John Laing
Mrs Frank Cant	Madame Gabriel Luizet x Baronne Nathalie de Rothschild
Mrs George Dickson	Madame Clémence Joigneaux x unknown
Mrs Harkness	Sport of Heinrich Schultheis
Mrs Harry Turner	Charles Lefebvre x Alfred de Rougemont
Mrs Hovey	r.setigera x unknown
Mrs Jessie Fremont	Duchesse de Brabant x unknown
Mrs John Laing	François Michelon x unknown
Mrs Oliver Ames	Sport of Madame Cusin
Mrs Paul	Madame Isaac Pereire x unknown
Mrs Pierpoint Morgan	Sport of Madame Cusin
Mrs Rumsey	Sport of Mrs George Dickson
Mrs W C Whitney	Mme Ferdinand Jamin x Souvenir d'Un Ami
Mrs W J Grant	La France x Lady Mary Fitzwilliam
Mrs W J Grant, Climbing	Sport of Mrs W J Grant
Mrs William Watson	Madame Vidot x Merveille de Lyon
Modèle de Perfection	Louise Odier x unknown
Mogador	Sport of Rose du Roi
Mohrenkoenig	Souvenir de William Wood x unknown
Monseigneur Touchet	Niphetos x Madame Chédane-Guinoisseau
Monsieur Albert Patel	Ma Capucine x Beauté Inconstante
Monsieur Barillet-Deschamps	Comte Bobrinsky x unknown
Monsieur Barthélemy Levet	Victor Verdier x unknown
Monsieur Bonçenne	Général Jacqueminot x Géant des Batailles
Monsieur Cordier	Géant des Batailles x unknown
Monsieur de Morand	Sport of Général Jacqueminot
Monsieur Désir	Gloir de Dijon x unknown (possibly Général Jacqueminot)
Monsieur Druet	Duchesse de Cambacérès x unknown
Monsieur Émile Lelong	Général Jacqueminot x unknown
Monsieur Joseph Chappaz	Sport of Jules Margottin
Monsieur Jules Lemaître	Madame Isaac Pereire x unknown
Monsieur Jules Maquinant	Jules Margottin x unknown

Monsieur Jules Monges   Souvenir de la Reine d'Angleterre x unknown
Monsieur Lapierre   Géant des Batailles x unknown
Monsieur le Préfet Limbourg   Pierre Notting x unknown
Monsieur Louis Ricard   Simon St Jean x Abel Carrière
Monsieur Nomann   Jules Margottin x unknown
Monsieur Rosier   Mademoiselle Mathilde Lanaerts x unknown
Monsieur Roubaud   Golfe Juan x unknown
Monsieur Séringe   Géant des Batailles x unknown
Moschata Grandiflora   r.moschata x r.multiflora
Mosella   Mignonette x (Mme Falcot x Shirley Hibberd)
Mossy Rose de Meaux   Sport of Rose de Meaux or Pompon de Mai
Muriel Grahame   Sport of Catherine Mermet
Mutabilis   Possibly a sport of r.chinensis spontanea

Nancy Lee   Madame Bravy x Edward Morren
Nanette   Possibly syn with Manette from Lecoffé
Nardy   Gloire de Dijon x unknown
Nardy Frères   Madame Boll x unknown
Noisette à grands fleurs   Believed to be a hybrid from Sempervirens
Nymphaea Alba   Mademoiselle Eugène Verdier x Gloire de Dijon

Odéric Vital   Sport of Baronne Prévost
Oeillet Parfait   Possibly a Gallica x Damask hybrid
Old Red Boursault   Probably original typical form of r.lheritieranea
Olivet   De La Grifferaie x Madame Baron Veillard
Oriflamme de St Louis   Général Jacqueminot x unknown
Ornement des Jardins (Rambaux)   Polyantha x unknown
Oskar Kordel   Merveille de Lyon x André Schwartz

Pallida (HFt)   r.foetida bicolour x unknown
Panachée (M)   Sport of Old White Moss or White Bath
Panachée de Luxembourg   Sport of Docteur Arnal
Panachée de Lyon   Sport of Rose du Roi
Panachée d'Orléans   Sport of Duchesse d'Orléans or sport of Baronne Prévost
Panachée Langroise   Sport of Jules Margottin
Panachée pleine (M)   Sport of White Bath
Papa Gontier   Duchess of Edinburgh x unknown
Papa Lambert   (White Lady x Marie Baumann) x Oskar Kordel
Paquerette   Seedling of seedling of r.multiflora polyantha
Paul Marot   Baronne Adolphe de Rothschild x Souvenir de Victor
                                 Hugo
Paul Neyron   Victor Verdier x Anna de Diesbach
Paul's Carmine Pillar   Gloire de Margottin x unknown
Paul's Early Blush   Sport of Heinrich Schultheis
Paul's Himalayan Musk Rambler   r.brunonii x unknown
Paul's Himalayica Alba Magna   Form of r.brunonii
Paul's Himalayica Double Pink   Form of r.brunonii
Peach Blossom   Jules Margottin x unknown
Pearl   Adam x Comtesse de Serenye
Pearl Rivers   Devoniensis x Madame de Watteville
Perfection de Montplaisir   Canari x unknown
Perle Blanche   La Reine x unknown
Perle de Feu   Madame Falcot x Claire Falcot
Perle des Blanches   Blanche Lafitte x unknown

Perle des Jardins	Sport of Madame Falcot seedling
Perle des Jardins, Climbing	Sport of Perle des Jardins
Perle d'Or	Polyantha Alba Plena x Madame Falcot
Perpétuelle	Athalin x unknown
Petit Constant	Mignonette x Luciole
Petite Léonie	Mignonette x Duke of Connaught
Petite Lisette	Probably a hybrid of an Alba and a Damask Perpetual
Philadelphica	Sport of r.banksiae lutea
Pierre Guillot	Madame Falcot x unknown HP
Pierre Notting	Alfred Colomb x unknown
Pink Léda	Sport of Léda or vice-versa
Pink Roamer	r.wichurana x Cramoisi Supérieur
Pink Soupert	Clothilde Soupert x Lucullus
Placidie (A)	Sport of Great Maiden's Blush
Polliniana	r.arvensis x r.gallica
Perle des blanches	Madame Blancje Lafitte x Sapho (DP)
Polyantha Grandiflora	Probably r.multiflora hybrid x r.moschata hybrid
Pompon de Paris, Climbing	Sport of pompon de Paris
Pompon Mousseux (M)	Sport of Rose de Meaux or Pompon de Mai
Pompon Rouge	Reverence x Miracle
Pompon Jaune	Sport of r.hemispherica
Premier Essai	r.roxburghii x Reine de la Lombardie
Président de la Rocheterie	Sport of Baron G B Gonella
Président Lenaerts	Duhamel du Monceau x unknown
Président Léon de St Jean	Charles Lefebvre x unknown
Président Mas	Triomphe de l'Exposition x unknown
Président Rodolphe Burgles	Jules margottin x Jean Bart
Président Thiers	Victor Verdier x unknown
Pride of Reigate	Sport of Comtesse d'Oxford
Pride of Waltham	Sport of Comtesse d'Oxford
Prince Albert (HP)	Gloire des Rosamanes x a Damask Perpetual
Prince Albert (B-Paul)	Comice de Seine-et-Marne x unknown
Prince Arthur	Général Jacqueminot x unknown
Prince Camille de Rohan	Possibly Général Jacqueminot x Géant des Batailles
Prince Charles d'Arenberg	Dupuy Jamain x Madame Sévigné
Prince Prosper d'Arenberg	Madame Bérard x unknown
Prince Theodore Bonney	Bon Silène x William Francis Bennett
Princess Alice	Poupre du Luxembourg x unknown
Princess Bonnie	Bon Silène x William Francis Bennett
Princess Louise	Madame Vidot x Virginal
Princess Mary of Cambridge	Duchess of Sutherland x Jules Margottin
Princess May	Gloire de Dijon x unknown
Princess of Wales	Adam x Elise Sauvage
Princesse Charles d'Arenbourg	Dupuy Jamain x Madame de Sévigné
Princesse de Béarn	Duc de Cazes x unknown
Princesse Elizabeth Lancelotti	Mignonette x William Allen Richardson
Princesse Étienne de Croy	Comtesse de Labarthe x Mme Eugène Verdier
Princesse Henriette de Flandre	Mignonette x Marquise de Vivens
Princesse Impériale de Brésil	Antoine Verdier x unknown
Princesse Joséphine de Flandres	Mignonette x Marquise de Vivens
Princesse Louise	r.sempervirens x Parson's Pink
Princesse Marguerite d'Orléans (T)	Papa Gontier x Isabelle Nabonnand
Princesse Marie Adélaïde de Luxembourg	Mignonette x unknown
Princesse Marie Dolgorouky	Anna de Diesbach x unknown

Princesse Ouroussof	Paul Nabonnand x Madame Falcot
Princesse Royale	Ponctuée x Tuscany
Princesse Stéphanie	Gloire de Dijon x unknown
Princesse Théodore Galitzine	Madame Caro x Georges Farber
Princesse Wilhelm von Preussen	Général Jacqueminot x unknown
Princesse Wilhelmine des Pays-Bas	Mignonette x Madame Damaizin
Principesea di Napoli	Duc de Magenta x Safrano
Professeur Jules Courteis	Général Jacqueminot x unknown
Progress	Madame Béard x Marie van Houtte
Proteiformis	r.rugosa alba x unknown
Psyche	Turner's Crimson Rambler x Golden Fairy
Purity	Said to be Devoniensis x Madame Bravy
Purpurea (N)	Possibly a Boursault x Noisette hybrid
Purpurea (Misc)	r.roxburghii x unknown
Quatre Saisons Blanc Mousseux	Sport of Autumn Damask
Queen of Bedders	Sir Joseph Paxton x unknown
Queen of Queens	La Reine x Maiden's Blush
Queen of Queens, Climbing	Sport of Queen of Queens
Queen of the Prairies	r.setigera x a Gallica
Queen Victoria (HP)	La Reine x unknown
Rainbow	Sport of Papa Gontier
Raoul Chauvry	Madame Lombard x unknown
Ravel	Le Géant x unknown
Red Dragon	Charles Lefebvre x unknown
Regierungsrat Stockert	Dupuy-Jamain x Madame de Sévigné
Reichsgraf E von Kesselstatt	Pcse Alice de Monaco x Duchesse Marie Salviati
Reine Blanches (HP-Damaizin)	La Reine x unknown
Reine des Amateurs (HP) (Oger)	Mademoiselle Eugénie Verdier x unknown
Reine des Belges (Ayr)	Mixed parentage of r.sempervirens, r.arvensis & a China
Reine des Belges (HCh)	Globe Hip x r.chinensis
Reine des Blanches (HP-Avoux or Pernet)	La Reine x unknown
Reine des Blanches (HP-Crozy)	Victor Verdier x unknown
Reine des Violettes	Pius IX x unknown
Reine du Midi	La Reine x unknown
Reine Maria Pia	Gloire de Dijon x unknown
Reine Marie Henriette	Madame Bérard (T) x Général Jacqueminot (HP) or Gloire de Dijon
Reine Nathalie de Serbie	Madame Lombard x Sulfureux or Bon Silène x William Francis Bennett
René Denis	Sport of Madame Bérard
Rêve d'Or	Madame Schultz x Gloire de Dijon
Reverend T C Cole	Chromatella x Maréchal Niel
Reynolds Hole (HP)	Duke of Edinburgh x unknown
Rivers' George IV	Thought to be Damask x r.chinensis
Roger Lambelin	Sport of Fisher Holmes
Roi des Aunes	De La Grifferaie x unknown
Rosa barbierana	r.wichurana x Turner's Crimson Rambler
Rosa x engelmannii	r.nutkana x r.acicularis
Rosa kotschyana	Natural hybrid of r.orientalis
Rosa macounii	A form of r.woodsii
Rosa macrocarpa	Possibly synonymous with r.odorata gigantea
Rosa x spinulifolia	Natural hybrid of r.pendulina x r.tomentosa

Rosalie (T)   Marie Van Houtte x unknown
Rosalie de Wincop   Général Jacqueminot x unknown
Rose de Meaux White   White form of r.centifolia pomponia
Rose d'Italie Blanc   Sport of Rose d'Italie Rose
Rose Edouard   Tois-les-Mois (DP) x Parsons' Pink
Rosea   r.banksiae alba-plena x unknown garden variety
Rosemary   Boule de Neige x unknown
Rosier de Bourgon   Rose Edouard x unknown
Rosieriste Chauvry   Victor Verdier x unknown
Rosieriste Max Singer   Polyantha Alba Plena Sarmentosa x Général Jacqueminot
Rosomane Hubert   Gloire de Dijon x unknown
Rosy Morn   Victor Verdier x unknown
Rouge Captain Christy   Sport of Captain Christy
Royal Scarlet   Madame Rady x Cheshunt Scarlet
Rubin   Daniel Lacombe x Fellemburg
Ruby Queen   r.wichurana x Cramoisi Supérieur
Ruga   Thought to be r.arvensis x r.odorata

Safrano à Fleurs Rouges   Sport of Safrano
Santa Rosa   Hermosa x Bon Silène (or seedling thereof)
Scharnkeana   Natural hybrid of r.californica x r.nitida
Schloss Luegg   De La Grifferaie x unknown
Schneelicht   r.rugosa x r.phoenicia
Secrétaire Général Delaire   Baronne A de Rothschild x Alphonse Soupert
Sémonville   Evratina x unknown
Sénateur Vaisse   Général Jacqueminot x unknown
Senator McNaughton   Sport of Perle des Jardins
Setina   Sport of Hermosa
Seven Sisters   Natural cross of r.multiflora carnea x r.rugosa
Shailer's Provence   r.centifolia x r.lheritierana
Shailer's White Moss   Sport of Common Moss
Shirley Hibberd   Madame Falcot x unknown
Sidonie   Belle de Trianon x unknown
Siegfried   Gloire de Dijon x unknown
Silver Queen   Sport of Queen of Queens
Sir Garnet Wolseley   Prince Camille de Rohan x unknown
Sir Robert Duff   Gloire de Dijon x unknown
Sir Rowland Hill   Sport of Charles Lefèbvre
Smith's Yellow China   Blush Noisette x Parks' Yellow Tea-scented China
Soeur Bernède de St-Vincent de Paul   Jules Margottin x unknown
Soeur des Anges   Duchesse d'Orléans x unknown
Soleil d'Or   Antoine Ducher x r.foetida persiana
Solfaterre   Lamarque x unknown
South Orange Perfection   r.wichurana x Cramoisi Supérieur
Souvenir d'Adolphe Thiers   Victor Verdier x unknown
Souvenir d'Arien Bahivet   Comtesse d'Oxford x unknown
Souvenir d'Arthur de Sansal   Jules Margottin x unknown
Souvenir de Christophe Cochet   R x kantchatka 'Alba Simple' x Comte d'Epremesnil
Souvenir de Gonod   Baronne Adolphe de Rothschild x unknown
Souvenir de la Malmaison, Climbing   Sport of Souvenir de la Malmaison
Souvenir de la Reine d'Angleterre   La Reine x unknown
Souvenir de l'Ami Pancher   Triomphe de l'Exposition x unknown
Souvenir de Léon Lille   Géant des Batailles x unknown
Souvenir de Lucie   Fellemberg x Ernestine de Barante

Souvenir de Madame Berthier	Victor Verdier x Jules Margottin
Souvenir de Mme Eugène Verdier (P-D)	Lady Mary Fitzwilliam x Mme Chedane-Guinoisseau
Souvenir de Mme Eugène Verdier (HP)	Baronne de Rothschild x unknown
Souvenir de Madame Hélène Lambert	Beauté de l'Europe x unknown
Souvenir de Madame Jeanne Balandreau	Sport of Ulrich Brunner fils
Souvenir de Madame Joseph Métral	Madame Bérard x Eugene Fürst
Souvenir de Madame l'Advocat	Sport of Duarte de Oliviera
Souvenir de Madame Léonie Viennot	Gloire de Dijon x unknown
Souvenir de Madame Levet	Madame carot x Madame Eugène Verdier
Souvenir de Madame Robert	Jules Margottin x unknown
Souvenir de Madame Sablayrolles	Devoniensis x Souvenir de l'Elise Vardon
Souvenir de Madame Sadi Carnot	Madame Victor Verdier x unknown
Souvenir de Madame William Wood	Général Jacqueminot x unknown
Souvenir de Monsieur Claude Dupont	Souvenir de Victor Hugo x unknown
Souvenir de Paul Neyron	Orphirie x unknown or Devoniensis x Souvenir de la Malmaison
Souvenir de Philémon Cochet	Sport of Blanc Double de Coubert
Souvenir de Pierre Dupuy	Général Jacqueminot x unknown
Souvenir de S A Prince	Sport of Souvenir d'un Ami
Souvenir de Spa	Madame Victor Verdier x unknown
Souvenir de Thérèse Levet	Adam x unknown
Souvenir de Victor Hugo (HP)	Ambrogio Maggi x unknown
Souvenir de Victor Hugo (T)	Duchesse de Brabant x Regulus
Souvenir de William Wood	Général Jacqueminot x unknown
Souvenir de Yeddo	r.rugosa x a Tea
Souvenir du Baron de Sémur	Charles Lefèbvre x unknown
Souv du Centenaire de Lord Brougham	r semperflorens (de Pronville) x a China x r indica (de Pronville)
Souvenir du Docteur Jamain	Charles Lefebvre x unknown
Souvenir du Président Carnot	Lady Mary Fitzwilliam x unknown
Souvenir du Président Porcher	Victor Verdier x unknown
Souvenir du Prince Charles d'Arenberg	Rêve d'Or x Duchesse d'Auerstädt
Souvenir du Prince Royal de Belgique	Triomphe de l'Exposition x unknown
Souvenir du Rosiériste Rambaux	Bon Silène x unknown
Souvenir of Wootton	Bon Silène x Louis van Houtte
Souvenir of Wootton, Climbing	Sport of Souvenir of Wootton
Spectabilis (HSem)	Possibly r. sempervirens x Noisette hybrid
Spenser or Spencer	Sport of Merveille de Lyon
Stanwell Perpetual	Duchess of Portland x r.spinosissima
Stéphanie et Rudolfe	Madame Barthélemy Levet x unknown
Sultan of Zanzibar	Duke of Edinburgh x unknown
Sunrise	Sport of Sunset
Sunset	Sport of Perle des Jardins
Suzanne-Marie Rodocanachi	Victor Verdier x unknown
Tamagled	Rosa rugosa x Étoile de Lyon
Tartarus	Erinnerung an Brod x Souvenir de Dr Jamain
Tatiana Onéguine	Elisabeth Vigneron x unknown
Thalia	r.multiflora x Pâquerette
The Bride	Sport of Catherine Mermet
The Garland	r.moschata x r.multiflora
The Puritan	Mabel Morrison x Devoniensis
The Sweet Little Queen of Holland	Céline Forestier x Madame Hoste
Thérèse Lambert	Madame Lambard x Socrate

Thusnelda   r.rugosa alba x Gloire de Dijon
Thyra Hammerich   Duchesse de Sutherland x unknown
Triomphe de Bolwyller   Apparently a hybrid of r.sempervirens x a Tea
Triomphe de Guillotière (S)   Probably r.roxburghii x r.odorata
Triomphe de Pernet père   Monsieur Désir x Général Jacqueminot
Triomphe de Rennes   Lamarque x unknown
Triomphe des Beaux Arts   Général Jacqueminot x unknown
Triomphe des Noisettes   Général Jacqueminot x Ophirie
Triumphant   r.setigera x unknown
Turenne (HP)   Sport of Général Jacqueminot
Tuscany Superb   Tuscany x unknown

Ulrich Brunner Fils   Sport or seedling of Paul Neyron or Anna de Diesbach x
                                       unknown
Una   Gloire de Dijon x r.canina
Unique de Provence   Centfeuilles Unique x unknown
Unique Moss   Sport of Unique Blanche
Unique Panachée   Sport of Unique Rouge
Universal Favorite   r.wichurana x Pâquerette

V Viviand-Morel   Safrano â Fleurs Rouges x unknown
Vainqueur de Solférino   Géant des Batailles x unknown
Varin   Pompon Varin x unknown
Venus (HP)   Général Jacqueminot x Princesse de Béarn
Vick's Caprice   Sport of Archiduchesse Elisabeth d'Autriche
Vicountess Falmouth   Adam x Soupert & Notting's Perpetual Moss
Victoire Fontaine   Catherine Guillot x unknown
Victor Hugo (HP)   Charles Lefèbvre x unknown
Victor Pulliat   Mélanie Willermoz x unknown
Victor Verdier (HP)   Jules Margottin x Safrano
Victor Verdier (Cl HP)   Sport of Victor Verdier
Ville de Saint Denis   Sport or seedling of La Reine
Violette Bouyer   Jules Margottin x Mademoiselle de Sombreuil or
                                       Sombreuil (different roses)
Viviand-Morel   Safrano à Fleurs Rouges x unknown

Waban   Sport of Catherine Mermet
Waitziana   r.canina x r.gallica
Weisser Herumstreicher   Daniel Lacombe x Pâquerette
White Baroness   Sport of Baronne Rothschild
White Bath   Sport of Common Moss
White Lady   Sport of Lady Mary Fitzwillam
White Maman Cochet (T)   Sport of Maman Cochet
White Pearl   Sport of Perle des Jardins
White Pet   Sport of Félicité-Pérpetue
White Pet, Climbing   Sport of White Pet
White Provence   Sport of r.centifolia
White Rose of York   r.gallica x r.canina
Wilberforce   Probably r.centifolia x r.gallica
William Allen Richardson   Rêve d'Or x unknown
William Francis Bennett   Adam x Xavier Olibo
William Jesse   Probably Madame Desprez x uncertain
William Warden   Sport of Madame Clémence Joigneaux
Winnie Davis   Devoniensis x Madame de Watteville

Wodan   Gloire des Rosomanes x possibly r.multiflora

Xavier Olibo   Sport of Général Jacqueminot

York and Lancaster   Sport of r.damascena

Zigeunerblut   r.pendulina x a Bourbon

Key to Entries

Classifications

A	Alba
Alp	Alpina
Arv	Arvensis
Ayr	Ayrshire
B	Bourbon
Bcr	Bracteata
Bks	Banksian
Bslt	Boursault
C	Centifolia
Can	Canina
Ch	China
D	Damask
E	Eglanteria
G	Gallica
HArv	Hybrid Arvensis
HBc	Hybrid Bracteata
HBl	Hybrid Blanda
HBslt	Hybrid Boursault
HCan	Hybrid Canina
HCh	Hybrid China
HEg	Hybrid Eglanteria
HFt	Hybrid Foetida
HG	Hubrid Gigantea
HMac	Hybrid Macrantha
HMcr	Hybrid Microphylla
HMsk	Hybrid Musk
HMult	Hybrid Multiflora
HP	Hybrid Perpetual
HRg	Hybrid Rugosa
HSem	Hybrid Sempervirens

HSet	Hybrid Setigera
HSpn	Hybrid Spinosissima
HT	Hybrid Tea
HWich	Hybrid Wichurana
LCl	Large-flowered Climber
M	Moss
Min	Miniature
Misc	Miscellaneous
N	Noisette
P	Portland
Pol	Polyantha
Pom	Pomifera
Rbf	Rubrifolia
Rg	Rugosa
S	Shrub
Sp	Species
T	Tea
H	Hybrid
Cl	Climbing

Colour Classification

As per Modern Roses 12 with amendments

ab	apricot and apricot blend
dp	deep pink
dr	deep red
dy	deep yellow
g	green
lp	light pink
ly	light yellow
m	mauve and mauve blend
mp	medium pink
mr	medium red
my	medium yellow
ob	orange and orange blend
op	orange pink and orange pink blend
or	orange red and orange blend
p	pink
pb	pink blend
r	red or russet
rb	red blend
w	white, near white and white blend
y	yellow
yb	yellow blend

Bloom

s	single
s-d	semi-double
dbl	double
vdbl	very double
f	full
vf	very full

Size

s	small
s-m	small to medium
m	medium
m-l	medium to large
l	large
vl	very large

Growth

wk	weak
m	moderate
vig	vigorous
vvig	very vigorous
sp	spreading

Scent

s	slight fragrance
m	moderate fragrance
f	fragrant
vf	very fragrant

NAMES	TYPE	YEAR	RAISER	COLOUR	BLOOM	SIZE	GROWTH	SCENT
À Aiguillons Flexibles	HSpn							
À Balais	C	c 1810	Descemet	mp	f	s		
		syn	Comtesse de Chamois					
À Bois Brun	HMult	1849	Vibert	mp	f			
À Bois et Feuilles Panachées	C							
À Bois Jaspé	HP	1877	Brassac	dr	f			
À Bois Panaché	Ch			p				
À Bois Strié	Ch	Pre 1834		p		m		
À Bois Violet	M	1827	Mauget	w				
À Bordures	C	c 1810	Descemet	mp	f	s		
		syn	Comtesse de Chamois					
A Bouquet	T	1873	Liabaud	w	f	l	m	
À Bouquets	D	Pre 1811	syn Argentée	lp		m		
À Bouquets	Ch	Pre 1820		w	vdbl			
À Boutons d'Unique	HSpn	1821						
À Boutons Jaunes	HSpn	1821						
À Boutons Penchés	HBslt	Pre 1820	Boursault / Vibert	p	vdbl	m	vig	f
À Boutons Renversés	Bslt	c 1810	syn Boursault Rose	mp	s-d			
À Boutons Verts	A	Pre 1830	Prévost	w	f	m		
À Bractées	Sp	1793	Wendland	w	s			
			syn r.bracteata					
À Calice Hispide	HBslt		Wild					
À Cinq Couleurs	G			y,r,m	f	l	vvig	
À Coeur Jaune	A	c 1810	Descemet	w	vdbl	s	m	
À Coeur Jaune	N	1825	Prévost	yb	dbl	s-m		f
À Coeur Vert	A	Pre 1820		w	f	s		
À Douze Pétales	C	1807	Charpentier	mp	s	s		
		syn À	Fleurs Presque Simples					
A Drawiel	HP	1887	Lévêque	dr	dbl	l		
À Feuilles à Nerves Jaunes	G/C	1827	Prévost	lp	f	m		f
À Feuilles Bipennées	C	Pre 1802	Thory	lp	f	m		
		syn	r.centifolia bipinnata					
À Feuilles Bleuâtres	A	1822		p				
À Feuilles Bullées	C	1809	syn Bullata	mp	vdbl	vl		vf
À Feuilles Cloquées	C	1809	syn Bullata	mp	vdbl	vl		vf
À Feuilles Crénelées	C	Pre 1804	Dupont	lp	f	s		m
À Feuilles Crépues	C	1809	syn Bullata	mp	vdbl	vl		vf
À Feuilles Crispées	C	Pre 1802	Thory	lp	f	m		
		syn	r.centifolia bipinnata					
À Feuilles de Bengale	HCan	Pre 1815	Descemet					
À Feuilles de Céleri	C	Pre 1802	Thory	mp	f	l		
		syn	r.centifolia bipinnata					
A Feuilles de Chanvre	C	Pre 1811		lp	dbl	m		
À Feuilles de Chanvre	A	1807	Flobert / Pelletier	w	dbl	s		
			syn Cymbaefolia					
À Feuilles de Chanvre Ovales	A	1826	Lecomte	w				
À Feuilles de Chêne	C	Pre 1811	Trianon	mp	vf	m	wk	
À Feuilles de Chou	C	1809	syn Bullata	dp	vdbl	vl		vf
À Feuilles de Fraxinelle	HCan	1815	Descemet					
À Feuilles de Frêne	S	Pre 1770	syn Turneps	dp	dbl	m-l		
À Feuilles de Frêne	HArv	1819	Vibrt	mp	dbl	m		f
À Feuilles de Frêne	Alp	Pre 1830		lp	s	m		
À Feuilles de Groseiller	C	Pre 1802	Thory	lp	f	m		
		syn	r.centifolia bipinnata					
À Feuilles de Laitue	C	1809	syn Bullata	mp	vf	vl		vf
À Feuilles de Pêcher	A	1810	Pelletier	w	f	m		
À Feuilles de Pêcher	Ch	Pre 1830	Vibert	lp	dbl	s		
		syn	À Feuilles de Saule					
À Feuilles de Persil	C	Pre 1802	Thory	lp	f	m		
		syn	r.centifolia bipinnata					
À Feuilles de Pimprenelle	HSpn	1820	Vibert	w	s	m		
À Feuilles de Pimprenelle	Alp	Pre 1830		mr	vdbl	s		f
À Feuilles de Sauge	M	Pre 1834	Lancezeur	dp		m		
À Feuilles de Saule	Ch	Pre 1830	Vibert	lp	dbl	s		
À Feuilles de Sorbier	HEg	Pre 1830	Vibert	lp	dbl	m		
		syn	Eglantier à Feuilles de Sorbier					
À Feuilles de Sorbier	HSpn			w				
À Feuilles d'Épine	Sp	1788	(Michaux)Bommueller	yb	s	s		
			syn Hulthemia Persica					
À Feuilles d'Orme	G	Pre 1820	Descemet	lp				
À Feuilles et Fleurs Marbrées	A	Pre 1830	Vibert	w	vdbl	s	m	
		syn	À Coeur Jaune (Des)					
À Feuilles Étroites	Pom	Pre 1830	Prévost	lp	dbl	m		
À Feuilles Gaufrées	C	1809	syn Bullata	mp	vf	vl		vf
À Feuilles Glauques	A	1819						
À Feuilles Luisantes	M	1843	Vibert	lp	f	m		f
		syn	Rose à Feuilles Luisantes					
À Feuilles Luisantes	Ch	Pre 1830	Vibert	lp	dbl	s		
À Feuilles Marbrées	HSpn		Bozérian	p				

Name	Class	Date	Raiser / Synonym					
À Feuilles Marbrées	A							
À Feuilles Molles	Pom			r				
À Feuilles Odorantes	HSpn	Pre 1820	Poilpré	p	dbl			
À Feuilles Panachées	HBc			w				
À Feuilles Penchées	Sp	Pre 1817	syn r.chinophylla	w		vl		
À Feuilles Presque Glabres	Can /Sp	Pre 1830		mp	dbl	m		
À Feuilles Rondes Crénelées	C	Pre 1804	Dupont syn À Feuilles Crénelées	lp	f	s		m
À Feuilles Rudes	Pom			r				
À Feuilles Soyeuses	HSpn	1823	Vibert	p				
À Feuilles Velues	HSpn	1825	Hamon	mp				
À Filets	T	Pre 1834		yb		l		
À Fleur d'Anénome	M	1824	Lemeunier syn De La Flèche	dr	dbl			
À Fleur Double	P	Pre 1820	syn La Moderne	lp	s-d	l		
À Fleur Double	HEg	1822	Prévost	mp	dbl	m		f
À Fleur Double	Can /Sp	Pre 1830		mp	dbl	m		
À Fleur Double	Ch	Pre 1830	Prévost syn À Fleur Pleine	lp	dbl	m		
À Fleur d'un Rouge Pâle	G	Pre 1811	syn Agathe Incarnata	lp	vdbl	m		vf
À Fleur Jaune	Misc	Pre 1830	Lindley	my	dbl	m		
À Fleur Multiple	B	Pre 1830	Laffay syn Perpétuelle	mp	dbl	m		
À Fleur Multiple	Can	Pre 1830		lp	dbl	m		
À Fleur Pleine	B	Pre 1830	syn Dubreuil	lp	f	m-l		
À Fleur Pleine	Ch	Pre 1830	Vibert	mp	vdbl	m		
À Fleur Pourpre	HCh	Pre 1830	Vibert	mr	dbl	l		
À Fleur Simple	Alp	Pre 1830		lp	s	s		
À Fleurs Blanches	A			w	f	s		f
À Fleurs Blanches	B	1829		w	f	m		
À Fleurs Blanches	Bks	Pre 1830		w	f	s		
À Fleurs Blanches Doubles	HMult	Pre 1870	Prévost	w		s		
À Fleurs Carnées	HMult	1804	Evans	lp	f	s		
À Fleurs Chagrinées	HCh	Pre 1830	Vibert	lp	dbl	m		f
À Fleurs Changeantes	N	Pre 1830		pb		s		
À Fleurs Comprimées	G/C	1822	Vibert	lp	vdbl	m		
À Fleurs Crispées	C	Pre 1830	Vibert syn Cent feuilles Veinée Marbrée	lp	dbl	m-l		
À Fleurs d'Anénome	M	1844	Mauget syn Anénome	mp	dbl			
À Fleurs d'Anénome	G			w	f	s		
À Fleurs de Junon	HCh		Hardy	p				
À Fleurs de Ronces	HMult			rb				
À Fleurs de Rose Trémière de Chine	G/C	Pre 1828	Pelletier	dp	vdbl	l	m	
À Fleurs de Seringat	Bks	Pre 1870		w	s	s		
À Fleurs Doubles	M			p				
À Fleurs Doubles	HMsk	Pre 1629	syn Double White	w	s-d	m		
À Fleurs Doubles	A	Pre 1770	syn Plena	w	s-d			
À Fleurs Doubles	HEg	c 1810	Redouté / Lahaye syn Petite Hessoise	mp	s-d	s		
À Fleurs Doubles	HSpn	Pre 1818 syn	Descemet Double White Burnet	w	dbl	m	vig	vf
À Fleurs Doubles	Pom	1819	Prévost	lp	dbl	m		
À Fleurs Doubles	B	1827	Vibert	pb		m		
À Fleurs Doubles Rouges	HSpn			r				
À Fleurs Doubles Violettes	Ch	Pre 1818		m				
À Fleurs Doubles Violettes	C			m	f	m		m
À Fleurs et Feuilles Marbrées	G	1832	Vibert	dr	s-d	m		
À Fleurs Frisées	G							
À Fleurs Gigantesques	G	1813		dp	vdbl	l		vf
À Fleurs Jaspées	Pom	Pre 1830		lp	dbl	m		
À Fleurs Jaunes	Bks	Pre 1830		y	f	s		
À Fleurs Jaunes	A			y		s		
À Fleurs Marbrées	G	Pre 1754	syn Marmorea	rb	s-d	m		
À Fleurs Marbrées	HMult	Pre 1830	Laffay syn Gay	pb	vdbl	m		
À Fleurs Multiples	B			p				
À Fleurs Pales	M			lp				
À Fleurs Panachées	C	c 1845	syn Variegata	pb	vdbl			
À Fleurs Panachées	D	Pre 1830	Girardin	w	dbl	m		
À Fleurs Perpétuelles	HSem	1820						
À Fleurs Pleines	HBc	Pre 1870		w		l		
À Fleurs Pleines	Ayr			w	dbl	m		f
À Fleurs Pleines	Ch	Pre 1834	Laffay	lp		m		
À Fleurs Pleines	T	Pre 1830	Calvert	lp	f	m		
À Fleurs Pourpres	N	1825	Vibert					
À Fleurs Pourpres Panaché Blanche	G	1825	Vibert					
À Fleurs Presque Simples	C	1807	Charpentier	mp	s			
À Fleurs Presque Violettes	D		Ternaux	dr				
À Fleurs Prolifères	HSpn	1820						
À Fleurs Roses	HMult		Laffay	lp				
À Fleurs Roses	HSem		Laffay	lp	dbl		vvig	
À Fleurs Roses	Alp	Pre 1810	Charpentier	lp	f	m		

			syn Elise					
À Fleurs Rouges	HEg	Pre 1826	Prévost	mp	dbl	m		
À Fleurs Rouges	P	1828	Dubreuil / Vibert	mr	dbl	m-l		
À Fleurs Rouges	D			r				
À Fleurs Rouges Cramoisi	G	1826	Prévost	dr				
À Fleurs Rouges Doubles	Alp			lp				
À Fleurs Rouges Doubles	D	Pre 1789	syn Red Damask	mr	dbl	m		vf
À Fleurs Semi-Doubles	HSpn	1825		y				
À Fleurs Semi-Doubles	Misc	1823	Cugnot	rb				
À Fleurs Simples	Ayr			p				
À Fleurs Simples	A		Vibert	lp				
À Fleurs Simples	T	Pre 1830	Vibert	mp	s	m		
À Fleurs Simples	Pom		Prévost					
À Fleurs Simples	C	Pre 1804	Dupont	mp	s-d	m		
À Fleurs Simples	Pom	Pre 1830	Prévost	lp	s	s		
À Fleurs Simples Couleur de Cire	Sp	Pre 1542	Herrmann	my	s		vig	m
			syn r.foetida					
À Fleurs Très Simples	Ch							
À Fleurs Variables	N			lp				
À Fleurs Vertes	Ch	1856	Bambridge & Harrison	g	s-d	m		
			syn Viridiflora					
À Folioles Crénelés	C		Dumont de Courset	p				
À Folioles Fermes	A	1819	Vibert					
À Folioles Lancéolées	Can /Sp	Pre 1830		lp	s	m		
À Folioles Ovales et À Pédoncules Glabres	Can /Sp	Pre 1830		lp	s	m		
À Folioles Ovales et À Pédoncules Velus	Can /Sp	Pre 1830		lp	s	m		
À Fruit Aplati	Pom							
À Fruit Déprimé	Pom	1819	Vibert					
À Fruit en Calebasse	Alp	Pre 1830	Vibert	lp	s-d			
À Fruit en Poire	G/C	1826	Prévost	lp	dbl	l	vig	
À Fruit Glabre	Pom	1817						
À Fruit Globeux	Pom		Bozérain					
À Fruit Langéniforme	Alp	Pre 1830	Prévost	lp	s	m	vig	
À Fruit Pendant	Alp	1818	Vibert	mr	s			
À Fruit Rouge	HSpn	1827	Tontain	mp				
À Geoffrey de St Hilaire	HP	1878	Verdier E	r	dbl	m		vf
À Grand Cramoisi	C	Pre 1818	Trianon	m	s-d			
À Grand Fleur	HSem	1829	Vibert	w		m		
À Grandes Corymbes	G	1835	Joly	pb				
À Grandes Feuilles	G		Lelieur	dp				
À Grandes Feuilles	Ch		Noisette L	dp	dbl		vig	
À Grandes Feuilles	HMult			dr				
À Grandes Fleurs	HSpn	1817	Noisette L	lp	dbl	l		f
À Grandes Fleurs	P	Pre 1834	Prévost	dp		vl		
À Grandes Fleurs	T	Pre 1834		w		l		
À Grandes Fleurs Carnées	HSpn	1826	Nicolle	lp	dbl	l		
À Grandes Fleurs Lilas	N							
À Grandes Fleurs Pleines	A			w	f			
À Grandes Fleurs Pourpres	N							
À Grandes Fleurs Simples	N	Pre 1830	Dubreuil	mp	s	l		
À Gros Cul	Misc	Pre 1629	Muenchhausen	m	dbl	m-l		
			syn r. x francofurtana					
À Gros Cul de Franckfort	G			pb				
À Long Fruit	Alp	1819		mr	s			
À Longs Pédoncules	Ch	Pre 1830	Noisette L syn Cerise	dp	dbl	m		
À Longs Pédoncules	M	1854	Robert	lp	dbl	s	vig	
A M Ampère	HP	1881	Liabaud	dr	f	m	vvig	
À Odeur d'Amande	HCh	Pre 1846		dr				vf
À Odeur d'Ananas	Ch	1825	Margat	rb	f	m-l	vvig	vf
À Odeur d'Anisette	HCh	Pre 1834	Vibert	dp	f	m		vf
À Odeur de Capucine	Ch	1817	Godefroy	dr	dbl	s-m		f
À Odeur de Dragées	P	Pre 1830	Laffay	lp	f	l		vf
À Odeur de Framoise	Ch	1817	Prévost	dr	dbl	s-m		f
		syn	À Odeur de Capucine					
À Odeur de Jacinthe	Ch	c 1825	Noisette L syn below	lp	f	m		m
À Odeur de Noisette	HCh	c 1825	Noisette syn Thisbé	lp	f	m		m
À Odeur de Noyer	Misc	1827	Prévost	lp	dbl	m		f
À Odeur de Pomme de Reinette	Sp	Pre 1551	syn r.rubiginosa	lp	s			
À Odeur de Punaise	C	Pre 1810	Dupont	mp	f	m		m
			syn Le Rire Niais					
À Odeur de Térébenthine	Pom			rb				
À Odeur de Thé	T	Pre 1830	Prévost	lp	dbl	l		
À Odeur de Thé	Ch		Laffay	dp				
À Odeur Ingrate	C	Pre 1810	Dupont	mp	f	m		m
			syn Le Rire Niais					
À Ovaire Lisse	Misc		Prévost					
À Pédoncule et Ovaire Hispides	Alp	Pre 1830	Joret Frères	mr	s			

Name	Type	Date	Raiser / Note					
À Pédoncules Courbées	G	Pre 1829	Coquerel	lp	vdbl	s		
À Pétale Teinté de Rose	D		Redouté	w	s			
		syn	r. x damascena subalba					
À Pétales Frangées	Ch	1831	Jacques	pb	f			sf
			syn Serratipetala					
À Pétales Frangées	Pom		Vibert					
À Pétales Mucronées	T	1827	Reveillère	lp	vdbl			
À Pétales Réfléchies	N	1825	Vibert	dp	vdbl	s		
À Pétales Roulées	Misc			r & w				
À Pétales Striées	Ch	1826	Noisette L	dr	f	m		
À Pétales Variés	D	Pre 1551	(Monardes)	pb	dbl			m
			syn York & Lancaster					
À Petites Feuilles	HMcr	Pre 1830		lp	f		vvig	
À Petites Fleurs	G	c 1802	syn Enfant de France	m	f	m		
À Petites Fleurs	N	1823	syn Noisette Pourpre	lp	vdbl	s		
À Petites Fleurs	HArv		Jacques	p	s			
À Petits Fruits	Pom							
À Poil de Boue	Alp							
À Rameaux Géminés	Misc	Pre 1834		p		m		
À Rameaux Horizontaux	Min		Laffay	lp				
À Rameaux Inclines	N		Noisette L	lp				
À Rameaux Sarmenteux	G	1845	Robert	pb	s-d	m		
À Rameaux Velus	Alp	1826	Prévost	dp	s	m		
À Sept Pétales	C	1807	Charpentier	mp	s	s		
		syn	À Fleurs Presque Simples					
À Tige Faible	Alp		Vilmorin	r				
À Tiges sans Épines	HSpn	Pre 1824	Nestler/De Candolle	mr	s			
			syn Inermis					
À Trois Feuilles	Misc	1822	Prévost syn Rosa Nivea	w	s	l		
Abaçon	T	1858	Schultz	y	f	l	vvig	
Abacy	HP	1847	Goudreau	dr	f		vvig	
Abadie de Rougement	HP	1854	Lartay	dr	f	m	vvig	
Abailard	G	Pre 1826	Sommesson	lp	vdbl	m		
Abaillard	G	1845	Robert	pb	f	m		
Abatucci	G	1820	Vibert	rb	f	l		
Abbé Baynal	HP	1853	Sortet	dr	f	m	vig	
Abbé Berlèze	G	Pre 1845	Baumann	w	dbl			
Abbé Berlèze	HP	1864	Guillot Fils	rb	f	l	vig	
Abbé Bramerel	HP	1864	Guillot Fils	dr	dbl	l	vig	f
Abbé de la Croix	Ch	Pre 1870		dp	f	m		
Abbé de la Haye	Ch	1854	Robert	p				
Abbé de la Haye	HT	1855	Bourbin	dp	f	l		
Abbé de l'Epée	G	1854	Robert	dr	f	l		
Abbé Feytel	HP	1857	Ducher	dp	f	vl		
Abbé Girardin	B	1881	Bernaix A	mp	f	l	vig	f
Abbé Giraudier	HP	1869	Levet	p	dbl	vf	vig	
Abbé Loury	HP	1864	Trouillard	dr		m		f
Abbé Marcelin	T	1854	Pradel	dp	vdbl	l		
Abbé Miolan	T			dr	vdbl			
Abbé Miolan	Ch	1839		m	dbl	m	m	
Abbé Plantier	B	Pre 1846		dp		l		
Abbé Reynaud	HP	1863	Guillot Fils	m	f	l	m	
Abbé Robert	G	1833	Vibert	dr	f	m		
Abbé Roustan	T	1878	Nabonnand	lp		l		
Abbé Thomasson	T	1888	Schwartz Vve	lp	f	m	vig	f
Abbé Vénière	HP	1865	Guillot Fils	mp	vdbl	m		
Abbesse	G	Pre 1848	Miellez	dr	f	m		
Abd-el-Kader	HP	1861	Verdier	pb	s-d	l	vvig	
Abdul Hamid	HRg	Pre 1848		r				
Abel	T		Van Houtte	p				
Abel Carrière	M	1856	Portemer	rb	f	m	vig	
Abel Carrière	HP	1875	Verdier E	dr	dbl	l	vig	
Abel Grant	HP	1865	Damaizin	dp	dbl	l	vig	vf
Abelard	G/C	Pre 1836		lp	vdbl	m		
Abondance	G			p				
Abondance	G		see Van Huyssen	r				
Abraham Lincoln	HP	1865	Ducher	dr	f	vl		
Abraham Zimmermann	HP	1879	Lévêque	mr	dbl	l	vvig	
Abranella	HP			p	f		m	
Abricotée	T	1843	Dupuis	ab	dbl	l	vig	
Acanthe	Ch		Laffay					
Acceptor	Misc			r				
Achille	G	Pre 1810	Miellez	dr	dbl	m		f
Achille Cesbron	HP	1894	Rousset	mr	dbl	vl		
Achille Constant	HP	1853	Lartay	dr	vf	m	vig	
Achille de Harlay	G	1855	Robert	m				
Achille de Saint-Ange	HP	Pre 1870		mr				
Achille Gonod	HP	1864	Gonod	mr	dbl	l	vig	vf
Achilles	HMult	Pre 1846		mp				
Aciculaire	Misc	Pre 1830	Lindley / Pronville	lp	s		m	
Acidalie	B	1833	Rousseau	w	f	l	vig	vf
Aculeata Incarnata	A			lp				

Name	Type	Date	Breeder					
Adalida	HT			lp	vf	l	vig	
Adam	T	1833	Adam	mp	f	vl	vig	vf
Adam Paul	HP	1852	Laffay	lp	f	vl	vvig	vf
Adanson	HP	1875	Schwartz	rb	f	l	m	
Adda	A	1825	Vibert	lp		s		
Adelaïde	G	Pre 1846		dp		s		
Adélaïde Bougère	B	1852	Bougère	m	f	l		
Adélaïde de Meynot	HP	1882	Gonod	dp	f	l	vig	f
Adélaïde de Savoie	HP	1864	Moreau-Robert	p				
Adélaïde d'Orléans	HSem	1826	Jacques	lp	s-d	m	vig	
Adélaïde d'Orléans	HP	Pre 1870	Robert	lp	f	l		
Adélaïde Dufrenois	HP	1875	Moreau-Robert	lp	f	vl		
Adélaïde Fontaine	HP	1856	Fontaine	mp	f	l	vig	
Adélaïde Pavie	N			w				
Adèle	G	Pre 1815	Descemet	mp	f	m		
Adèle	P	1828	Prévost	lp		m-l		
Adèle Angeli	HT			pb	f	m		
Adèle Bécart	HCh	1847	Laffay	p	f	l	vig	
Adèle Bernard	N			w	f	m		
Adèle Bougère	HT	1852	Robert	dr	f		m	
Adèle Bourdeau	B	1873	Vigneron	p	f	m	vvig	
Adèle Courtoise	G	Pre 1842		dp	f	m		
Adèle de Bellabre	T	1888	Pernet-Ducher	r & y	f	l	vig	
Adèle Descemet	G	Pre 1814	Descemet					
Adèle de Seringes	C			lp	f	m		
Adèle Dufresnoy	HP	1876	Moreau-Robert	lp	f	vl	vig	
Adèle Fragans	T	1888		ly				f
Adèle Gérard	G			w	f	l		
Adèle Heu	G	1816	Vibert	dp	vdbl	l		m
Adèle Huzart	HP			pb	vdbl	m	vig	
Adèle Jourgant	T		Lédéchaux	y	vdbl	m		
Adèle Jussieu	HP	1853	Robert	pb	f	l	vvig	
Adèle Launay	HP	Pre 1870		dr	f	l		
Adèle Lepetite	G			r	f	l		
Adèle Mauzé	HP	1847	Vibert	lp	f	m		
Adèle Pavie	M	1850	Vibert	lp	dbl	m		
Adèle Pavié	N	1858	Moreau-Robert	pb	f		vig	
Adèle Pellerin	A	1820						
Adèle Perrin	A	1850	Vibert	lp				
Adèle Plantier	B	Pre 1846		dr				
Adèle Pradel	T		syn Madame Maurin	p				
Adèle Prévost	G	Pre 1836	Prévost	lp	f	l	vig	f
Adelina	G		Miellez	p				
Adelina Patti	HP	1878	Fontaine	dp		l	vig	
Adeline	C	1830	Vibert	pb	f		sp	
Adeline	Ch	Pre 1834		w		m		
Adeline	G	Pre 1834		lp	dbl	m		
Adeline Bordeau	Ch			rb				
Adeline Camille	T	Pre 1846		w	f	l		
Adeline de Come	T	Pre 1846		w	f	s	m	
Adieu de Bordier	G			mr	vdbl			
Adine	HT	1897	Guillot P	op	f	l		
Admirable	G	Pre 1787		mr	f			
Admirable Bordé de Rouge	G	1826		w		m		
Admirable Panaché	G	1827	Lecomte syn Comte Foy	lp	dbl	vl		sf
Admiral de Rigny	N	Pre 1844		mp				
Admiral Dewey	HT	1899	Taylor	mr	dbl	l		
Admiral Nelson	HP		see Amiral Nelson	mp	dbl	l	vig	
Admiration	G		Miellez	lp				
Admiration	D		Prévost	lp				
Admiration	HP			dr				
Adolphe	HP			pb	f	m	m	
Adolphe Bossange	HP	1858	Touvais	rb	vdbl	l	wk	
Adolphe Brogniard	M	1868	Margottin	lp	f	m	wk	
Adolphe Cachet	G			mp	f	m		
Adolphe Cachet	HT			mr				
Adolphe Cochet	HT		(? same as above)	mp	vf		m	
Adolphe de Tarlé	T	1889	Tesnier	w		l	vig	f
Adolphe Noblet	HP	1862	Lédéchaux	dr	f	m		
Adolphe Poulain	HP			r				
Adolphe Soupert	HP		see Alphonse Soupert					
Adolphine	T			pb	f	l	m	
Adolphine de Volsange	G	Pre 1848		lp	dbl	m		
Adonis	G	Pre 1814	Descemet	dp	f	m		
Adonis	G	Pre 1829	Vibert	lp	f	m		
Adonis	HP	1835	Verdier V	pb	f	l		
Adrien Brogniard	C			mp	f	m		
Adrien de Jussieu	HP	1853	Robert	pb	f	l	m	
Adrien de Montebello	HP	1868	Margottin	lp	f	m	vig	
Adrien Marx	HP	1865	Granger	mr	f	l	m	
Adrien Schmitt	HP	1881	Schmitt	mr	dbl	l		

Adrienne Christophe	N	1868	Guillot Fils	ab	f	l	vig	
Adrienne de Cardoville	B	1845	Guillot Père	lp	f	m	m	
Adrienne Lecouvreur	HP	1826	Vétillard	lp				
Adrienne Lecouvreur	G	1830	Vibert	mr	f	m		
Adsire	Ch		Laffay	lp				
Aégeria	IIT	1878	Bennett	dr	t	l		
Aennchen von Tharau	HMult	1886	Geschwind	w	dbl	m		
Affre	T			lp	f	l		
Afghan Yellow	HFt	1885	Keer	y			vig	
Afranie	T	Pre 1830	Laffay	w	vdbl	m		
Africaine	M			pb				
Africaine	Ch		Vibert	dr				
Africaine	G	Pre 1838	Prévost	dr	vf	s		
Agamide (Agemede)	G	1836	Vibert	dp	f	m		
Agar	G	1836	Laffay					
Agar	G	1843	Vibert	pb	dbl	m		
Agar	B	1853	Robert	p			vig	
Agatha	G	Pre 1818		lp	dbl	l	vig	f
Agathe	G			lp				
Agathe Abondante	G			dr				
Agathe à Dix Coeurs	G	Pre 1830	Lahaye Père	lp	vf	m		
Agathe Admirable	G	c 1860?	Miellez	p				
Agathe à Feuilles Glauques	G	Pre 1836	Noisette E	dp	f	m		
Agathe Agnes Sorel	G		Miellez	p				
Agathe Agréable	D	Pre 1814	Descemet	mp				
Agathe Agréable	G	c 1860?	Miellez	mp				
Agathe Agrippa	G							
Agathe à la Mode	G			r				
Agathe Albine	D							
Agathe Alibert	D		Laffay					
Agathe Alzire	D			r				
Agathe Amédée	G	1827	Desportes	mp				
Agathe Amélie d'Orléans	G	1825	Cartier	lp				
Agathe Amusante	G	c 1860?	Miellez	mp				
Agathe Anaïs	G	1819	Vibert	m	f			
Agathe Anaïs	G	1827	Noisette	p				
Agathe Anastasia	D	1823	Toutain	dr				
Agathe Anénome Argent	G			dr				
Agathe Angelina	G	1824	Vibert					
Agathe Anna	G	Pre 1840	Vétillard	mp				
Agathe Antilope	G		Vibert	dr				
Agathe Antonia	G	1823	Vibert					
Agathe Archiduchesse Henriette	D							
Agathe Argentine	G	1823	Vibert					
Agathe Aristide	G	1823	Garilland		m			
Agathe Armande	G		Lahaye	dr				
Agathe Aspasie	G	1829	Vibert	dr				
Agathe Athala	G	Pre 1840	Garilland	op				
Agathe Atalante	G	1818	Vibert					
Agathe Augustine Bertin	G	1818	Vibert	lp				
Agathe Azelia	G		Miellez	p				
Agathe Bécourt	G	c 1860	Baumann					
Agathe Boursault	G	1827	Noisette	lp				
		syn	Mlle Boursault					
Agathe Brigitte	G	1821	Vibert	m				
Agathe Carnée	G	Pre 1813		lp				
Agathe Cécile	G	1825	Leroy					
Agathe Chérie	G		Miellez	mr				
Agathe Clarisse	G	1824	Hardy	lp				
Agathe Couronnée	D	c 1811	syn Marie Louise	lp	vdbl	m		
Agathe Crépue du Roi	G			p				
Agathe Crépue du Roi	G			w				
Agathe de Bruxelles	G/C	Pre 1830	Miellez	lp	f	s-m		
		syn	Dchesse d'Angoulème					
Agathe de Constance	G			mp	f	m		
Agathe de Constantine	G			mp				
Agathe de Corne	G			lp	f	l		
Agathe de Couleur de Soie	G	1836	Miellez	lp	f	m		
Agathe de Frankfort	G	Pre 1820		lp	vdbl			
Agathe de la Malmaison	G	Pre 1813	Pelletier	lp	f	m-l		
Agathe de Montmorency	G			w	f	m		
Agathe de Provence	G			lp				
Agathe de Rome	G	1825		lp	vf	m		
Agathe du Brésil	G			lp	vdbl	m		
Agathe Élégante	G	1823	Hardy	lp				
Agathe en Plummet	G	Pre 1836	Miellez	mp	dbl	l		
Agathe Eulalie	G		Miellez	p				
Agathe Fatime	G	Pre 1815	Descemet	dp	dbl			
Agathe Favorite	G	Pre 1834	Prévost	mp	f	s		
Agathe Félicie Boitard	G			lp	f	m		
Agathe Gentilhomme	G		Gentilhomme	p				

Name		Date	Breeder / Synonym					
Agathe Grande	G	Pre 1834		lp				
Agathe Grande Nouvelle	G	Pre 1820	Descemet	lp				
Agathe Hybrida Revoluta	G		Descemet					
Agathe Hyon	G			lp	f	m		
Agathe Incarnata	G	Pre 1811		lp	vdbl	m		vf
Agathe Incomparable	G/C	Pre 1830	Prévost	dp	vf	s		
Agathe Magnifique	G	Pre 1830	Lahaye Père	dp	vf	m		
			syn Jeanne Gray					
Agathe Majestueuse	D	Pre 1830	syn Le Triomphe (D)	lp	f	m		
Agathe Manchette	D	Pre 1830		mp	vf	m		
Agathe Marie Louise	G/C	Pre 1830	Miellez	lp	f	s-m		
		syn	Dchesse d'Angoulème	lp				
Agathe Nankin Derlin	G			mp	f	m		
Agathe Nouvelle	G	Pre 1814	Descemet	lp	f	m-l		vf
			syn Nouvelle Héloïse					
Agathe Ombrée	G	Pre 1830	Lahaye Père	dp	vf	m		
			syn Jeanne Gray					
Agathe Petite Agathe	G	syn	Renoncule Violette	dr				
Agathe Porcelaine	G	Pre 1830	Prévost	lp	vf	s		
Agathe Précieuse	G/C	1827	Miellez	lp	f	s-m		
		syn	Dchesse d'Angoulème					
Agathe Prolifère	G	Pre 1820	Prévost	mp	f	s		
Agathe Pyramidale Agréable	G		Robert	mp	f	m		
Agathe Rose	D	c 1811	syn Marie-Louise	lp	vdbl	m		
Agathe Rose	G	1823	Hardy	lp				
Agathe Royale	G	1817	Godefroy	mp	f	s	vig	
Agathe Sommesson	D	Pre 1830	Pelletier	lp	f	s		
Agathe Toujours Verte	HCan	Pre 1830	Prévost	lp	vdbl	s		
Agathe Volumineuse	D			lp				
Agathoïde	HP	1860	Lebreton	pb	f	l	vig	
Agénor	G	1832	Vibert	m	f	m		
Agénor	B	1852	Robert	rb	f	m		
Aglaée Adanson	G/C	1823	Vibert	lp	f	m		
Aglaée Adanson	HP	1852	Robert	lp	f		vig	
Aglaée de Marcilly	G	1822	Vibert	lp	vf	m		
Aglaée Loth	T	Pre 1846		w	f	s		
Aglaia	C	Pre 1811	Descemet (?)	lp	f			m
Aglaia	G	Pre 1813		lp				
Aglaia	HMult	1895	Schmitt	ly	dbl	m	vig	vf
			syn Yellow Rambler					
Agmète	G			lp	f	m		
Agnes Emily Carman	HRg	1898	Carman	mr	dbl	l	vig	
Agnes Sorel	G/C	1833	Vibert	lp	f	l		
Agnodice	G	1820	Vibert	dr	f	m		
Agnodice	M			lp				
Agréable	A			w				
Agremont	G	Pre 1846		mp				
Agrippina	Ch	1832	Coquereau	mr	dbl	s	vig	
		syn	Cramoisi Supérieur					
Ahasuerus	G/C	Pre 1848		dr				
Ahaverus	HP	1862	Granger	dr	dbl	l	m	
			syn Le Juif Errant					
Aigle Bleu	G	Pre 1830		rb				
Aigle Brun	G	Pre 1811	Godefroy	dr	dbl	m		
Aigle Brun Maculé	G	Pre 1830	Coquerel	dr	s-d	l		
			syn Grande Maculée					
Aigle de Meaux	T			lp	f	m		
Aigle de Prusse	G	Pre 1830	syn La Veuve (2)	pb	f	m		
Aigle du Sérail	G			dr	f	m		
Aigle Noir	G	1818	Godefroy	dr	dbl	m		
			syn Aigle Brun					
Aimable Amie	G	Pre 1813	Trianon	dp	dbl	m		f
Aimable Eléonore	G/C	Pre 1828	Coquerel	dp	f	m		
Aimable Emma	G	Pre 1830	Calvert	pb	vdbl	l		
			syn Clémence Isaure					
Aimable Étrangère	HSpn	1819	Vibert	w	dbl	m	vig	
Aimable Fanny	G			dp	f	m		
Aimable Félicie	T	1858	Lutz	pb	f	l	vig	
Aimable Félix	A	Pre 1830	Jacques	w				
Aimable Henriette	G	1842	Vibert	dp	f	m		
Aimable Hortense	G	Pre 1830	Vibert syn Hortense	lp	f	m		
Aimable Lieutot	G			p	f	m		
Aimable Pourpre	G	Pre 1811		dr		m		
Aimable Queen	G	Pre 1848		dr	vdbl	m	vig	
Aimable Rose	G	1819	Vibert	p		m		
Aimable Rosette	HSpn			p				
Aimable Rouge	G	1817	Vibert	dp	vdbl	m	m	m
Aimable Rouge	G	Pre 1820	Godefroy	mp	f	m		
Aimable Sophie	G	Pre 1830	Vibert	lp	s-d	l		
			syn Clémence Isaure					
Aimable Tastu	G	Pre 1848		m	vf			
Aimable Tastu	M	1851	Robert	rb	f		vvig	

Name	Class	Date	Raiser / syn					
Aimable Violette	G							
Aimable Virginie	G			lp	f	m		
Aimée	G	1823	Vibert	rb	f	m		
Aimée Belle Violette	N			rb	vdbl	s		
Aimée Desprez	N	c 1830	Desprez	dr	f	s		
Aimée Plantier	T			ab	s-d	m		
Aimée Roman	G	Pre 1830	Prévost	dr	vf	m		
Aimée Vibert	N	1828	Vibert	w	dbl	m	vig	vf
Aimée Vibert, Climbing	N	1841	Curtis	w	dbl	m	vig	vf
Aimée Vibert à Feuilles Marginées	N	1878	Schwartz	w				
Ainé	N	Pre 1846						
Aïxa	M	Pre 1870	Laffay	lp	f	m		
Ajax	T	1852	Oger	y	f	m	vig	
Alain Blanchard	G/C	Pre 1830	Coquerel / Vibert	m	s-d	l	vig	f
Alba	C	Pre 1775		w	f	l		
Alba	M		syn White Bath	w				
Alba	Bks	1807	Keer	w	f	vs		f
Alba	HCh	Pre 1846		w	dbl	m	m	
Alba	T	1863	Pradel	w				
Alba	HMult	1888		w	vdbl	s		
Alba Bifera	P	Pre 1830	Mauget	lp	vdbl	m		
Alba Bifera	A	1843	Augeul	w	vf			
Alba Carnea	HP	1867	Touvais syn Maiden's Blush	lp	f	m	vig	
Alba Floribunda	HP	1869	Touvais	pb	f	m	vig	
Alba Foliacea	A	1824		w	vf	m		
Alba Grandiflora	Bks	Pre 1846		w		vl		
Alba Hybrida cum Bifera	D	Pre 1830	Vibert syn Petite Lisette (Vib)	lp	vdbl	m		
Alba Hybrida Glaucophylla	A	Pre 1830	Godefroy syn Centfeuilles de Hesse	lp	f	s		
Alba Inermis	A		Noisette	w			vig	
Alba Italica	D			w	dbl	m		
Alba Maxima	A	Pre 1596		w	dbl	l	vig	m
Alba Monstrualis	M			w	f	l		
Alba Mutabilis	HP	1866	Verdier E	pb	vf	l	vig	
Alba Nova	M			w	vf	m		
Alba Nove Celestis	A	Pre 1830	Vibert	w	f	m		
Alba Odorata	HBc	1834	Mariani	w	f	l		m
Alba Odorata	HBc	1875	Levet	w		l		
Alba Perpetue	HP		Moulins	w	f	m		
Alba Plena	T			w	f	m		
Alba Plena	HSem	1861	Freundlich	w	f			
Alba Plena	D			w				
Alba Regia	A	Pre 1830	Prévost	lp	f	m		
Alba Regia Aureata	G			pb				
Alba Rosea	A	Pre 1810	syn Celestial	lp	dbl	l	vig	
Alba Rosea	A	Pre 1813	syn Beauté Tendre	lp	f	vl		
Alba Rosea	T	1862	Lartay / Schwartz syn Mme Bravy	w	f	l	vig	f
Alba Rosea Carnea	T			lp	vdbl	m	vig	
Alba Rubigens	A	Pre 1830		lp	vdbl	m		
Alba Sauveolens	A	Pre 1750		w	s-d			
Alba Scandens	T			w	s	m		
Alba Semi-plena	A	Pre 1596		w	s-d	m		vf
Alba Simplex	HBc	1888		w	s	l	vig	
Alba Subviridis	G			lp				
Alba Venusta	HBc			w				
Alba Victoria	A	Pre 1830	Mauget	w	f	s	vig	
Alba Vix Bifera	P	Pre 1830	Mauget / Vibert syn Alba Bifera	lp	vdbl	m		
Alba White	Ch			w		s		vf
Albanne d'Arneville	N	1885	Schwartz	lp	f	m	vig	
Albert de Stella	HP	1858	Guillot Père	mr		m	vig	
Albert de Stella	HP			w	f	l		
Albert Dureau	HP	1869	Vigneron	dr		l		
Albert Fourès	T	1899	Bonnaire	rb	f	l	vig	
Albert la Blotais	HP	1881	Moreau-Robert	dr	dbl	m	vig	f
Albert la Blotais, Climbing	Cl HP	1888	Pernet	mr	vdbl	l		
Albert Payé	HP	1873	Touvais	lp	f	l	vig	
Albert Stopford	T	1899	Nabonnand	lp				
Albertine	G	1827	Prévost	mp	dbl	m		
Albertine Borguet	T	1894	Soupert	yb				
Albida	C			w	f	m		
Albion	HP	1870	Liabaud	mr	f	l	vig	
Albion	T			w	f	m		
Albo Novo Pleno	Misc	Pre 1846						
Alboni	HP	1851	Foulard	mp				
Alcibiade	G			mp	f	m		
Alcide Vigneron	HP	1862	Vigneron	w	f	l		
Alcime	G	1845	Vibert	m				

Alcime	M	1861	Robert & Moreau	mr	f	m		
Alcina	M		Vibert	dp	f	l	vig	
Alcindor	HP	1863	Lartay	pb	f	l	m	
		syn	Belle du Printemps					
Alcine	G	1834	Vibert	dp	dbl	l	vig	
Alcine	Ch	Pre 1846		dr				f
Alcione	G	1826	Descemet	p		l		
Aldégonde	G	1817	Godefroy	m	f	m		
			syn Rouge Formidable					
Aldégonde	G	Pre 1820	Vibert	lp	f	m		
Aldégonde	G			dr				
Alector Cramoisi	G	Pre 1811	Dupont	dr	dbl	l		m
Alette	G/C	1845	Vibert	lp	f	l		
Alexander Dickson	HP	1873	Dickson	dr	f	l	vig	
Alexandre Breton	HP	1858	Touvais	dr	f	m	vig	
Alexandre Chatry	G			dr		l		
Alexandre Chomer	HP	1875	Liabaud	dr	f	l	vig	
Alexandre Damaizin	HP	1861	Damaizin	dr				
Alexandre de Humboldt	HP	1869	Verdier Ch	lp	f	l	vig	f
Alexandre Delmas	M		see Alfred de Dalmas					
Alexandre Dumas	HP	1861	Margottin	dr	dbl	m		
Alexandre Dunant	HP		Margottin	lp				
Alexandre Dupont	HP	1892	Liabaud	dr	dbl	vl	vig	
Alexandre Dutitre	HP	1878	Lévêque	lp	f	l	vig	
Alexandre Feodorowna	HP			lp	f	s		
Alexandre Fontaine	HP	1861	Fontaine	dp	f	l		
Alexandre Laquement	G	Pre 1885		m	f	m		vf
Alexandre Lemaire	HT	1897	Godard	y				
Alexandre Pelletier	B	1880	Duval H	dp	f	m	vig	
Alexandre Rohan	T			lp	f	m		
Alexandrine	G			dr				
Alexandrine Bacmeteff	HP	1852	Margottin	mr	f	l	vig	
Alexandrine Bruel	T	1885	Levet Père	w				
Alexandrine de Belfroy	HP	1859	Fontaine	op	f	vl		
Alexina	HP	1854	Lartay	lp		m		
Alexina	Ch	Pre 1846	Beluze	w	vf	l		
Alexis Galtier	HP			p				
Alexis Lepère	HP	1875	Vigneron	mr	dbl	vl		
Alfieri	G	1833	Vibert	m	f	m		
Alfieri	T			mr	f	m		
Alfred Aubert	Ch			dr			vig	
Alfred Colomb	HP	1852	Ducher	dr	f	l	vig	
Alfred Colomb	HP	1865	Lacharme	dp	f	l	vig	vf
Alfred Daney	M	1888	Bernède	lp				
Alfred de Dalmas	M	1855	Laffay	lp	dbl	s	vig	f
Alfred de Rougemont	HP	1863	Lacharme	dr	f	vl	vig	
Alfred Dubois	HP		see Alphée Dubois					
Alfred Dumesnil	HP	1879	Margottin Fils	rb	f	l		f
Alfred K Williams	HP	1877	Schwartz J	mr	f	l	vig	
Alfred Leveau	HP	1880	Vigneron	mp	f	l	vig	
Ali Pacha Chériff	HP	1886	Lévêque	mr	f	l	vvig	
Ali Pacha Shériff	M		Parmentier	rb				
Alice	B			mp	f	l		
Alice	A	c 1830	Parmentier	w	f	m		
Alice	HCh			lp				
Alice Aldrich	HRg	1899	Lovett	lp	dbl	l		
Alice Dureau	HP	Pre 1870		dp	f	l	vig	
Alice Fontaine	B	1879	Fontaine	op	f	m	m	f
Alice Furon	HT	Pre 1899		w		l	vig	
Alice Gray	Ayr	Pre 1804	see Scandens	w	s-d		m	vf
Alice Hoffmann	Ch	1897	Hoffmann	rb	f	m		
Alice Lafite	HP	1853	Pradel	lp	f	l		
Alice Lavenant	HP	Pre 1870		mp	f	m		
Alice Leroy	M	1842	Vibert	pb	dbl	vl	vig	
Alice Vena	G	Pre 1827		m				
Alice Vibert	M	1855	Robert	mp	f	m		
Alice Vigneron	HP		see Alcide Vigneron					
Aline	Ch		Laffay	dr	s-d			
Aline	T		Vibert	p	vf	m-l		
Aline	G	1816	Vibert	w	f	m		
Aline	Ch			dr	vdbl	s		
Aline de Beaulieu	B			p	vdbl	m		
Aline de Beauvalon	HP	1879		lp				
Aline Gibbon	HP	1853	Laffay	mp				
Aline Pierron	B	1858	Guillot Père	w	vf	m	vig	
Aline Rozey	N	1884	Schwartz	lp	f	m	vvig	
Aline Sisley	T	1874	Guillot Fils	dr	f	l	vig	
Alister Stella Gray	N	1894	Gray A H	ly	f		vig	f
Alix	G	Pre 1830	Sommesson	lp	f	vl		
			syn Diadème de Flore					
Alliance Franco-Russe	T	1899	Goinard	my	dbl	l	vig	
Alloa	HSpn	Pre 1846						

Name	Type	Date	Raiser					
Alpaïde de Rotalier	HP	1863	Campy	lp	f	l	vig	
Alpenfee	HSet	1890	Geschwind	lp	vdbl	m		
Alphée Dubois	HP	1881	Fontaine	rb		m-l	vvig	vf
			syn Préfet Limbourg					
Alphonse Bélin	HP	1863	Gautreau	mr	f	l		
Alphonse Damaizin	HP	1861	Damaizin	rb	f	m	m	
Alphonse de Coster	G			rb	f	m		
Alphonse de Lamartine	HP	1853	Ducher	lp	f	m	m	
Alphonse de Lamartine	G			lp	f	m		
Alphonse Fontaine	HP	1868	Fontaine	mp	f	l	vig	
Alphonse Karr	HP	1845	Portemer	dr				
Alphonse Karr	HP	1847	Feuillet	lp	vf	l		
Alphonse Karr	HP	Pre 1870	Cherpin	mp	f	l		
Alphonse Karr	HP	1878	Nabonnand	rb	vdbl	l		
Alphonse Karr	T	1878	Nabonnand G	m	dbl	l	vig	f
Alphonse Maille	HCh	1825	Boutigny	dr	f	l	vig	
Alphonse Maille	HT	1830	Laffay	mp				
Alphonse Maille	B	Pre 1899		mr	f	l	vig	
Alphonse Mortelsmans	T	1876	Ducher Vve	pb	f	l		
Alphonse Soupert	HP	1883	Lacharme	mp	dbl	l	vvíg	m
Alphonsine	G	1824	Laffay	pb	f	m		
Alsace-Lorraine	HP	1879	Duval	dr	f	l		f
			syn Directeur Alphand					
Altaïca	HSpn	c 1820	Bean	w	vdbl	s		
		syn	r.spinossisima altaica					
Altesse Impériale	HP	1858	Damaizin	rb	f	m	vig	
Althéer	C			mr	f	m		
Althénor	G			m	f	m		
Altonia	Sp	1835		mp	s-d			
Alupka	N	Pre 1900		w	dbl	m		m
Alvarez	G	Pre 1848		dr	f	m		
Alzais	B	Pre 1846						
Alzand	N	Pre 1846						
Alzina	B	Pre 1846						
Alzina	M	1860	Robert & Moreau	mp	f	l		
Alzine	HCh			dp	f	m		
Alzonde	N		Laffay	w	vf	s		
Amasilis	Ch	Pre 1820		w				
Amabilis	G	Pre 1845		m	f			
Amabilis	T	c 1850	Robert	mp				
Amabilis	T	1856	Touvais	mp	f	l	vig	
Amabilis	T	1857	Lartay	mp	f	l		
AmableM 1851 Robertrb								
Tastu								
Amable Tastu	G			dr				
Amadis	HMult			rb				
Amadis	HCh		Laffay	rb	vdbl	l		
Amadis	Bslt	1829	Laffay	dr	s-d	l	vig	
Amanda	G	1830	Vibert	lp	f	m		
Amanda Casado	T	1891	Pries	y				
Amanda Patenotte	P	1845	Vibert	mp	f	l		
Amandine	HP	1846	Vibert	dp	f	l		
Amarante	Ch		Laffay	dr	f	m		
Amarante	G			mr	f	m		
Amarante	B	1859	Page	dr	f	m		
Amarantine	B	Pre 1846		dr				
Amarelle	D			rb	f	s		
Amaryllis	G	1818						
Amazone	T	1873	Ducher	my	f	l	vig	f
Ambassadeur	G		Miellez	dr	vf	l		
Ambrogio Maggi	HP	1879	Pernet Fils	mp	dbl	vl	vig	
Ambroise Paré	G	1846	Vibert	m	dbl	m	vig	f
Ambroise Paré	T	1865	Moreau-Robert	lp		l	vig	
Ambroise Verschaffelt	HP	1858	Vindrin	dr	f	l	vig	
Ambuchetet	HSpn			lp	s	m		
Amédée	T			mp	f	l		vf
Amédée	G	1827	Desportes	mp				
Amédée de Langlois	B	1872	Vigneron	m	f	m		
Amédée Fouquier	T			pb				
Amédée Philibert	HP	1879	Lévêque	m	f	vl	vvig	
Amélia	A	1823	Vibert	mp	dbl	l		f
Amélia	G	Pre 1830	Prévost	mp	vdbl	m-l		
Amelie	Ch	Pre 1834		w		s		
Amélie de la Chapelle	B	1870	Jamain H	lp	f	l		
Amélie de Mansfield	G	Pre 1842		mp	dbl	m		
Amélie de Marsilly	A	1818	Vibert	lp				
Amélie d'Orléans	G	1825	Cartier	dp	s-d	l		
Amélie Guerin	HCh	1830	Vibert	w		m		
Amélie Halfen	HP		see Emilie Halphen	dp	f	l		
Amélie Hoste	HP	1874	Gonod	lp	f	l	vig	

Name	Class	Date	Breeder					
Amélie Laxton	HP	see	Mlle Emélie Laxton					
Amélie Mountclare	M	1862	Moreau & Robert	lp	f	m	vig	
Amélie Polonnais	T	1896	Nabonannd	mp	f	l		
Amélie Suzanne Morin	Pol	1899	Soupert and Notting	w		m	vig	vf
Amélie Tastu	G		see Amable Tastu	rb	f	m		
Aménaïde	B	Pre 1846	Robert	lp	f	m		
Amenia	N	Pre 1846						
America	N	1859	Page	ly	f	vl	vig	f
America	HRg	1894	Garđen / Paul & Son	mr	s	l	vig	
American Banner	T	1879	Cartwright	pb	s-d	s		
American Beauty	HP	1875	Lédéchaux	dp	f	l	vig	f
		syn	Mme Ferdinand Jamin					
American Beauty	HP	1886	Henderson	dr		vl		f
American Belle	HP	1893	Burton J	mp				
American Roseate	HEg	c 1840	Prince Nursery	dp	s-d		vig	
American White	HEg	c 1840	Prince Nursery	w	s-d		vig	
Améthyste	HCh			mr	vf	m		
Ami Aminta	G	Pre 1814	Descemet					
Ami Derair	G			rb	f	m		
Ami Devostre	HCh			rb	f	m		
Ami Stécher	T	1899	Weber	dr		l	vig	
Aminta	G	Pre 1834	Descemet					
Amiral Avellan	HP	1893	Lévêque	mr				
Amiral Cécile	HP	1850	Debeaumont	m	f	m-l		m
Amiral Coligny	G			lp	f	l		
Amiral Courbet	HP	1884	Dubreuil	mr	f	m	vig	vf
Amiral de Joinville	HP	1885	Verdier E	rb	f	l	vvig	f
Amiral de Rigny	Ch	Pre 1830	Laffay	lp	vf	s		
Amiral de Rigny	G	1827	Noisette L	w	vdbl		vig	
Amiral d'Estaing	HP	1846		pb				
Amiral Duperré	Ch	Pre 1834		dr	f	s		
Amiral Gravina	HP	1860	Moreau-Robert	m	f	m		
Amiral Lapéyrouse	HP	1863	Guillot Fils	rb	f	l	vig	
Amiral Nelson	HP	1859	Ducher	mp	dbl	l	vig	
Amiral Seymour	HP	1882	Verdier E	rb	f	l	vig	
Amitié	D	Pre 1813	Stegerhock/Dupont	lp	s-d	l		
			syn L'Amitié					
Amneris	HMult	1890	Geschwind	lp				
Amœna	T			mp	f	m		
Amœna	HP	1878	Soupert & Notting	rb	f	l	vig	
Amour des Dames	T	1851	Lartay	mp	f	m		
Amourette	B	Pre 1846		mp		s		
Amourette	Ch			mp		l		
Amoureuse	G	Pre 1830	Vibert	mp	vdbl	l		
Amphitrion	G			mr	f	m		
Amphirtite	G	Pre 1830	Vibert	mp	f	l		
Amphitrite	C	Pre 1834		lp		l		
Amphitrite	Ch	1853	Robert	m	f	m		
Amphytrite	Ch		Laffay	m				
Amurensis	Sp			mp	s-d	l		
Amy Robsart	HEg	1894	Penzance	dp	s-d	l	vig	f
Anacréon	G	1828	Vibert	mp	vdbl	m-l		f
Anacréon	HP	1854	Robert	rb	f	l		
Anacréon	HP	1876	Schwartz	dr				
Anaïs	HSpn	1823	Bizard	dp				
Anaïs	G	1829	Vibert	lp	f	s		
Anaïs	B			mp				
Anaïs Segalas	G	1837	Vibert	pb	dbl	l	vig	m
Ananas	Ch	Pre 1830	Calvert syn Ternaux	rb	vdbl	m		
Anarelle	D	1819	Vibert	mr	f	s		
Anarelle	G/C	Pre 1834		p		l		
Anastasia	D	1823	Toutain	mr				
Anastasie	Rbf	Pre 1830	Vibert	mr	f	m		
Anathalie Chantrier	HP	1854	Cherpin	w	f	m		vf
Anatole	G	1827	Noisette L	mr	vf	m		
Anatole de Montesquieu	N	1830	Jacques	m	f	m		
Anatole de Montesquieu	HSem	Pre 1852	Van Houtte	w	vdbl	s		
Ancelin	G	1829	Noisette E	dp	dbl	vl	vvig	
Ancelin	A			dr	f	l		
Ancien	HMac	Pre 1870		dy	dbl	ll		
Ancien	N		Dubreuil	dr				
Ancien Diadême de Flore	G		Vibert	pb	f	m-l		
Anderson's Double Lady's Blush	HSpn	c 1810	Anderson G	ly				
Andor	HMult	1890	Geschwind	dp				
André	G			rb	f	m		
André Chénier	HP	1851	Robert	m	f	m		
André de Garnier de Garets	HT	1899	Buatois	pb		m		
André Desmoulins	HP	1899	Lévêque	lp				
André Desportes	HP	1862	Standish	mr	f	m		
André Desportes	HP	1876		rb		l		
André Durand	HP	1871	Schwartz	lp	f	l	vig	

André Fouquier	G			mr	vf	l		
André Fresnoy	HP	1868	Pernet Père	rb	f	vl	m	
André Gille	HP	1883	Verdier E	rb	f	l	vig	f
André Leroy	HP	1860	Pradel	lp	f	l	vig	f
André Leroy d'Angers	HP	1866	Trouillard	mr	f	l	vig	
		syn Souvenir	dc Louis van Houtte					
André Nabonnand	T	1879	Nabonnand	dp	vdbl	l	vig	
André Schwartz	T	1883	Schwartz J	mr		m	vig	f
André Sibourg	T	1894	Reboul	pb				
André Thouin	T			lp	f	l		
André Thouin	G	Pre 1834	Prévost	rb	dbl	m		
André Thouin	M	1852	Robert	m	f	m		
André Vilnat	HP	1863		m	f	l		
Andrecelle	N	Pre 1846		lp	f	m		
Andrewsii	M	Pre 1806		mp	dbl	m		
Andrieux	B	1828	Vibert	dp		m		
Andromaque	G	1816	Vibert	mp	f	l		
Andromaque	C	1819	Vibert syn Arthémise	lp	dbl	m		
Andromaque	G	Pre 1839	Hardy	dp	vdbl	l		
Andromaque	M	1864	Moreau-Robert	lp				
Anemœniflora	Bks	Pre 1860		w			vig	
Anemonaeflora (Climbing)	HSem	1860	Van Houtte	w	f	s	vig	
			syn La Chinoise					
Anemonaeflora	Ch	1845	Lindley	w	f	s		
Anemonaeflora de Chine	HArv		Van Houtte	w	f	s		
Anémone	M	1824	Lemeusnier	dr				
			syn De La Flèche					
Anémone	T	1827	Péan	p				
Anémone	M	1844	Mauget	mp	dbl			
Anemone	G	Pre 1846		lp				
Anemone	S	1895	Schmidt J C	lp	s	l	vig	f
Anémone Ancienne	G	1825	Godefroy	lp	vdbl	s		
Anémone Argentée	G	Pre 1826	Barrier	m				
Anémone Cramoisie	Ch		Laffay	pb	dbl	s		
Anémone du Luxembourg	G		Hardy	dr	f	m		
Anémone Olry	HCh	1826	Mme Olry	p				
Anémone Rose	Ch		Laffay	p				
Anémone Sanguinea	M	1840	Vibert	pb	f	m		
Anémone Thea Rosa	T			p	f	m		
Anemonoides	C	1814	Poilpre	mr				
Angela Desportes	HP							
Angèle	D	Pre 1846		lp	vdbl	vl		
Angèle Fontaine	HP	1878	Fontaine	lp	f	m-l	vig	
Angèle Jacquier	T	1879	Guillot Fils	pb	f	l	vig	vf
Angèle Mousseuse	M	1853	Laffay	lp		l		
Angelica Minor	A			w	dbl			
Angelina	G	1824	Vibert	dp	f	m		
Angelina Granger	HP	1850	Granger	dr	f	l		
Angélique	G	c 1820	Descemet	mr	vf	l		
Angélique	A			rb	vf	l		
Angélique Quétier	M	1839	Quétier	lp	f	m	vig	
Angevin	Ch			w				
Angevine	N		Buret	w				
Angiola	HSem	1833	Vibert	w		m		
Angiola	G/C	1846	Vibert	w	f	m		
Anglaise	Misc	Pre 1830	Vibert	lp	dbl	m		
			syn Courtney					
Angle	Ayr	Pre 1848		lp	s-d	l		
Anicet Bourgeois	HP	1880	Moreau-Robert	mr	f	l	vig	
Animating	Ch	1817	Boursault	mp	f	m		f
			syn Bengale Animée					
Anisette	T			w				
Anna	Ch		Laffay	pb	f	s		
Anna Alexieff	HP	1858	Margottin	mp	dbl	l	vig	
Anna Benary	Pol			lp	f	s		
Anna Blanchon	HP	1875	Liabaud	dp	f	l	vig	
Anna Chartron	T	1896	Vve Schwartz	w		l	vig	
Anna Czartoriska	G	1845	Vibert	pb	f	l		
Anna de Bretagne	Ch			mp				
Anna de Diesbach	HP	1857	Lacharme	dp	vdbl	vl	vig	vf
Anna de Melun	HP	1849	Vibert	dp	f	m		
Anna Gerval	HP							
Anna Geschwind	HP	1882	Geschwind	lp	dbl			
Anna Maria	HSet	1843	Feast syn Anne Marie	dp	dbl	l		
Anna Moreau	HP	1884	Moreau-Robert	lp	vf	vl	vvig	
Anna Olivier	T	1872	Ducher	pb	f	l	vig	f
Anna Scharsach	HP	1890	Geschwind	mp	dbl	l		vf
Anna von Baden	G			lp	f	l		
Ännchen von Tharau	HMult	1886	Geschwind	w	vdbl			m
Anne Béluze	Ch/B	Pre 1846	Béluze	pb	l	m		
Anne de Boleyn	G	1829	Girardon	lp	s-d	l		
Anne de Bretagne	Ch	Pre 1836	Laffay	mp	dbl	m		

Name	Type	Year	Breeder					
Anne de Bretagne	HP	1849	Vibert	lp	f	l		
Anne Marie	HSet	1843	Feast	dp	dbl	l		
Anne-Marie Côte	N	1875	Guillot Fils	w	s-d	m	vvig	
Anne Marie Danloux	B	1877	Vigneron	w	f	m		
Anne-Marie de Montravel	Pol	1879	Rambaux Vve	w	dbl	s	m	f
Anne of Geierstein	HEg	1894	Penzance	dr	s	m	vig	m
Annette Gusel	Ch			w	dbl	m		
Annette Murat	T	1885	Levet Père	y			vvig	
Annette Séaut	T	1870	Levet	ob	f	l	vig	
Annie Cook	T	1888	Cook J	rb				
Annie Laxton	HP	1869	Laxton	mp	vdbl	m	vig	
Annie Vibert	N	Pre 1871	Vibert	w		m		m
Annie Wood	HP	1867	Verdier E	mr	dbl	l	vig	vf
			syn Mlle Annie Wood					
Anomalia	B	1838	Bizard	mp	f	m		
Ansegise	B	Pre 1846		lp				
Anténor	G		Parmentier	dp	f	l		
Anthéros	HP	1839	Lepage	mp		l		
Anthéros	T	Pre 1846		yb	f	l		
Antigone	G	1818	Vibert	lp	f	m		
Antigone	HP	Pre 1870	Vibert	lp	f	l		
Antinoüs	HP			dr	f	l		
Antinoüs	B	Pre 1846		dp	s	m		
Antione	G			pb	f	m		
Antiope	G	Pre 1815	Descemet	pb	f	m		
Antiope	HCh	1826	Vibert	dr	vdbl	m		
Antoine	N	Pre 1834		w		l		
Antoine Alléon	HP	1879	Damaizin	mr	f	l	vig	
Antoine Castel	HP	1873	Verdier E	pb	f	m		
Antoine Chantin	HP	1882	Verdier E	rb	f	l	vig	
Antoine Devert	T	1880	Gonod	w	f	l	vig	
Antoine Ducher	HP	1866	Ducher	dp	f	l	vig	f
Antoine Gaunet	T	1892	Reboul	dp				
Antoine Mercier	T	1853	Pradel	lp	f	m		
Antoine Mermet	T	1883	Guillot Fils	mp	f	l	vig	vf
Antoine Mouton	HP	1874	Levet	mp	s-d	vl	vvig	vf
Antoine Quihou	HP	1879	Verdier E	m	f	l	vvig	
Antoine Rivoire	HP	1889	Liabaud	rb				
Antoine Rivoire	HT	1895	Pernet-Ducher	lp	dbl	l	vig	f
Antoine Schurz	HP	1882	Geschwind	lp	vdbl	vl		m
Antoine Verdier	HP	1871	Jamain	pb	dbl	l	m	
Antoine Weber	T	1899	Weber	mp	dbl	l		
Antoine Wintzer	HP	1884	Verdier E	mr	f	l	vig	
Antoinette	A	Pre 1826	Descemet	w	f	m		
			syn Alba Victoria					
Antoinette Bouvagne	T	1842	Béluze	w	f	l		
Antoinette Cuillerat	Ch	1898	Buatois	w	s-d	l	vig	
Antoinette d'Orgot	Ch			w	f	m		
Antoinette Durieu	T	1890	Godard	dy				
Antonia	B			w	vdbl	m	vig	
Antonia	N			y	f	m		
Antonia Decarli	T		Levet	ob	f	m		
Antonia d'Ormois	G	1835	Vibert	lp	f	m	vig	f
Antonine	Ch	1830	Vibert	lp		s		
Antonine	N	Pre 1846		y	vdbl			
Antonine Verdier	N			y				
Antonine Verdier	HT	1872	Jamain	lp	f	l		
Apaïde de Rotailler	HP	Pre 1870		lp	f	l		
Apeta	M			dr				
Aphrodite	G	Pre 1838	Noisette L	rb	f	m		
Aphrodite	Ch		Laffay	lp				
Apolline	B	1848	Verdier V	mp	f	l	vvig	
Apolline	Ch			p	f	m		
Apolline Laffay	N		Laffay	lp	f	m		
Apollon	G	Pre 1848	Robert	dr	f	l		
			syn Superbe Cramoisie					
Apollonie	N	Pre 1830	Laffay					
Apothecary's Rose	G	Pre 1600		dp	s-d			vf
Apple Blossom	HMult	1890	Dawson	lp				
Apples	HRg	1896	Paul G	r				
Arabella	T			w	f	m		
Arabelle	N		Verdier C	lp	f	m		
Aramis	G	1845	Vibert	pb	f	m		
Aramis	B	1849	Boyau	dp	dbl	m		
Arance de Navarre	T	Pre 1846		lp	f	m		
Archduke Charles	Ch		see Archiduc Charles					
Archevêque de Besançon	G/Ch	Pre 1848		pb	f	l		
Archevêque de Cambrai	B	1851	Guillot	dr	f	m		
Archevêque de Malines	G	1825		pb	f	m		
Archevêque de Paris	HP	1862	Touvais	rb	vdbl	m		
Archidamie	G	1825	Hardy	dr	f	l		
Archiduc Charles	G	Pre 1830	Vibert / Noisette L	lp	vdbl	l		

Name	Type	Year	Breeder	Color	Fullness	Size	Vigour	Fragrance
			syn Clémence Isaure					
Archiduc Charles	Ch	Pre 1837	Laffay	rb	f	vl		m
Archiduc Joseph	T	1892	Nabonnand G	pb			vvig	
Archiduchesse Dorothée	G			dr	f	l		
Archiduchesse Elisabeth d'Autriche	HP	1881	Moreau-Robert	mp	dbl	vl	vvig	f
Archiduchesse Elisabeth-Marie	Pol	1898	Soupert & Notting	ly	f	m	vig	vf
Archiduchesse Maria Immaculata	T	1887	Soupert & Notting	mr	f	l		f
Archidsse Marie-Dorothée-Amélie	HT	1892	Balogh	yb				
		syn	Erzherzogin Marie-Do	rothea				
Archiduchesse Marie Marguerite	HT	1889	Balogh	dp	f	l		
Archiduchesse Thérèse-Isabelle	T	1834	Barbot	w	f	l		
Archimède	HP	1852	Laffay	w	vdbl	m		
Archimède	T	1855	Robert	mp	f	l	vig	f
Arctic Rose	Sp	1805	Lindley	dp			vig	m
			syn r.acicularis					
Ardoisée	G	Pre 1834		dr	dbl	l		
Ardoisée de Châtelet	HP	1865	Verdier E	dr	f	l		
Ardoisée de Lyon	HP	1858	Damaizin	m	f	vl	vig	f
Ards Rover	Cl HP	1898	Dickson A	dr	dbl	l		vf
Aréthuse	G	1819	Vibert	dp	f	s-m		
Aréthuse	Ch		Laffay	lp				
Aréthuse	M	1852	Robert	mp	f	l		
Argentea	Pom			w	dbl	m		
Argentea	D			w		m		
Argentée	Ch		Laffay	m	dbl	m		
Argentée	HSpn			w				
Argentée	C			lp	vdbl			sf
Argentée	D	Pre 1811	see Centflles Argentée	lp	vdbl	s		
Argentine	G	1823	Vibert					
Argus	G			dp	f	m		
Ariadne	G	1828	Vibert syn below?	mr		m		
Ariane	G	1818	Vibert	mr	f	m		
Ariane	A	1818	Vibert					
Ariane de Vibert	G	c 1835	Vibert	dp	vf	vl		
Aricia	G			pb	f	l	vvig	
Aricie	G	1826	Vibert	dr	f	m-l		
Aricie	HP	1839	Plantier	lp	f	l		
Ariel	G	Pre 1848		pb	f	m		
Ariel	N			lp	f	m		
Arielle	P	1845	Vibert	lp	f	s		
Aristide	G	1823	Garilland	m				
Aristide	N	1857	Robert	ly	f	l		
		Syn	Mademoiselle Aristide					
Aristide	M	Pre 1870		mr	f	m		
Aristide Dupuy	HP	1866	Trouillard	dp	f	l	vig	
Aristides	B	Pre 1846		lp				
Aristides	HSpn	1888		w				
Aristobule	M	1849	Foulard	dp	f	l		
Arkinto	T	Pre 1846		lp		l		
Arlequin	G	Pre 1821	Vibert	rb	f	s-m	wk	
			syn Bizarre Changeant					
Arlequin	HP	1872	Taillandier	rb				
Arlès Dufour	HP	1862	Liabaud	m	f	l		vf
Arlinde	D	1831	Vibert	lp	f	m		
Armand Carrel	B			lp	f	l		
Armand Marrast	B			mr	f	m		
Armand Patenotte	HP							
Armande	G		Lahaye	m				
Armantine	A	1824	Vibert	lp	f	s-m		
Armantine	B			dp	f	m		
Armide	A	1817	Vibert	lp	dbl	m		
Armide	N	Pre 1836	Laffay	mp	dbl	m		
Armide	P	1847	Vibert	mp		l		
Armide	HP	1858	Margottin	mp	f	l		
Armosa	Ch	Pre 1834	Marchesau	lp	f	m	m	f
			syn Hermosa					
Arnault	Ch		Laffay	m				
Arnold	HRg	1893	Dawson	mr	s		vig	
Arpajon	HCh			mp	f	l		
Arsénie	Ch	Pre 1834		lp		s		
Arsinoë	Ch	Pre 1846		pb				
Arsinoë	G	1829				m		
Artémise	HP	1851	Robert	dp				
Arteresea	HSpn			pb				
Arthémise	C	1819	Vibert	lp	dbl	m		
Arthémise	G	1819		dp				
Arthémise	HP	1876	Moreau-Robert	dp		l	vvig	

Name	Class	Year	Raiser					
Arthur Chiggiato	T	1899	Ketten	ob				
Arthur de Sansal	HP	1855	Cochet Sc	m	dbl	m	vig	vf
Arthur Oger	HP	1875	Oger	m	f	vl		
Arthur Young	M	1863	Portemer	m	f	l	vig	
Arvensis Flore Pleno	HArv			lp				
Arvina	G			dp				
Aschersoniana	S	1880	Münden	m		s		
Asepala	M	Pre 1837	Foulard	w	f	s		
Asmodée	G	1849	Vibert	mr	f	l		
Asmodée	B		Vibert	dr				
Aspasie	G/C	1819	Vibert	lp	f	m	m	
Aspasie	HP	1867	Touvais	mr	f	l	m	
Aspidie	HCh			mr	f	m		
Assemblage des Beautés	G	1823	Delaage	dr	dbl	m		vf
Assuerus	Ch	Pre 1846		dr				
Assuerus	HT			pb				
Astarade	G			m	f	m		
Astaroth	HCh			dp	vf	m		
Astéroïde	B	Pre 1846		lp	vdbl			
Astéroïde	G/HCh	Pre 1848		dp	f	m		
Astra	HT	1890	Geschwind	lp	dbl	l	vig	
Astrée	A	Pre 1842		mp	vdbl	vl		
Astrée	Ch		Laffay	w				
Astrée Blanche de Neige	A			w	f	m		
Astrolabe	HMult	1825	Garilland/Laffay	mr				
Astrolabe	HArv		Musqué	lp	f	vl		
Atala	D	Pre 1830	Vibert	lp	f	m-l		
Atala	G		Garilland	lp				
Atalante	G	1818	Vibert	lp				
Atalante	M	1853	Robert	lp	f	l		
Atar Gull	HP	1858	Avoux & Crozy	mp	f	m	vig	
Athalie	G	Pre 1830	Vibert	dp	vdbl	l		
Athalie	P	1851	Robert	lp	f	m		
Athalin	B	1830	Jacques	mr	dbl	l		
Athanase Coquerel	B	1853	Pradel	m	f	m	vig	
Athelin	G			dp	f	m		
Athénaïs	C			pb	f	m		
Athénaïs	G	1818	Vibert	lp	f	m-l		
Athol	HSpn	Pre 1846		pb		s		
Atrolutea Plenissima	Bks			y	vf	s		
Atronigra	Ch	1820	Godefroy syn below	dr	vdbl	s-m		
Atropurpurea	Ch	Pre 1830	Vibert syn Exubérant	dr	vdbl	s-m		
Atropurpurea	HRg	1899	Paul G	mr	s		vig	
Atrorubens	C			dr	f	m		
Atrovirens	HSem		syn Sempervirens	pb				
Attala	A	Pre 1834		mr		m		
Attala	G/C	1845	Vibert	mp	f	l		
Attila	A	Pre 1846		dp	s-d	l		
Attraction	HT	1886	Dubreuil	lp	f		vig	
Aubernon	HP	1840	Duval	dp	f	l		
Auberon	HP			mp	f	m		vf
Aubert	G		Parmentier	pb	f	m		
Audubon	HP	1856	Robert	p				
Augusta	N	1853		y				
Auguste André	HP	1886	Schwartz	mp	f	l	vig	
Auguste Buchner	HP	1880	Lévêque	m	f	l	vig	
Auguste Comte	T	1896	Soupert & Notting	mp	dbl	l	vig	
Auguste de Chalogne	B			mp	f	m		
Auguste de Ségur	HCh			m	f	l		vf
Auguste Fontaine	N			dp				
Auguste Guinoiseau	HP	1853	Guinoiseau	dr	f	l		
Auguste Mie	HP	1851	Laffay syn Madame Rivals	mp	vdbl	l	vvig	
Auguste Neumann	HP	1870	Verdier E	mr	f	l	vvig	
Auguste Oger	T	1855	Oger	pb	f	l		
Auguste Perrin	HP	1887		m	f	l		
Auguste Pujol (or Pajol)	HP	1854	Pradel	dp	vdbl	l		
Auguste Rigotard	HP	1871	Schwartz	mr	f	l	vig	
Auguste Rivière	T	1853	Lacharme	yb				
Auguste Rivière	HP	1863	Verdier E syn Souvenir d'Auguste Rivière	rb	f	l		
Auguste Thouvenel	HP			r		l		
Auguste Vacher	T	1853	Lacharme	yb	f	m	vig	f
Auguste Wattine	T	1896	Soupert & Notting	rb				
Augustine	G		Godefroy	lp				
Augustine Bertin	G/C	1818	Vibert	dp		l		
Augustine Fauvel	Ch			w	s	s		
Augustine Guinoiseau	HT	1889	Guinoiseau Fils	lp	f	l	vig	f
Augustine Halem	HT	1891	Guillot	dp	dbl	l		f
Augustine Hersent	Ch	Pre 1846		dp	f	l		
Augustine Lelieur	B	Pre 1870		dp	f	l		

Name	Class	Date	Raiser / Synonym					
Augustine Margat	B	Pre 1846		mp	vf	m		
Augustine Miellez	HP			dp	f	l		
Augustine Mouchelet	HP	1840	Mouchelet	pb	f	l		
Augustine Petite	B			w	f	m		
Augustine Pourprée	D	c 1811	syn Marie-Louise	lp	vdbl	m		
Augustine Pourprée	G	Pre 1830	Pelletier	m	dbl	l		
Augustine sans Épines	G		Godefroy	m	s-d	l		
Aurantiaca	E			ob	s	m		
Aurelia Liffa	HSet	1886	Geschwind	mr	dbl	l		f
Aurélie	G/C	1833	Vibert	lp		m		
Aurélie	HP	1849	Vibert	mp	f			
Aurélie Delamarre	G	1847	Verdier V	pb	f	m		
Aurélie Lemaire	G	Pre 1848		dp	f	m		
Aurélie Lemarc	G	Pre 1846		lp	dbl	m		
Aureny Zeb	B	Pre 1846		lp				
Aureus	T	1873	Ducher	yb	f	m		
Aurora	HCh	Pre 1846		dp	f	l		
Aurura	T	Pre 1860		w	dbl	l		f
Aurora	HT	1898	Paul W	op	f	l	vig	vf
Aurore	N		Laffay	pb		s	vig	
Aurore	T	Pre 1834		yb	f	l	vvig	
Aurore	HP	1861	Laffay	mp				
Aurore	HP	1861	Touvais	rb	f	l		
Aurore	HP	1866	Oger	rb	f	l		
Aurore	Ch	1897	Schwartz Vve	yb				
Aurore	C		syn Purpurascens	rb	f	s		
Aurore	HSpn							
Aurore	P			lp				
Aurore Boréale	HP	1865	Oger	mr	f	l	vig	
Aurore de Guide	B	1849	Thomas	dr	f	m	vig	
Aurore de Mons	HP	1865	Oger	dr				
Aurore d'Enghien	G	c 1830	Parmentier	m	f	m		
Aurore du Matin	HP	1857	Roland	mr	dbl	l		
Aurore Helvetia	G		Laffay	m	f	l		
Aurore Poniatowska	D		Redouté	pb				
Ausone	P	1861	Robert & Moreau	pb				
Austriaca	G	Pre 1806	syn Rosier d'Amour	m				
Austriaca	Sp			yb	s	m		
Austriaca Lutescens (Austrian Copper)	Sp	c 1596	syn r.foetida bicolor	rb	s	m		
Austrian Brier	Sp	Pre 1545	syn r.foetida	my	s			
Austrian Copper	HFt	c 1596	see above	rb	s	m	vig	f
Austrian Yellow	Sp	Pre 1542	syn r.foetida	my	s		vig	f
Auteuil	C			dp	f			
Autumn Damask	D	Pre 1700		mp	dbl			m
Autumnal Pompon	Ch			lp	f	s		
Autumnalis	Sp	1540	syn r.moschata	w				
Aux Cents Écus	HSpn	1817	Dupont / Vibert syn Belle Laure	w	s			
Auzou	HCh	c 1825	Cartier syn Couture	m	vf	m		
Avenant	G	Pre 1848		dp	vdbl	l		
Avenir	B	1858	Lartay	mp	f	l		
Avocat Adolphe Canler	HP	1885	Singer	dr	f	l	vig	
Avocat Duvivier	HP	1875	Lévêque	m	dbl	vl	vig	
Avocat Laloup	G	Pre 1848		rb	f	m		
Avocat L Lambert	HP	1884	Besson	mp	f	l	vig	
Axmannïï	G			lp				
Ayez	HSem	Pre 1832	syn Spectabilis	m	dbl	m	vig	
Ayrshire	Ayr			w	s-d		vvig	
Ayrshire	Ayr			lp	vdbl	m	vig	
Ayrshire Queen	Ayr	1835	Rivers	dr	s-d			
Ayrshire Rose	Ayr	1790	R arvensis hybrid	pb	dbl	m	vvig	
Ayrshire Splendens	Ayr	1835	R arvensis hybrid	w	s-d / dbl	m		vf
Azaïs	Ch			m	f	m		
Azélie	G/C	Pre 1838	Miellez	lp	dbl	s-m		
Azélie Imbert	T	1871	Levet	yb	f	l	vvig	
Azéma	G	1823	Vibert	lp	f	m		
Azurella	M		Foulard	pb		m		

NAME	TYPE	YEAR	RAISER	COLOUR	BLOOM	SIZE	GROWTH	SCENT
Babet	D	Pre 1838	Miellez	lp	f	m		
Bacchante	G	Pre 1811		dr	vdbl			m
Bacchus	HP	1855	Paul W	mp	f	m		
Bacchus	HP	1895	Paul G	mr	f	m-l		
Bachelier	G			pb	f	m		
Bacou	G			p	f	l		
Badensis	C			p	f	m		
Bailly de Suffren	C			lp	f	m		
Balbise	G	1827	Noisette	pb				
Balduin	HT	1896	Lambert P	pb	dbl	l	vig	f
Ball of Snow	HP	1887	Henderson	w	dbl	l		
Balsamine	D		Miellez	lp				
Baltimore	HT	1898	Cook J	lp				
Baltimore Belle	HSet	1843	Feast	lp	f	m	vig	m
Balusiana	G	c 1845		m				
Bambolina	G	1823	Noisette	dr				
Bance	G			pb	f	m		
Bandeau de Soliman	G	Pre 1826	Descemet	mr				
			syn Charles X					
Banestu	G	c 1845	Calvert	m				
Banff	HSpn	Pre 1846						
Bank's Rose	Sp	1796	Aiton syn r.banksiae	w or y		vs		sf
Banksiae Alba	Sp	1807	Aiton	w	dbl	s		
			syn r.banksiae banksiae					
Banksian Rose	Sp	1796	Aiton syn r.banksiae	w or y		vs		sf
Banse	Ch		Laffay	lp				
Baptiste Desportes	HP	1864	Trouillard	mr	f	l		
Baraguay	G	1819	Hardy	lp				
Barbanègra	G	1820	Vibert	m	f	l		
Barbot	T	Pre 1846		yb	f	l	vig	f
Bardon	T	1829		lp	f	m		
Bardon	Ch	Pre 1830	Laffay	w				
Bardou Job	B	1887	Nabonnand G	dr	s-d	l	vig	
Barillet	M	1850	Verdier V	mr	dbl	m		
Barillet Deschamps	HP	1867	Vigneron	rb	f	l		
Barlow	HP	1860	Ducher	dp				
Báró Natália Majthényi	HSet	1887	Geschwind	m	f	l		
Baron Adolphe de Rothschild	HP	1862	Lacharme	m	f	l	vig	
Baron Alexandre de Vrints	HP	1880	Gonod	pb	f	m	vig	m
Baron Bacchiochi	HP			p				
Baron Chaurand	HP	1869	Liabaud	mr	f	l	vvig	
Baron Cuvier	G	Pre 1848		pb	vdbl	l		
Baron de Bonstetten	HP	1871	Liabaud	dr	dbl	l	vig	f
Baron de Cressac	G							
Baron de Girardot	HP	1885	Marmy	rb				
Baron de Houlley	HP	1876	Vigneron	m	f	l	vvig	
Baron de Rothschild	HP	1862	Guillot Fils	m	f	vl	vvig	
Baron de Saint-Albe	HP	1895	Schwartz Vve	dr				
Baron de Saint-Trivier	T	1882	Nabonnand	pb	s-d	vl	vvig	
Baron de Warez	G			dr	f	m		
Baron de Wassenaer	M	1854	Verdier V	dp	dbl	m	vig	f
Baron de Wolseley	HP	1882	Verdier E	rb	f	l	vig	
Baron Elisi de Saint-Albert	HP	1893	Schwartz Vve	dr	f	vl		
Baron Ernest Leroy	HP	1875	Garçon	dp				
Baron G B Gonella	B	1859	Guillot Père	pb	f	l	vig	mf
Baron Girod de l'Ain	HP	1897	Reverchon	rb	dbl	l	vig	f
Baron Haussmann	HP	1867	Lévêque	mr	f	l	vig	
Baron Heckeren de Wassenaer	HP	1852	Margottin	mp	f	l		
Baron Larrey	HP	1854	Portemer	pb	f	l	vig	
Baron Larrey	HP	1856	Robert	pb	f	l		
Baron Lassus de Saint Geniez	HP	1865	Granger	mr	f	l	vvig	
Baron Louis	G	Pre 1830	Vibert	lp	f	m	vig	
Baron M de Lostende	HT	1893	Puyravaud	m				
Baron N de Rothschild	HP	1882	Lévêque	mp	f	l		
Baron Nathaniel de Rothschild	HP	1882	Lévêque (as above ?)	mr	f	l	vvig	
Baron Peletan de Kinkelin	HP	1864	Granger	dr	dbl	l		
Baron Raoul Chandon	HP	1896	Lévêque	dr				
Baron Taylor	HP	1880	Dugat	mr	dbl	l		
Baron T'Kind de Roodenbecke	HP	1897	Lévêque	m	dbl	m		
Baroness Rothschild	HP	1867	Pernet Père	lp	dbl	l	vig	
Baronne Ada	T	1897	Soupert & Notting	w	f	l		vf
Baronne Adolphe de Rothschild	HP	1867	Pernet Père	lp	dbl	l	vig	
		syn	Baroness Rothschild					
Baronne Athalin	HP	1862	Vigneron	rb	f	l		
Baronne Berge	T	1892	Pernet Père	pb	f	l	vig	vf
		syn Mme	la Baronne Berge					
Baronne Charles de Gargan	Cl T	1894	Soupert & Notting	ly	f	l	vig	m
Baronne Charles de Taube	T	1896	Ketten	yb	f	vl	vig	f

Name	Class	Year	Breeder					
Baronne Daumesmil	B	1863	Thomas	mp	f	l		
Baronne de Beauverger	HP	1867	Cochet	mr				
Baronne de Belleroche	HP	1897	Dubreuil	mr	f	l	m	
Baronne de Blochausen	HP	1884	Ketten	rb	vf	l	m	
Baronne de Cressac	Ch		Laffay	lp	f	s		
Baronne de Fonvielle	T	1886	Gonod	rb	f	l		vf
Baronne de Hoffmann	T	1887	Nabonnand	rb	f	l		
Baronne de Kermont	HP	1852	Lebougre	dp	f	m		
Baronne de Lage	Ch	Pre 1846		dr	f	m		
Baronne de Lostende	HP	1892	Puyravaud	p				
Baronne de Maynard	N	1864	Lacharme	w	f	m	vig	
Baronne de Medem	HP	1876	Verdier E	mr	f	l	vvig	
Baronne de Montarieu	B		Pradel	w	f	m		
Baronne de Morel	HP	1851	Quettier	lp	f	m	vig	
Baronne de Noirmont	B	1861	Granger	mp	f	m	vvig	m
Baronne de Prailly	HP	1871	Liabaud	mr	f	vl	vig	vf
Baronne de Rothschild	HP	1867	Pernet Père	lp	dbl	l	vig	
		syn	Baroness Rothschild					
Baronne de Rothschild à Fleurs Blnchs	HP			w				
Baronne de Saint-Cyr	G		Guérin	dp	f	m		
Baronne de Saint-Didier	HP	1886	Lévêque	mr	f	vl		
Baronne de Savigny	T	1854	Desprez	mp	f	l	vig	
Baronne de Sinety	T	1881	Gonod	yb	f	l	vvig	
Baronne de Staël	G	1820	Vibert	ob	f	m-l	vig	
Baronne d'Erlanger	T	1892	Lévêque	pb				
Baronne d'Ivry	G			w	vf	m		
Baronne F Van der Noot	T	1896	Ketten	yb				
Baronne Gaston Chandon	T	1894	Lévêque	yb	dbl	l	vig	
Baronne G de Noirmont	HT	1891	Cochet Sc	pb	f	l	vig	
Baronne Gustave de Saint Paul	HP	1894	Glantenet	lp	dbl	l	vig	
Baronne Hallez de Claparède	HP	1849	Lebougre	dr	vf	l		f
Baronne Haussmann	HP	1867	Verdier E	mr	f	l	vvig	
Baronne Henriette de Loew	T	1888	Nabonnand G	w	f	m	vig	f
Baronne Henriette Snoy	T	1897	Bernaix A	pb	dbl	l	vig	f
Baronne Jard Panvilliers	HP	1880	Duval	mp	f	l	vvig	
Baronne J-B de Morand	T	1892	Schwartz Vve	pb				
Baronne Lassus de Saint Geniez	HP	1862	Granger	rb	vdbl	m		
Baronne Louise Uxkull	HP	1871	Guillot Fils	pb	f	vl	m	f
Baronne Maurice de Graviers	HP	1866	Verdier E	rb	f	m	vvig	
Baronne M de Tornaco	T	1896	Soupert & Notting	w				
Baronne M Werner	T	1884	Nabonnand	pb	vf	vl		
Baronne Nathalie de Rothschild	HP	1885	Pernet Père	lp	vdbl	vl	vig	
Baronne Peletan de Kinkelin	HP	1863	Granger	dr	f	l		
		syn	Baron Peletan de Kink elin					
Baronne Prévost	HP	1842	Desprez	mp	f	vl	vig	f
Baronne Prévost Marbré	HP	1864	Van Houtte	mp				
Baronne Travot	HP	1884	Verdier C	mp	f	l	vig	
Baronne Vitat	HP	1873	Liabaud	mp	f	vl	vvig	
Barthe	A			m	s-d	vl		
Barthélémy Joubert	HP	1877	Moreau-Robert	mr	f	l	vvig	
Barthélémy Levet	HP	1878	Levet	pb	f	l	m	
Basile Dolgorouky	HP	1868	Margat	mp	vdbl	l		
Bassompière	HP	1853	Lartay	dr	f	l	vig	
Batard du Roi	Misc		Transon	r				
Batarde du Roi	Pom	Pre 1830	Prévost	mp	f	l		
Baucis	G	1832	Vibert	pb	f	m		
Baucis	B	1853	Robert	dr	f	m		
Baumann	N	Pre 1834		w	s			
Bause	T			yb	f	m		
Bause	Ch			pb	f	m		
Bayard	M	1855	Robert	yb	f	vl		
Bayard	Ch		Miellez	dp				
Bazaris	G	Pre 1830	Vibert	lp	vf	s-m		
Béatrix	B	1865	Cherpin	mr	f	l		
Béatrix	HP	Pre 1870		mp	f	l		
Beau Carmin	Ch	Pre 1810	Descemet	pb	f	m		
Beau Carmin du Luxembourg	Ch	Pre 1870		rb	f	m		
Beau Narcisse	G	Pre 1828	Miellez	m	dbl	vl		
Beaulieu	HP	1883	Moreau & Robert					
Beauregard	G		Miellez	dr	f	m		
Beaurepaire	M	1855	Robert	pb	f	vl		
Beauté (or Beauty)	Ch		Laffay	lp	f	m		
Beauté Brillante	G		Miellez	rb				
Beauté Choisie	G			rb				
Beauté Cramoisie	G	1816						
Beauté de Billard	HMult	Pre 1855	Dr Billard	mr	f	m	m	
Beauté de Crémone	N			pb				
Beauté de Grange de Héby	HT	1890	Ducher f	w				
Beauté de la Malmaison	G	Pre 1885		dr	f	m		

Name	Type	Date	Raiser / Synonym					
Beauté de l'Europe	T	1881	Gonod	op	dbl	l	vig	vf
Beauté de Lyon	T	syn	Beauté Inconstante					
Beauté de Roulers	HP	1860	De Cock	mp				
Beauté de Royghem	HP	1858	Robichon	pb	f	m	vig	
Beauté de Versailles	B	1842	Souchet	dp	f	l	vig	
			syn Georges Cuvier					
Beauté des Prairies	HSet	syn	Beauty of the Praires					
Beauté du Jour	G	Pre 1834	Miellez	dp	f	m		
Beauté du Printemps	HP			pb				
Beauté Fine	G		Miellez	p				
Beauté Flatteuse	G		Miellez	r				
Beauté Française	HP	1863	Lartay	mr	f	l	vvig	
Beauté Frappante	G			m				
Beauté Incomparable	G	Pre 1834		dp		m		
Beauté Incomparable	D	1860	Miellez	mr				
Beauté Inconstante	T	1892	Pernet-Ducher	ob	s-d	l	vig	m
Beauté Insurmountable	G	Pre 1811		dp	dbl	s		
Beauté Lyonnaise	HP	1851	Guillot Père	dp	f	m		
Beauté Lyonnaise	HT	1895	Pernet-Ducher	w	f	l	m	
Beauté Merveilleuse	G	Pre 1834		mp		l		
Beauté Pâle	T	1825	Laffay					
Beauté Pâle	G		Miellez	lp				
Beauté Panachée	C			pb	f	m		
Beauté Parfaite	G	Pre 1834		m	f	m		
Beauté Pourpre	G	Pre 1834		dr	dbl	m		
Beauté Rare	G	1818	Vibert syn Sapho	pb	f	m		
Beauté Renommée	G	Pre 1811		mr				
Beauté Riante	G	Pre 1830	Calvert	dp	vf	s-m		
Beauté sans Pareille	C			dr	f	m		
Beauté Sauvage	G			p	f	m		
Beauté Séduisante	B	1861	Touvais	dr	f	m	wk	
Beauté Superbe	G			rb				
Beauté Superbe Agathée	G	Pre 1811		lp	vdbl	s		m
Beauté Suprême	C	Pre 1846		m	f	m		
Beauté Surprenante	G	Pre 1820	Descemet / Vibert	w	f	m		
Beauté Tendre	G	Pre 1810	Dupont	dp	vdbl	l		
Beauté Tendre	A	Pre 1813	Vibert	lp	f	l		
Beauté Tendre Cramoisie	G			rb	vdbl	l		
Beauté Touchante	G	Pre 1813	Miellez	mr				
Beauté Violette	D	1827	Laffay	m				
Beauté Virginale	D	Pre 1811	Descemet	w	f	m		
Beauté Vive	Ch		Laffay	rb				
Beauty Bouquet	HCh	Pre 1846		w				
Beauty of Beeston	HP	1882	Frettingham	dr	f	s		f
Beauty of Billiard	HCh	Pre 1846		dr				
Beauty of Glasenwood	T	1876	Woodthorpe	ob	vf			
		see	also Fortune's Double	Yellow				
Beauty of Greenmount	N	1854	Pentland	dp	f	m		
Beauty of Stapleford	HT	1879	Bennett	rb	dbl	m	m	
Beauty of the Prairies	HSet	1843	Feast	pb	dbl	m	vig	
Beauty of the Thames	HP	1876	Walker	mp	f	l	vig	
Beauty of Waltham	HP	1862	Paul W	mp	dbl	l	vig	f
Beauty of Westerham	HP	1864	Cattell	mr	f	l	vig	
Beauvelours	G		syn Passevelours	rb				
Beck	D	Pre 1846	Laffay	lp		l		
Becquet	HCh	Pre 1846		dr				
Bedford Belle	HT	1884	Laxton	mr	vf	l		
Belby	M			rb				
Belgica Rubra	G	1817	Godefroy	dp	dbl	l		
Belgique	D			mp				
Belgique Minor	C	Pre 1846		lp		s		
Belgique Rose	D	Pre 1830	Prévost	lp	dbl	m		
Belisaire	D	Pre 1829	Hardy	lp	vdbl	m	vig	
Belisar	D			pb	f	m		
Bella	T	1890	California Nursery Co	w		l		
Bella Donna	D	Pre 1844		lp	vdbl	l		vf
Bella Victoria	G			rb				
Bellard (Bellart)	G	Pre 1842		lp	vdbl	vl		m
Belle Abellina	G		Miellez	lp				
Belle Actrice	G			dr				
Belle Actrice	A		Miellez	lp				
Belle Adelaïde	G	Pre 1834	Miellez	dp	f	m		
Belle Adèle	G							
Belle Africaine	G	Pre 1830	Prévost syn Africaine	dr	vf	s		
Belle Agathe	G			p				
Belle Agathe Carnée	C	Pre 1830	Pelletier	rb	f	s		
Belle Aimable	G	Pre 1811		rb	dbl	s		
Belle Alice	G		Parmentier	lp	f	m		
Belle Alix	N		Laffay	pb				
Belle Allemand	T	1841	Béluze	lp	vdbl	l	vig	vf
Belle Alliance	G	Pre 1821	Stegerhoek	rb	vdbl	s		
			syn Tricolore					

Name	Type	Date	Raiser / syn					
Belle Amante	G			rb				
Belle Amarante	G							
Belle Amazone	G		Miellez	r				
Belle Américaine	HP	1837	Boll D	dp	f	m		
Belle Amour	A	Pre 1867		lp	s-d			m
Belle Andalouse	HP	1852	Fontaine	mr	f	m	vig	
Belle Angevine	HP	1856	Robert	pb	f	l	m	
Belle Anglaise	HP	1856	Ducher	mr	vdbl	m	vvig	f
Belle Antide	C		Roeser	w	vdbl	m	vig	
Belle Antoine	N			lp	f	m-l		
Belle Archinto	T			lp	f	m		
Belle Arsène	G		Miellez	r				
Belle Aspasie	N	Pre 1836	Laffay	dp	f	m		
Belle Aspasie	T	Pre 1836	Coquerel	m	s-d	vl		
Belle Aspasie	G	Pre 1830	Coquerel	m	dbl	vl		
Belle Astelle	HSpn		Vibert					
Belle Auguste	G	1817	Vibert	lp	f	l		
Belle Auguste	D	Pre 1824	Descemet / Vibert	lp	f	l		
Belle Auguste Lee	G			lp	vf	l		
Belle Aurore	A	Pre 1810	syn Celestial	lp	s-d to dbl	l	vig	
Belle Aurore	A	1815	Vibert	lp	dbl	l		
			syn Ex Alba Rosea					
Belle Aurore	G	Pre 1830	Vibert	lp	vf	m		
Belle Bertholet	T		Robert	pb				
Belle Biblis	G	1815	Descemet	m	dbl	l		m
Belle Bigottini	T	1825	Laffay	lp				
Belle Blonde	A	1823	Cartier	w				
Belle Bouquetière	G			dp				
Belle Bourbon	G	Pre 1811	syn Rouge Formidable	mr	vdbl	m		
Belle Brun	G	Pre 1811		dr	s-d	l		
Belle Brune	HP	1861	Lartay	rb	f	l		
Belle Brunette	G		Miellez	rb				
Belle Camélia	G			rb				
Belle Camille	G	Pre 1820	Descemet	pb	s	m		
Belle Catalani	G	1826		pb	vdbl	l		
Belle Cerise	G	c 1810	Descemet	mr				
Belle Charlotte	G			dr				
Belle Chartronnaise	G			m				
Belle Chartronnaise	T	1861	Lartay	pb	f	l		
Belle Chinoise	Ch	Pre 1846						
Belle Clarissima								
Belle Clementine	A	Pre 1845		lp				
Belle Couronnée	D		syn Celsiana					
Belle Cramoisie	G		Robert	m	f	m		
Belle Cramoisie Formosa	G		Calvert					
Belle Cuivrée	T	1867	Pernet Père	yb	f	l		
Belle Damas	M		Noisette E	rb	vf	vl	vvig	
Belle d'Aulnay	G/C	Pre 1824	Barrier	mp	dbl	vl		m
Belle d'Auteuil	D	Pre 1826	Prévost (?)	pb	vf	m-l		
Belle d'Auteuil	M		Prévost	pb	f	m-l		
Belle de Baltimore	HSet	see	Baltimore Belle					
Belle de Bordeaux	B	1861	Lartay	pb	f	l	vig	
Belle de Bordeaux	T	1861	Bernède	pb	f	vl	vvig	f
			syn Gloire de Bordeaux					
Belle de Bourg-la-Reine	HP	1859	Margottin	mp	f	m	vig	
Belle de Cels	C	Pre 1830	Pronville	lp	dbl	l		
			syn Grande Couronnée					
Belle de Charonne	G			m				
Belle de Crécy	G	Pre 1829	Roeser	m	f	l		f
Belle de Damas	D			lp	f	l		
Belle de Florence	Ch	Pre 1846		lp	s-d	l	m	
Belle de Fontenay	G	Pre 1828	Boutigny	mp	f	m		vf
Belle de Fortenay	G			lp	f	m		
Belle de Hesse	G	Pre 1813	Godefroy	lp	f	m		
	syn La	Glorieus	e & La Gracieuse					
Belle de Hesse	G	Pre 1820	Descemet	pb	f	m		
			syn Illustre					
Belle de Hesse	A		Godefroy	w				
Belle de Humboldt	HCh			dp	f	m	vig	
Belle de la Gard	G	Pre 1830						
Belle de Lille	Bslt	Pre 1824	syn Blush Boursault	lp	f	vl	vig	
Belle de Marly	G			dp	f	l		
Belle de Monza	Ch	c 1825	Villares / Noisette	mr	f	m		
			syn De Florence					
Belle de Monzard	G	Pre 1830	Prévost	mp	f	m-l		
Belle de Normandy	HP	c 1890	California Nursery Co	mp		vl		
Belle de Parabère	N			rb	f	m		
Belle de Parny	HCh			m	f	m	vvig	
Belle de Pierrefitte	G	Pre 1834		lp		l		
Belle de Plaisance	Ch	1825	Vibert	rb	f	m-l	vvig	vf
			syn Centfeuille Pourpre					
Belle de Rosny	N			a		l		

Name	Class	Date	Raiser					
Belle de Saint Cyr	B	Pre 1846		mp				
Belle de Ségur	A	Pre 1828	Vibert / Lelieur	lp	dbl	m	vig	
Belle de Stors	G	c 1836	Lahaye Père	m	f	m		
Belle de Trianon	G	Pre 1826	Prévost	lp	vdbl	m		
Belle de Vaucresson	C	Pre 1830	Prévost	lp	vf	m		
Belle de Vernier	HCh	Pre 1827		pb	f	m		
Belle de Yèbles	G	1830	Desprez	mr	dbl	m		
Belle de Zarskoë	HSpn	1861	Freundlich	a				
Belle des Jardins	G	1872	Guillot Fils	m	dbl	m-l	vig	vf
Belle des Massifs	HP	1862		mp	vdbl	m		
Belle des Moulins	T	1852	Florins	lp	f	l	vvig	
Belle des Prairies	HSet	1843	Feast	pb	dbl	l	vig	m
		syn	Queen of the Prairies					
Belle d'Esquermes	N	Pre 1846	Miellez	dp	f	m	vig	
Belle d'Hyvrée	G			m	f	vl		
Belle Desbrosses	G	Pre 1834		dp	f	l		
Belle Dévise	G			pb	f	m		
Belle Diane	G		Miellez	dr				
Belle Didon	G			rb				
Belle Dijonnaise	B	1867	Bizot	mp			vig	m
			syn Zéphirine Drouhin					
Belle Distinctive	Misc			rb				
Belle Distinguée	C			rb	f	m		
Belle Ditte	Ch							
Belle Donna	Ch			w	f	m		
Belle Doria	G	Pre 1847	Parmentier	pb	f	m		
Belle d'Orleans	HP	1851	Vigneron	m				
Belle Dorothée	G			dp	f	m		
Belle Donaisienne	G		Miellez	mr				
Belle du Printemps	HP	1862	Damaizin	pb	vdbl	l	vvig	
			syn Alcindor					
Belle Écossaise	G			rb	f	s		
Belle Eléonore	G	1824 see	Princesse Eléonore	rb				
Belle Elisa	A	Pre 1830	Prévost	lp	f	l		
Belle Elise	Ch	Pre 1834		lp	f	m		
Belle Elise	T	1825	Laffay	lp	dbl	m	vig	vf
Belle Elodie	G			pb	f	m		
Belle Emilie	G	Pre 1830	Boutigny	lp	f	m		
Belle Emilie	T	Pre 1834		lp		l		
Belle Emilie	G	Pre 1838	Miellez	rb	vf	m		
Belle Emilie	Ch	Pre 1899		w	dbl	l	m	
Belle Emilie d'Arlon	G	1839	David	lp	f	l	vig	
Belle Esquermoise	G	Pre 1830	Miellez	rb	f	m-l		
Belle Estelle	HSpn	1824	Vibert syn Estelle	lp	s-d	m		
Belle Faber	P	Pre 1830	Prévost	p	vf	vl		
Belle Faber	HP	Pre 1834		dp	f	l	vvig	
Belle Fabert	P	Pre 1825	Fabert	dp	f	vl		
Belle Fédore	T			lp	f	m	vig	
Belle Félix	Ch			pb	f	m		
Belle Feronnière	Ch	Pre 1846		lp	vf	vl	vig	
Belle Fille du Printemps	HP	1862	Touvais	rb	f	m	vig	
Belle Fille Normande	HP	1852	Vigneron	w				
Belle Flamande	D	c 1811	Pelletier	lp	vdbl	m		
		syn	Agathe Couronnée					
Belle Flamande	N			pb	vdbl	l	vvig	
Belle Fleur	D	Pre 1830	syn La Divinité	lp	vf	m		
Belle Fleur d'Anjou	T	1873	Touvais	lp	f	vl	vig	
Belle Flore	G	Pre 1813	Descemet	dr	vdbl	l		m
Belle Florentine	G	Pre 1829	Boutigny	mp	f	l		
Belle Florine	G		Miellez	r				
Belle Fontagnes	N			yb	f	m		
Belle Forme	G			dp	f	m		
Belle Forme	N	Pre 1834		lp		s		
Belle Forme	T			pb	vf	l	vig	
Belle Gabrielle	G	Pre 1834	Laffay	lp	f	m		
Belle Galathée	G	Pre 1813	Descemet	lp		m		
Belle Gantoise	B	1878	Van Houtte	pb				
Belle Gris de Lin	G		Miellez					
Belle Havraise	G			dr	f	m		
Belle Hébé	Ch	Pre 1815	Descemet	lp	f	m	vig	
Belle Hébé	G	Pre 1836	Laffay	mp		l		
Belle Hélène	G	Pre 1815	Vibert	dp	vf	m		
Belle Hélène	G	Pre 1818	Descemet	m	vdbl	l		
Belle Hélène	G	1820	Vibert	lp	vdbl	l		
			syn Clémence Isaure					
Belle Hélène	Ch	c 1835	Laffay	w				
Belle Hélène	C	1825	Boutigny	mp	f	vl		
Belle Hélène	T			lp	f	l	vig	
Belle Héloïse	Ch		Laffay	pb	f	l		
Belle Henriette	G	1825	Vibert	lp	dbl	m		
Belle Henriette	HP			dr	f	m	vig	
Belle Henriette	M	Pre 1830	Vibert	w	s	m	vig	vf

Name	Type	Date	Breeder / syn					
Belle Henriette Rose	M	Pre 1830	Vibert	lp	s	m		f
Belle Henriette Rose Double	M	Pre 1830	Vibert	lp	f	l		f
Belle Hermance	HSpn			p	f	s		
Belle Herminie	G	1819	Coquerel	lp	f	m		
Belle Herminie Double	G	1824	Vibert	dp	dbl	s-m		
Belle Herminie I	G	1822	Vibert	mp	s-d			
Belle Herminie II	G	1822	Vibert	dr		l		
Belle Herminie III	G	1823	Vibert	m		l		
Belle Herminie IV	G	1823	Vibert	pb				
Belle Herminie V	G	1829	Vibert	lp	s-d	l		
Belle Herminie VI	G	1830	Vibert	mr		l		
Belle Herminie VII	G	1826	Vibert	mr	s-d	vl		
Belle Hollandaise	G		Miellez	P				
Belle Hortense	G		Miellez	pb				
Belle Hortense	M	Pre 1870		dr	f	m		
Belle Hyacinthe	G		Miellez	p				
Belle Illirienne	Ch			dr	f	s		
Belle Impératrice	G			p				
Belle Incarnata	G			lp				
Belle Inconnue	HSpn							
Belle Iphigénie	D	1825	Boutigny	lp	f	m		
Belle Isidore	Ch	Pre 1846		mp	f	m		
Belle Isis	G	1845	Parmentier	lp	dbl	m		
Belle Italienne	D	Pre 1830	syn Achille	dr	vf	m		
Belle Italienne	HP			lp	f	m		
Belle Ivryenne	HP	1891	Lévêque	dp	dbl	l		
Belle Jardinière	HP	1853	Avoux & Crozy	lp				
Belle Jules	G	1826	Vétillard					
Belle Julie	HP			m	f	l		
Belle Junon	G	Pre 1830	Prévost syn Rouge Agréable	lp	f	m		
Belle Junon	G	Pre 1811	Dupont syn Junon	dp	f	l		sf
Belle Kallos	G			w				
Belle Laura	HSpn			w	f	m		
Belle Laure	Ch	Pre 1870	Miellez	lp				
Belle Laure	HSpn	1817	Dupont / Vibert	w	s	s		
Belle Laure II	HSpn	1818	Descemet / Vibert	w	s	s		
Belle Laure III	HSpn	1822	Vibert	w	s	s		
Belle Laure IV	HSpn	Pre 1830	Vibert	rb	s			
Belle Laure V	HSpn	Pre 1830	Vibert	w	s	s		
Belle Laure à Feuilles Rapprochées	HSpn	1828	Prévost	pb	s	l		
Belle Laure à Fleur Double	HSpn	Pre 1830		pb	dbl	m		
Belle Lawrence	Ch	Pre 1846		lp				
Belle Léonide	C	1823	Bizard					
Belle Léonie	HCh							
Belle Léopoldine	G	Pre 1829	Boutigny	mp				
Belle Liliputienne	Min		Laffay	dp	f	s		
Belle Lilloise	G		Miellez	lp				
Belle Lise	G			dp				
Belle Louise	G			dp	f	m		
Belle Lucile	G	Pre 1810	Descemet					
Belle Lyonnaise	HP	1854	Lacharme	mp		m	vig	
Belle Lyonnaise	Cl T	1869	Levet F	ly	dbl	l	vig	m
Belle Maconnaise	T	1870	Ducher	mp	f	l	vig	f
Belle Magdeleine	G	1823	Duranche					
Belle Marbrée	G			lp	f	m		
Belle Marguerite	G			pb				
Belle Marguerite	T	Pre 1846		pb	f	l		
Belle Marie	D	Pre 1830		lp	f	m		
Belle Marie	HCh	Pre 1846		dp				f
Belle Marie	T	1851	syn La Belle Marie	dp	f	l	vig	m
Belle Marley	G	Pre 1860		dp	vdbl			
Belle Marseillaise	N	Pre 1846		mp				
Belle Marseillaise	Ch	1857	Fellemberg syn Fellemberg	dp	f	l	vvig	
Belle Mathilde	HSpn	1816 syn	Descemet / Vibert La Belle Mathilde	w	s-d	m-l	vig	f
Belle Mathilde	Pom			lp	vdbl	l		
Belle Mélanie	Ch	Pre 1846		dp	f	m		f
Belle Ménès	Ch	Pre 1846		mp	f	m		
Belle Merveilleuse	G		Miellez	lp	f	m		
Belle Mignonne	G	Pre 1819	Prévost syn Petite Louise	lp	dbl	s		
Belle Mode	G		Miellez	dr		m-l		
Belle Nanon	B	1872	Lartay	dp				
Belle Ninon	G	Pre 1821	Boutigny	dp	f	m		
Belle Noisette	N	Pre1834		lp		s		
Belle Normande	HP	1864	Oger syn De Vierge	w	f	l		
Belle Octavie	G			lp	f	m		
Belle Octavie	T			lp	f	l		

Belle Olry	Ch	1826	Olry	w				
Belle Olympe	G	Pre 1820	Descemet	mr				
Belle Orléanaise	N			dr	f	m		
Belle Panachée	G			rb				
Belle Parade	G	Pre 1811		m	vdbl	l		
Belle Parure	G	Pre 1834	Miellez	mp		m		
Belle Poitevine	HRg	1894	Bruant	mp	dbl	l	vig	sf
Belle Pourpre	G	Pre 1813		m				
Belle Pradher	N		Laffay	rb	f	m		
Belle Rosalie	Ch	Pre 1846		lp				
Belle Rosalie	M	Pre 1846		dp	f	l		
Belle Rosalie de la Croix	G			r	vf	s		
Belle Rose	HP	1864	Touvais	mp	f	vl	vig	
Belle Rosine	S	Pre 1820	Descemet	dp	dbl	l		
Belle Rosine (see also Amelia)	A	1825	Descemet	mp				
Belle Rosine	G	1830	Vibert syn Amelia (G)	mp	vdbl	m-l		
Belle sans Flatterie	G	Pre 1806	Godefroy	lp	f	m		
Belle sans Pareille	G	Pre 1845		mp				sf
Belle Sarah	N			lp	f	m		
Belle Satinée	G							
Belle Ségur	A		Lelieur	lp	f	m		
	see	also	Joséphine de Beauh-	arnais				
Belle Ségur	G			w	f	l		
Belle Siebrecht	HT	1894	Dickson A	lp	dbl	l	vig	vf
		syn	Mrs W J Grant					
Belle Singulière	Ch		Noisette	p				
Belle Sophie	T			lp	f	m		
Belle Splendens	G	Pre 1820	Descemet					
Belle Stéphanie	D	1825	Boutigny	lp	f	m		
			syn Belle Iphigénie					
Belle Sultane	G	Pre 1801	syn La Belle Sultane	dr		s		
Belle Sylvain	G	Pre 1846		w				
Belle Ternaux	G	c 1825	Boutigny	m	f	s-m		
Belle Théophile	G	Pre 1830	Prévost	mp	f	m		
Belle Thérèse	A	Pre 1830	Prévost	lp	dbl	m-l		
Belle Thérèse (same as above)	A	Pre 1830	Vibert	lp	dbl	m-l	vvig	
Belle Thérèse	C			rb	f	m		
Belle Thérèse	G			m				
Belle Thurette	HP			dr	f	m		
Belle Traversi	T	Pre 1830		w		m		
Belle Traversi	Ch	Pre 1846		w				f
Belle Travestie	T			w	f	m		
Belle Vichysoise	N	1895	Lévêque syn Cornélie	lp	dbl	m	vig	
Belle Victorine	C	Pre 1815	Descemet	lp	f	m		
Belle Victorine	G	Pre 1830	Vibert	lp	f	m		
Belle Villageoise	G	1839	Vibert	pb	dbl	l		sf
			syn Panachée Pleine					
Belle Villoresi	Ch	Pre 1830	Vibert	dr	f	m		
Belle Violette	HCh	Pre 1830	De Vergnies	m	f	m		
Belle Violette	N			m	f	s	vig	
Belle Violette	G	1845	Vibert (Robert)	m	f	m		
Belle Violette de Lille	G							
Belle Violette Foncé	G	Pre 1815	Descemet	m				
Belle Virginie	G	1814		m	f	m		
Belle Yvrienne	HP	1890	Lévêque	rb	vf	vl		
Belle Zaïre (Belizar)	T			lp	f	l		
Bellina Guillot	HMult	1889	Schwartz Vve	w				
Bellone	G		Miellez	lp				
Bellotte	G	Pre 1826	Vibert	mp		m		
Bellotte	HP	1862		lp	f	m		
Belmont	HCh	1846	Vibert	lp				m
			syn Indica Major					
Belphegor	T	Pre 1846		rb				f
Béluze	B	c 1840	Béluze	mr	f	m		
Belvedere	HSem	1829	Jacques	mp	f	m		
Belzunce	HP	1884	Moreau-Robert	rb	f	vl	vvig	
Bengal Crimson	Ch	Pre 1818	syn Sanguinea	dr	s			sf
Bengal Florida	Bslt	Pre 1824	syn Blush Boursault	pb	vdbl	vl	vig	
Bengale	Ch	Pre 1830		pb	dbl	m-l		
Bengale Animée	Ch	Pre 1817	syn Animating	mp		s		
Bengale Blanc	Ch	Pre 1830	Prévost	w	s-d	m		
Bengale Blanc, Climbing	Cl Ch	Pre 1830	Vibert	w	dbl	l	vig	
Bengale Borderouge	Ch			m	f	s		
Bengale Centfeuilles	Ch	1804	Noisette	pb	f	m		
Bengale Cerise	Ch	1820	Hardy	mr				
Bengale Cypress	Bslt			pb				
Bengale d'Automne	Ch	1825	Laffay	dp	vdbl	l		f
Bengale Ducher	Ch	1869	Ducher	w	vdbl	m	vig	
Bengale Formidable	Cl N	Pre 1846		lp	f			
Bengale Gontier	Cl HCh			dp	dbl		vig	
Bengale Hollandaise	Bslt		syn Maheca	pb				
Bengale Jaune	T		Laffay	yb				

Bengale Nabonnand	Ch	1886	Nabonnand	dr				
Bengale Pourpre	Ch	1827	Vibert syn Pourpre	m	f	m	vvig	
Bengale Rouge	HCh	1781		dr	s-d	s		
Bengale Sanguinaire	Ch	1838	Desprez	mr	vdbl	s		
Beniowski	G	Pre 1830	Coquerel	mr	f	m		
Benjamin Constant	G		Garilland	p				
Benjamin Drouet	HP	1878	Verdier E	dr	f	l	vvig	
Benjamin Mary	G			rb	f	l		
Bennett's Seedling	Ayr	1840	Bennett	w	f	m	vvig	vf
Ben Lomond	HSpn	1827		lp	s-d	s		
Benoist Pernin	HP	1889	Myard	mp				
Benoit Broyer	HP	1874	Gonod	dr	f	m	vig	
Benoit Comte	HP	1884	Schwartz	rb	f	l	vvig	
Benoit Cornet	HP	1863	Ducher	mr	f	l		
Bérangère	G	Pre 1846	Garilland	dp	f	vl		
Bérangère	HCh	Pre 1830		mp	f	s		
Bérangère	M	1849	Vibert	lp	dbl	l		
Berberifolia	HBc		Hardy	yb	f	s		
Berberifolia Hardii	HBc	Pre 1899		y	s	s		
Berceau Imperial	HP	1856	Vigneron	mp	f	l		m
Beremie	G			rb	f	m		
Bérénice	G	1818	Vibert	rb	f	l	vig	vf
Bérénice	Ch		Laffay	lp				
Bérénice	C	Pre 1829	Racine	lp	f	m		
Bergemann	T			lp	f	l		
Berlèse	G	1832	Vibert	dr		m		
Berléze	G	Pre 1846	Robert	m	f	m		
Bernard	P	1836	syn Madame Ferray	op	f	m		
Bernard	D	1846		op	dbl	m		f
Bernard Palissy	B	1847	Vibert	mp	f	l		
Bernard Palissy	HP	1863	Margottin	mp	vf	vl	vvig	
Bernard Verlot	HP	1874	Margottin	rb	f	l	vig	
Bernard Verlot	HP	1874	Verdier E	rb	f	l	vig	
Bernardin de St-Pierre	B	1848	Oger	m	f	m		
Berryer	G			lp	f	m		
Berthe Baron	HP	1869	Baron-Veillard	lp	f	l		m
Berthe Bozterais	HP	1869	Fontaine	dr	f	l		m
Berthe Chanu	HP	1867	Fontaine	dp	f	l		
Berthe de Sansal	HP	c 1850	De Sansal	mp	f	m		
Berthe du Mesnil de Mont Chauvau	HP	1876	Jamain	lp	dbl	m		
Berthe Gemen	HP	1898	Gemen Bourg	w	f			f
Berthe Lévêque	HP	1866	Céchet Père syn Mlle Berthe Lévêque	w	f	l	vig	
Berthe Thouvenot	T	1898	Ketten	y				
Berthet	G	Pre 1827	Cartier	m				
Bertholet	T	1855	Robert	lp	f	m	vig	
Bertin	N	c 1836	Bertin	mp	f	l	vig	
Bertrand	T	Pre 1870		dp		m		
Berwick	HSpn			pb	s-d	l		
Beryl	T	1897	Dickson A	dy		s		
Besnier	T			dr	f	m		
Bessie Brown	HT	1899	Dickson A	ly	vdbl	l	vig	sf
Bessie Johnson	HP	1873	Curtis	lp	vdbl	l	vig	f
Bessie Johnson, Climbing	Cl HP	1878	Paul G	dp				
Betzi	Pom	Pre 1830	Vibert	lp	f	m-l		
Beurre Frais	T			yb	vdbl	vl	vig	
Bianqui	T	1871	Ducher	w	f	l		
Biblis	G		Descemet					
Bichon	Ch	1826	Vibert syn À Odeur de Capucine	rb	f	s		vf
Bichonne	Ch	Pre 1820	Noisette / Laffay	rb				vf
Bicolor	N	Pre 1846		lp				
Bicolor	M	1855	Lacharme	pb				
Bicolore	HP	1877	Oger	w	f	l	m	
Bicolore	M	Pre 1870	Laffay	pb	vf	m	vig	
Bicolore Incomparable	HP	1861	Touvais	pb	f	m		
Bicolore Puniceo Subrubra	HFt			rb	s	m		
Bien-Aimée	G	Pre 1845		mr	f			m
Bienaimé Hain	T			pb	vf	s	vig	vf
Bifera	HSpn							
Bifera Italica	G	Pre 1811		lp	dbl	m		
Bifera Pumila	Misc		Noel	lp				
Bifera Venusta	P	Pre 1830	Descemet	lp	f	m		
Bifère	D			p	dbl			
Bifère à Fleurs Blanches	P	syn	Perpétuelle Blanches	w	vdbl	m		
Bifère à Fleurs Roses	P	Pre 1830	Perpétuelle à Fl Roses	lp	dbl	m		
Bifère Presqu'Inerme	P	Pre 1830	Vibert syn Quatre Saisons moins Épineux	lp	dbl	m		
Bigard	HP			lp	f	m		
Bignonia	N	1874	Levet	yb	f			
Bigottini	Ch	Pre 1830	Laffay	pb	dbl	m-l		

Name	Class	Date	Raiser/Syn					
Bijou	Misc	Pre 1846						
Bijou de Couasnon	HP	1886	Vigneron	dr	f	l		
Bijou de Lyon	HMult	1882	Schwartz	w	f	s	vvig	
Bijou de Parade	Misc	Pre 1846						
Bijou de Royat-lès-Bains	Ch	1891	Veysset	mp	dbl	m		
Bijou des Amateurs	G	Pre 1830	Jacquemot-Bonnefont	dr	f	vl		
Bijou des Prairies	HSet	1880	Schwartz J	dp	dbl	m	vvig	
		syn	Gem of the Prairies					
Bijou d'Enghien	G			p	f	m-l		
Bijou Royal	Misc	Pre 1846						
Billard	HP	Pre 1845	Billard	op	vf	l		m
Billard et Barré	Cl T	1898	Pernet-Ducher	my	dbl	l	vig	vf
Billiard	HP	Pre 1834		lp		m		
Bipenné	C			p				
Bipinnata	C	Pre 1802		lp	f	m		
		syn	r.centifolia bipinnata					
Bipinnata à Feuilles de Céleri	C			lp	f	m	vig	
Bishop Rose	G	Pre 1790	syn L'Évêque	m	dbl			m
Bisson à Odeur d'Anisette	Ch	Pre 1846						
Bisson d'Angers	Ch		Mme Herbert	lp				
Bizard Royal	Misc	Pre 1846						
Bizarine	B	Pre 1846		dp				
Bizarre	G	Pre 1830	Calvert	dp	f	s-m		
Bizarre Ardoisée	G	syn	Bizarre Triumphant	dr				
Bizarre Changeant	G	Pre 1830	Vibert	rb	vf	s-m		
		syn	Pourpre Marbrée					
Bizarre de la Chine	HCh	Pre 1830	Vibert	rb	vdbl	s-m		
Bizarre de la Chine	Ch	Pre 1834	Laffay	rb		m		
Bizarre Flammée	G	1822		rb		m		
Bizarre Incomparable	HCh	Pre 1830	Prévost	mr	dbl	m		
Bizarre Marbrée	G	Pre 1846		rb	f	m		
Bizarre Pintade	G	1823	Toutain	m				
Bizarre sans Fruit	G	1835	Joly	rb	dbl		vvig	
Bizarre Triumphant	G	Pre 1813	Descemet	dr	f	m		
Black	Ch			dp	f	s		
Black Fringed	C			dr	f	m		
Black Merice	Misc	Pre 1846		dr		vl		
Black Prince	HP	1866	Paul W	dr	f	l	vig	vf
Black Ranunculus	Ch			dr	f	m		
Bladud	HP	1896	Cooling	pb	f	l	m	
Blairii No 1	HCh	1844	Blair	mp	s-d	l		vf
Blairii No 2	HCh	1845	Blair	lp	dbl	l	vig	m
Blairii No 3	HCh	1845	Blair	mp				
Blanc	G			w	f	s		
Blanc	Ch	1804	Cels	w				
Blanc	Pom		Lemeusnier	w		vs		
Blanc	Min	Pre 1834	Laffay	w		vs		
Blanc	P			w				
Blanc	Pom		Noisette					
Blanc à Feuilles Lisses	Ch		Vibert	w				
Blanc à Feuilles Luisantes	Ch		Vibert	w	s-d	s-m		
Blanc à Fleur Simple	A	1826	Prévost	w	s	s-m	vig	
Blanc à Fleurs Doubles	HSpn	Pre 1817	Descemet	w	f	vl		
			syn Pompon Blanc					
Blanc à Fleurs Pleines	HSem	Pre 1830	Laffay M syn Pleine	lp	dbl			
Blanc à Grandes Feuilles	Ch	1827	Mauget	w				
Blanc à Petites Fleurs	Bks			w				
Blanc Ancien	Sp	1807 syn	r.banksiae banksiae	w	dbl	s	vig	
Blanc Carné	M		Shailer syn Blanche	lp	f	l		
Blanc de Neige	Sp	1803	syn r.laevigata	w	s		vig	
Blanc de Vibert	P	1847	Vibert	w	dbl	s		m
Blanc Double	Bks	1807	Keer	w	dbl	s	vig	f
Blanc Double à Onglets Jaunes	N	1827	Laffay	yb				
Blanc Double de Coubert	HRg	1892	Cochet-Cochet	w	dbl	l	vig	vf
Blanc Épineux	Bks	Pre 1846		w				
Blanc Mauget	T	Pre 1834		w		m		
Blanc Parfait	A	1876	Verdier E	lp	dbl	s		vf
		syn	Pompon Blanc Parfait					
Blanc Pur	N	1827	Mauget	w	dbl	l		m
Blanc Sarmenteux	Ch	Pre 1834	Vibert	w	s-d	l		
Blanc Unique	Ch			w				
Blanche	A	c 1810	Descemet	w				
			syn À Coeur Jaune					
Blanche	M	Pre 1870		w	f	m		
		syn	Shailer's White Moss					
Blanche	A		Jacques	w				
Blanche	HSpn	Pre 1834		w		s		
Blanche Agréable	A			w	f	m		
Blanche Carnée	HSpn	1820	Vibert	lp		s		
Blanche de Bath	M	1817	Salter	w	f	l		
		syn	White Bath					
Blanche de Beaulieu	HP	1850	Margottin	w	f	m	vvig	

Name	Class	Year	Breeder					
Blanche de Belgique	A	1817	Vibert	w	dbl	vl		
Blanche de Bernède	HP	1852	Bernède	w	f	l		
Blanche de Castille	G/C	1822	Vibert	lp	f	m	vig	
Blanche de Chatenay	N		Vibert	w	f	m		
Blanche de Chine	Ch			w				
Blanche de Forco	T	1891	Dubreuil	w				
Blanche de Lamoureux	HP			dp	f	m		
Blanche de Méru	HP	1869	Verdier C	w	f	m	vig	
Blanche de Parmentier	HP	1856	Robert	lp	f	m	vig	
Blanche de Portemer	HP	1851	Portemer	lp	f	l	vig	
Blanche de Soleville	T	1854	Pradel	w	f	l	vig	
Blanche de Suchet	T			w	f	m		
Blanche d'Avillers	D	Pre 1846		w	f	m		
Blanche d'Italie	M	c 1835	Prévost	w	dbl	m		m
Blanche d'Orléans	N	Pre 1834		w	f	m	vig	
Blanche Double	C	Pre 1775	syn Alba	w	f	l		
Blanche Double	M	1820	Vibert	w	dbl	m	vig	
Blanche Double	HSpn	Pre 1834	Prévost	w		s		
Blanche Double	HMult	Pre 1830	syn Multiflore Blanche	w	dbl	vs		
Blanche Double	D			w				
Blanche Double Superbe	Bks			w	f	s		
Blanche du Roi	B			w	f	m		
Blanche du Roi	D	1849	Dubos	w				vf
			syn Célina Dubos					
Blanche Duranthon	T		Nabonnand	w	dbl	m		
		see Mm	e Lucien Duranthon					
Blanche Durschmidt	N	1877	Guillot Fils	w	f	m	vvig	
Blanche et Rose	HP	1852	Oger	w	f	l	vig	
Blanche Foliacée	A	Pre 1830	Vibert	w	dbl	s-m	vig	
Blanche Globuleuse	HSpn	1822	Prévost	lp				
Blanche Lafitte	B	1851	Pradel	lp	f	m	vig	m
		syn	Mlle Blanche Lafitte					
Blanche Moreau	M	1880	Moreau-Robert	w	dbl	l	vvig	m
	syn	Mlle	M-Louise Bourgeois					
Blanche Mousseuse	M	1850	Shailer	w	dbl	m		
			syn White Bath					
Blanche Multiple	A	Pre 1830		w	dbl	m	vig	f
Blanche Nabonnand	T	1883	Nabonnand G	w	dbl	vl	vig	f
Blanche Nouvelle	M		syn White Bath	w				
Blanche Perfection	HP	1849	Oger	lp	f	l		
Blanche Pleine	HSpn	1820	Vibert	w				
Blanche Rebatel	Pol	1888	Bernaix A	pb	f	s	m	
Blanche Semi-Double	HSpn	Pre 1819	Vibert	w	s-d			
Blanche Semi-Double	A	Pre 1830	syn Blanche Multiple	w	dbl	m	vig	f
Blanche Simon	M	1862	Moreau-Robert	w	dbl	l	vig	
Blanche Simple	N	1825	Vibert	w	s	m		vf
Blanche Simple	G		Prévost	w				
Blanche Superbe	A	syn	Blanche de Belgique					
Blanche Unique	M	see	White Provence (C)	w	f	m		
Blanche-Vibert	P		Vibert	w	f	m	vig	
			syn Blanc de Vibert					
Blanchefleur	C	1835	Vibert	w	dbl	m	vig	vf
Blanchette	D	1845	Vibert	w	f	m		
Blanda	Misc	Pre 1846						
Blandford Rose	G	c 1791		mp				
Blandine	N	1829	Vibert	w		s		
Blandine	G/C	1846	Vibert	w	f	l		
Blandine	N		Miellez	lp				
Bleu	G		Descemet	m				
			syn Charles de Mills					
Bleu Céleste	A	Pre 1810	Dupont syn Celestial	lp	s-d	l	vig	
Bleu de la Chine	Ch	Pre 1830	Vibert	m	f	m		
Bleu Rougeâtre de Flettbeck	C			pb	vdbl	m		
Blondel de Vienne	G		Parmentier	lp	f	m		
Blood	G	Pre 1819	syn Hector	m	dbl	s		
Bloomerick	G	Pre 1845	Calvert	m	f	m		
Blücher	G			lp	f	m		
Blush	M	Pre 1838	Hooker	m	dbl	m	m	f
Blush	HSpn	Pre 1846		lp				
Blush	Arv	Pre 1846		lp				
Blush Belgique	C	Pre 1846		lp	dbl	l		
Blush Bengal	N	Pre 1846						
Blush Boursault	Bslt	Pre 1824		lp	vdbl	vl	vig	
Blush Damask	D	1759		lp	dbl	s		m
Blush Favorite	Ayr	Pre 1846						
Blush Hip	A	c 1840		lp	dbl	m	vig	
Blush Moss	M	Pre 1844		lp	dbl	l	m	
Blush Noisette	N	1817	Noisette	w	s-d	m	vig	m
Blush Tea	T	1789	syn Odorata	lp				
Blush Virgin	Ayr	Pre 1846						
Bobelina	HCh	1827	Laffay	pb	f	m		
Boccace	HP	1859	Robert & Moreau	dp	f	l	vig	

Name	Type	Date	Breeder / syn					
Boccage	T	Pre 1846		w	f	l		f
Boïeldieu	G	1828	Prévost	lp	f	l		
Boïeldieu	HP	1877	Garçon / Margottin	mp	vf	vl	vig	
Boileau	HP	1883	Moreau-Robert	mp	f	l		
Boisdoré	Ch							
Boisdron	Ch	Pre 1846		w	f	l		f
Bois Jaune	A		Bizard	yb				
Boisnard	T	Pre 1846		yb	f	l		vf
Bolivar(d)	Ch			rb	vdbl	m		
Bon Silène	T	1835	Hardy	dp	dbl	l	vig	m
Bon Silène Blanc	T	1885	Morat	ly		l		
Bona Weillschott	HT	1889	Soupert & Notting	dp	f	l		m
Bonamour	T	1897	Liabaud	pb		l		vf
Bonheur du Jour	G			dr	f	m		
Bonheur du Jour	Ch			pb	f	m		
Bonne de Bordeaux	C			dp	f	m		
Bonne Geneviève	HCh	1826	Chevrier / Laffay	dr	f	l	vig	
Bonnie Prince Charlie's Rose	A	Pre 1596	syn Alba Maxima	w	dbl			m
Bordeaux	C	Pre 1820		mp	s-d	m		f
Bordé de Blanc	Pom			p	s-d	m		
Bossuet	HP/B	c 1836	Vibert	pb				
Bossuet	G	Pre 1846		mr	f	m		
Botzaris	D	1824	Laffay	w	vdbl	m		f
Botzaris	D	1856	Robert (syn above?)	w		l	vig	
Bouclier d'Astolphe	G	Pre 1830	Lecomte	mr	vdbl	m-l		
Bouclier d'Astolphe	G		Savoureux	mr				
Bouflers	C		Vibert	lp				
Bouflers	HP	1856	Robert	lp				
Bougainville	N	1822	Cochet P	pb	vdbl	s	vig	sf
Bougainville	N	Pre 1830	Vibert	lp	f	m		
Bougère	T	1832	Bougère syn Clothilde	op	f	l	vig	f
Boulanger	M			dp	f	l		
Boule de Nanteuil	G	1834	Roeser	m	f	l	vvig	
		syn Comte	Boula de Nanteuil					
Boule de Neige	C	1825	Vibert see Globe White Hip	w	dbl	l		
Boule de Neige	N	Pre 1830	Laffay	w				
Boule de Neige	B	1867	Lacharme	w	dbl	m	vig	m
Boule d'Hortensia	D	1819/20	Godefroy syn Aimable Rouge	lp	f	m		
Boule d'Or	T	1860	Margottin	yb	f	vl	vig	
Boulogne	N	Pre 1846		dr	f	s	vig	
Boulogne	T			pb	f	l		
Boulotte	Pom			w				
Boulotte	Ch	Pre 1846	Laffay syn Africaine	m	f			
Bouquet	T	1873	Liabaud	w	f	l	vvig	
Bouquet Blanc	Pom			w				
Bouquet Blanc	N	1830	Vibert	w		s		
Bouquet Blanc	HP	1856	Robert	w	dbl	m		
Bouquet Blanche	A	Pre 1846		w	dbl			
Bouquet Charmant	HSet	c 1810	Descemet	lp				
Bouquet Charmant	G	Pre 1811	Guerrapain syn Venus Mère	mp	f	m-l		
Bouquet de Dame	Ch			lp	f	m		
Bouquet de Fleurs	N			pb	f	l	vig	
Bouquet de Flore	B	1837	Bizard	mr	dbl	vl	vig	f
Bouquet de la Mariée	N	1858	Damaizin syn Bouquet de Marie	w	dbl	m	vig	
Bouquet de Marie	HP	1858	Damaizin	w	dbl	m	vig	
Bouquet de Miellez	G		Miellez	dr				
Bouquet de Mühlenheck	G	c 1860	Baumann					
Bouquet de Vénus	G	Pre 1814	Lerouge	lp	vdbl	s		
Bouquet de Vierge	B	1874	Soupert & Notting	pb	f	s	m	
Bouquet d'Or	N	1872	Ducher	yb	dbl	l	vvig	f
Bouquet d'Otto	G	Pre 1860	Baumann					
Bouquet Joli	G		Lerouge					
Bouquet Parfait	G	Pre 1811	Godefroy syn Royale	lp	dbl	m		
Bouquet Parfait	G	1817	Godefroy syn Agate Royale	mp	f	s		
Bouquet Parfait	A	1826	Vibert	mp	f	s		
Bouquet Parfait	HMult	1898	Lille	lp				
Bouquet Pourpre	G	1814	Vibert syn Mine d'Or	rb		s-m		
Bouquet Rose	G	Pre 1834		mp		m		
Bouquet Rose	HP	1871	Touvais	rb	f	m	vig	
Bouquet Superbe	G	Pre 1830	Vibert syn Venus Mère	mp	f	m-l		
Bouquet Tendre	G		Lerouge					
Bouquet Tout Fait	D	Pre 1789	syn Red Damask	mr	dbl	m		vf
Bouquet Tout Fait	N	1836	Laffay	w	f	m		vf

Bouquet Triomphant	G		Miellez	p				
Bourbon	G	Pre 1811		pb	s-d	m		m
Bourbon	T	Pre 1830	Laffay	w		l		f
Bourbon	B	Pre 1846	Rameau / Jacques	lp				
Bourbon Nigra	G			dr	f	m		
Bourbon Queen	B	1834	Maugct	pb	dbl	l		
		syn	Queen of Bourbons					
Bourbon Rose	B	1817		dp	s-d		vig	m
Bourduge	Ch	Pre 1830	Vibert	rb	vdbl	s	wk	
Bourgmestre Victor Carbonnelle	HP	1885	Singer	rb	f	l		
Boursault	Bslt		Laffay	dr				
Boursault à Fleurs Doubles	HBslt		Laffay	rb				
Boursault à Fleurs Pleines	HBslt		Cartier	mp				
Boursault Pleine	HBslt	Pre 1830		mp	f	m		
Boursault Rose	HBslt	Pre 1810	Cugnot (?)	mp	s-d			
Boursier de la Rivière	M	Pre 1870	Laffay	rb	f	l	vig	
Boutelart (ud)	T	1829	Vibert	lp	vf	vl		
Bouton de Flore	HP			p	vf	l		
Bouton d'Or	T	1866	Guillot Fils	dy	vf	m	vig	f
Bouton Jaune Nouveau	N			w	vdbl	m		
Bouton Nankin	N			lp	f	m	vig	
Boutons d'Unique	HSpn	1821	Cartier	mp				
Boutrand	T	Pre 1846		mp				f
Bouvet	D		Vibert	dr	f	l		
Bracelet d'Amour	G	Pre 1830	Calvert	lp	vf	m		
Bracteata	HBc	1797	Wendl syn Macartney	w	s	m		
Bracteata à Feuilles Penchées	HBc			w				
Bradwardine	HEg		syn Rose Bradwardine	mp				
Bramante	M	1856	Robert	rb	f	m		
Brave Depute	HCh			m	f	l		
Brawinii	Cl			w				
Brémontier	HP	1872	Lartay	mr				
Brenda	HEg	1894	Penzance	lp	s	s	vvig	fol f
Brennus	HCh	1830	Laffay	dr	dbl	l	vig	
Bréon	G			rb	f	m		
Briard	E	1828	Vibert	lp	f	s		
Bride de Lille	D		see Pride of Lille					
Bride of Abydos	T	Pre 1846		w				f
Bridesmaid	T	1893	Moore F L	lp			vig	
Bridesmaid, Climbing	Cl T	1893	Dingee & Conard	lp				
Brightness of Cheshunt	Cl HP	1881	Paul G	mr	f	m		
Brighton Beauty	T	1891	Bragg	mr				
Brigitte	G	1821	Vibert	m	f	s-m		
Brillant	Ch	Pre 1830	Vibert syn Splendens	lp	s-d	m		
Brillante	G	c 1810	Descemet	mp	f	l		
Brillante	B	Pre 1846		mp				
Brilliant	M	Pre 1846	Lee	mp	s-d			
Brilliant	HP	1886	Paul W	rb		m		
Briseïs	C	1817	Vibert	lp	f	m-l		
Briseïs	Cl Ch	Pre 1846	Vibert	lp	f	m		
Brissac	B	1849	Lacharme	rb	f	m	vvig	
Britannicus	G		syn Manteau Impérial	m				
Broune (Brown)	HCh	Pre 1830	Calvert / Vibert	mr	f	l		f
Bruce Findlay	HP	1891	Paul G	rb		l		
Brun	Pom			dr				
Brune Magnifique	G			rb	f	l		
Brunette	G	c 1810	Descemet	dr				
Brunoniana	M	Pre 1889		w	s		vig	f
Brunonii	M	Pre 1846	Lindley	w	s	m		
Brunonii à Fleurs Doubles (Flore Pleno)	M	1895	Cochet	w	f	m	vig	
Bruny	HP	1858	Avoux and Crozy					
Buffalo-Bill	HP	1889	Verdier E	lp	f	l		
Buffon	P	Pre 1821		lp	vdbl	l		
Buffon	G	Pre 1848	Vibert	m	f	l		
Buffon	HP	1859	Guillot Fils	mr	f	m	m	
Buisson	C			mp				
Buissonfleurs	HCh		Guérin	p				
Bullata	C	1809		mp	vdbl	vl	vig	vf
Bunnert Fridolin	T	1885	Bernaix	pb	f	m	vig	f
Burdin	T			lp	f	m	vig	
Burdin	HCh							
Buret	T	Pre 1846	Buret	m	f	m	vig	f
Buret	Ch		syn Louis-Philippe	rb	f	m		
Burgermeister Carl Müller	HP	1873	Soupert & Notting	rb	f	l	vig	f
Burgundian Rose	G	Pre 1650		pb	dbl	s	s	
Burgundy	Pom	Pre 1846		lp	dbl	vs		
Burke	P	1860	Robert-Moreau	m				
Burnet Double Pink	HSpn	Pre 1650		p	dbl			
		syn	Double Blush Burnet					

Burnet Double White	HSpn	Pre 1650		w	dbl			vig	vf
		syn	Double White Burnet						
Burnet Marbled Pink	HSpn	Pre 1650	syn Double Marbrée	p	dbl	s			
Burnet Rose	Sp	Pre 1600	syn r.spinosissima	w	s				
Burret's Angarne	N			rb	f	l	vig		
Busard Triomphant	G	Pre 1790	syn Charles de Mills	dr	vdbl	m			sf
Button	HRg	1886	Veitch	p					
Byron	C	1825	Vibert	rb	vdbl	m			

NAME	TYPE	YEAR	RAISER	COLOUR	BLOOM	SIZE	GROWTH	SCENT
Cabbage Rose	C	Pre 1596	see also Communis	mp	vdbl	l	vig	vf
Cadisché	G	1830	Vibert	dp	f	l		
Cadot	N	Pre 1834		dp	f	s		
Cadoudal	HCh			w	f	m		
Caecilie Scharsach	HP	1887	Geschwind	lp	vdbl	l		vf
Calife de Bagdad	G		Miellez	lp	f	m		
California Wild Rose	Sp	1878	syn r.californica	mp	s			
Calliope	T	Pre 1846		w				
Calliope	HP	Pre 1846		dr		s		
Calliope	HP	1853		pb	vf	m		
Calliope	HP	1879	Moreau-Robert	mp	f	l	vvig	
Calocarpa	HRg	1894	Bruant	mp	s	s	vig	
Calvert	C	Pre 1826	Lee syn Globe White Hip	w	f	m		
Calvertia Purpurea	Ch	Pre 1834		dr		s		
Calypso	G	Pre 1813	Descemet	mp	vdbl	vl		
Calypso	HBslt	1826	Noisette syn Blush Boursault	pb	vdbl	vl	vvig	
Calypso	D	Pre 1846	Vibert	lp	dbl	l		
Calypso	Ch	1894	Noisette L	dr				
Calypso Petite	C	Pre 1820	Descemet	mp	vdbl	vl		
Camaïeux	G	1830	Gendron	m	dbl	s	vig	vf
Cambaut	T			lp	f	m	vig	
Cambronne	G			dr	f	m		
Caméléon	Ch	c 1827	Desprez	mr	f	l	vig	
Caméléon	T	c 1830	Laffay	pb	f	m	vig	m
Caméléon	Ch	Pre 1834		pb	f	m		
Camélia	Pom			w				
Camélia	Ch	1820	Laffay	rb	dbl	m		
Camélia	HSpn		Vibert	w				
Camélia	N	1827	Mauget	w				
Camélia	A	Pre 1830	Prévost	w	vdbl	s-m	m	
Camélia	Ch	Pre 1834		mp		m		
Camélia	Ch	Pre 1834	Lelieur	w	f	s		
Camélia Blanc	T	Pre 1834	Olry, syn Olry	w	vf	m	vig	f
Camélia Panaché	Ch	Pre 1846		dr	f	m		
Camélia Rose	N	c 1830	Prévost see also Camellia Rose	lp	dbl	m	vig	m
Camélia Violet	Ch	1827	Mauget	m				
Cameliaeflora	A	Pre 1846		w		s		
Cameliaeflora	Ch			pb	vdbl	m		
Cameliana	N			w				
Camellia	Ch		Prévost	lp	s-d	m		
Camellia Rose	HBslt	1830	Prévost	lp	vdbl	m		
Camellia Rouge	N	Pre 1834		lp	f	s		
Camille Bernardin	HP	1865	Gautreau	mr	dbl	vl	vvig	vf
Camille Bouland	A	Pre 1826	Prévost	lp	vdbl	m		
Camille de Chateaubourg	B	1864	Fontaine	m	f	l		
Camille Desmoulins	G			rb		l		
Camille Duclos	B	1853	Varangot	pb	f	m	vvig	
Camille Roux	T	1885	Nabonnand	mr	f	l	vig	
Camoëns	HT	1881	Schwartz J	mp	f	vl	m	m
Campanulé	G		Cugnot	w				
Campsey	HSpn	Pre 1846						
Camuzet	HCh	Pre 1829	Camuzet	m				
Camuzet Carné	HCh	1829	Camuzet	op	f	l		
Canari	T	1852	Guillot Père	my	f	m	wk	
Canaris	G	1826	Vétillard	m				
Canary	T	1852	Guillot Père	my	f	m	wk	
Candeur	HCh	Pre 1846		lp				
Candide	C	1820	Vibert	w	f	s-m		
Candide	Ch			w	f	m		
Candide	A	1831	Vibert	lp	f	m		
Candide	B	1857	Robert-Moreau	lp	f	m		
Candide	HP	1858	Touvais	lp				
Canelle	Alp	Pre 1830	syn Du St-Sacrement & r.cinnamomea	lp	vdbl	s		f
Cannabina	C			p				
Cannabina	A	Pre 1830	De Pronville syn À Feuilles de Chanvre	w	dbl	s		
Cannes la Coquette	HT	1878	Nabonnand	op	f	l	vig	
Canning	G		Parmentier	pb	f	m		
Capitaine A Milabran	T	1894	Tesnier Fils	pb				
Capitaine Barry	Cl			p				
Capitaine Basroger	M	1890	Moreau-Robert	rb	f	l	vvig	
Capitaine Charpine	HP	1851	Moreau-Robert	rb	f	l		
Capitaine Christy	HT		see Captain Christy					
Capitaine Christy à Fleurs Rouges	HT	1899	Perrier	dp				

Name	Type	Year	Breeder					
Capitaine John Franklin	HP	1853	Margottin	dr	f	l	vig	
Capitaine John Ingram	M	1854	Laffay	m	f	m	vig	m
Capitaine Lamure	HP	1873	Levet	m	f	l	m	
Capitaine Lefort	T	1888	Bonnaire	dp		vl	vig	f
Capitaine Louis Frère	HP	1883	Vigneron	dr				
	syn M-	onsieur	le Capitaine Louis Frè	re				
Capitaine Patrizzi	HP		see Cardinal Patrizzi					
Capitaine Paul	HP	1867	Boyau	mr	f	l	vig	
Capitaine Peillon	HP	1893	Liabaud	m	dbl	l		
Capitaine Rénard	P	Pre 1843		pb	vf	l		
Capitaine Rognat	HP	1864	Guillot Père	mr	f	l		
Capitaine Sissolet	HCh	Pre 1841		mp	vdbl	l	vig	
Capitaine Williams	G	Pre 1843		dr	vdbl	m		m
Capreolata	HArv		syn Ayrshire Rose	pb	vdbl	m		
Capreolata Ruga	Misc	1820		mp				
Caprice	B	1832	Vivian Faivre	p				
Caprice de Vick	HP		see Vick's Caprice					
Caprice de Zéphir	G		syn Agathe Rose	lp				
Caprice des Dames	HCh	Pre 1831	Miellez	dp	f	vs		
Caprice du Zéphyre (Zéphir)	D	c 1811	Prévost (?)	lp	vdbl	m		vf
			syn Marie-Louise					
Capricieuse	Misc		Pernet D	yb				
Capricorn	G	1819	Miellez	dp	f	m		
Capricorne	G	Pre 1830	Vibert	mp	vdbl	s-m		
Capricornus	C	Pre 1811		mr	vdbl			
Captain Christy	HT	1873	Lacharme	lp	f	l	vvig	sf
Captain Christy, Climbing	Cl HT	1881	Ducher	lp	f	l		vf
Captain Christy Panaché	HT	1896	Letellier	pb				
Captain Hayward	HP	1893	Bennett	dp	dbl	l	vig	vf
Captain Philip Green	T	1899	Nabonnand	pb	f	l	vig	
Capuchonnée	D	1820	Bozérian	mp				
Capucine	HFt	1768	Miller syn r.punicea	ly	s		vvig	
Capucine Harrissonii	HFt	1830	Harrisson	yb				
Capucine Liabaud	HP	1881	Liabaud	yb				
Capucine Orange	HFt			yb				
Capucine Ponctué	HFt	Pre 1846		yb	s			
Capucine Rouge	HFt							
Carache	B			lp				
Caradori Allan	HArv	Pre 1846		dp	vdbl	m		
Caravane de Nimes	HP	Pre 1870	Damaizin	dr	f	l		
Carbonara	HSem	Pre 1830	Prévost	lp	vdbl	m	vvig	
Cardinal	Misc	Pre 1846						
Cardinal Alberoni	G		Flon	r				
Cardinal d'Amboise	G			rb	f	m		
Cardinal de Bonnald	G		Parmentier	dr	f	m		
Cardinal de Chevérus	G	1845	Robert	m	f	l		
		see	Cardinal de Chevreuse					
Cardinal de Chevérus	B	1852	Pradel	m	f	m	vig	
Cardinal de Chevreuse	G		Vibert	m				
Cardinal de Richelieu	G	1840	Laffay	m	vdbl	s	vvig	m
Cardinal de Richelieu	G	Pre 1847	Parmentier syn above?	m	vdbl	s		
Cardinal de Richelieu	HP	1857	Trouillard	dp				
Cardinal Fesch	M			dp	s-d	m		
Cardinal Fesch	B	Pre 1846		rb	vf	m	vig	
Cardinal Patrizzi	HP	1853	Trouillard	dr	vf	m	vig	f
Cardon	HCh	Pre 1830	Cardon	m				
Carina	N	1830	Vibert	dp		s		
Carl Coërs	HP	1865	Granger	rb	f	l	vig	
Carl of Pembrocke	HP	1882	Bennett	rb	dbl	l	vig	
Carlin	Ch/T	Pre 1846		dp	f	l	vig	f
Carmen	Cl T	1888	Dubreuil	lp	vdbl	l	vig	f
Carmen Sylva	HT	1891	Heydecker	yb	dbl	l		
Carmin Amoureux	G			pb	f	m		
Carmin Brillant	G	Pre 1813		mr	vdbl	m		
Carmin Brillant	HP			pb	f	m		
Carmin Brillant	Ch		Laffay	dr				
Carmin d'Yèbles	Ch	1839	Desprez	mr	f	m		m
Carmin Liseré	G	Pre 1830	syn La Majestueuse	mr	f	m		
Carmin Multiflora	HSpn	1861	Freundlich	pb				
Carmin Multiplex	HSem			lp				
Carmin Royal	HP			pb	f	m	vig	
Carmin Superbe	Ch	Pre 1846		mr				
Carmin Vélouté	Ayr	Pre 1846		mp	vf	m	vvig	
Carmin Virginalis	D			lp				
Carminata Lutescens	Misc	1892	Brun					
Carmine	HEg	Pre 1846		mr				
Carmosina	G	Pre 1830	Calvert	mr	vdbl	m		
		see	Admirable & Cramois	ie				
Carnation	HEg	Pre 1846		lp				
Carné	Pom			lp				
Carné	HMult			lp				
Carné	HMcr			p				

Name	Class	Date	Raiser / Synonym	Colour	Form	Season	Vigour	Scent
Carné	A		Syn Maiden's Blush	w	dbl	m		
Carné	C			lp				
Carné	N	1814	Noisette P	lp				
Carné	P			lp				
Carné	M	Pre 1870	Robert	lp	f	m		
Carné Amabilis	A			lp	f	l		
Carné de Boisjeloux	HCh			lp	f	m		
Carné de Montmorency	B			mp	f	m		
Carné de Pelletier	Pom		Pelletier	lp	vdbl	l		sf
Carné d'Edenberg	A			pb	f	l		
Carné Grandiflora	HArv			lp	f	l		f
Carné Humilis	A			lp	f	s	vig	
Carné Millefolia	A			lp		m		
Carné Parviflora	G	1826	Lemeusnil					
Carné Plena Arvensis	HArv			lp	f	m	vig	
Carné Regalis	A	syn	Sophie de Bavière	dp	f	m		
Carné Simple	T		Laffay					
Carnea	C	Pre 1811	Volmorin syn Unique Carnée	lp	f	l		
Carnea	Pom	Pre 1838	syn Carné	lp	vf	m		
Carnea Hispida	HSpn	1861	Freundlich	w				
Carnea Maxima	HSpn	1861	Freundlich	pb				
Carnea Virginalis	D	Pre 1811	Descemet syn Beauté Virginale	w	f	m		
Carnée	B	Pre 1830	Laffay	lp	dbl	m		
Carnée Double	HSpn	Pre 1826	Prévost syn Double Carnée	w	dbl	s		
Carnot	T	1825	Laffay	dp				
Carnot	B	1851	Pradel	m	f	m		
Carolina Rose	Sp	1826	syn r.carolina	mp				
Caroline	T	1829	Guérin	lp	f	m		m
Caroline Bank	HMult	1890	Geschwind	lp	dbl	m		
Caroline Carré	D							
Caroline Cook	T	1871	Cook	ab				
Caroline d'Angleterre	A	1822	Calvert	lp	f	s		
Caroline d'Arden	HP	1887	Dickson A	lp	dbl	vl		vf
Caroline de Berri	C	Pre 1808	syn Foliacée	dp	f	l	vig	
Caroline de Berry	Ch	Pre 1846		w	f	m		f
Caroline de Brunswick	Ch		Laffay	w				
Caroline de Sansal	HP	1849	Desprez	mp	vdbl	l	vig	
Caroline d'Erard	B	1850	Cochet P	w	f	m	vig	
Caroline Fochier	T	1896	Liabaud	pb		vl		f
Caroline Joly	G	1822	Vibert					
Caroline Kuester	N	1872	Pernet Père	yb				
Caroline Maille	P	1825	Boutigny / Prévost	w	f	m		
Caroline Marniesse	N	1848	Roeser syn D'esse de Grammont?	w	dbl	m	vig	sf
Caroline Mittchell	D		Laffay	w				
Caroline Nilson	HP	1853	Guillot Père	lp	f	m		
Caroline Ohl	HP			lp	f	vl		
Caroline Riguet	B	1857	Lacharme	lp	f	m		
Caroline Schmitt	N	1882	Schmitt syn Mme Caroline Schmitt	yb	f	m	vig	
Caroline Superbe	B			pb	f	l		
Caroline Swailes	HP	1885	Swailes	lp	f	l		
Caroline Ternaux	N	c 1840	Laffay	w	f	l	vig	
Caroline von Braunschweig	Ch		Laffay	w	f	l		
Caroline Walner	C	Pre 1846		lp	f	s		
Carré de Boisgeloup	HCh	Pre 1846						
Carriage Dorizy	B	1849	Dorizy	m	f	m		
Cartier	D	1821	Vibert	mp	f	m		
Cartier	HSpn							
Caryclée	Ch		Laffay	lp				
Caryophilla	Ch			lp	f	s		
Caryophilla	D			rb	f	s		
Caryophilla Alba	D			w	f	s		
Casimir Bonjour	G			r	f	l		
Casimir Delavigne	D		Laffay	lp	f	l		
Casimir Delavigne	P	1848	Vibert	mr	f	l		
Casimir Delavigne	P	1851	Robert & Moreau	lp				
Casimir Périer	G	Pre 1830	Lambert / Savoureux	rb	f	l		
Casimir Périer	N	1851	Schmitt	mr				
Casimir Périer	HP	1874	Schwartz	dr	vf	l	vig	
Casimo Ridolphi	G	1842	Vibert	dr				
Casseret Foncé	G			pb	vf	l		
Cassius	T			lp	f	m	vig	
Castalie	N			lp	vf	m	vig	
Catel	A	Pre 1830	Vibert	lp	f	l		
Catel	HCh	Pre 1846		dp				
Catharina Gerchen Freundlich	T	1896	Ketten	pb				
Catherine II	T	Pre 1830	Laffay	lp	f	l		
Catherine Bell	Cl HP	1877	Bell & Son	pb	f	l	vig	f

Name	Class	Year	Raiser					
Catherine Bonnard	B	1871	Guillot Fils	dp	f	m	vvig	
Catherine d'Albret	B			pb				
Catherine de Médici	G		Miellez	r				
Catherine Ghislaine	D	1885		lp	s-d	s		m
Catherine Guillot	B	1860	Guillot Fils	dp	dbl	l	vig	f
Catherine Mermet	T	1869	Guillot et Fils	lp	dbl	l	vig	f
Catherine Mermet Blanche	T		see The Bride					
Catherine Seyton	HEg	1894	Penzance	lp	s		vig	m
Catherine Soupert	HP	1879	Lacharme	w	f	l	vvig	f
Catherine von Wurtemberg	M	1843	Robert	mp	vdbl	m	vig	
Catinat	G	1838	Vibert	m	f	m		
Catinat	G	Pre 1846	Robert	mr	vdbl		vig	
Catinat	HP	1874	Oger	mr	vdbl	l	vig	
Catuelle	G		Vibert	p				
Catuelle	D	1855	Robert	rb		l		
Caule Inermis Foliis Aculeatis	A	Pre 1830	Godefroy	lp	dbl	m	vig	
	syn		Herissée Presque Inerm	e				
Caura	G			m	f	s		
Cécile Berhod	T	1871	Guillot Fils	yb	vf	m	vig	
Cécile Binard	B		see Céline Binard					
Cécile Brunner	Pol	1881	Ducher V, & Pernet	lp	dbl	s		m
	syn		Mme Cécile Brunner					
Cécile Brunner, Climbing	Cl Pol	1894	Hosp	lp	dbl	s	vig	vf
	syn		Mme C Brunner, Clg					
Cécile Loisiel	A	1825	Loisiel	w	f	s		
Cecilia	C							
Cecilie Scharsach	HP	1887		w	f	l		
Cecilie Sergent	T	1899	Weber	w				
Celamire (Célanire)	A	Pre 1826	Cottin	lp	f	m	vig	
			syn Sophie de Bavière					
Céleste	HT			lp	f	l		
Céleste	Pom			w	vdbl	m		
Céleste	A	Pre 1759	syn Celestial	lp				
Céleste	G	Pre 1820	Descemet	lp	f	vl		
			syn Grand Sultan					
Céleste	A	Pre 1830	Vibert	w	f	m		
Celestial	A	1797	Kew	lp	dbl	l	vig	vf
Celestial	HCh	Pre 1830		lp	f	vl		vf
Celestial	HEg	Pre 1846		lp				
Celestial	HSpn	c 1854		lp	dbl	s		vf
Célestine	Ch	c 1825	Laffay	w	f	m		
Célestine	D	Pre 1826	Coquerel	lp	f	l		
Célestine	G	1822	Vibert	lp	vdbl	m-l		
Célestine	HP	Pre 1846		mp	f	m	vvig	
Célestine Pourreaux	HP	1873	Fontaine	dr	f	l	vig	
Celicel	HCh	Pre 1846						
Célie	P		Parmentier	dp	f	m		
Célimène	B	Pre 1846		lp	f	vl	vig	
Célina	M	Pre 1843	Hardy	m	dbl	m	m	
Célina Dubos	HP	1849	Dubos	w	f	m		vf
Célina Noirey	T	1868	Guillot Fils	pb	vf	l	vig	
Céline	B	1825	Laffay	mp	dbl	l	v vig	
Céline	M			mp	f	l		
Céline	HCh	1855	Robert	m				
Céline Binard	B	1853	Varangot	dp	f	m	vig	
Céline Bourdier	P	1851	Robert	mr	f	m	vig	
Céline Briant	M	1853	Robert	lp	f	l		
Céline Capella	B	1851	Pradel	dr	f	m	vig	
Céline d'Ortega	G		Parmentier	lp	f	m		
Céline Forestier	N	1842	Trouillard	ly	dbl	l	vig	m
Céline Gonod	B	1861	Gonod	mr	f	m	vig	
Célinette	Pom			lp	f	s		
Célinette	HSpn	1827		lp		s		
Célinette	C	1832	Vibert	lp		l		
Célinette Chataigné	B	1880	Brassac	mp	f	l		
Cellier	G			mp	f	l		
Cels	D		syn Celsiana	lp				
Cels Double	D		Laffay	lp				
Cels Multiflore	Ch	1836	Hardy / Cels	lp	f	l	m	
Cels Pleine	C	Pre 1830	Laffay	lp	f	l		
Celsiana	D	Pre 1750		lp	s-d	l	vig	m
Cendres de Napoléon	B	1841	Béluze	m	f	m		
Cénomane	HSpn	Pre 1846		w	f	l		
Cent Feuille	C	Pre 1596	syn Cabbage Rose	mp	vdbl	l		
Centfeuille	C	Pre 1846	Noisette L	pb				
Centfeuille d'Avranche	D	Pre 1830	syn Dsse de Grammont	mp	f	vl		
Centfeuille de Bordeaux	C	Pre 1820	syn Bordeaux	lp	s-d	l		f
Centfeuille de Hesse	A	Pre 1830	Godefroy	lp	f	s		
Centfeuille Pourpre	Ch	1826	Noisette L	dr	f	m-l	vvig	vf
	syn		Belle de Plaisance					
Centfeuilles	B	Pre 1846		lp				
Centfeuilles Argentée	C	Pre 1830	Pelletier	mp	f	m		f

Name	Class	Date	Breeder / syn					
Centfeuilles d'Anjou	C	Pre 1830	Vibert	mp	f	l		
Centfeuilles d'Auteuil	G	Pre 1830	Laffay	dp	f	l		
Centfeuilles de Bordeaux	C	Pre 1830	Vibert	mp	f	s		
Centfeuilles des Pleintres	C	Pre 1830		mp	vdbl	l		
Centfeuilles Descemet	C	Pre 1814	Descemet	lp	dbl	l		f
Centfeuilles Robin	C	Pre 1830		lp	dbl	l	vig	
Centfeuilles Rouge	C	Pre 1834		mr		l		
Centifolia Alba	M			w	f	l		
Centifolia Apelata	M			dp	f	m		
Centifolia Foliacee	C	Pre 1808	syn Foliacée	mp	dbl	vl		
Centifolia Incarnata	D	1825	Pronville syn Dsse de Grammont	mp	f	vl		
Centifolia Major	C	Pre 1830	syn Centfeuilles des Peintr-es	lp	vdbl	l	vvig	f
Centifolia Minor	C			lp				
Centifolia Muscosa	M	Pre 1596	syn Communis and r x centifolia muscosa					
Centifolia Rosea	HP	1863	Touvais	mp	f	l	vig	f
Centifolia Speciosa	Ch			m	f	l		
Centifolia Ulmifolia	C			p	f	l		
Centifolia Variegata	C	1845	syn Variegata	pb	vdbl			
Centimane	Pom			lp	f	m		
Céphise	D	1824	Guérin					
Ceres	HP			rb				
Ceres	B	Pre 1846		p				
Ceres	T	1853	Oger	lp	vf	l		
Ceres	B	1896	Schwartz Vve	p				
Cerisea Superba	T			yb	f	l		
Cerise	Ch	Pre 1830	Vibert	dp	dbl	m		
Cerise	G	Pre 1830	Vibert syn Amelia	mp	vdbl	m-l		
Cerise	T	Pre 1846		pb	f	l	vvig	
Cerise d'Angers	Ch	c 1834						
Cerise d'Enghein	G	c 1830	Parmentier	mp	f	m		
Cerise d'Orlin	G			dp	s-d	m		
Cerise Éclatante	Ch							
Cerise Parfaite	G	Pre 1834		mr		s		
Cerise Pourpre	T	1851	Robert	dr	vf			
Cerise Superbissima	G			rb	f	m		
Cerisette	HCh	Pre 1846		dr				
Cerisette	B	1851	Pradel	rb	f	l		
Cerisette la Jolie	G	Pre 1811	syn Surpasse Tout	mr	f	m		m
César Beccaria	G	1855	Moreau-Robert	w	dbl	l		
César Cardet	Ch	Pre 1846		lp	f	m		
César Jules	B	1865	Verdier E	dp	f	l		
Césarine Souchet	B	Pre 1870		lp	vf	l	vvig	
Césonie	P	Pre 1836	Vibert	dp	f	l		
Césonie	HCh	Pre 1846						
Césonie	D	Pre1848		dp	f	l		
Césonie	M	1859	Moreau-Robert	dp	dbl	m		
Chabrant	G			m	f	m		
Chaillot	B			dp	f	m		
Chambrière	G		Miellez	p				
Chamnagana	N		Hardy	mp				
Chamois	C	Pre 1824	Mme Chamois	mp				
Chamois	N	1829	Vibert	yb		s		
Chamois	T	1870	Ducher	ly	s-d	m	m	
Champion	G	1831	Vibert	dr	f	m		
Champion of the World	HP	1894	Woodhouse	mp	dbl	l	vig	f
Champnagana Nova	Misc	Pre 1834		lp		m		
Champneys' Bengal Rose	Ch	c 1800	Champneys	mp				
Champneys' Pink Cluster	N	1810	Champneys	lp	dbl	s	m	m
Champs de Mars	HP	1868	Verdier E	pb	f	l		
Chancelier d'Angleterre	G	Pre 1830	Calvert	mr	f	m		
Chancellor	Misc	Pre 1846		dr				
Changeante	G		Miellez	rb				
Chapeau de Napoléon	C	1827	syn Crested Moss	mp	vf	m	vig	vf
Chapeau Noir	G		Miellez	m	f	m		
Chapeau Rouge	G		Miellez	dr				
Chapelain d'Arenberg	G	Pre 1847		mp	f	m		
Chaptal	A	1823	Vibert	mp	f	m		
Charlemagne	HP	1836	Dorisy	dp	dbl	l	m	
Charlemagne	HP	1863	Oger	mr	f	l		
Charlemagne	B	Pre 1870		lp				
Charlemagne	G	1888	Dubreuil syn Président Dutailly	m	dbl	l	vig	vf
Charles-Anaïs	C	1824	Bizard					
Charles Auguste	G	1824	Paillard	lp	f	l		
Charles Baltet	HP	1877	Verdier E	mp	f	l	vig	vf
Charles Boissière	HP	1850	Granger	mr	vdbl	l		
Charles Bonnet	HP	1884	Bonnet	dp	dbl	m		
Charles Capella	HP			rb	f	l		
Charles Darwin	HP	1879	Laxton Bros.	mp	f	l	vig	

Name	Type	Year	Breeder					
Charles de Franciosi	T	1890	Soupert & Notting	yb	f	l		
Charles de Legrady	T	1884	Pernet-Ducher	dr	f	l	vvig	vf
Charles de Mills	G	Pre 1790		dr	vdbl	m		sf
Charles de Thézillat	T	1888	Nabonnand	yb	f	vl	vig	f
Charles Desprez	B	1831	Desprez	dp	f	m		
Charles Dickens	HP	1886	Paul W	mp	f	l	vig	
Charles Duval	B	1841	Duval	mp	f	l	vig	
Charles Duval	HP	1847	Laffay	mr	f		vig	
Charles Duval	HP	1877	Verdier E	rb	dbl	l	vig	
Charles Fauquet	HP	1883	Lévêque	mr	f	l	vig	
Charles Fontaine	HP	1868	Fontaine	dr	f	l	vig	
Charles Fouquier	HCh	Pre 1846		m		vl		
Charles Gater	HP	1893	Paul G	mr	dbl		vig	f
Charles Getz	Bks	1871	Cook	lp				
Charles Gillemot	HT	see	Charlotte Gillemot					
Charles Girard	HP			pb				
Charles Lamb	HP	1884	Paul W	mr	f	l		
Charles Laporte	M		Vibert	mp				
Charles Laporte	HP	1856	Robert	p	f			
Charles Lawson	B	1853	Lawson	dp	dbl	l	vig	
Charles Lee	HP	1869	Gautreau	dp	f	l	vig	
Charles Lefèbvre	HP	1861	Lacharme	dr	f	l	vig	vf
Charles Lefèbvre, Climbing	Cl HP	1875	Cranston	dr				
Charles Lemayeux	G	Pre 1885		dp	f	l		
Charles Lemoine	G	Pre 1885		m	f	m		
Charles Lévêque	T	1884	Nabonnand	dr	f	l	vvig	
Charles Louis	HP	Pre 1800	Guinoisseaux	mr	s-d	l		
Charles Louis I	HCh	1840	Foulard / Verdier	mr	f	l		m
Charles Louis II	HCh	Pre 1846		lp				
Charles Margottin	HP	1864	Margottin	mr	dbl	vl	vig	vf
Charles Martel	G	1840	Parmentier	pb	f	l		
Charles Martel	B	1847	Guillot Père	mr	f	l		
Charles Martel	HP	1876	Oger	dr	vdbl	vl		
Charles Quint	G	1880	Moreau-Robert	m	dbl	m		
Charles Ravolli	T		Pernet Père	dp		m		
Charles Reybaud	T	Pre 1846	Robert & Moreau	mp	f	l	vig	
Charles Reybouth (Rimbault)	T	Pre 1870		lp	f	l		
Charles Robin	B	1853	Vigneron	mp	f	m		
Charles Rouillard	HP	1852	Laffay	lp	f	l	vig	
Charles Rovelli	T	1876	Pernet Père	rb	f	m		
Charles Souchet	B	1842	Souchet	dp	f	m	vig	
Charles Turner	HP	1867	Verdier E	mr	f	vl	vig	
Charles Turner	HP	1868	Margottin	mr	dbl	l	vig	
Charles V	T			mp	f	l	vig	
Charles Verdier	HP	1867	Guillot Père	mp	f	vl	vig	
Charles Wood	HP	1864	Portemer	rb	f	l	vig	
Charles X	G	Pre 1826	Descemet	mr				
Charles X	N	1825	Vibert	dr	f	l	vig	
Charles X	Ch	1827	Mauget	dr				
Charlotte	HSpn	Pre 1830	Noisette	lp	s-d	l	m	
Charlotte	A	Pre 1830	Mauget	w	dbl	m-l		
Charlotte Corday	HP	1863	Joubert	dr	f	l	vig	
Charlotte Corday	G			w	f	l		
Charlotte Dandasme	B	1865	Vigneron	dp	f	l		
Charlotte de Lacharme	G	1822	Vibert	pb	vdbl	m		
Charlotte de Soers	M	1843	Vibert	p	vdbl	m		
Charlotte Gagneau	HP	1869	Duval	mp				
Charlotte Gillemot	HT	1894	Guillot P	pb	f	l		m
Charlotte Séguier	HP	1849	Béluze	lp	f	l	vig	
Charmante	N	Pre 1846						
Charmante Louise	G			dr				
Charmante Isidore	G	Pre 1830	Boutigny	mp	vdbl	m		
Charmante Violette	G			lp				
Charming Beauty	Misc	Pre 1846						
Charpentier	HSpn	Pre 1830	Prévost syn Estelle	mp	dbl	l		
Chaste Suzanne	G			mp	f	m	vig	
Chastleton	HP	1800		lp	vdbl	l		
Châteaubriand	G			lp	f	s		
Châteaubriand	C	Pre 1834		dr	f	m		
Châteaubriand	HCh	1827	Noisette	lp				
Châteaubriand	HP	1852	Portemer	mp	vdbl	m		
Château de Brussow	HP			lp	f	vl		
Château de Namur	G	Pre 1842	Quétier / Parmentier	pb	f	m		
Château des Bergeries	T	1886	Ledéchaux Vve	ly	vf	l		
Château d'Ourout	T	1896	Ketten	rb	f	l	vig	f
Château Luegg	HMult		see Schloss Luegg					
Châtelain	B	Pre 1846	Laffay	lp	f	l	vvig	
Châtelain	N			lp				
Châtelain d'Eu	HP	1885	Verdier E	rb				
Chatenay	B	Pre 1846		lp	f	l	vig	
Chaussée	A	Pre 1830	Vibert	lp	f	m		
Chauvineau	N	Pre 1846		m				

Name	Class	Year	Breeder/Synonym					
Chedanne Guinoisseau	HRg	1896	ChedanneGuinoisseau	lp	f	l		
	syn	Mons.	ChedanneGuinoisseau					
Chénédolé	HCh	c 1840	Thierry	or	dbl	s	vig	m
Chénédolé	HCh	Pre 1846		dp		vl		f
Chénier	HCh	c 1825	Laffay	mp	vf	m		
Chéreau	HP	1849	Thomas	rb	f	m		
Chérence	N	1826	Vibert	w	vdbl	m	vig	f
Chérie	N		Laffay	lp				
Chérie	G		Lerouge					
Chérie	D		Miellez	p				
Cherokee Rose	Sp	1803	syn r.laevigata	w	s			
Cheshunt Hybrid	Cl HT	1872	Paul	mr	f	l	vig	
Cheshunt Scarlet	HP	1888	Paul G	mr	s-d			
Chestnut Rose	Sp	Pre 1814	syn r.roxburghii	mp				
Chevalier Angelo Ferrarro	T	1895	Bernaix	dr	f	l	vig	
Chevalier d'Amour	T	Pre 1846		w	f	m	vig	
Chevalier de Colquhoun	HP	1878	Nabonnand	rb	s-d	vl	vig	
Chevalier Nigra	HP	1865	Damaizin / Verdier C	lp	f	l		
Chevreul	M	1887	Moreau-Robert	mp	f	l	vig	
Chévrier	HCh	c 1825	Laffay (Vibert?)	m	vdbl	s		
			syn Miralda					
Chickasaw Rose	Sp	1793	syn r.bracteata	w				
Chiffonnée	Ch	1836	Joly	p	dbl	m		
Chifone Très Double	Ch							
Chilcote Rose	Sp	Pre 1814	syn r.roxburghii	mp				
Child of France	G	c 1802	syn Enfant de France	m	f	m		
Childling	C	Pre 1759		mp		l		
Chimène	N		Laffay	lp				
China Rose	Sp	1759	syn r.chinensis	mr				
Chinese	HEg	Pre 1846		dp				
Chinese Monthly Rose	Ch	1790 syn	Slater's Crimson Ch.	mr				
Chinquapin Rose	Sp	Pre 1814	syn r.roxburghii	mp				
Chloë	N	Pre 1834		lp	f	m	vig	
Chloris	A	Pre 1814	Descemet	lp	dbl	m	vig	
Chloris	N	Pre 1846		rb	f	m		
Chloris	HT	1890	Geschwind	mr	vdbl	l		
Chlose	N		Laffay	w				
Chou	C	Pre 1596	syn Cabbage Rose	lp	f	vl		
Chou	G			lp	vf	m		
Chou Rouge	C			lp	f	l		
Chréau	HP		see Chéreau					
Chremesina Scintilland	G	Pre 1787	syn Admirable	mr	f			
Christeis	HCh	1852	Ducher	mp	f	l		
Christian Püttner	HP	1862	Oger	m	f	l	vig	
Christian IX	B	1864	Pradel	w	f	l	m	
Christina Nilsson	HP	1861	Jamain	mr	f	vl		
Christina Nilsson	HP	1867	Lévêque	mr				
		syn	Mlle Christina Nilson					
Christine de Bisan	C	Pre 1846		lp	f	m		
Christine de Noué	T	1890	Guillot	mr	f	l	vig	m
			syn Mlle C de Noué					
Christine Mester	T	1861	Soupert & Notting	yb				
Christophe Colombe	P	1854	Robert	m	f	vl		
Chromatella	N	1843	Coquerau	ly	vdbl	l	vig	m
Chrysocome	T	Pre 1846		pb	f	l		
Chrystalline Cluster	N	Pre 1846						
Cibles	HRg	1893	Kaufmann	mr	s	m	vig	
Cicéron	B	1854	Ducher	w		l	vvig	
Cicéron	HP			dr				
Cicéron	G	Pre 1846	Vibert	rb	dbl	l	vig	
Cicris Rose	G	Pre 1830	Vibert syn Créralis	dr	vf	m		
Cimabue	B	1857	Moreau-Robert	dr				
Cinderella	N	1859	Page G	pb	f	m		
Cinnamon Rose	Sp	Pre 1600	syn r.cinnamomea	m				m
Cinthie	G		Descemet	m				
Circassienne	G	1821	Vibert	mp		l		
Circé	M	1855	Robert	pb	f	l		
Cire d'Espagne	G	Pre 1834	Miellez	mr		m		
Cisaque de Sibérie	G			dr				
Cisteri	Ch							
Citoyen des Deux Mondes	Ch	Pre 1846	Lacharme	dr	f	m		
City of Portland	HT	1890	Pernet-Ducher	mp	dbl	vl	vig	m
		syn	Mme Caroline Testout					
Ciudad de Oviedo	C	Pre 1824		mp	s			
Claire	C	1822		mp	f	s		
Claire	HMult	Pre 1866		mp				
Claire	HArv	Pre 1846		dr	s	s		
Claire	D	syn	Roi des 4 Saisons	lp	f	l		
Claire Carnot	N	1873	Guillot Fils	yb	f	m	vvig	f
Claire de Cressac	Ch		Laffay	rb				
Claire d'Olban	D	1825	Vibert	dp	f	m		
Claire Duchatelet (du Chatelet)	HP	Pre 1834	Robert	mp	f	m		

Claire Godard	T	1894	Godard	w	f	l		
Claire Jacquier	N	1887	Bernaix A	ly	s-d	s	vvig	m
Claire Merle	T	1885	Nabonnand	lp	f	m	vvig	
Claire Renard	HP	1867	Oger	mp	f	l	vvig	
Claire Thierry	HP	1875	Oger	rb	s-d	l	vig	
Claire Traffaut	B	1887	Verdier E	lp				
Claire Wendel	N			w	f	l	vig	vf
Claisigny	G	1826		rb				
Clara	G	Pre 1830	Vibert / Miellez	dp	vdbl	m		
			syn Maximus					
Clara	Ch		Laffay	pb				
Clara Barton	HT	1898	Van Fleet	ab	dbl			m
Clara Cochet	HP	1885	Lacharme	lp	dbl	vl	vvig	m
Clara Pfitzer	Pol	1887	Soupert & Notting	pb		s		
Clara Pries	T	1887	Pries	w		s		
Clara Sylvain	T	1838		w	f	l		
Clara Watson	HT	1894	Prince G	w	dbl		vig	f
Clara Wendel	N	Pre 1846		yb		m		
Clarinde	G			lp	f	l		
Clarisse	D	1816	Vibert	lp	f	l		
Clarisse	Ch	Pre 1846	Laffay	lp				
Clarisse	T							
Clarisse Harlowe	N	Pre 1846		w	f	m		
Clarisse Jolivet	C		Vibert	w	f	l		
Clarisse Manson	G	1816	Vibert					
Claude Bernard	HP	1878	Liabaud	dp	f	l		
Claude Jacquet	HP	1892	Liabaud	dr	dbl	vl	vig	
Claude Levet	HP	1872	Levet	mr	f	l	vig	vf
Claude Lorrain	Ch/B	Pre 1846		dp	f	m		
Claude Million	HP	1863	Verdier E	dr	f	l		
Claudia Augusta	N	1858	Damaizin	w	f	l	vig	
Claudine	Pom			rb				
Claudine	A	1823	Vibert	w	dbl	s		
Claudine Gourd	T	Pre 1846		mp	f	vl	vig	
Claudius Levet	T	1886	Levet	pb	f	l		f
Clef d'Or	HCh							
Clélie	G			mp		vl		
Clélie	C	1825	Vibert	lp	f	vl		
Clémence Beaugrand	M	1851	Laffay	mp	dbl	l	vig	
		Syn Mme	Clémence Beaugrand					
Clémence Delarue	HP	1856	Fontaine	pb	f	l		
Clémence Isaure	G	Pre 1830	Vibert	lp	f	l		
Clémence Isaure	HP	1851	Robert	op	f	m	vig	
Clémence Isaure	HEg		Trattinick (syn Jay)	pb	s	m		
Clémence Joigneaux	HP	1861	Liabaud	mr	f	vl		
Clémence Lartay	HP	1860	Lartay	lp	f	m		
Clémence Mallet	Ch			pb	f	m	m	
Clémence Patenotte	HP	1849	Vibert	lp	f	l	vig	
Clémence Raoux	HP	1869	Granger	mp	f	l	vig	m
Clémence Robert	M	1863	Robert & Moreau	mp	f	m	vig	vf
Clémence Thierry	HP	1880	Oger	pb	vdbl	m	vvig	
Clément Marot	HP	1860	Oger	m	vdbl	l		
Clément Nabonnand	T	1877	Nabonnand	yb	f	l	vig	
Clémentine	G	1818	Vibert	mp	f	m		
Clémentine	HEg	Pre 1824	Descemet	pb	s-d	m		
Clémentine	B	Pre 1846		mp				
Clémentine Duval	G			lp				
Clémentine Duval	HP	Pre 1846		mp	f	m		
Clémentine Duval	B	1847	Laffay	mp	f	m	vig	
Clémentine Séringe	HP	1840	Wood	mp	f	l	vvig	vf
Cléobuline (or Cléodoxe)	G	1820	Vibert					
Cléodone	G		Hardy	dp				
Cléonice	D	1821	Vibert	lp	f	m		
Cléonice	N		Laffay	lp				
Cléopatra	T	1889	Bennett	pb	f	l	m	f
Cléopatre	C	1816						
Cléopatre	C	1819	Vibert	lp	f	m		
Cléopatre	T/N	Pre 1846		lp	f	m		
Cléopatre	M	1853	Verdier V	lp	f	m	vig	
Cléopatre	HP	Pre 1870		mp	f	m		
Cléosthène	HP	Pre 1866		m	f	vl		
Clintonia	Ch	Pre 1846						
Clio	Ch			dr	f	m		
Clio	G	Pre 1820	Descemet	mr		m		
Clio	HP	1894	Paul W	lp	vdbl	l	vig	f
Clitus	Ch	1853	Bernède	m	f	l		
Cloebert	G							
Clorinde	G	Pre 1834	Miellez	lp	vf	l		
Cloris	A	Pre 1830	Descemet	lp	vdbl	s-m		
Cloth of Gold	N	1843	Coquerau	ly	vdbl	l	vig	m
			syn Chromatella					
Clothilde	G	1827	Noisette	mr				

Name	Type	Year	Raiser					
Clothilde Pfitzer	Pol	1899	Soupert & Notting	w				
Clothilde Roland	HP	1867	Roland	rb	f	l	vig	
Clothilde Soupert	T	1883	Levet	mp	vf	l		
Clotilde	G	Pre 1830	Coquerel	lp	f	m		
Clotilde	T	1867	Roland	mp	f	vl	vig	
			syn Bougèrc					
Clotilde Perrault	B	Pre 1870		lp	f	m		
Clotilde Soupert	Pol	1888	Soupert & Notting	w	dbl	l	vig	m
Clotilde Soupert, Climbing	Cl Pol	1896	Berckmans P J Co	w	dbl	m		m
Clovis	G		Miellez	p				
Clovis	HP	1868	Ledéchaux	m				
Cluster	HEg	Pre 1846		lp				
Cluster of Maidenblush	A							
Clynophylla	Misc		Dupleix	w		s		
Cocarde	G	Pre 1790	Descemet	lp	f	m		m
			syn Majestueuse					
Cocarde	A	c 1810	Descemet	mp				
Cocarde	T			w	f	m		
Cocarde Jacobée	G	1824		mr				
Cocarde Pâle	G	Pre 1813	Pradel	lp				
Cocarde Rouge	G	c 1825	Vibert	mp	vdbl	vl		
Cocarde Royale	G	Pre 1818	Hardy	lp	f	l		
			syn Grand Monarque					
Cochiné	HMult	Pre 1830	syn Rouge	mp	vdbl	s		
Coccinea	HBc	Pre 1835		dr				
Coccinea	T	c 1840	Cels	m	f	m		vf
Coccinea	HMult	1843	Legris	pb	f	s		
Coccinea Superbe	HCh		syn Vingt-Neuf Juillet	dr	f	l	vvig	
Cochineal	G	Pre 1846		mr				
Coerulescens Marmorata	G	1852	Verdier V	rb	f	m		
Coeur Aimable	G	c 1860	Miellez	m	f	m		
Coeur de Lion	HP	1866	Paul W	mp	vdbl	l	vig	
Coeur Noir	G	c 1860	Miellez	dr				
Coeur Tendre	D	c 1860	Miellez	dp				
Colardeau	HP	1859	Vibert	lp	f	l		vf
Colbert	B	1859	Robert & Moreau	dr				
Colbert	Ch		Laffay	m				
Col de Berry	A	Pre 1830	Sommesson	lp	f	s-m		
Colette	G	1827	Noisette	pb				
Colibri	Cl			m	f	s	vig	
Colibri	Pol	1898	Lille	ly	dbl	m	vig	
Coligny	C	Pre 1846		mr		l		
Collet	M			lp	vf	m		
Colmar	M	1846						
Colocotroni	Ch		Péan S	m	f	m	vvig	
Colomba	HCh			lp	f	l		
Colombine	HCh			dp	f	l		
Colonel Combe	B	Pre 1846	Pradel	m		m		m
Colonel de Cambriels	HP	1859	Robert & Moreau	mp	f	l	vig	
Colonel de Rougement	HP	1853	Lacharme	pb	f	vl	vig	
Colonel de Sansal	HP	1875	Jamain	mr	f	l		
Colonel Fabvier	HCh	1832	Laffay M	dp	f	l		
Colonel Félix Breton	HP	1883	Schwartz	rb	f	l	vig	
Colonel Foissy	HP	1849	Margottin	mp	dbl	m		
Colonel Juffé	T	1893	Liabaud	mr	f	m	m	
Colonel Lory	HP	Pre 1870	Pouillaux	rb	f	m		
Colonel Mignot	HP	1894	Puyravaud	lp				
Colonel Poissy	HP	Pre 1870		mr	f	m		
Colonel Robert Lefort	M	1864	Verdier E	dr	f	vl	vvig	vf
Colonel Souflot	HP	1862	Vigneron	mr				
Colonel Tillier	B			m	f	m		
Colonial White	LCl	c 1880		w	vdbl			sf
Columbia	HP	1887		w				
Columbienne	HCh	Pre 1846						
Columella	G	Pre 1841	Vibert	dr	f	m		
Columelle	G	1860	Robert & Moreau	m	f	l		
Comble de Gloire	Ch	Pre 1846		dp	f	l		
Comice de Marseilles	HP	1847	Pelisson	mp	f	m		
		syn	Victoire d'Austerlitz					
Comice de Seine-et-Marne	B	1842	Desprez	mr	f	m	vig	
Comice de Tarn-et-Garonne	B	1852	Pradel	mr	f	m		vf
Commandant Beaurepaire	G	1874	Moreau-Robert	pb	dbl	l	vig	f
Commandant Fournier	HP	1846	Laffay	rb	f	l		
Commandant Fournier	HP	1884	Moreau-Robert	dr	f	l	vvig	
Commandant Larrey de la Malignie	HP	1890	Moreau-Robert	rb	f	l	vvig	
Commandant Mansuy	HP	1869	Vigneron	mr	f	l	vvig	
Common Blush China	Ch	1751	Parsons syn Old Blush	mp	s-d	m	vig	vf
Common Centifolia	C	Pre 1596	syn Cabbage Rose	mp	vdbl	l		m
Common China	Ch	1751	Parsons syn Old Blush	mp	s-d	m	vig	vf
Common Michigan	HSet	Pre 1846		mp	s			
Common Monthly	Ch	1751	Parsons syn Old Blush	mp	s-d	m	vig	vf

Name	Class	Date	Raiser / Synonym	Col	Form	Size	Vigour	Frag
Common Moss	M	Pre 1596	syn Communis	mp	vdbl	l	vig	vf
Common Pink China	Ch	1751	Parsons syn Old Blush	mp	s-d	m	vig	vf
Common Pompon	C	Pre 1814	syn Rose de Meaux & r.centifolia pomponia	dp	vdbl	s		m
Common Provence	C		syn Communis	p				
Common Purple Boursault	Bslt	c 1810	Vilmorin syn Reversa	m	s-d	m		
Common Red China	Ch	1790 syn	Slater's Crimson Ch.	mr	dbl	l	m	
Common Tea	T	Pre1834		lp		m		
Common White	A	Pre 1846		w				
Commun	Ch			p				
Commune	N			p				
Commune	C			p				
Communis	C			p	f	l		
Communis	M	Pre 1596	see Cabbage Rose	mp	vdbl	vl	vig	vf
Communis Alba	C			w	f	l		
Communis Nova	C			mp	vdbl	l		
Compton	Misc	Pre 1830	Noisette	lp	dbl	l		f
Comte Adrien de Germiny	HP	1881	Lévêque	mr	f	l	vvig	
Comte Alphonse de Serenyi	HP	1865	Touvais	pb	f	l		
Comte Boula de Nanteuil	G	1834	Roeser	m	dbl	l		
Comte Carneval	HP			mp	f	m		
Comte Cavour	HP	1856	Vigneron	mp	f	l		m
Comte Cavour	HP	1859	Liabaud	pb	f	m		
Comte Chandon	T	1894	Soupert & Notting	my	f	l		
Comte Charles d'Harcourt	HP	1897	Lévêque	mr	f	l		
Comte de Beaufort	HP	1858	Boyau	m	f	m	vig	
Comte de Bobrinsky	HCh	1849	Marest	dp	dbl	m	m	
Comte de Boubert	B	Pre 1855		lp	f	l	vig	
Comte de Bourmont	HP	1851	Oger	lp	f	l	vig	
Comte de Breteuil	HCh	1827	Hardy	dp	f	m		
Comte de Chambord	HP			lp	dbl	m	wk	
Comte de Chambord	P	1860	Robert & Moreau	pb	vdbl		vig	vf
Comte de Chambord	B			dr	f	m		
Comte de Charny	B	Pre 1870		mr		m		
Comte de Colbert	G			m	f	m		
Comte de Colbert	B	1853	Pradel	mp	f	l		
Comte de Coutard	B		Noisette E	m	vf	m		
Comte de Durais	HP	1856	Robert	r	f			
Comte de Falloux	HP	1863	Standish	dp	f	m	m	
Comte de Flandres	HP	1881	Lévêque	dr	f	vl	vvig	
Comte de Foix	HCh							
Comte de Grassin	HP	1890	Corboeuf	dp	f	l		
Comte de Grivel	T	1871	Levet	ly	vdbl	l	vig	
Comte de Lacépède	G	1830	Vibert	lp	f	l		
Comte de Montalivet	HP	1846	Mondeville	m	f	l		
Comte de Montebello	HP	1896	Lévêque	rb				
Comte de Montessier	HP	1852	Berger	mp				
Comte de Montijo	B	1855	Fontaine	mr	f	m	m	
Comte de Mortemart	HP	1880	Margottin Fils	mp	f	l		vf
Comte de Murinais	G	Pre 1846		dr		l		
Comte de Nanteuil	G	1834	Roeser	m	dbl	l		m
Comte de Nanteuil	B	Pre 1846		dr				
Comte de Nanteuil	HP	1852	Quétier	mp	dbl	l	vig	
Comte de Paris	HP	1839	Laffay	m	f	vl		
Comte de Paris	T	1839	Hardy	lp	f	vl	m	m
Comte de Paris	HP	Pre 1846		lp				f
Comte de Paris	HP	1864	Verdier C syn Général Hudelet	dp	f	l		
Comte de Paris	HP	1886	Lévêque	rb	f	l		
Comte de Pembroke	HP	See	Earl of Pembroke					
Comte de Rambuteau	B	1842	Souchet	dp	f	l	vig	
Comte de Rambuteau	HP			pb	f	l	vig	
Comte de Ribeaucourt	HP	1870	Gémaux	dp	f	l	vig	
Comte de Sembui	T	1874	Ducher Vve syn Jean Ducher	op	f	l	vig	m
Comte de Taverna	T	1872	Ducher	ly	vf	l	vig	
Comte d'Egmont	HP			mp	f	l		
Comte d'Epernon	G			rb		l		
Comte d'Epresmesnil	HRg	1882	Nabonnand	m	s-d	l	vig	vf
Comte d'Eu	B	1844	Lacharme	mr	f	l	m	
Comte d'Osmond	T	Pre 1846		pb	vf	l	m	
Comte Derby	HP		Vibert	lp	f	l	vig	
Comte Florimond de Bergeyck	HP	1879	Soupert & Notting	rb	vf	l	vvig	vf
Comte Foy	G	1827	Lecomte	lp	f	vl		sf
Comte Foy de Rouen (syn Comte Foy)	G	Pre 1836	Savoureaux	lp	dbl	vl		
Comte Frédéric (François) de Thun	T	1893	Soupert & Notting	dr	f	l	vig	f
Comte Frédéric de Thun-Hohenstein	HP	1880	Lévêque	dr	f	l	vvig	m
Comte G de Roquette-Buisson	B	1887	Nabonnand	mp	vf	l		m
Comte Henri Rignon	HT	1885	Pernet-Ducher	yb	f	vl	vig	

Comte Horace de Choiseul	HP	1879	Lévêque	rb	f	l	vig	m
Comte H de Choiseul	HFt	1894	Pernet-Ducher	op	f	l		
Comte Jaubert	HP		see Comtesse Jaubert					
Comte Lelieur	P		see Rose du Roi					
Comte Litta	HP	1867	Verdier E	rb	f	l		
Comte Odart	HP	1850	Dupuy-Jamain	mr	f	l	vig	
Comte Orloff	N		Vibert	lp				
Comte Plater	C	Pre 1860		w				
Comte Raimbaud	HP	1867	Rolland	mr	dbl	l	vig	
Comte Raoul Chandon	HP	1896	Lévêque	rb	f	l		
Comte Walsch	G			mp	f	m		
Comtesse A de Germiny	HP			rb				
Comtesse Alban de Villeneuve	T	1881	Nabonnand	pb	f		vig	
Comtesse Almaviva	G	Pre 1860		dr	vf	vl		
Comtesse Anna Thun	T	1887	Soupert & Notting	yb	f	l	vig	vf
Comtesse Antonia Migazzi	HP	1889	Benko	mp	f	l		
Comtesse Bardi	T	1896	Soupert & Notting	yb	dbl	l		m
Comtesse Bathiany	HP	1850	Laffay	dp	f	l		
Comtesse Bertrand de Blacas	HP	1888	Verdier E	mp	f	l	vig	f
Comtesse Branicka	HP	1888	Lévêque	lp	dbl	l	vvig	
Comtesse Cahen d'Anvers	HP	1885	Ledéchaux	mp	dbl	l	vig	m
Comtesse Caroline Radzinski	T	1886	Soupert & Notting	pb				
Comtesse Cécile de Chabrillant	HP	1858	Marest	pb	dbl	m	vvig	vf
Cmtse Cécile de Chabrillant Blanche	HP			lp				
Comtesse d'Alvilliers	G			lp	f	m		
Comtesse Daru	N		Laffay	w				
Comtesse de Baillet	G	1827		w	f	m		
Comtesse de Barbentane	B	1851	Guillot Père	lp	f	vl	vig	
Comtesse de Beaumetz	N	1876	Nabonnand	y	f	l	vig	
Comtesse de Bernis	HP	1890	Liabaud	pb				
Comtesse de Bethford	G			mr				
Comtesse de Bouchaud	N	1890	Guillot et Fils	my		vl		
Comtesse de Bresson	HP	1873	Guinoisseau B	lp	dbl	l	vvig	
Comtesse de Bréteuil	T	1892	Pernet-Ducher	lp				
Comtesse de Brossard	T	1863	Oger	my	f	m	vig	f
Comtesse de Camondo	HP	1880	Lévêque	mr	f	vl	vig	
	syn	Mme La	Cmtse de Camondo					
Comtesse de Caraman	T	1893	Godard	rb	vf	l	vvig	
Comtesse de Caserta	T	1877	Nabonnand G	mr	s-d	l	vig	vf
Comtesse de Casteja	HP	1884	Fontaine	dr	vf	l	vig	vf
Comtesse de Chabrillant	HP	1858	Marest	p	f	l	vig	
Comtesse de Chabrillant Blanche	HP	1870	Oger	op	f	l		
			syn Mme Lefrançois					
Comtesse de Chabrol	Misc							
Comtesse de Chamoïs	C	c 1810	Descemet	mp	dbl	s-m		
Comtesse de Choiseul	HP	1878	Motteau J	mr	f	l	vvig	
			syn Mlle Marie Rady					
Comtesse de Colbert	B	Pre 1846		m	f	m		
Comtesse de Coursy	HP	1862	Lévêque	dp				
Comtesse de Coutard	HCh	1829	Noisette M	mp	vdbl	l	vvig	
Comtesse de Crillon	T			m	f	m		
Comtesse de Falloux	HP	1867	Trouillard	mp	vf	vl		
Comtesse de Flandres	HP	1878	Verdier E	lp	dbl	l	vig	
Comtesse de Fresnel	N	Pre 1830	Prévost	m	dbl	m		f
Comtesse de Fressinet de Bellanger	HP	1885	Lévêque	lp	f	vl		
Comtesse de Frigneuse	T	1885	Guillot et Fils	my	dbl	l	vig	f
Comtesse de Galard-Béarn	N	1894	Bernaix A	ly	dbl	l	vvig	vf
Comtesse de Ganay	HP	1895	Lévêque	rb				
Comtesse de Genlis	G	1817	Vibert	w				
Comtesse de Glasgow	Pom			dr	dbl	s		
Comtesse de Grailly	T	1895	Puyravaud	w				
Comtesse de Greffulhe	HP	1896	Lévêque	pb	f	l		
Comtesse de Jaucourt	HP	1866	Desmazures	mp	vf	l	vvig	vf
	syn	Mme	La Cmtse de Jaucourt					
Comtesse de Kinnoul	Pom			dr	f	s		
Comtesse de Labarthe	T	1857	Bernède	lp	vdbl	m	vig	
		syn	Duchesse de Brabant					
Comtesse de Lacépède	G/Ch	1840	Duval / Verdier	lp	dbl	l	m	
Comtesse de Langeron	P	1820	Vibert	lp	f	m		
Comtesse de Leusse	T	1878	Nabonnand	mp	dbl	l	vig	
Comtesse de Limerick	T	1878	Nabonnand	w	f	l	vig	
Comtesse de Ludre	HP	1879	Verdier E	mr	f	vl	vvig	vf
Comtesse de Mailly-Nesle	HP	1882	Lévêque	lp	f	l	vig	
Comtesse de Marnes	HP	1854	Desprez	pb	f	l	vig	
Comtesse de Maussac	HP	1874	Vigneron	mp	f	l	vig	
Comtesse de Medina Coeli	HP	1864	Marest	mr	f	l		
Comtesse de Mélores	G			dr	f	s	vig	
Comtesse de Ménou	T	1890	Liabaud (syn Curiace)	w				

Name	Type	Year	Breeder					
Comtesse de Mercy d'Argentine	HP	1895	Lévêque					
Comtesse de Montalivet	G			pb	f	m		
Comtesse de Mosbourg	B	1861	Pradel	mp				
Comtesse de Murinais	M	1843	Vibert	w	dbl	l	vig	f
Comtesse de Murinais	G	1843	Robert	lp	f	l		
Comtesse de Nadaillac	T	1871	Guillot Fils	ab	f	s	vig	f
Comtesse de Nantes	HP							
Comtesse de Nassau	HArv							
Comtesse de Noë	M	1846	Portemer	m	vf	m		
Comtesse de Palikao	HP	1865	Pernet Père	lp	f	l	vvig	
Comtesse de Panisse	T	1878	Nabonnand	mr	f	l	vig	f
Comtesse de Paris	HP	1864	Verdier E	pb	f	l	vig	
Comtesse de Paris (re-introduced)	HP	1882	Lévêque syn above	pb	f	l	vig	
Comtesse de Polignac	HP	1862	Granger	dr	dbl	m	vig	
Comtesse de Rambuteau	HP			mp				
Comtesse de Rességuier	B	1842	Béluze	mp	f	m		
Comtesse de Rocquigny	B	1874	Vaurin	lp	f	m		
Comtesse de Roquette-Buisson	HP	1888	Lévêque	lp		vl		
C'se de Rosemond-Chabeau de Lussay	T	1887	Chauvry	op	f	l		
Comtesse de Saint-Andéol	HP	1889	Renaud G	pb				
Comtesse de Saint-Venant	B			lp	f	m	m	
Comtesse de Séguier	HP	1848	Verdier V	mr	f	l		
Comtesse de Séguier	HP	1861	Samson	mr				
Comtesse de Ségur	C	1848	Verdier V	lp	f	m	vig	
Comtesse de Seraincourt	T	1852	Pradel	mp	f	l		vf
Comtesse de Serenye	HP	1874	Lacharme	lp	f	vl	vvig	
Comtesse de Tolosan	N			w	f	l	vig	
Comtesse de Turenne	HP	1853	Oger	lp				
Comtesse de Turenne	HP	1867	Verdier E	lp	f	l	vig	
Comtesse de Vallier	HP	1866	Damaizin	m	f	m		
Comtesse de Vitzthum	T	1890	Soupert & Notting	my	f	l		
Comtesse Desroys	HP	1859	Moreau-Robert	dp				
Comtesse d'Eu	HP	1888	Verdier E	dr	f	l	vig	
Comtesse d'Eu	T	1893	Lévêque	mp				
Comtesse d'Eu	HP	1894	Lévêque	yb				
Comtesse d'Indre	HP							
Comtesse d'Oettingen	Pom	1826	Baumann	lp	f	s		
Comtesse Doria	M	1854	Portemer Fils	m	dbl	m		
Comtesse d'Orléans	HP	1854	Descemet	w	f	m		
Comtesse d'Orloff	N	1824	Vibert	dp	dbl	l		
Comtesse d'Oxford	HP	1869	Guillot Père	mr	dbl	l	vig	f
Comtesse d'Oxford, Climbing	HP	1875	Smith	dp				
Comtesse Duchatel	HP	1842	Laffay	mp	vf	m-l		
	see	Cmtse	Tanneguy Duchatel					
Comtesse Dusy	T	1893	Soupert & Notting	w	f	l	vig	m
Comtesse Eva Starhemberg	T	1890	Soupert & Notting	yb	f	l	vig	
Comtesse Félicie Morgues	HP	1866	Pernet Père	mp	f	l	vig	
Comtesse Festétics Hamilton	T	1892	Nabonnand	pb	f	l	vig	
Cmtse Frédéric de Thun-Hohenstein	HP	see	Comte Fr de Thun-H					
Comtesse Fressinet de Bellanger	HP	1886	Lévêque	mp	dbl	vl		
Cmtse Georges de Roquette-Buisson	N	1885	Nabonnand	my	dbl	m		
Cmtse Georges de Roquette-Buisson	HP	1899	Lévêque	mp	dbl	m		
Comtesse Hélène Mier	HP	1876	Soupert & Notting	lp	f	l	vig	
Comtesse Henriette Combes	HP	1881	Schwartz	pb	f	l	vig	vf
Comtesse Horace de Choiseul	HP	1878	Moreau	rb	f	l	vig	
Comtesse Horace de Choiseul	T	1886	Lévêque	pb	f	l		f
Comtesse Jaubert	HP	1847	Laffay	lp				
Comtesse Julie de Schulenburg	HP	1888	Soupert & Notting	dr	f	l		m
Comtesse Julie Hunyady	T	1888	Soupert & Notting	yb	f	l		
Comtesse Langeron	C		Vibert	lp	f	m		
Comtesse Lily Kinsky	T	1896	Soupert & Notting	w	f			
Comtesse Livia Zichy	T	1894	Soupert & Notting	yb				
Comtesse Louise de Kergolay	HP	1843	Touvais	m	f	l		
Comtesse Marie de Bourges	HP	1853	Cherpin	mp	f	l	vig	
Comtesse Mathide d'Arnim	HP	1875	Soupert & Notting	rb			vig	
Comtesse Molé	Ch/B	Pre 1846		mp	f	l	vvig	
Comtesse Nathalie de Kleist	HP	1880	Soupert & Notting	op	f	l		
Comtesse Odouard	D			lp	f	m		
Comtesse O'Gorman	HP	1888	Lévêque	rb	f	l		
Comtesse O'Gorman	T	1892	Nabonnand	pb	dbl	m		m
Comtesse Ouwaroff	T	1861	Margottin	lp	f	l	vig	f
Comtesse Platen	M			w	f	m		
Comtesse Platen	Ch	1842	Vibert	lp	f	l	vig	
Comtesse Plater	HP	1842	Vibert	w				
Comtesse Renée de Béarn	HP	1896	Lévêque	dr	f	l		

Name	Class	Date	Raiser	Col 1	Col 2	Col 3	Col 4	Col 5
Comtesse Renée de Mortemart	T	1893	Godard	w	f	l		m
Comtesse Riza du Parc	T	1876	Schwartz J	mp	dbl	l	vvig	f
Comtesse Saubert	HP			lp	s-d	m	vig	
Comtesse Tanneguy-Duchatel	HP	1843	Laffay	dp	f	vl	vvig	
Comtesse Théodore Ouwaroff	T	1897	Soupert	pb	f	vl		f
Comtesse Vaillant	HP	1854	Margottin	m	f	l		
Comtesse Vally de Serenye	HP	1875	Fontaine	rb	f	l	vvig	
Comtesse Vitalli	T	1899	Nabonnand	w				
Comtesse Woronzoff	T			pb	f	vl	vig	
Concha Bolin	T	1887	Pries	w				
Condesa da Foz	N	1885	Da Costa	yb	f	l	vvig	
			syn Rêve d'Or					
Conditorum	G	1629		dr	s-d	l		
Condorcet	M	Pre 1846		lp				
Confucius	Ch	Pre 1846		lp	f	l		
Congrès de Gand	G			mp	f	m		
Conque de Vénus	N	Pre 1846		lp	f	m		
Conquête de Jacques	Ch			m				
Conquête Heureuse	Ch	Pre 1846		mr				
Conrad Ferdinand Meyer	HRg	1897	Müller F	lp	dbl	l	vig	vf
Conseiller Jourdeuil	HP	1853	Lacharme	lp	f	m		
Constance	C	Pre 1830	syn Dsse de Grammont	mp	f	vl		
Constance Zacharius	G	Pre 1830	Coquerel					
Constant de Rébecque	N	1825	Vibert	mp	s-d	l		
Constant Lusseau	HP	1854	Trouillard	mp	f	m		
Constantin	G	Pre 1838	Vibert	mp	vdbl	l		
Constantin Petriakoff	HP	1878	Jamain	rb	f	l	vvig	vf
Constantine	G	Pre 1834	Vibert (syn Idalise)	mp	vf	l		
Contarini	G		Parmentier	lp	f	m		
Cooper	HFt			rb	s	m		
Coq de Biez	G			lp	f	m		
Coq de Village	G			dr	f	l		
Coquelicot	G	1820						
Coquereau	G	Pre 1834		mp	f	l		
Coquerel	G	Pre 1834		dr		m		
Coquette	Misc	Pre 1846						
Coquette Bordelaise	HP	1896	Duprat	pb	dbl	vl		
Coquette d'Angers	HP	1854	Robert	dp			vig	
Coquette de Bellevue	Ch			dr	f	s		
Coquette de Bellevue	HP	Pre 1846		dp			vig	
Coquette de Lyon	HP	1859	Lacharme	lp				
Coquette de Lyon	T	1870	Ducher	ly	f	m	m	f
Coquette de Melun	B	Pre 1846	Varengot	lp	f	m		
Coquette de Meudon	HP			dp	f	m	vig	
Coquette de Montmorency	HP	Pre 1846		m	f	m		
Coquette de Normandie	HP	1872	Oger	w	f	m	vvig	
Coquette de Saint-Marceau	HP	Pre 1870		mr		s		
Coquette des Alpes	B	1867	Lacharme	w	f	m	vig	
Coquette des Blanches	B	1871	Lacharme	w	dbl	m	vig	m
Cora	G	1827	Lecomte	m	f	s	m	
Cora	HP	1859	Guillot Père	mp	f	m	vig	
Cora	G	Pre 1885	Savoureux	m	dbl	s	m	
Cora	Ch	1899	Schwartz, Vve	yb	f	m	vig	f
Cora à Pétales Variés	Misc	Pre 1819		yb		l		
Cora L Barton	N	1840	Buist	lp		l		
Coralie	N	1827	Vibert	lp	dbl	l		f
Coralie	D	Pre 1846		lp	vdbl	m	vig	m
Coralie	M	c 1860	Miellez	lp	dbl	m		
Coralie Punctuée	G			lp	f	l		
Coralloïde	D		Bozérain					
Corcelles	T		Laffay	dr				
Cordon Bleu	G	Pre 1830	Lille / Miellez	dr	f	m-l		
Cordon Bleu de Baltet	G	Pre 1830	Calvert	mr	f	m-l		
			syn Grande Bichonne					
Cordon Double	G			lp				
Cordon Rouge	G	Pre 1830	Racine					
Corine	G	1818	Vibert	lp	f	s		
Corine	C	1832	Vibert	lp		m		
Corinna	T	1893	Paul W	pb	dbl	m	vig	f
Corinna	Ch			lp	f	m		
Coriophylla	C							
Cornelia	G			dr	f	l		
Cornelia Cook	T	1855	Cook	w	dbl	vl	vig	m
Cornélie	C	1819						
Cornélie	G	1830	Vibert	mp	f	m		
Cornélie	N	1855	Robert & Moreau	mp	f	m		
Cornélie	G		Garilland	mp				
Cornélie	Bks			mp				
Cornélie	G		Prévost	lp				
Cornet	C			lp				
Cornet	HP	1845	Lacharme	m	vdbl	vl	vig	m
Coronet	HT	1897	Dingee-Conard	lp	f	vl		vf

Name	Class	Date	Breeder / Synonym					
Coronis	N			lp	f	m		
Corporal Johann Nagy	HSet	1890	Geschwind	dp	dbl	m		
Coruscans	Rg	1897		lp				
Corvisart	HCh	1825	Laffay	mp	vf	m		
Corymbifère	D							
Corymbosa	N			w			vig	
Corymbosa Fulgens	N		Mme Herbert	m				
Corymbosa Plena	N		Laffay	lp				
Cosaque de Siberie	G	Pre 1830						
Cosimo Ridolfi	G	1842	Vibert	m	f	m		
Cotoneux	Pom	Pre 1830		lp	s	m	vig	
Cotoneux Hybride à Petites Feuilles	Pom	1823	Vibert	lp	dbl		vig	
Cottage Maid	G	1845	Vibert G	m	dbl	s	m	m
		syn	Perle des Panachées					
Couleur à la Mode	G			rb				
Couleur de Brennus	G	Pre 1857		mr	dbl	m		
Couleur de Bronze	G		Descemet					
Couleur de Chair	C	c 1805	Vilmorin syn Vilmorin	lp	f	m-l		
Couleur de Chair	N	1827	Mauget					
Couleur de Cuivre	Alp	Pre 1830	Vibert	mr	s			
Couleur de Feu	C	Pre 1886		or	f	m	vig	
Couleur de Mérise	G		Vibert	dr				
Couleur de Sang	G	Pre 1787	syn Admirable	mr	f			
Couleur d'Hortense	Ch			mr	f	m		
Couleur Lilas	G		Descemet					
Coulure	HCh	Pre 1846						
Countess of Caledon	HT	1897	Dickson A	lp	f	l	vig	
Countess of Crilon	N	Pre 1846						
Countess of Fresnel	N	Pre 1846						
Countess of Glasgow	HSpn	Pre 1817		dr				
Countess of Lieven	Ayr	Pre 1846		w	s-d	m	vvig	
Countess of Limerick	T	see	Comtesse de Limerick					
Countess of Oxford	HP	see	Comtesse d'Oxford					
Countess of Pembroke	HT	1882	Bennett	pb	vdbl	l	vig	f
Countess of Roseberry	HP	1879	Portans	mr	f	l		
Coupe d'Amour	HCh	Pre 1846	Laffay	lp	f	m		
Coupe de Cynthie	B			mp	f	m		
Coupe d'Hébé	B	1840	Laffay	dp	vdbl	l	vig	vf
Couronné Blanche	D		Miellez	w				
Couronné d'Amour	G			lp	f	m		
Couronné d'Ariane	G	Pre 1830	Racine	lp	f	m-l		
Couronné de Béranger	P	Pre 1846		lp	f	m		
Couronné de Brabant	G			lp				
Couronné de Salomon	G	Pre 1819		dp	vdbl	l		
Couronné de Vibert	HCh	1825	Bizard	mp				
Couronné des Parterres	HP	1861	Touvais	mr	f	m	vig	
Couronné des Pourpres	Ch	Pre 1846		m		m		
Couronnée	G	c 1811		lp	dbl	l		
Couronné Impériale	G	c 1810	Descemet	m	f	m		
Couronné Royale	G	Pre 1830		mp	f	m		
		syn	Empereur Couronné					
Courtin	G	1824	Cartier	lp				
Courtisan	Ch		Laffay	lp	f	s		
Courtney	Misc		syn Anglaise	lp				
Coutard	HCh	Pre 1846	Laffay	lp		l		
Couture	HCh	c 1825	Cartier	m				
Couturier-Mention	Ch	see Mm	e Couturier-Mention					
Couvrier	B	Pre 1846						
Craighall Climbing Rose	Ayr	1828		w	dbl			
Cramoisi	C	Pre 1629	syn Rubra	mr	dbl			sf
Cramoisi	G	Pre 1650	syn Burgundian Rose	pb	dbl			
Cramoisi	C	Pre 1820		dr	vdbl			
Cramoisi	M	Pre 1827	Tinwell / Lee syn Tinwell Moss	dp	dbl	l		
Cramoisi	N		Laffay	dr				
Cramoisi	M		Laffay	dr				
Cramoisi	HBc			mr				
Cramoisi	C			lp	s-d	m		
Cramoisi	HArv							
Cramoisi à Fleurs Simples	M	1856	Rivers	dr	s	m		
Cramoisi Bedder	HP		see Crimson Bedder					
Cramoisi Boursault	HCh			dr	f	m		
Cramoisi Brillant	G		syn Temple d'Apollon	dr	s-d	l		
Cramoisi de Meaux	M		syn Little Gem	dp				
Cramoisi des Alpes	G	Pre 1829	Trébucien	mr	f	m		
Cramoisi Double	Ch	Pre 1830	Prévost syn Sanquin	dr	vdbl	m	wk	
Cramoisi Éblouissant	Ch	Pre 1834	Laffay (?)	dr	dbl	s	m	
Cramoisi Feu	Ch		Laffay	dr	dbl			
Cramoisi Foncé Velouté	M		Laffay	dr				
Cramoisi Formosa	G	Pre 1830	Calvert	dr				
Cramoisi French	M			rb				

Name	Type	Date	Breeder / Syn					
Cramoisi Globe	M		see Crimson Globe					
Cramoisi Globe	B		syn Dr Rocques	dr	f	m		
Cramoisi Incomparable	G	Pre 1811	syn Velours Pourpre	dr	vdbl		s	
Cramoisi Majeur	G	Pre 1819	syn Hector	m	dbl	s		
Cramoisi Moss	M		syn Little Gem	dr				
Cramoisi Nuance	G	1822	Vibert	dr	s	m		
Cramoisi Panache	Ch	1820	Laffay	rb	f	m	vig	
Cramoisi Picoté	G	1834	Vibert	rb	vf	m		m
Cramoisi Pompon	M							
Cramoisi Ponctuée	G	Pre 1830	Prévost	dr	dbl	m		
Cramoisi Royal	G	c 1810	Descemet					
Cramoisi Superbe	HP			dr	f	m		
Cramoisi Supérieur	Ch	1832	Coquereau	mr	dbl	s	vig	
Cramoisi Supérieur, Climbing	Cl Ch	1885	Couturier	mr	s-d	m	vig	
Cramoisi Tinwell	M		syn Tinwell Moss					
Cramoisi Violet	G	1819	Vibert					
Cramoisie	G	Pre 1791		dr	dbl	m		
Cramoisie	HSpn	Pre 1846		mr				
Cramoisie Éblouissante	G	Pre 1811		dr	vdbl			
Cramoisie Enflammé	G	Pre 1846		dr				
Cramoisie Triumphante	G	Pre 1811		dp				m
Cramoisissimo Amplo	G		De Pronville, syn Temple d'Appolon					
Crême	S	1895	Geschwind	lp	s-d	s		vf
Crenata	C	Pre 1804	Dupont, syn À Feuilles Crénelées	lp	f	s		m
Crepe Rose	HP	1870	Levet syn Paul Perras	lp	vdbl	l		
Crépue à Feuilles Ondulées	G		Descemet	dr				
Creralis	G	Pre 1830	Calvert	mr	vf	m		
Crested Moss	C	1827	Vibert	mp	vf	l	vig	vf
Cricks	C	Pre 1821	syn Yorkshire Provence	mp				
Crignon de Montigny	G	Pre 1842		dr	f	m		
Crillon	HP	1834	Vibert	lp	f	m	vig	
Crimean Sweetbrier	Sp	1796	syn r.horrida	w				
Crimson	Arv	Pre 1846		dr				
Crimson	M	Pre 1827	Tinwell / Lee, syn Tinwell Moss	dp	dbl	l	vig	
Crimson Bedder	HP	1874	Cranston	mr	dbl	m	vig	
Crimson Bedder	HMult	1896	Cooling	mp	s			
Crimson Boursault	Bslt		see Amadis					
Crimson China Rose	Ch	1790	syn Slater's Crimson Ch.	mr	dbl		m	
Crimson Globe	M	1890	Paul W	dr	f	l	vig	
Crimson Mme Desprez	B	Pre 1846		dr		l		
Crimson Moss	M	Pre 1846	Lee	rb	dbl		vig	
Crimson Moss of Meaux	M		See Cramoisi de Meaux					
Crimson Perpetual	P			dr				
Crimson Pompone	M	Pre 1846		dp			s	
Crimson Queen	HP	1890	Paul W	dr	dbl	vl	vvig	
Crimson Rambler	HMult	1893	Turner	mr	dbl	s	vvig	
Crimson Superb	P	Aft 1810	Descemet, syn Mogador	dp	f	m		
Crimson Superbe	HCh			dr				
Crispée	M		see Cristata					
Cristalline	Ch			w	f	l	vig	
Cristata	C	1827	Vibert, syn Crested Moss and Chapeau de Napoleon	mp	vf	l	vig	vf
Crivalis	G	Pre 1846		dp				
Crivelli	HMult	Pre 1846		mr				
Croix d'Honneur	G	c 1830	Prévost	mr	f	s		
Croix d'Honneur	HCh	1852	Dorisy	w	dbl	l		
Crown	T		See Louis Philippe					
Crown Prince	HP	1880	Paul W & Son	rb	dbl	l	vvig	f
Cuisse de Nymphe	A	1597	Dumont de Courset, syn Great Maiden's Blush	lp	dbl	m	vig	
Cuisse de Nymphe à Ovaire Lisse	A	1802	Dumont de Courset, syn Maiden's Blush	w	dbl	m		m
Cuisse de Nymphe Émue	A	1802	Dumont de Courset, syn Maiden's Blush	w	dbl	m		m
Cuisse de Nymphe Grande	A	Pre 1738	syn Great Maiden's Blush	w	dbl	m		
Cuivré	Sp	c 1596	syn r.foetida bicolor	rb	s			
Cumberland	C	Pre 1818	Prévost	lp	dbl	l		
Cupid	Misc	Pre 1846						
Cupidon	N	1825	Laffay	rb	f	m		
Cupidon	G		Miellez	mp	f	l		
Cupidon	Ch	Pre 1830	Laffay	m	vdbl	s		
Cupidon de Cumberland	G		Prévost	lp				
Curé de Biez	G			lp				
Curé de Charentay	HP	1868	Ducher	dr	f	vl	vig	

Name	Class	Year	Breeder / Reference				
Curiace	T	1860	Bernède	yb	f	m	
Curidos	HMult			lp			
Curled	C	Pre 1846		mp			
Cuvier	G	1843	Vibert	lp	f	l	
Cybèle	G	Pre 1830	Racine	mr	f	m-l	
Cyclop	T	1890	Geschwind	rb	dbl	m	
Cymbaefolia	A	1807	Flobert / Pelletier	w	dbl	s	
		see	À Feuilles de Pêcher				
Cymedor	HP	1846	Guillot Père	dr	f	m	vig
Cymodécée	HCh			lp	f	l	
Cymodée	G			dr	f	m	
Cynthie I	G	Pre 1815	Descemet	lp	dbl	l	m
Cynthie II	G	Pre 1820	Descemet / Vibert	m	f	l	
Cypris	Bslt	Pre 1824	syn Blush Boursault	pb	vdbl	vl	vvig
Cyrus	G	Pre 1846		lp		l	
Cythère	B			w	f	m	vig
Cytherée	B	Pre 1846		mp			

NAME	TYPE	YEAR	RAISER	COLOUR	BLOOM	SIZE	GROWTH	SCENT
D'Aguesseau	G	1832	Vibert	mr	dbl	s		m
D'Amitié	D							
D'Amour	G			lp	f	m		
D'Anderson	HSpn			mp				
D'Andigné de la Blanchaie	HCh	Pre 1846		m	f	m		
D'Angers	HP	Pre 1846		lp				
D'Anjou	C	Pre 1834		dp	f	l		
D'Anjou	HP			dr	f	m		
D'Arago	G			lp	f	m		
D'Arcet	M	1851	Robert	dr	dbl	l		
D'Arcole	B		Vibert	lp	f	m		
D'Artagnan	B	1847	Vibert	lp	f	m		
D'Arzens	HP	1861	Ducher	op	s-d	l		
D'Assas	HP	1850	Vibert	pb	dbl	m	vig	
D'Assas	G	Pre 1846		m	f	m		
D'Aubenton	G			mp	vf	vl		
D'Aubenton	B		Laffay	mr				
D'Aubenton	M	1854	Robert	dp	f			
D'Audigné de la Blanchaie	HCh	Pre 1864	see D'Andigné above					
D'Auteuil	Misc		Laffay	dr				
Dahlia	T			mp	f	m	vig	
Dahlia Monstreux	HP	See	Damas Monstreux					
Dahlia Rose	Ch		Laffay	mp	dbl	m		
Dahliensis	T			dp	f	l	m	
Daisy	HT	1899	Dickson A	mp	f	l		m
Dalbret	B		see Jeanne d'Albret					
Dalbret	N		Laffay	lp	dbl	m		
Dalinde	Ch	Pre 1846		dr				
Dalkeith	HSpn	Pre 1846						
Dalrymple	HSpn	Pre 1846						
Damas Franklin	D	1853	Robert	pb				
Damas Monstreux	D	Pre 1834		lp		vl		
Damas Monstreux	P	1845	Vibert syn Arielle					
Damas Mousseux	M	Pre 1827	Tinwell / Lee syn Tinwell Moss	dp	dbl	l		
Damas Panache	D							
Damas Pourpre	D	Pre 1834		m	f	m		
Damas Violacé	D	1820	Godefroy	lp	vf	m		
Damascena	D	1768	Miller	lp	f	l	vig	
Damascena Petala Variegata	D	1551	Monardes syn York & Lancaster	pb	dbl	m		m
Damask Monthly	D	Pre 1700	syn Autumn Damask	mp	dbl			m
Damask Rose	D	Pre 1600	syn Summer Damask	lp	dbl	m		m
Damassine	HFt		Noisette	dp				
		syn	Parnassina de Pronv.					
Dame Blanche	D	Pre 1830	Miellez	w	f	l		
Dame Rose	HP			lp	f	l		
Damème	HP	1842	see Madame Damème	mp	f	l		
Dames Patronesses d'Orléans	HP	1877	Vigneron	dr	f	l	vig	
Danaé	G	1854	Robert	lp	f	m	vig	
Danaé	HP	1865	Touvais	pb	f	l		
Daniel Lacombe	HMult	1885	Allard	yb	dbl	m	vig	
Danmark	HT	1891	Zeiner-Larsen	mp	dbl	l		
Danville	M	Pre 1870		mr	vdbl	l	m	
Danzille	T		syn Mme Bravy	lp				
Daphne	HSpn	Pre 1817		dp		l		
Daphné	G	1819	Vibert	dp	dbl	m		
		syn	Nouveau Triomphe					
Daphné	HCh	1855		dp	f	m	vig	
Darius	Ch	1827	Laffay	mp	vdbl	m		sf
Darius	G			mr	dbl	l		
Dark Damask	Misc	Pre 1846						
Dark Mottled	Misc	Pre 1846		dr				
Dark Purple	Ch			dr	f	s		
Dark Shell	Misc	Pre 1846						
Dark Velvet	Misc	Pre 1846						
Darret	M	Pre 1870		mr	f	m		
Darzens	HP	1860	Ducher	op				
Dauphin	Ch	1827	Mauget	mr				
Dauphine	G	1814		lp				
Dauphine	Ch	1827	Mauget	lp	g	l	vvig	
David	Ch			lp	f	m		
David Lazard Sichel	HP	1885	Singer	m	f	l		
David Pradel	T	1851	Pradel	m	f	vl	m	vf
David Stard	HP			mr				
Davoust	HCh	Pre 1834	Laffay	lp	vdbl	m		
Dawn	Cl HT	1898	Paul G	mp	s-d	l		
Dawson	HMult	1888	Dawson	mp	s-d	s	vig	m
D'Ecosse	HSpn	Pre 1830		lp	s			

Name	Class	Date	Raiser / Synonym					
D'Esquermes Royale	HP			mp	f	l		
De Bar-sur-Aube	C							
De Belon	Pom		Lemeusnil	p				
De Bordeaux	C	Pre 1791	syn Petite de Hollande	mp	dbl	m		m
De Bordier	G			mr	f	l		
De Bourgogne	Pom	1735	syn Burgundy	lp				
De Bourgogne à Fleur Blanche	Pom			w				
De Brown	HCh	Pre 1830	syn Du Népaul	lp		l		
De Candolle	HSpn	c 1830	Prévost	w	s			
De Candolle	HCh	c 1845	Calvert	m	f	l		
De Candolle	M	1857	Portemer Fils	lp	s-d	l		
De Carlsruhe	C			p				
De Cels	HCh		syn À Fleurs Blanches					
De Cels	D			lp				
De Chartres	HCh	Pre 1820	Laffay syn Nain and Laurentia Nain	lp	dbl	s		
De Chartres	C			pb				
De Chatenay	D		syn Argentée					
De Chelles	C			lp				
De Chou	C		syn Ordinaire	dp				
De Colmar	M							
De Cornouailles	G		Sommerlich	m				
De Cumberland	C			p				
De Damas	D		syn Mme Hardy	w				
De Ferrière	N			lp				
De Flandre	G	Pre 1811	syn Agathe Incarnata	lp	vdbl	m		
De Florence	Ch	Pre 1830	Noisette L syn Belle de Monza	m	f	m		
De Fontenelle	M	Pre 1870		dp	vdbl	m		
De France	G							
De France	HP	1893	Verdier E	dp				
De Gontille	G			p	f	m		
De Granval	Ch							
De Hollande	G	Pre 1790	Majestueuse	lp	f			m
De Jéricho	G			dp				
De Jessaint	C		Girardon	m				
De Kingston	Pom			mr				
De la Baie d'Hudson	Alp	Pre 1830	Lindley	mp	s	l		
De la Baie d'Hudson	Misc	Pre 1830	Vibert	dp	s	m		
De la Baie d'Hudson	Misc	Pre 1830	Vibert	dp	s-d	m		vf
De Laborde	HCh	Pre 1830	Laffay	lp	f	m		
De Laborde	G			m	f	m		
De la Chine à Feuilles Longues	HSem			w				
De la Croix	HCh		Noisette M	dp	vdbl	m		
De Laffay	HSem			lp				
De la Flèche	M	1824	Lemeunier	dr	dbl	m		
De la Grifferaie	HMult	1845	De Grille / Vibert Robin	dp	dbl	m	vvig	m
De la Haie	Pom							
De la Hogue	C	Pre 1834	syn Robin	lp		l		
De la Maître d'École	G	1831 syn Rose	Coquereau de la Maître d'École	m	dbl	vl		
De la Malmaison	G	Pre 1826	Pelletier	lp	f	m - l		
De Lamartine	B	Pre 1846		m				
De la Mothe	HP	1858	Avoux / Crozy	mp	vf	vl	vig	
De la Queue	N	1827		mr				
De la Reine	G	Pre 1791	syn Regina Dicta	m	f	m		
De la Reine	HP	1842	Laffay	lp				
De la Reine	HP	1846	Portemer syn Reine des Fleurs	mr	f	l		
De la Reine à Fleurs Blanches	HP			w				
De la Tour	HCh		Noisette M	mr	dbl	l	vvig	
De Lawrence	Min	1810	Sweet	mp				
De l'Est	Ch	syn	L'Astrolabe & Rose de l'Est	lp				
De l'Ile	Bslt	Pre 1824	syn Blush Boursault	pb	vdbl	vl		
De l'Ile Bourbon	B		syn Edward	dp				
De l'Ile de France	B	1826	Vibert syn Dubreuil	lp	f	m-l		
De Mahon	HSem							
De Mai	Pom			mp				
De Malte	D			lp				
De Marienbourg	HSpn	1826	Vibert	w	s	m		
De Meaux	C	1789	Sweet	dp	vdbl	s		m
De Messine	G	1823	Sommerlich	lp				
De Metz	M			mp				
De Millepied	C			mp				
De Millet	D	Pre 1830	Prévost	lp	vdbl	m		
De Misson	G			mp	f	m		
De Mon Fils	A	Pre 1815	Descemet	mp				
De Montebello	HP	Pre 1870		mr	f	l		
De Montmorency	HP	Pre 1846		dr	f			
De Montseignat	B	see	Mme de Montseignat					
De Moyenna	Ch		Noisette L	m				

Name	Class	Date	Breeder / syn					
De Nancy	C	Pre 1834	syn De Chelles	dp		l		
De Naples	P	c 1810	Descemet					
De Neige	M	Pre 1830	Vibert; syn Belle Henriette	w	s	m	vig	vf
De Neuilly	P	1835	Verdier V; syn Perpétuelle de Neuilly	mp				
De Pensylvanie Double	Misc		Prévost					
De Pensylvanie à Fleur Pale	Misc		Prévost					
De Pléville	G							
De Port Royal	C			mp				
De Portugal	D			mr				
De Pronville	G			mr				
De Provence	C							
De Puteaux	P		syn Rose de Puteaux					
De Reims	C	c 1850	Robert; syn Petit St François	m	f			
De Rennes	Ch	Pre 1830	Prévost syn Grandval	mr	vf	m-l		
De Roxburgh	HMult		Laffay; syn De Gréville	w				
De Sabine	Alp							
De Saint Barthélemy	P	1820	Delaâge	m	dbl	m		
De Sainte-Aldegonde	G		Parmentier	dp				
De Schelfhout	G	1840	Parmentier	lp	dbl	m		
De Schrimacker	G		Parmentier					
De Soie	HP		Miellez	pb	f	m	vig	
De Suez	HP			dp	f	m		
De Tourville	B	Pre 1870	syn Tourville	dr		m		
De Tous les Mois	P	Pre 1830	Vibert; syn Du Calendrier	lp	dbl	m		
De Tous Mois	HMsk	Pre 1828	Vibert	w	s-d	m		
De Transylvanie à Fleurs Doubles	Misc			mp				
De Transylvanie à Grandes Fleurs Pâle	Misc			lp				
De Trianon	HP	1846	Guillot Père	lp				
De Van Eeden	G	1810	Van Eeden; syn L'Obscurité	m	dbl	m		
De Veillard	M		De Veillard					
De Vergnies	HCh	1824	Vibert	m	f	m		
De Vierge	HP			w				
De Vinck	M			lp	f	m		
De Wissous	Ch	1835	Joly	dp	vdbl	l	vvig	
De Woods	Alp		syn Sabine	mr				
De Yebles	B			dr	f	m		
Dean of Windsor	HP	1878	Turner	mr	f	l	vvig	m
Décoration de Geschwind	HMult	1885	Geschwind; syn Geschwinds Orden	lp	vdbl	m	vig	
Déesse Flore	D	1827	Vibert	lp	f	m		
Deiphille	D	Pre 1830	Prévost; syn Soeur Josephe	lp	vdbl	s		
Déjanire	C	Pre 1830	Robert	lp	f	m		
Delaage	HCh	Pre 1846	Vibert; syn Général Delaage	dr	vf	m-l		
Delâge	Ch			dp	vdbl	m		
Delambre	P	1863	Moreau-Robert	dp	dbl	m		m
Delaunay	G			lp	f	l		
Delcourt	HP	1827	Vibert	lp		l		
Delicata	HRg	1898	Cooling	lp	s-d	l	vig	m
Délicate	G	Pre 1827	Dubourg	mr				
Délicatesse	D	Pre 1846	Miellez	lp		m		
Délice de Plantier	T	Pre 1846		lp				
Délices de Flandres	C	Pre 1834	Vibert	lp	f	l		
Délices de Flandres	G		Miellez	lp				
Délices de Flore	G	Pre 1830				m		
Délices de la Guillotière	T			ly	f	l		
Délices du Printemps	HSpn	Pre 1830	Vibert	lp	dbl	m-l		
Délicieuse	G	c 1830	Vibert	mp	f	m		
Delille	G	1822	Vibert	mr	f	m-l		
Delille	M	1852	Robert	w	s-d			
Delille	B			mp	f	m		
Delille	M	Pre 1870		mr	f	m		
Delphine	N			lp			vig	
Delphine	T	Pre 1860		w		l		f
Delphine Bernard	Ch			w	f	m		
Delphine de Chambaron	HP	1853	Pradel	lp	f	l		
Delphine Gaudot	T	1840	Béluze	w	f	m		f
Delphine Gay	G	c 1820	Vibert	m	f	m		
Delphine Gay	D	1823	Vibert	lp	f	m-l		
Delphine Gay	HP	1847	Vibert	w				
Delphiniana	G	c 1802	syn Enfant de France	m	f	m		
Delphinie	M	Pre 1846		mp	dbl	s		
Delton	Ch			dr				

Dembroski	HP	1849	Vibert	dr	dbl	m		
Dembroski	B			rb	f	l		
Démétrius	N	1827	Laffay	w	f	m		
Denis Cochin	HP	1885	Verdier E	mr				
Denis Hélye	HP	1864	Gautreau	mr	dbl	l	vig	f
Denis Hélye	M	1864	Lévis	m	f	l		
Denis Papin	HP	1852	Laffay	mr	f	l	vvig	
Denise de Reverseaux	T	1855	Cook syn Cornelia Cook	w	dbl	vl	vig	m
Denise Cramoisi	Misc		Descemet					
Denon	Ch		Laffay	lp	f	s		
Député Montaut	HP	1895	Vilin	mr				
Des Alpes à Feuilles de Pimprenelle	HSpn			rb				
Des Alpes Double	Alp			lp				
Des Alpes sans Épines	G	Pre 1811	syn Bourbon	pb	s-d	m		m
Des Alpes Simple	G			lp				
Des Champs	Arv	Pre 1830		w	s	s		vf
Des Champs à Sépales Appendicées	Arv	Pre 1830		w	s	s		vf
Des Collines à Fleurs Doubles	HCan		Prévost	lp				
Des Collines à Flles Preque Glabres	HCan		Prévost	mp				
Des Jardins	C			mp				
Des Palais	N			mp				
Des Papes	D							
Des Parfumeurs	G			lp				
Des Peintres	M	Pre 1777	syn Rubra	mr	dbl	m		
Des Peintres	C	Pre 1806	syn Rose des Peintres	mp	f	vl	vig	f
Des Poëtes	D	c 1825	Cartier	mp				
Des Princes	D	Pre 1830	Prévost syn Argentée	lp	dbl	m		f
Des Pyrennées	Alp	Pre 1830		mp	s	m		
Des Pyrennées à Rameaux Velus	Alp	1826	Prévost	mr	s	m		
Des Quatre Saisons	Pom		Vibert	lp				
Des Rouges	T			mp	f	l		
Désaix	HCh	Pre 1830	Laffay	lp	f	s-m		
Désaix	G	1844	Vibert	dr				
Desbordes-Valmore	HP			mr			vig	
Desbordes-Valmore	G			lp	f	l		
Desbrosses	G	Pre 1830		mp	vdbl	s	vig	
Descartes	HCh	1846	Vibert	m	f	m		
Descemet	C	Pre 1820	Descemet	mp	dbl	vl		
Descemet	G	Pre 1830	Prévost syn Parfaite Agathe	lp	f	m		
Descemet (same as above)	G	Pre 1830	Vibert syn Didon & Parfaite Agathe	lp	f	m		
Descemet	HCh	Pre 1830	Vibert syn Zulmé	mr	vdbl	s-m		
Descemet	B	1847	Vibert	w		m		
Deschamps	G	c 1830	Charpentier	pb	f	m		
Deschamps	N	1877	Deschamps syn Longworth Rambler?	mr	dbl	l	vig	
Descrivieux	B/HP	Pre 1846		mp	f	m	vig	
Desdémona	P	1841	Vibert	mr	dbl	m		
Désespoir des Amateurs	C	1832	Foulard	mp	f		vig	f
Desfontaines	G	c 1825	Cartier	mp	dbl	m		
Desfontaines	T	Pre 1846		w			m	f
Desfossés	HCh	1826	Laffay	lp	f	s		
Desgaches	B	1840	Desgaches	mp	f	l		
Desgaches	HCh	1850	Gantin	lp	f	l	m	
Desgaches	HP	1850	Lacharme	mr	f	m	vig	
Deshoulières	G	1812	Prévost	mr	vdbl	m		
Désirée	G	1835	Joly	mp	vdbl	m	vig	
Désirée	Pom			w	f	m		
Désirée Fontaine	HP	1884	Fontaine	dr	f	l	vig	
Désirée Giraud	HP		syn Mme D Giraud					
Désirée Lancezeur	HP		Lancezeur	dr	f	s		
Désirée Parmentier	G	Pre 1841	Parmentier	lp	dbl	l		
Désirée Roussel	N	Pre 1846		mp	f			
Desmarchaise	Ch			lp	vf	l		
Despong	Misc	Pre 1846						
Desprez	N	Pre 1834	Desprez	op	f	m	vvig	
Desprez à Fleurs Jaunes	N	1830	Desprez syn Jaune Desprez	yb	f	l	vig	m
D'Esquermes	HP	Pre 1846		mp				
Destigny	HP	1852	Laffay	dp			vig	
Desvaux	Ch	1827	Guérin	lp	f	m		
Deuil	G	Pre 1830	Prévost syn La Veuve	m	vdbl	m		
Deuil de Colonel Denfert	HP	1878	Margottin Père	dr	f	l	vig	f
Deuil de Docteur Reynaud	B	1862	Pradel	dp	vdbl	l	vig	vf

Name	Class	Date	Raiser					
Deuil de Duc d'Orléans	B	1845	Lacharme	m	vdbl	l	vvig	
Deuil de Dumont d'Urville	B/HP	Pre 1846		m			vig	
Deuil de Dunois	HP	1864	Verdier E	r	dbl	m		
Deuil de Dunois	HP	1873	Lévéque	dr	dbl			
Deuil de Frédéric Willermoz	HP	1854	Lacharme	yb	dbl	m		
Deuil de la Duchesse d'Orléans	B	1845	Pradel	m				
Deuil de l'Amiral de Dumont d'Urville	HP	see	Deuil de D d'Urville	m				
Deuil de l'Archevêque de Paris	B	1849	Oger	dr	f	m		
Deuil de la Reine des Belges	HP	Pre 1870		dr	f	l		
Deuil de l'Empereur Maximilien	HP	Pre 1870		dr	f	l		
Deuil de l'Empereur du Mexique	HP	1867	Cordier	m				
Deuil de Lord Raglan	B		Pradel	dr	f	l		
Deuil de Louis Philippe	B	1851	Pradel	dr			vig	
Deuil de Paul Fontaine	M	1873	Fontaine	rb	dbl	l	vig	
Deuil de Robert Peel	B	1851	Fontaine	pb	f	m		
Deuil de Willermoz	HP	Pre 1870		dr	f	m		
Deuil du Maréchal Mortier	HCh	Pre 1841		dr	f	l		
Deuil du Prince Albert	HP	1862	Lapente	dr	f	m	vig	m
Deuil du Prince Jérôme	HP			dr				
Deuil Duc d'Orléans	B	Pre 1846		dr				
Devaux	Ch		Laffay	lp	dbl	m		
Devienne-Lamy	HP	1868	Lévéque	mr	dbl	l	m	
Devoniensis	T	1838	Forester	w	dbl	vl	vvig	vf
Devoniensis, Climbing	Cl T	1858	Pavitt	w	f	vl	vig	vf
D'Evrat	A	1809	Bosc syn Evratina	dp	vdbl	s	vig	
D'Halingen	N			lp	f	l	vig	
Diadème	Bks			w				
Diadème de Flore	A	1825	Sommerlich	lp				
Diadème de Flore	G	1825	Descemet / Vibert	lp	l	m-l		
Diadème de Flore	G	Pre 1830	Sommesson	lp	vl	m-l		
Diadème Superbe	G	Pre 1846		mr		s		
Diana	HP	1874	Paul W	dp	f	l	vig	
Diana de Colmar	M	1846						
Diane	G	Pre 1830		dr				
Diane de Bollwiller	T	Pre 1834		w		m		
Diane de Bollwillers	T	Pre 1884	Baumann	w	f	l		
Diane de Castro	M	1853	Robert	lp	f	l		
Diane de Poitiers	A	1818	Vibert	lp	dbl	m		
Diane de Poitiers	M	1845	Vibert	lp	f	l		
Diane de Windsor	HP		see Dean of Windsor					
Dianthaeflora	C	1789	Poilpré syn Oeillet	lp	dbl	s	vig	m
Dianthiflora	HRg	1891	Morlet syn Fimbriata	lp	dbl			vf
Diaphane	M		see La diaphane					
Diderot	G			dr	f	l		
Didier Erasme	M	1857	Robert & Moreau	mp	f	l	vig	
Didon	M	1854	Robert	lp	f	m		
Didon	G	Pre 1830	Vibert syn Parfaite Agathe	lp	f	m		
Didon	Ch		Laffay	lp	f	m		
Die Berühmte	G	Pre 1820	Descemet syn Illustre	pb	f	m		
Dieudonné	HCh	Pre 1830	Paillard	m	dbl	m		
Dieudonné	Min	Pre 1834		mp		vs		
Dieudonné	HCh	1827	Mauget	dr				
Dijonensis	Pom		see Centifolia minor					
Dingee et Conard	HP	1875	Verdier E	mr	f	l	vig	m
Dinsmore	HP	1888	Henderson	mr				
		Syn	Mme Charles Wood					
Diodore	HP	1851	Laffay	mp	f	l		
Directeur Alphand	HP	1883	Lévêque	m	dbl	l	vvig	
Directeur Constantin Bernard	HT	1885	Soupert & Notting	m	vf	l		
Directeur N Jensen	HP	1883	Verdier E	m	dbl	l		
Directeur René Gérard	T	1892	Pelletier	yb	f	l		
Directeur Tisserand	HP	1887	Lévêque	dr	f	l	vig	
Discolor	Pom			dr	s-d	s		
Distinction	HT	1882	Bennett	ab	dbl		vvig	
D'Italie	HSem	Pre 1834		lp		l		
D'Italie Blanche	D	1812	Carlet / Coquerel	w	dbl	m		f
D'Italie Blanche Simple	D		Garilland	w				
D'Italie Rose	D	Pre 1830	Godefroy	mp	dbl	m		f
Divinité	D		Prévost syn Bellefleur	lp	f	s		
Docteur Berthet	B	1858	Damaizin	mr	f	l	m	
Docteur Berthet	T	1879	Pernet Père	mp	f	l	vig	
Docteur Brière	B	1860	Vigneron	pb	f	l		m
Docteur Leprestre	B	1852	Oger	dr	f	l	vvig	
Docteur Marjolin	HP	1842	Laffay	mr	vf	m	vig	
Docteur Marjolin	M	1860	Robert & Moreau	mr	f	m	vvig	
Docteur Petit	N	Pre 1870		lp				

Name		Date	Breeder/Synonym					
Docteur Reymont	Pol	1888	Alegatière	mr	f	m	vig	vf
			syn Doctor Raimont					
Doctor Adolphe Eisl	HP	Pre 1870		rb	f	l		
Doctor Alphonse Schlumberger	T	1893	Soupert & Notting	mp				
Doctor Andry	HP	1864	Verdier E	mr	dbl	m	vig	f
Doctor Antoine Carlès	T	1885	Nabonnand	my				
Doctor Antonin Joly	HP	1886	Besson	op	vdbl	l	vig	
Doctor Arnal	HP	1848	Roeser	mr	f	l		
Doctor Auguste Krell	HP	1877	Verdier E	rb	f	l	vig	
Doctor Baillon	HP	1878	Margottin Père	dr	f	l	vig	
Doctor Bastien	HP	1890	Verdier E	rb				
Doctor Billard	Ch		see Beauté de Billard					
Doctor Blandin	B			lp	f	s		
Doctor Branche	HP	1890	Liabaud	mp				
Doctor Brechemier	HP	1873	Vigneron	mr	f	l		
Doctor Bretonneau	HP	1858	Trouillard	m	dbl	m		
Doctor Buisson	HP	1865	Pradel	mp	f	l	vig	
Doctor Caviole	B	1853	Pradel	mr	f	m	vig	
Doctor Cayrade	HP	1865	Pradel	mp	f	vl	vig	
Doctor Cazeneuve	HP	1899	Dubreuil	dr	dbl	l		
Doctor Chaillot	B			mp	f	m		
Doctor Chopard	B	1890	Verdier E	mp				
Doctor Danguet	HP	1852	Robert	m	f	l	vvig	
Doctor de Chalus	HP	1871	Touvais	mr	f	vl	vig	
Doctor de Henri IV	T			lp	f	m		
Doctor Dielthem	G	Pre 1848		mp	vf	l	vig	
Doctor Dor	HP	1885	Liabaud	mr	f	vl	vvig	f
Doctor Dorothea Söffker	Misc	1899	Welter					
Doctor Douet	HP	1889	Tesnier	dr				
Doctor Dusillet	T	1890	Reboul	mp				
Doctor Gales	Ch			dr	f	m		
Doctor Garnier	HP	1882	Robert & Moreau	mr	f	vl	vvig	
Doctor Grandvilliers	T	1893	Perny	pb	dbl	m		
Doctor Grill	T	1885	Bonnaire	op	dbl	m	m	f
Doctor Guépin	HCh	Pre 1846		m				
Doctor Guépin	HP	1872	Moreau-Robert	dr	f	l	m	m
Doctor Hardouin	B			mp	f	m	vig	
Doctor Hénon	HP	1855	Lille	w	f	m	vig	
Doctor Hogg	HP	1880	Laxton	dr	dbl	m	vig	
Doctor Hooker	HP	1876	Paul G	mr	f	l	vig	
Doctor Hurta	HP	1867	Geschwind	m	f	l		
Doctor Jaeger	HP			mr				
Doctor Jamain	HP	1851	Jamain	mr	f	m	vig	
Doctor Jenner	HP	1878	Margottin	dr	f	l	vig	
Doctor Jobert	HP			mr				
Doctor Juillard	HP	1851	Lacharme	dr	f	l	vig	
Doctor Jules Lisnard	T	1883	Nabonnand	lp	s-d	l	vvig	
Doctor Kane	N	1856	Pentland	my		l		
Doctor Larrey	HP	1866	Moreau-Robert	m	f	m	vig	
Doctor Lemée	HP	1871	Touvais	dr	f	l	m	
Doctor Lindley	HP	1866	Paul W	dp	f	l	vig	
Doctor Marx	HP	1842	Laffay	mr	f	l	vvig	
Doctor Néran	B	1856	Bernède	mr				
Doctor Parnot	HP	1864	Pradel	m	f	l	vig	
Doctor Pasteur	HT	1887	Moreau-Robert	dp	f	l	vig	
Doctor Pinel	HP	1885	Moreau-Robert	dr	f	l	vig	
Doctor Pouleur	T	1897	Ketten Bros	rb	f	m	vig	m
Doctor Raimont	Pol	1888	Allégatière	mr	f	m	vig	m
Doctor Ramsay	HP							
Doctor Raymond	HP			dp				
Doctor Raynaud (or Reynaud)	HP	1863	Pradel	mp	f	vl	vig	
Doctor Reignier	HP							
Doctor Rocques	B	1839	Desprez	mp	f	m		
Doctor Rouges	Cl T	1893	Schwartz Vve	rb	dbl	m		m
Doctor Ruschpler	HP	1856	Ruschpler	dp	f	l		vf
Doctor Sewell	HP	1879	Turner	mr	f	l	vvig	f
Doctor Spitzer	HP	1862	Geoffre	pb	f	l		
Doctor Tisl	HP	1859	Soupert & Notting	mr		l	vvig	
Doctor Valentin Teirich	B	1890	Geschwind	dr				
Doctor Varennes	HP	1872	Oger	dr	f	l	vvig	
Doctor Verthet	B		syn Doctor Berthet					
Doctor Vingtrinier	HP	1863	Fontaine	dp	f	l		
Doctor Wilhelm Neubert	HP	1873	Soupert & Notting	dr	f	l	vig	
Dog Rose	Sp	Pre 1737	syn r.canina	lp	s			
D'Oldenbourg	G							
Dollon	HCh			lp	f	m		
Dometil Beccard	G/C	1845	syn Variegata	pb	f	l	vig	m
Domingo Aldrufen	HP	1877	Pernet Père	lp	f	l	vig	
Dominic Boccardo	G/C	1845	syn Variegata	pb	f	l	vig	m
Dominie Sampson	HSpn	Pre 1848		lp	s-d			
Dominique	D		Delaage					

Name	Class	Date	Notes	Colour	Form	Size	Vigour	Scent
Dominique Daran	HP	1860	Touvais	m	f	l	m	
Don Alvarès	B	1842	Boyau	mp	f	m		
Don Alvarez	Pom			mp		m	m	
Don Carlos	Ch	Pre 1846		w	vf	l		
Don de Guérin	G	Pre 1846		dp	f	l		
Don de l'Amitié	G	1819	syn Daphné	lp				
Don Juan	B			rb				
Don Pedro	D	Pre 1811		lp	dbl			m
Doña Elvira	T			w	f	m		
Dona Isaura Alexandrina	HP	1891	Alexandrino					
Doña Maria	HSem	1828	Vibert	w	s-d	s		m
Doña Maria	N							
Doña Maria	Ayr		Laffay	w	f	s		
Doña Maria	A			w	f	m		
Doña Sol	G	1830	Vibert	w		m		
Doña Sol	G	1842	Vibert	rb	f	m		
Donna Maria	N	Pre 1846		mp	f			
Donna Marie (a)	HSem	1830	Vibert	w	vdbl	s		m
Dora	HMult	1887	Geschwind					
D'Orbessan	Misc	1815		my				
D'Orbessan	G			lp				
D'Orléans	HSem	syn	Adélaïde d'Orléans	w				
D'Orléans	M							
Dorothea Krey	HP			lp	f	l	vig	
Dorothée (or Descemet)	G	Pre 1830	Hardy	mr	f	m		
Dorothée (or Dositée)	G		Noisette L	dr		m	vvig	
D'Orsay Rose	Misc	Pre 1850		dp	dbl			f
Double	HSem	1825	Vibert	w				
Double	P			mr				
Double	A	Pre 1770	syn Plena (A)	w	s to s-d			
Double	Min	Pre 1834		mp		vs		
Double Ancien	M	Pre 1870		w		m		f
Double Ancienne	HSem			ly	f	m		
Double Blanche	HSpn	syn	Double White Burnet	w	s-d		vig	vf
Double Blush	HFt	Pre 1846	Guérin syn Victoria	yb	s-d	l		
Double Blush Burnet	HSpn	Pre 1821		pb	f	m		
Double Brique	G	1830		pb	dbl	m		
Double Carnée	HSpn	Pre 1826	Prévost	w	dbl	s		
		syn	Double Blush Burnet?					
Double Cherokee	Misc	1840	syn Fortuniana	w	dbl			
Double Cinnamon	Sp	1596	syn r.majalis	m	dbl			m
Double Dark Marbled	HSpn	Pre 1822	Brown	rb	s-d	s		
Double Dark Velvet	Ch	Pre 1846						
Double French	Sp	Pre 1600	syn r.gallica officinalis	dp	s-d			m
Double Jaune	Misc	Pre 1629	syn Multiplex	my	vdbl	vl		
Double Marbrée	HSpn	Pre 1770	syn Maculata	w	s-d	s		
Double Panachée	G			dr				
Double Pink Memorial Rose	HWich	1898	Horvath	mp	dbl		vig	m
			syn Universal Favorite					
Double Pourpre	Pom			dr	s-d	m		vf
Double Pourpre	HSpn		Calvert	m				
Double Purple	HSpn	Pre 1820		rb	s-d			
		syn	Dbl Dark Marbled?					
Double Red	HSpn	c 1808	Descemet syn Rouge	mp	dbl	m		
Double Red	HEg	c 1820		mr	dbl	s		f
		syn	La Belle Distinguée					
Double Scarlet	HEg	Pre 1896		mr	dbl		wk	vf
Double Scarlet Sweet Briar	HEg	c 1820		mr	dbl	s		f
		Syn	La Belle Distinguée					
Double Scotch White	HSpn	Pre 1818		w	s-d		vig	vf
		Syn	Double White Burnet					
Double Velvet Rose	G	Pre 1629		dr	dbl			
		Syn	Holoserica Multiplex					
Double Violet	HSpn		Prévost	m				
Double White	HMsk	Pre 1629		w	s-d	m	vig	
Double White	HBc	Pre 1835		w				
Double White	HEg	Pre 1896		w	dbl		vig	
Double White	Ayr		syn Elegans	w	s-d		vig	
Double White Altaica	HSpn	Pre 1818		w	s-d		vig	vf
		syn	Double White Burnet					
Double White Burnet	HSpn	Pre 1818		w	s-d		vig	vf
Double White Lady Banks Rose	Sp	1807		w	dbl	s		
		syn	r.banksiae banksiae					
Double White Memorial Rose	HWich	1899	Horvath	w	vdbl		vvig	
			syn Manda's Triumph					
Double White Moss	M	1788	Shailer	w	dbl	l		
		syn	Shailer's White Moss					
Double White Noisette	HSem	Pre 1830	Laffay M	lp	dbl			
			syn Plena (HSem)					
Double White Striped Moss	M	Pre 1844	Robert?	w	f	m		
			syn Panachée Pleine					

Name	Type	Date	Breeder/Notes	Col	Form	Size	Vigour	Frag
Double Yellow	HFt	Pre 1819		my	dbl	m	m	vf
		syn Will	iam's Double Yellow					
Double Yellow Plena	HSpn	See Will	iam's Double Yellow	my	dbl	m		
Double Yellow Scots Rose	HFt	Pre 1819		my	dbl	m	m	vf
		syn Will	Iam's Double Yellow					
All Double Roses		see also	Scotch Roses					
Douce Mélie	P		Lelieur	lp				
Douceur	D		Miellez	lp				
Douglas	Ch	1848	Verdier V	dr	f	m	vig	
Doux Espoir	Ch			pb	f	m		
Dowager Duchess of Marlborough	HP	1890	Paul G	mp		l		f
Dragon Wings	Sp	1890		w			vig	m
		syn	r.sericea pteracantha					
Drap d'Or	N							
Drémont	Ch	Pre 1834		lp		s		
Drémont	T	Pre 1846		w				vf
Drummond's Thornless	Alp	Pre 1846		pb	s-d	l		
Dryade	HBslt	1891	Geschwind	pb				
Du Calendrier	P	Pre 1830	Vibert	lp	dbl	m		
Du Japon	M			dp				
Du Japon	Pol			w				
Du Japon	Rg							
Du Luxembourg	N	1829	Hardy	m	f	l	vvig	vf
Du Luxembourg	HBc							
Du Luxembourg	D	Pre 1830	Prévost	lp	vdbl	m		
Du Luxembourg	HCh	Pre 1834	Hardy	dr	vdbl	m		
Du Luxembourg	Pom			pb				
Du Luxembourg	HSpn			lp				
Du Luxembourg	S	1888		dp	f	l	m	
Du Luxembourg	T			rb				
Du Maître d'École	G	1831	Coquereau	m	dbl	vl		vf
		syn Rose	de La Maître d'École					
Du Matin	A	Pre 1830	syn Cloris	lp	vdbl	s-m		
Du Népaul	HCh	Pre 1830		lp		l		
Du Pont	G	Pre 1811	syn Rouge Formidable	mr	vdbl	m		
Du Roi	P	1819	Souchet syn Lelieur	mr				
Du Roi	Pom			mr				
Du Roi à Long Pédoncule	P			dp				
Du Roi Blanc	P		syn Coelina Dubos	w				
Du Roi Moyenne	HP	Pre 1846		mr				
Du Roi Pourpre	P		syn Mogador	dr				
Du Roi Strié	P			lp				
Du Saint-Sacrement	Sp	1596	syn r.majalis	lp	dbl			f
Duarte de Oliviera	N	1879	Brassac	op	f	m-l	vvig	m
Dubocage	HCh	1827	Prévost	lp	f	m	vvig	f
Dubois Dessausais	C	1842	Vibert	lp	vf	l		
Dubost	B			mp				
Dubourg	HCh	1826	Dubourg	w	vdbl	vl		
Dubreuil	B	1826	Vibert	lp	f	m-l		
Dubreuil	Ch	Pre 1834	Neumann	lp	f	m		
Duc d'Alençon	HP	Pre 1846		mp	f	m	vvig	
Duc d'Angoulême	C	1821	Vibert	dp	f	m		
Duc d'Angoulême	G	1835	Vibert	dr	dbl	m	m	
Duc d'Anhalt	G		Parmentier	dr	f	m		
Duc d'Anjou	HP	1862	Boyau	dr	f	vl	vig	
Duc d'Arcourt	HP	See	Duchesse d'Harcourt					
Duc d'Arenberg	G	Pre 1836		m	f	l		
Duc d'Audiffret Pasquier	HP	1887	Verdier E	rb	f	l	vig	
Duc d'Aumale	HP	Pre 1846		dr				f
Duc d'Aumale	B	1858		dp	f	l		
Duc d'Aumale	HP	1876	Verdier E	dr	f	l	vvig	
Duc d'Avray	Ch			mp	f	l		
Duc de Bassano	G			dr	f	l		
Duc de Bassano	HP	1862	Portemer	dp	f	l	vig	
Duc de Bavière	G	1824		dp	f	l		
Duc de Bavière	G	Pre 1860	Miellez	lp	dbl	m	m	
		syn Duch	esse d'Angoulême					
Duc de Bavière	C	1821	Godefroy	mp	f	m-l		
			syn Duc d'Angoulême					
Duc de Beaufort	G	1825		pb	f	m		
Duc de Beaujolais	B	1862	Robert & Moreau	dr	f	m		
Duc de Berry	G	Pre 1830	Prévost	m	vf	m		
Duc de Bordeaux	G	1820	Vibert	lp	f	l		
Duc de Bordeaux	Ch	1825	Mauget	dr				
Duc de Bordeaux	C			rb	f	l		
Duc de Boufflers	N	Pre 1830	Miellez	lp	f	s		
Duc de Brabant	C	Pre 1842		mp	dbl	l	vig	
Duc de Bragance	HP	1886	Verdier E	mp	dbl	vl		
		Syn	Duchesse de Bragance					
Duc de Broglie	B			rb	f	m		
Duc de Broglie	N	Pre 1834		lp	f	s		

Name	Type	Date	Raiser					
Duc de Cambridge	D	Pre 1841	Laffay	m	dbl	l		
Duc de Cambridge	HP	1865	Margottin	dr	f	l	m	
Duc de Caylus	T	1896	Schwartz Vve	lp				
Duc de Cazes	B	Pre 1848		m	vf			
Duc de Cazes	Ch	c 1850		dr	f	l		
Duc de Cazes	HP	1861	Touvais	m	dbl	l	vig	f
Duc de Chartres	D	1820	Godefroy	lp	f	m		
Duc de Chartres	HCh	1827	Hardy	mr				
Duc de Chartres	HP	1876	Verdier E	dr	f	l	vvig	
Duc de Chartres	B/HP	Pre 1846		mp				
Duc de Choiseul	HCh	1825	Vibert	lp	f	l	vvig	vf
Duc de Choiseul	C	Pre 1830	Lecomte	mp	vdbl	l		
Duc de Clarence	C			mr	f	l		
Duc de Constantine	Ayr	1857	Soupert & Notting	mp	f	l	vvig	
Duc de Crillon	B	1860	Robert & Moreau	mr	f	l	vig	
Duc de Danemark	HP			lp				
Duc de Devonshire	Ch	1852	Laffay	pb	f	l	vig	
Duc de Devonshire	HP	1857	Vibert	mp				
Duc de Fitzjames	G	Pre 1835		dr	f	vl		vf
Duc de Grammont	T	1825	Laffay	pb	f	l	vig	
Duc de Grammont	HCh	Pre 1834		rb	f	m		
Duc de Guiche	G	1821	Prévost	m	dbl	vl		m
Duc de Lorraine	G			rb				
Duc de Luxembourg	G			w	f	m		
Duc de Luxembourg	A	Pre 1846		lp				
Duc de Magenta	T	1859	Margottin	ab	dbl	l	m	f
Duc de Malakoff	HP	1856	Avoux	rb	f	m	vig	f
Duc de Marlborough	HP	1884	Lévêque	dr	f	l	vvig	
Duc de Montpensier	HP	1875	Lévêque	dr	dbl	l	vvig	m
Duc de Nassau	HP	1873	Pradel	dr	f	l	m	
Duc de Némours	N			lp	f	l		
Duc de Némours	G	Pre 1846	Robert	lp	f	s		
Duc de Northumberland	G		Vétillard	m				
Duc de Richemond	B			mr				
Duc de Richelieu	Ch	Pre 1846		mp	f	l		
Duc de Rohan	HP	1861	Lévêque	mr	f	vl	m	
Duc de Sussex	Ch	Pre 1846		dr	f	l		
Duc de Sussex	D	Pre 1841	Laffay	lp	dbl	l		
Duc de Tarante	B			rb	f	l		
Duc de Trévise	G	Pre 1834		dr	f	m		
Duc de Valmy	G	Pre 1860		m	dbl	l		
Duc de Wellington	HCh	Pre 1830	Calvert syn L'Africaine	mr	vdbl	m		
Duc de Wellington	HP	1864	Granger syn Duke of Wellington	dr	dbl	l	vig	
Duc de Wellington	C			mp	f	l		
Duc de Wurtemberg	HP	1853	Robert	mr	f	l	vvig	
Duc des Centfeuilles	C	Pre 1846		p	f			
Duc d'Elchingen	B		Moulie	dr				
Duc d'Enghien	HP	Pre 1846		lp	vf	m	vvig	
Duc d'Enghien	G	c 1830	Parmentier	mr	f	m		
Duc d'Estrée	B	1845	Lacharme syn Henri Lecoq	dp				
Duc d'Harcourt	HP	1863	Moreau-Robert	mr	dbl	l	vvig	
Duc d'Isly	HP	1845	Lacharme	rb	s-d	l		
Duc d'Orléans	G	1831	Vibert / Calvert syn Adèle Heu	pb	vdbl	l		
Duc d'Orléans	T	Pre 1846		mr				
Duc d'Orléans	HP	1888	Verdier E	mr	f	l	vig	f
Duc d'Ossuna	HP	1855	Avoux & Crozy	dr	f	m	m	
Duc du Roi	C			dr				
Duc d'Uzés	HP	1893	Lévêque	dr				
Duc d'York	A	Pre 1818	Miellez	w	dbl	l		
Duc d'York	Ch		see Duke of York					
Duc Engelbert d'Arenberg	HT	1899	Soupert & Notting	w	f	vl		m
Ducher	Ch	1869	Ducher	w	dbl	m	vig	f
Duchesne	B	Pre 1846		mr		vl		
Duchess of Albany	HT	1887	Paul W	dp	f	vl	vig	vf
Duchess of Bedford	HP	1879	Postans R B	mr	dbl	l	vig	
Duchess of Bedford	HSpn	1888		dp				
Duchess of Cambridge	HP			dr				
Duchess of Connaught	HT	1879	Bennett	pb	vdbl	l		vf
Duchess of Connaught	HP	1882	Standish & Noble	dr	f	l	vig	m
Duchess of Edinburgh	T	1874	Nabonnand G	dr	dbl	l	m	
Duchess of Edinburgh	HP	1874	Bennett	lp	f	l	vig	
Duchess of Edinburgh	HP	1875	Schwartz	lp	f	l		
Duchess of Edinburgh	T	1875	Veitch	dr	dbl	l	vig	
Duchess of Edinburgh	HT			dr				
Duchess of Fife	HP	1876	Schwartz	lp	dbl	l		vf
Duchess of Fife	HP	1893	Cocker	lp	dbl	l	vig	vf
Duchess of Kent	Ch	1840	Laffay?	w	f	s	m	
Duchess of Leeds	HP	1887	Mack	dr			vig	

Name	Type	Year	Breeder					
Duchess of Norfolk	HP	1853	Margottin	mp	f	m	m	
Duchess of Portland	P	c 1770		mr	s-d	l	m	m
Duchess of Sutherland	HP	1839	Laffay M	lp	dbl	l	vig	f
Duchess of Westminster	HT	1879	Bennett	pb	dbl	l	m	sf
Duchess of York	HP	1897	Cocker	op				
Duchesse Antonine d'Ursel	HP	1883	Soupert & Notting	mr	f	vl		
Duchesse d'Abrantes	M	1851	Robert	lp	dbl	l		
Duchesse d'Alençon	HP	1861	Robert & Moreau	mr				
Duchesse d'Angoulême	G	Pre 1811	Hardy	lp	vdbl	m		m
			syn Agathe Incarnata					
Duchesse d'Angoulême	G/C	1821	Miellez	lp	f	s-m		
		syn	Duc d'Angoulême					
Duchesse d'Angoulême	C	Pre 1830	Vibert	lp	f	m		
Duchesse d'Angoulême	G	Pre 1860	Miellez	lp	dbl	m	m	
Duchesse d'Aoste	HP	1867	Margottin	mr	vdbl	l	vig	m
Duchesse d'Arenberg	G			m	f	l		
Duchesse d'Auerstädt	N	1887	Bernaix A	my	vf	l	vig	m
Duchesse d'Avranches	G	Pre 1860						
Duchesse de Berry	G	1820	Vibert	pb	f	vl		
Duchesse de Berry	Ch	1827	Mauget	dp	f			
Duchesse de Berry	T			lp	f	m		
Duchesse de Brabant	T	1857	Bernède	lp	dbl	l	vig	vf
Duchesse de Bragance	HP	1886	Verdier	mp	dbl	vl		
Duchesse de Buccleugh	G	1837	Vibert	rb	dbl	l	vig	m
Duchesse de Cambacèrés	HP	1854	Fontaine	mp	dbl	l	vvig	f
Duchesse de Campagne	T			w	vdbl	m		f
Duchesse de Caylus	HP	1864	Verdier C	dp	f	l	m	f
Duchesse de Chartres	HP	1875	Verdier E	mp	f	vl	vig	
Duchesse de Clermont-Ton.	C	1827	Noisette	dr				
Duchesse de Collé	G	Pre 1830	Vibert	lp	f	l		
Duchesse de Cornouailles	G	Pre 1830	Calvert syn Salamon	dr	f	m-l		
Duchesse de Coutard	C	Pre 1885		lp	f	m		
Duchesse de Danemark	HP							
Duchesse de Dino	HMult	Pre 1860	Baumann	lp	s-d	m		
Duchesse de Dino	HP	1889	Lévêque	dr	dbl	vl		
Duchesse de Galliera	HP	1847	Portemer	pb	dbl	l		
Duchesse de Galliera	HP	1887	Verdier E	mp	f	l	vig	
Duchesse de Grammont	D	1825	Cels	mp	f	vl		
		syn Cent-	feuilles d'Avranches					
Duchesse de Grammomt	N	Pre 1838		w	dbl	s		m
Duchesse de la Vallière	T	Pre 1834		lp	dbl	m		
Duchesse de Leeds	HP		see Duchess of Leeds					
Duchesse de Lorge	T	1894	Vigneron	mr				
Duchesse de Magenta	HP	1859	Guillot Père	lp	f	m	m	
Duchesse de Mecklenburg	T	Pre 1846		ly	s-d	l		
Duchesse de Medina Coeli	HP	1864	Marrest	mr	f	l	vig	
		syn	Comtesse de Medina Coeli					
Duchesse de Montebello	HCh	1824/5	Laffay	lp	vdbl	m		m
Duchesse de Montmorency	P	1844	Lévêque R	mp	dbl	l		
Duchesse de Montpensier	HP	1846	Margottin	lp	f	l		f
Duchesse de Morny	HP	1863	Verdier E	mp	dbl	l	vig	
Duchesse de Némours	HP	1841	Laffay	mp	f	l	vig	
Duchesse de Némours	G			p	f	m		
Duchesse de Normandie	B	1846	Oudin	dr	f	m		
Duchesse de Parme	Ch	Pre 1830	Vibert	dr	f	m		
Duchesse de Polignac	HP			dr				
Duchesse de Praslin	HP	Pre 1870		lp	f	l	vvig	
Duchesse de Reggio	HCh	Pre 1830	syn De Vergnies	m	f	m		
Duchesse de Reggio	G	Pre 1811	Descemet	mp	f	l		m
			syn Fanny Bias					
Duchesse de Richmond	G			lp	f	m		
Duchesse de Rohan	HP	Pre 1848		pb	dbl	l	vvig	
Duchesse de Saint-Quentin	HP			lp	f	m		
Duchesse de Sutherland	HP	1839	Laffay	lp	f	l	vig	f
		syn	Duchess of Sutherland					
Duchesse de Thuringe	B	1847	Guillot Père	w	f	l		
Duchesse de Vallambrosa	HP	1875	Schwartz J	ab	dbl	l	vvig	
Duchesse de Vallambrosa	T	1878	Nabonnand	pb	f	vl	vig	f
Duchesse de Verneuil	M	1856	Portemer Fils	pb	dbl	l	vig	
Duchesse de Wurtemberg	HP	1862	Pradel	lp	vf	l	vig	
Duchesse d'Edimbourg	HP	1874	Bennett	lp	f	l	vig	
Duchesse d'Edimbourg	T	1875	Veitch	dr				
		see also	Duchess of Edinburgh					
Duchesse d'Harcourt	HP	1873	Oger	lp	f	l	vig	
Duchesse d'Istria	M	1855	Portemer	dp	dbl	m		
			syn William Lobb					
Duchesse d'Oldenbourg	G	Pre 1830	Calvert syn Esther	lp	f	l		
Duchesse d'Orléans	G	Pre 1790	syn Lustre d'Église	mp	dbl	s		vf
Duchesee d'Orléans	G	1821	Laffay	mp				
Duchesse d'Orléans	C	1837	Vibert	lp	f	l	m	
Duchesse d'Orléans	N	Pre 1846						
Duchesse d'Orléans	HP	1851	Quettier	m	vf	l	vvig	

Name	Class	Date	Raiser	col	form	size	vig	frag
Duchesse d'Orléans	T	c 1860	Robert	w	vf	l		
Duchesse d'Orléans	HP	1886	Schwartz	dp	vdbl	l	vig	
		syn	Jean-Baptiste Casati					
Duchesse d'Ossuna	HP	1876	Jamain	dp	f	l	vvig	
Duchesse d'Ursel	C			w	s-d	l		
Duchesse Hedwige d'Arenberg	HT	1899	Soupert & Notting	mp	f	vl		m
Duchesse Lavalière	Ch			lp				
Duchesse Marie Salviati	T	1890	Soupert & Notting	ob	f	l	m	m
Duchesse Mathilde	T	see Gr-	ossherzogin Mathilde	w	f	l	m	
Ducis	HCh	Pre 1830	Laffay	m	vdbl	m		
Ducis	M	1857	Robert & Moreau	lp	f	l	vig	
Ducreux	N			m	vdbl	l		
Dudéffant	Ch	1827	Péan	w				
Dudley Baxter	HP	1879	Dudley Baxter	dr	f	l		
Dufresnoir (noye)	N	1825	Vibert	lp	f	s		
Dugay Trouin	M	1855	Robert	lp				
Dugnati	Ch			dp	f	m		
Duguesclin	G	1841	Vibert	m	f	m		
Duguesclin	HP	1853	Oger	dp				
Duguesclin	HP	1875	Moreau-Robert	rb	f	vl	vig	
Duhamel Dumonceau	HP	1872	Vilin	mr	dbl	l	vig	m
Duke of Albany	HP	1882	Paul W	dr	vf	vl	vig	
Duke of Connaught	HP	1875	Paul W	rb	dbl	l	vig	vf
Duke of Connaught	HT	1879	Bennett	mr	dbl	vl	m	
Duke of Devonshire	HCh	Pre 1846		lp		l		
Duke of Edinburgh	HP	1868	Paul W	dr	dbl	l	vig	f
Duke of Fife	HP	1892	Cocker	dr	f	l		
Duke of Teck	HP	1880	Paul G	dp	dbl	l	vig	m
Duke of Wellington	HP	1864	Granger	dr	dbl	l	vig	vf
Duke of Wellington	HP	1880	Ducher Vve	mr	f	l	vig	
Duke of York	Ch	1894	Paul W	pb	dbl	l	vig	
Dulce Bella	T	1890	Bennett	op	f	l		
Dulcinée Double	Rbf	1826	Vibert (Garilland)	lp		s		
Dulcinée Semi-Double	Rbf	1818						
Dumas	G		Parmentier	dp	f	m		
Dumnacus	HP	1880	Moreau-Robert	mp	f	vl	vvig	
Dumont de Combert	A			lp				
Dumont de Courset	B	1842	Souchet	dr	f	vl		
Dumont Durville	G			mp	f	m		
Dumortier	G	Pre 1843	Parmentier	pb	vdbl	m		
Dunbarton Blush	HSpn	Pre 1846		lp				
Dundee	HSpn	Pre 1832	Austin R	w	dbl	s	m	
Dundee Rambler	Ayr	Pre 1837	Martin	lp	dbl	m		sf
Dunkelrote Hermosa	B	1899	Geissler	dr				
Dunois	HP	1864		mr	f	l		
Dupetit Thouars	B	1844	Portemer	mp	f	l	vvig	vf
Duplessis Mornay	HP	1850	Vibert	mp	f	l		
Duplex	A	Pre 1754	syn Alba Semi-Plena	w				sf
Duplex	Misc	Pre 1770		mp	s-d	m		sf
Duplex No 1	Pom	Pre 1830	Vibert	mp	dbl	m		sf
Duplex	Misc	1888	syn Rose d'Amour	dp	s-d	l	m	m
Dupontii	Misc	1817		w				sf
Dupont Laroussière	HP			dp				
Dupuy-Jamain	HP	1868	Dupuy C	mr	dbl	l	vig	f
Dupuytren	G	1823	Cartier	dr	f	m		
Duquesne	HP	1858	Robert & Moreau	dr				
Duroc	HCh	Pre 1830	Laffay	lp	f	m		
Dutch Bengal	Bslt	c 1815	Noisette	m	s-d	m		
			syn Maheca					
Dutch Blush	Misc	Pre1846						
Dutch Cinnamon	Misc	Pre 1846						
Dutch Provence	C	1583 syn	r.centifolia batavica	dp				
Dutch Red Musk	Misc	Pre 1846						
Dutch Tree	Misc	Pre 1846						
Duvivier	HCh							
Dwarf Austrian	G	Pre 1806	Crantz?	m		l		m
			syn Rosier d'Amour					
Dwarf Bicolor	Pom			dr	s-d	vs		
Dwarf China	Min							
Dwarf Proliferous	Misc	Pre 1846						
Dybowski	HP	1892	Lévêque	dr				
D'Yebles	T	Pre 1846		lp	f	l		f
D'Yèbles	B	c 1830	Desprez	m	f	m		

NAME	TYPE	YEAR	RAISER	COLOUR	BLOOM	SIZE	GROWTH	SCENT
E Asmus	HT		Pernet Fils	lp				
E Veyrat Hermanos	Cl T	1895	Bernaix A	pb	dbl	l	vvig	vf
E Y Teas	HP	1874	Verdier E	mp	f	l	m	vf
Earl Gray	B	Pre 1846		lp		l		
Earl of Beaconsfield	HP	1880	Christy	dr	f	l		
			see Lord Beaconsfield					
Earl of Dufferin	HP	1887	Dickson A	dr	f	vl	vig	f
Earl of Eldon	N	1872	Eldon / Coppin	ob	dbl	l	vig	m
Earl of Pembroke	HP	1882	Bennett	mr	dbl	l	vig	
Earl Talbot	HP	Pre 1846		dp		l		
Ebène	HP	1844	Boyau	m	f	m	wk	
Eblouissante (see also	Ch	Pre 1830	Laffay	mr	vdbl	m		
L'Éblouissante)								
		syn	Cramoisi Superieur					
Eblouissante de la Queue	G	Pre 1860		dr	vdbl	l		
Ecarlate	M	Pre 1846		mp				
Éclair	HP	1883	Lacharme	dr	dbl	l	vig	f
Éclair de Jupiter	HP			mr	f	l	vig	
Éclaireur	HP	1895	Vigneron	dr	dbl	l	vig	m
Eclat des Roses	G			dp	f	l		
Éclatant	Ch	Pre 1830	Prévost	mp	dbl	m-l		
Éclatant	Pom	1825	Vibert					
Eclatante	M	Pre 1846		dp	dbl	l	vig	
Éclatante	G	c 1860	Miellez	mr				
Éclatante	HP	1862	Guillot	rb	f	m		
Edelmonde	B			dr	vdbl	m	vig	
Edemberger	Misc	Pre 1846		dp				
Edgar Jolibois	HP	1883	Verdier E	mr	f	l	vvig	
Edina	B	1849	Boyau	mp	f	m	m	
Edith Bellenden	HEg	1895	Penzance	mp	s	s	vig	fol f
Edith de Murat	B	1858	Ducher	w	f	m	vig	
Edith Turner	HP	1898	Turner	lp				
Edmond Bernède	HP			mr				
Edmond de Biauzat	T	1885	Levet Père	op	f	l		f
Edmond Duval	G	c 1835	Parmentier	mp	f	m		
Edmond Garret	N	Pre 1846		m	f	m	vig	
Edmond Sablayrolles	T	1888	Bonnaire	pb		m	vig	f
Edmond Wood	HP	1875	Verdier E	mr	f	l	wk	vf
Edouard André	HP	1880	Verdier E	dr	f	l	vvig	
Edouard Delair	B	Pre 1846		lp		l		
Edouard Desfossés	B	1840	Renard	lp	f	l	vig	
Edouard Dufour	HP	1861	Verdier E	dr	vf	m	vig	vf
			syn Prince Camille de	Rohan				
Edouard Dufour	HP	1877	Lévêque	dp	f	l	vvig	m
Edouard Fontaine	HP	1878	Fontaine	mp	f	l	vig	
Edouard Gautier	T	1884	Pernet-Ducher	yb	f	l	vig	f
Edouard Hervé	HP	1884	Verdier E	dr	f	l	vig	vf
Edouard Jessie	HP			dr	f	m	vig	
Edouard Lefèbvre	HP	1877	Oger	dr	f	m	vig	
Edouard Lefort	HP	1886	Verdier E	mr	vf	l		
Edouard Michel	HP	1888	Verdier E	dp	f	l	vig	
Edouard Morren	HP	1869	Granger	dp	f	vl	vig	
		not syn	with Edward Morren					
Édouard Ory	HP	Pre 1870		mr	f	l		
Edouard Pailleron	T	1887	Nabonnand	pb	f	l	vig	
Edouard Pinaert	HP	1877	Schwartz	dr	f	l	vig	
Edouard Van Malen	HCh			mr	f	l		
Eduard von Lade	T	1895	Soupert & Notting	pb	dbl	l	vig	
Edward	B	Pre 1830	syn De l'Ile Bourbon	dp	dbl	m		
Edward Jesse	B	c 1840	Laffay	m	dbl	m		
Edward Morren	HP	1868	Granger	mr	dbl	l	vig	
Edward Morren, Climbing	HP	1879	Paul & Son	mr	f	l	vig	
Edwin Fuller	B	1853	Robert	lp	f	m	vig	
Egeria	HP	1874	Paul W	lp	f	l		
Egeria	HP	1878	Schwartz	lp				
Egérie	N	Pre 1846	Vibert	lp	f			
Egérie	A	1819	Vibert	lp	dbl	m		
Egérie	HP	1851	Quettier	dp	f	m	vig	
Egilda	D		Laffay					
Égine	Misc	Pre 1830	Racine	lp	vf	s		
Egine	T	1852	Vibert	lp	f	l	vig	f
Eglanteria Lutea	Sp	Pre 1542	syn r.foetida	my	s			m
Eglanteria Pumila	HCan	Pre 1830	Godefroy	lp	f	vs		
			syn Petite Duchesse					
Eglanteria Punicea	Sp	c 1596	syn r.foetida bicolor	rb	s			m
Eglantier	Sp	1762	syn r.arvensis	w				sf
Eglantier à Feuilles Marginées	HEg	Pre 1846	Lee syn Hebe's Lip	w	dbl	m	vig	m
Eglantier à Feuilles de Sorbier	HEg	Pre 1830	Vibert	lp	dbl	m		

Eglantier à Fleur Marginée	HEg	Pre 1830	Lee syn Margin Hip	w	dbl	m			f
Eglantier à Fleurs Écarlates	HEg	Pre 1830	Prévost	dr	s-d	m			
Eglantier à Fleurs Roses Double	HEg			lp					
Eglantier de l'Ile Bourbon	HEg		Laffay	dr	dbl	l			f
Eglantier Double Odorant	HEg	1820	Godefroy	dp	s-d	m			f
Eglantier Odorant Très Épineux	HEg			mp					
Eglantier Rouge	Sp	Pre 1551	syn r.rubiginosa	lp	s				
Eglantier Semi-Double à Fruit Rond	HEg	Pre 1830	Vibert	mp	dbl	m			
Eglantine	Sp	Pre 1551	syn r.rubiginosa	lp	s				
Eglé	G	1822	Vibert	dp	f	m			
Eifel	HMult	1892	Lévêque	yb					
Eisenkammer	HP	1885	Singer	dr	f	l	vig		
Elaine Greffulhe	T	1892	Cochet S	w	vf	l	vig		
Elbfex	HMult	1890	Geschwind	m					
Elegans	Bslt	Pre 1844		rb	s-d	m			
Elegans	HSet	Pre 1846		mp	dbl				
Elegans	Ayr			w	s-d		vvig		
Elegans	HMult	1888		mp	f		s		
Elegans Rosea	N	Pre 1846		mp					
Élégant	HCh	c 1825	Prévost syn Roxelane	mp	dbl		s		
Elégant	HSpn		Goupil	dp					
Elégant à Fleurs Pleines	HCh	Pre 1830	Prévost	lp	vf		s		
Élégante	G	Pre 1820	Hardy	lp			vl		
Élégante	HP	1847	Laffay	lp	f	l			
Élégante	HMult	1859	Laurentius	mr					
Élégante	T	1882	Guillot	pb	dbl	m-l			
Eléonide	N		Laffay	mp	dbl	m			
Elevé	G		Dupont	lp					
Elia	Ch		Laffay	dr	dbl	m			
Elie Beauvillain	Cl T	1887	Beauvillain	mp	dbl	l	vig	m	
Elie de Beaumont	HP	Pre 1870		mr	f	l			
Elie Lambert	HP	1897	Lambert E	mr	f	l			
Elie Morel	HP	1867	Bouchalat	lp	f	vl	m		
Elina-la-Jolie	G	Pre 1815	Descemet	mr					
Elisa	A	Pre 1810	Charpentier	lp	f	l			
Elisa	G	Pre 1830	syn Agate Porcelaine	lp	vf	s			
Elisa Blanche	A	Pre 1810	Hardy syn Elisa	lp	f	l			
Elisa Boëlle	HP	1869	Guillot Père	w	f	m	vig		f
Élisa de Chénier	B	Pre 1870		mp	f	m			
Elisa Descemet	G	c 1810	Descemet	lp	vdbl	l			
Elisa Fenning	HP		Laffay	lp	f	s			
Elisa Fougier	T	1890	Bonnaire	w	vf	vl			
Elisa Leker	C	1839	Vibert	dp	f	m			
Elisa Masson	HP		Robert	dp					
Elisa Mercoeur	HCh	1842	Vibert	mp	f	l		m	
Elisa Mercoeur	P	1858	Robert & Moreau	lp					
Elisa Miellez	HP			mp	f	l			
Elisa Renou	HCh	Pre 1846		lp	f	l			
Elisa Roucolle (Bancolle)	T	Pre 1870	Pradel	ly	f	l			
Elisa Walker	D	1820	Prévost	lp	vdbl	l			
Elisabeth Barbensien	T	1883	Stammler syn M Furtado	my	vf	l	m	f	
Elisabeth Brow	M		see Elizabeth Rowe						
Elisabeth de la Rochetterie	HP	1881	Vigneron	lp	f	vl	vig		
Elisabeth Guizot	G	1827	Guillot	mr					
Elisabeth Roussel	Misc								
Elisabeth Schwartz	HP	1866	Guillot Père	w					
Elisabeth Vigneron	HP	1865	Vigneron	lp	vf	vl	vig		f
Elise	A	Pre 1846		lp	f	m			
Elise Balcombe	HP	Pre 1846		lp	f	s	vig		
Elise Cambier	HP			dr	f	l	vig		
Elise Chabrier	HP								
Elise Chatelard	Pom			dr					
Elise d'Auteuil	G			lp	f	m			
Elise d'Oazon	T			lp	f	l			vf
Élise Flory	Ch	Pre 1870		lp	f	m			
Elise Fry	Ch			dp	vf	l			
Elise Heymann	T	1891	Strassheim	yb	f	vl			
Elise Lemaire	HP	Pre 1886		lp	f	m	vig		
Elise le Mesle	G/C	1832	Vibert	w	f	l			
Elise Masson	HP	1849	Vibert	dp	f	m	vvig		
Elise Morel	HP		see Elie Morel						
Elise Rovella	G	Pre 1842	Roseraie de l'Hay	mp	dbl	m			
Elise Raynaud	B		Pradel	w			m		
Elise Sauvage	T	1838	Miellez	yb	f	l			f
Elise Stchegoleff	T	1881	Nabonnand	lp	vf	l	m		
Elise Vardon	T			lp	f	l	vig		
Elise Voïard	G	1827	Noisette	lp					
Eliza Balcombe	HP	1842	Laffay	w					

Eliza Le Maire	N	Pre 1846		w		s		
Eliza Werry	M	Pre 1846		w				
Elizabeth Plantier	B	Pre 1846		mr				
Elizabeth Rowe	M	Pre 1870		lp	dbl	vl		m
Ella Gordon	HP	1883	Paul W	mr	f	l	vig	
Ella May	T	1890	May	ab	f	l		m
Ellen Drew	HP	1896	Dickson A	lp	f	l		
Ellen Willmott	HT	1898	Bernaix A	lp	dbl	l	vvig	
Elodie	G	1827	Vibert	lp				
Elodie	D	1853	Robert & Moreau	lp		vl		
Elongata	D	Pre 1811	syn Argentée	lp		m		
Elphège	G	1827	Noisette	mr				
Else Schüle	HT	1892	Geisler	mr				
Elvina	T	1825	Laffay	w				
Elvinie	Ch		Laffay	lp	dbl	m		
Elvira	HEg			lp	s-d	m	vig	
Elvira	Ch	1843	Verdier V	dp	f	m		f
Elvire	HEg	1821	Cartier syn Poniatowsky	lp	s-d	m		
Elvire	D	1831	Vibert	lp		m		
Elvire Laffay	Ch		Laffay	mp	dbl	m		f
Elyse Flory	Ch	1851	Guillot Père	lp	f	m-l		
Elysian	Misc	Pre 1846						
Emélie Fontaine	HP	1881	Fontaine	pb	vf	l		
Emerance	C	Pre 1846	Vibert	w	f	m		m
Emerance	M	1858	Robert & Moreau	lp				
Emile Audusson	T	1842	Audusson					
Emile Bardiaux	HP	1889	Lévêque	dp	f	l		
Emile Courtier	B	1837	Portemer	mp	f	m	vvig	
Emile Dulac	HP	1862	Guillot Fils	dp	f	l	vig	
Emile Jourdan	HP	1887		mr	f	l	vig	
Emile Lévêque	T	1897	Pernet-Ducher	op				
Emile Varangeot	B							
Emilia Plantier	N	1878	Schwartz	ly	dbl	m-l	vvig	
Emilie	M	Pre 1885	Roseraie de l'Hay	w	f	s		
Emilie d'Abancourt	T			w	f	m	vig	
Emilie Dupuy	Cl T	1870	Levet	op	dbl	l		m
Emilie Duval	HP			p	f	m		
Emilie Gonin	T	1896	Guillot Père	w	f	vl	vig	m
Emilie Halphen	HP			lp				
Emilie Hausburg	HP	1868	Lévêque	m	dbl	l		m
Emilie la Jolie	G	1827	Boutigny syn Belle Emilie	lp	f	m		
Emilie Laxton	HP	see	Mlle Emilie Laxton & Emily Laxton					
Emilie Lazard	T	1885	Singer	mp	f	l	vig	
Emilie Lesourd (or Lesourt)	Ch			lp	f	s		
Emilie Levert	Ch		Laffay	dr	dbl	s		
Emilie Mauget	P	Pre 1830	Mauget / Prévost syn Alba Bifera	lp	vdbl	m		
Emilie Miret	B	1854	Pradel	dp	f	l	vig	
Emilie Peel	N		see Lady Emily Peel					
Emilie Plantier	B	c 1845	Plantier	mp	f	l	vig	
Emilie Verachter	G	1840	Parmentier	mp	f	m		
Emilie Verdier (N B Emile or Emilie in some cases)	HP		Verdier E	dp	f	l	vig	
Emily Laxton	HP	1878	Laxton	mr	f	l	vig	
Emin Pascha	HT	1894	Drögmüller	dp	dbl	l		
Emma Dampierre	HP	Pre 1846		lp	f			
Emmanuel Geibel	T	1897	Hedlund	yb				
Emmanuel Singer Senior	HP	1885	Singer	dr	f	l	vvig	
Emmelina	Ch		Laffay	lp				
Emmeline	HEg	Pre 1810	Prévost	w	s-d	m		f
Emmeline	HCh	Pre 1829	Boutigny	w	dbl	s		
Emmeline	M	1859	Robert & Moreau	w	f	s		
Emmeline	HP		Vibert	lp				
Emmeline	HCh	1888	syn Madeleine	lp	vdbl	l	vig	
Emolenila (Emonelina)	Ch			dp	f	m		
Emotion	B	1862	Guillot Père	w	f	m	m	f
Emotion	B	1879	Fontaine syn Alice Fontaine	pb	vdbl	l		m
Empereur	G	Pre 1810		dr				
Empereur Alexandre III	HP	1885	Soupert & Notting	dp	vf	vl	vvig	vf
Empereur Couronné	G	Pre 1830	syn Couronné Royale	mp	f	m		
Empereur de Russie	G	Pre 1830	Prévost	mp	f	m-l		
Empereur des Nègres	G	Pre 1830						
Empereur du Brésil	HP	1880	Soupert & Notting	rb	vf	vl	vvig	
Empereur du Maroc	HP	1858	Guinoisseau	dr	dbl	s	vig	m
Empereur du Mexique	HP	1865	Pernet Père	rb	f	l	vig	
Empereur Frédéric	T		see Kaiser Friedrich					
Empereur Napoléon	HP	1854	Granger	dr	f	l	vig	

Name	Type	Year	Raiser / Syn					
Empereur Napoléon III	HP	1855	Granger	dr		vl		
Empereur Wilhelm	T		see Kaiser Wilhelm					
Emperor	M	Pre 1846		dp				
Emperor	HP	1883	Paul W	dr	f	s		
Empress	HP	1884	Paul W	w		s		
Empress Alexandra of Russia	T	1897	Paul W	rb	f	l	vig	vf
Empress Eugénie	B	Pre 1860		lp	f	l	vig	
Empress Josephine (Francofurtana)	Misc	Pre 1770		mp	s-d	l		
Empress Josephine	G	Pre 1815	Descemet	pb	dbl			
Empress Marie of Russia	T			my		l		f
Empress of China	Cl Ch	1896	Jackson	mp	dbl	m	vvig	sf
Empress of India	HP	1876	Laxton	dr	f	m		m
Empress of the North (Russia)	Sp	c 1880	syn r.rugosa plena	m	dbl			
Enchanteresse	G	Pre 1824	François syn L'Enchantresse	mp	dbl	l		
Enchantress	T	1896	Paul W	w	f	l	vig	f
En Corymbes	D							
Enfant d'Ajaccio	B	Pre 1846 syn	Souvenir d'Anselme	dp	dbl	l	vvig	
Enfant d'Amenguy	HP	1867	Ducher	lp	f	l	vig	
Enfant de Chatillon	HP	1869	Fontaine	dr	f	l	vig	vf
Enfant de France	G	1802	Hardy	m	f	m		
Enfant de France	G	Pre 1810	Dupont syn Beauté Tendre (G)	dp	vdbl	l		
Enfant de France	A	Pre 1813	Descemet syn Beauté Tendre (A)	lp	f	m		
Enfant de France	G	Pre 1820	Prévost syn Roi de Rome	lp	f	s-m		
Enfant de France	HP	1860	Lartay	lp	vdbl	vl		m
Enfant de France Nouveau	G	Pre 1830	Pelletier syn Tout Aimable	r	f	s		
Enfant de l'Ouragan	G			p	f	l		
Enfant de Lyon	T	1859	Avoux & Crozy syn Narcisse	my	dbl	l	vvig	f
Enfant du Mont Carmel	HP	1851	Cherpin	mr	f	l		
Enfant du Nord	G			dp	f	m	vig	
Enfant Trouvé	T	1861	Lartay	mp				
Ennemond Boule	HP	1879	Liabaud	mr	f	m-l	vvig	
Epineux à Fleur Pleine	Bks	Pre 1846		w				
Epineux de la Chine	Misc	1840	syn Fortuniana	w	dbl			
Éponine	G	Pre 1829	Coquerel	m	vf	m		
Eponine	HMsk	Pre 1835		w	dbl	m		m
Eponine	M	Pre 1846		w				f
Erbprincessin von Ratibor	T	1893	Türke	rb				
Erdelinde	G	1824	Toutain	pb				
Erebus	HSpn	Pre 1846		dr				
Erebus	B	1890	Geschwind					
Eremit de Granval	Ch	c 1840	Prévost syn De Rennes	m	vf	m-l		
Erigone	G	1822	Vibert	dr	f	m		
Erikonig	HMult	1886	Geschwind see Roi des Aunes	m				
Erinnerung an Brod	HSet	1886	Geschwind	rb	dbl	l	vig	m
Erinnerung an Meine Mutter	B	1887	Geschwind	m		l	vig	
Erinnerung an Meinen Vater	HArv	1888	Geschwind	w				
Erinnerung an Schloss Scharfenstein	HT	1892	Geschwind	m	dbl	l		vf
Ermite	G		Miellez	dr				
Ermite	Ch	Pre 1830	syn Granval	mr	vf	m-l		
Ermite de Remistan	Ch	Pre 1846		dr				
Ernest Bachelier	G			mr	dbl	l		
Ernest Bergman	HP	1856	Quettier	dp	f	l		
Ernest Bonçenne	HP	1868	Cherpin / Liabaud	mp	f	m	vvig	
Ernest Feray	B/HCh	Pre 1846		dr	f	l		
Ernest Herger	T	1874	Pradel	mr		m		
Ernest Herger	HP	1873	Verdier E	dr	f	l	vig	
Ernest Metz	T	1888	Guillot J B	mp	f	l	vig	f
Ernest Morel	HP	1898	Cochet P	dr	f	l		
Ernest Prince	HP	1881	Ducher	mr	f	vl	vvig	
Ernestella Bracteata	HBc							
Ernestine	Ch		Girardon	lp				
Ernestine	G		Lerouge					
Ernestine Audio	D	Pre 1842	Audio	m	f			m
Ernestine de Barante	HP	1843	Lacharme	mp	f	s		
Ernestine Miellez	G			dp	vf	m		
Ernestine Odiot	HP			dp	f	l		
Ernestine Tavernier	T	1861	Pradel	pb				
Ernestine Tavernier	T		Touvais	w	f	l	vig	
Ernst G Dörell	HMult	1887	Geschwind	dp	dbl	m		
Ernst Willner	HT	1888	Geschwind					
Erubescens	A	Pre 1810	syn Celestial	lp	dbl	l	vig	vf
Erythrine	G	1827	Vétillard	dr				

Erzherzog Franz Ferdinand	T	1892	Soupert & Notting	pb	f	l	vig	f
Erzherzogin Marie Dorothea	HT	1892	Balogh	yb	vf	l		
Esmeralda	B	Pre 1846		dr	f			
Esmeralda	A	1847	Verdier V	lp	f	m		
Esmeralda	HP	1862	Fontaine	mp	f	m		
Esmeralda	HT	1888	Geschwind	w	f	l		
Espalais	N		see Des Palais					
Espartero	N			my	f	vl	vig	
Esponia	G		syn Charles X	dp				
Esquerme	HP			dr				
Estelle	G	Pre 1810		mp	vdbl	m		vf
Estelle	HSpn	Pre 1820	Vibert	lp	s-d	m		
Esther	C	1819	Vibert	lp		l		
Esther	G	Pre 1830	Vibert	lp	f	l		m
		syn Du-	chesse d'Oldenbourg					
Esther Pradel	T	1860	Pradel	ab	f	m	vig	
Étendard de Jeanne d'Arc	N/T	1882	Garçon / Margottin	w	vf	vl	vvig	
			syn Jeanne d'Arc					
Étendard de Lyon	HP	1885	Gonod	mr	f	l	vig	
Étendard de Marengo	HP	1848	Armand	mr	vf	l		
Étendard de Sébastopol	HP	1856	Ducher	dr	vdbl	m	vig	
Étendard de Grand Homme	HP			mr	vdbl	m		
Étendard des Amateurs	HP	1854	Oger	dr	f	m	vig	
Ethel	HP	1829						
Ethel Brownlow	T	1887	Dickson A	op		l		
Ethel Richardson	HT	Pre 1899		w			vig	
Étienette Desbrosses	D	c 1828						
Étienne	Ch	Pre 1846	Laffay	w	dbl	l		f
Étienne Dubois	HP	1873	Damaizin	dr	dbl	l	vig	
Étienne Dupuis (Dupuy)	HP	1873	Levet	mp	f	l	vig	
Étienne Levet	HP	1871	Levet Père	mr	dbl	vl	vig	
Etna	Ch	1825	Laffay	dr	vf	m		
Etna	M	1845	Vibert	dr	vdbl	m		m
Étoile d'Angers	T	1890	Tesnier	rb				
Étoile de la Gironde	B							
Étoile de la Malmaison	A	Pre 1844		lp	f	m-l	vig	
Étoile de Lyon	T	1881	Guillot Fils	my	dbl	l	vvig	f
Étoile de Mai	Pol	1893	Gamon	ly	dbl	s	vig	vf
Étoile de Marie	HP							
Étoile de Marle	HP			lp				
Étoile de Portugal	HG	1898	Cayeux	dp	dbl	l		
Étoile d'Or	Pol	1889	Dubreuil	yb	dbl	l	vig	
Étoile du Berger	B	1841	Béluze	w	f	m	vig	
Étoile du Matin	B	1851	Bernède	dp	f	m		
Étoile du Nord	B	1854	Fontaine	mr	f	m		
Étoile du Nord	HP	1859	Bernède	dr				
Étoile Polaire	T	1891	Tesnier	pb				
Étoilée	Ch		Mme Olry	m		vf	vig	
Eucharis	G	1815	Descemet	dp	dbl	l		
Eucharis	G	1822	Vibert	dp	f	l		
Eudoxia (e)	N	Pre 1870	Léon Lille	lp	f	m		
Eudoxie	G	Pre 1820	Descemet	dp		m		
Eudoxie	D	Pre 1848		mp	dbl	l	vig	
Eugène	G	1825	Boutigny	lp	f	m		
Eugène Alary	HP	Pre 1870	Pradel	dr	f	vl		
Eugène Appert	HP	1856	Trouillard	dr	f	m	vig	
Eugène Bourcier	HP	1861	Verdier E	dr	s-d	m	vig	
Eugène Bourgeois	N	1897	Denis syn René Denis	ly				
Eugène Bréon	B	1847	Paillet	op	f	l		
Eugène de Beauharnais	Ch	1838	Hardy	dr	dbl	l	m	m
Eugène de Luxembourg	HP	1864	Moreau & Robert	dr				
		syn	Prince	Eugène de Beauharn-	ais			
Eugène de Rogerie	B			pb				
Eugène de Savoie	M	1860	Moreau-Robert	lp	dbl	m	m	vf
Eugène Delaire	HP	1879	Vigneron	mr	dbl	l	vvig	
Eugène Delamarre	B	1873	Gautereau	mp	f	m	m	
Eugène d'Orléans	HSem	Pre 1829	Jacques	lp	dbl	m	vvig	
Eugène Fürst	HP	1875	Soupert & Notting	dr	dbl	l	vvig	f
Eugène Guinoisseau	HT			lp	f	m		
Eugène Janvier	G			dp	dbl	m		
Eugène Jardine	N	1898	Conard & Jones	w	f	l		m
Eugène Labruyère	HP		Labruyère	mr				
Eugène Maille	G	c 1825	Boutigny	mp	f	vl		
Eugène Mallet	N	1873	Nabonnand	yb				
Eugène Meynadier	T	1884	Nabonnand	m	vf	vl	vig	
Eugène Patette	T	1883	Nabonnand	m	vf	l	vvig	
Eugène Perrier	HP	1888	Perrier	dp	f	l		vf
Eugène Petit	HP	1862	Touvais	mr	f	l		
Eugène Pirolle	N	Pre 1844	syn Admiral de Rigny	mp	f	m		
Eugène Poitteaux	HP	1854	Morlet	dp	f	l	vvig	
Eugène Savary	HP	1875	Gonod	mp	f	l		
Eugène Scribe	HP	1866	Gautreau	mr	f	l		

Eugène Sue	HP	1852	Laffay	dp	f	l		vf
Eugène Transon	HP	1881	Vigneron	mr	f	l	vvig	
Eugène Vavin	HP	1869	Duval	mr	f	l		
Eugène Verdier	HP	1863	Guillot Fils	m	f	l	vig	
Eugène Verdier	M	1872	Verdier E	dp	vdbl	m	vig	vf
Eugénie	G	1818	Vibert	lp		m		
		syn	Nouveau Triomphe					
Eugénie Bourgeois	T	1897	Bourgeois	w	f	l		
Eugénie Desgaches	T	1835	Plantier	lp	f	l	vig	f
Eugénie Dubourg	N			lp	f	l		
Eugénie Frémy	HP	1885	Verdier E	dp	vf	vl	vvig	
Eugénie Grandet	B		Pradel	mp				
Eugénie Guinoisseau	B	1860	Guinoisseau	mp	vf	m		
Eugénie Guinoisseau	M	1864	Bertrand Guinoisseau	mr	dbl	m	vig	
Eugénie Hardy	Ch	Pre 1846		lp	vf	m		
Eugénie Jouvain (Jauvin)	T	1830	Desprez	w	f	l		
			syn Madame Roussel					
Eugénie Lamesch	Pol	1899	Lambert P	yb	dbl	m	vvig	m
Eugénie Lebrun	HP	1860	Fontaine	dr	f	l		
Eugénie le Prévost de Launay	HP	1856	Pradel					
Eugénie Napoléon	G			dr		m		
Eugénie Poileau	HP	1857	Poileau	dr			m	
Eugénie Rogery	B	1857	Pradel	dr				
Eugénie Verdier	HP	1869	Guillot Fils	dp	f	l	vig	
Eugénie Wilhelm	HP	1874	Soupert & Notting	dr	f	m	m	
Eugenius	HSpn	1888		p				
Eulalia de la Falconnière	B	1854	Dorizy	dr	f	l		
Eulalie	G	1826	Vibert	mp		m		
Eulalie Lebrun	G	1844	Vibert	w	dbl	m	m	
Euphémie	B	1847	Vibert	lp	f	l		
Euphrasie	G	1845	Vibert	lp	f	m		
Euphrasie Rousseau	HP	1863	Rousseau	mp	f	l		
Euphrosine	G	Pre 1830	Prévost	mp	dbl	l	vvig	
Euphrosine	HCh	1826	Vibert	lp	vf	m-l		
Euphrosine	N	Pre 1846		yb	f	l		
Euphrosine l'Élégante	C	Pre 1811	Descemet	dp				
Euphrosyne	HMult	1895	Schmidt	mp	dbl	s	vig	m
Euripides	HSpn	1888		m				
Euryanthe	HP	1866	Peters	dr	dbl	l		
Eurydice	G			lp	f	l		
Eurydice	P	1823	Vibert					
Eurydice	HP	1854	Robert	mp	f	m		
Eurydice	HSet	1886	Geschwind R	pb				
Eusèbe de Salverte	T		Duval	w	vf			
Eutaxie	G	1827	Noisette	mr				
Eva	N		Laffay	dp	vf	m		
Eva Corinna	HSet	1843	Feast	dp	dbl	m	m	
Eve	HSem	Pre 1830	Vibert	dp	f	m		
Eve	N		Laffay	dp	vdbl	m		
Eveline	G							
Eveline Turner	HP	1876	Verdier E	mp	f	vl	m	
Évêque	G	Pre 1790		m	dbl	l		
Évêque de Luxembourg	HP	1878	Soupert & Notting	rb	f	m	vig	
Évêque de Meaux	HP	1855	Quettier	dr	f	l		
Évêque de Nimes	HP	1856	Plantier / Damaizin	dr	f	l		
Everaerts	G			lp	f	m		
Evergreen Gem	HWich	1899	Horvath	w	dbl	m	vig	m
Evergreen Rose	Sp	1629	syn r.sempervirens	w	s			m
Evratina	A	1809	Bosc	dp	vdbl	s	vig	
Ex Alba Inermis Violacea	G	Pre 1814	Descemet	m				
Ex Alba Rosea	A	Pre 1830	Vibert	lp	dbl	l		
Ex Alba Violacea	G	Pre 1830	Noisette	dp	dbl	vl		
Ex Alba Violacea Crispa	G	Pre 1846	Descemet					
Exadelphé	T	1885	Nabonnand	my	f	l		vf
Exposition de Brie	HP	1861	Granger	mr	dbl	l	vig	vf
		syn	Maurice Bernardin					
Exposition de Provins	N	1895	Cochet-Cochet	mr	f	l		
Exposition de Toulouse	HP	1873	Brassac	mr				
Exposition du Havre	HP	1870	Gautreau	dr	f	l	vig	
Exquisite	HT	1899	Paul W	rb	f	l		
Extra de Gossart (d)	HCh		Gossart (d)	m	vdbl	m		
		syn	Triomphe d'Orléans					
Exubérant	Ch	1820	Godefroy	dr	vdbl	s-m		
Eymin Pacha	HT	1894	Drogmüller	mr				
Eynard	B	1828	Vibert	mp		m		
Eynard	HCh	Pre 1846	Laffay	dr	f	l		
Eyriés	HCh	Pre 1830	Calvert	m	f	m-l		
Ezard	T			lp	vdbl	l		

NAME	TYPE	YEAR	RAISER	COLOUR	BLOOM	SIZE	GROWTH	SCENT
F J Pfitzer	HP	1876	Verdier E	mr				
F L Segers	T	1899	Ketten Bros	pb	vf	l		m
F M Vos Santos Viana	T	1881	Nabonnand	lp	vf	l	vig	
F R C Sutton	HP	1884	Frettier	mp				
Faber	P							
Fabvier	Ch	1832	Laffay M	mr	s-d	m	m	f
Fafait	B			dp	f	l		
Fafait	T			w	f	vl		
Fair Berthe (Fairy Berthe)	B	1851	Foulard	lp			vig	
Fair Rosamund	HCh	1890	Paul W	lp				
Fairy	Ch	1888		lp				
Fairy Queen	T	1884	Ellwanger & Barry	dr				
Fairy Rose	Sp	1815	syn r.chinensis minima	w,p,r	s-d			
Fakir	T	1825	Laffay	dp	s-d	m		f
Fanny	A	Pre 1848		pb	f	l		
Fanny Bias	G	Pre 1811	Descemet	mp	f	l		m
Fanny Bias	G	1819	Vibert	lp		l		
Fanny Boydt	T	Pre 1844	Burel A	w	f	m		
Fanny Dupuy	T	Pre 1889	syn Abricotée	ab	dbl	l	vig	f
Fanny Duval	Ch	Pre 1870		w	f	l	vig	
Fanny Elssler	G	1835	Vibert	mp	vf			m
Fanny Geefs	G		Parmentier	rb	f	l	vig	
Fanny Giron	HP	1882	Schmitt	lp	f	l	vvig	
Fanny Marschall	G			lp	f	l		
Fanny Parissot	G	Pre 1811	Descemet	mp	f	l		m
			syn Fanny Bias					
Fanny Pavetot	G	1819		mp	vdbl	l		m
Fanny Petzhold	HP	1865	Fontaine	lp	f	l		
Fanny Rousseau	A	1817	Vibert	lp	f	m		
Fanny Sommesson	A	Pre 1826	Vibert	lp	f	m	vig	
Fanny Stollwerck	T	1896	Nabonnand	yb				
Fanta	HP			lp				
Fantasca	HMult	1890	Geschwind	pb				
Fantesse	D	Pre 1846		lp				f
Fantin-Latour	C	Pre 1900		lp	dbl	m	vig	m
Farnesse	A	Pre 1834		w		m		
Fasciculée	C	c 1810	Descemet	mp	f	s		
		syn	Comtesse de Chamois					
Fashionable	Misc	Pre 1846		dp				
Fastigiata	C		Descemet	mp				
		syn	Comtesse de Chamois					
Fata Morgana	T	1893	Drögemüller	mp	f	l		
Father Hugo's Rose	Sp	Pre 1899	Hemsley syn r.hugonis	my	s	m		
Fatime	G	Pre 1815	Descemet	dp	vdbl	m		sf
Fatime	Ch	1828	Vibert	lp		s		
Fatime	HCh	1854	Robert	dp	f	m	vig	
Fatinitza	HMult	1886	Geschwind	pb	s-d	m		
Faucheux	Ch							
Fausse Unique	D	Pre 1818	Prévost	w	f	l		
Faustine	B/D/M		Noisette	dr	vf	m		
Faustine	G	Pre 1830	Vibert	m	dbl	s		
Faustine	B	Pre 1834	Laffay	lp	f	m		
Faux Thé Rouge	Ch	1824	Noisette L / Vibert	mp	f	m		f
Favaricus	Misc	Pre 1846						
Favart	T	Pre 1846		lp				
Favier	C		Baumann					
Favilla	T	1856	Robert	dr	f			
Favorite	G		Vilmorin					
Favorite Agate	Misc	Pre 1846		lp				
Favorite (des Dames)	D	Pre 1830	Vibert	lp	f	s		
			syn La Favorite					
Favorite Purple	G	c 1836	Lahaye	m	f	m		
			syn Belle de Stors					
Féburier	HP	Pre 1834		lp	f	m		
Fedanne	N	1858	Robert & Moreau	lp				
Fedora	B	Pre 1846		dr	f	m		
Fedtschenkoana	Sp	1876	syn r.fedtschenkoana	w	s		vig	
Fée Opale	N	1899	Bruant	ly	f	l		
Felicia	N	Pre 1834	Duval	mp		s		
Félicie	N			lp	vf	m	vig	
Félicie	G	1820	Vibert	m	dbl	s		m
Félicie Boitard	HP	1827	Noisette L	lp	vdbl	l		
Félicien David	HP	1872	Verdier E	m	vf	l	m	
Félicité	D	Pre 1846		mr				
Félicité	A	Pre 1896		lp				
Félicité Bohain	M	Pre 1866		dp	vf	l		m
Félicité Lagrange	Ch			lp	f	l		
Félicité Parmentier	A	1834	Parmentier	lp	vdbl	m	vig	vf
Félicité-Perpétue	HSem	1827	Jacques	lp	vdbl	m	vvig	vf

Name	Type	Year	Raiser					
Félicité Rigault	HP	1853	Fontaine	lp	f	l		
Félix	Ch	Pre 1830	Vibert	dp	dbl	m		
Félix Dorizy	B	1852	Dorizy	dr	f	m	vig	
Félix Généro	HP	1866	Damaizin	m	f	l	vig	
Félix Mousset	HP	1884	Verdier E	m	f	l	vig	f
Félix Parmentier	G			dp	f	m		
Félix Peretti	HP	1856	Robert	lp	f	m		
Félix Ribeyre	HP	1888	Verdier E	mp	f	m	vig	vf
Fellemberg	N	Pre 1835	Fellemberg	mr	dbl	l	vig	m
Fénélon	Ch	Pre 1830	Laffay	m	f	s		
Fénélon	G	Pre 1838		dr	vf	l		
Fénélon	HP	1852	Rousseau	dr	vf	l		
Fenon Rouge Agathé	G			mr				
Ferdinand	HP	1852	Bernède	mr	f	m	vig	
Ferdinand Batel	HT	1896	Pernet-Ducher	yb	dbl	m	m	
Ferdinand Chaffolte	HP	1878	Pernet Fils	mr	vdbl	vl	vvig	m
Ferdinand de Buck	G	Pre 1842		mp	dbl	m		
Ferdinand de Lesseps	HP	1869	Verdier E	ob	dbl	l	vig	f
		see	Maurice Bernardin					
Ferdinand Deppe	HP	1852	Laffay	m	f	l		
Ferdinand Deppe	B	1854	Verdier E	rb	f	m	vvig	
Ferdinand de Sicile	D			w	f	m	vig	
Ferdinand Jamin	HP	1888	Lévêque	mr	f			
Ferdinand Jamin	HT	1896	Pernet-Ducher	op	f	l		
Ferdinand Lafite	B	1851	Pradel	dr	f	m		
Ferdinand I	HCh			lp	f	l		
Ferdoucy	M		Moreau-Robert	dp				
Fernande de la Forest	HP	1872	Damaizin	lp	f	l	vig	
Fernand Lemarchand	HP	1878	Margottin	mp				
Feroce (Ferox)	Misc	Pre 1830	Hérisson	dp	s	l	vig	
Ferox	HEg	1826	Vibert	mp	dbl	m		
Ferox	A	Pre 1844		w	vdbl	m	vig	
Ferox	D	Pre 1846		dr	f	l		f
Ferox	P			mr				
Ferret	HP	Pre1846		op	f			
Ferret	P			mp				
Ferrières	Alp			lp				
Ferruginea	M			dr				
Ferrugineux du Luxembourg	M	Pre 1834		mr	f	m	vig	
Feu Amoureux	G	Pre 1811		m	dbl	l		
Feu Brillant	HP	1865	Moreau-Robert	mr	f	l		
Feu Brillant	G	1819	Vibert	dr	f	m		
Feu Brillant	G	Pre 1830	Prévost	mr	s-d	l		
Feu Carmin	G	Pre 1834		mr		m		
Feu de Buck	G		syn Ferdinand de Buck	dr	f	m		
Feu de Vesta	G	Pre 1829	Coquerel	mr	dbl	l		
Feu d'Enghein	C			dp	s-d	m		
Feu d'Inkermann	HP		Moreau-Robert	dr				
Feuerkugel	B	1895	Geschwind		dbl	l		f
Feunon Rouge	G	Pre 1811		mr	vdbl	m		m
Feu Panaché	G	Pre 1830	Prévost	dr	vdbl	s		
Feu Royal	G							
Feu Turc	G		Miellez	dr		m		
Fiammetta	B	1887	Geschwind					
Fiammetta Nabonnand	T	1894	Nabonnand	w	dbl	l	m	f
Fiançailles de la Princesse Stéphanie et de l'Archiduc Rodolphe	N	1880	Levet	ob	f	m		
Fiançailles de Stéphanie	T	see	Princesse Stéphanie					
Fidèle	G		Miellez	lp	vdbl	vl		
Fidelia	G	Pre 1830	Prévost	lp	f	m		f
Fidélité	HCh	1843	Vibert	p	f	m		
Fidouline	HP	Pre 1846		lp	f			
Field Rose	Sp	Pre 1650	syn r.arvensis	w				sf
Fiery	Misc	Pre 1846						
Filius Strassheim	Pol	1892	Soupert & Notting	lp	dbl	s	vig	vf
Fille du Printemps	HP	see Bel-	le Fille du Printemps					
Fils Flon-Flon (Flonflon)	T			lp	f	m		
Fimbriata	HRg	1891	Morlet	lp	dbl	m	vvig	vf
Fimbriata à Pétales Frangées	HCh	1831	Jacques syn Serratipetala	dp	f	m	m	
Fina Soestmans	G			lp	f	m		
Fintelmans	G			dr	f	m		
Firebrand	HP	1872	Paul W	mr	f	vl	m	vf
Fisher Holmes	HP	1865	Verdier E	dr	f	l	vig	f
Fitemi's Rose	Cl Pol	1894	Hosp	lp	dbl	s	vig	vf
		syn	Mlle Cécile Brunner,	Clg				
Five-coloured China Rose	Ch	Pre 1620	syn Wu Se'Quaing Wei	r, p, w				
Flagellipetala	M			lp	f	m		
Flag of the Union	T	Pre 1882	Hallock & Thorpe	pb				
Flamande	G	Pre 1811	syn Agathe Incarnata	lp	vdbl	m		vf
Flamboyante	G	Pre 1815	Descemet	mr				

Name	Class	Date	Breeder					
Flamboyante	G	c 1820	Godefroy	m	f	s-m		
Flamboyante	B	1852	Viviant-Faivre	mr	f	m		
Flamme de Vésuve	G		Miellez	dr				
Flanders	Misc	Pre 1846						
Flava (Flavescens)	Pom			w	s-d	m		
Flavescens	HSpn	Pre 1824		ly				
Flavescens	T	1824	Parks	my	dbl	l		
		syn	Park's Yellow Tea-Scented China					
Flavia	G	c 1810	Descemet					
Flavia	HCh	c 1825	Laffay	dr	f	m		
Flavien Budillon	T	1885	Nabonnand	lp		l		vf
Flèche Scarlet	M		see De la Flèche	dr	f	m		
Fléchier	B	1853	Robert	lp	f	m	vvig	
Flesh-Coloured Noisette	N	Pre 1817	Noisette	w	s-d	m	vig	m
			syn Blush Noisette					
Fleur d'Amour	G	Pre 1830		dr		l		
Fleur de Cypres (Cypris)	T	Pre 1846		lp		m		
Fleur de Parade	Misc	Pre 1846						
Fleur de Passe Rose de la Chine	G	1827	Pelletier	lp				
Fleur de Peltier	G	1824	Roseraie de l'Hay	pb				
Fleur de Soufre	Ch		Laffay	ly	dbl	l		
Fleur de Vénus	Ch	Pre 1813	Descemet	w	f	m	vig	
Fleur des Pois	A			w	s	m	vig	
Fleur du Jeune Âge	N	Pre 1846		lp			vvig	
Fleur Plate	D			mp				
Fleurette	Bslt	Pre 1824	syn Blush Boursault	pb	vdbl	vl		
Fleurette	HCh	1829	Vibert	lp	f	m		
Fleurs Bombées	G	1827	Noisette	mp				
Fleurs Comprimées	G	1822	Vibert					
Fleurs d'Anémone	M	Pre 1846	Vibert	dr	f	m	vig	f
Fleurs de Centfeuille	D	1823	Toutain	dp				
Fleurs de Cypris	T			lp	f	m		
Fleurs de Matricaire	N			w	f	s		
Fleurs de Nerium	HCh		syn Neriiflora	mr				
Fleurs de Passion	G	1827	Pelletier	lp				
Fleurs de Pêcher	HP	1877	Paul W	pb	f	l		
			see Peach Blossom					
Fleurs de Pelletier	G	Pre 1842	Pelletier	dp	vdbl	m		
Fleurs de Pommier	G	Pre 1830		lp	f	m		
Fleurs et Feuilles Marbrées	G			dr	f	s	m	
Flocon de Neige	Ch	1898	Lille	w	vf	s		
Flon	D	1845	Vibert	mr		l		
Flora	HArv	1829		dp	f	l		
Flora	C	Pre 1846	Vibert	lp	f	m		
Flora	Ch			dp		vl	vig	
Flora	Pol	1888	Schwartz Vve	w	f	l	vig	
Flora McIvor	HCh	Pre 1846		lp		vl		
Flora McIvor	HEg	1894	Penzance	pb	s	s	vig	vf
Flora Nabonnand	T	1877	Nabonnand	mp		l		
Flora Nigricante	Misc	Pre 1846						
Flora Prévost	G			dp	f	m		
Floralie	T	1838	Coquereau	w	f	m	vig	
Flora's Riches	C	Pre 1846		dr				
Flore	HSem	1829	Jacques	mp	dbl	m	vvig	m
Flore Magno	C	Pre 1808	syn Foliacée	mp	dbl	vl		
Flore Pallido	M	c 1805	Vilmorin syn Vilmorin	lp	f	m-l		
Flore Pallido	HFt	1824	Souchet	ly				
Flore Plena	A	Pre 1770	syn Plena	w	s-d			
Flore Rubro	Misc	Pre 1846						
Floreat Etona	HP	1872	Knight	op	f	m-l		
		syn Pri-	ncesse Louise Victoria					
Florence	Ch							
Florence de Colquhoune	T	1880	Nabonnand	mr	s-d	l	vig	
Florence Paul	HP	1886	Paul W	mr	f	l		
Florent Pauwels	HP	1879	Soupert & Notting	dr	f	vl	vig	
Florentine	Misc	Pre 1846						
Florian	HP	Pre 1870		mp	f	m		
Floribunda	HMult	Pre 1846		lp				
Floribunda	HSpn	Pre 1846		lp				
Floribunda	Pol	1885	Dubreuil	lp	vdbl	m	m	m
Florida	HP		Laffay	lp				
Florida	Bslt	Pre 1824	syn Blush Boursault	pb	vdbl	vl		
Florida	Ch	1894	Noisette L syn Calypso	dr	f	vl		
Florinda	HSet	Pre 1846		lp	f	vl		
Florine	A		Jacques	lp	f			f
Florine	G	Pre 1834	Lerouge	mr		m		
Foetida Alli	HFt		syn Lutea	my				
Foliacée	C	Pre 1808	(Holland)	mp	dbl	vl		
Foliacée	C	1810	Descemet syn above?	dp	f	vl	vig	f
Foliacée de Fleury	A		Fleury	w				
Folie de Bonaparte	D	c 1810	(Belgium)	mr				
Folio Variegata	D	1551	Monardes	pb	dbl	m		m

syn York & Lancaster

Name	Type	Date	Raiser / Synonym					
Foncée	M			lp	f	l		
Foncier	Ch		Foncier	w				
Fontaine	M		see La Fontaine					
Fontaine Yolande	HCh			m	f	m		
Fontenelle	G	Pre 1830	Tributien	dp	f	m-l		f
Fontenelle	M	1849	Vibert	mp				
Fontenelle	HP	1877	Moreau-Robert	mr	dbl	vl	vig	vf
Forella	HSpn			m				
Forges de Vulcain	G		Miellez	dr				
Formidable	Ch	Pre 1846		mr				
Formosa	G	Pre 1811	syn Bourbon	pb	s-d	m		m
Formosa	Ch			dr	f	l		
Fornarina	G	1826	Vetillard	dr	dbl	m		
Fornarina	G	1841	Vibert	pb	f	m		
Fornarina	M	1862	Moreau-Robert	mp	f	s	vig	
Forster	HP	1864	Joubert	dr	f	l	vig	
Forstmeister's Heim	HSet	1886	Geschwind	mp	dbl	m		
Fortuneana	Bks	1840	Fortune syn Fortuniana	w	dbl	l		vf
Fortuneana Blanche à Grandes Fleurs	Bks			w				
Fortunée Besson	HP	1881	Besson	lp	vf	vl	vvig	vf
		syn	Mme Fortuné Besson					
Fortune's Double Yellow	T	1845	Fortune	yb	dbl	m	vvig	m
Fortune's Five-Coloured Rose	T	1844	Fortune	w	dbl	l		
Fortune's White	N	Pre 1860		w				
Fortune's Yellow	Bks	Pre 1870	Fortune	yb	s-d	l		
Fortuniana	Bks	1840	Fortune	w	dbl	l		vf
Fortunii	Bks	Pre 1860		w	dbl	vl	vig	
Foucheaux	G	Pre 1846		mr	f	m		
Foucher	G	1828	Vibert	lp	f	l		
Four Seasons Rose of Paestum	D	Pre 400	syn Quatre Saisons	mp	dbl			vf
Fourreau de Chataigne	HMcr			dr				
Fragolette	Ch	Pre 1846	syn Roi des Belges	lp	f	l	vig	f
Fragrans	HMult	1843		mp				
Fragrant	Ch		syn L'Odorante	mr	f	m	vig	vf
Fraiche Mignonne	HCh			dr	f	m		vf
Fraicheur de 15 Ans	D							
Frame Blanche	T			ly	f	l		
France Blanche	HT	see Mlle	Augustine Guinoisse-	au				
Frances Bloxham	HP	1892	Paul G	op	dbl	m		
Francesco Dona	HSet	1895	Geschwind	m	vdbl			vf
			syn Himmelsauge					
Francesco Ingegnoli	HMult	1888	Bernaix	rb	s-d		vig	
Frances E Willard	T	1899	Good & Reese	w		l		m
Francfort Agathé	G	Pre 1827		lp	dbl			
Francis B Hayes	B	1892	May	mr				
Francis Dubreuil	T	1894	Dubreuil	dr	dbl	m	vig	f
Francisca Krüger	T	1879	Nabonnand G	op	vdbl	l	vig	m
		syn	Mlle Francisca Krüger					
Francisca Pries	T	1888	Pries / Ketten Bros	pb	f	m	vig	m
Francisque Barillot	HP	1873	Damaizin	mr	f	l	vig	
Francisque de Foix	A			lp	vdbl	m		
Francisque Rive	HP	1884	Schwartz	mr	f	l	vvig	vf
Francofurtensis	Misc	Pre 1629	Munchhausen	m	s-d			
			syn r. x francofurtana					
François Arago	HP	1858	Trouillard	dr	dbl	m		
François Coppée	HP	1895	Lédéchaux	dr	dbl	l	vig	f
François Courtin	HP	1873	Verdier E	rb	f	l	vig	vf
François David	HP	1887	Pernet Père	mr	f	l		
François de Salignac	M	1854	Robert	mp	f	l	vig	
François Dubois	HP	1866	Damaizin	dp	f	l	vig	
François Dugommier	B	1873	Moreau-Robert	dr	f	l	vig	
François Fontaine	HP	1867	Fontaine	mr	f	m	vig	
François Fouquier	G	Pre 1885		dp	f	vl		
François Gaulain	HP	1878	Schwartz	dr	f	l	vig	
François Goeschké	HP	1865	Soupert & Notting	dr				
François Herincq	B	1853	Verdier E	ob	f	m		
François Herincq	HP	1878	Verdier E	mr	f	m	vig	m
François I	HP	1859	Trouillard	mr	f	l		
			syn François Premier					
François Jongleur	D	1825	Loisiel	lp	f	m-l	vig	
François Joseph Pfister	HP	1877	Verdier E	dr	f	l	vig	
François Lacharme	HP	1861	Verdier V	mr	f	m-l	vig	
François Levet	HP	1880	Levet A	dp	dbl	m	vig	
François Louvat	HP	1861	Touvais	pb	f	l	vig	
François Michelon	HP	1870	Levet A	dp	dbl	l	vig	
François Olin	HP	1881	Ducher	dp	f	l	vig	
François Premier	HP	1859	Trouillard	mr	f	l	m	
François Rougier	HP			rb				
François Treyve	HP	1866	Liabaud	mr	f	l	vig	
Françoise de Foix	HP		Laffay	lp	f	m		

Name	Type	Date	Breeder / syn						
Françoise de Foix	M	1855	Robert	rb					
Françoise de Foix	N		Parmentier						
Françoise de Kerjégu	T	1894	Lévêque	w					
Frangé	HCh	Pre 1846	Hardy	mr					
Frankfort	G			mr					
Frankfort Agathé	G	Pre 1827		dp	dbl				
Frankfurt	Misc	Pre 1629	Muenchhausen	m	s-d				
			syn r x francofurtana						
Franklin	D	Pre 1846	Robert	mr	vf	l			
Franz Degen Junion	N	Pre 1900		w					
Fraser's Pink Musk	N	1818	Fraser	lp	s-d		m		vf
Fratelli Ingegnoli	HMult	1889	Bernaix	pb					
Frau Dr E Skibinska	HP	1888	Geschwind						
Frau Geheimrath von Boch	T	1897	Lambert	w	f	l			vf
Frau Syndica Roeloffs	B	1898	Lambert P	pb	f		m	vig	vf
Frau Therese Glück	T	1896	Glück	rb					
Frau Viktoria von Thusansky	HT	1888	Geschwind						
Frédéric Bihorel	HP	1865	Damaizin	dr	f	l			
Frédéric d'Eu	HP	1862	Verdier E	dp					
Frédéric II de Prusse	HCh	1847	Verdier V	m	dbl	l		vig	m
Frédéric Schneider II	HP	1885	Ludovic	dp	dbl	l			
Frédéric Soullier	M	1854	Laffay M	rb	dbl	l	m		
Frédéric von Schiller	HP	1881	Mietzsch	dr	vf		m		vf
Frédéric Weber	Ch			lp	f		m		
Frédéric Woeber	T	Pre 1846							
Frédéric Wood	HP	1874	Verdier E	mr	f	l		vig	
French Crimson	M	Pre 1846		dp		l			
French Pure White	N	Pre 1846		w					
French Rose	Sp	Pre 1500	syn r.gallica	dp			m		
Frère Marie Pierre	HP	1891	Bernaix	mp	vdbl	l		vig	f
Frères Soupert & Notting	T	1871	Levet	w	f	m			
Fridolin Bunnert	T	1888	Bernaix	mr	f	m			
Friedrich von Schiller	HP	1881	Mietzsch	dr	vf	m			
Frilet	B	1854	Pradel	dr	f	m			
Fringed	M	Pre 1846		w					
Frisée	Ch			w					
Froissard	HP	1865	Liabaud	mp	f	l			
			syn Mrs Standish						
Fudide Lisky	Misc	Pre 1846							
Fujiyama Rose	Sp	1894		dp	s				
		syn	r.acicularis nipponensis						
Fulgens	G	1830	Vibert	dp	s-d		m		
Fulgens	HCh	c 1830	Guérin syn Malton	mr	f		m	vig	vf
Fulgens	Sp	Pre 1830	Madame Hébert	mr	dbl	l			
			syn r.corymbosa						
Fulgens	HSpn		Malton	m	s-d		m		
Fulgorie	HP	Pre 1840		mp	f	vl			
Full White	Pom			w	f	vl			
Fun Jwan Lo	S	Pre 1811		w	dbl		m	vvig	
Fürst Bismark	T	1886	Drögemüller	dy	vdbl	l			m
Fürstin Bismark	T	1887	Drögemüller	mr	vdbl	l			f
Fürstin Infantin von Hohenzollern	T	1898	Brauer P	m	dbl	m			
Fürstin Johanna Auersberg	HP	1884	Soupert & Notting	or	f	l		vig	
Furtado	Ch			dp	f	m			
Fusca	HSem		syn Sempervirens	mp					

NAME	TYPE	YEAR	RAISER	COLOUR	BLOOM	SIZE	GROWTH	SCENT
G W Watkins	HT	1890	Williams A	lp				
Gabina	G	Pre 1830	Calvert	m	vf	m		
Gabriel Fournier	HP	1877	Levet	dr	f	l		sf
Gabrielle	HCh	Pre 1829	Coquerel	lp	f	l	vvig	
Gabrielle	N	Pre 1846		m	f	m		
Gabrielle de Perrony	HP		Lacharme	dr	f	l	vig	
Gabrielle d'Estrées	A	1819	Vibert	lp	f	m-l		
Gabrielle Levainville	HP	1863	Pradel	lp				
Gabrielle Martel	T	1874	Levet	m	f	l		
Gabrielle Mérite	HP	1881	Vigneron	lp	f	m	vig	
Gabrielle Morfan	B	1853	Pradel	lp	f	l	vig	
Gabrielle Perronny	HP	1863	Lacharme	mr	f	l		
Gabrielle Tournier	HP	1876	Levet A	dr	f	l	vig	
Gaillarde Marbrée	G	Pre 1810	Dupont	dr	vdbl	m-l		
			syn Noire Couronnée					
Galande	HSem		see Garland					
Galatée	G	Pre 1820	Dubourg	lp	f	m		
		syn	Nouveau Triomphe					
Galathée	G	Pre 1830	Parmentier	lp	f	m		
Galathée	Ch		Robert	rb				
Galathée	HT			mp	f	l		
Galaxie	Ch	1827	Vétillard	w	f	m		
Galilée	G		Robert & Moreau	lp				
Gallait	HP		Parmentier	lp	f	l		
Gallande	HSem	c 1830	Jacques	mp	dbl			
Gallica Alba	G	Pre 1811		w	dbl			m
Gallica Alba Flore Plena	G	Pre 1811		w	vdbl			
Gallica Macrantha	G	Pre 1750		w				
Gallica Maheca	G	c 1795	syn La Belle Sultane	dr		m		
Gallica Maxima Gigantea	G	Pre 1830	Thory	lp	f	vl		
Gallica Vermilion	G	1823		lp	vf			
Gallique Panache (Gallica Versicolor)	G	Pre 1830	Prévost	w & dp	dbl	l		
Gallique Presque Blanc	G			lp				
Gallique Simple	G	Pre 1830	Godefroy	mp	s	m-l		
Gamma	T	Pre 1846		lp	f	l		
Ganganelli	G	Pre 1830	Lahaye	lp	f	m		
Gantin	B	Pre 1846		mr	vf	l		
Garden Favourite	HP	1884	Paul W	lp	f	m		
Gardenia	HT	1898	Soupert & Notting	w	f	l		m
Gardenia	HWich	1898	Horvath/Manda W A	w	vdbl	l	vvig	f
Garibaldi	HP	1859	Damaizin	dp	f	l		
Garibaldi	B	1860	Pradel	rb	f	l		
Garilland	G	Pre 1830	Vibert	lp				
Garland	HSem		Wells	lp	s	m		
			syn Spendens Garland					
Garlin	Ch							
Garnet	Misc	Pre 1846						
Garnet Striped Rose	Sp	Pre 1581	syn r.gallica versicolor	pb	s-d			m
Garnet Wolseley	HP	see	Sir Garnet Wolseley					
Garnier	Ch	Pre 1846	Laffay	mr				
Gaspard Monge	C	1854	Robert	m	dbl	m		vf
Gaspard Monge	HP	1874	Moreau-Robert	mr	f	l	vig	
Gassendi	G	1827	Hardy	dp	vdbl			
Gaston Chandon	HT	1881	Schwartz	pb	dbl	m		
Gaston de Panck	B	Pre 1846		lp				
Gaston Lévêque	HP	1878	Lévêque	mr	f	vl	vig	vf
Gay	D	Pre 1830	Hardy	mp	vdbl	l		
Gay à Fleurs Marbrées	D	Pre 1830		dp	vdbl	m		
Gaymard	G							
Gazelle	G	Pre 1843		lp	f	l	vig	
Géant des Batailles	HP	1845	Nérard / Guillot Père	mr	vf	l	m	vf
Géant des Batailles à Fleurs Roses	HP	1868	Carré	dp	f	l	vig	
Géant des Batailles Panaché	HP	1853	Cherpin	rb	f	m		
		syn	Marguerite Lecureaux					
Gelbe Malmaison	B	1887 syn	Kronprincessin V v P	w				
Gelon	B	1895	Geschwind	dp	dbl	l		
Gem of the Prairies	HSet	1865	Burgess A	dp	f	l	vig	sf
Général Allard	B	1835	Laffay M	dp	f	m	m	
Général Annenkoff	HP	1894	Lévêque	dr			vig	
Général Appert	HP	1884	Schwartz	dr	f	l	vvig	f
Général Baron Berge	HP	1892	Pernet Père	mr	vf	l	vig	vf
Général Barral	HP	1867	Damaizin	m	f	m		
Général Bedeau	HP	1851	Margottin	mr	dbl	m	vvig	
Général Bernard	HP	Pre 1845		pb	f	m	vig	
Général Bernardin	HP			mr				
Général Bertrand	G	1845	Vibert	rb	f	m		

Général Billot	T	1896	Dubreuil	dr	f	m	m	
Général Blanchard	B	Pre 1870		lp	f	m	m	
Général Browne	HSpn	1860		w	dbl	m		m
Général Brune	M	1863	Robert & Moreau	dr				
Général Bülow	G	Pre 1845		mp	f			
Général Canrobert	B	c 1860	Pradel	mr	f	l	vig	
Général Cavaignac	HP	1848	Foulard	mr	dbl	l		
Général Cavaignac	HP	1849	Margottin	mr	f	l		
Général Championnet	HP	1866	Moreau-Robert	dr	f	l	vig	
Général Changarnier	HP	1847	Laffay	dr	f	l		
Général Changarnier	HP	1847	Moulin	m	f	l	vvig	
Général Chassé	Ch			dp	f	m		
Général Chassé	T	Pre 1846		dr	f	l		
Général Chevert	HP	1876	Moreau-Robert	mr	f	vl	vig	
Général Christiani (y)	G			mr	f	l		
Général Clerc	M	1845	Laffay M	dr	f	m		
Général D Mertschansky	T	1890	Nabonnand	mp	f	l	vvig	
Général Damrémont	G		Portemer	dr	f	m-l		
Général Daumesnil	HCh			m	f			
Général de Bréa	G			dr	f	l		
Général de Bréa	HP	1870	Lebougre	dr	f	l		
Général de Bréda	HP	Pre 1870	Robert	mr	f	l		
Général de Castellane	HP	1851	Guillot Père	mr	f	vl	vvig	vf
Général de Cissey	HP	1875	Verdier E	mr	vf	l	vig	
Général de la Martinière	HP	1869	De Sansal	rb	f	vl	m	
Général de la Martinière	HP	1870	Jamain	dr	f	l	vig	
Général de Lamoricière	HCh	Pre 1866		m	f	m		
Général de Mirandol	HP	1864	Oger	dr	f	l	vig	
Général de Miribel	HP	1893	Lévêque	dp				
Général Decaen	HP	see Mm-	e la Générale Decaen					
Général Delaage	HCh	1826	Desportes	dr	vf	m-l		
Général Delaage	HP	1851	Robert	dp	f	l	vvig	
Général Désaix	G	Pre 1829	Boutigny	dp	f	m		
Général Désaix	HP	1867	Moreau-Robert	mr	f	l	vig	
Général Desjardin	M	1852	Robert	dp	f	m	vvig	
Général d'Hautpoul	HP	1864	Verdier E	mr	vdbl	m	vig	
Général Donadieu	G	Pre 1835		mr	vdbl	l		
Général Drouot	M	1847	Vibert	m	dbl	m	vig	
Général Dubourg	HP	Pre 1846		lp	f	l		
Général Duc d'Aumale	HP	1875	Verdier E	dr	dbl	l	vig	
Général Dumouriez	HP	1873	Moreau-Robert	mr	f	l	vig	
Général Evian	G		Parmentier	dr	f	m		
Général Forey	HP	1859	Robert & Moreau	dr	f	l	vvig	
Général Foy	D	1825	Boutigny	mp	f	s		
Général Foy	G	1827	Pelletier	mr	f	vl		
Général Foy	G	1844	Vibert	pb				
Général Galliéni	T	1899	Nabonnand G	rb	f	l	vig	m
Général Gilbert	HP							
Général Gordon	T	1885	Bennett	w	dbl	m		
Général Grant	HP	1869	Verdier E	mr	f	l		
Général Hoche	B			dp	vf	m		
Général Hudelet	HP	1852	Crousse syn Comte de Paris	pb	f	l	vig	
Général Jacqueminot	HCh	1846	Laffay	dr	vdbl	l	vvig	
Général Jacqueminot	HP	1853	Roussel syn above?	mr	dbl	vl	vig	vf
Général Junot	G			dr	f	l		
Général Kléber	HCh	Pre 1846		mp				
Général Kléber	M	1856	Robert	mp	f	l	vig	m
Général Kléber	HP	1872	Boyau	mr	f	l		
Général Korolkow	HP	1891	Lévêque	mr				
Général Kutusoff	Misc	Pre 1846		dr				
Général Lafayette	G			mr	f	l	vig	
Général Lamarque	N	1830	Maréchal syn Lamarque	w	dbl	m	vig	vf
Général Lawoestine	Ch	Pre 1846		dr	f	m		
Général Lery	G			lp	f	m		
Général MacMahon	HP	1857	Robert & Moreau	mp	f	l		
Général Merlin	HP	Pre 1846		p	f			
Général Miloradowitch	HP	1869	Louvat	mr	f	vl		
Général Morangiez	HP	1849	Portemer	lp	f	m	vig	
Général Moreau	G	Pre 1885	Moreau	m	f	m		
Général Négrier	HP	1851	Portemer	mp	f	l	vig	vf
Général Oudinot	B			dr	f	l	vig	
Général Oudry	Misc		Gauthier					
Général Pélissier	HP	1855	Ducher	mp	f	vl	vvig	vf
Général Pierce	HP	1853	Rémond	m	f	l		
General Robert E Lee	T	1896	Good & Reese	my				
Général Schablikine	T	1878	Nabonnand G	op	f	l	vig	f
Général Simpson	HP	1854	Lacharme	mp	f	m		
Général Simpson	HP	1856	Ducher	mr	vf	m	vvig	
Général Soyez	Ch	Pre 1846		dp	f	l	vig	
Général Tartas	T	1860	Bernède	dp	dbl	l		

Name	Class	Date	Breeder					
Général Taylor	B			mp	f	l		
Général Terwange	HP	1874	Gautreau	mr	f	l		
Général Thiard	HCh	Pre 1830	Laffay	dr	f	s		
Général Valazé	T	Pre 1835	Dubourg	w	f	l		
Général Vallé	T			lp	f	l		
Général von Moltke	HP	1873	Bell	rb	f	l	m	
Général Washington	T	1855	Page	mr				
Général Washington	HP	1860	Granger	dr	vdbl	l	m	m
Général Wolf	HP	1856	Pradel	mp	dbl	l		
Général Zachargewski	HP	1860	Ducher	pb				
Génie de Châteaubriand	HP	1852	Oudin	dr	f	l		
Gentil	G	1823	Gentil	mp	vf	m		
		syn	Les Trois Mages					
Gentil Bernard	D	1825	Bizard					
Gentilhomme	D	Pre 1846						
Gentiliana	HMult	1886	Bernaix	w	s-d	m		
		syn	Polyantha Grandiflora					
Geoffrin	Ch	1827	Péan	mp				
Geoffroy de Saint-Hilaire	HP	1878	Verdier E	dr	f	m-l	vig	vf
George Baker	HP	1881	Paul & Son	dp	vdbl		vig	
George IV	HCh	1830	Rivers	dr	dbl		vig	
		syn	Rivers' George IV					
George Peabody	Ch	1857	Pentland	m	f	l	m	
Georges Canning	M	1858	Laffay	lp	vf	m	vvig	
Georges Chevalier	HP	1877	Lemée	mr	f	l	vig	
Georges Cuvier	B	1842	Souchet	dp	f	l	vig	
Georges d'Amboise	HP	1853	Boyau	mr	f	l	vig	
Georges de France	T	Pre 1860		yb	f	m	vig	
Georges Dupont	B	1856	Lartay	mp				
Georges Farber	T	1889	Bernaix	dr			m	m
Georges IV	HCh	Pre 1834		m		m		
Georges IV	HSpn			lp				
Georges Lecamus	HP			dp	f	l	vig	
Georges Moreau	HP	1880	Moreau-Robert	mr	f	vl	vvig	f
Georges Patinot	HP	1879	Gautreau	mr	f	l	m	
Georges Paul	HP	1863	Verdier E	mp	f	l		
Georges Pernet	Pol	1887	Pernet-Ducher	mp		l	m	
Georges Prince	HP	1863	Verdier E	mr	f	m		
Georges Rouillard	HP	1853	Duval	mr	f	l		
Georges Rousset	HP	1893	Rousset	mr	f	vl		
Georges Sand	T			p	s-d	l	vig	
Georges Schwartz	HMult	1889	Schwartz Vve	mp		l	vig	
Georges Schwartz	T	1899	Schwartz Vve	my				
Georges Simon	HP	1863	Oger	dr	f	l		
Georges Vibert	G	1853	Robert	rb	dbl	m	m	m
Georgette	HP	1849	Vibert	lp	f		vig	
Georgette Mary	G		Parmentier	dp	f	m		
Géorgina	N	1827	Vibert	mp		s		
Georgina	D		Laffay					
Georgina Mars	G	Pre 1830	Lecomte	mr	f	s		
Georgine	HCh	Pre 1846		dr	f	m		
Geraldine	T	Pre 1846		lp				
Geranium	HT	1895	Geschwind	rb	dbl	l		
Gerardon	G			dp				
Gerbe de Roses	HP	1847	Laffay / Vibert	lp	dbl	m	vvig	
Germaine Caillot	HT	1887	Pernet					
Germaine de Marest	T	1891	Guillot Fils	w	f	l		
Germaine Molinier	T	1896	Schwartz Vve	mp				
Germaine Trochon	T	1897		yb				
Germania	HP	1889	Welter	dr	vdbl	l		
		syn	Gloire de Ducher					
Germanica	HRg	1890	Müller	mp	s			
Gertrude Bernard	G	1827	Noisette	mr				
Gervais Rouillard	HP/B	1853	Duval	dp	f	m	m	
Geschwind's Gilda	HMult	1887	Geschwind	dr	vf			m
Geschwind's Nordlandrose	HSet	1884	Geschwind	lp	vf	m		
Geschwind's Orden	HMult	1886	Geschwind	m	vdbl	m	vig	
Geuconditus	Misc	Pre 1846		lp				
Gewohnliche Moss Rose	M	Pre 1720	syn Communis	mp	dbl	l		
Giant of Battles	HP	1846	Nérard	mr	vf	m	m	vf
		syn	Géant des Batailles					
Giffard	HMult	1891	Lévêque					
Gigantea	Ch	Pre 1846						
Gigantea Blanc	LCl	1889	Collett	w		vl		
Gigantesque	G		Miellez	dp	f	m		
Gigantesque	T	1835	Hardy / Sylvain-Péan	lp	f	l		
Gigantèsque	T	1845	Odier	dp	f	l	vig	
Gil Blas	G	Pre 1843		pb	dbl	l		
Gil Blas	HSpn	Pre 1848		w				
Gilbert	HP	1882	Moreau-Robert	rb	f	l	m	
Gilbert Nabonnand	T	1888	Nabonnand	op	dbl	l	vig	m
Gilda	HMult	1887	Geschwind	m	f	m		

Gildippa	G		Miellez	mr	f	m		
Gipsy	HP	1885	Laxton	dr		s	vig	
Girardin	HP			dp	f	m	vig	
Girardon	D		Girardon	dp	f	l		
Girondet	G			dp	f	m		
Giselle	G	1843	Vibert	mp	f	m		
Giuletta	HP	1859	Laurentius	lp	dbl	m		
			syn Loevis					
Glabra	A			m				
Glandulose	C	Pre 1846		lp				
Glauca	M			mp				
Glauque	HCan			dr				
Glauque à Feuilles de Primprenelle	HSpn	Pre 1820	Redouté H	w	s	m		
			syn De Marienbourg					
Glauque à Feuilles Rouges	Rbf	Pre 1830		mr	s	s		
Glauque à Fleur Multiple	Rbf	Pre 1830	Laffay	mr	dbl	s		
Glauque Semi-Double	HCan			dr				
Glittering	Misc	Pre 1846		mr				
Globe Blanc	C	Pre 1826	Lee / Calvert	w	dbl	l		
			syn Globe White Hip					
Globe Céleste	C			lp	vdbl	vl		
Globe White Hip	C	Pre 1826	Lee / Calvert	w	dbl	l		vf
Globe Yellow	HFt	Pre 1846		my	f	l		
Globosa	HP	Pre 1870	Paul W	dp			m	
Globuleuse	M	1825	Vibert	mp	f	m		
Globuleuse	N	Pre 1830	Vibert	lp	dbl	m		
Globuleux	Ch	Pre 1834		lp	s-d	s		
Gloire d'Alger	B	Pre 1846		dp		m		
Gloire d'Angers	HP	1846	Boyau	m	s-d	f	m	
Gloire d'Auteuil	Ch			mr	f	m		
Gloire de Bordeaux	B	1861	Lartay	pb	dbl	l	vig	
		syn	Belle de Bordeaux					
Gloire de Bordeaux	T	Pre 1870		dr	f	l		
Gloire de Bourg la Reine	HP	1879	Margottin Pére	mr	f	l	vvig	f
Gloire de Bruxelles	HP	1889	Soupert & Notting	m	f	l	vig	f
Gloire de Charpennes	Pol	1898	Lille	mr	dbl	s		
Gloire de Chatillon	HP	1862	Fontaine	dr	f	vl	vvig	
			syn Madame Masson					
Gloire de Colmar	HCh	Pre 1848		dr	f	l		
Gloire de Couline	HCh	Pre 1846		dp				
Gloire de Deventer	T	1897	Soupert & Notting	ly	dbl	l		
Gloire de Dijon	Cl T	1850	Jacotot	op	dbl	vl	vvig	m
Gloire de Dijon à Fleur Rouge	Cl T	1878	Levet F	mr	dbl	l	vig	m
		syn	Reine Marie Henriette					
Gloire de Ducher	HP	1865	Ducher	dr	dbl	vl	vvig	f
Gloire de France	G	1828	Bizard	lp	vdbl	vl	vvig	vf
Gloire de France	HP	1853	Margottin	mr	f	l	wk	
Gloire de Guérin	HCh	1833	Guérin	dp	f	m		
Gloire de Hardy	T		Hardy	dp	f	l		vf
Gloire de la Guillotière	B	Pre 1846		lp		l		
		See Tri-	omphe de la Guillotiè-	re				
Gloire de l'Exposition de Bruxelles	HP	1889	Soupert & Notting	m	f	l	vig	f
		syn	Gloire de Bruxelles					
Gloire de Libourne	T	1887	Beauvillain	dy	vf	l	vvig	
Gloire de Lyon	HP	1857	Ducher	dr	f	m	vig	
Gloire de Margottin	HP	1887	Margottin	mr	f	l	vig	vf
Gloire de Montplaisir	HP	1866	Gonod	mr	f	l		
Gloire de Moulins	B			dp	f	m	vig	
Gloire de Paris	B	1842	Souchet	mr	vf	vl		
Gloire de Paris	HP	1858	Lacharme F	dp	dbl	l	vig	vf
			syn Anna de Diesbach					
Gloire de Parthenay	HP	1853	Jamain & Durand	lp	f	vl	vvig	
Gloire de Peley	Ch			m	f	s		
Gloire de Puy d'Auzon	T	1894	Nabonnand	mr				f
Gloire de Santenay	HP	1859	Ducher	m	f	l	vvig	f
Gloire de Thalwitz	HP	1866	Peters	mr	f	m-l		
			syn Rhum von Thalwitz					
Gloire de Thalwitz	HP	1867	Laurentius	dp				
Gloire de Toulouse	HP	1883	Brassac	mr	vf	vl		
Gloire de Vitry	HP	1854	Masson	mp	f	l	vig	
Gloire des Agathes	G	Pre 1830	Vibert	lp				
Gloire des Amateurs	HP			dp	f	l	vig	
Gloire des Brotteaux	B	1840	Renard	m	f	l		
		syn	Edouard Desfossés					
Gloire des Charpennes	Pol	1898	Lille L	dr	dbl	s	m	
Gloire des Cuivrées	T	1889	Tesnier	rb				
Gloire des Fleurs	D		syn Gloria Florum	mr	f	m		
Gloire des Héllènes	HCh	1825	Laffay	m	f	m	vvig	
			syn La Nubienne					
Gloire des Jardins	G	1815	Descemet	m	dbl	m		
Gloire des Lawrence(ana)s	Min	1837		mr		s		

Name	Type	Year	Breeder / Origin					
Gloire des Mousseu(x)ses	M	1852	Laffay	mp	dbl	l	vig	
Gloire des Perpétuelles	D	1845	Vibert syn Flon	mr				
Gloire des Polyantha	Pol	1887	Guillot et Fils	mp	dbl	s	vig	f
Gloire des Pourpres	G	Pre 1830	Vibert syn Volidatum	mr	vf	m		
Gloire des Rosomanes	B/Ch	1825	Vibert	mr	dbl	vl	vig	m
Gloire des Sans Épines	HP	1856	Guillot Père	mr		l		
Gloire d'Esquermes	T			dr	f	m		
Gloire d'Étampes	B	Pre 1870		mr	f	m		
Gloire d'Icarie	B			dr				
Gloire d'Isly	T			lp	vf	m	vig	
Gloire d'Olivet	B	1886	Vigneron	lp	f	l		
Gloire d'Orient	M	1856	Béluze	dr	f	m		
Gloire d'Orléans	HP	1879	Boitard	mp	f	l	vvig	vf
Gloire du Bouchet	HP	1885	De la Rocheterie	mr	f	vl		
Gloire du Sacré-Coeur	HP	1864	Pernet Père	lp	f	l	vig	
Gloire d'un Enfant d'Hiram	HP	1899	Vilin	mr	f		vig	f
Gloire d'un Parterre	HCh			mr				
Gloire Lyonnaise	HP	1884	Guillot et Fils	w	vf	vl	vvig	f
Gloria Florum	D		Prévost	mr	dbl	l		
Gloria Mundi	G	Pre 1820	Prévost	lp	f	m		
		syn	Nouveau Triomphe					
Gloria Mundi	G	Pre 1830	Calvert	m	vf	s		
	syn	La Plus	Belle des Violettes					
Gloria Nigrorum	G	Pre 1830	Calvert	m				
Gloria Rubrorum	G							
Glorietta	B	Pre 1860	Vibert	dr	f	m	m	
Gloriette	N	1836	Vibert	lp	f	s	m	
Gloriette	C	1854	Robert	lp	f	l	vig	
Gloriette	G	Pre 1885		op	f	l		
Glorieuse	G	Pre 1830	Calvert	dr	vf	s		
Glorieuse	G		Godefroy	lp	f	m		
Glorieux	B	Pre 1846		lp				
Gloriosa	HP	1874	Touvais	lp	f	m	vig	
Gloriosa Superba Noir	Misc	Pre 1846		dr	f			
Glory of Cheshunt	HP	1880	Paul & Son	dr			vig	
Glory of Edzell	HSpn	Pre 1900		pb	s	s	s	
Glory of Paris	HP	1858	Lacharme F	m	dbl	l	vig	vf
			syn Anna de Diesbach					
Glory of the Reds	Misc	Pre 1846		mr				
Glory of Waltham	HP	1865	Paul W	dr	vdbl	vl	vig	f
Glossy Rose	Sp	Pre 1724	syn r.virginiana	mp	s			
Glycère	C	Pre 1830	Vibert	mp	f	m		
Godecharles	G		Parmentier	dp	f	m		
Golconda	T	Pre 1846		lp				
Gold of Ophir	T	1845	Fortune	yb	dbl	m	vvig	m
		syn	Fortune's Double Yell ow					
Golden Chain	N	1869	Ducher Vve	my	dbl	m-l	vig	m
			syn Rêve d'Or					
Golden Fairy	Pol	1887	Bennett	ly		vs		
Golden Gate	T	1891	Dingee & Conrad	w	dbl	vl	vig	m
Golden Rambler	N	1894	Gray A H	ly	dbl		vig	m
			syn Alister Stella Gray					
Golden Rose of China	Sp	Pre 1899	syn r.hugonis	my	s	m		
Goldquelle	T	1899	Lambert P	ob				
Golfe-Juan	HP	1872	Nabonnand	mr	f	vl	m	
Goliath	C	1829	Girardon	lp	vf	l		
Goliath	HP	1861	Trouillard	lp	f	l	vig	
Gondouin	D		Goudoin	lp				
Gonsoli Gaetano	HP	1874	Pernet Père	mp	vdbl	vl	vig	f
Gonzalve	G	1835	Vibert	mr	f	m		
Gooseberry Rose	Sp	1897	syn r.stellata	m				
Gorge de Pigeon	HCh		Hardy	dr				
Gossart	D	1826	Gossart	dr	vdbl	m	vig	
Gottfried Keller	HFt	1894	Müller F	ab	s-d	m		m
Goubault	T	1843	Goubault	dp	dbl	l	vig	m
			syn Bon Silène					
Gouda (Gonda)	T			w	f	m	vig	
Gourdault	B	1859	Guillot Père	m	f	m-l		
		see	Monsieur Gourdault					
Gourgaud	D	1825	Laffay					
Goût du Jour	G		Miellez	mp				
Gouvion de Saint-Cyr	Ch	Pre 1834		mp	f	m	wk	
Governativa	T			pb	vdbl	l		
Grace Darling	HT	1884	Bennett	w	dbl	l	vig	f
Gracieuse	B			lp	f	l		
Gracieuse	HSpn	Pre 1830	Pelletier	lp	vdbl	s	vig	
Gracieuse	N		Noisette	lp	dbl		vig	
Gracieuse	A			lp	f	s		
Gracieuse	M	Pre 1829	Prévost syn Gracilis	dp	dbl	l	vig	
Gracieuse	HP	1849	Thomas	lp	f	m		
Gracieuse	T	1888	Perny	mp				
Gracieuse	D			lp				

Name	Type	Date	Raiser / Synonym					
Gracieuse	G		Miellez	mp				
Gracieuse Catherine	D	1825	Guérin					
Gracieuse Lofficial	D	1825	Guérin					
Gracieuse Pompon	D		Guérin					
Gracieux	HSpn	1827	Pelletier	lp				
Gracilis	Alp	1796	Shailer	fp	dbl	m		
Gracilis	A	1820	Calvert	lp	f	s		
Gracilis	M	Pre 1829	Prévost	dp	dbl	l	vig	
Gracilis	Bslt	1830	Wood	mp	s-d	m	vig	
Gracilis	G	Pre 1834	Vibert	w	f			
Gracilis	HCh	Pre 1834	Hardy	mp	dbl	s		
Gracilis	HSet	1841	Prince Nursery	mp	vdbl			
Graf Fritz Metternich	HP	1896	Soupert & Notting	dr	f	l		vf
Grain d'Or	G	Pre 1830	Prévost	dr	vf	s-m		
Grand Alexander	Misc	Pre 1846		dr				
Grand Alexandre	G	Pre 1820	Godefroy syn Évêque	m	dbl	l		
Grand Apollon	G	1824		m	dbl	vl		
Grand Bercam	C	Pre 1826	Prévost	mp	s-d	m-l		
Grand Capitaine	B	Pre 1846		dr	f	l	vig	
Grand Cels	C	Pre 1759	syn Childling	mp		l		
Grand Clovis	G	Pre 1820	Noisette L / Vibert syn Aldegonde	lp	f	m		
Grand Condé	G	1817	Godefroy syn Rouge Formidable etc	m	vdbl	m		
Grand Conquérant	HP	1851	Lartay	m	vf	l		
Grand Corneille	G	Pre 1829	Trébutien syn Cramoisi des Alpes	mr	f	l		
Grand Cramoisi de Trianon	C	Pre 1818	Trianon syn À Grand Cramoisi	m	s-d			
Grand Cramoisi de Vibert	G	1818	Vibert	mr	f	m		
Grand Czar	Misc	Pre 1846		dr				
Grand-Dauphin	G	Pre 1820	Prévost syn Roi de Rome & Enfant de France	lp	f	s-m		
Grand-Duc	Misc	1846		mp				
Grand-Duc Adolphe de Luxembourg	HT	1892	Soupert & Notting	rb	dbl	l	m	
Grand-Duc Alexis	HP	1892	Lévêque	mr	dbl	l		
Grand-Duc Héritier de Luxembourg	T	1879	Nabonnand G syn Mlle Franziska Krüger	op	vdbl	l		m
Grand-Duc Michel Alexandrowitsch	HP	1893	Lévêque	mr				
Grand-Duc Nicolas	HP	1877	Lévêque	mr	f	l	vig	
Grand-Duc Pierre de Russie	T	1885	Perny	pb		vl		
Grand Edouard	HP	1874	Verdier E syn La Souveraine	mp	f	vl		m
Grand Fulton	Misc							
Grand Hérit.Guillaime de Luxembourg	T	1892	Soupert & Notting	mp				
Grand Hercule	Ch			dr	f	l		
Grand Hubert	HCh			dp	f	l		
Grand Incas	G			m	f	m		
Grand Laeken	G			dp	vf	m		
Grand Lilas	G			lp	vdbl	l		
Grand Loewendal	G			rb	f	m		
Grand Mahomet	G	Pre 1830						
Grand Maman	C		Miellez	lp	f	l		
Grand Mexique	HCh			mp	f	l	vig	
Grand Mogol	G	Pre 1830	Prévost	dr	vf	m		
Grand Mogul	HP	1887	Paul W syn Jean Soupert	mr	f	l		
Grand Monarche	G	Pre 1818		lp	f	l		
Grand Monarque Nouveau	G	Pre 1830		mp	f	m		
Grand Montreuse	Misc	Pre 1846		mr				
Grand Napoléon	G	1809	Sevale & Haghen	m	vdbl	l		
Grand Palais	G	1824		mp		l		
Grand Palais de Fontainebleau	G			dp	f	vl		
Grand Palais de Laeken	G	1824		lp	f	m		
Grand Pandour	Misc	Pre 1846		dr		vl		
Grand Papa	G	Pre 1830	Prévost	dr	f	m-l		
Grand Papa Carré	HP			dp	f	m		
Grand Pompadour	G	Pre 1846	syn La Magnifique	dr	dbl	l		
Grand Pompée	G		Miellez	lp				
Grand Purple	Misc	Pre 1846		dr		l		
Grand Salomon	Ch		syn La Superbe	dr				
Grand Salomon	G		Miellez	mp				
Grand Souvarow	G			dr				
Grand Saint Francis	G	Pre 1790	syn Lustre d'Église	mp	dbl	s		vf
Grand Sultan	G	Pre 1815	Descemet syn Le Grand Sultan	m	vdbl	l		
Grand Sultan	G	Pre 1820	Descemet syn Céleste	lp	f	vl		

Name	Class	Date	Raiser / Syn	Colour	Form	Size	Vigour	Fragrance
Grand Tartare	D			lp				
Grand Triomphe	G	Pre 1820	Godefroy	lp	dbl	vl		
Grand Triumphant	Misc	Pre 1846						
Grand Turban	G	Pre 1820	Calvert syn Grand Sultan	lp	f	vl		
Grand Turkey	Misc	Pre 1846						
Grande Agathe	G	Pre 1810	Dupont syn Henriette	mr	f	l		
Grande Agathe Nouvelle	G	1816	Descemet syn Héloïse	lp	f	m-l		
Grande Ardoisée	G		Hardy	m				
Grande Beauté	G	Pre 1834						
Grande Bichonne	G	c 1815	Descemet	mr	f	m-l		
Grande Brique	G	Pre 1811		dp	dbl	vl		
Grande Brune	G	Pre 1811	syn Nouveau Monde	m	vdbl			
Grande Cels	C			lp				
Grande Centfeuille de Hollande	C	1840	Prévost	lp	vdbl	l		
Grande Centfeuilles de Hollande	C	Pre 1806	syn Rose des Peintres	mp	f	vl		
Grande Couronnée	C			lp				
Grande Cramoisie	G	1832	Vibert	dr		vl		
Grande Cuisse de Nymphe	A	Pre 1754	syn Great Maiden's Blush	w	dbl			vf
Grande Duchesse A de Luxembourg	T	1892	Soupert & Notting	ly				
Grande Duchesse A M de Luxembg.	T	1895	Soupert & Notting	pb				
Grande Duchesse Anastasie	T	1899	Nabonnand P C	dp	dbl	l	vvig	f
Grande Duchesse Mathilde	T	see Gro-	ssherzogin Mathilde					
Grande Duchesse Olga	T	1896	Lévêque syn Kai-serin Augusta Victoria	w				
Grande Engheinoise	G		Parmentier	dp	f	m		
Grande et Belle	G	Pre 1811	(Holland)	dp				
Grande Henriette	G	Pre 1824	François syn L'Enchantresse	mp	f	l		
Grande Héritière Hilda de Bade	T	1892	Soupert & Notting					
Grande Junon	G							
Grande Maculée	G	Pre 1829	Coquerel	m	dbl	l		
Grande Merveilleuse	C	Pre 1830	Vibert	lp	f	m-l		
Grande Obscurité	G	1818	Godefroy syn Passe Velours	mr	dbl	m		
Grande Pimprinelle	HSpn	1818	Vibert	w				
Grande Pivoine	G	syn Gr	Pivoine de Hollande	mp	dbl	l		
Grande Pivoine de Hollande	G	Pre 1830		mp	dbl	l		
Grande Pivoine de Lille	C	1820	Godefroy syn Le Triomphe	dr	f	l		
Grande Renommée	C		syn Belle de Cels	lp				
Grande Renoncule Violette	C	Pre 1885		mp	dbl	m		
Grande Souveraine	G	1825	Vibert	lp	f	l		
Grande Sultane	G	Pre 1820	syn Grand Sultan	lp	f	vl		
Grande Sultane	C	Pre 1818	Prévost syn Cumberland	lp	dbl	l		
Grande Tartare	D	Pre 1830	syn Agathe Manchette	mp	vf	m		
Grande Tige	C	1827	Noisette	mp				
Grande Victoria	C			dr	f	l		
Grande Violette Claire	G	c 1811		m	s-d	vl		
Grandes Divinités	G	1827	Vibert syn Pourpre sans Épines	m	f	m		
Grandes Feuilles	C		Lelieur	dp				
Grandesse Royale	G	Pre 1790	syn Lustre d'Église	mp	dbl	s		vf
Grandesse Royale	S	Pre 1799	syn Grosse Mohnkopfs Rose	dp	dbl			
Grandesse Royale	G	1817	Godefroy syn Great Royal	lp	f	vl		
Grandeur	HCh		Laffay	dr				
Grandeur of Cheshunt	HP	1883	Paul G	mr	f	vl	vig	
Grandeur Royale	G	1817	Godefroy syn Great Royal	lp	f	vl		
Grandeur Triomphante	C	Pre 1830	Prévost syn Cocarde Rouge	mp	dbl	vl		
Grandidentata	C	Pre 1811	Trianon syn À Feuilles de Chêne	mp	vf	m	wk	
Grandidier	T	Pre 1846		mp	f	l		
Grandidier	G	1826	Dubourg	m				
Grandiflora	Can		Lemeusnil	mp				
Grandiflora	M	Pre 1846		dp	f	vl		
Grandiflora	Bcr	Pre 1846		w				
Grandiflora	HMcr	Pre 1846	Rivers	lp		vl		
Grandiflora	N	Pre 1846		dp	f	m	vig	
Grandiflora	HP	Pre 1870		dr	f	vl		
Grandiflora	Pol	1887	Bernaix	w				
Grandiflora	T	Pre 1846		lp	s-d	l	m	

Name	Type	Date	Raiser/Syn					
Grandiflora I	Pom			mp				
Grandiflora II	Sp	c 1820		w	s			
		syn	r.spinosissima altaica					
Grandiflore	P		Hardy	mr				
Grandissima	G	Pre 1835	syn Louis-Phillipe	m	dbl	vl	m	
Granval	Ch	Pre 1834		dr	vf	m		
		syn	Eremit de Grandval					
Graulhié	HMult	Pre 1846	Van Houtte	w	dbl	s		
Graziella	HP	Pre 1870	Moreau-Robert	lp	f	m		
Graziella	HMult	1889	Geschwind	lp				
Graziella	T	1893	Dubreuil	lp	dbl	l		
Great Blush Mogul	Misc	Pre 1846		lp				
Great Crimson	Misc	Pre 1846		dp		l		
Great Double White	A	Pre 1867	syn Alba Maxima	w	dbl			m
Great Maiden's Blush	A	Pre 1738		w	dbl	l	vig	vf
Great Purple	Misc	Pre 1846						
Great Red Mogul	Misc	Pre 1846		mr		l		
Great Royal	G	Pre 1813		lp				
		possibly	syn Aimable Rouge					
Great Western	B	1840	Laffay M	m	dbl	l	vig	
Greatness	Misc	Pre 1846						
Green Rose	Ch	Pre 1845	Bambridge&Harrison	w	dbl	m	m	
Greenmantle	HEg	1895	Penzance	rb	s		vvig	fol
								vf
Greenock	HSpn	Pre 1846						
Grégoire Bordillon	HP	1863	Stand	dr	f	l		
Grégoire IV	HCh			lp	f	m		
Grelot	B			rb				
Grenadier	B	1843	Verdier V	dr	f	m		
Grenadine	G	1835	Joly	dr	s-d	l		
Gretry	Ch		syn La Superbe	m				
Grevery	E			lp				
Grevillei	HMult	Pre 1828		w	s			
Grevillei Alba	HMult	Pre 1846	Rivers	w				
Grevillei Grandiflora	HMult	Pre 1846		dp		vl		
Grevillei Minor	HMult	Pre 1846		lp				
Grevillia Rose	HMult	1815	syn Seven Sisters	pb			vig	m
Gribaldo Nicola	T	1891	Soupert & Notting	w	dbl	vl		m
Grilloni	HCh	Pre 1846		pb	f	l		
Grimpant Double Rose	HSem		Descemet					
Gris Cendré	HP			lp		m	vig	
Gris Cendré Petite	G			mp				
Grisdeline	Misc	Pre 1846						
Griseldis	LCl	1895	Geschwind R	mp	s-d	m		
Grison	T			dp	vf	vl		
Grison	Ch		Laffay	mp	dbl	l		
Groot Voorst	G	Pre 1846		dr		l		
Groslier	HMult		See Graulhier					
Gros Chalons	G	Pre 1799	syn Pourpre de Tyr	dr	f	m		
Gros Charles	Ch	Pre 1834		mp		m		
Gros Choux d'Hollande	C	Pre 1820	Prévost	lp	f	m	vig	vf
Gros Fruit	G			dr				
Gros Major	G	Pre 1830	Prévost	mr	vf	m-l		
Gros Pompon	C	Pre 1791	syn Petite de Hollande	mp	dbl	s		
Gros Pompon de Bourgogne	C		syn De Bordeaux	mp	dbl	s		m
Gros Provins Panaché	G	1866	Fontaine	m	f	l	vig	f
Grosse Centfeuilles de Hollande	C	Pre 1820	Prévost	lp	f	m	vig	vf
		syn Gro	s Choux d'Hollande					
Grosse Cerise	G	Pre 1810	Dupont	mr				
Grosse Hollande	Pom		Vibert	lp	f	m		
Grosse Mohnkopfs Rose	S	Pre 1799		dp	dbl			
Grosse sans Épines	G			m				
Grossherzog Carl Alexander	HP	1895	Schmidt	mr				
Grossherzog Ernst Ludwig von Hesse	Cl HT	1888	Müller	mp	vdbl	vl		vf
Grossherzogin Mathilde von Hessen	T	1861	Vogler	w	dbl	l	vig	
Grossherzogin Sophie-Louise	HP	1895	Schmidt	mp				
Grossherzogin Viktoria Melita von H	HT	1897	Lambert	w	f	vl		
Grotius	G			mr	f	m		
Gruss an Leipsik	HCh							
Gruss an Teplitz	HCh	1894	Geschwind R	mr	f	m	vig	vf
Gruss an Wein	HP	1889	Geschwind	m	dbl	l		f
Gudrum	HT	1897	Jacobs	mp				
Guenille	C	1789	Poilpré syn Oeillet	lp	dbl	s	vig	m
Guérin	HCh	Pre 1830	Vibert	m	vf	s		
Guérin de Donai (same as above?)	G	Pre 1846	Vibert	dp	f	l	vig	
Guerin's Gift	G	Pre 1860		mp				
Guilbert Slater	HP	1847	Vibert	dr	f	m		

Guillaume d'Orange	M	1856	Robert	lp	f	l	
Guillaume Gillemot	HP	1880	Schwartz	dp	f	vl	m
Guillaume Graziella	HP						
Guillaume Koelle	HP	1875	Verdier E	dr	f	l	vig
Guillaume le Conquérant	B	Pre 1870		lp	f	vl	
Guillaume Tell	G	Pre 1835		lp	f	l	
Guillaume Tell	HP	1852	Robert	m	f	l	vvig
Guillot	T	syn	Surabondant Boyron	mp			
Guindal	G			dp	f	m	
Gulistan	HP			lp	f	m	vig
Gustave Bonnet	N	1864	Lacharme	w	f	m-l	
Gustave Coraux	HP	1856	Robert	m	f	m	
Gustave Nadaud	T	1889	Soupert & Notting	dr			
Gustave Persin	HP	1865	Fontaine	dr	f	l	vvig
Gustave Piganeau	HP	1889	Pernet-Ducher	mr	dbl	vl	m
Gustave Régis	HT	1890	Pernet-Ducher	ly	s-d	l	vvig
Gustave Révilliod	HP	1876	Schwartz	mp	f	l	vig
Gustave Rousseau	HP	1862	Fargeton	m	f	l	
Gustave Thierry	HP	1881	Oger	dp	f		vig
Guyton de Morvau	M	1858	Robert & Moreau	dp			
Gypsy	HP	1885	Laxton				
Gypsy	HMult	1898	Lille	pb			

NAME	TYPE	YEAR	RAISER	COLOUR	BLOOM	SIZE	GROWTH	SCENT
H Plantagenet Comte d'Anjou	T	1892	Tesnier	mp				
Habit Épiscopal	G	Pre 1830						
Haileybury	HP	1896	Paul G	mr	vf	l		m
Hamilton	Ch	Pre 1846		lp				
Hamon	T	Pre 1834		lp	f	m	vig	vf
Hans Mackart	HP	1884	Verdier E	rb	dbl	m	vig	f
Hardii	Sp	1832	syn Hulthemia Hardii	yb	s			
Hardy	Ch	Pre 1834		w		m		
Hardy	N	Pre 1846		lp	s	m	wk	
Hardy	M	Pre 1846		mp	vl			
Hardy	T	Pre 1846		lp	f	m		f
Hardy	Pom			w	f	s		
Hardy	HSpn	Pre 1846	Girardon	w				
Hardy Cherokee	Sp	c 1820		w	s			
		syn	r.spinosissima altaica					
Hargita	HRg	1894	Kaufmann	mr				
Harisonii No 1	HFt	Pre 1846		ly	dbl	m	m	
Harisonii No 2	HFt	Pre 1848		yb	dbl	m	m	
Harison's Yellow	HFt	c 1824	Harison	dy	s-d	s		m
Harpagon	G			m	f	m	vig	
Harrison Weir	HP	1880	Turner	dr	f	l	vvig	f
Harrison's White	HSpn	Pre 1846		w				
Harry Laing	T	1895	Soupert & Notting	mp				
Hatchik Effendi	T	1897	Ketten Frères	yb	f	vl	vig	f
Hauptmann A Steinsdorfer	HT	1890	Geschwind					
Haute Jamain, Climbing	HP	1887	Paul G	dp				
Hay's Early Blush	Misc	Pre 1846		dp				
Hébé	HP	1883	Moreau-Robert	lp	f	vl	vvig	
Hébé	C	Pre 1830	Vibert	mr	dbl	m		
Hébé	G		Vibert	lp	f	l		
Hébé	D		Miellez	mp				
Hebe's Lip	HEg	Pre 1846	Lee	w	s-d		vig	m
Hector	G	Pre 1819	Racine / Parmentier	m	dbl	s		
Hedgehog Rose	Sp	Pre 1846	syn r.rugosa	m				
Heinrich Keller	S	1894	Müller	ly	s-d			
Heinrich Laurentius	HP	1863	Verdier	rb	f	l		
Heinrich Schultheis	HP	1882	Bennett	lp	dbl	vl	vig	vf
Helen Gould	HT	1896	Lambert P	pb	dbl	l	vig	f
			syn Balduin					
Helen Keller	HP	1895	Dickson A	dp	f		vig	f
Helen Paul	HP	1881	Lacharme	w	f	l		
Helena Williams	N	1825	Leloup	lp				
Hélène	G		Miellez	dr				
Hélène	N			lp	f	m	vig	
Hélène	HMult	1897	Lambert P	pb	s-d	m	vig	sf
Hélène de Lobkowitz	G			mr	f	m		
Hélène Maret(te)	HP	Pre 1846	Robert	w		l		
Hélène Mauget	M	Pre 1846		lp				
Hélène Puyravaud	T	1893	Puyravaud	dy	f	l		
Hélène Stewart	HP	see	Lady Helen Stewart					
Helfn (a?)	HP	1854		pb				
Héliodore Daullé	G			mr	vf	l		
Héliodore Dober	G			mr	f	l	vig	
Héliogabale	HP	1864	Guinoiseau	mr	f	l		
Helmonde	M	1854	Robert	lp	f	m		
Héloïse	Ayr		Laffay	lp	vdbl			
Héloïse	G	1816	Descemet	lp	f	m-l		f
Héloïse	G		Lerouge	m				
Héloïse	C	1818		lp		s		
Héloïse	T	1831	Vibert	w		m		
Héloïse	M	1845	Vibert (or Robert)	lp	f	m		
Héloïse Mantin	T	1895	Lévêque	yb				
Helvetia	T	1873	Ducher	op	f	l	vig	
Helvetia	Ch	1897	Schwartz Vve	yb				
			syn Aurore					
Helvetia	HRg	1899	Froebel	w				
Helvetius	G	c 1830	Desprez	rb	dbl	l		
Henard	Misc	1864						
Henderson	HP	1864		mp	dbl	l	m	
		syn Tri-	omphe de la Terre des	Roses				
Henneloup	Ch	Pre 1846		mp	f	m		
Hennequin	G	c 1830	Desprez	dr	f	m		
Hennequin	B	Pre 1846	syn Splendens	lp	f	l	vig	vf
Henri	N	Pre 1846		lp	f	m		
Henri Barbet	B/HCh	Pre 1846		dp			vig	
Henri Brichard	HT	1891	Bonnaire	w	vdbl	l		
Henri Clay	B	Pre 1846		dp	f	l		
Henri de Buck	G			dp	vf	vl		
Henri Foucquier	G	1811		mp	dbl	l		m

Name	Type	Date	Raiser					
Henri IV	G	1816	Vibert syn Adèle Heu	m	dbl	l		m
Henri IV	D	Pre 1829	Trébutien	mp	f	l	vig	
Henri IV	G	Pre 1830	Calvert	dr	vdbl	l		
Henri IV	B	Pre 1846		lp	f			
Henri IV	HP	1847	Vibert	dp	dbl	l		
Henri IV	HP	1862	Verdier E	dr	f	l		
Henri Lecoq	B	1845	Lacharme	dp	f	l		
Henri Lecoq	T	1871	Ducher	pb	f	l	vig	f
Henri Ledéchaux	HP	1868	Ledéchaux	mp	f	l	m	
Henri Lemain (ire)	G			mr	f	m		
Henri Martin	M	1863	Laffay	mr	s-d	m	vig	sf
Henri Meynadier	T	1885	Nabonnand	mp	f	l	vvig	
Henri M Stanley	T	1891	Dingee	mp				
Henri Pagés	HP	1870	Levet	mp	f	l	vig	
Henri Plantier	B	Pre 1846		dp	f	m		
Henri Puyravand	B	1892	Chauvry	pb	f	l		
Henri Quatre	G	1821	Calvert	dp	dbl	l		
Henri V	Ch	Pre 1846		dp	f	m	m	
Henri Vilmorin	HP	1879	Lévêque	dr	f	l	vvig	
Henri Ward-Beecher	HP	1874	Verdier E	m	f	l	vig	
Henriette	Ch			m	s-d	m		
Henriette	G	Pre 1810	Dupont	mr	f	l		
Henriette	G	Pre 1811	syn Bifera Italica	lp	dbl	m		
Henriette Boulogne	P	1795	Dupont	dp	s-d	m		m
		syn	Quatre Saisons d'Italie					
Henriette Campan	A	Pre 1830		m	f	m		
Henriette de Pansey	HP	1851	Robert	lp	f	l	vig	
Henriette Duval	HP	1879	Duval					
Henriette Grande Agathe	G			mr				
Henriette Laval	HP	1852	Guillot Père	dp	f	m	vig	
Henriette Petit	HP	1878	Margottin	rb	f	l	vvig	
Henriette Rose	M	1825	Vibert					
Henriette Wallner	D							
Henrion de Pansey	G	1851	Robert	dr	f	l		
		see	Henriette de Pansey					
Henry Bennett	T	1872	Levet	pb	f	m	m	vf
Henry Bennett	HP	1875	Lacharme	mr	f	l	vig	
Henry M Stanley	T	1891	Dingee & Conard	pb	vf			m
Henry V	Ch			rb	vf	l		
Henry's Crimson China	Ch	1885		dr	s	m	m	
		syn	r.chinensis spontanea					
Henscheler	G			dr	f	m		
Her Majesty	HP	1885	Bennett	mp	vdbl	vl	vvig	f
Héraclius	HCh		Hardy	lp	vf	m	vvig	
Herbemont's Caroline	N	Pre 1846						
Herbemont's Musk Cluster	N	Pre 1836	Herbemont	w	dbl	vl		
Hercule	G		Miellez	dp	f	m		
Hérissé	Alp							
Hérissé Presque Inerme	A	Pre 1830	Godefroy	lp	dbl	m	vig	
Herissonnée	HSpn	1818	Poilpré	pb				
Hermance	HP	1853	Robert	lp	f	l		
Hermance Louisa de la Rive	T	1882	Nabonnand	w	f	l	vig	
Hermann Kegel	M	1848	Portemer Fils	m	dbl	m	vig	
Hermine	Ch	Pre 1846		lp	f	m		
Hermine Madélé	Pol	1887	Soupert & Notting	w	f	s		
Herminie No 7	G	Pre 1830	Vibert	dr	dbl	m		
		syn	Cramoisi Ponctuée					
Hermione	G	1818		mp	f	m		
Hermosa	B/Ch	Pre 1834	Marcheseau	lp	dbl	s	vig	m
Hermosa, Climbing	Cl Ch	1879	Henderson	lp	f	m		m
			syn Sétina					
Hérodiade	N	1888	Brassac	yb	f	m-l	vig	
Héroïne de Vaucluse	B	1863	Moreau-Robert	mp	f	l	vig	f
Héroïque Commandant Marchand	T	1899	Buatois	yb	vf	l	vig	f
Hersilie	G	Pre 1846		lp				
Hersilie	B/HCh	Pre 1846		mp				
Hersilie	M	1851	Robert	lp	f	l		
Hervy	G	Pre 1830	Prévost	mr	vdbl	l		
Hervy à Fleurs Pleines	G		Hardy	mr	vf	l	vvig	
Herzblättchen	Pol	1887	Geschwind	dp	dbl	s		
Herzogin Marie von Ratibor	T	1897	Lambert	w		m		
Hespérie	G	Pre 1830	Racine					
Hessoise	HEg	Pre 1811	Schwarzkopf	mp	s-d			
Hessoise Anémone	HEg	Pre 1813	Vibert / Dupont	mp	dbl	m		vf
			syn Zabeth					
Hessoise à Feuilles Values Double	HEg		Vibert					
Hessoise à Feuilles de Chanvre	HEg	1821	Vibert	lp	dbl	m		
Hessoise à Gros Aiguillons	HEg	1819						
Hessiose Hybride à Fleurs Lilas	HEg	1827	Prévost	lp	f	s-m		f

Name	Type	Date	Breeder / Synonym					
Hessoise Nikita	HEg	1827	Vibert	dp	vdbl	m		
Hessoise Pourpre Double	HEg	Pre 1815	Descemet	m				
Hessoise Pourpre Pleine	HEg	1821	Vibert	dp	f	m		
Hessoise Rose Double	HEg	1817	Vibert	mp				
Hessoise Rose Foncé	HEg	Pre 1830	Vibert	dp	dbl	m	vig	
Hessoise Rose Foncé Pleine	HEg	1821	Vibert	lp	f	s		
Hétéroclite	T	Pre 1846		yb	f	l	vig	
Heterophylla	HRg	1899	Cochet-Cochet	w	s-d			
Heterophylla	HCan		Lemeusnil	lp				
Hétérophylle	Ch	Pre 1834		mp		m		
Heureuse Conquête	Ch			lp				
Heureuse Surprise	G	Pre 1834		dr	f	l		
Hibbertia	Ch	Pre 1846		dp				
Hibernica	HSpn	1802		lp	s			
Hildegarde	G	1827	Noisette	dr				
Hilltop Rose	Sp	Pre 1788	syn r.collina	mp				
Himalayan Musk Rose	Sp	1822	syn r.brunonii	w	s			
Hiamlayensis	HRg	1879	syn Kaiserin des Nordens	m	dbl	l		
Himmelsauge	HMult	1894	Geschwind	m	dbl	l		vf
Hippolyte	G	Pre 1842	Parmentier	m	dbl	m	vig	sf
Hippolyte	T	Pre 1846		w	f	m		f
Hippolyte Barreau	HT	1893	Pernet-Ducher	dr	f	l	m	vf
Hippolyte Flandrin	HP	Pre 1870	Damaizin	mp	f	l	m	
Hippolyte Jamain	B	1856	Pradel	m	f	l		
Hippolyte Jamain	HP	1869	Faudon	mp	f	vl	vig	
Hippolyte Jamain	HP	1874	Lacharme	mr	dbl	vl	vig	m
Hippolyte Jamain, Climbing	Cl HP	1885	Paul G	m				
Hippolyte Marchand	HP	1881	Vigneron	mr	f	vl	vvig	
Hispanica Moschata Simplex	HMsk	Pre 1629	syn Spanish Musk Rose	w	s	m		
Ho Hua Chiang Wei	Sp	1804	syn r.multiflora carnea	lp	dbl			
Hobold	HT		see Kobold					
Hofgartendirektor Graebener	HT	1899	Lambert P	lp	dbl	m		
Hollandaise	Bslt	c 1815	Noisette syn Maheca	m	s-d	m		
Hollandica	C	Pre 1695		dp	vdbl			m
Hollandica	HRg	c 1888		lp	vdbl			m
Holmes' Mandarin	HCh	Pre 1846						
Holopherne	N			lp	f	m		
Holoserica	G	Pre 1629		dr	dbl			
Holoserica Duplex	G	Pre 1629	syn Semi-Double Velvet Rose	dr	s-d			
Holoserica Multiplex	G	Pre 1629	syn Double Velvet Rose	dr	dbl			
Holoserica Regalis	G	Pre 1815	Schwarzkopf	m	dbl			
Holy Rose of Abyssinia	S	Pre 400	syn r.sancta	lp	s	m		
Homère	T	1858	Robert & Moreau	pb	dbl	l	vig	f
Hona d'Adorjan	HP	1874	Verdier E	lp	f	l	vvig	
Honneur de Flandres	G		Miellez	mp	vf	l		
Honneur des Jardins	G		Miellez	dr				
Honorable Edith Gifford	T	1882	Guillot et Fils	w	dbl	l	vig	f
Honorable George Bancroft	HT	1879	Bennett	rb	f	l	m	vf
Honorine	HCh	Pre 1834	Laffay	mp	dbl	m		
Honorine	HSpn		Goupil	mp				
Honorine	G	1818	Vibert	mp				
Honorine d'Esquermes	G	Pre 1834	Miellez	mp	f	vl		
Hoog's Straw coloured	HFt			yb				
Hooker's Blush	M	Pre 1846		lp				
Horace Vernet	HP	1866	Guillot et Fils	dr	dbl	l	vig	vf
Horatius	HCh	1830	Vibert	lp	f	m		
Horatius Coclès	G	Pre 1828	Miellez	mr	f	l		
Hortense	T	1871	Ducher syn Hortensia (T)	dr	f	l	vig	
Hortense	M							
Hortense	G	Pre 1830	Prévost syn Aimable Hortense	lp	f	m		
Hortense Blanchette	HP		Damaizin	w	f	m		
Hortense de Beauharnais	G	Pre 1848	Prévost	pb	f	m		
Hortense Dupré	HP	1885	Singer	mp	f	l		
Hortense Leroy	B/HCh	Pre 1846	Verdier V	lp	vf	m	vig	
Hortense Mignard	HP	1873	Baltet	rb	f	l	m	
Hortense Vernet	M	1861	Moreau-Robert	w	vdbl	l	m	
Hortensia	G	Pre 1813	Miellez syn GreatRoyal	lp	f	l		
Hortensia	Ch	1829	Vibert	mp		m		
Hortensia	T	1870	Ducher	mp	vf	l	m	
Hortensis	B/Ch	Pre 1846		dp				
Hortus Tolosanos	T	1881	Brassac	w	vf	l	vvig	m
Hospitalière	G/Ch	Pre 1946		dp	f	m		
Hovyn de Tronchère	T	1897	Puyravaud	rb	dbl	l		
Hudson's Bay Rose	Sp	1773	syn r.blanda	mp	s			
Huet	T			w	f	vl	vvig	
Hugh Low	HP	1864	Verdier E	m				

Name	Class	Year	Breeder / syn	Colour	Form	Size	Vigour	Scent
Hulda	C	1845	Vibert	dr	dbl	m		
Hulthemia Hardii	Sp	1832	Hardy	yb				
Hulthemia Persica	Sp	1788		yb				
Hume's Blush Tea-scented China	T	1809	Hume A	lp	dbl			vf
Hundred-Leaved Blush	C	Pre 1759		lp				
Hurdalsrosen	A	1860		mp				
Hyacinth	Misc	Pre 1846						
Hybrida cum Bifera	A	1817	Vibert syn Petite Lisette	dp	f			sf
Hybrida Nova	G	Pre 1830	Vibert / Descemet syn Ninon de l'Enclos	dp	vf	m		
Hybride à Bois Lisse	HP			lp				
Hybride à Fleurs Blanches	HP			w				
Hybride à Fleurs Roses	HCh		Hardy	mp				
Hubride à Fleurs Rouges	HEg		Prévost	dp				
Hybride à Fleurs Pourpres	HCh		Vibert	dr				
Hybride à Grandes Fleurs Carnées	HSpn		Nicolle	lp	s-d	l		
Hybride du Luxembourg	HCh	Pre 1830	Hardy	dp	f	s		
Hybride Glaucophylla	A		Prévost	lp				
Hybride Parfaite	Misc	Pre 1846		lp	f			
Hybride Stadtholder	HCh	Pre 1850		dp				
Hyménée	T	c 1820	Hardy	ly		l		
Hypacia	C	Pre 1844	Hardy	pb	dbl	l	vig	m
Hupocrate	HCh	Pre 1846		mp				

NAME	TYPE	YEAR	RAISER	COLOUR	BLOOM	SIZE	GROWTH	SCENT
Ianthe	HSpn	Pre 1846						
Ibara	HMult	syn Turn	er's Crimson Rambler	mr				
Icarie	T			lp	f	m	wk	
Icteros	Ch	Pre 1846		w	f	l		f
Ida	B	Pre 1846		mr				
Ida	T	1875	Ducher Vve	ly	f	m		
Ida	HMult	c 1890	Dawson	op				
Ida Percot	B	Pre 1846		pb	f	m		vf
Ida Sisley	B			dr	f	l	vig	
Idalise	G	Pre 1830	Vibert syn Constantine	dp	vf	m		
Idalise	M	1852	Robert	lp	f	l		
Idéalisée	G			dr	f	l		
Ignescens	Ch	Pre 1830	Laffay	mr	dbl	s		
Ildefonse	G	1827	Verdier L	dp	vf	vl	vig	
Ile Bourbon de Parmentier	B		Parmentier	lp	f	l		
Ilicifolia	C	Pre 1811	Trianon	mp	vf	m	wk	
		syn	À Feuille de Chêne					
Illustre	G	Pre 1820	Descemet	pb	f	m		
Illustre Beauté	D	Pre 1830	Vibert	mp	vf	m		
Illustre Beauté	D		Miellez	lp	f	m		
Illustre en Beauté	C		Miellez	mr	f	m		
Ilona d'Adorjan	HP	1874	Verdier E	lp	f	l	m	
Image du Bonheur	D		Miellez	lp				
Imbricata	S	1869	Ducher	lp	f	l	vig	
Immense	T							
Impératrice Alexandra Foedorowna	T	1897	Lévêque	yb				
	syn	Prince	Hussein Kamil Pacha					
Impératrice Augusta	T	1878	Soupert & Notting	my	f	l	vvig	
Impératrice Augusta Victoria	HT	see Kais	erin Augusta Victoria					
Impératrice Charlotte	HP	1867	Verdier E	dp	f	l	vig	
Impératrice de France	D	Pre 1846	Robert	mr	f	m	vvig	
Impératrice de Hollande	D	Pre 1826	syn Roi des Pays-Bas	dp	dbl	l	vvig	
Impératrice de l'Inde	HP		see Empress of India					
Impératrice de Russie	G	c 1825	Péan	dp	vf	l		
Impératrice des Français	HP	1855	Roger	lp	f	l		
Impératrice du Brésil	HP	1864	Pradel	dp	f	l		
Impératrice Elizabeth	B	1850	Lartay	lp	f	m	vig	
Impératrice Eugénie	T	1853	Pradel	my	vf	m		
Impératrice Eugénie	B	1855	Plantier	m				
Impératrice Eugénie	B	1855	Béluze	mp	f	m	vig	
Impératrice Eugénie	M	1855	Guillot Père	dp	dbl	m	vig	m
Impératrice Eugénie	HP	1856	Avoux and Crozy	w	f	m	vig	
Impératrice Eugénie	HP	1856	Oger	w	f	m	vig	
Impératrice Frédérick	T	see	Kaiserin Frederic					
Impératrice Joséphine	G	Pre 1815	Descemet	pb	dbl			
		syn	Empress Josephine					
Impératrice Joséphine	Ch	Pre 1846		dr	f	m		
Impératrice Joséphine	B	1842	Verdier V	lp	vf	m	vvig	
Impératrice Joséphine	HP	1852	Lartay	lp	f	l		
Impératrice Maria Alexandrina	HP	1862	Damaizin	w	f	m	wk	
Impératrice Maria Foedorowna	HP	1892	Lévêque	mp		l		
Impératrice M Foedorowna de Russie	T	1883	Nabonnand	ly	vf	vl	vvig	f
Imperial Beauty	Misc	Pre 1846		m				
Imperial Blush	C	Pre 1846		lp		l		
Impériale	G	Pre 1791	syn Regina Dicta	m	f	m		
Impériale à Plumet	G			lp				
Improved Rainbow	T	c 1896	Burbank	pb		vl		
Incarnata	C	Pre 1819		lp				
		syn	My Lady Kensington					
Incarnata	HSpn	Pre 1826	Prévost	w	dbl	s		
			syn Double Carnée					
Incarnata Major	A	Pre 1754	syn Gt Maiden's Blush	w	dbl			vf
Incarnata Maxima	D	Pre 1750	syn Celsiana	lp	s-d	l	vig	m
Incarnate	M	c 1805	Vilmorin syn Vilmorin	lp	f	m-l		
Incomparable	G	Pre 1813	(Holland)	dp				
Incomparable d'Auteuil	C	Pre 1826	Laffay	mp				
Incomparable de Lille	G	Pre 1830	Prévost	dp	f	m-l		
Incomparable en beauté	G		Miellez	dr				
Incomparable Purple	Misc	Pre 1846		m				
Incomparable Violet	Misc	Pre 1846		lp				
Inconnu	G			mp	f	m		
Indiana	G	1834	Vibert					
Indiana	Ch			m				
Indiana	M	1845	Vibert	mp	vdbl	m		
Indica Alba	Ch	1802		lp			vig	
Indica Major	S	Pre 1811	syn Fun Jwan Lo	w	dbl	m	vvig	
Indica Major	HCh	1823	Vibert	lp	vdbl	m		

Name	Type	Date	Raiser					
Indica Major, Climbing	Ch	Pre 1846	as above	lp				
Indica Maxima	Ch	Pre 1846		mr		l		
Indicella	Ch			dr	s-d	s		
Indigo	P	c 1830	Laffay	m	f	l		vf
Inépuisable	HMult	1898	Lille	mp				
Inermis	A			w				
Inermis	HSpn	Pre 1824	Nestler / De Candolle	mr	s			
Inermis	HP	1850	Lacharme	dp	f	m		
Inermis	HP	1851	Margottin	lp				
Inermis Flore Pleno	A			w				
Inermis Foliis Aculeatis	A			lp				
Inermis Morlettii	Bslt	1883	Morlet syn Morlettii	m	s-d	m		
Inermis Sub Albo Violacea	G	Pre 1811	syn Bourbon	pb	s-d	m		m
Ines de Castro	C			lp	f	m		
Ines de Castro	P	1858	Robert & Moreau	dr				
Infante	G	1829	Vibert	lp	f	l		
Infernal	Misc	Pre 1846		dr				
Infidèle	Ch	Pre 1870		lp	dbl	m		
Infidélité de Lisette	HCh	Pre 1846	syn Mme Bureau	w	vdbl	l		m
Inflexible	G			dr	f	m		
Inflexible	HP			mr	f	m		
Ingegnoli Prediletta	B	1868	Bizot syn Zéphirine Drouhin	mp				m
Ingegnoli Prediletta	T	1892	Bernaix	dp		m	vig	
Ingénieur Madèlé	HP	1874	Moreau-Robert	dp	f	vl	m	
Ingénue	G	1833	Vibert	w	dbl	m		
Ingrata	C	Pre 1810	Dupont syn Le Rire Niais	mp	f	m		m
Ingres	HP	1850	Pradel	lp	f	l		
Inigo Jones	HP	1886	Paul W	pb	f	l	vig	
Innocence	HT	1897	Pernet-Ducher syn L'Innocence	w	f	l		
Innocente Pirola	T	1878	Ducher Vve	w	f	m	vvig	f
Insigne Destècles (d'Estekies)	G	Pre 1846		mp	f	m-l		
Institutrice Moulins	Ch	1893	Charreton	dp	dbl	l	vvig	
Insurmountable Beauty	Misc	Pre 1846						
Intendant Général Périé	HP	see	M. l'Intendant Perier					
Intéressante	G	Pre 1830	Prévost	dr	f	m		
Intus Luride Flavescens	A			w	s-d	m		
Invincible	G	Pre 1819	Miellez	mr	dbl	s		
Invincible	D	Pre 1846	syn Nivalis	mp				
Involuta	HSpn							
Iolande d'Aragon	HP	Pre 1846		lp				
Iphigénie	Ch			w	f	s		
Iphigénie	G	1820	Vibert	mp	f	m		
Iphigénie	HP	1848	Vibert	dr	f	l	vig	
Ipsilanté	G	1821	Vibert	m	dbl	vl	vig	
Ipswich Gem	HP							
Irena	G	Pre 1830	syn Elisa Descemet	mp	vdbl	l		
Irène	N			w	f	l	vig	
Irène	C	Pre 1830	Laffay	mp	f	m		
Irène	HSpn	1823	Vibert	lp	dbl	m		
Irène Watts	HCh	1896	Guillot P	w	dbl	vl	vig	
Iris	HSpn			w	s-d	m		
Iris Noir	Misc	Pre 1846		m				
Iris Nova	G			pb				
Irma	Ch	1824	Laffay	w	dbl	m		
Irma	T	1835	Vibert	pb				
Irrlicht	Misc	1895	Geschwind		s-d	l		f
Isaac Demole	T	1895	Nabonnand	mp				
Isabella	G	1834		dp				
Isabella Gray	N	1854	Gray, A	dy	f	vl	vig	f
Isabella Sprunt	T	1865	Sprunt	my	dbl		m	f
Isabelle	G	Pre 1820	Descemet	dr	vf	s-m	wk	
Isabelle	G	Pre 1830	Calvert	dr	vf	s-m		
Isabelle	G	Pre 1830	Vibert syn Héloïse	mp	f	m-l		
Isabelle	Ch	Pre 1846	Laffay	lp	dbl	l		
Isabelle de Castille	HP	1852	Robert	lp	s-d	m	vig	
Isabelle de Lorraine	G	1843	Vibert	mp	f	l		
Isabelle de Montolieu	T	1826	Vétillard	w				
Isabelle d'Orléans	N	1824	Vibert	w	f	l		
Isabelle II	B	1853	Pradel	mp	f	l		
Isabelle Labie	HP	1852	Pradel	mp	f	m	vig	
Isabelle Latour	B			mr				
Isabelle Nabonnand	T	1873	Nabonnand	pb	dbl	l	vvig	f
Isabelle Rivoire	T	1897	Dubreuil	mp	f	l	vig	vf
Isabelle Sprungh	T	1866	Verschafelt	ly	s-d	l	vig	
		see also	Isabella Sprunt					
Isaline	C	1825	Vétillard	dp	f	l		
Isaline	D	Pre 1830	Vibert	mp	f	l		
Isaline	M	1852	Robert	dp				

Name	Class	Date	Breeder					
Isaure Labbé	HP	Pre 1846	Buchanan	pb	vf	m	vig	
Iselle Dubor	HP		Pradel	mp		vl		
Isidore	T	Pre 1834		lp	f	m		f
Isidore Malton	T	1846	Guillot Père syn Mme Bravy	w	dbl			
Isis	G		Parmentier	lp	f	m		
Isis	N	1853	Robert	w	f	l	vig	
Islay	HP			lp	s-d	m	vig	
Isle de Bourbon	B	Pre 1846		lp	f	m		
Isle de France	B			mr	f	l		vf
Ismaël	Ch		Laffay	lp	f	l		
Ismène	D	1845	Vibert	lp	f	l		
Ismène	N		Laffay	lp	f	s		
Ismène	M	1852	Robert	lp	f	l	vig	
Isménie	Misc	1823	Vibert	mp	dbl	m-l		
Isocrate	HP	1851		mp			m	
Isoline	G	1851	Robert	lp	f	l		
Isoline	HP	1852	Dupuy-Jamain syn Paul Dupuy	mr	f	l		
Ispahan	D	Pre 1832		mp	dbl	m		vf
Italian Four Seasons Rose	P	1795	Dupont syn Quatre Saisons d'Italie	dp	s-d	m		m
Italian Yellow	HFt	Pre 1846		ly				
Iver Cottage	HEg	Pre 1846		lp	s			
Iwara	HMult	Pre 1830		w	s	s		
Izayoi Bara	Sp	Pre 1814	syn r.roxburghii	mp	dbl			

NAME	TYPE	YEAR	RAISER	COLOUR	BLOOM	SIZE	GROWTH	SCENT
J A Escarpit	HP	1883	Bernède	m	vf	l	vig	vf
J B Varonne	T	1889	Guillot et Fils	dp	f	l	vig	vf
J Prowe	HP	1893	Lévêque	mr				
J Van den Merch Mertens	T	1881	Nabonnand	w	f	l	vvig	
Jack Rose	HP	1853	Roussel	rb	dbl		vig	vf
		syn	Général Jacqueminot					
Jacksonia	Ch	Pre 1846		mr				
Jacob	HP			mp	f	l	vig	
Jacob Pereire	HP	1869	Moreau-Robert	mr	f	l		
Jacquard	B	1842	Béluze	dp	f	m		
Jacques	N	Pre 1834	Laffay	lp	dbl	s	vig	
Jacques	Ch			mr	f	l		
Jacques Amyot	N	1844	Varangot	m	vdbl	m	vig	
Jacques Cartier	P	1868	Moreau-Robert	lp	vf	l	vig	m
Jacques Cartier Blanc	P	c 1870		w				
Jacques Dessailles	G			lp				
Jacques Lafitte	HP	1845	Vibert	dp	f	l	m	
Jacques Pereire	HP	1870	Moreau-Robert	mr	vf	l	vvig	
Jacques Plantier	HP	1872	Damaizin	pb	f	l	m	
Jacques von Baden	A			w	f	l		
Jacquin	Ch			mr	f	m		
Jacquinot	C	Pre 1848		pb	dbl	m	vig	
James Bourgault	HP	1887	Renauld-Guépet	w	dbl	m	vig	
James Brownlow	HP	1890	Dickson A	mp	f	vl		m
James Dickson	HP	1861	Verdier E	pb	dbl	l	m	
James Mitchell	M	1861	Verdier E	dp	dbl	m		vf
James Purple	HSpn							
James Sprunt	Cl Ch	1858	Sprunt	mr	dbl	m	vig	
James Veitch	HP	1851	Laffay	dp	f	l	vvig	
James Veitch	M	1864	Verdier E	m	dbl	m	m	
James Watt	HP	Pre 1846		lp		l		
James Watt	HP	1873	Moreau-Robert	rb	f	l	vig	
Jane	HSet	c 1846	Pierce	lp	vdbl	m		
Janet's Pride	HEg	Pre 1892	Paul syn Clémentine	pb	s-d	m	vig	vf
Japanese Rose	Sp	Pre 1846	syn r.rugosa	m				
Jason	G		Miellez	mp				
Jaunâtre	N	1832	Vibert	y		s		
Jaunâtre	T	1827	Vibert	ly	dbl	l		f
Jaunâtre	HSem	Pre 1834		y		s		f
Jaunâtre Pleine	Sp			my	dbl			
Jaune	Bks	Pre 1834	syn Yellow	y	f	s		
Jaune	HSpn		Descemet	y	f	l		
Jaune Ancien	Sp	Pre 1503	syn r.hemisphaerica	my	s			
Jaune Ancien	HFt	Pre 1629	syn Multiplex	my	vdbl	vl		
Jaune Ancienne	T	Pre 1870		my	f	l		
Jaune à Petite Fleur	Bks			y				
Jaune Bicolor	Sp	1633		yb	s	m	vig	
Jaune de Fortune	N		see Fortune's Yellow					
Jaune de Hollande	HFt			y				
Jaune de William	HFt	Pre 1819	Williams J	my	s-d			vf
		syn	Williams' Double Yell	ow				
Jaune des Anglais	HSpn			y				
Jaune Desprez	N	c 1830	Desprez	yb	f	l	vig	m
		syn	Desprez à Fleurs	Jaunes				
Jaune d'Italie	HFt	Pre 1846	(Italy)	ly	dbl			
Jaune d'Or	T	1864	Oger	ob	dbl	l	m	f
Jaune Double	HFt	Pre 1819	Williams J	my	s-d	m		vf
		syn	Williams' Double Yell	ow				
Jaune Double	Bks	1823	Damper	my	dbl	s	vig	vf
Jaune Double de Hollande	HFt			ly	vf	l		
Jaune Double des Anglais	HSpn			my	f	s		
Jaune Grande	Bks			y				
Jaune Lilacée Double	Pom		Goupil	lp				
Jaune Multiple	HSpn		Prévost	my				
Jaune Nabonnand	T	1890	Nabonnand	dy	dbl	l	vig	
Jaune of Smith	T	1834	Smith	dy	f	l		
		syn	Smith's Yellow China					
Jaune Pâle Semi-Double	HSpn		Vibert	ly				
Jaune Panache	T		Cels	ly	vf	l		
Jaune Plus Grand	Bks			y				
Jaune Serin	Bks	Pre 1846	syn Lutescens Spinosa	my	f	l		
Jaune Serin Double	HSpn	1825	Hardy	y				
Jaune Simple	HEg	Pre 1830		ly	s			f
Jaune Soufre	T	1827	Mauget					
Jaune Soufre	HSpn	Pre 1838	Hardy syn Sulphurea	ly	s-d	l		
Jay	HEg	1819	Vibert	w				
Je Ne Maintiendrai	G	Pre 1860		mp		l		
Jean	G			mr	vf	m		

Jean André	T	1893	Pelletier	yb	f	m		m
Jean Bach Sisley	Ch	1898	Dubreuil	pb	dbl		m	m
Jean-Baptiste Casati	HP	1886	Schwartz Vve	dp	vdbl	l		
Jean Baptiste Guillot	HP	1861	Verdier E	m	vf	vl	m	
Jean Baptiste Josseau	HP	1863	Rousseau	mp		l		
Jean Baptiste Varonne	T	1889	Guillot Fils	dp	f	l		
Jean Bart	P	Pre 1836	Trébucien	m	dbl	vl		m
Jean Bart	G	Pre 1830	Vibert	mr	vdbl	vll		
Jean Bart	HP	1860	Margottin	m	vdbl	l	vig	
Jean Bodin	M	1846	Vibert	lp	dbl	m	vig	vf
Jean Brosse	HP	1867	Ducher	dp	f	l		
Jean Cherpin	HP	1865	Liabaud	m	vdbl	vl	vig	
Jean Dalmais	HP	1873	Ducher	dp	f	vl	vig	
Jean Desprez	N	c 1820	Desprez	rb	f	m	vig	vf
Jean Dorizy	B	1850	Dorizy F	mp	f	l		
Jean Ducher	T	1873	Ducher	op	dbl	l	vig	m
Jean France	HP	1866	Levet	dr				
Jean Goujon (Coujon)	HP	1862	Margottin	mr	f	vl	vig	
Jean Hardy	N	1859	Hardy	yb	f	l	vig	
Jean Lambert	HP	1865	Verdier E	mr	f	l	vig	
Jean Lelièvre	HP	1879	Oger	dr	dbl	l	vig	m
Jean Liabaud	HP	1875	Liabaud	dr	vf	l	vig	f
Jean Lorthois	HT	1879	Ducher Vve	pb		l		
Jean Marie	Ch			mr			vig	
Jean Pernet	T	1867	Pernet Père	my	f	l	vig	f
Jean Rosenkrantz	HP	1864	Portemer Fils	or	dbl	l	vig	vf
Jean Sisley	HT	1879	Bennett	m		l	m	
Jean Soupert	HP	1875	Lacharme	dr	dbl	l		f
Jean Touvais	HP	1863	Touvais	m	f	l	vig	
Jeanne Abel	T	1882	Guillot Fils	lp	f	m-l	vig	vf
Jeanne Bouvet	HP	1884 syn Mlle	Bernède Jacqueline Bouvet	dr		m-l		
Jeanne Chevalier	HP	1879	Rambeaux Vve	mr		l	vig	
Jeanne Corbœuf	Pol	1899	Corbœuf	mr				
Jeanne d'Albret	G	1819	Vibert	dp	vdbl	l		
Jeanne d'Albret	B		Laffay	lp	dbl	m		
Jeanne d'Arc	A	1818	Vibert	w	vf	m-l	vig	vf
Jeanne d'Arc	N	Pre 1846		w			vig	
Jeanne d'Arc	HP	1847	Verdier V	w	dbl	l	vig	
Jeanne d'Arc	M	1858	Moreau-Robert	w				
Jeanne d'Arc	T	1870	Ducher	my	f	m	vvig	
Jeanne d'Arc	N	1882	Garçon/Margottin	mp	f	l		m
Jeanne Deans	Ch			lp	f	m		
Jeanne de Clisson	P	1852	Robert	lp	f	l	vvig	
Jeanne de la Noue	HP	1852	Robert	lp	vf	l	vig	
Jeanne de Laval	G	Pre 1846		dp	f	l		
Jeanne de Laval	HP	1865	Moreau-Robert	mp				
Jeanne de Montfort	M	1851	Robert	mp	s-d	l	vig	m
Jeanne de Nègre	T	1888	Perny	mp				
Jeanne Dickson	HP		see Jeannie Dickson					
Jeanne Drivon	Pol	1883	Schwartz J	w	vdbl	m		
Jeanne d'Urfé	C		Vibert	mp	f	l		
Jeanne Forgeot	T	1896	Forgeot Tardey	yb	vdbl	l	vvig	
Jeanne Gray	G	Pre 1830	Lahaye Père	m	vf	m		
Jeanne Gross	HP	1871	Damaizin	mp	f	l	vig	
Jeanne Guillot	HP	1869	Liabaud	mp	f	vl	vig	
Jeanne Hachette	P	Pre 1830	Coquerel	mp	f	vl		
Jeanne Hachette	D	Pre 1834				vl		
Jeanne Hachette	G	1842	Vibert	dp	dbl	l		
Jeanne Hachette	M	1851	Robert	m				
Jeanne Hachette	HP	1868	Oger	dp	f	l		
Jeanne Halphen	HP	1878	Margottin	mp	f	l	vig	
Jeanne Hardy	N	1859	Hardy syn Jean Hardy	yb			m	
Jeanne Hely d'Oissel	HP	1889	Ledéchaux	rb				
Jeanne Labbé	HP		see Isaure Labbé					
Jeanne Maillotte	G	Pre 1830	Miellez	lp				
Jeanne Masson	HP	1891	Liabaud	lp	dbl	m		m
Jeanne Massop (Mossop)	T	1879	Nabonnand	lp			vvig	
Jeanne Naudin	T	1879	Nabonnand	mp	f	l	vig	
Jeanne Renou	HP	1878	Oger	mp		l		
Jeanne Sellier	G			lp	f	m		
Jeanne Seymour	HCh			mr	f	m		
Jeanne Seymour	G	1829	Vibert	lp	f	l		
Jeanne Shore	Ch	1827	Péan	w	f	m	m	
Jeanne Sury	HP	1868	Faudon	dp	dbl	l	m	
Jeanne Vertpert	G			mr	f	m		
Jeanne Wannez	HP	1885	Singer	pb	vf	vl		
Jeanneton	G		Miellez	lp				
Jeannette	G	Pre 1815	Descemet	dp	dbl			
Jeannie Deans	T	Pre 1846		lp				f
Jeannie Deans	HEg	1895	Penzance	dr	s-d	m-l	vig	fol f

Jeannie Dickson	HP	1890	Dickson A	pb	f	l	vig	
Jefferson	G		Descemet	dr				
Jelina	HRg	1894	Kaufmann	dp	dbl	l		
Jenner	HCh	Pre 1830	Laffay	lp	f	m		f
Jenny	HSpn	Pre 1810	Dupont syn Estelle	lp	s-d	l		
Jenny	Min	Pre 1834		dr		vs		
Jenny	HCh	Pre 1836		dr				
Jenny Audiot	P	Pre 1836	Audiot	mp	f	l	vig	
Jenny Cherrie	B	Pre 1846						
Jenny Dauzac	T	1891	Reboul	my				
Jenny Delacharme	G	1827	Hardy	mp	vdbl	m		
Jenny Duval	G	1821	Duval	mp	dbl	l		vf
Jenny Gay	B	1865	Guillot Fils	w	f	m	m	
Jenny Jones	T	1890	Williams A					
Jenny Lind	M	1845	Laffay	mp	vdbl	s		
Jenny Varin	HP	Pre 1870		lp	f	m		
Jéricho	G	Pre 1811	syn Bourbon	pb	s-d	m		m
Jérome Graff	HP			mr	f	vl	vig	
Jersey Beauty	HWich	1899	Horvath / Manda W A	ly	s	l	vig	vf
Jessica	Ayr	Pre 1846	syn Angle	lp	s-d	l		
Jeune Âge	M			lp	f	m		
Jeune Âge (Arcole)	T			dr	f	m		
Jeune Âge Bergére	A			w	s-d	m		
Jeune Arcole	Ch	Pre 1846		lp	f			f
Jeune Bergére	A		Miellez	lp	dbl			
Jeune Henry	C	Pre 1815	Vibert	mp	dbl	m		
Jeune Henry	P	Pre 1815	Descemet	mr	f	l		
Jeune Panaché	T	Pre 1846		w				f
Jezabel	G	1826	Péan	dr	vdbl	m		
Joachim du Bellay	HP	1882	Moreau-Robert	mr	f	l	vvig	
Joan of Arc	B	Pre 1846		lp		l		
Joaquin Aldrufeu	HT	1897	Aldrufeu	m	dbl		m	sf
Joasine Hanet	HP	1846	Vibert	m	dbl	m		m
Jobez Desgaches	HP			lp	f	m	m	
Jocabelle	HP			rb	vdbl	m		
Johanna Lebus	HT	1894	Müller	pb	f	vl		vf
Johannes Wesselhöft	HT	1899	Welter & Hinner	my	f	l		
Johannet	HP		Van Houtte					
John Barnes	HP	1868		mp	vdbl	m		
John Bright	HP	1878	Paul & Son	mr	dbl	m		
John Cant	HEg	1895	Cant B R	dp	s-d	s		
John Cranston	M	1861	Verdier E	m	dbl	m	vig	
John D Pawle	HP	1888	Paul G	m				
John Franklin	HP			lp	f	l	vig	
John Fraser	M	1861	Lévêque	rb	dbl	l		
John Fraser	HP	1876	Verdier E	dr	vf	l		
John Gould Veitch	HP	1864	Lévêque	mr	f	l	vig	
John Grier	HP	1865	Verdier E	dp	f	l	vig	
John Grow	M	1859	Laffay M	mp	f	l		
John Harrison (Harisson)	HP	1873	Verdier E	dr	f	vl	vig	
John Hopper	HP	1862	Ward	pb	vf	l	vig	vf
John Keynes	HP	1864	Verdier E	dr	vf	l	vig	vf
John Kiniguy	B	1850	Oudin	mr	f	l		
John Laing	HP	1872	Verdier E	dr	dbl	m	m	
John Nesmith	HP	1863	Verdier E	dr	f	m		
John Saul	HP	1878	Ducher Vve	mr	f	vl	vig	vf
John Stuart Mill	HP	1875	Turner	mr	dbl	l	vig	
John Waterer	HP	1861	Portemer	mr	f	l		
Jolie Parmentier	G			m	f	l		
Jolie Rose Pierret	G	Pre 1811	syn Agathe Incarnata	lp	vdbl	m		vf
Joseph	Pom			my	f	m		
Joseph Bernacchi	N	1878	Ducher Vve	w	f	vl	vvig	f
Joseph Chappaz	HP	1883	Schmitt	pb	dbl	l	vvig	
		syn	Monsieur Joseph Chap	paz				
Joseph Decaisne	HP	1851	Margottin	mp	f	vl	vig	
Joseph Degueld	HP	1891	Soupert & Notting	mp				
Joseph Deschiens	Ch	Pre 1846		mr	f	m		
Joseph Durand	HP	1863	Ledéchaux	m	f	l	vig	
Joseph Fiala	HP	1863	Verdier E	rb	f	l	vig	
Joseph Fraser	HP	1876	Verdier E	dr	vf	l		
			syn John Fraser					
Joseph Gourdon	B	1851	Robert	pb	f	l		
Joseph Goujon	HP	1862	Margottin	mr	f	vl		
			syn Jean Goujon					
Joseph Metral	HP	1883	Liabaud	dr		l	vig	
Joseph Métral	T	1888	Bernaix	rb	vdbl	l	vig	f
Joseph Saladin	HP	1861	Moreau-Robert	mr				
Joseph Schmidt	B	1832	Pradel	mp	f	m		
Joseph Tasson	HP	1882	Soupert & Notting	dr	f	l		
Joseph Teyssier	T	1892	Dubreuil	mp				
Joseph Vernet	HP	1858	Robert & Moreau	mp	f	m		
Joseph Waterer	HP	1861	Portemer	mr	f	l		

			syn John Waterer					
Joseph Wattecamps	G			mp	f	l		
Joséphina	G	Pre 1813	Savoureux (?)	lp	dbl	m		
Joséphine	P	Pre 1821	syn Buffon	lp	vdbl	l		
Joséphine	G	Pre 1825	Boutigny	dp	s-d			
Joséphine	G	Pre 1829	Boutigny	mp	dbl	m		
Joséphine	G	Pre 1830	Vibert syn Ninon de l'Enclos	dp	vf	m		
Joséphine	P	Pre 1830	syn La Gracieuse	lp	vf	m		
Joséphine	A	Pre 1834		lp		m		
Joséphine	M	Pre 1846		dp	dbl	m		
Joséphine Antoinette	HP	Pre 1834	Hardy	mr	f	m		vf
Joséphine Antoinette	C		Péan	mp	vdbl	vl		
Josephine Burland	Pol	1888		w	dbl	m		
Joséphine Chambert	B	1853	Pradel	mp	f	l	vig	
Joséphine Clermont	B	1857	Guillot Père	mp	f	m		
Joséphine Dauphin	T	1896	Liabaud	w		vl		
Joséphine de Beauharnais	A	1823	Vibert	lp	vf	m	vig	
Joséphine de Beauharnais	HP	1865	Guillot Fils	lp	f	vl	vig	
Joséphine de Hohenzollern	D	Pre 1830	Prévost	mp	f	m		
Joséphine Fouquier	G			dp	f	m		
Joséphine Guyet	B	1873	Touvais	dr	f	m		
Joséphine Ledéchaux	HP	1855	Ledéchaux	ob	f	m	vvig	
Joséphine Maille	G	c 1825	Boutigny	mp	f	l		
Joséphine Malton	Ch	c 1830	Guérin	ab	f	l		
Joséphine Maltot	T	1846	Guillot Père syn Mme Bravy	w	dbl			
Joséphine Marot	HT	1894	Bonnaire	lp	f	l	vig	
Joséphine Morel	Pol	1892	Alégatière	dp	dbl	s		
Joséphine Oudin	G			ly	f	m		
Joséphine Parmentier	G	c 1840	Parmentier	mp	f	m		
Josephine Ritter	HMult	1899	Geschwind	mp	dbl	l		m
Joséphine Robert	HP	1848	Vibert	lp	f	l	vig	
Joubert	Ch			dr	f	m		
Juanita	G	1836	Vibert	pb	dbl	m		
Juanita	C	1855	Robert	pb		l		
Jubilee	HP	1897	Walsh	m	dbl	l	m	f
Judicelli	Ch		Laffay	m	s-d			
Jugurtha	HSpn	1846						
Juif Errant	HP			dr	f	l		
Juillet	HP			mr				
Jules Bagot	G	Pre 1860		dp	dbl	l		
Jules Barigny	HP	1886	Verdier E	mr	dbl	l		vf
Jules Bire	HP	1886	Bire	dp	f	vl		
Jules Bourgeois	HP	1867	Ledéchaux	dr	dbl	m	m	
Jules Bourquin	T	1892	Chauvry	yb	f	vl		
Jules Calot	HP	1866	Verdier E	pb	f	l	vig	
Jules César	B	1865	Verdier E	dp	f	l	m	
Jules Chrétien	HP	1869	Damaizin	mp	f	l	vig	
Jules Chrétien	HP	1878	Schwartz	mr	f	l		
Jules Dassonville	HT	1887	Soupert & Notting	p	f	m	vig	
Jules Deschiens	N			lp	dbl	m	m	
Jules Desmont	T			lp	s-d	m		
Jules Desponts (ds)	HP	1888	Liabaud	dp	f	l	vig	
Jules Dutertre	HP	1849	Margottin	mp	f	m	vvig	
Jules Felice	T			lp	f	m	m	
Jules Finger	T	1879	Ducher Vve	rb	dbl	vl	vig	f
Jules Jamain	Ch			mp	f	s	vig	
Jules Jürgensen	B	1879	Schwartz	m	f	l	vvig	m
Jules Lavay	HP	1864	Damaizin	mp	f	m	vig	
Jules Lesourd	P	1863	Robert & Moreau	mr	f	m		
Jules Maquinat	HP	1883	Vigneron	mr	f	l	vvig	
Jules Margottin	HP	1853	Margottin	mp	vf	l	vig	sf
Jules Margottin, Climbing	Cl HP	1874	Cranston	mr	vf	l	vig	vf
Jules Monges	HP		see M Jules Monges					
Jules Ravenel	HP	Pre 1870		mr	f	m	vvig	
Jules Roussignihol	HP	1864	De Sansal	mr	f	l	vig	
Jules Savary	HP							
Jules Seurre	HP	1869	Liabaud	mr	f	l	vig	
Julia Dante	N	Pre 1846						
Julia Dymonier	HP	1880	Gonod	lp	f	l		
Julia Festilla	HMult	1890	Geschwind	dr				
Julia Fontaine	B	1879	Fontaine	lp	f	m	vig	
Julia Mannering	HEg	1895	Penzance	lp	s-d	s	vig	m
Julia Touvais	HP	1868	Touvais	lp	f	vl	vig	
Juliana	M	Pre 1846		lp	s-d			
Julie	G	Pre 1860		mp		l		
Julie	T			w	f	m	vig	
Julie Barthère	HP		Lartay	dp	f	l		
Julie de Fontenelle	B	1855	Portemer	dp	f	m		f
Julie de la Bastide (de Labastide)	HP		Pradel	lp				

Name	Class	Date	Raiser					
Julie de la Roche (Delaroche)	HP	1847	Vibert	mp	f	m		
Julie de Loynes	B	1835	Desprez	lp	f	s		
Julie de Loynes	B	Pre 1846		w	f	s		
Julie de Mersan	M	1854	Thomas	mp	f	m	m	
Julie de Saint-Aignan	HP	1852	Pradel	lp	f	l		
Julie d'Etanges	G	1834	Vibert	m	dbl	l	vig	
Julie d'Etanges	M	1852	Robert	mr	f	m	vvig	
Julie Dugourd	HP							
Julie Dupont	HP	1841	Dupont	mp	f	m	vig	vf
Julie Everaertz	G			mr	f	l		
Julie Guinoisseau	HP	1854	Guinoisseau	mp		m	vig	
Julie Krüdner	P	1847	Laffay	lp	f	m	vvig	
Julie Mansais	T	1834	Mansais	w	f	vl	m	vf
Julie Moncey	T			w	f	l	vig	
Julie Sisley	B	Pre 1846		mp	f	l		
Julie Treyve	HP	1868	Liabaud	lp	f	l	vig	
Julienne Lesourd	N/Ch	Pre 1846		mp	f	m		
Juliette	G	1795	syn La Belle Sultane	dr		m		
Juliette	G	Pre 1828	Miellez	mr	dbl	m		
Juliette	N			w				
Juliette	HP	Pre 1853		mp				
Juliette	HP	1862	Lartay	mr	f	l	vig	
Juliette Doucet	T	1881	Bernède	w	f	l	vvig	
Juliette Halphen	HP	1869	Margottin Père	lp	f	l	vvig	
Julius Finger	HP	1879	Lacharme	op	f	l	vvig	f
Junia	N		Laffay	lp	f	m		
Juno	C	Pre 1832	Probably syn below	lp	vdbl	l		vf
Juno	HCh	1847	Laffay	lp	dbl	vl	vig	
Juno Rose	C	Pre 1820		lp	f	s		
		syn	Petite Junon de Hollan	de				
Junon	G	Pre 1811	Dupont	dp	f	l		sf
Junon	G	Pre 1811	syn Surpasse Tout	mr	f	m		m
Junon	G	Pre 1830	Prévost	mp	vdbl	s-m		
			syn Belle Junon					
Junon	Ch	Pre 1830	Vibert	mr	dbl	m		
Junon	HCh	Pre 1834	Hardy	dr		s		
Junon à Fleurs Pleines	G	Pre 1830	Prévost	mp	f	m		
Junon Argentée	C	Pre 1820	Prévost	lp	f	s		
		syn Pet-	ite Junon de Hollande					
Junonis	G	Pre 1811	Dupont syn Junon	dp	f	l		sf
Jupiter	B	1845	Verdier V	rb	f	m	vig	
Jury	B	1849	Guillot	mr	f	m	vig	
Just Detrey	HP	1884	Detrey	mr	f	m	vig	
Justine	T	1827	Foulard					
Justine	C	1828	Vibert	lp	vdbl	m		
Justine	B	1845	Rousseau	dp	f	m	vvig	
Justine Ramet	C	1845	Vibert	m	dbl	m	vig	f
Juturne	HP	1845	Vibert	dp				

NAME	TYPE	YEAR	RAISER	COLOUR	BLOOM	SIZE	GROWTH	SCENT
Kaiser Friedrich	T	1890	Drögemüller	pb	f	l		m
Kaiser Wilheim	T	1887		pb	f	l	vig	f
Kaiser Wilhelm der Siegreiche	T	1889	Drögemüller	pb	vdbl	l		m
Kaiser Wilhelm I	HP	1878	Ruschpler	m	dbl	l	vig	m
Kaiserin Augusta	T	1872	Elze	dr	f	l	vig	
Kaiserin Augusta	T	1878	Soupert & Notting	my	f	l	vvig	
		syn	Impératrice Augusta					
Kaiserin Auguste Viktoria	HT	1891	Lambert P	w	vf	l	m	vf
Kaiserin Auguste Viktoria, Climbing	Cl HT	1897	Dickson A	w	dbl	vl		
Kaiserin des Nordens	HRg	1879	Regel	m	dbl	l	m	
			syn possibly Taicoun					
Kaiserin Friedrich	Cl T	1889	Drögemüller	pb	vdbl	vl	vvig	f
Kakayan	Pol(?)	Pre 1867		w	s			
Kamtchatica	HRg	c 1800		dr	s	m	vig	
Karaïskaki	G	1827	Prévost	dr	f	m		
Karaïskaki (same as above?)	HCh	1827	Laffay	dr	f	m		
Karl Maria von Weber	T	1893	Türke	mr				
Karl Müller	HP	see	BurgomeisterC Müller					
Kate Hausburg	HP	1863	Granger	lp	f	vl	vig	
Katkoff	HP	1887	Moreau-Robert	mr	f	l	vig	
Kazanlik	D	Pre 1700		dp	f	m		vf
Kean	G	1843	Godefroy	m	f	m-l	vig	
Keller	G			mr	f	m		
Kellner	G			mp				
Kentucky Thornless	HSet	Pre 1846			s			
Kératry	HCh	1827	Péan	mr	f	m	vvig	
Kermesina	HSpn	1861	Freundlich	dr				
Kertly	G	Pre 1846		dp				
Ketten Frères	T	1882	Nabonnand	my	vf	vl	vvig	f
Killarney	HT	1898	Dickson A	mp	dbl	l	vig	vf
King	Misc	Pre 1846						
King George IV	HCh	1830	Rivers	dr	dbl		vig	
			syn Rivers' George IV					
King of Holland	C	Pre 1846		p				
King of Rome	Misc	Pre 1846		mr	f	l		
King of Sardinia	HP			lp	f	m		
King of Scots	HSpn	1803	Brown R	dp	s-d	m		
King of the Prairies	HSet	1843	Feast	mr				
King of the Purples	Misc	Pre 1846		dr		s		
King of the Reds	Misc	Pre 1846		r				
King's Acre	HP	1864	Cranston	rb	f	l	vvig	
Kingston	C	Pre 1846		lp	f	s		
Kingston de Portugal	C							
Kingstoniana	C			mp				
Kiska Rose	Sp	Pre 1846	syn r.rugosa	m				
Kleber	HCh	1872	Boyeau	mr	f	l	m	
Kleiner Liebling	Pol	1895	Schmidt J C	mp		m		
Kleiner Postillon	HMult	1886	Geschwind	lp	vdbl	s		
Klin	Ch		Laffay	dp	f	m		
Kobold	HT	1888	Geschwind	rb				
Köchling (Koechling)	G		Baumann	dp				
König Friedrich II von Danemark	HP	Pre 1840		dr	dbl	m		
König Friedrich II von Danemark, Clg	Cl HP	1840	Vogel	dr				
König Johann von Sachsen	HP	1877	Ruschpler	dp	f	m	vig	vf
König von Sachsen	G	1878	Ruschpler	mp			vig	
König von Sachsen	Ch			m	f	l		
König von Sachsen	T							
Königin Carola	HP	1890	Pollner	m				
Königin von Dänemark	A	1816	Booth	mp	vdbl	m	vig	vf
Koniginrosa	G	Pre 1791	syn Regina Dicta	m	f	m		
Kosciusko	M	1853	Robert	dr	f	m	vvig	
Kreinii	G			dr				
Kretly	G	1842	Bardou	m	f	m		
Krey	G			dr	f	m	vig	
Krinhilde	T	1893	Drögemüller	yb	f	l		m
Kronprincessin Viktoria von Preussen	B	1887	Volvert	w	vdbl	l	vig	vf
Kurtzii	T	Pre 1846						f

NAME	TYPE	YEAR	RAISER	COLOUR	BLOOM	SIZE	GROWTH	SCENT
La Bacchus	HEg	Pre 1830	Vibert	mp	vdbl	s		
		syn	Bouquet Charmant	(Descemet)				
La Bedoyère	B	Pre 1846		mr				
La Béguine	HCh	Pre 1834		m		m		
La Belle Africaine	G	Pre 1838	Prévost syn Africaine	dr	vf	s		
La Belle Auguste	D	Pre 1824	Descemet / Vibert	lp	f	l		
			syn Belle Auguste					
La Belle Distinguée	HEg	c 1820		mr	dbl	s		f
La Belle Egarée	HP	1859		lp				
La Belle Elize	G	Pre 1846		lp		l		
La Belle Marie	T	1856	Raynaud	dp		m	vig	m
La Belle Mariée	G	Pre 1846		mp	vf			
La Belle Marseillaise	N	1857	Fellemberg	dp	f	l	vvig	
		syn	Belle Marseillaise					
La Belle Mathilde	HSpn	1816	Descemet	w	s-d			m
La Belle Ninon	G	Pre 1821	Boutigny	m	f	m		
			syn Belle Ninon					
La Belle Sultane	G	1795		dr		m		
La Belle Villageoise	G	1839	Vibert	pb	dbl	s		sf
			syn Panachée Pleine					
La Belle Violette	G	Pre 1846		dr		l		
La Beresina	Misc							
La Betsi	C	1825	Vibert	lp				
La Biche	N	1832	Trouiller	w	vdbl	l	vig	vf
La Biche	T	1850	Robert	w	dbl	l	vig	
			syn Mlle de Sonbreuil					
La Bien Aimé	G	1821	syn Bien-Aimée	mr	f			m
La Bien-Aimée Hoin	N	1830	Vibert	w		s		
La Bien Trouvé	HEg	Pre 1846		w				vf
La Bonne Geneviève	HCh	1826	Chevrier / Laffay	m	f	m		
			syn Bonne Geneviève					
La Boule d'Or	T	1860	Margottin	dy	f	vl	vig	f
La Boulotte	HCh	Pre 1830	syn L'Africaine	dr	vdbl	m		
La Bouquetière	HP	1843	Laffay	lp	f	l	vig	
La Brillante	N	Pre 1846						
La Brillante	HP	1853	Roussel	rb	dbl	vl	vig	vf
		syn	Général Jacqueminot					
La Brillante	HP	1861	Verdier V	mr	dbl	l	vig	
La Brillante	Ch			dp				
La Brune	G							
La Bruyère	HP	1853	Robert	mr				
La Caille	M	1857	Robert & Moreau	mp	f			
La Calaisienne	C		Vibert	mp				
La Caleta	T	1893	Pries	mp				
La Candeur	HP	1849	Vibert	lp	f	m	vig	
La Capricienne	G	1831	Vibert	dp		m		
La Cendrée	HP			lp				
La Centfeuilles Prolifère Foliacée	C	Pre 1824		mp	f	l		vf
		syn	Prolifera de Redouté					
La Cerise	Misc	Pre 1846		mr				
La Chanson	T	1890	Nabonnand	lp				
La Charmante	Ch	Pre 1834	Laffay	mp	f	s	vig	
La Chérie	C			mp				
La Chérie	D	Pre 1846		lp				
La Chérie	HP	Pre 1870		mp	f	l		
La Chérie	N	Pre 1834		lp		s		
La Chinoise	Misc	1840	syn Fortuniana	w	dbl			
La Chinoise	Cl		syn Anemonaeflora	lp				
La Chinoise	Ch		Laffay	w				
La Circassienne	C	1821	Vibert	lp	f	l		
La Cocarde	G	Pre 1790	Descemet	mp	f	m		m
			syn La Majestueuse					
La Cocarde	G	Pre 1790	syn L'Évêque	m	dbl			m
La Comète	HP	Pre 1870		mp	f	l		
La Comtesse	G	Pre 1830	Prévost	dp	vf	m		
			syn La Terminale					
La Constance	D	Pre 1830	Vibert syn Constance	mp	f	vl		
La Constance	G	1817		lp				
La Convenable	G	Pre 1830		mp	f	m		
La Coquette	D	Pre 1750	syn Celsiana	lp	s-d	l	vig	m
La Coquette	G/C	Pre 1815	Descemet	lp	dbl	l		
			syn Porcelaine					
La Coquette	Ch		Laffay	mr	f	s		
La Coquette	HP	1864	Joubert	mp	f	m	vig	
La Coquette de Cannes	HP	see	Cannes la Coquette					
La Coquette de Lyon	T	1872	Ducher	ly		m		
			syn Coquette de Lyon					
La Coquette de Marly-le-Roy	B	1863	Cagneux	w				
La Coquette Heureuse	Ch			mp	f	m		

Name	Class	Date	Breeder / Syn					
La Coquille	C	Pre 1830	syn Anémone	lp	s-d	m		
La Couronne des Pourpres	Ch			dr	f	m		
La Couronne du Président	G			dr	f	l		
La Couronne Tendre	G			lp	dbl	s		
La Croix d'Honneur	HCh	1852	Dorisy syn Croix d'Honneur	w	dbl	l		
La Curieuse	T			ly	f	m	m	
La Dame Blanche	D	Pre 1834	Laffay	w				
La Dauphine	HCh	Pre 1846		lp		l		
La Délicatesse	M		Miellez	lp				
La Délicieuse	G	Pre 1830	Vibert	lp	dbl	m-l	vig	
La Delphinie	M	Pre 1846	syn Delphinie	mp	dbl	s		
La Désirée	G	c 1810	Descemet					
La Désirée	N	Pre 1846		w				
La Désirée	HCh	Pre 1848		mp	f	s		
La Diaphane	M	1848	Laffay	lp	vdbl	l	m	
La Digittaire	C	Pre 1759	syn Childing	mp		l		
La Digittaire	C	Pre 1824	Prévost syn Prolifera de Redouté	mp	f	l		vf
La Divinité	D	1820	Godefroy syn Damas Violacé	lp	vf	m		
La Dominante	G		Miellez	lp	f	l		
La Duchesse	G	1838		mp				
La Duchesse de Morny	HP	1863	Verdier E	mp	dbl	l	vig	
La Esmeralda	HP	1862	Fontaine syn Esmeralda	mp	f	m		
La Favorite	G	c 1815	Descemet	mr				
La Favorite (des Dames)	D	Pre 1830	Vibert	lp	f	s		
La Favorite	HP	1871	Guillot	lp	dbl	m		f
La Félicité	D	Pre 1810	Dupont	dp	s-d	m		
La Félicité	C		Prévost	w	s-d	m		
La Ferté	HP							
La Fiancée	D	Pre 1846	Robert	w	f	m		
La Fiancée d'Abydos	T			w	f	m	vig	
La Fidèle	C	Pre 1834		lp		l		
La Fille de l'Air	C	Pre 1846		lp		l		
La Flamboyante	G	Pre 1830	Godefroy	dr	f	s-m		
La Florifère	B	1846	Bougère	dp	f	m	vig	
La Florifère	M	1861	Robert & Moreau	mr				
La Florifère	B	1865	Soupert	mp				
La Florifère	T	1872	Ducher syn Le Florifère	mp	f	m	vig	
La Fontaine	G	c 1815	Descemet	mr	f	l		
La Fontaine	HCh			dr				
La Fontaine	D		Vibert	lp	f	s		
La Fontaine	HP	1845	Vibert	mr	f	m	wk	
La Fontaine	G	1846	Vibert	mp	dbl	m		
La Fontaine	HP	1847	Laffay	lp	f	m		
La Fontaine	M	1851	Robert	lp	f	l	vig	
La Fontaine	HP	1855	Guinoiseau	mp	f	l	vig	
La Fontaine	HP	1871	Guillot	mr	f	l	vig	
La Fontaine	HT	1899	Schwartz	mp	dbl	l		
La Fraîcheur	Ch	1858	Moreau-Robert	lp	s-d		m	
La Fraîcheur	HT	1891	Pernet-Ducher	w				
La France	HP	1867	Guillot et Fils	lp	f	vl	vig	vf
La France à Fleurs Blanches	HT	1889	Guinoiseau Fils syn Augustine Guinoiseau	lp	f	l		
La France à Fleurs Panachées	HT	1890	Veysset syn M me Angélique Veysset	pb	dbl	l		
La France à Fleurs Rouges	HT	1888	Paul W syn Duchess of Albany	dp	f	vl		
La France, Climbing	Cl HT	1893	Henderson P	lp	dbl	l	vig	vf
La France de Quatre Vingt Neuf (89)	Cl HT	1889	Moreau-Robert	mr	vdbl	vl	vvig	
La Gaillarde	C	Pre 1830	Vibert (syn Carnée)	lp	vdbl	m		
La Gaufrée	Ch	1823	syn À Petals Striées	mr	vdbl	m		
La Georgienne	C	Pre 1830	Laffay	lp	f	m		
La Georgienne	HCh	Pre 1830	syn Formidable	lp	vf	m-l		
La Glacée	G	Pre 1830	Vibert syn Uniflore	lp	f	m		
La Globuleuse	HP	1862	Crousse	lp	f	vl		
La Gloire des Jardins	G	1815	Descemet	m	dbl	l		
La Gloire des Laurencias	HCh	Pre 1829	Miellez	dr	f	s		
La Glorieuse	G	Pre 1820	Descemet syn Illustre	pb	f	m		
La Glorieuse (same as above?)	G	Pre 1830	Godefroy	lp	f	m		
La Glorieuse	G	Pre 1830	Calvert	m	vf	s		
La Gracieuse	G	Pre 1820	Descemet syn Illustre	pb	f	m		
La Gracieuse	P	Pre 1830		lp	vf	m		
La Gracieuse	M	Pre 1843	Hardy syn Celina	m	dbl	l		
La Gracieuse	B	Pre 1846		mp				
La Grand Obscurité	G	Pre 1820	Descemet syn Passe-Velours	m	dbl	m		
La Grande Junon	G	Pre 1811	Miellez syn Minerve	dp				

Name	Type	Year	Raiser / Synonym					
La Grande Violette	G	1811	syn Roxelane	dp	s-d			
La Grandesse	Misc	Pre 1846						
La Grandeur	HCh	Pre 1846		mp				
La Grandeur	T	1878	Nabonnand	m	f	vl	vig	
La Grandeur	HT	1894	Pernet-Ducher	my	dbl	vl		
La Guirlande	HSem			w				
La Haitienne	HCh		Laffay	dr	f	m		
La Jeune Fille	D		Vibert	w				
La Jeannette	G		Descemet					
La Jonquille	T	1871	Ducher	my	s-d	m	m	
La Juive	G			dp		l		
La Julie	G	Pre 1815	Descemet					
La Laitière	D		Miellez syn Petite Laponne	lp	f	m		
La Laponne	HCh	Pre 1829		mp		s		
La Libération	B	1872	Pradel	dr				
La Lilacée	HP		Lacharme	lp				
La Liliputienne	HCh	Pre 1829	Miellez	dp	f	s		
La Louise	C	Pre 1810	Dupont	m	s-d			
La Louise	G	1840	Parmentier	dr	f	m		f
La Lune	T	1878	Nabonnand	ly	dbl	vl	vig	
La Maculée	G	1810	Dupont	pb	s-d	m-l		f
La Madeleine	HP	1881	Nabonnand	dr	f	vl	m	
La Madeline	B	Pre 1846		w		l		
La Magnanime	HP		syn Monstreux					
La Magnifique	G	Pre 1811	syn Pourpre Charmant	m	dbl	vl		m
La Majestueuse	N			w				
La Majestueuse	G	Pre 1790	Vibert / Descemet syn La Cocarde	mr	f	m		m
La Majestueuse	Misc	Pre 1846		mp				
La Marseillaise	Misc			lp				
La Meldoise	HCh			mp	f	l		
La Mère de St Louis	HP	1851	Lacharme syn Mère de St Louis	w	dbl	m		
La Mère Gigogne	G	Pre 1815	Descemet					
La Mère Gigogne	C	c 1820	Vibert	lp	f	m		
La Mère Gigogne	Ch	c 1830	Vibert	dp	vf	m		
La Merveille	G	Pre 1820	Descemet					
La Mienne	HP	Pre 1834	Vibert syn Flon	mr		m		
La Mignonne	HP	1876	Soupert & Notting	mr				
La Minerve	G		Descemet					
La Miniature	Min	Pre 1834		dp		vs		
La Miniature	C/M	Pre 1830	Robert	lp		s		
La Moderne	P	Pre 1820	syn Portland à Fleur Dbl.	lp	dbl	l		
La Moskowa	G	Pre 1834		m		m		
La Mouche	HCh	Pre 1830	Miellez	dp	f	s		
La Nankeen	T	1871	Ducher	yb	f	l		
La Nantaise	HArv							
La Nantaise	HP	1885	Boisselet	dr	f	l	m	
La Napolitaine	G	Pre 1826	Calvert / Descemet syn Charles X	mr	f	m		
La Napolitaine	G	Pre 1838	Crammwell syn Ulysse	mr				
La Nationale	G	Pre 1835		pb	dbl	m		
La Négresse	G	Pre 1810	Dupont syn Superbe en Brun	m	dbl	m		
La Négresse	D	1842	Vibert	dr	f	m	s	
La Neige	HSpn	Pre 1846		w				
La Neige	G	1853	Robert	w	f		vig	f
La Neige	T	1888	Perny	w				
La Neige	Ch	1894	Reboul	w				
La Neustrienne	HP	1877	Oger	lp				
La Neuville	N			lp				
La Nina	G	c 1810	Descemet					
La Ninette	N	1894	Puyravaud	mp				
La Noble Fleur	G	c 1810	Vibert / Descemet syn Pelletier	lp	f	m		
La Noblesse	C	1856	Pastoret / Soupert	lp	dbl	l		vf
La Nouvelle Redouté	Misc	1818	Vibert	mr		l		
La Nuancée	T	1875	Guillot	w	f	m		
La Nubienne	HCh	1825	Laffay	m	f	m		
La Nymphe	T	Pre 1830	Laffay	lp	f	l		
La Nymphe Echo	N	Pre 1834		lp		s		
La Palée	Misc	Pre 1846						
La Panachée	Sp	Pre 1581	syn r.gallica versicolor	pb	s-d			m
La Parisienne	HP	Pre 1830		lp	f	m		
La Parisienne	G							
La Petite Duchesse	HEg	c 1820		mr	dbl	s		f
			syn La Belle Distinguée					
La Peyrouse	HP	1854	Robert	dr	f	l		

La Philippine	HCh	1816	Vibert	dr	s-d	m		
La Phocéenne	HP	1862	Geoffre	dp	f	l		
La Pivoine	HP	1862	Robert & Moreau	mr	f	l		
La Plaisante	HP			mp				
La Planète	A	Pre 1830						
La Plus Belle	Ch			mp				
La Plus Belle des Panachées	G		as below					
La Plus Belle des Ponctuées	G	1829		pb	dbl	m	vvig	f
La Plus Belle des Violettes	G	Pre 1830	Calvert	m	vf	s		
La Plus Élégante	G	Pre 1811		dp				m
		syn	Cramoisi Triumphante					
			Parmentier					
La Porte	G			mp				
La Possédée	G			dr				
La Précieuse	D			lp				
La Prédestinée	G	Pre 1820	Descemet syn Illustre	pb	f	m		
La Prédestinée (same as above?)	G	1825	Godefroy	dp	f	m		
La Princesse	G	Pre 1830	Prévost	mr	f	m		
La Princesse Vera	T	1877	Nabonnand	w	vf	l		
La Prospérine	HMult	1897	Ketten	op	dbl	m		m
La Provence	G	Pre 1819		dr				
La Pucelle	G	Pre 1811	Dubourg	r	f	s-m		
La Pucelle	G	Pre 1828	Miellez	pb	f	m-l		
			syn Pucelle de Lille					
La Pucelle d' Orléans	HP							
La Pudeur	B	Pre 1830	Laffay (syn below?)	lp	f	s-m		
La Pudeur	B	1853	De Fauw (syn above?)	w	f	l		
La Pyramidale	G/C	Pre 1815	Descemet	lp	dbl	l		
			syn Porcelaine					
La Quintinie	HCh	Pre 1848		m		vl		
La Quintinie	B	1853	Thomas	dp	f	l	vig	
La Quintinine	HCh	Pre 1846		lp				
La Ravissante	G			mp				
La Régulière	Ch	Pre 1830		mr		s		
La Reine	HP	1842	Laffay M	mp	f	l	vig	m
La Reine de la Pape	HP	1863	Guillot	m	vdbl	vl		
			syn Reine de la Pape					
La Reine de Provence	C	1824		mp	dbl	vl	vvig	m
		Syn	Reine de Centfeuilles					
La Reine des Primprenelles	HSpn	1821	Vibert	mp		s		
La Remarkable	A	Pre 1833		w	f	m		
La Renommée	T	Pre 1846		w				
La Renommée	Ch							
La Revenante	G	1825	Miellez	mp	dbl			
La Rochefoucault	G	1825	Coquerel	lp		l		
La Rochefoucault-Liancourt	HCh	1825	Vibert	mr	f	m		
La Rochefoucault-Liancourt	G	1825	Coquerel	pb	vf	vl		
La Rochefoucault-Liancourt	D	Pre 1830	Lecomte	dp	f	m	vvig	
La Rose de York	A	Pre 1600		w	s-d	m	m	
		syn	White Rose of York					
La Rosière	HP	1851	Lartay	w				
La Rosière	HP	1861	Verdier E	dr	vf	l	vig	vf
		syn Pri-	nce Camille de Rohan					
La Rosière	HP	1874	Damaizan	dr	dbl	m		
La Roxelane	G	1828	Vibert	m				
La Royale	A	Pre 1738		w	Dbl			vf
		syn	Great Maiden's Blush					
La Royale	A	Pre 1770	syn Plena	w	s-d			
La Royale	A	Pre 1830	Vibert	lp	f	m		
			syn Cuisse de Nymphe					
La Rubanée	G	Pre 1832	Vibert (?)	pb	vdbl			m
La Rubanée	C	1845		dr				
La Sanguine	Ch	Pre 1818	syn Sanguinea	dr	vdbl	m	wk/sp	
La Sarmenteuse	N	1827	Vibert	lp		s		
La Saumonnée	HCh	1877	Margottin Fils	op	f	l		
La Savannaise	HCh		Laffay	dr				
La Séduisante	A	Pre 1738		lp	dbl	m	vig	vf
		syn	Great Maiden's Blush					
La Séduisante	A	Pre 1830	Vibert	lp	f	m-l		
La Séduisante	HP	1850	Lacharme (Portemer)	mr				
La Séduisante	T	1888	syn Virginale	lp	f	m		
La Sentitienne	N		Laffay	w				
La Sirène	HP	1867	Soupert & Notting	m	dbl	l		
La Somptueuse	G		Racine	lp				
La Souveraine	HP	1874	Verdier E	mp	f	vl	vig	m
			syn Grand Edouard					
La Soyeuse	D			lp				
La Spaendonck	HCh	Pre 1830	Cels	m	vdbl	m		
La Splendeur	G	Pre 1846		mr				
La Sultane Favorite	Misc							
La Superbe	G	Pre 1830	Vibert	dp	f	m		
		syn	Couronne Impériale					

Name	Type	Date	Raiser / Synonym					
La Superbe	M		Miellez	mr				
La Superbe	Ch	Pre 1830		m				
La Superbe	B	Pre 1846		lp		l		
La Superbe	HP			mp				
La Surprise	G							
La Surprise	A	1823	Poilpré	w	vdbl	s		
La Sybille	B			lp				
La Sylphide	T	1838	Vibert	ly	s-d	l		
La Sylphide	T	1842	Boyau	m	s-d			f
La Syrène	HP	1874	Touvais	mr	f	l		
La Tendresse	G	Pre 1820	Dupont	m				
La Tendresse	HP	1864	Oger	mp	f	l		
La Tendresse	N			mp				
La Tenterelle	HCh		syn Belle de Parny	m				
La Terminale	G			dr				
La Terminale	Pom		Dupont	mr				
La Toulousaine	HP	1877	Brassac	lp	f	m		
La Tour d'Auvergne	G	1842	Vibert	rb	dbl	l		
La Tour de Crouy	HP	1862	Fontaine	lp	f	l		
La Tourterelle	HCh	Pre 1846		w				
La Transparente	C	Pre 1811	Vilmorin syn Unique Carnée	lp	f	m		m
La Très Haute	G	Pre 1811	syn Aigle Brun	dr	s-d			
La Très Sombre	G	1820						
La Triomphante	G	Pre 1820	Descemet syn Illustre	pb	f	m		
La Triomphante	Ch		syn La Superbe	m				
La Triomphante	C	Pre 1830	syn Justine	lp	vdbl	m		
La Tulipe	T	1868	Ducher	w	s-d	l	vig	f
La Vaillante Bergère	HP	1847	Cherpin	dp	f	m		
La Valoise	HP	1850	Vigneron	mp				
La Variable	C	Pre 1759	syn Childing	mp		l		
La Variable	Ch		Vibert	rb				
La Vénitienne	G	Pre 1830						
La Vestale	A	Pre 1830	Vibert	w	vdbl	m		
La Vestale	C	1831	Vibert	w		m		
La Veuve	G	Pre 1830	Prévost	dr	f	m		
La Victoire	G	Pre 1830	Vibert syn Uniflore	lp	f	m		
La Victoire	Ch	Pre 1834		dp		s		
La Victoire	HP	1862	Maréchal Vaillant	r				
La Victoireuse	N	Pre 1846		lp		m		
La Vierge	N	1829	Vibert	w		s		
La Vierzonnaise	HP	1893	André	lp				
La Villageoise	G	1823	Vibert	lp	dbl	l		
La Villageoise	G	1839	Vibert syn Panachée Pleine	pb	dbl	s		sf
La Ville de Bruxelles	D	1836	Vibert	mp	vdbl	m	vig	vf
La Ville de Gand	G		Robert	mp				
La Ville de Londres	G	Pre 1844	Vibert	dp	f	vl		
La Ville de Saint Denis	HP	1853	Thomas syn Ville de Saint Denis	mp	f	l	m	
La Vineuse	HEg	Pre 1830	Prévost syn La Bacchus	lp	vdbl	s		
La Virginale	A	Pre 1738	syn Great Maiden's Blush	w	dbl			vf
La Virginale	D	Pre 1811	Descemet syn Beauté Virginale	w	f	m		
La Virginale	HP	1858	Lacharme	w	dbl	m		
La Volumineuse	P	Pre 1835		lp		l		
La Volupté	G	Pre 1828	Bizard	dp	f	l	m	
La Zulinée	Misc	Pre1846						
L'Abbandonata	HMult	1846	Laffay M syn Lauré Davoust	lp	dbl	s		
Labbey de Pompières	G	1827	Prévost	mp	f	l		f
Labedoyère	HP	Pre 1870		dr	f	l	vig	
L'Abondance	HP	1864	Verdier E	mr				
L'Abondance	N	1877	Moreau-Robert	w	f	m		
L'Abondant	HP	1864	Trouillard	mp	f	l		
Laborde	G	1823	Vibert	lp		m		
Labrador Rose	Sp	1773	syn r.blanda	mp	s			
Lacépède	HP	1865	Verdier Ch	dp	f	l		
Lactance	HCh	1853	Robert	dr	f	l	vig	
Lactance	N	Pre 1846		w	f	m		m
Lactea	C			w				
Lactea Grandiflora	T			w				
Lactens	N	Pre 1870		w		m		
Lacteola	C	1775	Grimwood syn White Provence	w	dbl	l		m
Ladies' Favorite	Misc	Pre 1846						
L'Admirable	G/C	Pre 1787	syn Admirable	lp	f	m		
L'Admirable Blanc Bordé Rouge	G			w	f	m		
L'Admiration	D	Pre 1830	Vibert	lp	f	m		

L'Admiration	Ch	1856	Robert	mp	s		m		
Lady Alice	HT	1887	Paul G	lp					
Lady Alice Peel	HP	1842	Laffay	mr	f		l		vf
Lady Arthur Hill	HP	1889	Dickson	lp	f		l		
Lady Baillie	HSpn	Pre 1848	Lee	ly	s-d				
Lady Balcombe	Ch		Laffay	lp	dbl		l		
Lady Banks	HSpn			mp					
Lady Banks Rose	Sp	1807		w	dbl		s		
		syn	r.banksiae banksiae						
Lady Blusch	HSpn			mr					
Lady Brisbane	Ch	1832	Coquereau	mr	dbl		s	vig	
		syn	Cramoisi Supérieur						
Lady Brisbane, Climbing	Ch	1885	Couturier	mr	s-d		m		
		syn	Cramoisi Supérieur,	Climbing					
Lady Byron	N	Pre 1846							
Lady Canning	B	Pre 1846	Miellez	pb	f		l	vvig	
Lady Castlereagh	T	1887	Dickson	yb	f		vl	vig	
Lady Compton	HSpn			m					
Lady Dorothea	T	1898	Dunlop	pb					
Lady Einch Hatton	HSpn	see	Lady Finck Holton						
Lady Elphinstone	HP			mr	f		l	vig	
Lady Emily Peel	HP	1862	Lacharme	w	f		l	vig	
Lady Finck Holton	HSpn	1829		m	s-d		l		f
Lady Fitzgerald	G	1827	Noisette L	w	vdbl		l		
Lady Fitzharris	HCh		Laffay	pb	f		l		
Lady Fordwich	HP	1838	Laffay	mr	f		m	vig	
Lady Granville	B	Pre 1846		dp					
Lady Granville	HT			lp	f		m		
Lady Hamilton	B			m	f		l	vig	
Lady Helen Stewart	HP	1887	Dickson A	dr	dbl		s	vig	vf
Lady Henry Grosvenor	HT	1892	Bennett	lp	f		l	vig	
Lady Loch	HT	1885	Johnson						
Lady Macbeth	G		Parmentier	mp	f		m		
Lady Mary Fitzwilliam	HT	1882	Bennett	lp	f		l	wk	vf
Lady Milson	HP	1852	Ducher	m	f		m	vig	
Lady Milton	T			lp	f		m		
Lady Fitzgerald	D	Pre 1846		mp					
Lady Montague	B	1847	Laffay	mp	f		m	vvig	
Lady Montgomery	B	Pre 1846		lp			l		
Lady Morgan	G		Girardon	mp	vf		l	vvig	
Lady of the Lake	Ch	Pre 1846		w					
Lady of the Lake	HP	1884	Paul W	pb	f		l	vig	
Lady Penzance	HEg	1894	Penzance	op	s		m	vvig	f
Lady Roccoly	G		Parmentier	dr	f		m		
Lady Rollo	HSpn								
Lady Seymour	HP	1842	Vibert	mp	f		m		
Lady Sheffield	HP	1881	Postans	mp	f		l		
Lady Shelley	HP	1853	Mitchell	mr					
Lady Stanhope	N			lp	f		s		
Lady Stanley	B	1849	Dubos	dp	f		l		
Lady Stanley	T	1887	Nabonnand	m	dbl		vl		m
Lady Stuart	HCh	Pre 1846		dp					
Lady Stuart	HCh	1851	Portemer Fils	lp	vf		l	vig	
Lady Suffield	HP	1866	Paul W	dr	f		l	vig	
Lady Thenermill	G		syn Manteau Impérial	m					
Lady Warrender	T	1838	syn Clara Sylvain	w	f		l		
Lady Wynne	HSpn	Pre 1848		lp					
Lady Zoë Brougham	T	1886	Nabonnand	my	f		l		f
Laelia	HP	1844	Laffay	lp			m		
Laelia	HP	1857	Avoux & Crozy	mp			vl	vig	
Laetitia	G	Pre 1828	Bizard syn La Volupté	dp	f		l	m	
Laewis	Alp		syn Glabra	m					
Lafayette	N	Pre 1830	Laffay	dp	vdbl		m		
Lafayette Panaché	N		Laffay	mp	f		m		
Laffay	Ch	c 1825	Laffay	mr	f		m		
Laforcade	HP	1889	Lévêque	mr			vl		
L'Africaine	HCh	Pre 1830	Vibert	m	vdbl		m		
L'Aimable Beauté	G	Pre 1820	Prévost	lp	f		m		
			syn Nouveau Triomphe						
L'Aimable de Stors	G	1817	Vibert	dp	vf		m		
			syn Ninos de Lenclos						
L'Aimable de Stors	C	Pre 1846		mr					
L'Aimable Etrangère	HSpn	1819	Vibert	w	dbl		m		
			syn Aimable Etrangère						
Laïs	T	Pre 1870		yb	f		m		
L'Albane	D	1859	Robert & Moreau	lp					
Lamarque	N	1830	Maréchal	w	dbl		m	vvig	vf
Lamarque	HCh			mr					
Lamarque	N	Pre 1846		w	f		l	vvig	
Lamarque à Coeur Rose	N	Pre 1846		w			l		f
Lamarque Jaune	N	1869	Ducher	ly	f		m	m	
Lamartine	B	1842	Guillot	mr	f		m		

Name	Type	Year	Raiser					
Lamartine	HP	1890	Dubreuil	dp	f	m		
L'Amazone	G	Pre 1830						
L'Ambassadeur	G			mr				
L'Ami Boisset	T	1898	Puyravaud	mr				
L'Ami Devienne	HP		see Devienne Lamy					
L'Ami Loury	HP	1887	Verdier E	mr	f	l	vig	
L'Ami Maubray	HP	1890	Mercier	rb				
L'Ami Noël	HP	1886	Chauvry	mr				
L'Amitié	D	Pre 1813	Stegerhoek/Dupont	lp	s-d	l		
Lamotte Sanguin	HP	1869	Vigneron	mr	f	vl	vig	
L'Amoureuse	G	1820	Vibert	mp				
			syn Andromaque					
Lancel	M	Pre 1846	Robert	mr	f	m		
Landreth's Carmine Cluster	N	Pre 1846						
Lane	HP	1841	Laffay	dr	f	l		
Lane	M	1860	Robert	mr	f	l	vvig	
Lane	HP	Pre 1870		lp	vdbl	m		
Laneii	M	1845	Laffay	mr	dbl	l	vvig	
Languiewich	B	1863	Pradel	dr	f	m		
L'Angevine	N	Pre 1830	Vibert	lp	vdbl	vl		
Lansezeur	M	Pre 1846	Panaget	dp	f	m		
Laodicée	G	1823	Sommesson	mp	dbl	vl		
Laomédon	G		Miellez	mr	f	l		
L'Archevêque	G	Pre 1811	syn Pourpre Charmant	m	vdbl			m
Large Double Two-Coloured	HSpn	1803	Brown R	dp	s-d	m		
			syn King of Scots					
Large Fruited	M	Pre 1846		lp	s-d	l		
Large Provence	C	1583		dp				
		syn	r.centifolia batavica					
L'Argentière	Ch		Laffay	m				
Largilière	M	1855	Robert	m		vvig		
L'Arioste	N	1859	Robert & Moreau	lp		m		
Lartay	B	1851	Laffay	dr	f	m		
Lascaris	N			lp	vf	m		
Las-Casas	HCh	1828	Vibert	dp	f	l	vig	
Lass O'Gowrie	HSpn	Pre 1848		w	dbl	s	f	
Lasthénie	HCh	1829	Vibert	lp		m		
Lasthénie	A	1844	Vibert	lp	f	m	vig	
L'Astrolabe	Ch		syn Rose de l'Est	lp				
Latone	G	1829	Vibert	lp	vf	l		
Latone	M	Pre 1870	Paul W	dp	f	l	vig	
L'Attrayante	HP	1847	Laffay	lp	f	m		
Laura	C	Pre 1836		mp	f	l		
Lauré Audenet	G		Godefroy	lp				
Lauré Brémont	T	1884	Guillot	m	vf	l		
Lauré Davoust	HMult	1834	Laffay M	lp	dbl	s	vvig	f
Lauré de Fénélon	T	1884	Nabonnand	mr	dbl	l	vvig	
Lauré de Saint-Martin	T	1863	Pradel	lp	f	m		
Lauré Dubourg	B	1850	Pradel	mr	f	l		
Lauré Dupont	HSpn							
Lauré Fontaine	T	1867	Fontaine	w	f	l	vvig	
Lauré Nankin	HSpn			pb				
Lauré Ramaud	N	1849	Lacharme	lp	f	l		
Laurence	Misc	1826	Vétillard	m				
Laurence Allen	HP	1896	Cooling	mp	f	l	vig	vf
Laurence de Montmorency	HP	Pre 1846		lp	f	l	vvig	vf
Laurent Carle	HP	1889	Verdier E	mp				
Laurent de Rillé	HP	1885	Lévèque	mr	dbl	l	vig	m
Laurent Descourt	HP	1862	Liabaud	m	f	m	m	
Laurent Heister	P	1859	Robert & Moreau	mr				
Laurentia Double	Ch	Pre 1830	Vibert	mp	f	vs	wk	
Laurentia Nain	Ch	Pre 1830	Laffay	mp	vdbl	vs	wk	
Laurentia Simple	Ch	Pre 1830	Noisette L	mp	s	vs	wk	
Laurentiana Alba	Ch	1827	Mauget	w				
Laurentius	HP	1863	Verdier	dr	f	m		
Laurette	T	1853	Robert	lp	dbl	l	vig	
Lauriol de Barny	HP	1866	Trouillard	rb		l		
L'Aurore du Guide	B	Pre 1870		mr	f	m		
L'Aurore du Matin	HP	1867	Rolland	mp		vl		
Lavalette	D	1823	Vibert	dp	f	m		
Lavalette	G/C	Pre 1830	Cartier / Prévost	lp	f	m		
Lavallière	M	1851	Robert	lp				
Lavaquerie	HCh	1851	Robert	m				
L'Avenir	B	1858	Lartay syn Avenir	mp	f	l	vig	
Lavinie	G/C	1831	Vibert	lp		l		
Lavinie Dariule	T			w	f	l		
Lavinie d'Ost	B	Pre 1846		lp	vf	l	vvig	
Lavoisier	D	1857	Robert & Moreau	w				
Lavoisier	G/C	Pre 1830	Lecomte	m	f	m		
Lays	N	c 1860	Guillot	lp	f	m	wk	m
Lays	T	1863	Damaizin	my	f	m	vig	
Le Ballon	G	Pre 1830						

Name	Type	Date	Breeder / Synonym					
Le Baron de Rothschild	HP	1862	Guillot Syn Baron de Rothschild	m	f	l		m
Le Baron Louis	G	Pre 1846		dp				
Le Bengale à Bouquets	Ch	1770	Slater Syn Slater's Crimson China	mr	dbl		m	
Le Bienheureux de la Salle	B	1880	Garçon Syn Mme Isaac Pereire	dp	dbl	l	vig	vf
Le Bignonia	T	1873	Levet	ob				
Le Brun	B	Pre 1834		lp		m		
Le Cafre	G			dr	f	m		
Le Camée	B	1845	Béluze	m	f	m	vig	
Le Camoens	Ch	Pre 1846		lp				
Le Cordon Bleu	G			mr				
Le Deuil	G	Pre 1830	syn La Veuve	dr	f	m		
Le Deux Décembre	B	1852	Pradel	lp	f	m		
Le Diable Boiteux	G			lp	f	l		
Le Fakir	T	Pre 1830	Laffay	dp	dbl	m		f
Le Flavia Bleuatre	G	Pre 1846		lp				
Le Florifère	T	1872	Ducher	mp	f	m	vig	
Le Florifère	HP	1873	Faudon	dp				
Le Futur Empereur des Français	B			mr				
Le Géant	HP	1863	Bruant	dp	f	vl		
Le Goufre	Ch	syn	Cramoisi Supérieur	mr				
Le Grand Alexandre	G							
Le Grand Dauphin	G	Pre 1824	Prévost syn Enfant de France	lp	f	s-m		
Le Grand Lowendal	Misc	Pre 1834		dp		m		
Le Grand Sultan	G	Pre 1815	Descemet	m	vdbl	l		
Le Grand Sultan	C	Pre 1834	Robert	mp		vl		
Le Grand Triomphe	G	Pre 1818	Lille syn Nouvelle Pivoine	m		l		
Le Grand Triomphe	C	Pre 1830	Vibert syn Le Triomphe	mr	f	l		
Le Gras St Germain	A	Pre 1846 syn Mme Legras de St Germain		w	vdbl	l	vig	m
Le Grelot	B	1855	Robert	rb				
Le Grenadier	B	1843	Verdier V	mr				
Le Havre	HP	1870	Eudes	mr	dbl	l	vig	f
Le Jacobin	G	1898	Corboeuf-Marsault syn Marcel Bourgouin	m	dbl	l		vf
Le Jeune Âge	M		Robert	lp				
Le Jeune Roi Dauphin	G	Pre 1824	Prévost syn Enfant de France	lp	f	s-m		
Le Juif Errant	HP	1862	Granger	dr	f	l		
Le Khédive	HP	1882	Barrault / Verdier E syn Tewfik	rb	f	m-l	vig	
Le Lobèrde	M			mp	vdbl	m		
Le Loiret	HP	1882	Ribault	mr	f	vl	vvig	
Le Majestueuse	G	Pre 1790	syn Majestueuse	lp	f			m
Le Météore	HCh	Pre 1846	Thierry	mr	dbl	vl		
Le Mont Blanc	T	1870	Ducher	ly	f	l	m	
Le Mont d'Or	T	1863	Ducher	w	f	l	vig	f
Le Nankin	T	1871	Ducher	yb	vf	m	vig	f
Le Pactole	T	Pre 1841	Miellez	ly	dbl	l	m	
Le Pactole	HP			mp				
Le Pérou	G	Pre 1826	Gossard / Parmentier	dr	f	m		
Le Phoenix	G	1843	Vibert	mp	vdbl	l		
Le Phoenix	B			mr				
Le Président	Sp	1789	syn r.rubrifolia	mp				
Le Président	HArv			dp	f	s		
Le Président	T	1833	Adam syn Adam	mp	dbl			vf
Le Prince	G	Pre 1846	syn The Prince	mr				
Le Prince des Galles	P	Pre 1826		dp	f	m		
Le Prince de Salm Dick	P	1852	Robert	mr				
Le Prince Régent	G			dp				
Le Rhône	HP	1862	Guillot Fils	mr	f	l	m	
Le Rire Niais	C	Pre 1810	Dupont	mp	f	m		m
Le Roi de Siam	Cl T	1825	Laffay M syn Roi de Siam	lp	s-d	l		m
Le Roi des Pourpres	G		Descemet	mr	f	vl		
Le Roitelet	B	1869	Soupert & Notting	mp	dbl	s		
Le Rosier Aurore Poniatowska	A	Pre 1810	syn Celestial	lp	dbl	l	vig	vf
Le Rosier de Philippe Noisette	N	1814	Noisette syn r x noisettiana	w				
Le Rosier Évêque	G	Pre 1790 syn L'Évêque & The Bis-hop		m	vdbl	m		m
Le Rosier Pompon Blanc	C	Pre 1824 syn Rose de Meaux White		w				
Le Royal Époux	HP	1859	Damaizin syn Royal Époux	mp	f	l		
Le Seigneur d'Artzelane	Misc	Pre 1846		dr				

Name	Class	Date	Breeder / Syn					
Le Shah	HP	1874	Paul G syn The Shah	mr				
Le Soleil	G			mr	f	m-l		
Le Soleil	T	1891	Dubreuil	my	vf	vl	vvig	
Le Solitaire	G			lp	f	l		
Le Solitaire	N			lp				
Le Styx	G		Parmentier	dr				
Le Tasse	G		Parmentier	dr	f	m		
Le Titien	HP	1852	Miellez	mp	f	l		
Le Triomphe	D	Pre 1790	syn Majestueuse	lp	f	m		m
Le Triomphe	C	1817	Godefroy	m	f	l		
Le Triomphe	G	1819-20	Vibert syn Aimable Rouge	dp	vdbl	m	m	m
Le Triomphe de Lille	D	Pre 1830	Vibert	lp	f	m		
Le Triomphe de Saintes	HP	1885	Derouet	mr	vf	l		sf
Le Troubadour	HCh	Pre 1846		mr				
Le Vésuve	Ch	1825	Laffay M	dp	vdbl	l	vig	f
Le Vineux	HCh	Pre 1830	Cugnot syn Dieudonné	dp	dbl	m		
Le Vingt-Neuf Juillet	HCh	Pre 1836		dr	f	l	vig	
Léa	G	c 1825	Vétillard	dp	f	l		
Lea Lévêque	B	1887	Lévêque	w	f	l	vig	
Léandre	G	c 1825	Calvert syn Pelletier	lp	f	m		
Leatherleaf Rose	Sp	1878	syn r.coriifolia	lp				
Leblanc	D							
L'Éblouissante	Ch	1823	Vibert syn Cramoisi Éblouissante	mr	f	m	m	
L'Éblouissante (see Éblouissante)	Ch	Pre 1830	Laffay syn Cramoisi Supérieur	dr		s		
L'Éblouissante	HP	1852	Touvias	mp	f	l	vig	
L'Éblouissante	M	1853	Robert	mr	dbl	l		
L'Éblouissante de La Queue	G	c 1820		dr	vdbl	l		
Lebrun	Ch		Laffay	dp	f	m		
Lebrun	P	1862	Robert & Moreau	dp				
L'Écarlate	HP	1857	Margottin	m				
Lechenaultiana	HArv							
L'Éclair	B			mr				
Léclatant	Ch		Prévost	mr				
L'Éclatante	HP	1862	Guillot	rb	vdbl	m	vig	
Lecoq Dumesnil	HP	1882	Verdier E	mr	vdbl	vl	vvig	m
Lecomte-Bocquet	HP	1884	Singer	dp	f	l	vvig	
L'Écossaise	Ch		Laffay	m	f	s		
Léda	T			w	f	l		
Léda	D	1826	Deschiens	w	dbl	s	vig	m
Léda	D		(Pink sport of above)	lp	dbl	s	vig	m
Ledonneaux-Leblanc	G	Pre 1834		w	f	l		
Ledru-Rollin	B		Pradel	mr				
Lee	G	1823	Vibert	mp	f	l		
Lée	G	c 1825	Vetillard syn Léa	dp	f	l		
Lée	N	Pre 1830	Prévost	lp	vdbl	l	vvig	sf
Lee	P	1827	Vibert syn Perpetuelle earlier	lp	dbl	m		m
Leea Rubra	C	1899 or Pre 1846		w	f	l		
Lee's Blush Perpetual	B			mr				
Lee's Crimson Perpetual	P	1815	Lelieur-Souchet syn Rose du Roi	mr	s-d	l	vig	vf
Lee's Duchess	HEg	c 1820	syn La Belle Distinguée Noisette L	mr	dbl	m		m
Légère	N		Robert	w		s		
Legouvé	B	Pre 1846	Robert	mr	f	l		
Leila	D	1826	Deschiens syn Léda	w	dbl	m		m
L'Élégante	G		Hardy	lp	vdbl	l	vig	
L'Élégante	N	Pre 1830		mp		s		
L'Élégante	HP	1847	Laffay syn Élégante	lp	f	l		
L'Élégante	HP	1862		mp	f	m		
L'Élégante	T	1882	Guillot Fils	pb	f	m-l	m	f
Lelia	HP	Pre 1870		mp	f	l		
Lelieur	P	Pre 1830		mr	vdbl	m		
Lelieur	B/Ch	Pre 1846	Laffay	lp	dbl	m		
Lelieur	N	Pre 1846		rb	f	m		
Lelieur	D		Lelieur	lp				
Lemercier	Ch		Laffay	mr				
Lemesle	Ch	1825	Laffay M syn Le Vésuve	pb	vdbl	l	vig	
Léna Turner	HP	1869	Verdier E	rb	f	l		
L'Enchantée	G		Miellez	lp	f	vl		
L'Enchantresse	G	Pre 1824	François	mp	f	l		
L'Enfant de France	G	Pre 1824	Prévost syn Enfant de France	lp	f	s-m		
L'Enfant du Mont Carmel	HP	1851	Cherpin	dp	f	l		
L'Enfant Trouvé	T	1861	Lartay syn Enfant Trouvé & Élisa Sauvage	mp		l		

Lenfroy	G	1836	Joly	mp	s-d	l		
Leocadie	G		Hardy	lp	vdbl	l	vig	
Léon de Bruyn	T	1895	Soupert & Notting	ly	f	l		m
Léon Delaville	HP	1885	Verdier E	dr	f	l		
Léon de Saint-Jean	HP			mr				
Léon Duval	HP	1879	Lévêque	dr	f	l	vvig	
Léon Félix Bigot	T			mp	f	l		
Léon Haymann	HP	1855	Lartay	mp	f	l		
Léon Lecomte	D	c 1854		dp	f	l		m
Léon Legay	HP	1851	Marrest	dr	f	l		
Léon Oursel	B	1847	Oger	dp	f	l		
Léon Plée	HP	1852	Laffay	mp	f	m		
Léon Renault	HP	1878	Ledéchaux	mr	vdbl	vl	vig	
Léon Say	HP	1873	Lévêque	rb	f	vl	vig	m
		syn Souvenir	de Romain Desprez					
Léon X	G	Pre 1846		lp		vl		
Léon XIII	T	1892	Soupert & Notting	w	f	l	vig	
Léonard de Vinci	G	1861	Robert & Moreau	mp				
Léonce Bergis	B		Pradel	mp	f	m		
Léonce Moïse	HP	1859	Vigneron	mr	f	l		
Leonidas	G/Ch	Pre 1846	Sommesson	mp		l		
Léonide	G	Pre 1830		dr				
Léonide Leroy	HP		Vibert	mp				
Léonie	G			mp	f	m		
Léonie	HP	1864	Trouillard	rb				
Léonie Charmante	T	Pre 1846		w				
Léonie Lamesch	Pol	1899	Lambert P	ob	s-d	s	vig	f
Léonie Lartay	HP	1860	Lartay	mr	f	l		
Léonie Leroy	HP			w	f	m	vig	
Léonie Osterrieth	T	1893	Soupert & Notting	w	f	l		m
Léonie Verger	B	1846		mp	f	m		
Leonora (e)	HP	1848	Verdier V	mp	f	m		
Leonore d'Este	G		Vétillard	pb				
Leonore d'Este	HP	1849	Portemer	my	f	m	vvig	
Léontine	G	1823	Vibert	lp	f	l		
Léontine Fay	D	1831	Vibert	lp		m		
Léontine Laporte	T	1866	Pradel	yb	f	l		
Léopold de Beaufremont	HCh	Pre 1846		lp	f	m	vig	
Léopold Hausburg	HP	1863	Granger	pb	f	l	vvig	
Léopold Vauvel	HP	1889	Verdier E	mr				
Léopold I	HP	1863	Van Asche	dr	vdbl	vl	vig	
Léopold I	G			lp	f	l		
Léopold II	HP	1868	Margottin	lp	f	vl	vig	
Léopoldine	P	1826	Tontain	lp				
Léopoldine	M	1850	Robert	lp	f	m		
Léopoldine d'Orléans	HSem	1828	Jacques	lp	dbl	m	vig	
Lepida	Ch		Laffay	w	f	m		
L'Ermite	Ch	c 1826	syn below	mr	vf	m-l		
L'Ermite de Grandval	Ch	Pre 1830	Prévost syn De Rennes	mr	vf	m-l		
L'Ermite du Mont Cindre	Ch			dr	f	s		
Leroux	HP		Leroux	lp	vdbl	vl		
Les Trois Mages	G	1823	Gentil	mp	vf	m		
Lesbie	N	1824	Vibert	lp	dbl			
Lesbie	HP		Vibert	lp				
Leschenault's Rose	Sp	1830	Wight & Arnott	w				
			syn r.leschenaultii					
L'Espérance	HP	1871	Lartay	pb	dbl	l	vig	
Lesponda	G	Pre 1826	Descemet	mr				
			syn Charles X					
Lesueur	P	1853	Robert	m	f	l	vvig	
L'Étincelante	HP	1875	Verdier E	mr	f	vl	vig	
L'Étincelante	HP	1891	Vigneron	mr	f	l	vig	f
Letitia	HP	1859		dp				
L'Etna	Ch	1825	Laffay M syn Etna	mp	vdbl	m		
L'Etna	M			mr	f	l		
L'Etoile	T			m				
L'Etoile	A		Soupert & Notting	lp				
Letty Coles	T	1876	Keynes	lp	dbl	l		f
Leuchtstern	HMult	1899	Kiese/Schmidt J C	pb	s	m	vvig	sf
Leukoskiorhodon	T			w				
L'Évêque	G	Pre 1790		m	dbl			m
Leweson Gower	B	1845	Béluze	op	dbl	vl		
L'Héritiana	A	1817	Vilmorin	mp	f	l	vig	
L'Héritier	A	1817	Vilmorin	dr				
L'Héritier	Ch	Pre 1830	syn Violet	m	s-d	m		
L'Héritier	Ch	Pre 1830	Desportes	dr				
Lhertieranea	Bslt	c 1810	syn Boursault Rose	mp	s-d		m	
L'Hombre	M	1853	Robert	rb	s-d	m		
L'Hospitalière	G	Pre 1846	Vibert	mp				
L'Hospitalière	G	1852	Robert	lp	f	m		
Liberty	HT	1897	Dickson A	dr	dbl	l	vig	vf
Licelle	Misc			m				

Name	Class	Year	Origin / syn	Colour	Form	Size	Vigour	Fragrance
Lichas	B	1845	Guillot Père	mr	f	l		
L'Idéale	N	1887	Nabonnand G	mr	s-d	l	vig	vf
Lidorie	C			mp				
Lie de Vin	G	Pre 1815	Descemet	dr				
Liésis	N	1842	Trouillard	ly	dbl	l	vig	m
			syn Céline Forestier					
Lieter	C			lp				
Lilac Queen (?)	HCh	Pre 1846						
Lilacé	HP	1824	Vétillard	lp	f	m		
Lilacé Variegata	C	Pre 1846		lp				
Lilacea Grandiflora	B	Pre 1846		lp		vl		
Lilacina	T	Pre 1846						f
Lilas	T	Pre 1830		lp	f	m		
Lilas à Grandes Fleurs	N	Pre 1830		lp				
Lilas Double	N	Pre 1834		lp	dbl	s		
Lilas Foncé	N		Laffay	lp				
Lilas Rosé	B			lp				
Lili Dieck	HRg	1899	Dieck	mr				
Lilian Nordica	HT	1898	Walsh	w	dbl	l	vig	f
Lilliput	Cl Pol	1897	Paul G	mr	dbl	s		
Lily Mertschersky	N	1878	Nabonnand	m	vf	m		
Lincelle	G	1826	Dubourg	m	vf	m		
L'Incomparable de Lille	G	Pre 1830		lp	f	m-l		
		syn	Incomparable de Lille					
Lindley	HP	1866	Paul W	dp	f	l		
			syn Docteur Lindley					
L'Infante d'Espagne	G	Pre 1811		dp		s		m
		syn	Cramoisie Éblouissante					
L'Inflexible	HP	1847	Lacharme	mp				
L'Ingénue	C	1832	Vibert	w	f	m	wk	
Linné	HP	1878	Margottin	dr	f	l	vig	
Linnean Hill Beauty	HSet	Pre 1846		lp	f			
Linneanhall Beauty (? Same as above)	Ayr	Pre 1866		lp	vf			
L'Innocence	HT	1897	Pernet-Ducher	w	f	l	vig	
L'Intéressante	G	Pre 1830	syn Intéressante	mr	f	m		
L'Invincible	G	Pre 1819	Miellez	mr				
			syn Invincible					
L'Invincible	G/C	Pre 1830	Vibert	dp	vf	s		
		syn	Agathe Incomparable					
Lion des Combats	HP	1850	Lartay	mr	dbl	l	vig	
Lionel de Moutiers	G			lp	f	m		
Lios Alpha	HSem	1886	Geschwind	lp	vdbl	m		
Lisbeth	G/C	1832	Vibert	lp	f	m		
Lisbon	Misc	Pre 1846						
Lisdana	B	1895	Geschwind	lp	dbl			
Lise Boucot	C	1832	Vibert	lp	f	m		
Lise Deville	HSpn	1827	Noisette	lp				
Lisette de Béranger	HP	1867	Moreau F/Guillot Fils	mp	f	m	vig	
Lisirmin	P			mp				
Lisse	Misc	Pre 1820		w				
Little Dot	Pol	1887	Bennett	lp				
Little Gem	M	1880	Paul W	dp	dbl	s		vf
Little Gem	Pol	Pre 1896	Alderton	lp				
Little White Pet	Pol	1879	Henderson	w	dbl	s	vig	sf
			syn White Pet					
Little White Pet, Climbing	Cl Pol	1894	Corboeuf	w				
			syn White Pet, Climbg					
Little Woods Rose	Sp	Pre 1840	Nuttall	lp	s			
			syn r.gymnocarpa					
Livida	Alp			dr				
L'Obscurité	G	Pre 1820	Van Eeden syn Cora	m	f	s		
L'Obscurité	G	Pre 1830	Prévost	dr	dbl	m		
L'Obscurité	M	1848	Lacharme	dr	dbl	l		
L'Obscurité	HCh	1851	Robert	dr				
Loddiges	N			w	l	s		
Lodoïska	G	1820	Vibert	lp		m		
Lodoïska Marin	P	Pre 1830	Prévost	lp	f	l		
L'Odorante	Ch		Laffay syn Odorant	pb	dbl	m		vf
Loelia	Hp	1888		lp		vl	vig	f
Loisel	G	1826	Prévost	dp	f	l		
L'Ombre	G	1820						
L'Ombre	M	Pre 1870		mr	f	m		
L'Ombre Panachée	Misc	Pre 1846						
L'Ombre Superbe	Misc	Pre 1846		dr				
Longfellow	HP	1884	Paul G	dr				
Longworth Rambler	LCl	1880	Liabaud	mr	s-d	m	vig	
			syn Deschamps (N)?					
Lord Bacon	HP	1883	Paul W	dr	dbl	l	vig	
Lord Beaconfield	HP	1878	Christy	dr	f	l	vig	
Lord Belphleger	Ch			lp	f	l		
Lord Byron	T	Pre 1830	Laffay	lp	f	m		sf

Name	Type	Year	Breeder					
Lord Byron	G			lp	f	l		
Lord Clyde	HP	1863	Paul	dr	f	l	vig	
Lord Derby	N			lp	f	m	vvig	
Lord Eldon	N	1872	Eldon	ob	dbl			m
			syn Earl of Eldon					
Lord Elgin	HP	1858	Guillot Père	dr	vf	m	vig	
Lord Frederick Cavendish	HP	1883	Frettingham	mr	dbl	l	vig	
Lord Gray	B			m	f	l		
Lord Herbert	HP	1863	Paul W	dp	f	l	m	
Lord John Russel	Ch	Pre 1846	Laffay	w	f	l	vvig	
Lord Keith	HCh	Pre 1846		m		vl		
Lord Knight	HCh							
Lord Londonderry	G			mr	f	m		
Lord Macaulay	HP	1863	Paul W	dr	f	l	vig	
Lord Napier	HP	1874	Paul W	dp	f	m	vig	
Lord Nelson	HCh	Pre 1846		dr	f	m		
Lord Palmerston	HP	1857	Margottin	mr	f	m	vvig	
Lord Penzance	HEg	1894	Penzance	yb	s	s	vvig	m
Lord Raglan	HP	1854	Guillot Père	dr	vf	vl	vvig	vf
Lord Tarquin	T	1841	Bougère	w	dbl	l	vig	vf
			syn Niphetos					
Lord Wellington	G	Pre 1830	Vibert	m	f	m		
Loreley	HCh	1887	Geschwind	lp				
L'Orientale	G	Pre 1829	Coquerel	m	vf	m		
L'Orléanaise	Bslt	1899	Vigneron	lp	vf	l		
Lorna Doone	B	1894	Paul W	mr	f	l	m	vf
Louis Barlet	T	1876	Ducher Vve	w	f	l	vig	
Louis Béluze	B	c 1840	Béluze	mp	f	m		
Louis Bonaparte	HP	1839	Laffay	mr	f	l	vvig	
Louis Bonaparte	HP	Pre 1870		mp	vdbl	m		
Louis Brassac	HP	1872	Brassac	mp	f	l	vig	
Louis Bulliat	HP	1867	Gonod	mr	f	l	vig	
Louis Calla	HP	1885	Verdier E	m	dbl	l		
Louis Carlier	G			dr	f	m		
Louis Cazas	D	1850		lp	vf	m		m
Louis Chaix	HP	1857	Lacharme	mr	f	l	m	
Louis Charlin	HP	1871	Damaizin	pb	f	vl	m	
Louis Corbie	HP	1871	Corbie	mr	f	l		
Louis d'Autriche	HP	1858		m	f	l		
Louis de Bouchard de Bussy	B			mp				
Louis de la Poyade	T	1899	Puyravaud	w				
Louis Donadine	HP	1887	Gonod	dr	f	vl	vig	
Louis Doré	HP	1879	Fontaine	mr	f	l-vl	vig	
Louis Foucquier	G			mr	f	l		
Louis Gigot	T	1871	Ducher	w	f	l		
Louis Gimard	M	1877	Pernet Père	mp	dbl	vl	vig	
Louis Gontier	T	1883	Nabonnand	mr	vf	vl	vvig	
Louis Guillaud	T	1888	Nabonnand	pb	f	vl	vig	f
Louis Gulino	HP	1859	Guillot Fils	dr	f	m	vig	vf
Louis Labie	HP	1853	Pradel	mp	f	m		
Louis Lazard	T	1885	Singer	lp	f	l	vvig	
Louis Le Grand	G		Miellez	mr				
Louis Lévêque	T	1892	Soupert & Notting	pb	f	l		
		syn	Erzherzog Franz Ferd-	inand				
Louis Lévêque	T	1894	Lévêque	yb				
Louis Lille	HP	1887	Dubreuil	mr	f	vl	vig	
Louis Neyret	T	1894	Reboul	pb				
Louis Noisette	HP	1864	Ducher	mp	f	l	vig	
Louis Odier	HP	Pre 1870		mp	f	l		
Louis Parmentier	G		Parmentier	mp	f	l		
Louis-Philippe	G	1824	Hardy	m	dbl	vl	m	
Louis-Philippe	Ch	1834	Guérin	rb	dbl	m	m	f
Louis-Philippe	B	1835	Miellez	dr	vdbl	l		
Louis-Philippe	HP	Pre 1846		m				
Louis-Philippe	T		Cels	mp	f	l		
Louis Philippe Albert d'Orléans	HP	1884	Verdier E	mr	f	l	vig	
			syn L P d'Orléans					
Louis-Philippe d'Angers	Ch	1834	Guérin	rb	dbl	m	m	f
		syn	Louis-Philippe (Ch)					
Louis Philippe d'Orléans	HP	1884	Verdier E	mr	f	l	vig	
Louis-Philippe I	P	1832	Duval C	dr	f	vl		vf
Louis Puyravaud	N	1896	Puyravaud	my	f	l		
Louis Richard	T	1873	Ducher Vve	op	f	l	vig	f
			syn Helvetia					
Louis Rollet	HP	1886	Gonod	dr	f	l		
Louis Spaeth	HP	1877	Soupert & Notting	lp	f	vl	vvig	
Louis Van Fitt	G							
Louis Van Houtte	HP	1861	Margottin					
Louis Van Houtte	HP	1863	Granger	dp	f	l	vvig	
Louis Van Houtte	HP	1869	Lacharme F	dr	vf	l	vig	vf
Louis Van Tyle	G	Pre 1846		m	s-d	s		

Name	Class	Date	Raiser / syn					
Louis XII	G	Pre 1829	Coquerel	m	f	m		
Louis XIV	G	1824	Hardy	lp	f	l		
Louis XIV	B	Pre 1846		mp				
Louis XIV	Ch	1859	Guillot et Fils	dr	dbl	m	m	vf
Louis XIV	HP	Pre 1870		dr	f	l		
Louis XVI	M			mp	f	m		
Louis XVI	D	Pre 1810	Miellez syn Achille	dr	vf	m		
Louis XVIII	T			mp	vdbl	vl		
Louis XVIII	G	Pre 1830	Prévost	lp	f	vl		
Louis XVIII	Ch	1827	Mauget	m				
Louis XVIII Nouveau	G	1826		m	vdbl	l		
Louisa Turner	HP			mp				
Louise	C	Pre 1810	Dupont syn La Louise	m	s-d			
Louise	G	c 1840	Parmentier syn La Louise (G)	dr	f			
Louise Aimé	P	1845	Aimé					
Louise Béluze	B	c 1840	Béluze	dp	f	m		
Louise Bordillon	HP		Vibert	mp	f	l		
Louise Bourbonnand	T	1892	Nabonnand	mp				
Louise Boyer	HP	1881	Bernède	dp	f	vl	vig	
Louise Clément	T	1856	Guillot	w	f	m	vig	
Louise Collet	M	1840	Vibert	mp	f	l		
Louise Damaizin	HP	1864	Damaizin	w	f	m	vig	
Louise d'Arzens	HP	1861	Lacharme F	w	f	s	m	
Louise d'Autriche	HP	1856	Fontaine	m	f	l	vvig	
Louise de Chateaubourg	HP	1853	Fontaine	mr	vf	l	vvig	vf
Louise de Savoie	T	1854	Ducher	ly	f	vl	vig	vf
Louise Dutard	D	1825	Vétillard	mp				
Louise Favre	HCh	1846	Lacharme	m	f	m		
Louise Labadie	T			mp				
Louise Leclerc Thouin	HP			lp	f	m	vig	
Louise Leneveu (x)	G	1836	Joly	mp	f	s	vig	
Louise Magnan	HP	1855	Fontaine	w	dbl	m	wk	
Louise Margottin	B	1862	Margottin	lp	f	m	vig	
Louise Marie	B		Pradel	m				
Louise Méhul	G		Parmentier	pb	f	l		
Louise Muller	HP	1897	Muller	mr				
Louise Odier	B/HP	1851	Margottin	dp	dbl	m	vig	
Louise Pagnon	HP		Fontaine	w	vf	vl		
Louise Peyronny	HP	1844	Lacharme F	dp	dbl	vl	m	m
Louise Puget	HP	1842	Vibert	w	f	m	vvig	vf
Louise Thiébault	M		Robert	mp				
Louise Verger	M	1860	Moreau-Robert	mp	dbl	m		
Louise Wood	HP	1869	Verdier E	mp	dbl	l	vig	
Lovely Rambler	Arv	Pre 1846		mp				
Lovely Violet	Misc	Pre 1846		lp				
Loyalist	A	Pre 1738	syn Great Maiden's Blush	w	dbl			vf
Lubec	Misc	Pre 1846		dr				
Lucette Delman	Ch			lp				
Lucida	Ch		Prévost	w				
Lucida Duplex	HBc	Pre 1846		w	s-d			
Lucie Ashton	G			w				
Lucie Astraix	HCh			mp	f	m		
Lucie de Barante de Montozon	HP	1850	Pelissier	mp	f	m		f
Lucie Dubourg	T			lp	f	m	vvig	
Lucie Duplessis	M	1853	Robert	lp	f	m		
Lucie Faure	T	1898	Nabonnand	w	f	l		
Lucie Mathieu	C			lp	f	vl		
Lucien Duranthon	HP	1894	Bonnaire	mp	dbl	l	vvig	
Lucile	Ch	Pre 1830	Vibert	w				
Lucile Dubourg	G	1826	Dubourg	m				
Lucile Duplessis	G	1836	Vibert	dp	f	m		
Lucile Lafitte	T		Pradel	w				
Lucilla Hybrida	HCh	Pre 1860		m				
Luciole	T	1886	Guillot et Fils	dp	f	l	vig	vf
Luckner	B	1860	Robert & Moreau	rb				
Lucrèce	G	Pre 1790	syn La Majestueuse	mp	f	m		m
Lucrèce	HCh	c 1830	Laffay	lp	f	m		
Lucrèce	A	1847	Vibert	lp	dbl	vl		
Lucrèce	T	1866	Oger	op	f	l		
Lucullus	Ch	1854	Guinoiseau-Flon	dr	vdbl	m	vvig	
Lucy Ashton	HEg	1894	Penzance	w	s	m	vvig	f
Lucy Bertram	HEg	1895	Penzance	rb	s		vvig	f
Lucy Canergie	T	1898	Nabonnand P C	dp	dbl	l	vvig	
Ludovic Létaud	HP	1849	Cherpin or Ducher	dp	f	m		
Ludovic Marin	HP		Marin	mp	f	l		
Ludovicus	G	Pre 1830	Calvert	m	f	m		
Luisante Nouvelle No 1	Misc	Pre 1830	Vibert	mp	vdbl	l	vig	f
Luisante Nouvelle No 2	Misc	Pre 1830	Vibert	mp				
Luisante Nouvelle No 3	Misc	Pre 1830	Vibert	lp	dbl	m		
Luisante Semi Double	Misc	Pre 1830	Vibert	mp	vdbl	m		

Name	Type	Date	Breeder / Notes	Color	Form	Size	Vigor	Frag
Luisante Simple	Misc	1826	Vibert	mp	s	m		
Lully	Ch		Laffay	mr	f	s		
Lunel	M	1854	Robert	lp	f	m		
Lusiadas	N	1885	Da Costa	yb	f	l	vvig	vf
			syn Céline Forestier					
Lusignan	Ch	1854	Robert	mr	f	l		
Lusseldemberg	B	Pre 1846		lp		l		
Lustre d'Eglise	G	Pre 1790	(Holland)	mp	dbl	s		vf
Lutea	Sp	1823	Damper	ly	dbl	l	vvig	
			syn r.banksiae lutea					
Lutea Alba Plena	HArv			w				
Lutea Flora	T	1874	Touvais	my	f	l	m	
Lutea Flore Pleno	Misc	Pre 1629	syn Multiplex	my	vdbl	vl		
Lutea Fortunei	N			my				
Lutea Maxima	HSpn			my	s			f
Lutea Nova	T	1824	Parks	my	dbl			
		syn Park's	Yellow Tea-Scented	China				
Lutea Plena	HSpn	Pre 1838	Hardy syn Sulphurea	ly	s-d	l		
Lutea Simplex	Sp	c 1816		my	s			
		syn	r.banksiae lutescens					
Lutea Striata	T			w	f	l	vvig	
Lutea Sulphurea	HSpn			ly				
Luteola	HFt	Pre 1821		ly	s			
Lutescens	HEg	Pre 1846		ly	s	s		
Lutescens Flavescens	T	1824	Parks	my	dbl	l	vig	
		syn Park's	Yellow Tea-Scented	China				
Lutescens Grandiflora	T	Pre 1846		y		l		
Lutescens Marginata	HCh							
Lutescens Mutabilis	T	Pre 1834		y	f	m		
Lutescens Simplex	Sp	c 1816		my	s			
		syn	r.banksiae lutescens					
Lutescens Spinosa	Bks	1887		my	f	l		
Lutin	HP		see Kobold					
Luxembourg	M	Pre 1834	Hardy	mr	f	m		
		syn	Ferrugineux du Luxem bourg					
Luxembourg	N	Pre 1846		m				
Luxembourg	M	1848	Hardy	m	dbl	m		m
		syn	Pourpre du Luxembou rg					
Luxembourg Hybrid	HMcr	Pre 1846		mp			vig	
Lycoris	M			mr	f	m		
Lycoris	G	1835	Vibert	pb	dbl	l		
Lydia	N	1892	Geschwind	lp	dbl	m		
Lydia de Forbin	G	1827	Noisette	mr				
Lydia Marty	HP	1878	Liabaud	lp	f	l	m	
Lyonnais	T	Pre 1846		lp				
Lyonnais	HP	1872	Lacharme	mp	dbl	l	vig	
Lyonnaise	HP	1854	Lacharme	mp				
			syn Belle Lyonnaise					
Lycoris	G	Pre 1846		dp				
Lyre de Flore	G	Pre 1811	Hardy	dp	f	s		
		syn	Beauté Insurmontable & Phénix					

NAME	TYPE	YEAR	RAISER	COLOUR	BLOOM	SIZE	GROWTH	SCENT
M Freundlich	HSpn		Freundlich					
Ma Capucine	T	1871	Levet	yb	dbl	m	m	f
Ma Clochette	G	Pre 1834		m	f	l		
Ma Favorite	D		Mieller	mp				
Ma Fillette	Pol	1895	Soupert & Notting	ab		s	m	vf
Ma Frisée	HP	1876	Vigneron	mr	f	l	m	
Ma Mousseuse	M		syn Ordinaire	mp				
Ma Paquerette	Pol	1875	Guillot Fils	w	vdbl			
			syn Paquerette					
Ma Petite Andrée	Pol	1898	Chauvry	dr	dbl	l	m	
Ma Pivoine	HP	1864	Levet	dr	f	l		
Ma Pivoine Rose	HP	1848	Verdier V	mp				
Ma Pivoine du Roi	G	1810	Descemet	dp	f	l		
Ma Ponctuée	M	1858	Guillot Père	pb	dbl	m	vig	m
Ma Ponctuée Semi-Double	M	1850	Moreau & Robert	rb	s-d			
Ma Pupille	HCh	Pre 1830	Lecomte	m	f	s		
Ma Surprise	S	1872	Guillot Fils	w	dbl	vl	vvig	f
Ma Surprise	HP	1884	Levet A	dr		m	vig	
Ma Tante Aurore	T	Pre 1846	Robert	mp				
Ma Tulipe	HT	1899	Bonnaire	mr	s-d	l		
Mabel Morrison	HP	1878	Broughton	w	dbl	vl	vig	
Mably	HCh	Pre 1830	Laffay	m	f	s		
Macarthy	T	Pre 1846		dp				
Macartney	Sp	1793	syn r.bracteata	w	s			
MacGregor's Damask	P	1846	Vibert	m	dbl			m
			syn Joasine Hanet					
Maclovie	Ch		Laffay	w				
MacMahon	HP	1872	Verdier E	dp	f	l	vig	
Macrantha Rubicunda	G	Pre 1877		mr	vdbl	l		
Macrophylla	N							
Macrophylla	Pom			w				
Macrophylla Bisserulata	A	1828	Prévost	lp	s-d	vl	vig	
Macrophylla Scandens	Ayr	Pre 1804	syn Scandens	w	s-d		m	vf
Maculata	HSpn	Pre 1770		w	s-d	s		
Maculata	G	Pre 1815	Dupont	pb	s-d	m		
			syn La Maculée					
Madame A Etienne	T	1886	Bernaix	dp	f	l	vig	vf
Madame A Labbey	HP	1843		pb	f	m		
Madame A Schwaller	HT	1886	Bernaix	mp	f	l		
Madame Abel Chatenay	HT	1894	Pernet-Ducher	pb	dbl	m	vig	f
Madame Ada Carmody	T	1898	Paul W	w	f	l	vig	
Madame Adélaïde Côte	HP	1881	Schmitt	mr	f	l	vig	vf
Madame Adélaïde de Meynot	HP	1882	Gonod	mr				
Madame Adélaïde Fontaine	B		see Angèle Fontaine					
Madame Adélaïde Ristori	B	1861	Pradel	dp	f			
Madame Adèle de Murinais	HP	1876	Schwartz	lp	f	l	vvig	
Madame Adèle Huzard (Hazard)	HP	1868	Verdier	mp	f	m	vig	
Madame Adèle Launay	HP	1863	Boyeau	lp	f	l		
Madame Adolphe Aynard	HP	1893	Liabaud	lp				
Madame Adolphe de Tarlé	T	1889	Tesnier	w				
Madame Adolphe Loiseau	HT	1897	Buatois	lp	vf	vl		
Madame Agathe Nabonnand	T	1886	Nabonnand G	lp	f	vl	vig	f
Madame Agathe Roux	T	1887	Nabonnand	lp	f	l	vig	
Madame Aimée	HP			mp	f	l		
Madame Albani	HP	1877	Verdier E	dr	f	m-l	vvig	
Madame Albert Bleunard	T	1893	Tesnier	w				
Madame Albert Fitler	HP	1873	Faudon	mp	f	l	vig	
Madame Albert Patel	T	1893	Godard	w				
Madame Alboni	M	1850	Verdier V	lp	f	m		
Madame Alégatière	Pol	1888	Alégatière	dp	dbl	m	m	vf
Madame Alexandre Bernaix	HT	1877	Guillot Fils	pb	f	l	m	m
Madame Alexandre Danowski	T	1894	Soupert & Notting	yb				
Madame Alexandre Jullien	HP	1882	Vigneron	lp	f	l	vvig	
Madame Alexandre Pommery	HP	1882	Lévêque	mp				
Madame Alexandrine Bruel	T	1884	Levet	w				
Madame Alfred Bleu	HP	1884	Verdier E	dp	f	m	vig	
Madame Alfred Carrière	N	1879	Schwartz J	w	dbl	l	vvig	vf
Madame Alfred de Rougemont	HP	1862	Lacharme	lp	f	m	vig	m
Madame Alfred Leveau	HP	1880	Vigneron	mp	f	l		
			syn Alfred Leveau					
Madame Alice Alatine	HP	1888	Nabonnand	dr				
Madame Alice Dureau	HP	1867	Vigneron	lp	f	l	vig	vf
Madame Alice Van Geert	HP	1883	Lévêque	pb	f	l	vvig	
Madame Aline Lavenant	HP	1852	Laffay	mr	f	m		
Madame Alphonse	HP			mr	f	l		
Madame Alphonse Aubert	HP	1876	Fontaine	mr	f	l	vvig	
Madame Alphonse Lavallée	HP	1863	Baumann	mr	f	l	vig	m
			syn Marie Baumann					

Madame Alphonse Lavallée	HP	1878	Verdier E	rb	f	l	vig	
Madame Alphonse Seux	HP	1887	Liabaud	mp	f	vl	vig	
Madame Amadieu	T	1880	Pernet Père	pb	dbl	vl	vig	vf
Madame Amandinoli	T	1881	Brassac	lp				
Madame Ambroise Triollet	HP	1869	Moreau-Robert	op	f	l	m	
Madame Ambroise Verschaffelt	HP	1864	Verdier E	lp	f	l		
Madame Amédée Despeyre	HP	1863	Pradel	w	f	l		
Madame Amélie Baltet	HP	1878	Verdier E	lp	f	l	vig	
Madame Anaïs Cabrol	T	1851	Pradel	mp	f	l		
Madame Anatole Leroy	HP	1892	Leroy A	lp	dbl	l	vig	
Madame André Duron	HT	1887	Bonnaire	mr	f	vl		
Madame André Leroy	HP	1864	Trouillard	mp	dbl	l	vig	
Madame André Thouin	M		see André Thouin					
Madame Andry	HP	1850	Verdier V	mp	f	vl	vvig	
Madame Angèle Dispott	HP	1869	Dauvesse	mr	f	m	m	
Madame Angèle Favre	HT	1888	Perny	op				
Madame Angèle Jacquier	T	1879	Guillot Fils	pb	f	l	vig	vf
Madame Angèle Jacquier	T	1890	Veysset	pb				
Madame Angélina	B	1844	Chanet	my	vf	m	m	
Madame Angélique Veysset	HT	1890	Veysset	pb	dbl	l		
Madame Anna Bugnet	HP	1866	Gonod	lp	f	l		
Madame Anna de Besobrasoff	HP	1868	Gonod	mr	f	l	vvig	
Madame Anna de Besobrasoff	HP	1877	Nabonnand	w	f	l	vig	m
Madame Anna Gérold	HP	1882	Soupert & Notting	mp	f	l		
Madame Anna Kleinnickel	HP	1888	Kleinnickel	mp				
Madame Anna Moreau	HP	1883	Moreau-Robert	lp	vf	vl	vig	
Madame Anne Béluze	B	c 1840	Béluze	mp		m		
Madame Antoine Rivoire	HP	1894	Liabaud	lp	dbl	vl		
Madame Antoinette Chrétien	HP	1897	Liabaud	lp	f	l		
Madame Apolline Foulon	HP	1882	Vigneron	pb	f	l	vvig	
Madame Arntzenius	HP	1874	Soupert & Notting	mr	f	l	vig	
Madame Arsène Bonneau	HP	1871	Bonneau	mr				
Madame Arthur Oger	Cl B	1899	Letellier	mp	vdbl	vl	vvig	
Madame Asselin	G			lp	f	m		
Madame Aubis	B			mp				
Madame Aubry	HP			mp				
Madame Aude	B	1839	Desprez	m	f	l		
Madame Audot	A	1844	Verdier V	lp	f	m	vig	
Madame Audot	HP		Vibert	lp				
Madame Auguste Odier	HP	1877	Fontaine	lp	f	l	vig	
Madame Auguste Perrin	N	1878	Schwartz J	lp	vf	m	vig	m
Madame Auguste Rodrigues	B	1897	Chauvry	mp	vf			m
Madame Auguste Sommereau	HT	1892	Corboef-Marsault	lp	f	l		m
Madame Auguste van Geert	HP	1861	Robichon	pb	f	m		
Madame Augustine Bardiaux	T	1893	Lévêque	yb	dbl	l	vig	
Madame Augustine Hammond	HT	1897	Vigneron	mp	dbl	vl		
Madame Augustine Margat	HCh			dp				
Madame Azélie Imbert	T	1870	Levet	yb	f	l	vvig	f
Madame Badin	T	1897	Croibier	pb	f	m	vig	f
Madame Badoud	HT	1890	Godard	mp				
Madame Baptiste Desportes	HP	1865	Trouillard	mr	f	l		
Madame Barillet-Deschamps	T	1853	Bernède	w	f	l	vig	
Madame Barny	HP	1868	Trouillard	mp		m	vig	
		syn Mm	e Lauriol de Barny					
Madame Barret	T	1898	Liabaud	my				
Madame Barriot	HP	1867	Damaizin	dp	f	vl	vig	
Madame Baron-Veillard	B	1889	Vigneron	lp				
Madame Barthélemy Levet	T	1879	Levet	ly	f	l	vvig	f
Madame Baulot	HP	1885	Lévêque	mp	dbl	l		
Madame Belfort	HP							
Madame Bellender Kerr	HP	1867	Guillot Père	w	f	m	m	m
Madame Bellon	HP	1871	Pernet Père	mp	f	vl	m	
Madame Bennet	HP	1876	Nabonnand	mp		l	vig	
Madame Benoist	HP	1891	Moreau-Robert	mp				
Madame Benoit Desroches	T	1877	Nabonnand	mp		l	vig	
Madame Benoit Rivière	T	1891	Liabaud	ab				
Madame Bérard	Cl T	1870	Levet F	ob	dbl	l	vvig	m
Madame Berger	HP	1853	Ohl	dp	f	m		
Madame Berkeley	T	1898	Bernaix Fils	pb	dbl	l	m	m
Madame Bernard	T	1875	Levet	yb	f	l	vig	
Madame Bernède	T	1856	Bernède	pb	f	l		
Madame Bernutz	HP	1873	Jamain H	mp	f	vl	vig	
Madame Bertha Mackart	HP	1883	Verdier E	mp	f	vl	vvig	
Madame Berthe Fontaine	HT	1898	Buatois	mp	vf	vl	vig	m
Madame Bertrand	HP	1889	Pernet Père	dp				
Madame Bessemer	HT	1898	Conard & Jones	op	vf	l		
Madame Bessonneau	T	1891	Moreau-Robert	ly				
Madame Betty Hendlé	HP	1892	Boutigny	dr	f	l		
Madame Bijou	HP	1886	Chauvry	dr	f	l		
Madame Blachet	T	1859	Boyau	mp	f	l		
Madame Blondel	HT	1899	Veysset	mp	dbl	vl		m

Madame Boegner	HP	1888	Vigneron	mr	f	l	vig	
Madame Bois	HP	1886	Levet Père	lp				
Madame Boissière	HP	1859	Pradel	mp		l		
Madame Boll	HP	1843	Boll, D	dp	dbl	l	vig	vf
Madame Bonnet-Aymard	T	1875	Pernet Père	w	f	m	vig	
Madame Bonnet des Claustres	T	1891	Reboul	w	f	vl		
Madame Bonnin	HP	1877	Cochet S	op	vf	l	vvig	
Madame Borriglione	T	1895	Nabonnand	mp				
Madame Boucher	M		Guinoiseau	dp	f	m		
Madame Bourjade	T	1858	Pradel	w	f	l		
Madame Bourgeois	HP							
Madame Boutin	HP	1861	Jamain	mr	f	vl	vig	
			syn Christina Nilsson					
Madame Bouton	M	1851	Robert	dp	f	m		
Madame Brassac	T		Nabonnand	dr	f	l	vvig	
Madame Braux (Brault)	HP	1891	Lévêque	lp				
Madame Bravy	T	1846	Guillot Père	w	dbl	m	m	f
Madame Brémont	T	1866	Guillot Fils	dr	f	m-l	m	
Madame Bréon	Ch	1841	Verdier V	dp	f	l		
Madame Bréon	B	Pre 1846		mp		l		
Madame Briançon	HP	1862	Fontaine	rb	f	l		
Madame Brice	HP	1863	Moreau-Robert	lp				
Madame Brosse	HP	1886	Brosse	mr	f	l		
Madame Brunner	N	1890	Brunner	ly				
Madame Bruny	HP	1858	Avoux & Crozy	m	f	m	vvig	
Madame Bureau	HCh	Pre 1846		w	f	l		m
Madame Buzo	T	1894	Liabaud	my				
Madame Byrne	N	1840	Buist	w	dbl	l		
Madame C P Strassheim	T	1897	Soupert & Notting	my	f	l	vig	vf
Madame Cadeau-Ramey	HT	1896	Pernet-Ducher	op	f	l	vig	m
Madame Cadel	HP	1873	Levet	mp				
Madame Caillat	HP	1861	Verdier E	mr	f	l	vig	
Madame Calot	B	1850	Miellez	dp				
Madame Camille	T	1871	Guillot et Fils	lp	f	l	vig	f
Madame Camille Bigotteau	HP	1883	Vigneron	mr				
Madame Campan	A	Pre 1846		lp				
Madame Campan	G	Pre 1848		mr	f	m	wk	
Madame Campbell d'Islay	HP	1847	Schneider	lp	f	l	vig	
		syn	Triomphe de Valenciennes					
Madame Caradori-Allan	HMult	1843	Feast	lp	dbl	m		
Madame Carle	HP	1887	Bernaix	mr	f	m	vig	
Madame Carmen	T	1888	Dubreuil	lp	f	m	vig	f
Madame Carnot	N	1889	Moreau-Robert	yb	vdbl	l	vvig	f
Madame Carnot	T	1893	Pernet Père	w		l	vig	
Madame Caro	T	1880	Levet	yb	vf	m	wk	
Madame Caroline de Sardoux	T	see Mar-	ie Caroline de Sartoux					
Madame Caroline Küster	N	1872	Pernet	yb	dbl	m	vig	
Madame Caroline Schmitt	N	1878	Schmitt	yb	dbl	m-l		
Madame Caroline Testout	HT	1890	Pernet-Ducher	mp	dbl	vl	vig	m
Madame Carré	D	Pre 1885		w	f	m		
Madame Catherine Fontaine	T	1892	Liabaud	dp	s-d			
Madame Cécile Berthod	T	1871	Guillot Fils	dy	vf	m-l	vig	sf
Madame Cécile Morand	HP	1890	Corboeuf	dr	vf	l		
Madame Céline Noirey	T	1868	Guillot et Fils	lp	vdbl	l	vig	f
Madame Céline Touvais	HP	1859	Touvais	mp	dbl	l		
Madame Céphalie Laurent	HP	1894	Boutigny	mp				
Madame César Brunier	HP	1887	Bernaix	mp	vdbl	l	vig	m
Madame Chabal	HP	1889	Schwartz V	mp				
Madame Chabanne	T	1896	Liabaud	yb	f	l	vig	
Madame Chabaud de St-Mandrier	N	1881	Nabonnand	lp	vf	vl	vig	
		syn	Madame Gustave Gossart					
Madame Chalonge	N	Pre 1846		lp				
Madame Chaplet	HP	1862	Avoux					
Madame Charles	T	1864	Damaizin	yb	f	l	m	f
Madame Charles Baltet	B	1865	Verdier E	lp	vf	l	vig	vf
Madame Charles Boutmy	HT	1892	Vigneron	lp	f	vl		
Madame Charles Crapelet	HP	1858	Fontaine	pb	f	l	vig	m
Madame Charles de Rostang	HP	1890	Tesnier	mp				
Madame Charles Détraux	B	1895	Vigneron	mr		l		
Madame Charles Franchet	T	1894	Liabaud	pb				
Madame Charles Frédéric Worth	HRg	1889	Schwartz Vve	dp	s-d	l	vig	m
Madame Charles Genoud (Gonod)	N	1891	Godard	ly				
Madame Charles Lavot	HP	1881	Vigneron	lp	f	l	vig	
Madame Charles Levet	T	1870	Levet	op				
Madame Charles Meurice	HP	1878	Meurice	dr	dbl	l	vig	f
Madame Charles Roy	HP	1862		mp	f	l		
Madame Charles Salleron	M	1867	Fontaine	mr	f	l		
Madame Charles Séguret	B	1861	Pradel	mr				
Madame Charles Truffaut	HP	1878	Verdier E	lp	f	l	vig	

Name	Class	Year	Breeder					
Madame Charles Verdier	HP	1863	Lacharme	mp	f	l	vig	m
Madame Charles Wood	HP	1861	Verdier E	mr	dbl	l	m	f
Madame Charlet	T	1856	Corbie	yb	s-d	l		
Madame Charlotte Wolter	HP	1887	Moreau-Robert	mp	f	l	vig	
Madame Chaté	HP	1871	Fontaine	rb	f	l	vig	
Madame Chauvel	HP	1855	Chauvel	dp	f	l		
Madame Chauvry	T	1886	Bonnaire	yb	f	l	vvig	f
Madame Chavant	Ch	Pre 1846		lp	f	l		
Madame Chavaret	T	1872	Levet	yb	vf	l	m	m
Madame Chédanne-Guinoisseau	T	1880	Chédanne-Guinoisseau	ly	f	l	vvig	f
Madame Chevalier	B	1886	Pernet Père	mp	dbl	l	vig	
Madame Chevrier	B	1888	Vigneron	mp	f	m	vig	
Madame Chevrot	HP	1878	Pernet Père	mp	f	l	vig	
Madame Chierot	HP	1877	Pernet Père	dp	f	l	vig	
Madame Chignard	HP	1877	Vigneron	dr	f	vl	vig	
Madame Chirard	HP	1867	Pernet Père	mp	f	vl	vvig	m
Madame Christine Meister	T	1861	Soupert & Notting	my	f	l		
Madame Christophe	G	Pre 1830	Calvert syn Nigretiana	dr	f	m		
Madame Claire Jaubert	T	1887	Nabonnand	yb	s-d	vl	vig	f
Madame Claire Mathieu	HP	1874	Vigneron	lp		m	vig	
Madame Claudius Gaze	T	1894	Godard	mp				
Madame Clavel	HP	1849	Lacharme	mp	f	m	wk	
Madame Clémence Beauregard	M	1851	Laffay	mp	f	l		
Madame Clémence Joigneaux	HP	1861	Liabaud	pb	dbl	vl	vvig	
Madame Clémence Marchix	T	1899	Bernaix P	rb				
Madame Clément Massier	N	1884	Nabonnand	mp	vf	m-l	vvig	
Madame Clert	HP	1868	Gonod	op	f	l	vig	
Madame Clorinde Leblond	HP	1870	Dauvesse	dr	dbl	m		
Madame Clothilde Perrault	B	1863	Vigneron	dp	f	m-l		
Madame Collet	B	1864	Liabaud	lp	f	m	vig	
Madame Collet	HP	1864	Liabaud	pb	f	l	vig	
Madame Compatier	B							
Madame Compton	T			mr	f	m		f
Madame Comtesse	B	1857	Margottin	lp	f	m		
Madame Corboeuf	HT	1895	Corboeuf	mr	s-d	l		
Madame Cornélissen	B	1865	Cornélissen	lp	vdbl	l	m	m
Madame Cornet	HP			mp				
Madame Corvassier	T	1895	Lévêque	y				
Madame Cottin	G			dp	f	l		
Madame Coudret	HP			w	f	m		
Madame Coulombier	HP	1883	Lévêque	mr	f	l	vvig	
Madame Cousin	B	1849	Margottin	dp	f	l		
Madame Couturier-Mention	Cl Ch	1885	Couturier	mr	s-d	m	vig	
Madame Créqui	Ch			dp	f	m		
Madame Crespin	HP	1862	Damaizin	m	f	m		
Madame Creux	T	1890	Godard	op	dbl	l		m
Madame Creyton	HP	1868	Gonod	rb	f	l	vvig	
Madame Crombez	T	1888	Nabonnand G	op	dbl	vl	vig	m
Madame Crozy	HP	1881	Levet	mp		l		
Madame Cusin	T	1881	Guillot et Fils	rb	dbl	m	vig	f
Madame D Wettstein	HP		Verdier V	mr	f	l	vig	
Madame Dacier	G			mr	f	l		
Madame Damaizin	T	1858	Damaizin	w	dbl	vl	vvig	f
Madame Damême	HP	1842	Cochet P	mp	f	l	vvig	
Madame Damoreau	Misc							
Madame d'Arblay	HMult	1835	Wells	w	s-d	m	vvig	m
Madame Daru	T	1858	Morlet	mp	f	l		vf
Madame Daurel	HP	1884	Bernède	rb	f	l	vig	
Madame David	T	1895	Pernet Père	lp	vdbl	m		m
Madame de Baux	T			w				
Madame de Bertot	T			w				
Madame de Cambacérès	HP	Pre 1860		mp	f	m		
Madame de Canrobert	HP	1862	Liabaud	m	f	l	m	
Madame de Canrobert	HP	1868	Gonichon	mr	vf	m	vig	
Madame de Chalonges	T	Pre 1841	Miellez syn Le Pactole	ly	dbl	l		
Madame de Corval	HP	1868	Pernet Père	mp	f	l	vig	
Madame de Coster	G			dp				
Madame de Cousté	HP			lp	vdbl	l	vig	
Madame de Creguy	Ch	Pre 1846		dp				
Madame de France	B		Pradel	w	f	m	m	
Madame de Grandpré	B	1856	Pradel	lp		m		f
Madame de Guizard	HP	1856	Pradel	lp		l		
Madame de la Bastie	HP	1894	Liabaud	mp				
Madame de la Boulaye	HP	1877	Liabaud	op	f	l	vig	
Madame de la Collonge	HT	1889	Levet Père	dp				
Madame de la Rôchelambert	M	1851	Robert	m	f	l	m	vf
Madame de la Rocheterie	HP	1880	Granger	lp	f	l	m	
Madame de Lamoricière	HP	1849	Portemer	pb	f	m	vig	
Madame de Lamou	HP	1861	Lartay	mr				
Madame de Loeben-Sels	HT	1879	Soupert & Notting	w	vf	l		

Name	Type	Date	Breeder	Colour	Form	Size	Vigour	Scent
Madame de Maintenon	D	Pre 1846		p				
Madame de Mannel	HP	1852	Lacharme	mp	f	l	vig	
Madame de Moidrey	T	1896	Schwartz V	mp				
Madame de Montchauveau	HP	1888		lp	dbl	vl		
Madame de Montseignat	B	1861	Pradel	dr				
Madame de Nanteuil	N							
Madame de Narbonne	T	1872	Pradel	my	f	l	m	
Madame de Plantamour	HRg	Pre 1900		m				
Madame de Pontbriant	HP			mr				
Madame de Reydellet	B	1897	Lapierre	mp				
Madame de Reyniès	T	Pre 1870		w	f	l		
Madame de Ridder	HP	1871	Margottin	dr	f	l	vig	m
Madame de Richter	HP	1872	Faudon	dp				
Madame de Rochefontaine	B	1885	Vigneron	lp				
Madame de Rohan	B	Pre 1846		lp				
Madame de Rohan	Ch	Pre 1846		w				
Madame de Saint Fulgent	HP	1872	Gautreau	dr	f	m		
Madame de Saint Genest	HP			m				
Madame de Saint Georges	HP			mr				
Madame de Saint Hermine	HCh	Pre 1846		dp				
Madame de Saint Joseph	T	Pre 1846		lp	dbl	l	m	vf
Madame de Sancy de Parabère	see	Madame	Sancy de Parabère					
Madame de Sansal	P	c 1850	De Sansal	mr				
Madame de Selve	HP	1886	Bernède	mr		vl		
Madame de Sertot	T	1846	Guillot Père syn Madame Bravy	w	dbl	l		
Madame de Serval	HP	1854	Desprez	rb	f	m		
Madame de Sévigné	B	1874	Moreau-Robert	pb	dbl	l	vig	f
Madame de Stael	M	1857	Moreau-Robert	lp	f	m		
Madame de Stella	B	1863	Guillot Père	lp	dbl	m	m	
Madame de Tartas	T	1859	Bernède	mp	dbl	l	vig	sf
Madame de Terrouenne	HP	1887	Vigneron	rb	f	l	vig	
Madame de Tressan	D	1822	Sommesson	mp	f	l		
Madame de Trotter	HP	1854	Granger	r	dbl	m	vig	
Madame de Vatry	T	1855	Guérin	dp	dbl	l	vig	f
Madame de Villars	M	1847	Béluze	mp				
Madame de Ville-Mareuil	HP	1853	Carré	w	f	l		
Madame de Valembourg	HP	Pre 1870		mr	f	l		
Madame de Watteville	T	1883	Guillot et Fils	lp	dbl	l	vvig	vf
Madame Debray	HP	1884	Ribault	dp				
Madame Decour	HP	1869	Pernet Père	mp	vdbl	vl	vvig	
Madame Delacour	HP			mp				
Madame Delaville	T	1873	Oger	w	vdbl	m		
Madame Dellespaul	T	1886	Schwartz V	w	f	l		f
Madame Dellevaux	HP	1883	Besson	mp	f	l	vvig	
Madame Delville	HP	1889	Schwartz V	pb	f	l	vig	
Madame Denis	T	1853	Guillot	w	vf	m-l	vig	
Madame Denis	T	1872	Gonod	w	f	l	wk	
Madame Deparchy	HP	1897	Lévêque	lp				
Madame Depuis	T	Pre 1846		w				
Madame Derepas-Matrat	T	1897	Buatois	dy	dbl	l	vig	
Madame Derouet	HP	1885	Derouet	w	f	l		
Madame Derreult-Douville	HP	1863	Lévêque	mp	f	l	vvig	
Madame Desbordeaux	HP	1873	Oger	mp	f	l	m	
Madame Descamps	T	1863	Pradel	mr	f	l		
Madame Desgaches	B			w	f	s	vig	
Madame Desgaches	HP	Pre 1846		lp	f	m-l	vig	
Madame Deshouillères	G			mr	f	m		
Madame Désir	HP	1886	Pernet Père	op	dbl	l		
Madame Désir Vincent	T	1898	Marqueton	yb	f	l		
Madame Désirée Giraud	HP	1854	Van Houtte	pb	f	m	m	
Madame Deslongchamps	N	1850	Lévêque	w	f	m	vig	
Madame Desmoutiers	G			dr	f	m		
Madame Desprez	B	1831	Desprez	mp	dbl	m	vig	
Madame Desprez	N		see Desprez					
Madame Desprez	Ch	c 1835	Desprez	w	vdbl	l		m
Madame Desrougé (Desrongé)	Ch			dr	f	m		
Madame Desse	HP	1891	Desse	mp				
Madame Desseilligny	T	1873	Pradel	lp	f	l	m	
Madame Devert	HP	1876	Pernet Père	pb	f	vl	vvig	
Madame Devoucoux	T	1874	Ducher Vve	my	dbl	m	vig	
Madame d'Hébray	C	Pre 1820	Chausée, Mme syn Unique Panachée	w	dbl	l	vig	f
Madame Docteur Jutté	T	1872	Levet	yb	f		vig	vf
Madame Docteur Wettstein	HP	1884	Levet	mr	f	l	vig	
Madame Domage	HP	1853	Margottin	mr	dbl	l	vig	vf
Madame Domoran	G			mp	f	l		
Madame Doré	B	1863	Fontaine	lp	dbl	l	m	m
Madame Dorgère	T	1890	Tesnier	lp				
Madame Dorlia	HP	1878	Fontaine	dr	f	l	vig	
Madame Dos Santos Vianna	HP	1882	Soupert & Notting	mr	f	l		
Madame Doublat	HP	1878	Margottin	mr				

Madame Dubarry	G	Pre 1866		mp	f	m		
Madame Dubois	HP	1866	Fontaine	mr			wk	
Madame Dubos	HP	Pre 1870		mr	f	l		
Madame Dubost	B	1890	Pernet Père	lp	f	m		
Madame Dubroca	T	1882	Nabonnand G	pb	dbl	l	vvig	
Madame Dubuisson	HP	1861	Baudry	mp	f	l	vig	
Madame Ducamp	HP	1863	Fontaine	m	f	l	vig	
Madame Ducher	HP	1851	Cordier / Ducher	mr				
Madame Ducher	T	1869	Ducher	ly	f	m	vig	f
Madame Ducher	HP	Pre 1870		lp	f	l		
Madame Ducher	HP	1878	Levet	rb	f	vl	vig	
Madame Duparchy	HP	1898	Lévêque	mp	f	l		
Madame Dupin	HP	1850	Foulard	lp	f	l		
Madame Durand	T	1890	Moreau-Robert	dy	f	l		
Madame Durieu	T	1889	Godard	mp				
Madame Dustour	HP	1869	Pernet Père	pb	f	vl	vig	
Madame E A Nolte	Pol	1892	Bernaix	ly	dbl	m	m	
Madame E Forgeot	HP	1890	Vigneron	mr				
Madame E Souffrain	N	1897	Chauvry	yb	vf	l		
Madame Edmond Cavaignac	T	Pre 1870	Pradel	lp		m		
Madame Ed de Bonnières de Vrières	HP	1887	Lévêque	mp				
Madame Edmond Fabre	HP	1884	Verdier E	mp	dbl	l		
Madame Edmond Laporte	B	1894	Boutigny	pb		vl		
Madame Edouard Dubreuil	B	1850	Pradel	lp	f	l		
Madame Edouard Helfenbein	T	1893	Guillot P	yb	f	l	vig	
Madame Edouard Michel	HP	1886	Verdier E	dp	f	vl		
Madame Edouard Michel	HP	1891	Liabaud	mp				
Madame Edouard Ory	M	1854	Robert-Moreau	dp	dbl	m	vig	m
Madame Edouard Raynaud	B	1856	Pradel	dr	f	m	vig	
Madame Elie Lambert	T	1890	Lambert E	w	vf	vl	m	
Madame Elisa Chabria	HP	Pre 1870		mr	f	l		
Madame Elisa Jaenisch	HP	1869	Soupert & Notting	rb	f	l	vig	
Madame Elisa Reboul	T	1887	Reboul	w		m		vf
Madame Elisa Tasson	HP	1879	Lévêque	mr	f	vl	vvig	
Madame Élisa Vilmorin	HP	1864	Lévêque	mr	dbl	l		
Madame Elisabeth Schwarz	HP	1866	Guillot Père	w				
Madame Elise de Chénier	B	1858	Touvais	dp	f	m	wk	
Madame Elise Stegoleff	T	1881	Nabonnand	lp	vf	l		
Madame Emain	HP	1862	Pernet Père	m	f	l	vig	
Madame Emile de Girardin	M	1853	Robert	lp	f	m		
Madame Emile Duneau	N	1879	Nabonnand	lp	vf	vl	vvig	
Madame Emile Metz	HT	1893	Soupert & Notting	lp				
Madame Emilie Boyau	HP	1864	Paul W	lp	f	l	vvig	
Madame Emilie Charrin	T	1895	Perrier	mp	dbl	l	vvig	
Madame Emilie Dunair	N	1879	Nabonnand	lp		m	wk	
Madame Emilie Dupuy	T	1870	Levet	mp	f	l	vig	f
Madame Emilie Vloeberghs	T	1888	Soupert & Notting	yb	f	m		f
Madame Emma Combey	HP	1872	Cordier / Gonod	mp	f	l	vig	
Madame Emma Dampierre	HP	1842	Desprez	mp	f	m	vig	
Madame Emma Grimm	HP			mr				
Madame Ernest Calvat	B	1888	Schwartz Vve	mp	dbl	vl	vvig	f
Madame Ernest Dréolle	HP	1861	Grujoire	m	f	m		
Madame Ernest Piard	HT	1887	Bonnaire	dp	dbl	vl		
Madame Ernestine Verdier	T	1894	Perny / Aschery	pb	vf	vl		
Madame Errera	T	1899	Soupert & Notting	ob	f	l	vig	vf
Madame Escallier	HP	1878	Margottin	lp				
Madame Etienne	T	1887	Bernaix A	mp			vig	
Madame Etienne Levet	HT	1878	Levet	mr	dbl	l	vig	m
Madame Eugène Appert	HP	1866	Trouillard	op	f	l	vvig	
Madame Eugène Cavaignac	HP	1851	Laffay	lp	f	l		
Madame Eugène Chambeyran	HP	1878	Gonod	pb	f	l	vvig	
Madame Eugène Jouvin	T			lp				
Madame Eugène Labruyère	HP	1882	Gonod	mp	f	l	vig	
Madame Eugène Mallet	N	1875	Nabonnand G	yb	dbl	m	vig	f
Madame Eugène Résal	Ch	1894	Guillot P	pb	dbl	l	vig	f
Madame Eugène Sebille	HP	1890	Vigneron	mp				
Madame Eugène Sudreau	HP	1857	Bernède	dp				
Madame Eugène Verdier	HP	1859	Guillot Père	mp	f	l	vig	m
Madame Eugène Verdier	HP	1875	Verdier E	lp	dbl	l	vig	m
Madame Eugène Verdier	T	1882	Levet	my	f	l		m
Madame Eugénie Boullet	HT	1897	Pernet-Ducher	pb	dbl	l	m	f
Madame Eugénie Bréon	B	1847	Belet	my				
Madame Eugénie Dubus	HP	see	MmeHippolyte Dubus					
Madame Eugénie Frémy	HP	1884	Verdier E	dp	vdbl	l	vvig	
Madame Eugénie Savary	HP	1872	Gonod	w	f	l	vig	
Madame Faber	P			mr				
Madame Falcot	T	1858	Guillot Fils	my	dbl	l	vig	m
Madame Fanny de Forest	N	1882	Schwartz J	lp	dbl	vl	vig	
Madame Fanny Giron	HP	1882	Schmidt	mp	f	l	vvig	
Madame Fanny Pauwels	T	1884	Soupert C	yb	f	m		
Madame Farfouillon	HP	1869	Liabaud	op	f	l		

Name	Class	Year	Breeder					
Madame Fauchère	HP	1871	Pradel	mp				
Madame Fauconnier	HP	1878	Fontaine	dr	f	l	vig	
Madame Fauvennier	HP	1878	Fontaine	lp		l	wk	
Madame Feburier	HP			mp	f	l		
Madame Félicité Trouillet	B			lp	s-d	l		
Madame Félix Faure	HP	1899	Veysset	mr				
Madame Fellier	HP							
Madame Ferdinand Jamin	HP	1875	Ledéchaux	dp	f	vl	vig	vf
			syn American Beauty					
Madame Ferray	P	1836	syn Bernard	op	f	m		
Madame Feuchère	HP			mp				
Madame Fey-Pranard	P	1869	Cherpin	lp	f	l		
Madame Fillion	HP	1865	Gonod	op	dbl	l	vig	
Madame Florentin Laurent	HP	1870	Granger	dp	vf	l		
Madame Flory	HP	1850	Guillot Père	mp	f	l		
Madame Flory	HP	1872	Levet	lp				
Madame Fontaine	G			mp	f	m		
Madame Fontaine	B	1852	Fontaine / Paul	mr	f	m		
			syn Prince Albert					
Madame Forcade La Roquette	HP	1891	Gautreau	rb	f	l	vig	
Madame Fortuné Besson	HP	1881	Besson	lp	vf	vl	vvig	vf
Madame Francis Buchner	HP	1884	Lévêque	lp	f	l	vvig	
Madame Francisque Morel	T	1888	Liabaud	w	f	l	vig	f
Madame François Brassac	T	1884	Nabonnand	rb	vdbl	l	vvig	
Madame François Bruel	HP	1882	Levet	mp	f	l	vig	
Madame François Janain	T	1872	Levet	ob	f	m	m	m
Madame François Pittet	B	1877	Lacharme F	w	vdbl	m	vig	
Madame Fray Panard	HP	1869	Cherpin	lp				
Madame Fréderic Daupias	T	1899	Chauvry	yb	f	l		
Madame Fréderic Daupias	HT	1899	Soupert & Notting	pb	f	vl		
Madame Fréderic Weiss	Pol	1892	Bernaix	rb				
Madame Freemann	HP	1862	Guillot Père	w	f	m	wk	
Madame Freemann	T	1874	Nabonnand	w	f	l	vig	
Madame Frémoin	HP	1853	Margottin	mr	f	m		vf
Madame Fresnoy	HP	1865	Pernet	mr	f	l		
Madame Fresnoy	HP	Pre 1870		lp	f	m		
Madame Freulon	T	1892	Moreau-Robert	w				
Madame Fries-Morel	Ch	Pre 1846		w	vf	m		
Madame Fuller	HP	1853	Robert	mr	f	l	vig	
Madame Furtado	B	1852	Bélot-Défougères	dp	f	l		
Madame Furtado	HP	1860	Verdier V	dp	vf	vl	m	f
Madame Furtado-Heine	HP	1887	Lévêque	pb	f	l	vig	
Madame Gabriel Luizet	HP	1865	Liabaud	lp	f	l	vig	m
Madame Gabriel Méritte	HP	1881	Vigneron	lp	f	m	vig	
Madame Gadel	HP	1872	Pernet Père	m	f	l	vig	
Madame Gaillard	B	1866	Pradel	mp		m	vig	
Madame Gaillard	T	1870	Ducher	op	f	l	m	
Madame Galet	T	Pre 1846		w	f	l		
Madame Galli-Marié	HCh	1876	Verdier E	mp	f	m	vig	
Madame Gaston Allard	T	1893	Cailleau	w		m		
Madame Gaston Anouilh	N	1899	Chauvry	w	dbl	m		vf
Madame Gensoul	B			mr				
Madame George Paul	HP	1886	Verdier E	mr	f	l		
Madame Georges Bouland	T	1894	Lévêque	ob				
Madame Georges Bruant	HRg	1887	Bruant	w	s-d	l	vig	m
Madame Georges Desse	HP	1897	Desse / Duprat	pb				
Madame Georges Durrschmidt	T	1894	Pelletier	mp				
Madame Georges Halphen	T	1899	Lévêque	op		l		
Madame Georges Paul	HP	1866	Verdier E	mp	f	l	vig	
Madame Georges Perrin	HP			lp				
Madame Georges Schwartz	HP	1871	Schwartz	mp	f	vl	vvig	
Madame Georges Vibert	HP	1879	Moreau-Robert	mp	f	vl	vvig	
Madame Gerberon	HP			mr		m-l		
Madame Gévelot	T	1897	Lévêque	mp	f	vl	vig	
Madame Gomot	HP	1885	Liabaud	mp	vdbl	vl		
Madame Gonod	HP	1867	Moreau-Robert	mp	f	l	wk	
Madame Goubault	T	Pre 1846				l		
Madame Grandin-Monville	HP	1875	Verdier E	rb	f	l	vig	
Madame Granla	T	1860	Lartay	dr	f	m		
Madame Grawitz	HP	1878	Soupert & Notting	lp	f	l	vig	vf
Madame Grenville Gore Langton	T	1896	Nabonnand	pb				
Madame Grondier	HP	1867	Gonod	op	f	l	vig	
Madame Gros	B	Pre 1846						
Madame Guérin	T	Pre 1846		w				
Madame Guérin	HP			w	f	m		
Madame Guillaume Koelle	HP	see	Guillaume Koelle					
Madame Guillot	HP	1851	Guillot Père	mp	f	m	vig	
Madame Guinoisseau	HP	see	Auguste Guinoisseau	mp	vf	l		
Madame Gustave Bonnet	HP	1864	Lacharme	mp	f	l	m	
Madame Gustave Bonnet	B	1868	Bizot	mp		vl	vig	m
			syn Zéphirine Drouhin					

Name	Type	Year	Raiser					
Madame Gustave Fintelmann	HP	1853	Baumann	mp	f	l		
Madame Gustave Gossart	N	1889	Godard	lp				
Madame Gustave Henry	T	1899	Buatois	op	dbl	vl	vig	
Madame Gustave Jourdan	B	1852	Pradel	mp				
Madame Gustave Pierret	HP	1884	Vigneron	lp	f	l	vig	
Madame Guyot de Montfavet	HP	1871	Gonod	lp	f	l	vig	
Madame Guyot de Villeneuve	HP	1873	Gautreau	lp	f	l		
Madame H de Potworowska	T	1899	Bernaix	dp	dbl	m		
Madame Haimnan	HP	Pre 1870		lp	f	l		
Madame Hardon	HP	1897	Cochet P	mp				
Madame Hardy	D	1832	Hardy	w	f	l	vig	vf
Madame Hardy du Thé	Pol	1890	Soupert & Notting	w	vdbl	l		m
			syn Clothide Soupert					
Madame Harriet Stowe	HP	1852	Laffay	lp	f	l		
Madame Hébert	G	1828	Mme Hébert	m	vdbl	l	vig	f
			syn Président de Sèze					
Madame Hector Jacquin	HP	1852	Fontaine	pb	f	l	wk	
Madame Hélèna Fould	HP	1878	Lévêque	dr		vl	vvig	
Madame Hélène de Lüsemans	HP	1883	Soupert & Notting	mr	f	l	vig	
Madame Hélène Michel	HP	1883	Vigneron	dr				
Madame Hélène Schirmer	HP	1852	Ohl	mr	f	m		
Madame Helfenbein	B	1852	Guillot Père	m	f	l		
Madame Hélody	HP	1856		lp				
Madame Hélye	HP	1862		mp	f	l	vig	
Madame Hénon	HP	1852	Lille	lp	f	l		
Madame Henri Bennett	T	1872	Levet	lp	f	m		
Madame Henri de Vilmorin	T	1881	Nabonnand	yb	f	l	vig	
Madame Henri Graire	T	1895	Lévêque	pb	f	l	vig	
Madame Henri Gréville	T	1892	Tesnier	my				
Madame Henri Pereire	HP	1887	Vilin	mr	dbl	l		f
Madame Henri Perrin	HP	1892	Schwartz Vve	pb		l		
Madame Henriette	C			pb	f	vl		
Madame Henriette Dubus	HP	1861	Fontaine	dp				
Madame Henriette Vapereaux	HP	1872	Pradel	mr	f	l	vig	
Madame Hérault	HP	1856	Ducher	mp	f	vl	vig	f
Madame Hérivaux	HP	1875	Hérivaux	pb	f	l		
		syn	Mme Charles Crapelet					
Madame Hermann	N	1861	Avoux / Crozy	op	f	m	vig	
Madame Hermann Stenger	HP	1864	Gonod	mp	f	m	wk	
Madame Hersilie Ortgies	B	1868	Moreau-Robert	w		l	vig	
Madame Hersilie Ortgies	HP	1868	Soupert & Notting	lp	f	m	vig	
Madame Hilaire	HP	1850	Verdier V	lp	f	l		
Madame Hippolyte Jamain	T	1869	Guillot Fils	yb	f	l	vig	f
Madame Hippolyte Jamain	HP	1871	Garçon	w	vf	l	vig	
Madame Hitz	HP	Pre 1870		lp	f	m		
Madame Hobetz	B			mp	f	m		
Madame Hoche	M	1859	Robert & Moreau	lp	f	m		
Madame Honoré Defresne	T	1886	Levet F	my	dbl	l	vig	vf
Madame Hortense de Montefiore	HT	1890	Soupert & Notting	w				
Madame Hoste	HP	1865	Gonod	lp	f	m	vvig	
Madame Hoste	T	1887	Guillot et Fils	w	f	vl	vig	f
Madame Huet	C	Pre 1846		lp	f	l		
Madame Humboldt	HP	1850	Ducher	lp	f	l		vf
Madame Hunnebelle	HP	1872	Fontaine	mp	f	vl	vig	
Madame Husson	T	1899	Reboul	w				
Madame Huvette	G			mp	vf	l		
Madame Immerwahr	HP	1885	Singer	mp	f	l	vvig	
Madame Ingrès	B		Pradel	mp				
Madame Isaac Periere	B	1880	Garçon	dp	dbl	l	vig	f
Madame Iwens	HP			lp				
Madame J Bonnaire Pierre	HP	1892	Bonnaire					
Madame J F Trievoz	T	1894	Schwartz Vve	yb				
Madame J M Gonod	HP	1875	Gonod	dr	f	vl		
Madame Jacques Charreton	T	1897	Bonnaire	ab	f	l	vig	f
Madame Jacqueminot	T	1846	Laffay	w	f	l		f
Madame Jacquier	HP	1869	Guillot Fils	m	f	vl	m	
Madame James Gross	HP	1864	Baumann	mp	f	l		
Madame James Hennessy	HP	1879	Duval	mp	f	vl	vvig	
Madame Janin	HP							
Madame Jard	B	1857	Guillot Fils	mr		m	vig	
Madame Jean André	T	1894	Pelletier	mp				
Madame Jean Bansillon	T	1893	Godard	ly				
Madame Jean Sisley	Ch	1884	Dubreuil	w	f	m	vvig	
Madame Jeanne Bouvet	HP	1887	Bernède	lp		m		
Madame Jeanne Bouyer	HP	1877	Gonod	mp	f	vl	vvig	
Madame Jeanne Cuvier	T	1887	Nabonnand	mp	f	l	vig	f
Madame Jeanne Joubert	HCh	1888		dr		l		
Madame Jeannine Joubert	B	1877	Margottin Fils	dp	f	m	vig	
Madame Jelye	HP	Pre 1870		mr	f	l		
Madame Jenny de Forest	N	1882	Schwartz	w				
		see	Madame	Fanny de Forest				

Name	Class	Year	Raiser					
Madame Jenny Varin	HP	1858	Touvais	mp	f	m	vvig	
Madame Jessie Frémont	T	1891	Dingée					
Madame Jobez Desgaches	HP	see	Madame Desgaches					
Madame John Taylor	T	1876	Nabonnand	w	f	l	m	
Madame John Twombly	HP	1881	Schwartz	dr	f	l	vvig	
Madame Jolibois	HP	1879	Verdier E	pb	f	l	vig	
Madame Joly	B	1859	Oger	mp				
Madame Joseph Bonnaire	HT	1891	Bonnaire	pb	vf	vl	vig	
Madame Joseph Bouvet	HP	1886	Bernède	w				
Madame Joseph Combet	HT	1894	Bonnaire	pb	vdbl	l	vig	
Madame Joseph Desbois	HT	1886	Guillot et Fils	w	f	l	m	
Madame Joseph Godier	T	1887	Pernet-Ducher	pb	vf	l		m
Madame Joseph Halphen	T	1858	Margottin	pb	f	m	m	f
Madame Joseph Laperrière	T	1899	Laperrière	lp				
Madame Joseph Linossier	HP	1890	Liabaud	lp				
Madame Joseph Schwartz	T	1871	Schwartz J	w	dbl	m	vig	
Madame Joséphine Guyet	B	1873	Touvais	dr	f	m		
			syn Joséphine Guyet					
Madame Joséphine Mühle	T	1867	Oger	yb	s-d	m	m	f
		syn	Safrano à Fleurs Rou-ges					
Madame Joséphine Mühle	T	1887		pb	vdbl		vig	
Madame Jourdan	B	1851	Pradel	lp	f	m		
Madame Jouvain	N			mr	f	l	vvig	
Madame Jouvain	M	1863	Robert & Moreau	lp				
Madame Jules Caboche	HP	1875	Vigneron	lp	f	l	vig	
Madame Jules Cambon	T	1888	Bernaix	pb	f	m	m	f
Madame Jules de Malleville	B		Pradel	lp				
Madame Jules Finger	HT	1893	Guillot P	lp	f	vl	m	
Madame Jules Franke	N	1887	Nabonnand	w	vf	m	vig	
Madame Jules Girard	HT	1895	Godard	lp				
Madame Jules Grévy	HT	1881	Schwartz	pb	f	m-l	vvig	
Madame Jules Grolez	HT	1896	Guillot P	mp	f	l	vig	f
Madame Jules Margottin	T	1871	Levet	pb	f	m	vig	m
Madame Jules Siegfried	T	1894	Nabonnand	w	dbl	vl		
Madame Julia Daran	HP	1861	Touvais	dr	f	vl		vf
Madame Julie Gonod	HP	1875	Gonod	mr				
			syn Mme J M Gonod					
Madame Julie Labastide	HP			lp				
Madame Julie Lasseu	N	1881	Nabonnand	dp	vf	l	vvig	
Madame Julie Weidmann	HT	1881	Soupert & Notting	op	f	vl	m	
Madame Just-Détrey	B	1869	Just-Détrey	dp	f	l		
Madame Knorr	HP	1855	Verdier	lp	f	m	m	vf
Madame Knorr (same as above?)	P	1865	Verdier V	mp	f	m	vvig	f
Madame Krantz	B	1856	Pradel	mp				
Madame La Baronne Berge	T	1892	Pernet Père	pb	f	m-l	vig	vf
Madame La Baronne de Médem	HP	1876	Verdier E	mr				
Madame La Baronne de Wassenaer	M	1864	Verdier V	m				
Madame La Comtesse de Camondo	HP	1880	Lévêque	mr	f	vl		
Madame La Comtesse de Jaucourt	HP	1866	Desmazures Père	mp	vf			
Madame La Comtesse de Maussac	HP	1874	Vigneron	mp	f	l		
		syn	Comtesse de Maussac					
Madame La Générale Decaen	HP	1869	Gautreau	mp	f	l		
Madame La Générale Gourko	T	1892	Soupert & Notting	mp				
Madame La Marquise d'Hervey	HP	1877	Vigneron	mr	f	l	vig	
		syn	Marquise d'Hervey					
Madame La Moricière	HP	Pre 1870		mp	f	m		
Madame La Princesse de Radziwill	T	1886	Nabonnand	mr	dbl	l		
Madame La Vicomtesse de Terrail	B	1864	Vigneron	lp	f	l	vig	
		syn	Vicomtesse de Terrail					
Madame l'Abbey	C	Pre 1846		mp	f	l		
Madame Lacharme	B	Pre 1846		lp	f	m	vig	
Madame Lacharme	HP	1872	Lacharme	w	f	l	vig	
Madame Lacoste	HP	1856	Bernède	dp	f	m		
Madame Lacour-Jury	HP	1853	Guillot Père	lp	f	m		f
Madame Lacroix	N	1853	Guillot Père	w	f	m		
Madame Lafayette	HCh	Pre 1846		dp				
Madame Laffay	HP	1839	Laffay	mr	dbl	m	vvig	vf
Madame Lambard	T	1878	see Madame Lombard					
Madame Lambert	D	Pre 1848		mr	f	vl		
Madame Lambert-Détrey	M	1874	Moreau-Robert	mp				
Madame Lambert-Détrey	HP	1883	Detrey	mp	f	m-l	vig	vf
Madame Lamon	HP	1861	Lartay	mr		m	vig	
Madame Lamoricière	HP	1849	Portemer	mp	f	l		

Madame Landeau	M	1873	Moreau-Robert	rb	dbl	m	vvig	f
Madame Laporte	Misc		Boutigny					
Madame Laprade	Misc		Pradel	mp				
Madame Larivière	M	1860	Moreau-Robert	lp	f	m		
Madame Lartay	T	1856	Lartay	lp	vf	vl		
Madame Laurent	HP	1870	Granger	mp	vf	l	vvig	
Madame Laurent Simons	T	1894	Lévêque	op	vdbl	l	vig	m
Madame Laure Ramaud (Ramond)	N	1849	Lacharme	lp				
Madame Laurette Messimy	Ch	1887	Guillot et Fils	dp	dbl	l	vig	f
Madame Lauriol de Barny	B	1868	Trouillard	lp	dbl	l		f
Madame Laxton	HP	1875	Laxton	mp	f	l		vf
Madame Lazarine-Poizeau	T	1876	Levet	yb	f	m	vig	
Madame Leclerc Guillory	HP	1851	Robert	mp	f	vl		
Madame Lecomte-Bouquet	HP	1884	Singer	dr	f	l	vig	
Madame Lefèbvre	HP	1885	Moreau-Robert	mp	dbl	l		
Madame Lefèbvre Bernard	HP	1872	Levet	mp	f	m		
Madame Lefèbvre de St-Ouen	HP	1875	Vigneron	mr	f	l	vig	
Madame Lefrançois	HP	1870	Oger	op	f	l		
Madame Legrand	M	1863	Fontaine	pb	dbl	l		
Madame Legras de St Germain	A	Pre 1846		w	vdbl	l	vig	
Madame Lehardelay	T	1852	Oger	my	f	l		
Madame Lelièvre de la Place	HP	1882	Verdier E	mr	f	l	vig	sf
Madame Lemesle	HP	1890	Moreau-Robert	m	dbl	m		
Madame Léon	HBc							
Madame Léon de Malleville	HP		Pradel	mp	vf	l		
Madame Léon de Saint Jean	T	1875	Levet	m	f	vl	wk	
Madame Léon Février	T	1884	Nabonnand G	pb	dbl	vl	vig	vf
Madame Léon Halkin	HP	1886	Lévêque	mr	f	l		
Madame Léonard de Lille	HT	1880	Nabonnand	mr	f	m	vig	vf
Madame Léopold Moreau	HP	1882	Vigneron	mr	dbl	l	vvig	
Madame Létuvée de Colnet	B	1887	Vigneron	lp	f	vl	vig	
Madame Levainville	HP	1871	Pradel	mp	f	m		
Madame Levet	Cl T	1869	Levet	yb	vf	l	vig	f
Madame Liabaud	HP	1858	Lacharme F	w	dbl	m	vvig	
Madame Lierval	HP	1868	Fontaine	pb	f	l		
Madame Lilienthal	HP	1878	Liabaud	dp	f	l	vig	
Madame Limars	HP		Oger	mr	f	l		
Madame Livia Freege	HP	1872	Soupert & Notting	lp	f	l	vig	
Madame Loeben Sels	HT	1879	Soupert & Notting	w	dbl	l	m	
Madame Lombard	T	1877	Lacharme F	op	vdbl	l	vig	f
Madame Longeron	T	1889	Schmidt	my				
Madame Loriol de Barny	HP	1867	Trouillard	mp				
Madame Louis Blanchet	N	1894	Godard	m				
Madame Louis Donadine	HP	1878	Gonod	w	f	l	vig	
Madame Louis Gaillard	T	1892	Liabaud	w	f	l		
Madame Louis Gravier	T	1896	Gamon	op	f	l		m
Madame Louis Henry	N	1879	Ducher Vve	w	f	m	vvig	
Madame Louis Laurans	T	1894	Bonnaire	dr	f	vl	vig	m
Madame Louis Lévêque	HP	1873	Lévêque	dp	dbl	vl	m	sf
Madame Louis Lévêque	T	1892	Lévêque	yb	dbl	l	m	
Madame Louis Lévêque	M	1898	Lévêque	mp	f	l	vig	m
Madame Louis Paillet	HP	1873	Verdier E	lp	f	l	m	
Madame Louis Patry	T	1891	Tesnier	pb				
Madame Louis Poncet	T	1899	Guillot	rb	f	l	vig	m
Madame Louis Reydellet	B	1897	Laperrière	mp				
Madame Louis Ricard	B	1892	Duboc	lp	f	l		m
Madame Louise Carique	HP	1859	Fontaine	mr	f	m	vig	
Madame Louise Collet	M	1840	Vibert	dp	f	l		
Madame Louise Depeyre (Depaygne)	N	1861	Pradel	lp				
Madame Louise Garnier	HP	1871	Pradel	m				
Madame Louise Morin	N	1877	Nabonnand	dy	f	l	m	
Madame Louise Mulson	T	1897	Lévêque	yb	f	l		
Madame Louise Seydoux	HP	1867	Fontaine	lp	f	vl		
Madame Louise Thénard	HP	1850	Fontaine	m	f	l		
Madame Louise Vigneron	HP	1882	Vigneron	lp	f	l	vvig	
Madame Lucien Chauré	HP	1884	Vigneron	mr	f	l	vig	
Madame Lucien Duranthon	T	1898	Bonnaire	w		l		
Madame Lucien Linden	T	1897	Soupert & Notting	yb	dbl	l	vig	vf
Madame Lucile Coulon	T	1899	Schwartz Vve	lp				
Madame Luizet	B	1867	Liabaud	pb	f	l	m	
Madame Lureau-Escalais	HP	1886	Verdier E	mp	dbl	l		
Madame Macker	HP		Soupert & Notting	mp				
Madame Macker	HP	1863	Damaizin	lp	f	l	m	
Madame Macker	B	1868	Liabaud					
Madame Madèle	HP							
Madame Magonette	T	1884	Soupert & Notting	pb	f	m		f
Madame Malherbe	HP	1853	Oger	mp	f	m		
Madame Malibran	C			lp	f	l		
Madame Manoël	HP	Pre 1870		mp	f	l		
Madame Mantin	HP	1888	Vigneron	mp	f	l	vig	

Madame Marcel Fauneau	HP	1886	Vigneron	mr	dbl	l	vig	
Madame Marchal	B	1858	de Fauw	w	f	m	m	
Madame Margat	B	Pre 1846	syn Augustine Margat	mp				
Madame Margottin	T	1866	Guillot et Fils	yb	dbl	l	vig	f
Madame Marguerite de Soras	T	1890	Nabonnand	my				
Madame Marguerite Large	T	1886	Nabonnand	lp				
Madame Marguerite Marsault	HP	1894	Corboeuf	m	dbl	l		
Madame Marie Berton	T	1875	Levet	ly	f	vl		
			syn Marie Berton					
Madame Marie Bianchi	HP	1881	Guillot Fils	m	f	m-l	vvig	vf
Madame Marie Brémond	T	1866	Guillot	m	f	m-l		
Madame Marie Calvat	Ch	1899	Dubreuil	w				
Madame Marie Cirodde	HP	1868	Verdier E	dp	f	l	vvig	vf
Madame Marie Closon	HP	1882	Verdier E	lp	f	l	vvig	
			syn Mlle Marie Closon					
Madame Marie de Beaux	T	1846	Guillot Père	w				
Madame Marie Descamps	HP	1871	Pradel					
Madame Marie de Willeboissnet	HP			lp	f	l		
Madame Marie Dubourg	B	1851	Pradel	lp	f	m		
Madame Marie Duncan	HP	1873	Lacharme	mp	f	l	vig	
Madame Marie Finger	HP	1872	Lacharme	op	f	l	vvig	
Madame Marie Garnier	HP	1882	Gonod	lp	vf	vl	vig	
			syn Lyonnais					
Madame Marie Husser	T	1889	Nabonnand	mr				
Madame Marie Latone	HP	1861	Pradel	mr				
Madame Marie Lavallée	N	1881	Nabonnand G	pb	s-d	vl	vvig	
Madame Marie Legrange	HP	1882	Liabaud	mr	f	vl	vvig	
Madame Marie Manissier	HP	1876	Liabaud	mp	f	m		
Madame Marie Marivaux	Ch							
Madame Marie Pavie	T	1888	Nabonnand	lp	f	vl	vig	f
Madame Marie Röderer	HP	1881	Lévêque	dp	f	l		
Madame Marie Roussin	T	1888	Nabonnand	my	f	l	vig	f
Madame Marie Van Houtte	HP	c 1870	Van Houtte	lp	f	l		
Madame Marie Verdier	HP	1888	Verdier	mp	dbl	l	vig	
Madame Mariette Biolley	HP	1874	Gonod	mp				
Madame Marius Côte	HP	1872	Guillot Fils	dp	vf	vl	vvig	
Madame Marthe d'Halloy	HP	1881	Lévêque	mp	f	l	vig	
Madame Marthe Dubourg (du Bourg)	T	1890	Bernaix	w	f	l	vig	
Madame Martin Cahuzac	T	1892	Lévêque	yb				
Madame Martin de Bessé	HP	1866	Bernardin	w	f	l		
Madame Mary Bennett	HP	1884	Bennett	mp				
Madame Masset	B	1853	Lacharme	mp		l	vig	
Madame Massicault	HP	1884	Schwartz	lp	vdbl	m-l	m	
Madame Masson	HP	1856	Masson	dr	vf	vl	vig	m
Madame Massot	N	1856	Lacharme F	w	f	m	vig	
Madame Massot	B	1875	Lacharme	lp	f	m		
Madame Maurice Kuppenheim	T	1877	Ducher Vve	ab	dbl	l	vig	
Madame Maurice Rivoire	HP	1876	Gonod	lp	f	m	m	
Madame Maurin	T	1853	Guillot	w	vf	l	vig	f
			syn Madame Denis					
Madame Max Singer	T	1884	Singer	yb	f	vl	vvig	
Madame Maxime Bonnet	B	1861	Pradel	mr				
Madame Maxime de la Rocheterie	HP	1880	Granger	mp	f	m-l	vig	
Madame Mélanie	HP	1860	Pernet Père	m	vdbl	m		
Madame Mélanie Vigneron	HP	1882	Vigneron	m	vf	l	vig	
Madame Mélanie Willermoz	T	1845	Lacharme F	w	dbl	l	vig	m
Madame Millard	B		Pradel	lp	f	m		
Madame Miolan Carvalho	N	1875	Chedane-Guinoisseau	dy	f	l	vig	m
Madame Molin	T	1893	Liabaud	lp				
Madame Molroguier	HP			mp	f	l	vig	
Madame Montet	HP	1880	Liabaud	lp	dbl	vl	vvig	f
Madame Morane Jeune	HP	1878	Jamain	lp	f	l	vig	
Madame Moreau	HP	1864	Moreau	mr	vdbl	vl	vvig	f
Madame Moreau	M	1872	Moreau-Robert	pb	dbl	l	vvig	f
Madame Moreau	T	1889	Moreau-Robert	yb	f	vl		
Madame Morel	B	Pre 1846		mp				
Madame Moser	HT	1889	Vigneron	pb	dbl	l		
Madame Mulson	T	1895	Bernaix	pb	f	l		
Madame Musset	HP	1885	Liabaud	mr	f	vl		
Madame Nabonnand	T	1877	Nabonnand	w	f	vl		
Madame Nachury	HP	1873	Damaizin	mp	f	vl	vvig	
Madame Nancy Dubord	B		Pradel	w	f	m	vig	
Madame Nathalie Simon	HP	1882	Vigneron	mr	f	l	vig	
Madame Nérard	B	1838	Nérard	pb	f	l	vig	vf
Madame Neumann	HCh	Pre 1840	Marcheau syn Hermosa	lp	dbl	m	vig	m
Madame Nicholas Koechlin	C	c 1860	Baumann	mp				
Madame Nobécourt	B	1893	Moreau-Robert	lp	vdbl	vl	vvig	vf
Madame Noman	HP	1867	Guillot Père	w	f	s	m	
Madame Norman	HP	Pre 1867	Guillot	w	dbl	m		

Name	Type	Year	Breeder					
Madame Normand Néruda	HP	1884	Paul G	mp		m		vf
Madame Ocker Ferencz	T	1892	Bernaix A	yb	f	l	vig	
Madame Octave Depeyre	HP		Pradel	mp				
Madame Oger	HP	1851	Oger	mp	f	m		
Madame Ohl	Misc	1846		r				
Madame Olga	T	1889	Lévêque	w	f	l	vig	
Madame Olympe Térestchenko	B	1882	Lévêque	w	f	l	vig	
Madame Oscar	T	1882	Lautrec					
Madame Oswald de Kerchove	HP	1879	Schwartz	pb	vf	m	m	vf
Madame Oudin	HP			mr	F	m		
Madame Oudinette	G			mp	vf	m		
Madame Paul Desse	HP	1882	Duprat	mr				
Madame Paul Lacoutière	HT	1897	Buatois	op	s-d	l		
Madame Paul Marmy	T	1884	Marmy	yb	f	l	vvig	f
Madame Paul Tanche	HP	1893	Liabaud	mp	dbl	vl	vig	
Madame Pauline	T			mp				
Madame Pauline Labonté	T	1852	Pradel	op	dbl	l	vig	f
Madame Pauline Vilot	HP	1859	Marest	mr	f	l		
Madame Pauwert	Ch	1876	Rambaux	w	f	l	m	
Madame Payen	Ch			mr	f	m	vig	
Madame Pélisson	T	1891	Brosse	ly	dbl	m	vig	
Madame Pepin	HP	1848	Verdier V	lp	f	m		
Madame Pernet-Ducher	HT	1891	Pernet-Ducher	ly	s-d	l	vig	m
Madame (P) Perny	T	1879	Nabonnand	my	f	l	vig	
Madame Perrier	T	1897	Perrier	my	f	l		
Madame Ph. Dewolfs	HP	1885	Soupert & Notting	mp	f	l	vig	
Madame Phélip	HP	1852	Lacharme	lp	f	l	vig	
Madame Philémon Cochet	T	1887	Cochet S	lp	vdbl	m-l		m
Madame Philippe Kuntz	T	1889	Bernaix	pb	f	l		m
Madame Pierre Cochet	N	1891	Cochet S	yb	dbl	m	vig	vf
Madame Pierre de Beys	HP	1885	Soupert & Notting	dr				
Madame Pierre Guillot	T	1888	Guillot et Fils	ob	f	l	vig	f
Madame Pierre Liabaud	HP	1890	Liabaud	lp				
Madame Pierre Margery	HP	1881	Liabaud	mp	f	l	vig	
Madame Pierre Oger	B	1878	Oger C	pb	dbl	m	vvig	f
Madame Pierre Perny	T	1880	Nabonnand	ly	s-d	l	vig	f
Madame Pierre Pitaval	HP	1885	Liabaud	mr	f	l	vvig	
Madame Pierre Place	HP	1854	Margottin	mp	f	m	vig	
Madame Pierson	HP	1860	Fontaine	lp	f	l		
Madame Plantier, (Climbing)	A	1835	Plantier	w	vdbl	l	vig	m
Madame Plantier	M	Pre 1846		w				
Madame Plantier	HSem	Pre 1846		lp				
Madame Platz	M	1864	Moreau-Robert	dp	dbl	m	vig	vf
Madame Poignant	HP	1871	Pradel	mp	f	l	vig	
Madame Poncey	HCh			dr	f	l		
Madame Ponctuée	M			mp	f	m		
Madame Prosper Laugier	HP	1875	Verdier E	mr	dbl	l	vvig	m
Madame Prudhomme	HP	1872	Moreau-Robert	mr	f	l	vig	
Madame Puissant	HP	1861	Moreau-Robert	mr	f	l		
Madame Pulliat	HP	1866	Ducher	pb	f	l	vig	
Madame Quételet	G	1830	Parmentier	lp	f	s		
Madame Rambaux	HP	1881	Rambaux	dp	vdbl	vl	vvig	m
Madame Rameau	HCh	Pre 1860		dr	s-d	l		
Madame Raoul Chandon	HP	1884	Verdier C	lp	f	l	vig	f
Madame Raphaël de Smet	T	1885	Nabonnand	dp	vf	l		
Madame Ravary	HT	1899	Pernet-Ducher J	ob	dbl	l	vig	m
Madame Ravel	HP			dr				
Madame Rebatel	HP	1885	Liabaud	mp				
Madame Récamier	HP	1853	Lacharme	w	dbl	m	m	
Madame Rémond	T	1882	Lambert E	yb	f	m	vig	m
Madame Renahy	HP	1889	Guillot et Fils	dp	f	l		
Madame Renard	HP	1871	Moreau-Robert	op	dbl	vl	m	f
Madame Rendatler	HP	1853	Oger	dr	f	l		
Madame René de St Marceau	T	1898	Guillot P	yb				
Madame René Gérard	T	1897	Guillot P	yb	f	l		
Madame Renée Baltet	B	1865	Verdier	dr	f	l		
Madame Retornaz	T	1867	Guillot Père	yb	f	l	vig	
Madame Reyniès	T	1860	Pradel	w				
Madame Richaux	HP	1887	Liabaud	mp	f	l	vig	
Madame Richer	N		Laffay	mr				
Madame Richer	HP	1870	Faudon	dp	f	l		
Madame Richter	N	1883	Geschwind	pb				
Madame Ridder	HP	1871	Margottin	dr	f	l	vvig	
Madame Rigail de Lastour	HP		Pradel	mp				
Madame Rival	HP	1866	Gonod	lp	f	l	vig	sf
Madame Rival Verne	HP	1874	Liabaud	pb	f	l	vig	
Madame Rivers	HP	1850	Guillot Père	mp	f	m	vig	
Madame Rivière	B	1875	Verdier E	lp	f	vl	vig	
Madame Rocher	HP	1878	Cochet S	dr	vf	l	vig	
Madame Rochet	HP	1883	Liabaud	mp	f	l	vig	
Madame Roger	HP	1877	Moreau-Robert	lp	f	l	vig	
Madame Rohan	HP		syn Madame Bureau	w				

Madame Rohan	T	1888		lp	f	l		
Madame Roland	HP	1869	Roland	pb	f	l		
Madame Rolland	G	Pre 1835	Girardon	dp	dbl	l		f
Madame Rolland	HP	1867	Moreau-Robert	dp	f	vl	m	
Madame Rollet	HP	1875	Gonod	mp	f	vl		
Madame Rosalie de Wincop	HP	1881	Vigneron	mp	f	l	vvig	
Madame Rosa Monnet	HP	1885	Monnet	dp		l		m
Madame Rose Caron	HP	1899	Lévêque	mp		l		
Madame Rose Charmeux	HP	1875	Gautreau	dr	vf	m		
Madame Rose Chéri	M	1850	Laffay	mp	dbl	m	vig	
Madame Rose Romarin	T	1888	Nabonnand	rb	f	l	vig	m
Madame Rosine Cavène	T	1891	Reboul	w				
Madame Rouge	B	1882		dr				
Madame Rougier	HP	1875	Jamain	lp	f	l	vig	
Madame Roussel	T	1830	Desprez	w	f	l		
Madame Rousset	HP	1864	Guillot Fils	lp	f	l	vvig	
Madame Rozain-Boucharlat	T	1894	Liabaud	yb	f	l	vvig	
Madame S Mottet	N	1899	Cochet-Cochet	my				
Madame Sadi Carnot	T	1889	Renaud G	w				
Madame Saison Lierval	HP	1873	Verdier E	mr	f	vl	m	
Madame Salomé Barth	HP	1853	Ohl	lp	f	vl		
Madame Sancy de Parabère	Bslt	1874	Bonnet	mp	s-d	m	vvig	m
Madame Sandeur	G			lp	f	m		
Madame Sanglier	HP	1885	Vigneron	rb				
Madame Saportas	G			dp	dbl	l		
Madame Schmitt	HP	1854	Schmitt	mp	f	l	vig	
Madame Schultz	N	1856	Béluze	yb	dbl	m	vig	vf
Madame Schwaller	HT	1886	Bernaix	mp		l	vig	
Madame Scipion Cochet	HP	1872	Cochet S	rb	dbl	l	vig	
Madame Scipion Cochet	T	1886	Bernaix A	pb	dbl	l	vig	m
Madame Seigneur	HP	1851	Quettier	mp	f	l		
Madame Senez	T	1852	Pradel	ly	f	m		
Madame Simon	HP	1851	Oger	mr	f	l		
Madame Simon	T	1890	Moreau-Robert	w				
Madame Simon Delaux	T	1891	Degressy	yb				
Madame Simonne	HP			mp				
Madame Smith	HP			mp				
Madame Solignac	T	1889	Schmidt	w				
Madame Sommeson	G	Pre 1834		lp	f	m		
Madame Sophie Froppot	HP	1876	Levet	mp	dbl	l	vvig	
Madame Sophie Stern	HP	1887	Lévêque	dp	dbl	vl		
Madame Soubeyran	HP	1872	Gonod	dp	f	s	vig	vf
Madame Souchet	B	1843	Souchet	pb	vf	l	vig	f
Madame Soupert	M	1851	Moreau-Robert	mr	f	m	vig	
Madame Soupert	HP	1862	Portemer	w	f	m	vig	
Madame Soupert (?same as above)	HP	1864	Pernet	w	f	m		
Madame Souveton	P	1874	Pernet Père	pb	f	m	m	
Madame Standish	HP	1860	Trouillard	mp	f	m	vig	
Madame Stingue	HP	1884	Liabaud	dr	f	l	vig	
Madame Stolz	D	Pre 1848		ly	f	m		m
Madame Suzanna Schultheis	T	1880	Nabonnand	my	f	vl	vvig	
Madame Suzanne Chavagnon	HP	1887	Gonod	mp	f	vl		
Madame Sylvestre	T		Verdier E	w	f	m		
Madame Tellier	HP	Pre 1870		lp	f	m		
Madame Teyssier	T	1876	Pernet Père	mp	vdbl	vl	vvig	
Madame Thalberg	M			mp	f	m		
Madame Théobold Sernin	HP	1877	Brassac	mr	f	l	vig	
Madame Théodore Cornet	HP	1899	Bénard	mr				
Madame Théodore Delacour	HP	1884	Verdier E	mp	f	m	vig	
Madame Théodore Martell	HP	1854	Margottin	lp	vdbl	l	vig	
Madame Théodore Vernes	HP	1891	Lévêque	mp	f	l		
Madame Thérèse de Parieu	HP	1871	Gautreau	mp	f	l		
Madame Thérèse Deschamps	T	1888	Nabonnand	pb	s-d	l	vig	f
Madame Thérèse Genevay	T	1874	Levet	op	f	l	vig	f
Madame Thévenot	HP	1878	Jamain H	dr	vdbl	l	m	vf
Madame Thibaut	HP	1889	Lévêque	lp	dbl	l		
Madame Thiébaut Aîné	HP	1886	Lévêque	mp				
Madame Thiéran	M	1851	Foulard	mr	f	m		
Madame Thiers	B	1873	Pradel	pb	f	m	vig	
Madame Thirion	T	1894	Puyravaud	mp				
Madame Tissot	T			w	f	m	vvig	
Madame Tixier	T	1886	Tixier	lp				
		syn	Souvenir d'un Ami					
Madame Tony Baboud	HT	1895	Godard	my	s-d	l		
Madame Tressan	G	1822	Sommesson	mp	f	l		
			syn Mme de Tressan					
Madame Treyre Marie	HP	1886	Liabaud	mr	f	l	vig	
Madame Trifle	N	1869	Levet	yb	vdbl	l	vig	m
Madame Tripet	B	1845	Margottin	dp	vf	vl		
Madame Tronel	T	1876	Oger	pb	f	l	vig	
Madame Trudeaux	HP	1850	Boll	dp	f	l		

Name	Type	Year	Breeder					
Madame Ugalde	M	Pre 1870		lp		m		
Madame Vachez	B	1864	Ducher	lp		vl	m	
Madame Valembourg	HP	1863	Oger	m	f	l	vig	
Madame Van Houtte	HP	1857	Margottin	lp	f	m		
		see	also M-	me Marie Van Houtte				
Madame Varangeot	B			mr	f	l		
Madame Vasseur	HP	1852	Pradel	mr	f	l		
Madame Vauvel	HP	1885	Verdier E	lp				
Madame Verdier	HP	1840	Verdier V	w	f			
Madame Verlot	HP	1876	Verdier E	mp	vf	vl	vig	vf
Madame Verrier-Cachet	HP	1895	Chédane-Guinoisseau	mr	dbl	vl		
Madame Verschaffelt	HP	1864	Verdier E	lp	f	l		
Madame Veuve Alexandre Pommery	HP	1882	Lévêque	lp	vf	vl	vvig	
Madame Veuve Ménier	HT	1891	Schwartz Vve	lp	vf	l		
Madame Vibert	HP	c 1835	Vibert	dp	f	m		
Madame Victor Caillet	T	1891	Bernaix	pb	dbl	l		
Madame Victor Hovart	HP	1882	Vigneron	dr	f	l	vig	
Madame Victor Verdier	HP	1863	Verdier E	mr	vf	l	vig	vf
Madame Victor Wibaut	HP	1870	David	op	f	m		
Madame Vidot	HP	1854	Couturier; Verdier E	ab	f	m	vig	vf
Madame Vignat	HP	1892	Liabaud	lp				
Madame Vigneron	HP	1858	Vigneron	op	f	vl	vig	f
Madame Ville	G	Pre 1885		mp	f	m		
Madame Ville-Mereuil	HP	1853	Carré	lp	f	l		
Madame Villerin	T	Pre 1846		w				
Madame Villy	HP	1885	Liabaud	rb	f	l		
Madame Viviand-Morel	Ayr	1882	Schwartz	dp	f	m	vvig	f
Madame Viviand-Morel	HP	1887	Bernaix	mr	dbl	vl		
Madame Von Siemens	T	1895	Nabonnand	mp	f	vl		
Madame W C Whitney	HT	1894	May	lp		l		vf
			syn Mrs W C Whitney					
Mme Wagram, Comtesse de Turenne	T	1894	Bernaix A	pb	f	vl	vig	m
Madame Walton	B	1874	Nabonnand	mr	f	m	m	
Madame Ward	HP		Ward	mp	f	l	vig	
Madame Welche	T	1878	Ducher Vve	yb	f	l	vig	vf
Madame Wilfrid	HP			mp	f	m		
Madame William	T	1857	Lartay	ly	f	l	m	f
Madame William Bull	HP	1876	Verdier E	dp	f	m	vig	vf
Madame William Paul	HP	1862	Verdier E	m	f	l	vig	
Madame William Paul	M	1869	Moreau-Robert	dp	dbl	l	vig	
Madame William Wood	HP	1876	Verdier E	pb	vf	l	vig	
Madame Wilson	HP	1883	Vigneron	lp	f	l	vvig	vf
Madame Xé	HP							
Madame York	HP	1881	Moreau-Robert	dr	dbl	l	vig	vf
Madame Zöetmans	D	1830	Marest	w	vdbl	m	vig	m
Mmes Soeurs Chevandier	HP	1864	Pernet	dr		m		
Madeleine	HCh	1888	syn Emmeline	lp	vdbl	l	vig	
Madeleine Chomer	B	1876	Schwartz	lp	f	m	m	
Madeleine d'Aoust	T	1889	Bernaix	lp	f	l		
Madeleine de Vauzelle	B	1882	Vigneron	lp	f	l	vvig	
		syn Mlle	Madeleine de Vauzelle					
Madeleine Guillaumez	T	1892	Bonnaire	w		m	vig	
Madeleine Nonin	HP	1866	Ducher	mp	f	m	m	
Madelon Friquet	G	1842	Vibert	pb	vf	m		
Mademoiselle	G	1820	Vibert	lp	f	m		
Mademoiselle Adèle Bourdeau	B	1874	Vigneron	lp	f	l		
Mademoiselle Adèle de Murinais	HP	1877	Schwartz J	lp	f	l	vig	
Mademoiselle Adèle Jougant	Cl T	1862	Ledéchaux	my	dbl	m	vvig	
Mademoiselle Adèle Launay	HP	1863	Boyau	lp	f	l		
Mademoiselle Adelina Viviand-Morel	N	1890	Bernaix	ab	dbl	m-l		
Mademoiselle Adeline Outrey	HT	1889	Nabonnand	my				
Mademoiselle Adrienne Christophle	T	Pre 1870		ab	f	m		
Mademoiselle Alboni	M	1850	Verdier V	lp	f	m	m	
Mademoiselle Alice Furon	HT	1896	Pernet-Ducher	ly	f	l		
Mademoiselle Alice Leroi	M	1842	Vibert	m	dbl	m		
Mademoiselle Alice Leroy	HP	1855	Trouillard	lp	f	m	m	
Mademoiselle Alice Marchand	B	1891	Vigneron	lp	f	l		
Mademoiselle Alice Morhange	HP	1879	Bernède	dp	f	l	vvig	
Mademoiselle Aline Gilbon	HP	1853	Laffay	mp	f	m		vf
Mademoiselle Aline Pierron	B			w	f	m		
Mademoiselle Amanda (e)	T	1861	Lartay	mr	f	l		
Mademoiselle Amélie Halphen	HP	1864	Margottin	lp	vf	l		
Mademoiselle Anaïs Lorette	Misc			mp				
Mademoiselle Anaïs Molin	Pol	1895	Molin	w		s	m	
Mademoiselle Andrée Worth	B	1890	Lévêque	lp	f	l		
Mademoiselle Angeline Séringe	HP	1852	Bernède	mp	f	l		

Name	Type	Year	Breeder					
Mademoiselle Anna Chatron	T	1896	Schwartz Vve	yb	f	l	vig	
Mademoiselle Anne-Marie Côte	N	1875	Guillot Fils	w		l		
Mademoiselle Anne-Marie Danloux	HP	1877	Vigneron	lp	f	l	vig	
Mademoiselle Annette Gamon	HT	1889	Godard	lp				
Mademoiselle Annette Murat	T	1884	Levet	my	f	m	vvig	
Mademoiselle Annie de Varange	B	1851	Pradel	lp	f	m-l	vig	
Mademoiselle Annie Wood	HP	1866	Verdier E	mr	dbl	l	vvig	m
Mademoiselle Antonia Decarly	T	1873	Levet	dy	f	m		
Mademoiselle Antonine Veysset	T	1874	Veysset	yb				
Mademoiselle Aristide	N	1857	Robert	ly	f	l	vig	
Mademoiselle Aristide	M	1858	Laffay	dp	f	m		
Mademoiselle Augusta	HP			mr				
Mademoiselle Augustine Guinoisseau	HT	1889	Guinoisseau	pb	dbl	l	vig	
		syn	Augustine Guinoiseau					
Mademoiselle Berger	B	1884	Pernet Père	lp	f	m-l	m	
Mademoiselle Bertha Ludi	Pol	1891	Pernet-Ducher	w	f		m	
Mademoiselle Berthe Bazterais	HP	1869	Fontaine	mp	f	m	vig	
Mademoiselle Berthe Chanu	HP	1867	Fontaine	dp	f	l		
Mademoiselle Berthe Clavel	B	1891	Chauvry	w	f	l		
Mademoiselle Berthe Lévêque	HP	1865	Céchet Père	lp	f	s	vig	
Mademoiselle Berthe Levet	HP	1865	Cochet	mp	f	l	m	
Mademoiselle Berthe Lirique	HP	Pre 1870		lp	f	m		
Mademoiselle Berthe Saccavin	HP	1875	Verdier E	lp	f	l	wk	
Mademoiselle Betzi Haimann	HP			yb				
Mademoiselle Blanche	HP	1877	Guillot Fils	lp				
Mademoiselle Blanche Durrschmidt	T	1877	Guillot Fils	lp	dbl	m	vig	
Mademoiselle Blanche Lafitte	B	1851	Pradel	lp	dbl	m	vig	
Mademoiselle Bonnaire	N	1859	Pernet Père	w	dbl	l	m	
Mademoiselle Bonnaire	HP	Pre 1870		lp	f	l		
Mademoiselle Boursault	G		Noisette	w	vdbl	m		
Mademoiselle Brigitte Viollet	T	1878	Levet	m	f	l	vig	
Mademoiselle Camille Bigotteau	HP	1882	Vigneron	mr	f	l	vvig	
Mlle Camille de Rochetaillée	Pol	1886	Bernaix	w	f	m		m
Mademoiselle Cécile Brunner	Pol	1880	Ducher Vve	lp	dbl	s	vig	m
Mlle Cécile Brunner, Climbing	Cl Pol	1894	Hosp	lp	dbl	s	vig	vf
Mademoiselle Charlotte Card	HP	1876	Vigneron	mr	f	l		
Mlle Charlotte de la Trémoille	HP	1877	Chedane-Guinoisseau	lp	f	vl		vf
Mademoiselle Christina Nilson	HP	1867	Lévêque	mp	f	l	vvig	
Mademoiselle Christine de Noué	T	1890	Guillot et Fils	rb	f	l	vig	m
Mademoiselle Claire Jacquier	N	1888	Bernaix A	ly	s-d	m	vvig	m
			syn Claire Jacquier					
Mademoiselle Claire Mathieu	HP	1875	Vigneron	lp	f	m		
Mademoiselle Claire Merle	T	1885	Nabonnand	lp				
Mademoiselle Claire Truffaut	B	1887	Verdier E	lp	dbl	m	vig	vf
Mademoiselle Claudine d'Offroy	HP	1861	Touvais	mr		s	vig	
Mademoiselle Claudine Perreault	T	1885	Lambert E	mp	dbl	vl		
Mademoiselle Clémentine Ribault	HP	1885	Ribault	mr				
Mlle Clémentine de Fontenille	HP		Pradel	mr	vf	l		f
Mademoiselle Clothilde Perrault	B	1863	Vigneron	mr				
Mademoiselle Clothilde Soupert	T	1883	Levet	mp	vdbl	l		
Mademoiselle de France	Ch	1827	Mauget	w				
Mademoiselle de la Seiglière	HP	1886	Maindion	lp	f	l		
Mademoiselle de la Serna	G		Parmentier	lp				
Mademoiselle de Labarthe	T	1856	Bernède	lp	f	l	vig	vf
		syn	Duchesse de Brabant					
Mademoiselle de Salvandy	T			ly				
Mademoiselle de Sombreuil	T	1850	Robert	w	dbl	l	vig	f
Mademoiselle Denise de Reversaux	T	1855	Cook	w	dbl	vl	vig	m
			syn Cornelia Cook					
Mademoiselle Donadieu	HP			lp		l		
Mademoiselle Dubost	HP	1891	Pernet Père	lp				
Mademoiselle Duchesnois	G			lp	f	l		
Mademoiselle Dumaine	HP	1874	Pernet Père	lp	vdbl	l	m	
Mademoiselle Elénore Grier	HP	1876	Verdier E	dp	f	l	vig	
Mademoiselle Elisabeth de Grammont	T	1885	Levet Cl.	pb	f	l		f
Mlle Elisabeth de la Rocheterie	HP	1881	Vigneron	lp	f	vl		
Mademoiselle Elisabeth	T	1897	Liabaud	lp		vl		

Monod

Mademoiselle Elise Chabrier	HP	1867	Gautreau / Cochet S	lp	vdbl	l	vig	
		syn	Mlle Louise Chabrier					
Mademoiselle Emain	B	1861	Pernet	w	f	l		
Mademoiselle Emélie Fontaine	HP	1881	Fontaine	mr	vdbl	l	vvig	vf
Mademoiselle Emélie Verdier	HP	1875	Verdier E	mp	f	l	wk	m
Mlle Emélie Verdier, Climbing	Cl HP	1878	Paul G	lp				
Mademoiselle Emily Laxton	HP	1878	Laxton	lp				
Mademoiselle Emma Allen	HP	1877	Liabaud	mp	f	vl		
Mademoiselle Emma Hall	HP	1876	Liabaud	op	f	l	vig	
Mlle Eugénie Leprovost de Launay	HP	1856	Pradel		f			
Mademoiselle Eugénie Savary	HP	1872	Gonod	w	f	l	vvig	
		syn	Mme Eugénie Savary					
Mademoiselle Eugénie Verdier	HP	1859	Verdier E	lp	dbl	vl	vig	
Mademoiselle Eugénie Verdier	HP	1869	Guillot et Fils	mp	vdbl	l	vig	f
Mademoiselle Eugénie Verdier	HP	1872	Schwartz	mr		l	vig	
Mlle Eugénie Verdier, Climbing	HP	1887	Paul G	mp				
Mademoiselle Eugénie Wilhelm	HP	1873	Soupert & Notting	dr	vf	l		
Mademoiselle Faugel	HP	1857	Robert & Moreau	lp				
Mademoiselle Favart	B	1869	Lévêque	lp	f	m		
Mademoiselle Félicité Trouillot	B	1861	Verdier E	mp	s-d	m	vig	
Mademoiselle Fernande de la Forest	HP	1872	Damaizin	pb	f	l	vvig	
Mademoiselle Fernande Dupuy	Pol	1899	Vigneron	dp	dbl	s	m	
Mademoiselle Franziska Krüger	T	1879	Nabonnand G	op	vdbl	l	vig	m
Mademoiselle Gabrielle de Peronny	HP	1863	Lacharme	mr	f	l		
Mademoiselle Gabrielle Martel	T	1874	Levet	m	f	l		
			syn Gabrielle Martel					
Mademoiselle Gabrielle Touvais	HP			dp				
Mademoiselle Geneviève Godard	T	1889	Godard	yb	dbl	m		
Mademoiselle Geneviève Goujon	T	1891	Schwartz Vve	w				
Mademoiselle Germaine Caillot	HT	1887	Pernet-Ducher	op	f	vl		
Mademoiselle Germaine Molinier	T	1896	Schwartz Vve	ab	dbl	l	m	
Mademoiselle Germaine Raud	T	1894	Raud	w	vdbl	l		
Mademoiselle Germaine Trochon	Cl HT	1893	Pernet-Ducher	pb	f	l	vig	m
Mademoiselle Godard	HP	1857	Ducher	mp	f	l		
Mademoiselle Haymann	HP	1855	Lartay	mp	f	l	vig	
			syn Léon Haymann					
Mademoiselle Hélène Croissandeau	HP	1882	Vigneron	mp		vl	vig	
Mlle Hélène Gambier (Cambier)	HT	1895	Pernet-Ducher	op	dbl	l		vf
Mademoiselle Hélène Michel	HP	1883	Vigneron	dr	f	l	vvig	
Mademoiselle Henriette	HP	1857	Lartay	mp				
Mademoiselle Henriette de Beauvan	T	1887	Lacharme	my	f	l		vf
Mademoiselle Henriette Dubus	HP	1858	Fontaine	mr	f	s	m	
Mademoiselle Henriette Mathieu	HP	1884	Vigneron	mp				
Mademoiselle Henriette Vapereau	HP	1871	Pradel	mp				
Mademoiselle Honorine Duboc	HP	1894	Duboc	dp	dbl	vl		
Mademoiselle Hortense Blanchette	B	1860	Damaizin	w				
Mademoiselle Inola (e) d'Adorjan	HP	1874	Verdier E	mp	f	l	vvig	
Mademoiselle Jacqueline Bouvet	HP	1884	Bernède	dr	f	l	vvig	
Mademoiselle Jeanne de Gironde	T	1852	Pradel	lp	f	l		
Mademoiselle Jeanne Ferron	Pol	1887	Schwartz Vve	mp	f	l		
Mademoiselle Jeanne Guillaumez	T	1889	Bonnaire	dp	f	l	vvig	
Mademoiselle Jeanne Marix	HP	1866	Liabaud	m	f	l		
Mademoiselle Jeanne Naudin	T	1878	Nabonnand	w	f	l	vvig	
Mademoiselle Jeanne Philippe	T	1898	Godard	yb	f	vl		
Mademoiselle Jenny Gay	B	1865	Guillot Fils	w	f	m		
			syn Jenny Gay					
Mademoiselle Joséphine Burland	Pol	1886	Bernaix	w	vdbl	l		

Mademoiselle Joséphine Guyet	B	1863	Touvais	dr	f	m		
			syn Joséphine Guyet					
Mademoiselle Joséphine Violet	N	1890	Levet Fils	my				
Mademoiselle Jules Grévy	HP	1879	Gautreau	dr	f	l		
Mademoiselle Julia Dymonier	HP	1879	Gonod	lp	f	l	vvig	
			syn Julia Dymonier					
Mademoiselle Julia Touvais	HP	Pre 1870		lp	f	l		
Mademoiselle Julie Gaulain	HP	1883	Liabaud	op	vdbl	l	vvig	
Mademoiselle Julie Péréard	HP	1872	Pernet Père	mp	f	vl	m	
Mademoiselle Juliette Berthaud	B	1890	Schwartz Vve	my				
Mademoiselle Juliette Doucet	T	1881	Bernède	yb	f	l	vvig	
Mademoiselle Juliette Halphen	HP	1869	Margottin	lp	f	l	vig	
Mlle la Comtesse de Leusse	T	1878	Nabonnand	pb	dbl	l		
Mlle la Princesse de Bourbon	T	1878	Nabonnand	mp	vdbl	m		
Mademoiselle Laure Dubourg	B	1850	Pradel	mr	f	l		
			see also Laure Dubor					
Mademoiselle Lazarine Poizeau	T	1876	Levet	ob	f	m	vig	
Mademoiselle Léa Lévêque	HP	1883	Verdier E	lp	f	m	vig	
Mademoiselle Léonie Giessen	HP	1875	Lacharme	lp	f	l	vig	
Mademoiselle Léonie Persin	HP	1861	Fontaine	lp	f	l		
Mademoiselle Lobry	HP	1863	Guillot Père	w	vdbl	m	vig	
Mademoiselle Loïde de Falloux	HP	1864	Trouillard	w	f	l	m	
Mademoiselle Louise Aunier	HP	1883	Liabaud	mp		l	vvig	
Mademoiselle Louise Bourdin	B	1893	Vigneron	mr				
Mademoiselle Louise Boyer	HP	1881	Bernède	dp	f	vl	vvig	
Mademoiselle Louise Carique	HP			mr	f	m		
Mademoiselle Louise Chabrier	HP	1867	Cochet S	lp	dbl	l		
Mademoiselle Louise Chrétien	HP	1883	Liabaud	dp	f	vl	vvig	
Mademoiselle Louise Dessagre	B	1861	Pradel	w		l	vig	
Mademoiselle Louise Lion	B	1852	Pradel	dr	f	m	vig	
Mademoiselle Louise Margérand	HP	1876	Liabaud	lp	f	l	wk	
Mademoiselle Louise Morin	N	1878	Nabonnand	yb	f	l	vvig	
Mademoiselle Louise Oger	T	1895	Lévêque	w				
Mademoiselle Lucie Chauvin	T	1893	Moreau-Robert	op	f	vl		
Mademoiselle Lucie Faure	T	1898	Nabonnand	w		l	vig	
Mademoiselle Lucie Jolicoeur	T	1896	Soupert & Notting	pb	dbl	l	vig	f
Mademoiselle Lucile Lafite	T		Pradel	mp				
Mademoiselle Lydia Marty	HP	1878	Liabaud	lp	f		vvig	
Mlle Madeleine de Vauzelles	B	1881	Vigneron	lp	f	l		
Mademoiselle Madeleine Delaroche	T	1890	Corboeuf	lp	vf	l		
Mademoiselle Madeleine Nonin	HP	1866	Ducher	op	f	m		
Mademoiselle Malibraz	Misc	1877	Levet					
Mademoiselle Malvine Lartay	HP	c 1855	Lartay	mr	f	m		
Mademoiselle Marguerite Appert	HT	1896	Vigneron	mr	f	vl		
Mademoiselle Marguerite Boudet	HP	1888	Guillot Fils	op	f	l	m	
Mademoiselle Marguerite Chatelain	B	1880	Vigneron	lp				
Mademoiselle Marguerite de Thésillat	T	1883	Nabonnand	mr				
Mademoiselle Marguerite D'Ombrain	HP	1888		lp	f	vl	vig	vf
Mademoiselle Marguerite Fabisch	T	1889	Godard	mp				
Mademoiselle Marguerite Manein	HP	1879	Fontaine	dr	f	l		
Mademoiselle Marguerite Michon	HP	1882	Vigneron	dr	f	l	vig	
Mademoiselle Marguerite Preslier	T	1892	Ducher Fils	mr				
Mademoiselle Marie Achard	HP	1896	Liabaud	lp				
Mademoiselle Marie André	HP	1882	Soupert & Notting	mr	f	m		
Mademoiselle Marie Arnaud	T	1872	Levet	my	f	l	vig	m
Mademoiselle Marie Aviat	HP	Pre 1870	syn Marie Aviat	lp	f	m		
Mademoiselle Marie Bady	HP	Pre 1870		mr	f	l		
Mademoiselle Marie Berton	T	1876	Levet	ly	f	vl		
Mademoiselle Marie Brécy	B	1851	Pradel	lp	f	l	vig	
Mademoiselle Marie Castel	HP	1877	Verdier E	lp	f	m-l	vig	
Mademoiselle Marie Chauvet	HP	1881	Besson	dp	vf	vl	vvig	
Mademoisells Marie Closon	HP	1882	Verdier E	lp	vf	m-l		
			see Marie Closon					
Mademoiselle Marie Cointet	HP	1872	Guillot Fils	mp	f	l	m	
Mademoiselle Marie Crépey	T	1894	Pernet Père	my				
Mademoiselle Marie Dauphin	HP	1886	Liabaud	lp				
Mademoiselle Marie Dauvesse	HP	1859	Vigneron	mp	f	m		

Name	Type	Year	Breeder	col5	col6	col7	col8	col9
Mademoiselle Marie Debeaux	T	1846	Guillot Père	mp				
Mademoiselle Marie de la Villeboisnet	HP	1864	Trouillard	lp	f	vl	vig	
Mademoiselle Marie de Malleville	HP		Pradel	lp				
Mademoiselle Marie Descamps	HP	1871	Pradel	mp				
Mademoiselle Marie Digat	HP	1882	Levet Père	mr	f	l	vig	vf
Mademoiselle Marie Drivon	B	1887	Schwartz	pb	vdbl	m	vvig	
Mademoiselle Marie Ducher	T	Pre 1870		lp	f	l		
Mademoiselle Marie Gagnières	T	1879	Nabonnand	yb	f	vl	vig	f
		see	Marie Gagnières					
Mademoiselle Marie Garnier	HP			lp	f	vl		
Mademoiselle Marie Gaze	N	1892	Godard	pb	dbl	l		m
Mademoiselle Marie Gonod	HP	1871	Gonod	lp	f	l	m	
Mademoiselle Marie Halphen	HP			mp	f	l		
Mademoiselle Marie Liabaud	HP	Pre 1870		dp	f	m		
Mademoiselle Marie-Louise Bourgeois	M	1891	Corboeuf	w	f	l		
Mlle Marie-Louise de Vitry	HP	Pre 1870		mp	f	m		
Mlle Marie Louise Margerand	HP	1876	Liabaud	lp	f	l	vig	
Mademoiselle Marie-Louise Oger	T	1895	Lévêque	w		vl		
Mademoiselle Marie Louise Pagerie	T	1894	Chauvry	lp				
Mademoiselle Marie Magat	HP	1889	Liabaud	mr	dbl	l		
Mademoiselle Marie Métral	HP	1888	Liabaud	mp	f	l	vig	
Mademoiselle Marie Moreau	T	1879	Nabonnand G	w	f	m	vig	
Mademoiselle Marie Page	HP	1894	Corboeuf	lp	f	l		
Mademoiselle Marie Perrin	HP	1893	Perrin	lp				
Mademoiselle Marie Rady	HP	1865	Fontaine	mr	f	l	vig	
Mademoiselle Marie Roë	HP	1875	Liabaud	mp	f	l	vig	
Mademoiselle Marie Röderer	HP	1881	Lévêque	mp				
		syn	Mme Marie Röderer					
Mademoiselle Marie Sisley	T	Pre 1870		w	f	m		
Mademoiselle Marie Thérèse Coumer	B	1867	Liabaud	mp	f	l		
Mlle Marie Thérèse de la Devausaye	B	1895	Chédane-Guinoisseau	w	f	l		
Mademoiselle Marie Thérèse Molinier	T	1896	Schwartz Vve	lp				
Mademoiselle Marie van Houtte	T	1871	Ducher	pb	f	l	vvig	f
			syn Marie van Houtte					
Mademoiselle Marie Verdier	HP	1877	Verdier E	mp	f	vl	vig	m
Mademoiselle Marie Verlot	HP	1883	Verdier E	mp	f	l	vig	vf
Mademoiselle Marthe Hirigoyen	B	1899	P Marqueton	lp				
Mademoiselle Mathilde Lenaerts	T	1880	Levet	lp	dbl	l	vvig	
Mademoiselle Montesquieu	B	Pre 1846		w	f	m	vig	
Mademoiselle Montessu	G			lp	f	m		
Mademoiselle Nancy Laserre	B	1851	Pradel	mp	f	l		
Mademoiselle Nathalie Imbert	T	1883	Nabonnand	mp	f	l	vvig	
Mademoiselle Noelie Merle	T	1878	Nabonnand	my	f	vl		
Mademoiselle Pauline	N			my	f	m	vig	
Mademoiselle Pauline Chateau	HP	1856	Pradel	lp	f			
Mademoiselle Pauline Nodet	Pol	1892	Schwartz Vve	my				
Mademoiselle Philiberte Pelé	HP	1873	Gonod	dp	f	l		
Mademoiselle Polonia Bourdin	T	1854	Oger	mp	f	l	vig	
Mademoiselle Portier	HP	1864	Guillot Fils	lp	f	m	m	
Mademoiselle Quétel	HP		Oger	lp				
Mademoiselle Rachel	T	1860	Damaizin	w	f	vl		
Mademoiselle Rosa Bonheur	M	Pre 1870		p	f	l		
Mademoiselle Schwarz	HP	1867	Guillot Père	mp				
Mademoiselle Silvie de Cillard	B	1852	Oudin / Parmentier	lp	f	m	vig	
Mademoiselle Sontag	G			dp	f	m		
Mlle Sophie de la Villeboisnet	HP	1867	Touvais	mp	f	m	m	
Mademoiselle Suzanne Blanchet	T	1885	Nabonnand	mp	vf	l		vf
Mademoiselle Suzanne Bouyer	HP	1879	Gonod	mr	f	l	vvig	
Mademoiselle Suzanne Rodocanachi	HP	1880	Verdier E	mp	f	l	vig	vf
Mlle Suzanne-Marie Rodocanachi	HP	1883	Lévêque	mp	f	vl	vig	
		syn	Suzanne-Marie Rodo-	canachi				
Mademoiselle Thérèse Appert	HP	1855	Trouillard	lp	f	l		
Mademoiselle Thérèse Coumer	B	1867	Liabaud	mp	f	l		
Mlle Thérèse de la Devansaye	B	1895	Chedanne G	w				
		syn Kro-	npricessin Victoria					
Mademoiselle Thérèse Levet	HP	1864	Levet	mp	vdbl	l	vig	m
Mademoiselle Th. Raynaud	HP	1852	Liabaud	dp				

Mademoiselle Thirion Montauban	T	1891	Puyravaud	w				
Mademoiselle Victoire Hélye	HP	1878	Verdier E	pb	f	m-l	vig	vf
Mademoiselle Walton	N			lp				
Mademoiselle Wathély	B	1864	Cagnerre	mr				
Mademoiselle Yvonne Gravier	T	1894	Bernaix	yb	f	l		m
Madrée	G			lp				
Maffeis	P	Pre 1830	(Fromont)	dp				
Mages	G		Gentil	mr	vf	m		
Magdeleine Beauvillain	T	1887	Beauvillain	ly	f	l		f
Magdeleine de Chatelier	Pol	1894	Dubreuil	my			m	
Magna Charta	HP	1876	Paul W	mp	dbl	vl	vig	f
Magna Rosea	HCh	1888		lp		vl		
Magnanine	N	Pre 1846		w				
Magnifique à Fleur Cerise	G	Pre 1830	Prévost	rb	dbl	vl		
Magnifique sans Égale	C			mp	f	m		
Magnolia Rose	T	1838	Foster syn Devoniensis	w	dbl	vl	vvig	vf
Magnolia Rose. Climbing	Cl T	1858	Pavitt syn Devoniensis, Climbing	w	f	l	vig	vf
Magnus Ladulus	T			lp	f	l		
Mahaeca	G	1795	syn La Belle Sultane	dr		m		
Mahaeca de Dupont	G	Pre 1790	syn Charles de Mills	dr	vdbl	m		sf
Maheca	Bslt	c 1815	Noisette L	m	s-d	m		
Maheca	Ch	Pre 1834		dr		s		
Maheca Nova	G	1818	Godefroy	dr	dbl	m		
Maheck à Fleurs Simples	G	Pre 1629	syn Holoserica	ob	s-d			
Maheka	Misc	Pre 1846	Syn Purpurea	m	dbl			
Mahieux	C			mr	f	l		
Mahl	G			mr	f	m		
Mahoniaeflora	HP							
Mai Fleuri	T	1892	Tesnier	w	f	vl		
Maid of Honour	T	1899	Hofmeister	mp	f	l		
Maid of the Mist	HT	1890	Bennett	w				
Maid of the Valley	C	1821	Chaussée, Mme syn Unique Panachée	w	dbl	l	vig	
Maiden's Blush	A	Pre 1754	syn Gt Maiden's Blush	w	dbl	l	vig	vf
Maiden's Blush	A	1797	Kew	w	dbl	m	vvig	vf
Maiden's Blush	C	1818	syn Heloïse	lp	f	s		
Maiden's Blush	HSpn	Pre 1846						
Majestic	Misc	Pre 1846						
Majestueuse	G	Pre 1790	(Holland)	lp	f	l		m
Majestueuse	HP			or				
Majestueux	B	Pre 1846	Robert	mp				
Major	G	Pre 1811	Dupont syn Alector Cramoisi	dr	dbl	l		m
Major	Pom			w				
Major	HSem			w				
Major	C			mp				
Major Franz Teirich	B	1888	Geschwind					
Major Multiplex	C	Pre 1806	syn Rose des Peintres	mp	f	vl	vig	f
Malek-Adel	G			lp	f	l		
Malesherbes	G	1834	Vibert	m	vf	vl		
Malesherbes	HP	1862	Oger	mp				
Malfilâtre	HP	1872	Oger	dr	f	l	vig	
Malibran	T	Pre 1846		w	f	m	vig	
Malingre	HP			mr				
Malinoise	G			mp	f	m		
Malmaison Rose	B	1845	Béluze syn Leweson-Gower	op	dbl	vl		
Malmaison Rouge	B	1882	Gonod	dr	f	m		
Malmort	T	Pre 1834	Laffay	lp	dbl	m		f
Malton	HCh	1830	Guérin	mr	f	m	vvig	vf
Malvina	G	Pre 1811	Hardy syn Bourbon	pb	s-d	m		m
Malvina	B	1829	Vibert	dp		m		
Malvina	C	1841	Verdier V	lp	vdbl	l		
Malvina	M	Pre 1846		lp	f	m		
Malvina Grüneberg(er)	HP	1885	Singer	dr	f	l	vvig	
Maman Cochet	T	1892	Cochet S	pb	vdbl	vl	vig	m
Maman Cochet Blanche	T	1897	Lambert	w	dbl	l	vig	m
Maman Loiseau	T	1899	Buatois	yb		l	vig	
Manchu Rose	Sp	1820	syn r.xanthina	my	dbl	m		
Mandarin Chinois	HCh	1852	Guillot Père	dr	f	m		
Manda's Triumph	HWich	1899	Horvath	w	vdbl	m	vvig	
Manette	G	Pre 1820	Lecoffé	rb	vdbl	m	vig	
Manette	G	c 1835	Prévost	dp	f	m		
Manettii	N	1835	Manetti S	lp	s		vig	
Manettii Alba Rosea	Misc	1887	Geschwind	lp				
Manettii Floribunda	Misc	1887	Geschwind	w				
Manettii Purpurea	Misc	1887	Geschwind	m				
Manget	HP			lp	f	m		
Manning's Blush	HEg	Pre 1799	Manning	w	dbl	vs		fol

f

Name	Class	Date	Raiser / Synonym					
Manon	G		Miellez	lp		m		
Manouri	HP							
Mansais	T	Pre 1846	Mansais	pb	f	vl		vf
Mantault (or Manteau)	HCh	Pre 1846						
Manteau de Jeanne d'Arc	B	c 1840	Béluze	lp	vf	m		
Manteau d'Evêque	G	Pre 1819	syn Évêque	m	s-d	m		
Manteau d'Evêque	HCh			dr	f	l		
Manteau d'Evêque	HP	1853	Moulins	m	f	l		
Manteau Impérial	G	Pre 1830	Prévost	m	f	s		
Manteau Pourpre	G	Pre 1811	syn Rouge Formidable	mr	vdbl	m		
Manteau Pourpre	G	Pre 1811	Vibert	m	dbl	m		
Manteau Rouge	G	Pre 1811	syn Rouge Formidable	mr	vdbl	l		
Manteau Rouge	G	Pre 1811	syn Manteau Pourpre	m	dbl	m		
Manteau Royal	G	Pre 1820	Descemet	dr	vf	m		
Manteau Royal	G	Pre 1830	Vibert	mr	vdbl	m		
Marbled	G	Pre 1754	syn Marmorea	rb	s-d	m		
Marbrée	G	Pre 1754	syn Marmorea	rb	s-d	m		
Marbrée	HP			mp	f	vl		
Marbrée	HCh	1831	Vibert	mr		m		
Marbrée	Ayr	Pre 1846		mr				
Marbrée	A			w				
Marbrée	HSpn	Pre 1846	Prévost syn Belle Laure	dr				
Marbrée	P	1858	Robert & Moreau	rb	dbl	l		sf
Marbrée d'Enghien	HSpn	c 1830	Parmentier	w	dbl	m		
Marbrée d'Enghien	HP			mp	f	l		
Marbrée d'Enghien	M	c 1850	Robert	m				
Marbrée Semi-Double	M	Pre 1846	Robert – syn above?	mr				
Marc Aurèle	D	Pre 1846	Vibert	mp	f	m		
Marceau	G	1832	Vibert	mr		l		
Marceau	HP	1851	Vibert	mr			vig	
Marcel Bourgouin	G	1898	Corboeuf-Marsault	m	dbl	l		vf
Marcel Grammont	HP	1868	Vigneron	dr	f	l	vig	
Marcelin Roda	T	1873	Ducher	yb	vf	l	wk	f
Marcella	HP	1865	Liabaud	mp	f	vl		
Marchesa Boccella	HP	1842	Desprez	lp	dbl	l		m
Marchioness of Downshire	HP	1894	Dickson A	pb	f	l	vig	
Marchioness of Dufferin	HP	1891	Dickson A	mp	dbl	vl	m	
Marchioness of Exeter	HP	1877	Laxton	lp	f	l	vvig	m
Marchioness of Londonderry	HP	1893	Dickson A	lp	f	vl	vvig	m
Marchioness of Lorne	HP	1888	Paul W	pb	dbl	l	vig	vf
Marchioness of Salisbury	HT	1890	Pernet Père	dr	dbl	m		vf
Mardonius	HP	1845	Béluze	m	f	m		
Maréchal	N	1830	Maréchal	w	f	l		
Maréchal Bazaine	HP	1864	De Fauw	lp	f	m	vig	
Maréchal Bougeaud	T	1843		pb	f	l	vig	f
Maréchal Canrobert	HP	1863	Pernet Père	mr	f	m	vvig	
Maréchal d'Ancre	G		Parmentier	mp	f	m		
Maréchal Davoust	M	1852	Robert	mp	f	l		vf
Maréchal de Canrobert	HP	1885	Lévêque	pb	f	l		
Maréchal de Chateauroux	M	1858	Robert & Moreau	m				
Maréchal de la Brunerie	HP	1856	Robert	dp	f	m		
Maréchal de Tavannes	G		Parmentier	dr	f	l		
Maréchal de Villars	B	Pre 1846		dp	f	l		
Maréchal du Palais	B	1846	Béluze	lp	f	l		
Maréchal Duroc	HCh			m	f	m		
Maréchal Forey	HP	1862	Margottin	mr	vf	l	vig	
Maréchal Forey	HP	1863	Pradel	mp	f	l	vig	
Maréchal Gaspard de Vallières	HP	1851	Lartay	lp	f	l		
Maréchal Lannes	HCh			mr	f	m		
Maréchal Mortier	HCh	Pre 1841		dr	f	l		
		syn Deuil	du Maréchal Mortier					
Maréchal Ney	T			w	f	m		
Maréchal Niel	N	1864	Pradel	my	dbl	l	vvig	vf
Maréchal Niel à Feuilles Panachée	T	1895	Dienemann	yb				
Maréchal Niel Blanc de Deegen	T	1894	Deegen	w				
Maréchal Niel Rouge	T	1897	Muller	mr				
			syn Grossherzog Ernst Ludwig					
Maréchal Pélissier	HP			mr				
Maréchal Robert	T	1875	Ducher Vve	yb	f	vl	vig	f
Maréchal Serrurier	B			mr				
Maréchal Soult	HP	1838	Laffay	mr	f	m		
Maréchal Suchet	HP	1863	Guillot Fils	mr	f	l	m	
Maréchal Suchet	HP	1876	Damaizin	mp	f	vl	vig	
Maréchal Vaillant	HP	1861	Lecomte	mr	f	l	vig	
			syn Avocat Duvivier					
Maréchal Valée	T			mp	f	m		
Maréchale Niel	HP	1861	Pradel	lp				
Margaret Dickson	HP	1891	Dickson A	w	vf	l	vig	sf

Name	Class	Date	Raiser					
Margaret Haywood	HP	1888	Haywood / Paul & Son	lp	f	vl		
Margarita	N	1868	Guillot Fils	yb	f	m	vvig	
Margat Jeune	HCh	Pre 1850		mr	f	l	vig	vf
Margherita di Simone	T	1898	Guillot P	yb	f	l		
Margined Hip	HEg	Pre 1846	Lee syn Hébe's Lip	w	dbl	m	m	m
Margined Hip (same as above)	HEg	Pre 1846	syn Emmeline	w	dbl	m		
Marguerite	G	1827	Hardy syn Tricolore	dr	vdbl	s		
Marguerite	Ch		Laffay	lp				
Marguerite	T	Pre 1834		lp		m		
Marguerite	T	1868	Guillot	dp	f	m	m	
Marguerite Bonnet	B	1864	Liabaud	w	f	m	m	
Marguerite Boudet	HP	1897		lp				
Marguerite Brassac	HP	1874	Brassac syn Charles Lefèbvre	dr	f	l	vvig	vf
Marguerite Chatelain	B	1879	Vigneron	lp	f	l	vvig	vf
Marguerite d'Anjou	Ch	1827	Guérin	mp		s-m		
Marguerite d'Anjou	N	Pre 1834		lp		s		
Marguerite d'Anjou	HP	1847	Boyau	m	vf	vl		
Marguerite d'Anjou	HP	1862	Trouillard	rb		s	m	
Marguerite d'Anjou	B	1864	Moreau-Robert	mp				
Marguerite d'Anjou	HP	Pre 1870		lp	f	m		
Marguerite de Fénélon	T	1883	Nabonnand	pb	s-d	l	vig	
Marguerite de Flandre	C	Pre 1862		dr	f	l		
Marguerite de Flandre	D	Pre 1885		lp	f	l		
Marguerite de Roman	HP	1882	Schwartz J	w	f	vl	vig	m
Marguerite de Saint Amand	HP	1864	De Sansal / Jamain	mp	f	l	vig	
Marguerite de Soras	T	1890	Nabonnand	yb				
Marguerite de Valois	G	see	Marguerite Valois					
Marguerite de Vaubrun	HP	1853	Robert	mp	f	m		
Marguerite d'Ombrain	HP	1865	Verdier E	mp	vf	vl	vvig	vf
Marguerite Dubourg	B	1854	Pradel	mp	f	l		
Marguerite Hédouin	B	1847	Vibert	lp	f	m	vvig	
Marguerite Jamain	HP	1873	Jamain	lp	vdbl	l	vig	
Marguerite Ketten	T	1897	Ketten Bros	yb	f	l	vig	m
Marguerite Lanzeseur	G	Pre 1860		mr	f	m		
Marguerite Lartay	B	1855	Béluze syn Impératrice Eugénie	mp	f	m		
Marguerite Lartay	B	1873	Lartay syn Impératrice Eugénie	m	f	l	(Plantier)	
Marguerite Leblond	HP							
Marguerite Lecureaux	HP	1853	Cherpin	rb	f	m		
Marguerite Marchais	T	1879	Nabonnand	yb	vf	l	vig	
Marguerite Ramet	T	1886	Levet Père	mp				
Marguerite Valois	G	1829		dp	f	l		
Maria	T	Pre 1860		w				f
Maria Christina	T	1895	Aldrufeu, Joaquin	ob	f	m-l		
Maria Christina Reine d'Espagne	T	1894	Perny	mr	vdbl	m	vvig	
Maria Duckhardt	T	1897	Ketten	w	f	l		
Maria Fournier	Ch		Laffay	lp	dbl	m		
Maria Graebner	S	1880		mp	s	s		
Maria Leonida	HBc	1829	Lemoyne	w	f	l	m	vf
Maria Leonida Scarlet (Marie Léonie)	HBc			mr	f	l		
Maria Sage	Ch	1890	Dubreuil	mp				
Maria Scholtz	T	1891	Pries	dp				
Maria Stella	N	Pre 1846	Vibert	mp	vf	m		
Maria Thérésa	HP	1872	Ducher	lp	vf	m	vig	vf
Marianne	B	Pre 1846	Laffay	dp	f	m		
Mariano Vergara	T	1896	Aldrufeu	mr	dbl	l	vig	
Marie	B		Pradel	mr	f	l		
Marie	HCh		Noisette L	m	vdbl	m	vig	
Marie Accary	N	1872	Guillot et Fils	pb	f	s	vvig	
Marie Andresen	C			mp	f	m		
Marie-Antoinette	G	1829	Vibert	m	dbl	vl	vig	f
Marie Aviat	HP	1856	Rousseau	mr	f	m	vvig	
Marie Baumann	HP	1863	Baumann	mr	vf	l	vig	f
Marie Bennett	HP	1885	Bennett	mp	f	l		
Marie Berton	T	1875	Levet	ly	f	vl		
Marie Boissée	HP	1864	Oger	w	f	m	vig	
Marie Boyer	HP	1858	Lartay	dp				
Marie Brémont (d)	T	1866	Guillot Fils	dr		m	vig	
Marie Bret	T	1899	Nabonnand	pb				
Marie Caroline de Sartoux	T	1881	Nabonnand	w	f	l	vig	
Marie Chargé	N	1853	Desponds	yb	f	m		
Marie Closon	HP	1882	Verdier E	lp	vf	m-l	vig	vf
Marie Cointet	HP	Pre 1896	Bennett	lp				
Marie Cordier	HP	1874	Fontaine	dr	f	l	vig	
Marie de Beau	T	Pre 1870		w	f	l	vig	
Marie de Blois	M	1852	Robert	mp	f	vl	vig	
Marie de Bourges	HP	1853	Cherpin	dr				
		syn Co-	mptesse Marie de Bo-	urges				

Name	Class	Year	Breeder					
Marie de Bourgogne	A	Pre 1844	Vibert	pb	vdbl	m		
Marie de Bourgogne	M	1853	Robert	mp	dbl	m		f
Marie de Champlouis	HCh			yb	f	l	vig	
Marie de Chateauroux	M	1858	Robert	m	vf	l		
Marie de Goursac	HCh		Gonduin	mp	f			f
Marie de Médicis	T	Pre 1846		mp	f	l	vig	
Marie de Nerrea	N	Pre 1846		lp	dbl	l	m	
Marie de Saint-Jean	P	1869	Damaizin	w	dbl	s	vig	vf
Marie Denise	P	Pre 1834		p		m		
Marie Denise	P	Pre 1846	Portemer	mr	f	l		
Marie Dermar	N	1889	Geschwind R	ly	dbl	m		m
Marie Desfossés	B	1850	Desfossés	mp	f	l	vig	
Marie Desmazures	HP	1868	Desmazures	mp				
Marie Digat	HP	1882	Levet	mr		l	vig	vf
Marie d'Orléans	Bslt	1825	Boutigny	lp				
Marie d'Orléans	T	1883	Nabonnand G	mp	dbl	l	vig	f
Marie Ducher	T	1869	Ducher	lp	f	l	vig	m
Marie Duleau	B	c 1850	Desfossés	w	f	m		
Marie Finger	HP	1869	Guillot et Fils	mp	vdbl	l	vig	
		syn	Mlle Eugénie Verdier					
Marie Finger	HP	1873	Rambeaux syn above	mp	f	l	vvig	
Marie Fouquier	G			dr				
Marie Fournier	Ch		Laffay	lp	dbl	m		
Marie Gagnières	T	1878	Nabonnand	yb				
Marie Geschwind	T	1898	Geschwind	mr				
Marie Girard	HT	1898	Buatois	lp	dbl	l		m
Marie Guillot	T	1874	Guillot et Fils	w	dbl	l	vig	m
Marie Guillot, Climbing	Cl T	1898	Dingee & Conard	w	f	l		m
Marie Hartmann	HP	1894	Hartmann	mr				
Marie Husser	T	1887	Nabonnand	lp				
		see	Madame Marie Husser					
Marie Jaillet	T	1879	Ducher Vve	pb	f	l	vig	
Marie Joly	B	1860	Oger	lp	f	m		
Marie Joséphine	G	1828	Prévost	lp	f	s-m		
Marie Koenigin von Sachsen	HCh	1877	Ruschpler					
Marie Labie	HP		Pradel	mp		m	vig	f
Marie Lafon	HP	1861	Pradel	dr				
Marie Lambert	T	1886	Lambert E	w	dbl	m		f
Marie Larpin	B	1867	Guillot Fils	lp	f	m	m	
Marie Lecomte	T	1885	Singer	my	f	vl		
Marie Leczinska	HP	1847	Béluze	lp	f	m		
Marie Leczinska	M	1865	Moreau-Robert	dp	f	m		
Marie Liabaud	HP	1884	Liabaud	lp		l	vig	
Marie-Louise	D	c 1811		lp	vdbl	m		vf
Marie Louise de Vitry	HP	1856	Masson	dp	f	l		
Marie Louise Pernet	HP	1876	Pernet Père	dp	f	l	m	
Marie Louise Puyravaud	T	1895	Puyravaud	my	f	l		
Marie Malezon	HP	1854	Schmidt	lp		m	vig	
Marie Opoix	T	1874	Schwartz	w	f	l	wk	
Marie Page	T	1891	Perrier	pb				
Marie Paré	B	1880	Paré / Jamain	lp	f	m	m	
Marie Pavié (c)	Pol	1888	Alégatière	w	dbl	m	vig	
Marie Perrachon	HP	1864	Ducher	m		m	m	
Marie Pochin	HP	1881	Pochin	mr		m	m	
			syn Mary Pochin					
Marie Portemer	HP	1857	Portemer	m	f	l	vig	
Marie Rambaux	T	1880	Rambaux	w		m	vig	
Marie Robert	P	1850	Robert & Moreau	m	dbl	m		
Marie Robert	N	1893	Cochet Sc	pb	f	l		
Marie Roederer	HP	1881	Lévêque	mp	f	l		
		syn	Mlle Marie Roederer					
Marie Roland	T	1870	Roland	lp	s-d	vl		
Marie Salomon	HP			mp				
Marie Sage	Ch	1890	Dubreuil	mp				
Marie Scholtze	T	1891		mp				
Marie Sisley	T	1868	Guillot Fils	yb	f	l	vig	f
Marie Soleau	T	1895	Nabonnand	mp	f	l		
Marie Stella	HCh			mp	vf	m		
Marie Stuart	G	1820	Prévost	dr	f	m		
Marie Stuart	G	1820	Dubourg	dp	f	l		
Marie Stuart	Ch		Laffay	lp	f	m		f
Marie Stuart	T	Pre 1830	Guérin	pb	f	m	vvig	
Marie Stuart	Pom			yb				
Marie Thérése	Ch	Pre 1846						
Marie Thérése	C	1858	Robert & Moreau	mp				
Marie Thérése	HP	1872	Ducher	lp	vf	m	vig	vf
Marie Thérése Dubourg	N	1888	Godard	dy	dbl	m	vvig	
Marie Thierry	HP	1858		lp		m	m	
Marie Tout Court	B		Pradel	mr				
Marie Tudor	G	Pre 1835		dp				
Marie Van Baerle	G			mp	f	l		
Marie Van Houtte	T	1871	Ducher	pb	vdbl	l	vig	f

Marie Wolkoff	Ch	1896	Nabonnand	mr	vdbl	l		
Marie Zahn	HT	1887	Müller Dr F	lp	f	l		
Marietta de Besobrasoff	T	1879	Nabonnand	pb	f	m	vig	m
Mariette Biolley	HP	1874	Gonod	mr	f	l	m	
Marinburgensis	Pom		syn Major	w	f	s	vig	
Marinette	C	1819	Vibert	lp	vdbl	l		
Marion Dingee	HT	1889	Cook J	dr				
Mariquita	D	1860	Robert & Moreau	pb	f	l		
Maritorne	P	1851	Robert	lp	f	m		
Marjolin	G	1829	Hardy / Roeser	dr	vf	vl		
Marjolin	HP			mp				
Marjolin	Ch	Pre 1846	Desprez	dr	f	l		
Marjolin	HCh			lp	f	l	m	
Marjolin du Luxembourg	Ch	c 1830	Desprez	pb	vf	vl		
Marjorie	HT	1895	Dickson A	w	dbl	l	vig	
Marmontel	M	1855	Robert	mp	f	m	vig	
Marmorata	HSpn	Pre 1770	syn Maculata	w	s-d	s		
Marmorata Plena	Ayr			w				
Marmorea	G	Pre 1754		rb	s-d	m		
Marmorea Belgica	G			lp				
Marpha	G	syn l'H-	éroïne de Nowogorod					
Marques de Aledo	T	1899	Nabonnand	rb				
Marquis d'Ailsa	HP	1842	Laffay M	mr	f	vl	vig	
			syn Dr Marx					
Marquis d'Alex	HP	1880	Brassac	m	f	l		
Marquis d'Aligre	HP	1887	Lévêque	dr	f	l	vig	
Marquis de Dreux Brézé	G			dp	f	m		
Marquis de la Garde	T	1896	Chauvry	m				
Marquis de la Romana	G	Pre 1830	Prévost	mp	f	s-m		
Marquis de Montserrat	G			mr	f	l		
Marquis de Murat	HP		Ducher	lp	f	l	vig	
Marquis de Sanima	T	1876	Ducher Vve	mp	f	l	vig	f
Marquis de Vaubrun	M	1856	Robert	rb	f	m		
Marquie d'Ivry	B	Pre 1846		lp				
Marquis d'Osseroy	B			mr	f	m	vig	
Marquis of Salisbury	HP	1878	Paul G	mr	f	l		
Marquise Adèle de Murinais	HP	1873	Schwartz	mp	f	l	vig	
Marquise Bocella		syn	Marchesa Boccella					
Marquise d'Alex	T	1880	Brassac	w	vf	l	vvig	
Marquise de Balbiano	B	1855	Lacharme	m	f	m	vig	vf
Marquise de Béthisy	B	1853	Varangot	mr	f	l	m	
Marquise de Boxella	HP		Desprez	lp	f	m		vf
Marquise de Briges	HP	1863	Oger	mr				
Marquise de Castellane	HP	1869	Pernet Père	dp	dbl	l	m	m
Marquise de Chambon	B	1870	Gautreau	mp	f	l	vvig	
Marquise de Chaponnay	T	1897	Bernaix	yb	f	l		
Marquise de Chavaudon	HP	1853	Carré	pb	f	l		
Marquise de Forton	T	1889	Charreton	yb		m		
Marquise de Foucault	T	1860	Margottin	w	dbl	l	vig	f
Marquise de Gibot	HP	1868	De Sansal	lp	f	l	vvig	
Marquise de Ligneris	HP	1869	Genoux	lp	vf	l	vvig	
Marquise de Mac-Mahon	HP	1865	Pernet Père	mp	f	l	m	
Marquise de Marat	HP	1855	Ducher	lp	f	l	vig	
Marquise de Mortemart	HP	1868	Liabaud	w	f	l	vig	
Marquise de Moyriat	B	1845	Lacharme	mr	f	l		
Marquise de Paris	HP	1860	Quetier	mp		l		
Marquise de Pontois-Pontcarré	T	1894	Lévêque	pb	vdbl	m		
Marquise de Reynies	HP		Pradel	lp	vf	l		f
Marquise de Salisbury	HP	1888	Lévêque	lp				
Marquise de Salisbury	HT	1891	Pernet Père	dr	dbl	m-l	vig	
		syn Ma-	rchioness of Salisbury					
Marquise de Trazégnies	G			mp	f	l		
Marquise de Verdun	HP	1868	Oger	mp	f	l		
Marquise de Vivens	T	1886	Dubreuil	dp	dbl	l	vig	f
Marquise d'Exeter	HP	1877	Laxton	lp	f	vl		
Marquise d'Exeter	HP		Paul G	mp				f
Marquise d'Hervey	HP	1877	Vigneron	mr	f	l	vig	
Marquise d'Ivry	HT	Pre 1866		dp	f	vl	vig	
Marquise du Buisson	B	1852	Pradel	lp	f	m	vig	
Marquise Litta de Bréteuil	HT	1893	Pernet-Ducher	mr	vf	l	m	f
Marquisette	Ch	1872	Ducher	op				
Marrast	B		Foulard	mp	f	l		
Mars	Ch	Pre 1846		mp	vdbl	m	vig	
Marsais	T			yb				
Marshal Soult	HP	Pre 1846		dp				
Marshall P Wilder	HP	1885	Ellwanger & Barry	dr	f	l	vig	vf
Marshall Soult	B	Pre 1846	Hooker	mp				
Martha Washington	S	Pre 1900		mp				
Marthe d'Halloy	HP	1881	Lévêque	mp	f	l	vig	
Martin Cahuzac	HP	1889	Lévêque	mp		l	vvig	
Marvellous	Misc	Pre 1846						
Marx	HSpn	c 1825	Cartier	my	f	s		m

Mary Bennett	HP	1885	Bennett	dp	f	l		
Mary Lawrence's Shell Rose	Ch	1799		mr	f			
Mary Pochin	HP	1881	Pochin	mr		m		
Mary Washington	N	Pre 1891		w	dbl	m	vvig	vf
Massillon	HP	1863	Robert & Moreau	mr				
Masterpiece	HP	1880	Paul W	mp	f	vl		
Matherin Regnier	HP	1855	Lévêque	lp	f	m		
Mathieu Molé	G		Vibert	mr	f	l		
Mathilde	T	1841	Bougère syn Niphetos	w		l		vf
Mathilde	T	1877	Granger	lp	f	m	vig	
Mathilde Bernard	HP	1860	Bernêde	m	f	m		
Mathilde de Mondeville	HP	1858	Robert & Moreau	lp	f	m		
Mathilde Jesse	P	1847	Laffay	dp				
Mathilde Jourdeuil	HP	1846	Lacharme	lp	f	l		
Mathilde von Hessen	T	1869	Vogler	w				
Matthew's Surprise	T	1889	Matthews H	lp				
Maubach	HCh	1826	Vibert	dr	f	m		
Maud Little	T	1891	Dingee & Conard	mp	f			
Mauget	N	Pre 1834		lp		s		
Mauget	M	1840	Prévost	dp	f	m		
Mauget	G	Pre 1830		dr	vf	s		
Maupertuis	G	1858	Robert & Moreau	mp				
Maupertuis	M	1868	Moreau-Robert	mp	f	m	vig	
Maure de Venise	HCh	Pre 1828	Maure de Venise	m	f	m		
	syn	Othello	syn Mort de Virginie					
Maure de Virginie	G	Pre 1830	syn Mort de Virginie	m	f	m		
Maurice Bernardin	HP	1861	Granger	mr	dbl	l	vig	vf
Maurice L de Vilmorin	HP	1889	Lévêque	mp				
Maurice Lepelletier	HP	1868	Moreau-Robert	dr	dbl	l		
Maurice Perrault	HP	1869	Vigneron	dr	f	l	vvig	
Maurice Rouvier	T	1890	Nabonnand	pb	dbl	vl	vig	
Maurice Vilmorin	HP	1868	Lédéchaux	rb	dbl			f
Mauve	G	Pre 1811	syn Bourbon	pb	dbl	m		m
Mavourneen	HP	1895	Dickson A	lp	dbl	l	vig	
Mavrocordato	HSpn	1827	Laffay	m				
Max Buntzel	T	1899	Soupert & Notting	lp				
Maxence Lefebvre	B		Pradel	m	f	m		
Maxima	G	Pre 1790	syn Majestueuse	lp	f	l		m
Maxima	C	1829	Girardon syn Goliath	lp	vf	l		
Maxima	A	Pre 1867	syn Alba Maxima	w	dbl	l		m
Maxima	C	Pre 1885	syn Regina (C)	mp	vdbl	m	vig	vf
Maxima de Hollande	C			lp	vf	l		
Maxima Multiplex	C	Pre 1806	syn Rose des Peintres	mp	f	vl		
Maxima Multiplex	A	Pre 1829	Prévost	w		l		
Maxime	G	1827	Noisette	dr				
Maxime	HP	Pre 1860		dp				
Maxime de la Rocheterie	HP	1871	Vigneron	dr	f	l	vig	
Maximilien d'Aremberg	G			lp	f	l		
Maximilien Empereur du Mexique	HP	1858	Verdier V	mr	f	l	m	
Maximilien Roi de Bavière	HP	1865	Pernet Père	mr				
Maximilien II	HP	1858	Verdier V	dr		m	m	
Maximum	G			dr				
Maximus	G	Pre 1830		mp	vdbl	m		
Max Singer	HP	1885	Singer	rb	f	l	vvig	
Max Singer	HMult	1885	Lacharme	dr	dbl	m	vig	
May Queen	HWich	1898	Manda W A	mp	vdbl		vvig	f
May Queen	HWich	1898	Van Fleet	lp	s-d	l	vig	vf
May Quenell	HP	1878	Postans	mr	vf	l	vvig	
May Rivers	T	1890	Rivers	w	f	l		
May Turner	HP	1874	Verdier E	op	f	vl	vig	m
Mazeppa	G	Pre 1841		rb	dbl	m		vf
Mazerati (y)	HCh			dr	f	m		
Meadow Rose	Sp	1773	syn r.blanda	mp	s	m		
Mécène	G	1845	Vibert	pb	dbl	m	m	f
Méchin	N	Pre 1830	Prévost	w	vdbl	m		f
Medea	T	1890	Paul W	ly	vf	l	vig	f
Meg Merrilees	HSpn	1888		p				
Meg Merrilies	HEg	1894	Penzance	dp	s	s	vvig	vf
Mehemit Ali	B	Pre 1846		w		l		
Méhul	G	1826	Cartier	m	vdbl	l		
Méhul	B	1846	Guillot Père	mp				
Meigela	HMult	1895	Geschwind	pb		m		
Mélange de Beautés	G		Miellez	rb				
Mélanie	HCh	Pre 1830	Vibert	mp	f	s		
Mélanie Cornu	HP	1841	Cornu	p	f	l	vvig	
Mélanie de Montjoie	HSem	Pre 1829	Jacques	w	f	m	vig	
Mélanie Lemarié	B/Ch	1834-41	Marcheseau / Koenig syn Hermosa	lp	f		vig	m
Mélanie Oger	T	1851	Oger	w	f	m		
Mélanie Pantin	M	1850	Robert	dp	f	m		
Mélanie Soupert	T	1881	Nabonnand G	w	vf	l	vvig	

Name	Type	Year	Breeder / Note					
Mélanie Waldor	G	1836	Vibert	w	f	m		
Mélanie Waldor	M	1865	Moreau-Robert	m	f	m		
Melanocarpa	Pom		syn Microcarpa	dr	vdbl	s		
Melchior Salet	M	1854	Lacharme M syn Salet	mp	f	vl	vig	m
Meleagris	G	Pre 1817	Loiseleur-Deslongcha- syn Pintade	mps mp				
Mélina	Ch		Laffay	lp	vf	s		
Melisandre	B	1854	Robert	lp	f	l	vig	
Melpomène	G		Parmentier	mp	f	l		
Mélusine	G			mp	f	l		
Mélusine	M	1851	Robert	mr	f	l	vig	
Melville	T	1839		mp	f	l		
Memorial Rose	Sp	1886	syn r.wichurana	w	s	m		m
Ménage	A	1847	Vibert	w	dbl	m		
Ménage	M	1858	Robert & Moreau	mp	f			
Mendox	HArv			mp	f	m	vvig	
Menes	Ch	Pre 1870		lp	f	m		
Menoux	HMult	1845	Lacharme	lp	f	m	vig	
Menoux (same as above?)	HMult	1848	Jobert	dp	f	m		
Mercedes	G	1847	Vibert	lp	dbl	l	m	m
Mercedes	HMult	1886	Geschwind	lp	s-d	m		
Mère Brune	G		Miellez	dr				
Mère de Saint Louis	HP	1851	Plantier (Lacharme)	w	f	l	m	
Mère Gigogne	Ch	Pre 1820 syn	Vibert Prolifera de Redouté	mr	vdbl	m		vf
Mériame de Rothschild	T	1897	Cochet P	dp	dbl	m	vig	
Méris	B			mr	f	m		
Merlet de Laboulais	T	Pre 1846		dr	f	l		
Mermaid	HSet	1887	Geschwind	lp				
Mérope	HP	Pre 1846		lp	f	l		
Merrie England	HP	1897	Harkness	pb				
Merry England	HP	1897	Harkness	mr	dbl		vig	vf
Merveille d'Anjou	HP	1867	Touvais	m	f	vl	vvig	
Merveille de l'Univers	G	Pre 1827	(Belgium)	rb	vf	l		
Merveille de Lyon	HP	1882	Pernet Père	w	dbl	l	vig	f
Merveille des Blanches	HP	1894	Pernet Père	w	dbl	l	vig	
Merveille du Monde	D	Pre 1826	syn Roi des Pays-Bas	dp	dbl	l		
Merveille du Monde	G			dp				
Merveilleuse Beauté	G		Miellez	mp				
Merveilleuse de Noisette	G		Noisette	m				
Mesdames Soeurs Chevandier	HP	1864	Pernet Père	rb		m		
Meta	T	1898	Dickson A	rb	dbl	l	vig	f
Meteor	HT	1887	Bennett	mr	dbl			sf
Meteor	N	1887	Geschwind	dp	dbl	vl	vig	m
Metz	M	Pre 1846		mp				
Meunière	G		Parmentier	dr	f	m		
Meunière de Santis	G			mp	f	m		
Mexica Aurantia	G	1827	Lahaye Père syn Tricolore	pb	vdbl	s		m
Mexico	HP	1863	Bruant	m	f	l	vig	
Meyerbeer	G			mr	f	m		
Meyerbeer	HP	1867	Verdier E	dr	f	vl	vig	
Mezerai	E	1825	Vibert	lp	dbl	s-m		f
Miaulis	HCh	1825	Laffay	dr	vf	m		
Micaela	G	1864	Moreau-Robert	lp	vdbl	m		
Micaela	G		Vibert	lp	f	l		
Micaela	M	Pre 1870		mp	f	m		
Michael Saunders	HT	1879	Bennett	pb	vdbl	m	m	m
Michel Adamson	M	1852	Robert	mr	f	m	vvig	
Michel-Ange	A		Vibert	lp				
Michel-Ange	G	1847	Verdier V	mp	f	l	vig	
Michel-Ange	HP	1863	Oger	dp	f	m		
Michel Bonnet	B	1864	Guillot syn Catherine Mermet	dp	dbl	l	vig	
Michel Buchner	HT	1893	Soupert & Notting	mp				
Michel Dupré	HP	1876	Gonod	mr	f	l	vig	
Michel Strogoff	HP	1882	Barault	dr	f	m	vig	
Michigan	HSet	Pre 1870		lp		s		
Michigan Anna Marie	HSet	1843	Feast syn Anna Marie	dp	dbl	l		
Michigan Eva Corrina	HSet	c 1846	Pierce syn Eva Corinne	lp	dbl		m	
Michigan Milledgville	HSet	1842	see also Milledgeville	mp		m		
Michigan Perpetual	HSet	1843 syn	Feast Perpetual Michigan	m	f	l		
Michigan Rose	Sp	1810	syn r.setigera	dp	s	m		
Michigan Superba	Cl			lp	dbl	m		
Microcarpa	Pom			dr				
Microphylla Alba Odorata	HBc		see Alba Odorata					
Microphylla Bisserbulata	A	1828	Prévost	mp	dbl	vl	vig	
Microphylla Imbricata	HMcr		see Imbricata					
Microphylla Purpurea	HBc			dr				
Microphylla Rouge Violacé	HBc			m				
Miellez	T			w	f	m	vig	f

Name	Class	Date	Raiser / synonym	Colour	Form	Size		
Miellez	N			my				
Mignard	HP	1858	Baltet	mp				
Mignon	HSpn	1827	Cartier	mp				
Mignon	N	Pre 1846						
Mignon	Pol	1880	Ducher Vve syn Cécile Brünner	lp	dbl	s		m
Mignon, Climbing	Cl Pol	1894	Hosp syn Cécile Brünner, Climbing Cartier	lp				vf
Mignonne	Pom			mp	vdbl	s		
Mignonne	T	1879	Nabonnand	lp	f	s	vvig	
Mignonne Blanche Cendrée	Pom			w				
Mignonette	Pol	1881	Guillot et Fils	lp	dbl	s	m	
Mignonette	HP		Fontaine	mp				
Mikado	HRg	1888	Morlet	dr	f	l		
Milledgeville	HSet	1842		mp	vdbl	m	vig	
Mille	A	1826	Cartier syn Rose Mille	w	vdbl	m		
Miller-Hayes	HP	1873	Verdier E	mr	dbl	l	m	m
Miller's Climber (ing)	Ayr	Pre 1838		dp	s-d	m	vvig	
Millesi	B	Pre 1846		lp				
Milliez	Ch	Pre 1846		ly		l		
Mill's Beauty	Rbf		syn Miller's Climber	mp	s-d	l	vig	
Milton	N	Pre 1830	Laffay	lp	dbl	l		
Milton	HCh			mp	f	m		
Mine d'Or	G	Pre 1830	Laffay syn Bouquet Pourpre	rb		s-m		
Minerva	P	Pre 1846		dp	f			
Minerva	HSpn	1846						
Minerve	G	Pre 1811	Miellez	dp				
Minerve	HP	1868	Jamain	dp	f	m		
Minerve	HP	1869	Gonod	mr	f	l	vig	
Minette	A	1819	Vibert	lp	f	m		
Mimiata	Misc	Pre 1846		my				
Miniature	Pol	1884	Alégatière	lp	vdbl	vs	m	vf
Miniature Moss	M	Pre 1838	Rivers	lp	s-d	s		
Minima	B	Pre 1846		dp	f	s		
Ministre Jules Bara	HP	1885	Singer	dr	f	l	vvig	
Minna	HEg	1895	Penzance	w	s-d	l	vvig	f
Minnie Dawson	HMult	1896	Dawson	w				
Minor	C	Pre 1791	syn Petite de Hollande	mp	dbl	s		m
Minor	Pom	Pre 1806	syn Pompone Jaune	my	vdbl	s		
Minor	M	Pre 1829	Prévost syn Gracilis	dp	dbl	l	vig	
Minor	HSem	Pre 1846		lp				
Minor	Ayr			yb				
Minor des Français	M		Laffay	mp	f	l		
Minor Prolific	M			mp				
Minos	G		Robert	m				
Minutifolia Alba	HMult	1888	Bennett	w				
Mirabile	T	Pre 1846		my				
Mirabilis	G	Pre 1787	syn Admirable	mr	f			
Mirabilis	T	c 1845	Boyau	ab	f	m		
Miralda	HCh	c 1825	Laffay	m	vdbl	s	vig	
Miranda	T	Pre 1846		w	vdbl	l		
Miranda	D	1868		lp				
Miranda	P	1869	De Sansal	mp	s-d	l	m	m
Miranda	G		Parmentier	dr	f	l		
Miret	P		Robert					
Miroir	P	1826	Cartier					
Miroir de Perfection	B	1846	Armand	mp	f	m		
Miroir des Dames	D	Pre 1830		lp	f	m		f
Miroir des Dames	A		Prévost	w	f	m		f
Miss Chauncey	B	Pre 1846		mp				
Miss Compton	Ch		Laffay	m	dbl	s		
Miss de Misson	G							
Miss Edith Gifford	T	1882	Guillot et Fils syn Hon Edith Gifford	w	dbl	l		
Miss Ellen Wilmott	HT	1899	Bernaix	pb	dbl	l	vig	
Miss Ethel Brownlow	T	1887	Dickson A syn Ethel Brownlow	op		l		
Miss Ethel Richardson	HP	1897	Dickson A	w	dbl	vl		
Miss Fanny	B	Pre 1846		lp	f	m	vig	
Miss Glegg	N	1831	Vibert	w	f	s		
Miss Gunnell	HSet	c 1846	Pierce	lp	dbl	m		
Miss Hassard	HP	1874	Turner syn Madame Renard	lp	f	l	wk	m
Miss Hillier	HP	1873	Verdier E	mr		s	vig	
Miss House	HP	1838	House	w				
Miss Ingram	HP	1867	Ingram	w	f	l	vig	
Miss Jeanne C. Meymouth (Meymot)	HP	1850	Laffay	lp	f	l		vf
Miss Kate Schultheiss	Pol	1887	Soupert & Notting	w	f	s		
Miss Katherine G Warren	T	1894	Bernaix	mr	f	m	vvig	
Miss Kennedy	N			mp	f	m		

Name	Type	Year	Raiser					
Miss Lawrence	G	1825	Vibert	dp	dbl	m		
Miss Lawrence's Rose	Sp	1815	syn r.chinensis minima	w, p or r	s-d			
Miss Lizzie	T	1887	Nabonnand	w	f	l	vig	f
Miss Lowe	HCh	1887	Lowe	mr	s	s		
Miss Marston	T	1889	Pries / Ketten Bros	pb	f	l	vvig	m
Miss May Paul	T	1879	Levet A	m	f	l	vvig	m
Miss Poole	HP	1875	Turner	mp	f	l	m	
Miss Sargent	T	Pre 1846		lp				f
Miss Smithson	N	1828	Vibert	lp	f	s		
Miss Smithson	HSpn	1827	Dagonnet	m				
Miss Trotter	HSpn	1888		lp				
Miss Wenn	T	1890	Guillot et Fils	mp	f	l		
Miss Willmott	T	1899	Paul G	rb				
Miss Wood	M			dr	f	m		
Miss Wright	G	1825	Vibert					
Mister Gladstone	HP	1866	Paul G	mp	f	m	wk	
Mister John Barnes	HP	1866	Ward	dr	f	l	vvig	
Mister John Laing	HP	1887	Bennett	mp				
Mister Hamilton	Pom			dr	vdbl	s		
Mister Laxton	HP	1878	Laxton	mr	f	l	vvig	
Mister Sterling	Pom			mr	vdbl	l		
Mister Toronto	T	1892	Dunlop	my				
Mister Ward	HP			mp	f	l		
			see Mistress Ward					
Mister Woolfield	HP	1868	Guillot Père	mp	f	l	vvig	
Mrs Anthony Waterer	HRg	1897	Waterer	dr	s-d	l	vig	vf
Mrs Baker	HP	1876	Turner	mr	f	vl	m	m
Mrs Bosanquet	B/Ch	1832	Laffay M	lp	vdbl	l	vig	f
Mrs Bosanquet Blanche	B	1895	Freundlich	w				
Mrs Caroline Swailes	HP	1884	Swailes	lp	f	l		
Mrs Charles Wood	HP	1861	Verdier E	mr		s	vig	
Mrs Charlotte Guilfoyle	HT	1885	Johnson					
Mrs Clarendon	Ch			lp	f	m		
Mrs Cleveland	HP	1853	Roussel	rb	dbl	vl	vig	vf
		syn	Général Jacqueminot					
Mrs Cleveland	HP	1897	Gill	mr				
Mrs Cocker	HP	1899	Cocker	mp	f	l		vf
Mrs Cripps	HP	Pre 1845	Laffay	mp	dbl	l		
Mrs De Graw	B	1885	Burgess	op				
Mrs D'Ombrain	HP	1862	Trouillard	dr				
Mrs Edward Mawley	T	1899	Dickson A	pb	f	vl		m
Mrs Edworgt	Rbf			mp				
Mrs Elliott	HP	1840	Laffay	lp	f	l	vig	
Mrs F W Sanford	HP	1898	Curtis	lp	vdbl	l		m
Mrs Frank Cant	HP	1899	Cant F	mp	vf	l		
Mrs George Dickson	HP	1884	Bennett	mp	dbl	l	vig	
Mrs Harkness	HP	1893	Paul	lp	dbl	l	vig	vf
			syn Paul's Early Blush					
Mrs Harry Turner	HP	1880	Turner	mr	f	l	vig	
Mrs Henry Clay	HSet	Pre 1846		w				
Mrs Hovey	HSet	Pre 1846	Pierce	w	f	l		
Mrs Idon	N	Pre 1870		my	f	l		
Mrs J Berners	HP	1866	Ward	dp		s	vig	
Mrs J Pierpoint Morgan	T	1896	May J H	dp	vdbl	l	vig	
Mrs James Wilson	T	1889	Dickson A	yb	f	vl	vig	m
Mrs Jesse Fremont	T	1891	Dingee & Conard	w		m		
Mrs John Laing	HP	1887	Bennett	mp	f	l	vig	vf
Mrs John Laing (same as above?)	HP	1891	Dingee	w				
Mrs John Taylor	T	1887	Bennett	mp				
Mrs Jowitt	HP	1876	Nabonnand	mr				
Mrs Jowitt	HP	1880	Cranston	rb	f	vl	vig	f
Mrs Laing	HP	1872	Verdier E	mp	f	m	vig	
Mrs Laing	HP	1882	Cranston	mp				
Mrs Lane	B			w	f	m		
Mrs Laxton	HP	1875	Laxton	mp	vf	vl		m
Mrs Mirabel Grey	T	1894	Nabonnand	mr				
Mrs Oliver Ames	T	1898	Montgomery R	pb	f			
Mrs Opie	T	1877	Bell	op	f	m-l	vig	
Mrs Paul	B	1891	Paul	lp		l	m	m
Mrs Pierce	HSet	1850	Pierce	mp				
Mrs R G Sharman-Crawford	HP	1894	Dickson A	pb	vf	l	vig	m
Mrs Rivers	G	Pre 1846		lp	dbl	l		
Mrs Robert Garret (Garnett)	HT	1898	Cook J	mp	dbl	m	vig	
Mrs Robert Peary	Cl HT	1898	De Voecht; De Wilde	w	dbl	vl		
		syn	Kaiserin Auguste Vikt-	Oria, Clg				
Mrs Rumsey	HP	1899	Rumsey	mp				
Mra S G Crawford	HP	1897		mp				
Mrs Siddons	N	Pre 1846		ly	f	l		
Mrs Standish	HP	1853	Cherpin	mr				
Mrs Standish	HP	1865	Liabaud	lp	f	l		
Mrs Stirling	HSpn	1888		dp				

Name	Type	Year	Raiser					
Mrs Treseder	T	1889	Paul G	ly				
Mrs Veitch	HP	1872	Verdier E	mp	f	l	vig	sf
Mrs W C Whitney	HT	1894	May	lp		l		vf
Mrs W J Grant	HT	1895	Dickson A	lp	dbl	l		vf
Mrs W J Grant, Climbing	Cl HT	1899	E G Hill Co	lp	f	l		
Mrs Ward	HP	1866	Ward	mp		s	vig	
Mrs William Paul	HP	1863	Paul	mr	f	l	vig	
Mrs William Watson	HP	1890	Dickson A	m	f	l		
Mrs Wood	HP	1840	Wood	mp	dbl			
		syn	Clémentine Seringe					
Mrs Wood	M	Pre 1846		dp		s		
Mithridate	G	1824	Hardy	mr	dbl	l		
Modèle de Perfection	B	1859	Guillot Fils	mp	f	m	m	
Modeste Guérin	T	1855	Guérin	dp				
			syn Madame de Vatry					
Mogador	P	1819	Descemet	dp	f	m		
Mohelina (Mohelida)	B	1851	Robert	mr	f	m		
Mohrenkoenig	HP	1880	Vogt	dr	f	l	m	
Moiret	T	1843	Moiret	yb	f	l	vig	vf
Moïse	G	1828	Parmentier	m	dbl	l	m	
Moïse	G		Miellez	mr	f	l		
Molière	Ch	Pre 1830	Laffay	mp	vdbl	m-l		
Molière	B	1858	Robert & Moreau	lp				
Mollevaut	G	1827	Noisette	mr				
Momus	HP			mr	f	s	wk	
Mon Ami Jérôme	G		Parmentier	mr	f	m		
Mon Caprice	G		Miellez	mr				
Mon Gout	G							
Mon Hortense	G	1827	Vétillard	mp				
Mon Rêve	HP	1891	Vigneron	mp				
Mon Trésor	G	Pre 1830	Calvert	dr	f	m		
Monarchie	G			mr	f	l		
Mondor	T	Pre 1846		dp		vl		
Mondox	HMult			lp				
Monica	A	Pre 1838		lp	f	m		
Monime	G	Pre 1846		mp		m		
Monique	A	1828	Prévost	lp	vdbl	m		
Monplaisir	G	c 1845	Calvert	m				
Monplaisir	T	1868	Ducher	my	f	vl		
Monseigneur Fournier	HP	1875	Lalande	mr	f	vl		
Monseigneur Touchet	T	1895	Corboeuf-Marsault	w	f	l		
Monsieur	G	Pre 1830		dp	f	m		
		syn	Cramoisie des Alpes					
Monsieur A Maille	B	1889	Moreau-Robert	pb	f	vl	vvig	vf
Monsieur Aimé Colcombet	T	1891	Bernaix	mp		m	vig	
Monsieur Albert Dureau	HP	1869	Vigneron	dr		m	m	
		syn	Albert Dureau					
Monsieur Albert Patel	T	1895	Godard	mr	dbl	l	vig	f
Monsieur Alexandre Pelletier	B	1879	Duval H	mp	f	m		
Monsieur Alexis Lepère	HP	1875	Vigneron	mr		l	vig	
Monsieur Alfred Daney	M	1886	Bernède	dp	f	vl		
Monsieur Alfred Leveau	HP	1880	Vigneron	mp	f	l		
			syn Alfred Leveau					
Monsieur André Wilnat	HP	1865	Vigneron	m	f	vl		
Monsieur Auguste Perrin	HP	1887	Schwartz V	mr				
Monsieur Baconnier	HP	1893	Schwartz Vve	dr				
Monsieur Barillet-Deschamps	HP	1867	Vigneron	mr	f	l	vvig	
Monsieur Barthélemy Levet	HP	1878	Levet	mp	f	l		
Monsieur Benjamin Druet	HP	1878	Verdier E	dr	vdbl	vl	vig	
Monsieur Benoit Comte	HP	1883	Schwartz	my				
Monsieur Berthier	HP	1884	Vigneron	mr	f	l	vvig	
Monsieur Bonçenne	HP	1864	Liabaud	dr	f	l	vig	f
Monsieur Bonçenne, Climbing	HP	1885	Schwartz	rb	vdbl	l	vvig	
Monsieur Bunel	HT	1899	Pernet-Ducher	pb	f	vl	vig	
Monsieur Célestin Port	HP	1894	Tesnier	dr				
Monsieur Chabaud de St-Mandrier	T	1883	Nabonnand	dr	vf	vl	vvig	
Monsieur Chaix d'Est-Ange	HP	1866	Lévêque	mr	f	l		
Monsieur Charles de Thézillat	T	1888	Nabonnand	yb	f	vl	vig	f
Monsieur Chédane-Guinoisseau	HRg	1895	Chédane-Guinoisseau	lp	dbl	vl		
Monsieur Chevallier	HP	1887	Pernet Père	mr	vdbl	l	vig	
Monsieur Clerc	B	1894	Vigneron	mr				
Monsieur Cordeau	B	1892	Moreau	dp	vdbl	vl	vvig	vf
Monsieur Cordier	Cl HP	1871	Gonod	mr	f	vl		
Monsieur Curt Schultheiss	T	1881	Nabonnand	rb	vf	vl	vvig	
Monsieur de Linières	B	1862	Robert & Moreau	mr	f	l	vig	
Monsieur de Montigny	HP	1855	Paillet	dp	dbl	l	vig	
Monsieur de Morand	HP	1891	Schwartz Vve	rb	f	l	m	
Monsieur de Pontbriand	HP	1864	Damaizin	dr	f	l	vig	
Monsieur de Syras	HP	1894	Schwartz Vve	mp				
Monsieur Désir	Cl HT	1888	Pernet Père	dr	s-d	l	vvig	f

Name	Type	Year	Breeder					
Monsieur Dorier	T	1897	Croibier	dp	f	l		
Monsieur Drochard	Misc	1881	Brassac					
Monsieur Druet	HP	1876	Rambaux	mp			vvig	
Monsieur Dubost	B	1864	Vigneron	op				
Monsieur Dunand	HP	Pre 1870		mr	f	m		
Monsieur E Y Teas	HP	1874	Verdier E syn E Y Teas	mp	f	l		vf
Monsieur Edouard Detaille	HP	1893	Gouchault	m	dbl	l		
Monsieur Edouard Littaye	T	1891	Bernaix	pb	f			
Monsieur Edouard Ory	HP	1864	Moreau-Robert	mr	f	l		
Monsieur Emile Jourdan	HP	1887	Verdier Ch	mp				
Monsieur Emile Lelong	HP	1887	Bire	mp				
Monsieur Emile Masson	HP	1886	Liabaud	dr				
Monsieur Ernest Dupré	HP	1894	Boutigny	mr				
Monsieur Etienne Dupuy	HP	1873	Levet	lp	f	l		
Monsieur Eugène Delaire	HP	1879	Vigneron	mr	f	l		
Monsieur Eugène Petit	HP	1862	Touvais	mr	f	l		
Monsieur Figeron	HP	1854	Quettier	mr	f	l		
Monsieur Fillion	HP	1876	Gonod / Lévêque	mp	f	l	vig	
Monsieur Fournier	HP	1876	Lalande	mr	f	vl		
		syn	Monseigneur Fournier					
Monsieur Francisque Rive	HP	1883	Schwartz J	mr	f	l		
Monsieur François Ménard	T	1892	Tesnier	mr		l		
Monsieur Frédéric Daupias	T	1898	Chauvry	w	vf	vl		m
Monsieur Furtado	T	1866	Laffay	ly	vf	l	m	f
Monsieur G Niogret	HP	1887		mp	f	l	vig	
Monsieur Gabriel Tournier	HP	1876	Levet	dp	vf	l		
Monsieur Georges Chevallier	HP	1877	Lemée	mp	f	l	vvig	
Monsieur Gerberon	HP	1879	Vigneron	mr	f	m-l	vig	
Monsieur Gonin	HP	1895	Pernet Père	mr	dbl	l	vvig	f
Monsieur Gourdault	B	1859	Guillot Père	dr				
Monsieur Guillaume Popie	HP	1894	Corboeuf	mr	f	l		
Monsieur Henri Gréville	T	1892	Tesnier	my				
Monsieur Henschler	G			dr	f	m		
Monsieur Hippolyte Marchand	HP	1881	Vigneron	rb	f	vl		
Monsieur Hoste	HP	1884	Liabaud	mr	dbl	l	vvig	
Monsieur J Niogret	HP	1887	Liabaud	dr				
Monsieur Jacobs	HP	see	Rosiériste Jacobs	mp	f	l		
Monsieur Jard	B	1857	Guillot Père	m	f	l		
Monsieur Jean France	HP	1866	Levet	m				
Monsieur Joigneaux (P)	HP	1859	Liabaud	mr	f	l	vig	
Monsieur Joseph Chappaz	HP	1882	Schmitt	m	dbl	l	vvig	
Monsieur Joseph Métral	HP	1883	Liabaud	dr		l-vl	vig	
Monsieur Journeaux	HP	1868	Marrest	mr	f	l	wk	
Monsieur Jules Deroudilhe	HP	1886	Liabaud	m	dbl	m		
Monsieur Jules Lemaître	HP	1890	Vigneron	dp	dbl	vl		
Monsieur Jules Maquinant	HP	1882	Vigneron	mr	dbl	l		
Monsieur Jules Monges	HP	1881	Guillot Fils	mp	f	vl	vig	
Monsieur Jules Priou	HT	1899	Schwartz Vve	dr	dbl	l	vig	
Monsieur Just-Détrey	HP	1883	Just-Détrey	mp	f	m-l	vig	
Monsieur Krey	G			m	f	m		
Monsieur Lapierre	HP	1878	Gonod	dr		m-l	vig	
Monsieur Lauriol de Barny	HP	1866	Trouillard	dr	f	l	vig	
Monsieur le Capitaine Louis Frère	HP	1883	Vigneron	dr		l		
Monsieur le Docteur Koch	Misc	Pre 1886						
Monsieur le Préfet Limbourg	HP	1878	Margottin Fils	dr	dbl	l		
Monsieur Lierval	HP	1869	Fontaine	dr	f	l		
Monsieur l'Inténdant Périer	HP	1881	Vigneron	dr	f	l	vig	
Monsieur Louis Ligier	HP	1899	Berland	dr	f	vl		
Monsieur Louis Ricard	HP	1899	Boutigny P	mr	f	l	vig	f
Monsieur Mandet	HP			mr	f	l		vf
Monsieur Mathieu Baron	HP	1886	Schwartz Vve	dr	dbl	l	vig	
Monsieur Max Deegen	T			w				
Monsieur Michel Dupré	HP	1877	Gonod	mp				
Monsieur Montague (?)	Misc			dp				
Monsieur Moreau	HP	1864	Guillot Père	m	f	m		
Monsieur Moreau	HP	1885	Vigneron	mp	f	l		
Monsieur Nomann	HP	1866	Guillot Père	lp	f	l	vig	
Monsieur Paul Floret	T	1881	Nabonnand	m	f	l	vig	
Monsieur Pélisson	M	1848	Vibert syn Pélisson	dr	f	l	vig	
Monsieur Perrier	T	1894	Tesnier	y				
Monsieur Pierre Mercadier	T	1892	Ducher Fils	my				
Monsieur Pierre Migron	T	1898	Chauvry	yb	f	l		
Monsieur Pierson	HP	1864	Fontaine	mr	f	l		
Monsieur Plaisançon	HP	1866	Ducher	dp	f	l	vig	
Monsieur Pontbriant	HP	1864	Damaizin	rb	f	l	vig	
Monsieur Rambaux	HP	1872	Rambaux Vve	lp	vf	l		
Monsieur Ravel	HP	1866	Guillot Fils	dr	f	l	vig	
Monsieur Richard	HP	1886	Vigneron	mr				
Monsieur Richter	G			dr	f	m		
Monsieur Rosier	T	1887	Nabonnand	pb	f	l	vig	f
Monsieur Roubaud	HP	1878	Nabonnand	rb			vig	

Name	Type	Year	Raiser / Synonym					
Monsieur Séringe	HP	1856	Guillot Père	m		m	vig	
Monsieur Tallandier	HP	1872	Tallandier	mr				
Monsieur Thaes	HP	1874	Verdier E	mr	f	l		
Monsieur Thiers	HP	1866	Trouillard	mr	f	l	vig	
Monsieur Thouvenel	HP	1880	Vigneron	dr	f	m	vvig	
Monsieur Tillier	T	1891	Bernaix A	op	dbl	l	vig	
Monsieur Tony Baboud	HT	1895	Godard	mr				
Monsieur Trievoz	HP	1888	Schwartz Vve	mp	f	m	vig	
Monsieur Weeb	HP	1877	Nabonnand	m		l	vvig	
Monsieur Woolfield	HP	1868	Guillot Père	mp	f	l	vig	
Monstrueuse	C	1809	syn Bullata	mp	vdbl	vl		vf
Monstrueuse	N	Pre 1846		w	vf	m		
Monstrueuse	P	Pre 1846		lp		vl		
Monstrueuse	HEg	Pre 1846		r	s			
Monstrueux	D	Pre 1830		lp	f	l		
Monstrueux	HP							
Mont Blanc	T	1870	Ducher syn Le Mont Blanc	ly	f			
Mont d'Or	T	1863	Ducher syn Le Mont d'Or	w	f	l		
Mont Rosa	T	1872	Ducher	yb	f	m	vig	
Mont St Bernard	HCh			lp	f	m	vig	
Mont Vésuve	HP	1858	Ducher	dr	f	m	vig	
Montaigne	HP	1845	Vibert	mr	f	m		
Montalembert	G	1852	Robert & Moreau	m	f	l	m	
Montano	D	1827	Noisette	mp				
Monteau	HCh			dr	f	l		
Monte Cristo	HP	1861	Fontaine	dr	f	l	m	
Montebello	HP	1859	Fontaine	mr	f	m		
Montézuma	G	Pre 1830	Coquerel	m	f	l		
Montézuma	HEg	Pre 1846		lp	s			
Monthyon	G	1828	Vibert syn Crignon de Montigny	dp	f	m		
Montmorency	HP			mr	vf	l	vig	
Montpellier	Misc	Pre 1846						
Montplaisir	T	1868	Guillot Fils	yb	vf	vl		
Mordant	N	Pre 1834		lp		m		
Mordant à Fleurs Pleines	N	Pre 1834		lp				
Mordant Delaunay	HSem	Pre 1830	Laffay	lp	vdbl	m		
Moreau	T	1825	Foulard	w	vf	l		
Moreau	T	Pre 1830		dp		m		
Morin de Damas	G			mr				
Morletii	Bslt	1883	Morlet	lp	s-d			sf
Morphée	N			mp	f	m		
Morphée	HP	1887	Schwartz Vve	dr	f	l	vig	
Morpheus	T			m	f	vl		
Mort de Virginie	G	1824		m	f	m		
Moschata Grandiflora	HMult	1866	Bernaix A	w	s	l	vvig	vf
Moschata Nivea	M			w				
Moselblümchen	HCh	1889	Lambert	dp				
Mosella	Pol	1895	Lambert & Reimer	w	f	m	m	
Moser	HP	1888	Lévêque	dr				
Mossy	HEg	Pre 1846		lp				
Mossy Rose de Meaux	M	c 1813		mp	f	s		
Mottled Moss	M	Pre 1826	Philippe syn Prolifère (M)	dp	f	m		
Mouche	Min		Miellez see also La Mouche	lp				
Mountjoy	Sp	Pre 1840		lp	s-d			
Mousseline	T	1841	Bougère syn Niphetos	w		l		vf
Mousseline	M	1855	Portemer syn Alfred de Dalmas	lp	dbl	s	vig	
Mousseline	HP	1865	Pernet Père	mp	f	m		
Mousseline	M	1881	Moreau-Robert	w	f	m	vig	m
Mousseuse	Ch			mp	f	m		
Mousseuse à Feuilles de Chanvre	M	Pre 1830	(Lansezeur)	mp	f	m		
Mousseuse à Feuilles de Sauge	M	Pre 1830	syn above	mp	f	m		
Mousseuse à Fleurs Pales	M	Pre 1830	Vibert syn Muscosa Gracilis	lp	f	m-l		
Mousseuse Anémone	M	Pre 1830	see Anémone	dp	dbl	s		
Mousseuse Ancien	M	1825	Vibert	pb	vdbl	l		
Mousseuse Blanche	A	1788 syn	Shailer's White Moss	w	f	m	wk	
Mousseuse Blanche Nouvelle	M		see White Bath	w	vf	vl	vvig	
Mousseuse Carnée	M	Pre 1830		lp	f	l		
Mousseuse Commune	M	Pre 1830		lp	f	l		
Mousseuse de la Flèche	M	Pre 1830	see Mous. Anémone	dp	dbl	s		
Mousseuse Panachée	M	Pre 1830		w	s-d	m		
Mousseuse Partout	M	Pre 1846	syn Zoé	mp				
Mousseuse Pourpre	M	Pre 1830	syn Mosseuse Rouge	dp	dbl	m		
Mousseuse Presque Partout	M	Pre 1846		mp	vdbl			
Mousseuse Prolifère	M	Pre 1830	Philippe	mp	vf	l		

Name	Class	Date	Raiser / Syn					
Mousseuse Rose Foncé	M	Pre 1830		dp	dbl	m		
Mousseuse Rose Foncé, Pleine	M	Pre 1830		dp	f	m		
Mousseuse Rouge	M	Pre 1830	syn Mous. Rose Foncé	dp	dbl	m		
Mousseuse Semi-Double	M	Pre 1830	Vibert	mp	dbl	l		
Mousseuse Simple	M	Pre 1804		mp	s or s-d	m		
Mousseuse Vilmorin	M	Pre 1830	syn Mousseux Carnéc	lp	f	m	vig	
Mousseux	D		Vibert	mr				
Mousseux des Quatre Saisons Blanc	M			w	dbl	m		
Mousseux du Japon	M			m	s-d	m	m	f
Mousseux Ordinaire (or Ancien)	C			mp	vf	l		
Moyenne (Moyena)	HCh	Pre 1834		mp	f	m		
Moyse	G	Pre 1834		mr		l		
Mozard	Pom							
Multiflora	N	1849	Margottin	lp		m		
Multiflora	D		see Red Damask	mr				
Multiflora à Bois Bruni	Cl							
Multiflora Nana Perpetuelle	Pol	1893	Lille	lp	s	s		
Multiflore	C	Pre 1821		lp	s-d	l		f
Multiflore	Min	Pre 1846	syn Lawrence Double	dp		s		
Multiflore	Ch		Noisette	m				
Multiflore	M	1847	Vibert	p	f	s		
Multiflore à Fleur Marbrée	HMult		Laffay	pb	dbl	s		
Multiflore à Fleur Rose	HMult	Pre 1830		lp	f	vs		
Multiflore à Fleur Rose Foncé	HMult	Pre 1830	Vibert	dp	vdbl	vs		
Multiflore Blanc Simple	HMult	Pre 1830		mp	s	vs		
Multiflore Blanche Double	HMult	Pre 1830	Prévost	w	dbl	vs		
Multiflore de Hollande	C	Pre 1820 syn Gros	Prévost Choux d'Hollande	lp	f	m	vig	vf
Multiflore de Vaumarcus	N	1875	Menet	lp	vdbl	m		
Multiflore Élégante	HMult		Laffay	w	f	m	vig	
Multiflore Rouge à Petites Feuilles	HMult	Pre 1830	Laffay	mp	dbl	s		
Multiple Dominante	D		Miellez	w				
Multiplex	Misc	Pre 1629		my	vdbl	vl		
Mungo Park	HRg	1895	Paul					
Muriel Grahame	T	1896	Dickson A	yb	f	vl	wk	
Murillo	HP	1862	Fontaine	m	dbl	m-l	m	
Muscade	M			w	s or s-d			sf
Muscade à Bois Violet	M	1825	Vibert	m				
Muscade à Coeur Jaune	M	1825		yb		s		
Muscade Double	M	Pre 1830	Vibert	w	f	s-m		sf
Muscade Multiple	M	Pre 1830	Vibert	w	s-d			
Muscade Nain Simple	M		Mauget	w				
Muscade Noire	Misc							
Muscade Parviflore	M		Toutain	w				
Muscade Rouge	A	1809	Bosc syn Evratina	dp	vdbl	s	vig	
Muscade Semi-Double	M	Pre 1830	syn Muscade Multiple	w	s-d			
Muscade Semi-Double Rose	M		Dumont de Courset					
Muscade Simple	M			w				
Muscosa	M	Pre 1727		mp				vf
Muscosa	M	1854	Oger	mp				
Muscosa Alba	M	1788 syn	Shailer's White Moss	w	vdbl	m		
Muscosa Gracilis	M	Pre 1830	Prévost	lp	f			
Muscosa Japonica	M	Pre 1895		dp				
Muscosa Simplex	M	Pre 1807		mp	s			
Musquée Pleine	M	Pre 1830	Vibert syn Muscade Double	w	f	s-m		sf
Musquée Presque Inerme	M	1820	Prévost	w	s	m	vig	
Mutabilis	G			w				
Mutabilis	A	c1810	Descemet syn Cocarde	mp				
Mutabilis	N	Pre 1830	Calvert	my		s		
Mutabilis	HSem	Pre 1870	Calvert	lp		m	vvig	
Mutabilis	T	1889	Da Costa	my				
Mutabilis	Ch	Pre 1894		yb	s	l	vig	
Mutabilis Albissima	C			w	vf	m		
My Lady Kensington	C	Pre 1819		lp				
Myriacantha	HSpn			rb				
Myriacanthes	HSem	Pre 1846		lp				
Myriacanthes Renoncule	HSem			pb	dbl	l		
Myrrh Scented	Ayr	Pre 1835	syn Splendens	w	s-d			vf
Mystère	T	1877	Nabonnand	pb	f	vl	vig	
Myrtle Scented	Ayr	Pre 1870		dp		m		

NAME	TYPE	YEAR	RAISER	COLOUR	BLOOM	SIZE	GROWTH	SCENT
Nabab	Ch		Laffay	mr				
Nabonnand	Ch	1887	Nabonnand	dr	f	l	vvig	
Nabonnand, Climbing	Ch	1896	Camon	dr	dbl	l	vvig	
Nadine de Karadec	Ch	1852	Dorisy	w	f	m	vig	
Nadine Faye	HCh	1847	Bélot-Défougères	mp	vf	m		
Nadiska	B	1847	Vibert	mr	f	m		
Nadiska	C	1819	Vibert	mp	f	m		
		syn	Orpheline de Wilna					
Nain	G	Pre 1806	Crantz (?)	m	s	l		m
			syn Rosier d'Amour					
Nain	Ch	1812	Colleville	mp				
Nain	HCh	Pre 1820	Laffay	lp	dbl	s		
			syn De Chartres					
Nain	HMult	1895	Vigneron	pb	s			
Naine	B	1831	Vibert	lp		m		
Naissance de Vénus	A	1816	Booth	mp	vdbl	m	vig	vf
		syn K	önigin von Dänemark					
Nämenlose Schöne	T	1886	Deegen	w		l		f
Nana	Alp	Pre 1815		lp	s			f
Nana	C		syn Pumila	dy				
Nanako Rose	Pol	Pre 1867		pb				
Nancia (?)	Misc							
Nancy Lee	HT	1879	Bennett	dp	f	s	wk	vf
Nanette	G	Pre 1848		pb	vdbl	m	vig	
Nanine	G		Vétillard	lp				
Nankin	HSpn	Pre 1819	Descemet	w	s	m		
Nankin	N	Pre 1848		ly				
Nankin	T	1871	Ducher	my	vf	m	vig	
Nankin Double	HSpn	1827	Vibert	pb	dbl			
Nankin Nouvelle	T		Nankin		s-d	l		vf
Napoleon	G	Pre 1834	Hardy	m	dbl	vl	vig	
Napoléon	Ch	c 1835	Laffay	pb	dbl	l		
Napoléon Nouveau	HP			dr				
Napoléon III	B	1852	Bacot	mp				
Napoléon III	HP	1855	Granger	dr				
		syn E	mpereur Napoléon III					
Napoléon III	HP	1866	Verdier E	rb	f	l	vig	
Narcisse	T	Pre 1846	Avoux & Crozy	my	f	l	m	f
Narcisse	Ch	1845	Laffay	w	dbl	m		
Narcisse de Salvandy	G	1843	Parmentier/van Houtte	mp	dbl	l	sp	
Narcisse Desportes	HCh	Pre 1846						
Nardy	HP	Pre 1870		dp	f	l		
Nardy	T	1888	Nabonnand	dy	vf	vl	vig	f
Nardy Frères	HP	1865	Ducher	m	f	vl	m	
Narrow Water	N	1883	Daisy Hill Nursery	lp	s-d			sf
Nastarana	N	1879	Paul	w	s-d	m	vvig	vf
Natascha Metschersky	T	1878	Nabonnand	w	f	vl	vvig	
Nathalie	Ch	c 1835	Laffay	mr	f	s-m		
Nathalie	HCh	Pre 1846						
Nathalie	M	1849	Vibert	dp	f	m		
Nathalie Daniel	B	1845	Verdier V	pb	vf	m		
Nathalie de Marsac	HP		Pradel	lp				
Nathalie de Pronville	G	1824	Hardy	pb	s-d	l		
Nathalie Imbert	T	1884	Nabonnand	mp	dbl	m	vig	f
Nathalie Simon	HP	1882	Vigneron	mr	f	l	vig	
Nationale Tricolore	G	Pre 1836	syn La Nationale	pb	dbl	m		
Nausicae	G	1817	Vibert	mr	f	l		
Navarin	Ch	Pre 1834		mr		s		
Néala	G	1822	Vibert	dp	f	m		
Ne Plus Ultra	G	c 1810	Descemet	mp	f	l		
Ne Plus Ultra	N	Pre 1846		w	f	m		vf
Négresse	HP	1847	Vibert	m	vf	s	vig	
Négresse	G	syn	Perle de Veissenstein					
Négretienne	G	Pre 1811	syn Subnigra	m	s-d	m		
Négrette	G	Pre 1811	syn Subnigra	m	s-d	m		
Negro	Misc	Pre 1846		dr				
Negro Panaché	Misc	Pre 1846		dp				
Neige	Ch		Miellez	w				
Nelly	B		Lartay	w	f	m		
Nelly	G		Robert	lp	f	m		
Nelson	G	Pre 1846	Vibert	m	f	m		
Némésis	Ch	1836	Bizard	dr	dbl	s		
Némésis	N	Pre 1846		rb	dbl	s		
Némésis	HFt			mr	vdbl	m		
Némorin	G			mr	f	m		
Nemox (?)	Misc			dr				
Nenia	Misc		Da Costa	dr				
Nenoux	Cl			dp	f	m		
Néphis	HSpn	1825	Dagonnet	dp				

Name	Type	Date	Breeder / syn					
Neptune	HSpn	Pre 1848		dr	f	m		
Nérard	B			lp	f	m		
Néréïde	Ch		Laffay	w	f	m		
Néreïs	D	1828	Vibert	lp	f	m		
Nérestan	M	1854	Robert	pb	s-d	l		
Neriiflora	HCh			mr	f	l		
Nerina	G	Pre 1830	Racine					
Nerine	B	Pre 1846		dp				
Néron	G	1841	Laffay	rb	f	m		
Nerrière	HBc	Pre 1847	Vibert	w	f	l		
Nestor	G	1834		mr	dbl	m	vvig	
Neuman	B	1826	syn Dubreuil	lp	f	m-l		
New Blush Hip	A	Pre 1846	syn Blush Hip	lp	dbl	m		
New Cabbage Rose	C		syn Ranunculus	w				
New Celestial	D	Pre 1846		mp		l		
New Double	M	Pre 1846		w				
New Double	Misc			m				
New Dutch Virgin Blush	Misc	Pre 1846		lp				
New French Yellow	N	c 1830	Desprez	yb	f	l	vig	m
New Globe Hip	G	1829		w	vdbl	m		
New Village Maid	G	Pre 1846		w	f	m		
New White Moss	M		syn White Bath	w	f	l		
New Yellow	T			w	f	l-vl	vvig	
Newton	HCh		Laffay	w	f	m		
Newton	HP	1852	Robert	w				
Newton	HP	1869	Gonod	rb	f	vl	vvig	
Nias James	HP	1885	Singer	lp	f	l	vig	
Nicetas	Ch	1827	Péan	mp	vdbl	m	vig	
Nicette	Ch	1847	Vibert	lp	f	l		
Nickmene	N	Pre 1846		lp				
Nicolas Belot	HP			mp				
Nicolas d'Assas	HP	1854	Robert	mr	f	m		
Nicolas Flamel	M	1856	Robert	mp				
Nicolas Koechlin	G	c1860	Baumann	m				
Nicolas Leblanc	HP	1885	Moreau-Robert	mr		vl	vig	
Nicolas Rolland	B	1846	Dorizy	mp	f	m		
Nicolette	C			lp	f	m		
Nid d'Amour	T	Pre 1846		lp	vdbl	m-l		f
Nidia	Misc	1831	Vibert	mp		l		
Nigra	HCh	Pre 1835		m	f	s		
Nigrette	G	Pre 1811	syn Subnigra	m	dbl	l		
Nigretiana	G	Pre 1810	Dupont syn Superbe en Brun	m	dbl	m		
Nigretiana	G	Pre 1830	Coquerel	dr	f	m		
Nigritienne	G	Pre 1846		dr				
Nigrorum	G	Pre 1830	Calvert	m	f	s		
Nikita	HSpn		Vibert	dp				
Nimphea Alba	HT			w				
Nina	T	1828	Vibert	lp	f	l		f
Ninette	M	1857	Robert & Moreau	mr	f	m	vig	
Ninette	HP		syn Petite Ninette	lp				
Nini	Ch		syn Adeline Bordeau	rb				
Nini	T	1825	Barrier	mp				
Nini	Ch	Pre 1834	Barrier	mp	f	m		f
Ninon	HCh			m	f	m		
Ninon à Fleurs et Feuilles Panachées	G		Prévost	dp	vf			
Ninon de Lenclos	G	1817	Vibert (syn Joséphine)	dp	vf	m		
Ninon de Lenclos	B	Pre 1846		dp				
Niobé	G	1819	Vibert syn Nouveau Triomphe	lp	f	m		
Niobe	HT	1895	Geschwind	dr	dbl	m		
Niobée	HP	1819		lp	f	m	vig	
Niphetos	T	1841	Bougère	w	dbl	l	vig	vf
Niphetos, Climbing	Cl T	1888	Keynes,Williams &Co	w	dbl	l	vig	vf
Nisida	C	1822	Vibert	lp	dbl	m		
Nisida	G	1827	Noisette	mr				
Nisida	T	1840	Goubault	pb	f	m	m	vf
Nitida	T			w	f	m		
Nivalis	HSpn							
Nivalli	D	Pre 1846		mp				
Nivea	A			w	f	m		
Nivea	C	1775	Grimwood syn White Provence	w	dbl	l		m
Nivea	Sp	1803	syn r.laevigata	w	s	m		
Nivea	N	1828	Vibert syn Aimée Vibert	w	dbl	l	vig	vf
Nivea	M	Pre 1830	Dupont syn Belle Henriette	w	s	m	vig	vf
Noble Cramoisie	G		Robert	mr	f	m		
Noble Fleur	G	Pre 1834	Vibert	dp	f	m		
Noble Pourpre	G	1828	Vibert	dr	f	m-l		

Name	Class	Date	Raiser / syn	col	dbl	size	vig	fr
Noël	HP	Pre 1846		lp	f	m		
Noémie	HCh	c 1820	Hardy	m	vf	l		
Noémie	D	1845	Vibert	dp	f	l		
Noémie	HP	1845	Aubert	lp	f	m	vig	
Noémie	HP	1850	Foulard	mr	f	l		
Noémie Galtier	HP	1864	Pradel	lp				
No Ibara	HRg							
Noire	Ch		Laffay	mr				
Noire	G	Pre 1819	syn Hector	m	dbl	s		
Noire Couronnée	G	Pre 1810	Dupont	dr	vdbl	m-l		
Noire de Hollande	G	Pre 1811	syn Subnigra	m	s-d	m		
Noire Frisée	G							
Noire Pourpre Panachée	G	Pre 1811	syn Ombre Panachée	m	dbl	l		
Noisette à Grandes Fleurs	N		Noisette L	w	s-d	l		f
Noisette à Grandes Fleurs Simples	N		Dubreuil	m	s	l		sf
Noisette à Rameaux Inclinés	N		Noisette L	lp	dbl	m		
Noisette Angevine	N		Buret	w	dbl	l	vig	
Noisette Ayez	HSem	Pre 1832	Vibert syn Spectabilis	m	dbl	m	vig	vf
Noisette Blanche Semi-Double	N	Pre 1830	Vibert	w	dbl	s	vig	
Noisette Buret	N		Buret	rb	dbl		vvig	
Noisette Carnée	N	1817	Noisette Ph	lp	vdbl	m	vvig	
Noisette Chamnagana	N	1827	Vibert	lp	s-d	l	vig	sf
Noisette Cupidon	Ch	Pre 1830	Noisette L / Vibert syn Cupidon	mp	vdbl	s		
Noisette de l'Inde	N	1814	Noisette syn r x noisettiana	w				
Noisette Desprez	N	c 1830	Desprez syn Jaune Desprez	yb	f	l	vig	m
Noisette Gracieuse	N		Noisette L	lp	dbl		vig	
Noisette Jacques	N		Laffay	w	dbl	m	vig	
Noisette Jaune	N	c 1820	Desprez see Jean Desprez	rb	f	m		
Noisette Jaune	T	1834 syn	Smith Smith's Yellow China	dy	f	l		
Noisette Légère	N		Noisette L	w		s		
Noisette Lilas Foncé	N		Laffay	w	vdbl	s	wk	
Noisette Moschata	N	1873	Schwartz	w				
Noisette Ponctuée	N	1826		lp	s-d	s		
Noisette Pourpre	N	1823	Laffay	lp	vdbl	s		
Noisette Putaux	N		Putaux	mp	s-d		vig	
Noisette Rampante	N		Noisette M	w	dbl	m	sp	
Noisette Renoncule	N		Miellez	lp	dbl			
Noisette Rose	N	1814	Noisette syn r x noisettiana	w				
Noisette Rose	N	Pre 1830	Nicolle	mp	dbl	m		
Noisette Rouge	N	1824	Vibert syn Noisette Pourpre	lp	vdbl	s		
Noisette Sarmenteuse	N	Pre 1830	Vibert	lp	vdbl	m		
Noisette Sarmenteux	N	Pre 1830	Noisette L	lp	s-d	m		f
Noisettiana Repens	N	1829	Noisette, Marie	w	dbl			f
Nonesuch	Misc	Pre 1846						
Nonpareil	Misc	Pre 1846						
Nora	HT	1895	Geschwind	lp	dbl	l		
Normandica	C	Pre 1791	syn Petite de Hollande	mp	dbl	s		m
Northern Cherokee Rose	Sp	c 1820 Syn	r.spinosissima altaica	w	s	l		
Northern Light	HWich	1898	Van Fleet	lp	s	l		
Northern Praire Rose	Sp	1773	syn r.blanda	mp	s	m	vig	
Nosegay	Misc	Pre 1846						
Notaire Bonnefond	HP	1868	Liabaud	m	f	vl	vig	
Notre Dame de Fourvière	HP	1861	Ducher	lp	f	l		
N'veau Deuil de l'Archevêque de Paris	B	1853	Oger	dr	f	m		
Nouveau Duc d'York	G	1823	Sommaire					
Nouveau Grand Monarque	G			mp	f	m		
Nouveau Intelligible	G	Pre 1811		m	vdbl			
Nouveau Monde	G	Pre 1811		m	vdbl			
Nouveau Petite Serment	C	Pre 1811		m	vdbl	s		m
Nouveau Rouge	G	Pre 1811		dr	vdbl			m
Nouveau Triomphe	D	1820	Godefroy syn Duc de Chartres	lp	f	m		
Nouveau Triomphe	G	Pre 1825	Prévost	lp	f	m		
Nouveau Vulcain	G	1820		m	vdbl	m		vf
Nouvel Etendard du Grand Homme	HP	1854	Lartay	lp	f	l		
Nouvelle à Feuilles d'Orme	G	1822	Vibert	lp	dbl	m-l		
Nouvelle de Provence	C	Pre 1830	Vibert syn Justine	lp	vdbl	m		
Nouvelle Duchesse d'Orléans	G			w	f	l		
Nouvelle du Jour	G			dr	f	m		
Nouvelle Élégante	HP			mp	f	m		

Name	Type	Date	Breeder / Synonym					
Nouvelle Froment (Frommont)	T			w	f	l		
Nouvelle Gagnée	G	Pre 1813	Miellez	mp				
Nouvelle Héloïse	G	1816	Descemet syn Héloïse	lp	f	m-l		
Nouvelle Pavot	G		Miellez	mr	dbl	l		
Nouvelle Pivoine	G	Pre 1818	Lille	m	f	l		
Nouvelle Redouté	G			mp	f	m		
Nouvelle Redouté	HRg	1818	Vibert	mr	f	m		
Nouvelle Rose Marguerite	Ch			lp				
Nouvelle Rose Pavot	G		Miellez	mr				
Nouvelle Rubannée d'Enghien	G			rb	f	m		
Nouvelle Transparente	G	1835	Miellez	dp	f	l		vf
Nova	Ch		Vibert	lp				
Nova Coelestis	A	Pre 1810	syn Celestial	lp	dbl	l	vig	vf
Nova Incarnata	A	Pre 1810	Charpentier syn Elisa	lp	s-d	m		
Novatella	M	1860	Moreau-Robert	lp	f	m		
Nuancée de Bleu	A	Pre 1810	Dupont syn Celestial	lp	dbl	l	vig	vf
Nubienne	HCh	1825	Laffay syn Gloire des Hellènes & La Nubienne	dr	dbl	m		
Nuits de Young	M	1845	Laffay	dr	vdbl	m	m	m
Numa	Ch	Pre 1846		mr				
Nutka Rose	Sp	1876	syn r.nutkana	mp	s			
Nutkana	D		syn Pyramid Harbour	w				
Nuttaliana	Sp	1897		mp				
Nycetas	Ch		Péan	pb	vf	m	vig	
Nymphaea Alba	HT	1889	Drögemüller	w	dbl	m		
Nymphe	T	1825	Laffay	lp	f	l		
Nymphe de Mer	Cl	1886	Geschwind	lp				
Nymphe Echo	N			lp	vf	s	wk	
Nymphe Egeria	T	1892	Ketten	mp				
Nymphe Egeria	HMult	1892	Geschwind R	mp	dbl	m		
Nymphe Naine Émue	A	1802	Dumont de Courset syn Maiden's Blush	w	dbl	m		m
Nymphe Tepla	HMult	1886	Geschwind R	pb	vdbl	m		
Nypethos	T	Pre 1846		w				

NAME	TYPE	YEAR	RAISER	COLOUR	BLOOM	SIZE	GROWTH	SCENT
Oakmont	HP	1893	May	pb	dbl	l		
Oberlin	HP	1855	Robert	rb	f	s	vig	
Obscurité	G	Pre 1830	Prévost	m	dbl	m		
Ochroleuca	Pom			ly				
Octavie	G	1800	Coquerel	lp	f	m-l	vig	
Octavie	G	c 1810	Descemet	dp				
Octavie	G	c 1835	Vibert (same as above)	dp	vf	s-m		
Octavie	N	1845	Vibert	m	f	m		m
Octavie Choquet	HP	1868	Fontaine	lp	f	m		
Octavie Fontaine	B	1858	Fontaine	w	f	m	vig	
Odéric	G			dr	f	m		
Odéric Vital	HP	1858	Oger	lp	f	l		
Odesca	HP	1851	Vibert	lp	f	m	vig	
Odette de Champsdivers	G/C	Pre 1846		lp	f	m		
Odeur de Muscade	T			lp	f	m		f
Odeur de Pâte d'Amandes	HCh			dr				f
Odine	Ch	Pre 1830		lp				
Odorant	Ch		Laffay	pb	dbl	m		vf
Odorata	T	1809	Hume/Banks/Colville	lp	dbl	l		vf
		syn	Hume's	Blush Tea-Scented	China			
Odorata	HSem	Pre 1846		w		vl		
Odorata	HBc			w				
Odoratissima	Bks	Pre 1846		w				f
Odoratissima	T	Pre 1846		lp				f
Oeillet	C	c 1789	Poilpré	lp	dbl	s	vig	m
Oeillet	Ch		Redouté	dp				
Oeillet	D			mr				
Oeillet Blanc	D	Pre 1830	Prévost	lp	vdbl	s		
Oeillet Blanc	C		Prévost	w	dbl	s		
Oeillet de Saint-Arquey	Ch	1831	Jacques	pb	f			sf
			syn Serratipetala					
Oeillet Double	G	c 1835	Prévost	m				
Oeillet Fantaisie	HP	1871	Guillot Fils	dr	f	m	vig	
Oeillet Flamand	G	1845	Vibert	pb	vdbl	m	vvig	vf
Oeillet Flamand	B	1866	Oger	mp		m		
Oeillet Panachée	M	1888	Verdier C	pb	f	m	vig	m
Oeillet Parfait	D	1841	Foulard	pb	dbl	m	vig	f
Oeillet Parfait	G			p	f	m		
Oeillet Rose	D	Pre 1830	Prévost	lp	f	s	vig	
Oeillet sans Pétales	C	1798						
Officinal	D			p				
Officinalis	Sp	Pre 1600	syn r.gallica officinalis	dp	s-d			m
Offley Rose	Sp	Pre 1600	syn r.gallica officinalis	dp	s-d			m
Ohl	G	1830	Vibert	m	dbl	l	vig	f
Old Black	M	1845	Laffay M	dr	vdbl	m		m
			syn Nuits de Young					
Old Blush	Ch	1751	Parsons	mp	s-d	m	vig	sf
Old Cabbage Provence	C	Pre 1846		mp	vf	l		
Old Crimson	Ch	1790		mr	dbl	m	m	
			syn Slater's Crimson	China				
Old Crimson China	Ch	1790	syn Slater's Crimson	China mr	dbl	m	m	
Old Glory	Cl T	1853	Jacotot	op	dbl	l	vig	m
			syn Gloire de Dijon					
Old Pink Daily	Ch	1751	Parsons syn Old Blush	mp	s-d	m	vig	sf
Old Pink Monthly	Ch	1751	Parsons syn Old Blush	mp	s-d	m	vig	sf
Old Pink Moss	M	Pre 1720	syn Communis	mp	dbl	l		
Old Red Boursault	Bslt	c 1810		mr	s-d	m	vvig	
Old Red Pet	Ch	1854	Guinoisseau-Flon	dr	vdbl	m		
			syn Lucullus					
Old Spanish Rose	HMult	Pre 1826	Cormack & Sinclair	m	dbl	m	vig	m
			syn Russeliana					
Old Tuscan	G	Pre 1598	syn Tuscany	m	s-d	l	vig	
Old Velvet Moss	M	1855	Laffay M	m	s-d	l	vig	m
			syn William Lobb					
Old Velvet Rose	G	Pre 1598	syn Tuscany	m	s-d	l	vig	
Old White Moss	M	1798	Shailer	w	dbl	l		
		syn	Shailer's White Moss					
Old Yellow Tea	T	1824	Parks	my	dbl			
		syn	Parks'	Yellow Tea-Scented	China			
Olga	Pom			p				
Olga Marix	B	1873	Schwartz	lp	f	m	vig	
Olgerasie	HP	Pre 1846		lp	f			
Olivet	HMult	1892	Vigneron	mr	f	l		
Olivier Belhomme	HP	1861	Verdier V & C	mr	f	m	vig	
Olivier de Clisson	HP	1866	Moreau-Robert	mr	f	m	vvig	
Olivier de Serres	HP	1828	Menard	dp	f	l	vig	
Olivier Métra	HP	1884	Verdier E	mr	vf	l	vig	f
Olry	T	1888		w	vf	l	vig	f
Olympe	M		Vibert	lp	f	m		

Name	Type	Date	Raiser					
Olympe	Ch		Laffay	dr	f	l		
Olympe	N	1830	Vibert	lp		s		
Olympe	N		syn Paniculata Rubra	mr				
Olympe	D	1843	Vibert	dr	f	m		
Olympe Frécinay	T	1861	Damaizin	w	f	l	m	
Olympe Terestchenko	HP	1882	Lévêque	w	f	l	vvig	
Olympia	B	Pre 1846		lp				
Olympic	Ch	Pre 1846		lp				
Olympie	D	Pre 1830	Vibert	lp	f	m		
Omar Khayyám	D	1893	Simpson / Kew	lp	vf	s		m
Omar Pacha	B	1863	Pradel	mr	f	l	vig	
Omar Pacha	HP		Laffay	rb				
Ombre	G	1824	Vibert	m		m		
Ombre Panachée	G	Pre 1811		m	dbl	l		
Ombre Parfaite	G/C	1823	Vibert	lp		s	vig	
Ombre Précieuse	G	1843		r		m		
Ombre sans Pareille	G	Pre 1830	Prévost	m	f	s		
Ombre Superbe	G	Pre 1811	(Holland)	m	dbl	l		
Ombrée de Hollande	G	Pre 1834		m		m		
Ombrée Parfaite	G	1823	Vibert	m	f	m		f
Omniflore Marbrée	G	Pre 1846		mp				
Omphale	G	1820	Vibert	lp				
Omphale	G	1839	Vibert J P	mp	vdbl	l		
Ondine	Ch		Laffay	lp	vdbl	s		
Onguiculata Comophillata	C	1789	Poilpré syn Oeillet (C)	lp	dbl	s	vig	m
Onguiculé	Min		Noisette M	mr				
Onispertis	G	Pre 1830		dr				
Onvre de Montpensier	G	Pre 1860						
Oocarpa	Pom		syn Ochroleuca	ly				
Ophelia	T	Pre 1870	Ducher	ly	vf	m	vig	
Ophelia	N			my				
Ophir	HMsk	c 1835	Laffay	my	f	s		vf
Ophirie	N	1841	Goubault	op	vdbl	m	vig	f
Oracle du Siècle	G	Pre 1834	Miellez	mr		m		
Orange Incarnata	N	Pre 1870		y	dbl	m		
Orange Perfection	HP	1898	Manda	lp				
Orberin (Orbelin)	G			m	f	m-l		
Ordéric Vital	HP	1858	Oger syn Odéric Vital	lp	dbl	m		
Ordinaire	Ch	1789	Keer (Kerr) syn Pallida	lp	vdbl	m	vig	
Ordinaire	M	Pre 1870	syn Communis	mp	f	l	vig	vf
Ordinaire	G							
Orgueil de Lyon	HP	1886	Besson	mr	dbl	m		
Oriental Beauty	Misc	Pre 1846						
Oriflamme	G	Pre 1846		mr	f	m		
Oriflamme	D	1819	Bozérian	rb				
Oriflamme de Saint Louis	HP	1858	Baudry & Hamel	dp	f	vl	vvig	
Orleans	Bks	Pre 1846		dr				
Orloff	N	Pre 1846						
Ornement de Carafe	G	Pre 1811 syn	Descemet Ornement de Parade	dp	f	m		m
Ornement de la Nature	G	Pre 1813 syn	Toutain Anémone Ancienne	lp	vdbl	s		sf
Ornement de Parade	G	Pre 1811	Prévost	dp	f	m		m
Ornement des Bosquets	N	1860	Jamain H	dp	dbl	m		
Ornement des Jardins	HP	1855	Robert & Moreau	mr	f	m		
Ornement des Jardins	Pol	1882	Rambaux	lp				
Ornement des Rouges	G	1824	Hardy syn Abatucci	mr	f	l		
Ornement des Vierges	A	Pre 1830	Prévost syn Charlotte	w	dbl	m-l	vig	
Ornement du Luxembourg	HP	1840	Hardy	m	dbl	s		
Orphée	N		Laffay	dp	f	m		
Orphée	G	Pre 1830	Racine	rb	f	m-l		
Orphée de Lille	D	c 1811	Pelletier syn Marie-Louise	lp	vdbl	m		vf
Orpheline	T			w	f	m		
Orpheline de Guillotiére	Ch	Pre 1846		yb		l		
Orpheline de Juillet	G	Pre 1836	Parmentier or Vibert	m	vdbl	l	m	
Orpheline de Wilna	HCh			mp	f	m		
Orpheus	N			dp	f	m		
Orphirie	N	Pre 1846		mp				
Orphise	G	Pre 1826	Vibert	mr	f	l		
Oscar Cordel	HP	1897	Lambert P	mp	dbl	l	vig	f
Oscar II, Roi de Suède	HP	1888	Soupert & Notting	mr	vdbl	l	vig	m
Oscar Foulard	M		Robert syn Pompon Crimson	dr	f	s		
Oscar Lamarche	HP	1875	Schwartz	rb	f	l	wk	
Oscar Leclerc	B	1846	Verdier V	mr	f	l	vvig	
Oscar Leclerc	M	1853	Robert	dp	f	m		
Osiris	Ch		Péan	w	f		vig	

Oskar Kordel	HP	1897	Lambert P	mp		l	vig	m
Otaïtienne	G		Miellez	dr	f	vl		
Othello	G	Pre 1830	Trébucien	dr	f	m		f
Othello Maure de Venise	HCh	Pre 1828		m	f	m	wk	
Ourika	G	1825	Hardy	dr	f	m		
Ovid	HSet	1890	Geschwind R	mp	f	l		
Ovide	G	1853	Robert	lp	f	m		
Oxonian	HP	1876	Turner	mp	f	l	vig	f

NAME	TYPE	YEAR	RAISER	COLOUR	BLOOM	SIZE	GROWTH	SCENT
P Riffault	T	1888	Nabonnand	mp	f	l	vig	f
Paeonia	HP	1855	Lacharme	dr	dbl	l	m	vf
Paeoniflora	T	Pre 1846		mr				
Paeoniflora	C		syn Constance	mp				
Paestina	Misc	Pre 1846						
Paganini	G			mr	f	m		
Paillard	Ch		Vibert	dr				
Paillet	Ch			m	f	m		
Painted Damask	D	1826	Deschiens syn Léda	w	dbl	m	vig	m
Pair de France	T			dr	f	l	vig	
Pajol	Ch	1830	Vibert	mr	f	m	vig	
Palais de Cristal	HP	1851	Quettier	lp	vf	m	vvig	
Palais de Laeken	G	1824	syn Grand Palais de L	lp	f	m		
Palais de l'Industrie	HP		Pradel	mp				
Palavicini	Ch		Laffay	lp	dbl	m		
Pale Coloured	HSpn	Pre 1846						
Pale-Flowered	M	c 1805	Vilmorin syn Vilmorin	lp	f	m-l		
Pale Rouge Nouveau	G			rb				
Pale Rouge Panaché	G	Pre 1811	syn Belle Aimable	rb	dbl	s		
Pale Rouge Superbe	G	Pre 1811	synBouquet Charmant	mp	dbl	l		
Pale Violet	Misc	Pre 1846						
Palestro	HP	1859	Boyau	rb	f	m		
Palladens	Ch			mr		m		
Pallagi	Ch	Pre 1834		dr		l		
Pallagi Panaché	HCh	Pre 1846		mp	f	l		
Pallas	G	Pre 1811	Miellez	m	f	l		m
Pallas	M		Miellez	lp	vdbl	s		
Pallasii	Sp	c 1820		w	s	l		
		syn	r.spinosissima altaica					
Pallavicini	Ch	Pre 1834		w				
Pallida	Ch	1789	Kerr	mp	f	m		
Pallida	HFt	1824	Souchet	ly	s	m		
Pallida	HSet	1843	Feast	lp	dbl			
Pallidior	G	Pre 1811	syn Agatha Incarnata	lp	vdbl	m		m
Pallidior	C	Pre 1830	syn Belle de Cels etc	lp	dbl	l		
Palludia	M	1859	Robert & Moreau	mp	f	l		
Palmengarten Director Siebert	HT	1899	Welter	lp				
Palmyre	P	Pre 1830	Vibert	lp	f	m		
Palmyre	HP	1817	Vibert	lp	f	m		
Palmyre	D	1844	Laffay	lp				
Palmyre	B	1852	Lartay	mr	f	l		
Palmyre	HP	Pre 1870		lp	f	l		
Palo Alto	T	1898	Conard & Jones	ab	f	l		
Palotte Picottée	HP			lp	f	m		
Pamela	G	1821	Vibert	lp	f	m		
Panaché	Sp	Pre 1581		pb	s-d			m
		syn	r.gallica versicolor					
Panachée	G		Vibert	m	f	m		
Panachée	M	c 1818	Shailer	w	s-d	m		
Panachée	D	c 1820	Godefroy	pb	dbl	m		
Panachée	C	1825		lp	s-d	l		
Panachée	T			w	s-d	m	vig	
Panachée à Fleurs Doubles	G	1839	Vibert	pb	dbl	m		
Panachée à Fleurs Pleines	G	1839	Vibert	m				
Panachée à Petales Étroits	G		Robert	mp				
Panachée d'Angers	HP	1875	Moreau-Robert	pb	dbl	l	vig	f
		syn	Commandant Beaure-	paire				
Panachée de Blanc	G	1825	Vibert	m	dbl	m		f
			syn Ombrée Parfaite					
Panachée de Blanc et de Cramoisi	G	Pre 1581	syn r.gallica versicolor	pb	dbl			
Panachée de Bordeaux	HP	1898	Duprat	pb	dbl	vl		vf
		syn	Coquette Bordelaise					
Panachée de Girardon	HP		Girardon	pb	f	m		
Panachée de Luxembourg	HP	1866	Soupert & Notting	pb	f	m	vig	
Panachée de Lyon	P	1895	Dubreuil	pb	dbl	m	m	vf
Panachée d'Orléans	HP	1854	Dauvesse	pb	f	m	vig	f
Panachée Double	G	1832	Vibert (?)	pb	vdbl	l	m	m
			syn La Rubannée					
Panachée Double	G	1839	Vibert	pb	dbl	s		sf
		syn	Panachée Pleine (G)					
Panachée Double	M			w				
Panachée Langroise	HP	1873	Rimancourt	rb	f	l	vig	
Panachée Pleine	G	1839	Vibert	pb	dbl	s		sf
Panachée Pleine	M	Pre 1844	Robert (?)	w	f	m	vig	
Panachée Pleine à Petales Etroites	M	Pre 1844	Robert (?) syn above	w	f	m		
Panachée Semi-Double	M	Pre 1834	Vibert	lp	s-d	m		

Name	Type	Date	Breeder / syn					
Panachée Semi-Double	G	Pre 1830		pb	dbl	m		
Panachée Simple	Sp		Hardy	lp				
Panachée Superbe	G	1823	Hardy	dp	f	s		
		syn	Beauté Insurmontable					
Panachée Superbe	G	Pre 1811		dr	f			m
Panaget	M	Pre 1844	syn Lancezeur (?)	rb	dbl	m		
Pandore	HCh	1846	Vibert	dr	f	m	vvig	
Paniculata Rubra	N			mr				
Paniculé	Ch		Boursault	dr				
Paniculé	Alp			dr				
Paniculé	C			w				
Paniculé	Bslt	c 1810	Vimorin syn Reversa	m	s-d	m		
Paola	Ch		Laffay	lp	f	m		
Papa Gontier	T	1883	Nabonnand G	pb	s-d	l	vig	f
Papa Gontier, Climbing	Cl T	1898	Hosp	pb	dbl			
Papa Gontier à Fleurs Blanches	T	see	Fiametta Nabonnand					
Papa Lambert	HT	1899	Lambert P	mp	dbl	l		vf
Papverina Major	S	Pre 1799		dp	dbl	m		
		syn	Grosse Mohnkopfs Rose					
Papillon	Ch	c 1826	Dubourg	mr				
Papillon	T	1881	Nabonnand	op	s-d	m	vvig	sf
Pâquerette	Pol	1875	Guillot et Fils	w	vdbl	s	m	sf
Paquita	G	Pre 1841		m	f	m-l		
Paragon	Misc	Pre 1846						
Parfait	B			rb	f	m	vig	
Parfaite	N			lp				
Parfaite Agathe	G	Pre 1830	Prévost syn Didon	lp	f	m		
Parfum d'Ispahan	D	Pre 1832	syn Ispahan	mp	dbl			vf
Parigot	HCh	Pre 1846		mr				
Paris	T	Pre 1846		mp	f	l		
Parisian	Misc	Pre 1846						
Parisienne	G		Hardy	mr				
Parisienne	D			lp				
Parks' Yellow Tea-Scented China	T	1824	Parks	my	dbl			f
Parmentier	M	1847	Robert / Vibert	mp	dbl	l		
Parmentier	M	1860	Guillot et Fils	dp	f	m	vig	
Parnassina de Pronville	HFt		Noisette L	dp	f			
Parnassine	HRg	1825	Noisette E	m	dbl			
Parny	HCh	1826	Laffay	rb	f	m-l		
			syn Belle de Parny					
Parquin	B	Pre 1846		m	f	m		
Parsons' Pink China	Ch	Pre 1751	Parsons syn Old Blush	mp	s-d	m	vig	sf
Partout	M		syn Zoé	mp				
Parure de Flore	Ch			lp	f	m		
Parure des Vierges	D	Pre 1810	Prévost	w	dbl	m		
Parviflora	Pom			lp	f	s		
Parviflora	G	Pre 1650	syn Burgundian Rose	pb	dbl	s		
Parviflora	HSpn	1823	Vibert	lp	dbl	l		
Parvifolia	G/C	Pre 1650	syn Burgundian Rose	pb	dbl	s		
Parvula Nobis	HMult	1866	Cochet Sc.	m	f	s		
Pascal	B	1861	Robert & Moreau	mp				
Passé-Princesse	G	Pre 1813	Prévost	mp	f	vl		
			syn Grandesse Royal					
Passé-Velours	G	Pre 1820	Descemet	m	dbl	m		
Pasture Rose	Sp	1826	syn r.carolina	mp				
Patrick	HP	1854	Lartay	dr	f	l	vig	
Paul Bestion	B	1879	Nabonnand	mr	f	vl	vig	
Paul de Fabry	HP	1879	Liabaud	mr	vdbl	vl	vvig	
Paul de Fontainne	M	1873	Fontaine	m	dbl	l	vig	
		syn	Deuil de Paul Fontaine					
Paul de la Meilleraye	HP	1863	Guillot	mr	dbl	vl	vvig	
Paul Desgrand	HP	1862	Liabaud	m	f	m	vig	
Paul Dupuy	HP	1852	Dupuy-Jamain	mr	f	l	vig	
Paul Emile	HP	1860	Robert & Moreau	mp				
Paul et Virginie	B	1847	Oger	m	f	l		
Paul Féval	HP	1861	Guillot Fils	mp	f	l	m	
Paul Floret	T	1881	Nabonnand	m		l	m	
Paul Fontaine	HP	1851	Fontaine	m	f	m	vig	
Paul Foucher	G		Parmentier	pb	f	m		
Paul Hermann	D	1858	Robert & Moreau	mp				
Paul Jamain	HP	1861	Lacharme F	dr	f	l	vig	m
			syn Charles Lefèbvre					
Paul Jamain	HP	1878	Jamain	dr	f	l	vig	
Paul Joseph	B	1842	Lebougre	dr	f	m	m	
Paul Krüger	Cl T	1889	Keynes, Williams &Co	w		l	vig	vf
		syn	Niphetos, Climbing					
Paul Marmy	T	see	Madame Paul Marmy					
Paul Marot	HT	1892	Bonnaire	mp	f	l		
Paul Nabonnand	T	1877	Nabonnand G	mp	dbl	l	vig	f
Paul Neyron	HP	1869	Levet A	dp	f	vl	vig	f
Paul Neyron Panachée	HP	1896	Duprat	pb	dbl	vl		

Name	Type	Date	Raiser					
		syn	Coquette Bordelaise					
Paul Perras	B	Pre 1846		lp		l		
Paul Perras	B	1870	Levet	lp	vdbl	l	vig	
Paul Ricault	C	1845	Portemer Fils	mp	dbl	l		vf
Paul Richard	HP	1845	Portemer	mr	f	m	vig	
Paul Verdier	HP	1866	Verdier C	dp	dbl	l	vig	m
Paul Véronèse	M	1859	Robert & Moreau	mp	s-d	m		
Paulin Talabot	HP	1873	Verdier E	dp	f	l	m	
Paulina	G	Pre 1830	Mme Hébert	mp	f	m		
Pauline	C			lp				
Pauline	A	Pre 1830	Hardy	lp	f	s-m		
		syn	Col de Berry					
Pauline	Ch	1830	Vibert	w		s		
Pauline Bonaparte	B	1832	Laffay M	lp	vdbl	l	vig	f
		syn	Mistress Bosanquet					
Pauline Bonaparte	HP	1850		w	f	m		
Pauline Borghese	Ch		Laffay	lp	f	m		f
Pauline Brade	HP			mr	s-d	m		
Pauline Chateau	HP		Pradel	lp				
Pauline de la Gragne (ue)	Ch			w	f	m		
Pauline de Mondeville	HP			lp	f	m	vvig	
Pauline Dubreuil	P	1828	Dubreuil	lp	s-d	m		
Pauline Garcia	C	1844	Vibert	w	vf	l	vig	
Pauline Garcia	B	1851	Foulard	lp	f	l		
Pauline Girardin	B	1850	Vivian-Faivre	mr	f	m	vig	
Pauline Henri (y)	N	Pre 1846		lp	f	m		
Pauline Labonté	T	1852	Pradel	lp	f	l	vig	
Pauline Lancezeur	HP	1854	Lancezeur	dr	dbl	l	vvig	
Pauline Lansezeur	HP	1854	Lancezeur syn above	dr	dbl	m	vvig	
Pauline Leclerc	B			mr	f	m		
Pauline Levasseur (Levanneur)	HP			lp	f	m		
Pauline Nias	C			w	f	m		
Pauline Plantier	T	1841	Plantier	w	f	m	m	
Pauliska	HP	1856	Avoux et Crozy	lp	f	l	vig	m
Paul's Carmine Pillar	HMult	1895	Paul G	mr	s	l	vig	sf
Paul's Early Blush	HP	1893	Paul G	lp	dbl	l	vig	vf
Paul's Himalayan Musk Rambler	M	1899	Paul	lp	dbl	s		vf
Paul's Himalayica Alba Magna	Sp	1899	Paul	w	s-d			
Paul's Himalayica Double Pink	Sp	1899	Paul	lp	s-d			
Paul's Perpetual White	N	1883	Paul	w	s	m	vig	
		syn	Paul's Single White					
Paul's Single Crimson	HP	1883	Paul G	dr	s	l	vig	
Paul's Single White	HP	1883	Paul G	w	s	m	vig	
Paul's Single White Perpetual	HP	1883	Paul syn as above	w	s	m	vig	
Pavillon de Prégny	N	1863	Guillot Père	m	f	m	vig	m
Pavot	D		Prévost	dr	s-d	l		
Pavot	C		Miellez	mp	dbl	l		
Pavot	G		Labaye Père	lp				
Pavot	S	Pre 1799		dp	dbl	m		
		syn	Grosse Mohnkopfs Rose					
Pavot	C	Pre 1830	De Pronville	mr	f	l		
		syn	Le Triomphe					
Pavot	G	Pre 1830		mr	dbl	l		
Pavot Royal	G			lp	f	m		
Paxton	B	1851	Laffay M	dr	f	m	vvig	m
		syn	Sir Joseph Paxton					
Paysanne	C		syn Ordinaire	mp		l		
Paysanne en Toilette	G		Miellez	mr				
Pea-Fruited Rose	Sp	1877	syn r.pisocarpa	mp	s		wk	
Peach Blossom	HP	1874	Paul W	lp	f	l	vig	
		syn	Egeria (?)					
Peach Blossom	T	1890	Dingee & Conard	op				
Peach-Leaved Rose	Sp	1820		dp	s			
		syn	r.chinensis longifolia					
Pearl	HT	1879	Bennett	lp	vdbl	m	wk	m
Pearl Rivers	T	1890	Dingee & Conard	w				vf
Peddy	G	Pre 1830		dr	f	m		
Pedro Costa	HT	1889	Da Costa	yb				
Pélisson	M	1848	Vibert	dp	f	m		f
Pelletier	G	c 1825	Pelletier	lp	f	m		
Pelletier's Flesh Coloured	Pom			lp	vf	l		f
Pellonia	T	Pre 1846	Touvais	w	vf	l		vf
Pénélope	G	1818	Vibert	mr				
Pénélope	D	1818	Vibert	dp	vdbl	l		
Pénélope	Ch	Pre 1834		mr		m		
Pénélope	B	1851	Robert	mp	f	m		
Pénélope Mayo	HP	1864	Verdier C	dp	f	l	m	m
		syn	Duchesse de Caylus					
Pénélope Mayo	HP	1878	Davis	mr	f	l	vig	f
		syn	Marie Baumann					

Pennsylvania Dwarf	D	Pre 1846		lp				
Pensylvanie à Fleur Double	Misc	Pre 1830	Prévost	mp	f	s		
Pensylvanie à Fleur Simple	Misc	Pre 1830	Prévost	mp	s	m		
Pensylvanie à Grandes Fleurs Pâles	Misc	Pre 1830	Prévost	lp				
Pentland	HSpn	Pre 1846						
Peonia	HP	Pre 1870		mr	f	l		
Peonie	HP	Pre 1860		dp				
Pepin	Ch	Pre 1870		mr	f	m		
Pepin le Bref	T			mp	f	m		
Pépita	G	c 1850	Moreau	pb				
Perfect Ranunculus	Misc	Pre 1846						
Perfection	T	Pre 1846		mp				
Perfection	HP	1851	Miellez	mr				
Perfection	HP	1854	Lartay	dp	f	vl	vvig	
Perfection	B	1858	Laurentius	lp		l	vig	f
Perfection	HP	1866	Touvais	mp	f	l	vig	
Perfection de Lyon	HP	1868	Ducher	pb	f	vl	vvig	
Perfection de Montplaisir	T	1871	Levet	my	f	m	m	f
Perfection des Blanches	N	1873	Schwartz J	w	dbl	m	vig	
Perfection Orange	HWich	1899	Horvath	pb	dbl	s		m
	syn	South	Orange Perfection					
Pergolèse	P	1860	Robert & Moreau	m	vdbl	m		m
Périclès	D	Pre 1826	Vibert	dp	dbl	m		
Périclès	G/HCh	Pre 1830	Laffay	lp	f	m		
Perle Blanche	HP	1870	Touvais	w	f	l	vig	
Perle d'Angers	B	1879	Moreau-Robert	lp	vf	l	vvig	
Perle de Brabant	G			lp	f	l		
Perle de Feu	T	1893	Dubreuil	yb	dbl	m	vig	
Perle de France	A	1824	Dematra	w	f	m		
Perle de France	G	Pre 1830						
Perle de l'Orient	G	Pre 1811	Schwarzkopf	rb	s-d	m		
Perle de l'Orient	G	1817	Godefroy	dr	f	m		
Perle de l'Orient	HEg	Pre 1830	Vibert	mp	vdbl	s		
	syn		Bouquet Charmant	(Descemet)				
Perle de Lyon	T	1872	Ducher	dy	dbl	l	m	f
Perle des Blanches	N	1872	Lacharme F	w	f	m	vig	f
Perle des Jardins	T	1874	Levet F	ly	dbl	l	vig	vf
Perle des Jardins, Climbing	Cl T	1890	Henderson	ly	vf	vl	vvig	vf
Perle des Panachées	G	1845	Vibert	pb	vdbl	l	m	m
			syn La Rubanée					
Perle des Panachées	G/D	Pre 1846		w	f	m		
Perle des Rouges	Pol	1896	Dubreuil	dr	dbl	l	m	sf
Perle d'Or	Pol	1875	Rambaux; Dubreuil	yb	vdbl	m	vig	vf
Perle von Weissenstein	G	1773	Schwarzkopf	m	dbl	m		
Perle von Zerbst	B	1872	Elie	lp				
Perles d'Orient	HEg		Vibert	lp	s-d	s		
Perlet	M		Robert	w				
Pérou de Gossard	G	Pre 1826	Gossard/Parmentier	dr	f	m		
			syn Le Pérou					
Perpetual Michigan	HSet	1843	Feast	m	f	l		
Perpetual Scotch	HSpn	1819		lp	dbl	m-l		m
Perpetual White Moss	M	1835	Laffay M	w	dbl	m	vig	
	syn	Quatre	Saisons Blanc Mousseux					
Perpetuel	B	syn	À Fleurs Multiples					
Perpétuelle	HP	1827	Vibert	mp	s-d	m		
Perpétuelle	B	Pre 1830	Laffay	mp	dbl	m		
Perpétuelle	Pom			lp	f	l		
Perpétuelle	HEg			lp				
Perpétuelle à Fleurs Roses	P	syn	Bifera à Fleurs Roses	lp	dbl	m		
Perpétuelle à Fleurs Rouges	P	1828	Dubreuil / Vibert	mr	dbl	m-l		
			syn À Fleurs Rouges					
Perpétuelle Blanche	HP		syn Bifère Blanche	w				
Perpétuelle d'Angers	HP	Pre 1834		lp		m		
Perpétuelle d'Anjou	D	Pre 1845		lp				
Perpétuelle de Miellez	HP			lp				
Perpétuelle de Neuilly	B			mr	f	l		
Perpétuelle de Neuilly	HP	1834	Verdier V	mp	f	l		vf
Perpétuelle de Saint Barthélemy	HP	Pre 1834		lp		m		
Perpétuelle de St Ouen	HMsk	Pre 1828	syn De Tout Mois	w				
Perpétuelle de Vibert	HP	1827	Vibert					
Perpétuelle Indigo	HP		syn Indigo	dr				
Perpétuelle Mauget	M	1844	Mauget	mp	f	m	vig	
Perpétuelle Mousseuse	M		Pirolle	w	vf		vig	
Perpétuelle Mousseuse	M	1835	Laffay M	w	dbl	m	m	f
	syn		Rosier de Thionville					
Perpétuelle Pinck	Cl			lp				
Perpétuelle Poultier	HP			mp				
Perpétuelle Sapho	P	1847	Vibert syn Sapho	w	f	s		
Perpétuelle Semi-Double	P	Pre 1830	Vibert	lp	dbl	m		
			syn Du Calendrier					

Name	Class	Date	Raiser / syn					
Perruque	Misc	Pre 1846						
Persian Musk Rose	N	1879	Paul syn Nastarana	w	s-d	m	vvig	f
Persian Yellow	Sp	1837	Willock	my	s	m	vvig	
		syn	r. foetida persiana					
Persicifolia	A	Pre 1817	Pelletier	w	f	m	vig	
		syn	À Feuilles de Pêcher					
Pescherah	HMult	1890	Geschwind	dr				
Pétales Rayées	C			mr				
Peter Lawson	HP	1862	Thomas	dr	f	l	vig	
Petit César	C	1825		mp	dbl	m		
Petit Constant	Pol	1899	Soupert & Notting	mr	dbl	s	vig	vf
Petit Dragon	G		Miellez	mr				
Petit Hermite	Ch		Laffay	dr	vf	s		
Petit Jean	G		Miellez	mr				
Petit Louis	HP	1849		mp				
Petit Maître	G	Pre 1830	Prévost	mp	vdbl	s		
Petit Panaché	Misc	Pre 1846				s		
Petit Saint François	C	c 1850	Robert	dp	dbl	s		
		syn	Pompon de St-Françoi	s				
Petit Triomphe	Ch		Laffay	mr	f	s		
Petit Vermilion	G	c 1823		mr				
Petite	N			lp				
Petite Agathe	D	Pre 1820	Pelletier	mp	f	s		
			syn Sommesson					
Petite Aimée	G	Pre 1814	Descemet					
Petite Aïne	N	Pre 1834		mp		s		
Petite Amante	B	1866	Soupert & Notting	mp	f	m		f
Petite Anglaise	A	1802	Dumont de Courset	w	dbl	m		m
			syn Maiden's Blush					
Petite Auguste	HCh		Hardy	mr	dbl	s		
Petite Beauté	C			lp	f	m		
Petite Blush	Misc	Pre 1846		lp		s		
Petite Chalons	G	Pre 1650	syn Burgundian Rose	pb	f	vs		
Petite Cuisse de Nymphe	A	Pre 1830	Prévost	lp	vdbl	m	vvig	
			syn Alba Rubigens					
Petite de Hollande	C	Pre 1791		lp	dbl	s	m	m
Petite Duchesse	HCan	Pre 1830	Prévost	lp	f	vs		
			syn Petite Mignonne					
Petite Ecossaise	HSpn	Pre 1826	Vibert	lp	s-d	s	m	
Petite Ernestre	D		Descemet	lp				
Petite Ernestre	C	Pre 1820	Vibert	lp	f	s		
		syn Peti-	te Junon de Hollande					
Petite Étoilée	N		Laffay	lp	f	vs		
Petite Évéque	G	Pre 1815	Descemet					
Petite Herva	T			lp	f	m		Vf
Petite Hessoise	HEg	c 1810	Redouté / Lahaye	mp	s-d	s		
Petite Hollande	C	Pre 1791	Vibert	lp	dbl	s	m	m
		syn	Petite de Hollande					
Petite Indienne	T	1825	Laffay					
Petite Junon de Hollande	C	Pre 1820		lp	f	s		
Petite Lapone	Min							
Petite Léonie	Pol	1893	Soupert & Notting	w	dbl	s	vig	
Petite Lisette	D	1817	Vibert	dp	f	s		sf
Petite Lisette	D	Pre 1830	Vibert	lp	vdbl	m		
Petite Louise	G	Pre 1819	Prévost	lp	f	s		
			syn Belle Mignonne					
Petite Magnificence	D		Miellez	lp				
Petite Marie	HP	1847	Vibert	mp	f	m		
Petite Mignonne	Can	Pre 1830	Vibert	lp	f	vs		
Petite Négresse	HP		syn Négresse	r				
Petite Ninette	HP			lp				
Petite Nini Lourdeau	Ch	Pre 1870		pb	f	l	vig	
Petite Orléanaise	G	Pre 1843		mp	dbl	s	vig	
Petite Pierre	HCh	Pre 1846		lp				
Petite Provins	G	Pre 1806	Crantz(?)	m	s	l		m
			syn Rosier d'Amour					
Petite Red Scotch	HSpn	Pre 1822	Brown	rb	s-d	s		
		syn	Double Dark Marbled					
Petite Renoncule Violette	G	1823	Vibert syn Félicie	m	vf	s		m
Petite Rose de Mai	Pom			mp		s		
Petite Sophie	D	1820	Vibert	lp	f	s-m		
Petite Villageoise	G		Miellez	mr				
Petite Violette	G	Pre 1815	Descemet	m		s		
Pétrarque	G	1844	Vibert	dr	f	m		
Pétrarque	M	1859	Robert & Moreau	lp				
Pétronille	G	Pre 1811	Vibert	lp	vf	l		
		syn Be-	auté Superbe Agathée					
Phaedra	HT	1895	Geschwind	pb	dbl	l		
Phaéton	N		Miellez	lp	f	m	wk	
Phaéton	Ch	Pre 1834		dp		s		
Phaloé	G	Pre 1804	Calvert	lp	vf	m-l		
			syn Triomphe Royal					

Name	Type	Year	Breeder / syn					
Phaloé	N	1846	Vibert	yb	f	l	vig	
Phanaricus	G							
Pharaon	T	Pre 1846		mp		l		f
Pharaon	B	Pre 1889	Bernède	mr	f	l		
Pharericus	G	c 1829	Calvert	dp	f	m-l		
			syn Fleur d'Amour					
Phèdre	G	Pre 1830	Coquerel / Miellez	rb	f	m		
Phénice	B			dr	f	l		vf
Phénice	G	1843	Vibert	dp	dbl	m		
Phénix	G	1823	Hardy	dp	f	s		
Philadelphia	T	Pre 1846		lp				f
Philadelphica	Bks	Pre 1846		w	s			
Phileas	G	1827	Noisette L	dr	dbl	l		
Philémon	Ch	1821	Cochet P / Vibert	mp	f	m		
Philémon	N	1825	Vibert	mr		s		
Philémon	N	c 1835	Laffay	m	f	s		
Philémon Cochet	B	1895	Cochet S	dp	vf	vl	vvig	f
Philiba	G	1826	Vétillard	m				
Philibert Delorme	HCh			ob	f	l		
Philiberte Pellet	HP	1873	Gonod	dr	f	l	vig	
Philippe Bardet	HP	1874	Moreau-Robert	mr	f	vl	vig	
Philippe I	C		Duval	m	f	vl	vig	
Philippe I	Ch			mr				
Philippe I	T	Pre 1834		mp		m		
Philippe I	HP	Pre 1834		dr	f	m		
Philippe I	D	Pre 1846		mr				
Philippine	Ch		Laffay	dr	dbl	m		
Phillipart	B	Pre 1846		lp				
Philodamie	HP	1849	Vibert	lp	f	l		
Philomèle	G	Pre 1830	Hardy (Descemet)	dr	f	m		
Philomèle	N	1844	Vibert	lp	vdbl	s		
Philomene	C		Hardy	m				
Philomène Crozy	HP	1857	Avoux	m				
Phoebe's Frilled Pink	HRg	1891	Morlet syn Fimbriata	lp	dbl	m		vf
Phoebus	G	1818		mp				
Phoebus	HP	1837		mp	dbl	l		f
Phoebus	D	Pre 1848		m	f	l		
Phoenix	G	1843	Vibert	dp	dbl	s		
Phoenix	B	Pre 1846		dp				f
Picayune	Ch	Pre 1843		lp	dbl	s		
Picciola	M		syn Pompon Scarlet	mp	f	m		
Picotte	Pol	1890	Geschwind					
Pie IX	HP	1849	Vibert syn Pius IX	mp	vdbl	l	vig	vf
Pierian	G	Pre 1846		mr				
Pierre Ayrault	C		Vibert	mr	f	l		
Pierre Caro	HP	1879	Levet	dr	dbl	m	vig	vf
Pierre Corneille	G	Pre 1830	Tributien	mr	f	l		
Pierre de St Cyr	B	1838	Plantier	lp	vdbl	l	vig	
Pierre Dupont	HP	1861	Clément	dr	f	m		
Pierre Durand	HP	1881	Pernet Père	mp	dbl	l	vig	
Pierre Fitte	T			w	f	m	vig	
Pierre Guillot	HT	1879	Guillot Fils	rb	dbl	l	m	vf
Pierre Izambart (Jyambart)	HP	1871	Gautreau	mr	f	m	m	
Pierre Janssens	G	Pre 1860		mp	vf	m		
Pierre Le Grand	G	Pre 1830		rb	f	m		
Pierre l'Hermite	G		Parmentier	dr	f	m		
Pierre Liabaud	HP	1887	Liabaud	dr	f	l	vig	
Pierre Notting	HP	1863	Portemer Fils	dr	vf	l	vig	m
Pierre Seletzky	HP	1872	Levet	dr	f	l	vig	f
Pierre Simon	G		Parmentier	lp	f	m		
Pierre Sterkman	G			mr	f	l		
Pierre Storkmans	G			mr	f	l		
Pierret Rose	G	1819	Vibert	lp		m		
Pigeonnable	G		Miellez	dr				
Pigeron	B	1850	Berger	mr	f	l		
Pigeron	HP	Pre 1870		dp	f	l		
Pilar Domedel	T	1893	Pries	mp				
Pillar of Gold	Cl T	1895	Bernaix A	pb	dbl	l	vig	vf
		syn	E Veyrat Hermanos					
Pilosa	Pom			mp		s	wk	
Pimpernel Rose	Sp	Pre 1600	syn r.spinosissima	w	s			
Pimpinellifolia	Alp			mp				
Pimprenelle Blanche, Double	HSpn	Pre 1830		w	vdbl	m		
Pimprenelle Blanche, Globuleuse	HSpn	1822	Prévost	w	vdbl	m		
Pimprenelle Blanche, Pleine	HSpn	1827	Vibert	w	f	m		
Pimprenelle Blanche, Simple	HSpn	Pre 1830		w	s			
Pimprenelle Camillia	HSpn	Pre 1830	Vibert	w	dbl	m-l		
Pimprenelle Carnée, Double	HSpn	Pre 1830		lp	dbl	m		
Pimprenelle Grevery	E	Pre 1830	Grevery	mp	dbl	s		f
Pimprenelle Jaune, Pale	HSpn	Pre 1830	Vibert	ly	s-d	m		
Pimprenelle Jaune, Multiple	HSpn	Pre 1830	Vibert / Godefroy	ly	f	m		

Name	Type	Date	Raiser / Synonym	Colour	Form	Size	Vigour	Fragr.
Pimprenelle Jaune, Simple	HSpn	1823	Vibert	ly	s	l	vig	
Pinprenelle Nankin	HSpn	Pre 1830	Vibert	yb	s			
Pimprenelle Nankin, Double	HSpn	Pre 1830	Vibert	y	dbl	m		
Pimprenelle Pourpre Foncé	HSpn	Pre 1830	Vibert	mr	s	m		
Pimprenelle Pourpre Marbré, Simple	HSpn	Pre 1830		rb	s	m		
Pimprenelle Rose, Multiple	HSpn	1827	Prévost	lp	dbl	m		
		see also	Pimpernel Rose above					
Pimprenelle Violette, Double	HSpn	Pre 1830		mp	dbl	m		f
Pindare	G			m	f	m		
Pine-Scented Rose	Sp	1821	syn r.glutinosa	w		s		m
Pink Agatha	G	Pre 1811	syn Agathe Incarnata	lp	vdbl	m		vf
Pink Bourbon	B	1888	Schwartz Vve	mp	s-d	vl		
		syn	Mme Ernest Calvat					
Pink Cherokee	S	1896	Geschwind/Schmidt	lp	s	l	vig	m
			syn Anemome					
Pink Garland	HMult	Pre 1846		mp				
Pink Gloire de Dijon	T	Pre 1888		dp	dbl	vl	vvig	m
Pink Léda	D	Pre 1827		mp	dbl	m		vf
Pink Perle des Jardins	T	1891	Nantz	mp				
Pink Rambler	HMult	1895	Schmitt	mp	s-d	s	vig	m
			syn Euphrosyne					
Pink Roamer	HWich	1897	Horvath	pb	s	s	vig	m
Pink Rover	Cl HT	1891	Paul W	lp			vig	m
Pink Soupert	Pol	1896	Dingee & Conard	mp	f	m	vig	
Pinnatifide	S	Pre 1828		mp				
Pintade	G	Pre 1817	Loiseleur-Deslongcha-	mps mp				
Pio Nono	HP			mr				
Pirolle	HCh	1826	Laffay	m				
Pissardii	N	1879	Paul syn Nastarana	w	s-d	m	vvig	
Pitord	HP	1867	Lacharme	rb	f	l	vig	
Pius IX	HP	1848	Vibert	mp	vdbl	l	vig	vf
Pivoine	G	Pre 1790	syn Lustre d'Église	mp	dbl	s		vf
Pivoine	G	Pre 1834	Hardy syn Bourbon	pb		vl	vvig	
Pivoine de Lille	G	Pre 1818	Lille	m		l		
			syn Nouvelle Pivoine					
Pivoine des Hollandais	G	Pre 1813	syn Great Royal	lp	dbl	l		
Pivoine du Roi	G		Descemet	mr	f	l		
Pivoine Rose	HP	1848	Verdier	mp	f	l		
Placidie	A	1820	Prévost / Vibert	mp	dbl	s		
Placidie	G		Robert	mr	f	l		
Placidie	P		Vibert	mp				
Plantier	N		Vibert	w				
Plantier	Ch		Robert	dp	f	m	vvig	
Plato	HSpn	c 1850	Vibert	mr	dbl			
Platyphylla	HMult	1815	Thory	mp	vdbl	s	vig	m
			syn Seven Sisters					
Pleine à Corymbes	Misc		Laffay	lp				
Pleine Lune	G	Pre 1830	Prévost	rb	f	m-l		
			syn Cordon Bleu					
Plena	A	Pre 1770		w	s-d			
Plena	HSem	Pre 1830	Laffay M	lp	dbl			
Plena	HBc	Pre 1835	syn Double White	w				
Pletink	HCh			mp	f	m		
Plicate	Misc	Pre 1846						
Pline	HP	1865	Guillot Fils	rb	f	vl	vvig	
Plotine	G			mr	f	m		
Plotine	HCh	Pre 1830	Prévost	lp	vf	s		
		syn	Elégant à Fleurs Plein	-es				
Pluto	C	Pre 1799		dr				
Pluto	B	Pre 1846		dr				
Pluton	Ch	Pre 1834		mr	f	s		
Pluton	G		Miss Lawrence					
Pluton	C	1824	Toutain	mr				
Pluton	G	1843	Vibert	m	f	m		
Poilpré	G	Pre 1830		lp				
Pointed Damask	D		see Painted Damask					
Poiteau	HP	1855	Robert	dp	f	l		
Poiteau	G		Noisette	mp				
Polivities	Misc	Pre 1846						
Polliniana	Misc	1820		w		l		
Polonie Bourdin	N	Pre 1860		mp	f	m		
Polyantha	Sp	1784	syn rosa multiflora	w	f	s	vig	
Polyantha Double	HMult	1888	syn rosa multiflora	w	f	s	vig	
Polyantha Grandiflora	HMult	1886	Bernaix	w	s	m	vig	f
Polyantha Simplex	Sp	1784	syn rosa multiflora	w	f	s	vig	
Polyantha Single	HMult	1888	syn rosa multiflora	w	s			
Polybe	HP	1847	Laffay	lp	f	m		
Polynice	G	Pre 1830	Racine					
Pomifera	A	Pre 1846		p	s	m	vig	
Pomme de Grenade	A	Pre 1830	Godefroy	mp	dbl	m	vig	
		syn	Herissée Presque Inerm	e				

Name	Class	Date	Breeder / Synonym					
Pomme de Grenade	Pom		Vilmorin					
Pommée	C			mp				
Pommifère	Misc			w				
Pommifère à Fleur Double	Pom	Pre 1770	syn Duplex	mp	s-d	m		sf
Pomone	G		Miellez	mp				
Pompéïa	N	Pre 1834		mp		s		
Pompon	C	1755		mr	vdbl	s		
Pompon	C			dp	f	vs		
Pompon (or Mousseux de Meaux)	M	1814		rb	f	s		
Pompon	Ch	Pre 1830	Prévost	lp	dbl	s	wk	
Pompon	G	1835	Joly	dr				
Pompon	HP	1847	Vibert	mp				
Pompon	G	1857	Robert & Moreau syn Pompon Panachée	w	dbl	l	m	
Pompon à Fleur, Double	C	Pre 1830	Godefroy	lp	dbl	vs		
Pompon à Fleur, Semi-Double	C	Pre 1830	Vibert	lp	s-d	vs		
Pompon Agathe	Ch	1827	Mauget					
Pompon Ancien	Min		syn Pompon Bijou	lp				
Pompon Bazard	A	Pre 1830	Bazard	lp	f	s-m		
Pompon Bicolor	HCh			pb	f	m	vig	
Pompon Bijou	Min	Pre 1834	syn Pompon Ancien	lp		vs		
Pompon Blanc	C	Pre 1811	Mauget	w	vdbl	s		m
Pompon Blanc	HSpn	Pre 1817	Descemet	w	f	vl		
Pompon Blanc à Coeur Vert	A	Pre 1830		w	f	s		
Pompon Blanc des Hollandais	A	Pre 1830	(same as above)	w	f	s		
Pompon Blanc Parfait	A	1876	Verdier E	lp	dbl	s		vf
Pompon Brun	C	Pre 1830	Pelletier	mp	dbl	vs		
Pompon Brun	HFt			dr	f	s		
Pompon Carmin	B	Pre 1846	Lacharme	mr	f	s		
Pompon Carné	Min			lp				
Pompon Carné	Ch		Laffay	lp				
Pompon Carné	A	Pre 1830	Pelletier syn Pauline	lp	f	s-m		
Pompon Commun	C	Pre 1814	syn Rose de Meaux	dp	vdbl	s		m
Pompon Cramoisi	B			mp				
Pompon Crimson	M		Foulard	dr	f	s		
Pompon d'Angers	M	1846	Vibert	dr	vdbl	s		
Pompon d'Automne	Ch	Pre 1830	Vibert	lp	f	s		
Pompon de Bourbon	B		Laffay	lp				
Pompon de Bourgogne	G	Pre 1629	syn Burgundian Rose	pb	dbl	s		
Pompon de Bourgogne	C	Pre 1846		mp	f	vs		
Pompon de Bourgne à Fleurs Blanches	G	1827	Mauget	w	vdbl	vs		
Pompon de Kingston	C	Pre 1817		lp	f	s		
Pompon de la Queue	C	Pre 1846		mp				
Pompon d'Elisa	G	Pre 1830	Lecomte	lp	f	vs		
Pompon de Kingston	C	Pre 1830		lp	dbl	vs		
Pompon de Meaux	C	Pre 1814	syn Rose de Meaux	dp	vdbl	s		m
Pompon de Panachée	G	1857	syn Pompon Panachée	w	dbl			
Pompon de Paris	Ch	1839		mp	dbl	vs		
Pompon de Paris, Climbing	Cl Ch	c 1839		mp	dbl	vs		sf
Pompon de Saint-François	C	c 1850	Robert	dp	dbl	s	m	
Pompon de Wasemmes	B		Rameau	lp				
Pompon des Dames	C	Pre 1791	Vibert syn Petite de Hollande	mp	dbl	s		m
Pompon des Princes	D	Pre 1832	syn Isaphan	mp	dbl			vf
Pompon des Quartre Saisons	P	Pre 1830	Vibert syn Quatre Saisons Pompon	lp	vdbl	vs	vig	f
Pompon du Roi	C	Pre 1830	syn Pompon Nain	dp	dbl	vs		
Pompon Feu	M	Pre 1846	Robert	mr	f	m		
Pompon Jaune	HFt	Pre 1806	syn Pompone Jaunes	my	vdbl	vs		
Pompon Lillois	Misc		Miellez	lp				
Pompon Marbré	M			mp	f	l		
Pompon Moss	M	c 1813	syn Mossy Rose de Meaux	lp	f	s		
Pompon Mousseux	M	c 1813	syn Mossy Rose de Meaux	lp	f	s		
Pompon Nain	C	Pre 1830		dp	dbl	vs		
Pompon Nymphe	Ch	1827	Mauget					
Pompon Panachée	G	1857	Robert & Moreau	w	dbl			
Pompon Parfait	Ch	1876		mp	vf	s		
Pompon Perpetual	P	1836	syn Bernard	op	f	m		
Pompon Perpétuel	M	1849	Vibert	lp	f	m		
Pompon Pourpre	T	1827	Mauget					
Pompon Pulchella	Pom			mp	f	s	vig	
Pompon Quartre Saisons	P							
Pompon Rennois	M			mr				
Pompon Robert	G	1857	Robert syn Pompon Panachée	w	dbl			
Pompon Rose	C	Pre 1814	syn Rose de Meaux	lp	vdbl	vs		m
Pompon Royal	C	Pre 1830		lp	s-d	m		
Pompon Saint François	G	Pre 1830	syn Petit Chalons	rb	f	vs		

Name	Class	Date	Originator / Synonym					
Pompon Scarlet	M			mp	f	m		
Pompon Schwerin	M		Foulard	mr	vf	s	vig	
Pompon Spong	C	1805	Spong syn Spong	mp	vdbl	s		sf
Pompon Varin	C	1822	Calvert	mp	s-d	s		
Pompone	N	Pre 1846						
Pompone	Min	Pre 1846		lp				
Pompone Bicolor	HCh	Pre 1846		mp				
Pompone Elegante	HCh	Pre 1846		lp				f
Pompone Jaune	HFt	Pre 1806		my	vdbl	vs		
Pompone Violet	Ch	Pre 1846		dp				
Pomponia Muscosa	M	c 1813		mp	f	s		
		syn	Mossy Rose de Meaux					
Pomponnette	HP	1860	Robert & Moreau	w				
Pomponnette	B	1879	Soupert & Notting	lp	f	m-l	vig	
Poncheau-Capiaumont	HCh	Pre 1834		dr	f	m		
Poncey	HCh			dr				
Ponctué	HP	Pre 1845	Laffay	pb	dbl	m		
Ponctuée	G	1819	Coquerel	m	s-d	m		
			syn Belle Herminie					
Ponctuée	N	1826		lp	s-d	s		
Ponctuée	Ch	1826	Hardy	lp				
Ponctuée	M	1829	Mme Hébert	pb				
Ponctuée	M	1846	Laffay	pb	vdbl	l		
Ponctuée	M	1847	Moreau-Robert	pb	s-d	m	m	
Ponctuée	M	1857	Guillot Père	pb	dbl	m	m	
			syn Ma Ponctuée					
Ponctuée Semi-Double	M	Pre 1846	Moreau-Robert	rb	s-d			
Poniatowski	HEg	1821	Cartier	lp	vdbl	m		
Poniatowski	HP	Pre 1834	Robert	lp	f	m	vig	
Pony	G	Pre 1828	Deschiens	dr				
Pope	D	Pre 1844	Laffay	dr	f	vl	vvig	
Pope Pius IX	HP	1848	Vibert syn Pius IX	mp	vdbl	l	vig	vf
Poppy Rose	S	Pre 1799		dp	dbl	m		
		syn	Grosse Mohnkopfs Rose					
Porcelain à Bordre Blanc	Misc	Pre 1846		w				
Porcelaine	G/C	Pre 1815	Descemet	lp	dbl	l		
			syn Belle de Cels etc					
Porcelaine Royale	G	Pre 1830	Vibert / Miellez	m	f	s-m		
			syn Valentine					
Porcia	G	Pre 1811	syn Rouge Formidable	mr	vdbl	m		
Portland	P	Pre 1846		dp		l		
Portland à Fleurs Rouges Doubles	P	Pre 1830	Vibert	mr	dbl	m		
Portland à Grandes Fleurs	P	Pre 1830	Prévost	dp	dbl	vl		
			syn À Grandes Fleurs					
Portland Blanc	P	1836	Vibert	w	f	m		
Portland Crimson Monthly	P	c 1770	syn Duchess of Portld	mr	s-d	l		
		syn	Duchess of Portland					
Portland from Glendora	P	1846	Vibert	m	dbl	m		m
		syn	Joasine Hanet					
Portland Pourpre	P	c 1830	Prévost	dp	s-d	m		
Portland Rose	P	c 1770		mr	s-d	l	vvig	
		syn	Duchess of Portland					
Portlandica Carnea (Portland Carnée)	P	Pre 1830		mp	f	l		
Portuense	HP	1890	Da Costa	m				
Potager du Dauphin	HRg	1899	Graveraux	mp				
Potard	T	Pre 1846		lp	vf	m	vig	vf
Poteriifolia	HSpn							
Poultier	HCh			mr	f	m		
Pourpre	P			m				
Pourpre	M	Pre 1777	syn Rubra	mr	dbl	m		
Pourpre	N	1823	Laffay	m				
Pourpre	Ch	1827	Vibert	m	s	s		
Pourpre	M		Laffay	mp				
Pourpre	D	Pre 1830		mp	f	m		
Pourpre	HMult	Pre 1830		mp	vdbl	s		
		syn	Multiflore Rose Foncé					
Pourpre	HSpn	1827	Vibert	mr	s-d	s		
Pourpre Ancien	HMcr	c 1829		m	vf	l		
Pourpre à Onglet Blanc	T		Laffay	w				
Pourpre Ardoisée	G	Pre 1790	syn Charles de Mills	dr	vdbl	m		sf
Pourpre Belle Violette	G			m	vdbl			
Pourpre Brillant	G	Pre 1815	Descemet	m				
Pourpre Brillant	Ch	Pre 1834		mr		s		
Pourpre Brun	HCh	Pre 1844		dr	f	vs		
Pourpre Cendré	HP			m	f	m		
Pourpre Charmant	G	Pre 1811		m	vdbl	m		m
Pourpre Charmant Strié	G		Hardy	m				
Pourpre Clair	Ch	Pre 1830	Vibert syn Sanguin	mr	vdbl	m	wk	
Pourpre Couronné	G	1824	Hardy	m				
Pourpre Cramoisi	G	Pre 1811		mr	vdbl	m		

Name	Class	Date	Breeder / Syn					
			syn Rouge Formidable					
Pourpre de Corinthe	G	Pre 1830		mr	f	m		
Pourpre de La Reine	G	Pre 1830	Coquerel	dr	vdbl	l	vig	
Pourpre de Lelieur	Ch		Laffay	m				
Pourpre de Tyr	G	Pre 1799	Calvert	mr	f	m		
			syn Gros Chalons & Bizarre					
Pourpre de Tyr	N	Pre 1846		mp	f	m		
Pourpre d'Orléans	HP	1861	Dauvesse	m	f	m		vf
Pourpre Double	G	Pre 1790	syn Lustre d'Église	mp	dbl	s		vf
Pourpre Double	Ch	Pre 1828	Laffay	dr	vdbl	m	wk	
			syn Sanguin					
Pourpre du Luxembourg	M	1848	Hardy	m	dbl	m		m
Pourpre d'Yèbles	Ch	1830	Desprez	m				
Pourpre Éclatant	Ch							
Pourpre Elegans	Misc	Pre 1846		dp				
Pourpre et Violette	G							
Pourpre Favorite	G	c 1830	Lahaye Père	lp	f	s-m		
			syn Belle de Stors					
Pourpre Foncé	G	Pre 1815	Descemet	m	f	s		
Pourpre Foncé	HSpn	1819	Vibert	dr	s	s		
Pourpre Foncé à Petites Fleurs	N	1827	Vibert	mr	s	m		
Pourpre Holocericea	Pom							
Pourpre Holocericea	M							
Pourpre Holocericea	HBc							
Pourpre Marbrée	G	Pre 1821	Vibert	m	vf	s-m		
			syn Bizarre Changeant					
Pourpre Marbrée Simple	HSpn		Prévost	m				
Pourpre Noir	Ch	Pre 1830		m				
Pourpre Noir	G	Pre 1811	syn Ombre Superbe	m	dbl	l	m	
Pourpre Noir	Ch	1820	Godefroy	dr	vdbl	s-m		
			syn Atropurpurea					
Pourpre Noir Simple	Min	1826	Hardy					
Pourpre Nouveau	G							
Pourpre Oeillet	G							
Pourpre Obscur	G	1821	Godefroy	m	f	s		
			syn Manteau Impérial					
Pourpre Panaché	HCh	1827	Vibert	m	f	m		
Pourpre Parfait	B	Pre 1846		m	vdbl			
Pourpre Pivoine	G							
Pourpre Ponceau	G			m	dbl	l		
Pourpre Rouge	G	1816	Prévost(?)	dr	s-d	l		
			syn Temple d'Apollon					
Pourpre Royal	G	Pre 1834		mr		s		
Pourpre Royale	HP	1846	Laffay	m	f	l	vig	
Pourpre Sans Aiguillons	G	1827		mp	f	m		
Pourpre Sans Épines (same as above)	G	1827		mp	f	m		
Pourpre Sans Pareil	G							
Pourpre Semi-Double	Ch	Pre 1830	Prévost	mr	dbl	s-m	c	
Pourpre Simple	Ch	1827	Vibert	mr	s	s-m		
Pourpre Strié Blanc	G	Pre 1834		m	f	m		
Pourpre Triomphant	G	Pre 1830	Vibert	mr	f	m		
Pourpre Velouté	C	1820	Toutain					
Pourpre Violet	Ch	1827	Mauget					
Pourpre Violet	M	Pre 1862		m	f	m		
Pourpre Violet Marbré	G			m	vf	m		
Pourpre Violette	HP			m	f	l	vig	
Pourpre Violette	HSpn	Pre 1830	Laffay					
Powellii	B	Pre 1846						
Praire	HP							
Prairie Belle	HSet	1843	Feast	pb	dbl	l	vig	m
			syn Queen of the Prairies					
Prairie de Terrenoire	HP	1861	Lacharme	m	f	l	vig	
Prairie Reine (Queen)	HSet	Pre 1870		lp		s		
Prairie Rose	Sp	1810	syn r.setigera	dp	s	m		
Précieuse	G	Pre 1804	Dupont (?)	lp	vdbl	m		
			syn Prolifière					
Précieuse	G/C	Pre 1813	Hardy	mp	vdbl	m	wk	
Précieuse	G		Miellez	mr				
Précieuse	D			lp	vf	l		
Preciosa	HT	1896	Vieweg	dr				
Précoce	M	1843	Vibert	dp	dbl	m		
Predestina	Misc	Pre 1846						
Predominant	Misc	Pre 1846		mr				
Préfet Limbourg	HP	1878	Margottin Fils	dr	dbl	l	vig	
			syn Monsieur le Préfet Limbourg					
Préfet Rivaud	HP	1893	Pernet Père	mr				
Prémices de Pontoise	B			lp				
Prémices des Charpennes	B	1845	Cherpin	m	f	m	vvig	
Premier Essai	S	1866	Geschwind	w	f	m	vig	
Premier Noble	Misc	Pre 1846		dr				
Président	T	1833	Adam syn Adam	mp	dbl	l		vf

Name	Type	Date	Raiser					
President	HSet	c 1846	Pierce	dp	vdbl	s		
Président	T	1860	Paul A	mp	vf	l	vig	
Président Besson	HP			mr				
Président Carnot	HP	1891	Degressy	mp	f	l	vvig	f
Président Constant	T	1886	Nabonnand	rb				
Président de la Rocheterie	B	1891	Vigneron	m	dbl	vl		
Président de Lestrade	T	1892	Puyravaud	rb				
Président de Sèze	G	1828	Mme Hébert	m	vdbl	l	vig	f
Président d'Olbecque	Ch	1834	Guérin	rb	dbl	m	m	
			syn Louis-Phillipe					
Président Dutailly	G	1888	Dubreuil	m	vdbl	l	vig	vf
			syn Charlemagne					
Président Gausen	B	1862	Pradel	mr	f	l		
Président Grévy	HP	1872	Verdier E	mr	f	m	vig	f
Président Hardy	HP	1873	Verdier E	mr	f	l	m	
Président Joachim Crespo	HP	1884	Lévêque	mp	f	l	vvig	
Président Lenaerts	HP	1882	Soupert & Notting	r	f	l	m	vf
Président Léon de Saint-Jean	HP	1875	Lacharme	mr	f	l	vig	
President Lincoln	HP	1862	Granger	dr	dbl	l		sf
Président Mas	HP	1865	Guillot Fils	dr	f	l	vig	
Président Marx	N			m				
Président Menoux	HP	1854	Guillot Père	lp	f	l	vig	
Président Molé	B	Pre 1846		mp				
Président Myard	HP	1891	Renaud G					
Président Pierce	M	1852	Laffay	mp	f	l		
Président Porcher	HP	1866	Vigneron	lp	f	vl		
Président Rodolphe Burghes	HP	1886	Bire	mr	f	m		
Président Schlachter	HP	1877	Verdier E	m	dbl	l		
Président Sénelar	HP	1883	Schwartz	dr	f	l	vvig	
Président Thiers	HP	1871	Lacharme	mr	f	vl	vig	
Président Willermoz	HP	1867	Ducher	mp	f	vl	vig	
Presque Blanc	Ch	Pre 1830	Prévost	w	dbl	m		
Presque Bleu	G	c 1815	Descemet	dr				
Presque Partout	M	Pre 1850		dp	dbl	m	vig	
Préval	P	c 1821	Prévost	lp	vdbl	l		m
Préval Rose	C		Prévost	lp	vdbl	l		
Prickly Rose	Sp	1805	syn r.acicularis	dp	s	s	vig	m
Pride of Lille	D	Pre 1826	Vibert	lp	f	m		
			syn Triomphe de Lille					
Pride of Reigate	HP	1884	Brown J	rb	dbl			
Pride of the Valley	HP	1898	Curtis	lp				m
			syn Mrs F W Sanford					
Pride of Waltham	HP	1881	Paul W	mp	vdbl	l	vig	f
Pride of Waltham, Climbing	HP	1885	Paul & Son	mp	vdbl	l	vig	f
Pride of Washington	HSet	Pre 1846	Pierce	m	vdbl	m		
Primerose Dame	T	1887	Bennett	ab	f			f
Prince A de Wagram	HP	1891	Cochet S	m	vf	l	vig	
Prince Albert	HP	1837	Laffay	rb	f	l	vvig	f
Prince Albert	B	Pre 1846		lp				
Prince Albert	HP	1850	De Fauw	pb	f	l		
		syn	Souvenir de la Reine	des Belges				
Prince Albert	B	1852	Laffay	mr				
		syn Le	Future Empereur des	Français				
Prince Albert	B	1852	Fontaine / Paul A	mr	f	m	vig	
Prince Albert	B		Brentley (Brenchley)	lp	f	m	wk	
Prince Antoine d'Arenberg	G	c 1830	Parmentier	dr	f	m		
Prince Arthur	HP	1875	Cant B R	mr	vf	m	vig	vf
Prince Bazile Dolgorouki	HP	1860	Marrest	mp			vig	vf
Prince Bonaparte	HP			mr	f	l		
Prince Camille de Rohan	HP	1861	Verdier E	dr	vf	m	vig	vf
Prince Charles	G			dr	f	m		
Prince Charles	B	1842	Hardy	dp	s-d	m	vig	vf
Prince Charles	Ch	Pre 1846		dr	f	m		
Prince Charles d'Arenberg	HP	1887	Soupert & Notting	mp	f	vl	vig	
Prince Chipetouzihoff	HP	1853	Guinoisseau	m	f	l	vvig	
Prince Cretwertinsky	N	1888	Nabonnand	ly	f	l	vig	
Prince d'Aldobrandini	M		Parmentier	mp	vf	m		
Prince d'Arenberg	G	Pre 1836	syn Duc d'Arenberg	m	f	l		
Prince d'Esterhazy	T	Pre 1846		mp				vf
Prince d'Orange	D							
Prince de Beïra	HP	1888	Verdier E	mr	f	l	vig	vf
Prince de Carignan	G		Miellez	mr				
Prince de Chimay	G		Parmentier	lp	f	m		
Prince de Chimay	B	1855	Robert	rb	f	l	vvig	vf
Prince de Croy	B			lp	f	l		
Prince de Galles	P	Pre 1826	Blinière	dr	f	m		
Prince de Galles	HP	Pre 1846		lp	f	m		
Prince de Joinville	B	Pre 1846		dp				
Prince de Joinville	B	1867	Paul W	mr	dbl	m		
Prince de la Moskowa	G			mr				
Prince de la Moskowa	HP	1853	Thomas	mr	f	m		
Prince de Ligne	G			mp	f	l		

Name	Type	Year	Breeder					
Prince de Naples	HP	1897	Gaetano	mp				
Prince de Nassau	G		Miellez	dp				
Prince de Porcia	HP	1865	Verdier E	dr	dbl	l	vig	
Prince de Salerne	T	1826	Jacques	dp	f			f
Prince de Salm	B	Pre 1846		mp				
Prince de Salm-Dyck	D	1852	Parmentier	mp	f	m		
Prince de Salm-Dyck	P	1852	Robert	dp				
Prince de Vaudemont	M	1854	Robert	lp	f	m		
		syn	P'cesse de Vaudemont					
Prince des Asturies	HP		Pradel	m		l		
Prince Engelbert	G		Parmentier	lp	f	l		
Prince Esterhazy	T			m	f	m		
Prince Eugène	Ch	1838	Hardy	dr	dbl	l		m
		syn Eug-	ène de Beauharnais					
Prince Eugène de Beauharnais	HP	1864	Robert-Moreau	dr	dbl	m	vig	
Prince Fréderick	G	1840	Parmentier	mr	vdbl	l		f
Prince Friedrich von Preussen	G			lp	f	l		
Prince Henri des Pays-Bas	HP	1862	Soupert	mp	f	m	vig	
Prince Henri d'Orléans	HP	1886	Verdier E	dp	dbl	l		
Prince Humbert	HP	1867	Margottin	m	f	l	vig	
Prince Hussein Kamil Pacha	T	1893	Soupert & Notting	mp				
	syn Im-	peratrice	Alexandra Foedorow-	na				
Prince Impérial	HP	1856	Pradel	lp		l	m	
Prince Impérial	HP	1856	Granger	mp	vf	l	vig	
Prince Jacob von Baden	HP			w	f	l		
Prince Léon Kotschoubey	HP	1852	Marrest	mr	vf	vl	vvig	
Prince Léopold	HP	Pre 1888	Paul W	dr	f	l	vig	
Prince Napoléon	B	1864	Pernet Père	pb	vf	vl	vig	m
Prince Noir	HP	1854	Boyau	m	f	m	m	vf
Prince of Wales	HP	1867	Laxton	mr	f	l	m	
Prince of Wales	HCh			lp	f	l	vig	
Prince Paul Demidoff	HP	1873	Guillot Fils	lp	f	l	vvig	
Prince Prosper d'Arenberg	T	1880	Soupert & Notting	op	f	m	vvig	
Prince Regent	G	Pre 1860						
Prince Stirbey	HP	1871	Schwartz J	dp	f	l	m	
Prince Theodore Bonney	HT	1898	Dingee & Conard					
Prince Théodore Galitzine	T	1899	Ketten Frères	or	vf	l		f
Prince Trigiano	HP	1878	Margottin					
Prince Waldemar	HP	1885	Verdier E	rb	f	l		
Prince Wasiltchikoff	T	1874	Nabonnand	lp				
		syn Duc	hess of Edinburgh					
Prince's Pearl Color	N	Pre 1846	Prince	lp			vvig	
Prince's Superb White	N	Pre 1846	Prince	w			vvig	
Prince's Coral	N	Pre 1846	Prince	lp				
Princess	HCh	Pre 1846		dp				
Princess	HSpn	Pre 1846		lp				
Princess Alice	M	1853	Paul A	mp	f	m	vig	f
Princess Beatrice	HP	1872	Paul W	mp	f	l	vig	
Princess Beatrice	T	1887	Bennett	yb	f	l		m
Princess Bonnie	T	1896	Dingee & Conard	dr	s-d	l		vf
Princess Christian	HP	1870	Paul W	mp	f	l	vig	
Princess Louise	HP	1869	Laxton / Paul	w		m	vig	
Princess Mary of Cambridge	HP	1867	Paul G	lp	f	l	vig	
Princess May	HT	1893	Paul W	lp	dbl	l	vig	m
Princess of Neapel	HP	1899	Bonfiglioni	mp				
Princess of Ratibon	T	1897		dr				
Princess of Wales	HP	1864	Paul W	mr	vdbl	l	vig	
Princess of Wales	HP	1871	Laxton	lp	f	l	vig	vf
Princess of Wales	T	1882	Bennett	yb	dbl	m	vig	
Princess Radziwill	T	1886	Nabonnand	mr				
Princesse	G	1824	Hardy	dp	f	m		
Princesse Adélaïde	M	1845	Laffay	lp	dbl	l	vig	f
Princesse Adélaïde	T	Pre 1846		ly	f	l		vf
Princesse Adélaïde d'Orléans	HSem	1826	Jacques	w	s-d	l	vig	
		syn	Adélaïde d'Orléans					
Princesse Alice	G			w	f	l		
Princesse Alice	HP	1862	Ducher	lp		m-l		
Princesse Alice de Monaco	T	1893	Weber	yb		m	vig	
Princesse Amedée de Broglie	HP	1885	Lévêque	lp	f	l	vig	
Princesse Amélie	C	Pre 1830		mp	vdbl	l		
Princesse Amélie	D	Pre 1834		lp		vl		
Princesse Amélie	M	1851	Robert	m	dbl	l		
Princesse Amélie des Pays-Bas	HP	1872	Liabaud	dr		l	vig	
Princesse Amélie d'Orléans	HP	1884	Lévêque	lp	f	vl	vvig	
Princesse Anna Lœwenstein	T	1897	Soupert & Notting	mp	f	l		
Princesse Antoinette Strozzio	HP	1874	Verdier E	lp	f	l	m	
Princesse Bacchiochi	M	1866	Moreau-Robert	mp	dbl	m		m
Princesse Belgiojoso	HP	1847	Vibert	mp	f	l		
Princesse Blanche d'Orléans	HP	1877	Verdier E	dp	f	m	vig	vf
Princesse Caroline	C	Pre 1808	syn Foliacée	mp	dbl	vl		
Princesse Charles d'Arenberg	HP	1877	Soupert	pb	f	l		

Princesse Charlotte	G	Pre 1830	Prévost	dp	vf	m		
Princesse Charlotte	G/Ch	Pre 1838	Laffay	lp	dbl	l		
Princesse Charlotte de la Trémouille	HP	1877	Lévêque	lp	f	vl	vig	
		syn Mlle	Charlotte de la Trémouille					
Princesse Christine von Salm	HP	1897	Reverchon	rb	dbl	l		sf
		syn	Baron Girod de l'Ain					
Princesse Clémentine	C	1842	Vibert	w	f	l	vvig	
Princesse Clémentine	B	1842	Souchet	dr	f	m	vig	
Princesse Clémentine	HP	1876	Verdier E	lp	vf	m		
Princesse Clotilde	HP	Pre 1870		lp	f	m		
Princesse de Bessaraba de Bracovan	T	1890	Bernaix	pb	dbl	m	vig	
		syn	Mme la Princesse de Bessaraba de Bracovan					
Princesse de Béarn	HP	1885	Lévêque	mr	dbl	l	vig	f
Princesse de Bourbon	T	1877	Nabonnand	lp	f	m	vvig	
Princesse de Croi (y)	B	Pre 1846		mr		l		
Princesse de Galles	P	Pre 1830		dp	f	l		
Princesse de Joinville	B	1840	Poncet	mp		m		
Princesse de Joinville	HP	Pre 1870		lp	f	l		
Princesse de Lamballe	A	Pre 1830	Miellez	w	vdbl	m	vvig	
Princesse de Liévin	G		Parmentier	mp	f	m		
Princesse de Metternich	HP	1871	De Sansal	mp	f	l		
Princesse de Modena	B	Pre 1846		lp				
Princesse de Monaco	T	1892	Dubreuil	ly				
Princesse de Naples	HP	1897	Gaëtano/Bonfiglioli	lp	f	vl		
Princesse de Nassau	M	Pre 1830	Laffay M	ly	vdbl	m		m
Princesse de Nassau	G	c 1840	Miellez	dp				
Princesse de Portugal	G	Pre 1828	Pelletier	mp	f	vl		
Princesse de Sagan	T	1887	Dubreuil	dr	dbl	m	vig	
Princesse de Salerne	HP	1846		lp	f	m		
Princesse de Salm	G	1822	Vibert	lp	f	vl		
Princesse de Sarsina	T	1891	Soupert & Notting	ly				
Princesse de Siam	G			mr	f	l		
Princesse de Thuringe	Ch			lp				
Princesse de Vaudemont	M	1825	Vibert	lp	dbl	m	m	m
Princesse de Vaudemont	M	1854	Robert	lp	f			
Princesse de Venosa	T	1895	Dubreuil	w	vdbl	vl	vvig	
Princesse d'Esterhazy	T	Pre 1870		lp		l		
Princesse d'Orange	N	1825	Vibert	w	vf	m-l	vvig	vf
Princesse Eléonore	G	Pre 1826	Miellez	mr	dbl	l		
Princesse Elisabeth	Pom			mr	f	m		
Princesse Elisabeth Lancelotti	Pol	1893	Soupert & Notting	ly	dbl	l	m	vf
Princesse Etienne de Croy	T	1898	Ketten Bros	m	dbl	vl	vvig	vf
Princesse Guillaume	HP		Radig		s-d	m		f
		see	Prinzessin W von Hohenzollern					
Princesse Hélène	HP	1837	Laffay	dp	vdbl	m	vig	
Princesse Hélène	T	Pre 1846	(Luxembourg)	w	f	vl		f
Princesse Hélène	T	Pre 1846	(Modeste)	w				f
Princesse Hélène d'Orléans	HP	1886	Verdier E	mp	f	l		
Princesse Henri des Pays-Bas	HP	1867	Soupert	w	f	m	wk	
Princesse Henriette de Flandres	Pol	1887	Soupert & Notting	w	f	s	vig	f
Princesse Hohenzollern	T	1886	Nabonnand	rb	dbl	vl		
Princesse Impériale Clothilde	HP	1859	Verdier E	w	f	m	vig	
Princesse Impériale de Brésil	HT	1881	Soupert & Notting	mp	vf	l	vig	
Princesse Impériale Victoria	B	see	Kronprincessin Victoria					
Princesse Joséphine de Flandres	Pol	1887	Soupert & Notting	pb	f	s		
Princesse Joséphine de Hohenzollern	D	1840	Baumann	mp	f	m		
Princesse Julie d'Arenberg	T	1885	Soupert & Notting	yb	vf	l	vvig	
Princesse Lichtenstein	HP	1864	Paul W	w	f	m		
Princesse Lise Troubezkoi	HP	1878	Lévêque	lp	f	m	vig	
Princesse Louise	HSem	1829	Jacques	w	dbl	m		
Princeese Louise	HP	1869	Laxton; Paul G	w	f	m	vig	
			syn Princess Louise					
Princesse Louise, Climbing	Cl			lp	f	m		
Princesse Louise d'Orléans	HP	1886	Verdier E	mp	f	l		
Princesse Louise-Victoria	HP	1872	Knight	op	f	m-l		
Princesse Ma	T	1899	Ketten	w				
Princesse Marguerite d'Orléans	HP	1888	Verdier E	dp	f	vl	vig	
Princesse Marguerite d'Orléans	T	1890	Nabonnand	lp	f	vl		
Princesse Marianne	G	Pre 1830		mp	f	m		
Princesse Marie	HSem	1829	Jacques	mp	f	m	vvig	
Princesse Marie	T	Pre 1846		w	f	l		
Princesse M Adélaide de Luxembourg	Pol	1895	Soupert & Notting	w	f			
Princesse Marie Dagmar	T	1858	Moreau & Robert	pb	dbl	l		
			syn Socrate					
Princesse Marie de Lusignan	N	1888	Perny	y				
			syn Narcisse					
Princesse Marie de Roumanie	T	1895	Soupert & Notting	w				
Princesse Marie Dolgorouky	HP	1878	Gonod	lp	dbl	vl	vig	

Name	Class	Year	Breeder					
Princesse Marie d'Orléans	HP	1885	Verdier E	mp	f	l		
Princesse Mathilde	HP	1860	Liabaud	m	f	m	vig	
Princesse Metternich	HP	1871	Jamain	mp	f	m	vvig	
Princesse N Troubetzkoi	T	1899	Ketten	or				
Princesse Olga Allierii	T	1897	Lévêque	y		vl		
		syn	Duchesse Mathilde					
Princesse Olympie	HP	1858	Béluze	w	vf	l	vig	
Princesse Ourousof(f)	T	1895	Soupert & Notting	lp	dbl	l	m	
Princesse Nobilis	G			mr				
Princesse Portia	HP			mr	f	m		
Princesse Radziwill	HP	1883	Lévêque	mp	f	l	vvig	
Princesse Royale	M	1846	Portemer	mp	dbl	m	vig	
Princesse Royale de Portugal	Ch	1827	Guérin					
Princesse Stéphanie	N	1880	Levet	ob	f	m		
syn Fiançailles	de la	Princesse	Stéphanie et de l'Archi	duc Rodolp	he			
Princesse Stéphanie	T	1880	Levet A	op	dbl	l	vvig	f
Princesse Thérèse de Thurn et Taxis	T	1897	Soupert & Notting	dp	f	l		
Princesse Vera	T	1878	Nabonnand	w	f	vl	wk	
Princesse Wilhelmine des Pays-Bas	Pol	1885	Soupert & Notting	w	f	m	m	m
Princesse Wilhelm von Preussen	HP	1883	Radig	mr	f	m	m	vf
Principe da Beïra	HP	1890	Da Costa	m				
Principessa di Napoli	T	1898	Brauer / Ketten Bros	lp	f	l	vig	m
Prinz Friedrich Auguste von Sachsen	HP	1890	Pollner	dr				
Prinzessin W. von Hohenzollern	T	1887	Nabonnand	mr				
Priscilla	HSet	Pre 1846		lp				
Priscilla	T	1886	Lambert E	w	dbl			
			syn Marie Lambert					
Procera	Misc	Pre 1846			s			
Professeur Bazin	HP	1897	Lévêque	op	f	l		
Professeur Charguéreau	HP	1891	Lévêque	r				
Professeur Chevreul	HP	1884	Verdier Ch	dr	f	l	vig	
Professeur Duchartre	HP	1865	Verdier E	mr	f	l	vvig	
Professeur Edouard Regel	HP	1883	Verdier E	lp	f	l	vig	
Professeur Ganiviat	T	1890	Perrier	pb	vdbl	l	vvig	
Professeur Jolibois	HP	1888	Verdier E	dr	f	l	vig	
Professeur Jules Courtois	HP	1886	Bire	mr	dbl	m		
Professeur Koch	HP	1861	Verdier E	lp	f	m	vig	
Professeur Lambin	HP	1891	Lévêque	mr				
Professeur Maxime Cornu	HP	1885	Lévêque	mr	f	vl		f
Professor Dr Schmidt	Misc	1899	Strassheim					
Professor N E Hansen	HRg	1892	Budd	dr				
Professor Reinworth	Misc	1846						
Progrès Libéral	HP	1885	Singer	mr	f	l	vvig	
Progress	HT	1890	Drögmüller	pb	dbl	l		m
Prolifera	C	Pre 1759	syn Childing	mp		l		
Prolifera de Redouté	C	Pre 1824		mp	f	l		vf
Prolifère	C	Pre 1759	syn Childing	mp		l		
Prolifère	G	Pre 1804	Dupont (?)	lp	vdbl	m		
Prolifère	T			lp	f	m	vig	vf
Prolifère	M	Pre 1826	Philippe	dp	f	l	vig	
Prolifère	N	Pre 1830						
Prolifère	HCh	Pre 1846						
Prolifère à Odeur de Thé	N		Laffay	w				
Proliferous Carmine	Misc	Pre 1846		mr				
Prolific	M	Pre 1829	Prévost	dp	dbl	l	vig	
			syn Gracilis					
Prolific Agate	Misc	Pre 1846		lp	vf			
Prolific Red	HSpn	Pre 1846		r				
Promethée	D	Pre 1830	Vibert	lp	vdbl	m		
Promethée	HCh	Pre 1846						
Pronville	G			mr	f	m		
Properce	G		Vibert	m				
Proserpine	G	Pre 1830	Prévost	mr	vdbl	m		
Proserpine	B	1841	Mondeville /Verdier V	m	f	m		
Proserpine Nouvelle	G	Pre 1830	Racine	dr	f	m		
Prosper Laugier	HP	1883	Verdier E	mr	dbl	l	vvig	m
Prospérité	HP	1871	Lartay	mr	f	l		
Proteiformis	HRg	1894		w	s-d			
Protocolle	G			dr				
Provence à Fleur Comprimée	G	Pre 1830	Vibert	lp	vf	m		
Provence Éclatante	G			mr	f	l		
Provence Moss	M	1844	Robert	w	dbl	l		
			syn Unique Moss					
Provence Pink	C	1759		mp				
Provence sans Épines	C	Pre 1830						
Provincialis Hybrida	C	1805	Spong syn Spong	mp	vdbl	s		f
Provins	HSpn	1888		p				
Provins à Fleur Pourpre	G	1825	Vibert	m	dbl	m		f
			syn Ombrée Parfaite					
Provins à Fleur Prpre Violet,	G	1826	Prévost	dr	vf	m		

Marbrée

Name	Class	Date	Breeder / Syn					
Provins à Fleur Rouge Cramoisi	G	1826	Prévost	mr	f	m		
Provins à Grands Corymbes	G	1835	Joly	dp	dbl	vl	vvig	
Provins Blanc	D	Pre 1818	Prévost syn Fausse Unique	w	f	l		
Provins Double	G	Pre 1790	syn L'Évêque	m	dbl			m
Provins Éclatant	G	Pre 1834		dp		m		
Provins Marbré	G	Pre 1754	syn Marmorea	rb	s-d	m		
Provins Ordinaire	G			mr				
Provins Panaché	Sp	Pre 1581	syn r.gallica versicolor	pb	s-d			m
Provins Panaché	G	Pre 1834		mp	dbl	m		
Provins Panaché	B	c 1860	Fontaine	pb	dbl			vf
Provins Pompon	G	1835	Joly	mr	f	s	vig	
Provins Renoncule	G	Pre 1810	Cartier/Dupont	mp	vdbl			m
Provins Rose	Sp	Pre 1500	syn r.gallica	dp		m		
Provins Rose Feu	G	Pre 1830	Tributien	mp	dbl	vl		
Provins Semi-Double	G	1818	Godefroy syn Aigle Noir & Aigle Br	mr	dbl	m		
Prudence	G		Miellez	un				
Prudence Besson	HP	1865	Lacharme	mp	dbl	vl	vig	
Prudence Rœser	HP	1840	Rœser	mp	f	m		
Prudence Rœser	N			mp	vf	m	vvig	
Prudhomme	HP	Pre 1846		mp	f	m		
Psyché	G	1818	Vibert	lp	f	m		
Psyché	B	Pre 1846		lp				
Psyché	HMult	1898	Paul	mp	dbl			sf
Psyché	HP		Miellez	lp				
Pubescens	HEg	Pre 1819	Manning syn Manning's Blush	w	dbl	vs		
Pucelle	Pom			lp				
Pucelle de Bergham	G			lp			vig	
Pucelle de Bruxelles	G	Pre 1830	Paillard syn Reine des Roses	dr	f	s		
Pucelle de Cologne	G							
Pucelle de Jacques	G		Jacques	dr				
Pucelle de l'Est	G			lp	f	l		
Pucelle de Lille	G	Pre 1828	Miellez	pb	f	m		
Pucelle d'Enghien	G							
Pucelle Sadeur	G			mr	f	m		
Puebla	HP	1861	Rousseau syn Sénateur Favre	dr	f	l	vig	
Pulchella	B	Pre 1846		mp				
Pulchella	N	Pre 1846						
Pulchérie	HP	1829	Vibert	mr		m		
Pulchérie	D	Pre 1846		w				
Pulchérie	B	Pre 1846						
Pulchérie	HP		Robert	mr	f	l	vig	
Pulchra Marmorea	G			mr	f	m		
Pulmonaire	G	Pre 1815	Dupont syn La Maculée	pb	s-d	m		
Pulverulenta	Misc	1897		w	s			
Pumila	G	Pre 1806	Crantz(?) syn Rosier d'Amour	m	s	l		m
Pumila	Ch	c 1806	Colville	w	s-m			
Pumila	HFt			my				
Pumila	Pom			w	f	vs		
Pumila Alba	N	1847	Hardy	w	f	vs		
Pumila Alba	Ch			w	vdbl	m		
Punctata	G	1819	Coquerel syn Belle Herminie	m	s-d	m		
Punicea	Sp	c 1596	syn r.foetida bicolor	rb	s			
Purity	B	1898	Cooling	w		m		
Purple	Ch	1834	Guérin syn Louis-Philippe	rb	dbl			
Purple Bengal	Ch	1827	Vibert	dr				
Purple Leaved	M	Pre 1846		mr				
Purple Mignone	Misc	Pre 1846						
Purple Noisette	N	1822	Laffay M syn Purpurea	dr	s-d			
Purple Royal	Misc	Pre 1846						
Purple Scotch	Pom							
Purple Triumphant	Misc	Pre 1846						
Purple Velvet	Misc	Pre 1846		mr				
Purple Violet	Misc	Pre 1846		lp				
Purpur von Weilburg	Ch	1886	Jacobs	mp				
Purpurascens	C			dr				
Purpurea	G	Pre 1770	syn Purpurine de France	m	s-d			m
Purpurea	N	1822	Laffay	dr	s-d			
Purpurea	HMcr	Pre 1844	Buist	m		l		
Purpurea	Ch	Pre 1846		m				
Purpurea	HSpn	Pre 1846		m				

Purpurea Plena	Misc	c 1829	syn Pourpre Ancien	m	vf	l		
Purpurea Rubra	M	Pre 1870		m	dbl	l		vf
Purpurea Velutina Parva	G	Pre 1820	Van Eeden syn L'Obscurité	m	dbl	m		
Purpureo-Violacea Magna	G	Pre 1790	syn L'Évêque	m	dbl			m
Purpurine	HP	1848	Margottin	mr	f	m	vvig	
Purpurine	HP	1865	Liabaud	dr	f	l		
Purpurine de France	G	Pre 1770		m	s-d			m
Puteaux	N			lp	s-d		vig	
Putidula	C	Pre 1810	Dupont syn Le Rire Niais	mp	f	m		m
Pygmæa	G			dr				
Pyracantha	M		Laffay	dr	s	m		
Pyrame	G	Pre 1830	Racine	dr	f	m		
Pyramid Harbour	D		Presl syn Nutkana	w				
Pyramidale	G	Pre 1815	Descemet syn Porcelaine	lp	s-d	l		
Pyramide Agréable	D	Pre 1830	Miellez syn Miroir des Dames	w	f	m		f
Pyrenaïca	A			lp				
Pyrolle	Ch		Laffay	mp	f	m		
Pyrrhus	G			lp	f	l		
Pythagoras	HSpn	Pre 1848	Vibert (?)	pb	s-d			
Pythagore	M	1855	Robert	mp	f	vl		
Pythagore	Pom			mp				

NAME	TYPE	YEAR	RAISER	COLOUR	BLOOM	SIZE	GROWTH	SCENT
Quatre Saisons	D	Pre 400	syn Autumn Damask	mp	dbl	m		m
Quatre Saisons à Feuilles Bullées	P			mp	f	l		
Quatre Saisons à Feuilles Panachées	P							
Quatre Saisons Blanc	D	Pre 1830		w	vdbl	m		
		syn Bi-	fère à Fleurs Blanches					
Quatre Saisons Blanc Mousseux	M	Pre 1834	Laffay M	w	dbl	m	m	f
Quatre Saisons Blanche	D	1838	syn with above	w				
Quatre Saisons Continue	D	Pre 1849	syn Autumn Damask	mp	dbl			m
Quatre Saisons d'Italie	P	1795	Dupont	dp	s-d	m		m
Quatre Saisons Magnifique	P			w				
Quatre Saisons Moins Épineux	P	Pre 1830	Vibert	lp	dbl	m		
		syn	Bifère Presque Inerme					
Quatre Saisons Mousseux	M	syn	Perpetual White Moss	w				
Quatre Saisons Panaché	P	Pre 1830	Prévost	w	vdbl	m		
Quatre Saisons Pompon (Perpétuel)	P	Pre 1830	Vibert	lp	vdbl	vs		
Quatre Saisons Pompon Mousseux	M			lp				
Quatre Saisons Rose	D	1580		mp				
Quatre Saisons Rose	P	Pre 1830	Vibert C	lp	dbl	m		
		syn Perp	etuelle à Fleurs Roses					
Quatre Saisons sans Aiguillons	P			mp				
Quatre Saisons Tomenteux	P			lp				
Queen	Ayr	Pre 1846		dr				
Queen	B	1899	Paul	mp	f	l	m	
Queen Eleanor	HP	1876	Paul W	mp	f	l	vig	vf
Queen Mab	Ch	1896	Paul W	ab	dbl	l	m	
Queen of Autumn	HP	1887	Paul G	mr	f	m		
Queen of Beauty and Frangrance	B	1843	Béluze	lp	dbl	vl	vig	vf
		syn	Souv de la Malmaison					
Queen of Bedders	B	1871	Noble	dp	f	m-l	vig	f
Queen of Bourbons	B	1834	Bréon / Mauget	pb	dbl	l	vvig	vf
Queen of Denmark	A	1816	Booth	mp	vdbl	m	vig	vf
		syn	Königin von Dänema-	rk				
Queen of Denmark	D	1846	Vibert	lp				
Queen of Denmark	HP	1858		mr	f	l	vig	
Queen of Hungary	Misc	Pre 1846						
Queen of Moss	M	1845	Laffay	mr				
Queen of Naples	Ch	Pre 1846		dr				
Queen of Pearl	HWich	1898	Van Fleet	lp				
Queen of Queens	HP	1882	Paul W	pb	f	l	vvig	
Queen of Queens, Climbing	HP	1892	Paul W	mp		vl		
Queen of Roses	Misc	Pre 1846						
Queen of Scarlet	Ch	1832	Coquereau	mr	dbl	s	vig	
		syn	Cramoisi Supérieur					
Queen of the Belgians	Ayr	1832	Jacquea	w	vdbl	s		
			syn Reine des Belges					
Queen of the Prairies	HSet	1843	Feast	pb	dbl	l	vig	m
Queen of Waltham	HP	1875	Paul W	mr	f	l	vig	
Queen Olga of Greece	N	1881	Nabonnand	mr	dbl	l	vig	m
		syn	Reine	Olga de Wurtembourg				
Queen Olga of Greece	HP	1898	Paul W	rb	f	l	vig	
Quuen Olga of Wurtembourg	N	1881	Nabonnand	mr	dbl	l	vig	m
		syn	Reine	Olga de Wurtembourg				
Queen Victoria	HP	1830	Laffay M syn Brennus	dr	f	l		
Queen Victoria	T	1846	Bélot-Défougère	lp	dbl	vl	vig	vf
		syn	Souvenir d'un Ami					
Queen Victoria	HP	1850	Fontaine	lp	dbl	l	vig	
Queen Victoria	HP	Pre 1870	Margottin	lp		vl		
Queen Victoria	T	1872	Labruyère	lp				
Queen's Scarlet	Ch	1880	Hallock & Thorpe	mr	dbl	s		f
Quercifolia	C	Pre 1811	Trianon	mp	vf	m	wk	
		syn	À Feuilles de Chêne					
Quesné	G	1826	Prévost	dp	vf	m		
Quirinit	G		Parmentier	mp	f	m		
Quitterie	A	1820	Vibert	lp	s-d	l		
Quitterie	HCh	Pre 1846		lp		s		

NAME	TYPE	YEAR	RAISER	COLOUR	BLOOM	SIZE	GROWTH	SCENT
R B Cater	HP	1899	Cooling	dr				
R Dudley Baxter	HP	1879	Paul W	mr				
Rabelais	D		Laffay					
Rachel	C			lp	f	m		
Rachel	HP		Vibert	mp				
Rachel	G		Parmentier	mp				
Rachel	B		Pradel	mp				
Rachel Ruisch	HCh			lp	f	l	vvig	
Racine	HP	1867	Oger	mr	f	l	vig	
Racine	Ch		Laffay	lp	f	m		
Radamiste	T			lp	f	m		
Ragged Robin	Ch	1825	Vibert	mr	s-d	vl	vig	m
			syn Gloire des Rosomanes					
Rainbow	T	1889	Sievers	pb	dbl	m	m	m
Rainbow	HT	1891	Dingee & Conard					
Ramanas Rose	Sp	Pre 1846	syn r.rugosa	m		m		
Rameau	G		Miellez	mp	f	m		
Rampante	HSem	1830	Jacques / Noisette	w	f	s	vvig	
Rancourt	G		Calvert	mr	vdbl	m		
			syn La Napolitaine					
Range View Cream Tea	T	1838	Foster	w	dbl	vl	vvig	f
			syn Devoniensis					
Ranoncule Ponctuée	G	Pre 1846		mr				
Ranunculiflora	HSet	c 1846	Pierce	lp	vdbl	s		vf
Ranunculus	N			lp	f	m	vig	
Ranunculus	M	Pre 1846		w				
Raoul Chauvry	T	1896	Chauvry	yb	dbl	l		m
Raoul Guillard	HP	1885	Margottin	dr	f	l		vf
Raphael	M	1856	Robert	lp	f	m		
Raphael	HP		Oger	mr	f	vl	vvig	
Raphael	G		Verdier V	mp	f	l		
Raucourt	G	Pre 1830	Calvert	mr	f	m		
			syn La Napolitaine					
Ravel	HP	1866	Guillot Fils	mr	f	l		
Ravereau	G			mr	vdbl	vl		
Ravissante	D		Miellez					
Raymond	B							
Raynal	HP	1846	Laffay					
Rebecca	HP	Pre 1846	Trouillard	m	f	m	vig	
Reclinata	A		Bozérain	dr				
			syn Boursault					
Red Agate	Misc	Pre 1846						
Red Belgic	Misc	Pre 1759		mr	f			
Red Cabbage	C	Pre 1860	syn Cabbage Rose	mp				
Red Damask	Sp	c 1200	syn r.gallica officinalis	dp	s-d			m
Red Damask	D	1789		mr	dbl	m		vf
Red Dragon	HP	1878	Paul W	dr	vdbl	l	vig - cl	
Red Gauntlet	HP	1881	Postans	mr	vf	vl	vig	
Red Hermosa	Ch	1880	Hallock & Thorpe	mr	dbl	s		
			syn Queen's Scarlet					
Red La France	HT	1888	Paul W	dp	f	vl		
			syn Duchess of Albany					
Red Malmaison	B	1882	Gonod	dr	f	m		
			syn Malmaison Rouge					
Red Maréchal Niel	Cl HT	1888	Müller Dr F	mp	vdbl	vl	vf	
		syn Gro-	ssherzog Ernst Ludw-	ig von	sse			
			He-					
Red Mignone	Misc	Pre 1846						
Red Moss	M	1862	Laffay M	mr	s-d			sf
			syn Henri Martin					
Red Pet	Ch	1887	Parker / Paul G	dr	vdbl	s		
Red Provence	C	Pre 1629	syn Rubra (C)					
Red Robin	Ch	1825	Vibert	mr	s-d	vl	vig	m
		syn	Gloire des Rosomanes					
Red Rose	Sp	Pre 1500	syn r.gallica	dp			m	
Red Rose of Lancaster	Sp	c 1200	syn r.gallica officinalis	dp	s-d			m
Red Rover	HP	1864	Paul W	mr	f	m	vig	
Red Safrano	T	1867	Oger	yb	s-d	m		
		syn	Safrano à Fleurs Rou-	ges				
Red Soupert	Pol	1898	Chauvry	dr	dbl	l		
			syn Ma Petite Andrée					
Red Unique	Misc	Pre 1846						
Red Variegated	Misc	Pre 1846						
Red Velvet	Misc	Pre 1846						
Redouté	Rbf	1818	Vibert					
Redouté	HSpn	Pre 1820	Redoute H	w	s	m		
			syn De Marienbourg					
Redum Dentata Major								
Redutea Glauca	HSpn	Pre 1820	Redouté H	w	s	m		

			syn De Marienbourg					
Regalis	G	Pre 1811	Godefroy syn Royale	lp	dbl		m	
Regalis	G	Pre 1813	syn Great Royal	lp				
Regeliana	HRg		Regel	dr	s	l	m	
			syn Taïcoun					
Regeliana Flore Pleno	HRg	1879		m	dbl	l	m	
			syn Kaiserin des Nordens					
Regeliana Rubra	HRg	1879		m	dbl	l		
			syn Kaiserin des Nordens					
Regia	A	Pre 1813	Prévost	lp	f	vl		
			syn Beauté Tendre (A)					
Regia Purpurea	G	Pre 1830	Coquerel	m	f	m		
Regierungsrat Stockert	HP	1887	Soupert & Notting	lp	f	l	vig	m
Regina	C	Pre 1885	syn Maxima	mp	vdbl	m	vig	vf
Regina Dicta	G	1817	Godefroy	m	f	m		
Regina Nigrorum	G	Pre 1846		dr		l		
Régulus	G	Pre 1830	syn La Magnifique	mr	dbl	l		
Regulus	T	1860	Moreau-Robert	pb	vdbl	l	vvig	vf
Reichsgraf von Kessestadt	T	1898	Lambert	rb	vdbl	vl		
Reina Maria Christina	T	1894	Aldrufeu	ob	f	m-l	vvig	
			syn Maria Christina					
Reine Auguste Victoria	HT	Pre 1846	Lee	w			m	vf
			syn Kaiserin Auguste Vic-toria					
Reine Blanche	HEg	Pre 1846	Lee syn Hebe's Lip	w	s-d		vig	m
Reine Blanche	Ch	Pre 1870	Laffay	w	dbl	m		
Reine-Blanche	M	1857	Robert & Moreau	w	dbl	l	vig	
Reine Blanche	HP	1868	Damaizin	w	f	l	m	
Reine d'Angleterre	T			dp	vf	m	m	
Reine de Bassora	T	Pre 1846		lp		l		f
Reine de Belgique	HCh	Pre 1846		lp		l		
Reine de Castille	HP	1851	Lartay	dr	vf	l	vig	
Reine de Castille	B	1863	Pernet Père	lp	f	l	vig	f
Reine de Cythère	T			mp	f	m		
Reine de Danemark	D	1826	Miellez	lp	vdbl	l	vig	
			see also Königin v Dänemark					
Reine de Danemark	HP	1857	Granger	lp	f	l		
Reine de Fontenay	B	Pre 1846		mp				
Reine de Fontenay	HP	Pre 1846		mp	f	m		
Reine de France	HCh			lp	f	m		
Reine de Golconde	T	1825	Laffay	lp	dbl	l	vvig	
Reine de Golconde	D		Miellez	mp				
Reine de Hongrie	G			dr	f	m		
Reine de la Citée	HP	1858	Moreau & Robert	mp	f	m	vig	
Reine de la Guillotière	HP	1835	Plantier	lp	f	l	m	
Reine de la Lombardie	Ch	Pre 1835		dr	dbl	m		
Reine de la Pape	HP	1863	Guillot Père	m	f	l		
Reine de Laffay	HP	1843	Laffay	lp	f	vl		
Reine de Lombardie	Ch	Pre 1846		mr				
Reine de Lyon	HP			dr	f	l		
Reine de Nigritie	G	1825	Godefroy	m	f	m		
Reine de Pæstum	T			w				
Reine de Perse	G	Pre 1825		lp	f	m		vf
Reine de Portugal	T	1868	Guillot et Fils	yb	vdbl	l	m	f
Reine de Provence	C	Pre 1848		lp	vdbl	l	vig	
Reine de Prusse	C	1821	Hardy	mp	f	m-l		
			syn Duc d'Angoulême					
Reine de Prusse	G	1824	Asselin (?)	mr	f	m		
Reine de Prusse	G	Pre 1860	Miellez	lp	dbl	m	m	
			syn Duc -hesse d'Angoulême					
Reine de Saxe	C	Pre 1820		mp	dbl	m		m
Reine de Vibert	G	c 1835	Vibert	m				
Reine des Agathes	G			lp	vf	l	vig	
Reine des Amateurs	G	Pre 1829	Mme Hébert	m	vdbl	vl		
Reine des Amateurs	HP	1879	Oger	lp	f	l	vig	
Reine des Beautés	HP	1870	Gonod	lp	f	l	vvig	vf
Reine des Belges	B	1831	Jacques	lp	f	l		
Reine des Belges	HSem	1832	Jacques	w	vdbl		vig	sf
Reine des Belges	G	Pre 1846		w				
Reine des Belges	T	Pre 1846		w	vdbl	l		f
Reine des Belges	T	1862	Cochet	w	f	m		
Reine des Belges	HCh	1867	Cochet	w			vig	
Reine des Belges	HP		Vibert	w				
Reine des Blanches	HP	1868	Avoux or Pernet	w	f	l	m	
Reine des Blanches	HP	1870	Crozy	w	f	l	vig	
Reine des Cartes	D		syn René Descartes					
Reine des Centfeuilles	C	1824		mp	dbl	vl	vvig	m
Reine des Cerises	G			dr	f	m		
Reine des Fées	T	1884	syn Rosalie	mp	vf	m		m
Reine des Fleurs	HP	1846	Portemer	mp	f	l		
Reine des Français	HP	1842	syn La Reine	mp		l	vig	m
Reine des Francois	HSem	Pre 1846		mp	f			
Reine des Hybrides	HCh	Pre 1830	Prévost syn Vibert	dr	f	m		

Reine des Iles-Bourbon	B	1834	Bréon / Mauget	pb	dbl	l	vvig	vf
			syn Queen of Bourbons					
Reine des Massifs	T	1874	Levet	mp	f	l		
Reine des Mousseuses	M	1860	Moreau-Robert	lp	dbl	m		
Reine des Nègres	G	Pre 1810	Dupont	m	f	s		
			syn Superbe en Brun					
Reine des Noires	G		Parmentier	dr				
Reine des Pays-Bas	D			lp				
Reine des Pays-Bas	C			mp	f	m		
Reine des Pays-Bas	G	1824		dp		m		
Reine des Pays-Bas	T	1858	Fontaine	lp		m		
Reine des Pimprenelles	HSpn	1821	Vibert	lp	s-d	m-l		
Reine des Poêtes	D	c 1825	Cartier syn Des Poêtes	mp				
Reine des Pourpres	G	Pre 1811	Miellez syn Pallas	m	f	l		m
Reine des Prairies	HSet	1843	Feast	pb	dbl	l	vig	m
			syn Queen of the Prairies					
Reine des Perpetuelles	D	Pre 1846		w & p				
Reine des Reines	HP	1882	Paul W	pb	f	l		
			syn Queen of Queens					
Reine des Roses	G	Pre 1830	Vibert	m	f	s		
			Syn Pucelle de Bruxelles					
Reine des Vierges	B	1844	Béluze	lp	s-d	m		
Reine des Violettes	HP	1860	Mille-Malet	m	vdbl	m-l		vf
Reine d'Espagne	HP	1861	Fontaine	mr	f	m		
Reine d'Italie	Ch	1886	Perny	dr				
Reine du Congrès	B	1842	Béluze	lp	f	m		
Reine du Matin	HP	1845	Béluze	m	f	m		
Reine du Midi	HP	1867	Roland	lp	f	vl	vig	m
Reine Emma des Pays-Bas	T	1879	Nabonnand G	my	s-d	l	vig	
Reine Hortense	B	1852	Fontaine	lp	f	l	vvig	f
Reine Isabelle II	HP	1887	Lévêque	lp	f	l	vig	
Reine Marguerite	G	Pre 1821	Steigerhoek	rb	f	s		
			syn Tricolore					
Reine Maria Pia	T	1880	Schwartz J	dp	dbl	l	vig	f
Reine Marie Henriette	Cl T	1878	Levet F	mr	dbl	l	vvig	m
Reine Mathilde	HP	1849	Oger	lp	f	l	vig	
Reine Nathalie de Serbie	T	1885	Soupert & Notting	lp	f	l	vig	f
Reine Olga	T	1885	Nabonnand	mr				
Reine Olga de Wurtemberg	N	1881	Nabonnand G	mr	dbl	l	vvig	m
Reine Rémond	B			mr				
Reine Victoria	HP	1838	Laffay	dp	f	m		
Reine Victoria	T	Pre 1846		y		l		f
Reine Victoria	B	1872	Labruyère / Schwartz	mp	dbl	l	vvig	vf
			syn La Reine Victoria					
Remarquable	A			w	f	m		
Rembrandt	P	1883	Moreau-Robert	m	dbl	l	vvig	f
Remontante	HP			lp				
Rémond	B	Pre 1870	syn Sylvain Péan	mr	f	m		
Rene Daniel	HP	1868	Damaizin	dp	f	l	vig	
René d'Anjou	HT			mr	f	l	vig	
René d'Anjou	M	1853	Robert	lp	dbl	s	vig	
René Denis	T	1897	Denis	ly				
René Descartes	M	1854	Robert	mp	f	l	vvig	
Renestine Audio	D	Pre 1846		mr	f	l		
Renoncule	HP			dr	f	m		
Renoncule	Cl			lp				
Renoncule	N		Miellez	dp				
Renoncule	G	Pre 1810	Dupont	mp	vdbl	m		m
			syn ProvinsRenoncule					
Renoncule	T	1827	Miellez	lp				
Renoncule	N	Pre 1834		lp		s		
Renoncule Admire-Moi	G							
Renoncule Cartier	G		Cartier	dr				
Renoncule Marbrée	Ch		Laffay	dr				
Renoncule Noirâtre	G	Pre 1817	Vibert	dr	f	m		
			syn Roi des Pourpres					
Renoncule Noire	G	1825	Hardy	m	f	s		
Renoncule Olry	HCh	1826	Mme Olry	dr				
Renoncule Ponctuée	G/C	1833	Vibert	mr	dbl	m		
Renoncule Pourpre	G/Ch	Pre 1834	Laffay	dr		s		
			see Miss Wood					
Renoncule Rose	HCh	1825	Laffay	lp	f	s-m		
Renoncule Rose	G	Pre 1830	Vibert	lp	f	s		
Renoncule Rouge	G	1820	Godefroy	mr	vf	s-m		
Renoncule Violette	HCh	1824	Hardy					
Renoncule Violette Veloutée	G	Pre 1830	syn Manteau Impérial	dr	f	s		
Renufe d'Osmond	HP	Pre 1846		lp	f	m		
Repens	N	1828	Vibert	w	dbl	m	vig	vf
			syn Aimée Vibert					
Repens	Ayr	c 1835	syn Splendens	w	s-d	m		vf
Requien	HP	Pre 1846		lp	f	l		
Reseïs	HCh	1853	Robert	mp	f	m		

Name	Type	Year	Raiser					
Resplendent	HP	1896	Williams A	lp				
Resplendissante	HP	1875	Touvais	dp	f	l	vig	
Retour du Printemps	HCh	Pre 1835		dp	s-d	m		
Rêve de Bonheur	T	Pre 1846		mr	f	m		f
Rêve d'Or	N	1869	Ducher Vve	my	dbl	l	vig	m
Rêve du Bonheur	HP	1851	Lartay	mp	f	m		
Réveil	HP	1849	Lacharme	mp	f	m		
Réveil	B	1854	Guillot Père	rb	f	l	vig	
Réveil de l'Empire	HP	1852	Bernède	mp	f	l	vvig	vf
Réveil du Printemps	HP	1883	Oger	w	vf	l	vvig	
Reveillère	Ch			dp	f	m		
Revenante	G	1825	Miellez	mp	dbl			
			syn La Revenante					
Révérend	G			mp	f	vl		
Reverend Alan Cheales	HP	1894	Paul G	pb	dbl	vl	m	
Reverend H Dombrain	B	1863	Margottin	mr	dbl	l	vig	
Reverend James Sprunt	Cl HCh	1858	Sprunt	mr		l		
Reverend J B M Camm	HP	1875	Turner	mp		l	m	
Reverend T C Cole	Cl T	1880	Cole, Rev T C	dy				
Reverend Trautmann	HP	1877	Soupert & Notting	mp	f	l	vig	
Reversa	Bslt	c 1810	Descemet/Vibert	m	s-d	m		
Reversa Pourpre	Bslt	c 1815	Vibert syn Maheca	m				
Rex Nigrorum	G	Pre 1846		dr	f	s		
Rex Rubrorum	G			mp	f	l		
Reynard	B	1859	Robert & Moreau	mp				
Reynier de Toulouse	B			m				
Reynolds Hole	B	1862	Standish & Noble	mp	vdbl	m		
Reynolds Hole	HP	Pre 1870		mr	f	l		
Reynolds Hole	HP	1873	Paul G	rb	f	l	vig	f
Rhadamante	G	Pre 1830	Racine					
Rhadamis(te)	Ch	Pre 1834		dp	f	s		
Rheingold	T	1889	Lambert	my				
Rhodante	B	1859	Guillot Père	mr	f	l	vig	
Rhum of Thalwitz	HP	see	Ruhm von Thalwitz					
Riante	G		Miellez	mr				
Richard Laxton	HP	1877	Laxton	mr	f	l	vig	
Richard Lenoir	HP	1863	Robert & Moreau	dr				
Richard Smith	HP	1853	Roussel	rb	dbl		vig	vf
			syn Général Jacqueminot					
Richard Smith	HP	1861	Verdier E	dr	vf	m		
Richard Wagner	T	1892	Türke	y				
Richard Wallace	HP	1871	Lévêque	mp	f	l	m	f
Richelieu	HCh	1845	Verdier V	m	vdbl	l		
Richelieu	B	Pre 1846	Duval	mr				
Richer	N		Laffay	rb	f	s		
Richesse	G			lp	f	m		
Richesse de Couleur	HP	1861	Touvais	dr		l	vig	
Richter	G			dr	f	m		
Riégo	HCh	1831	Vibert	dp	f	l	vvig	vf
Rien Ne Me Surpasse	G	Pre 1830	Miellez	mr	f	m		
Rigoletto	B	1890	Geschwind	dr				
Rigoulot	G		Rigoulot	lp	f	vl	vig	
Ritay	HCh		Laffay	mp	f	m		
Rival de Paestum	T	1841	Béluze	w	dbl	l	m	f
Rival de Paestum	HCh	Pre 1848	Paul G	w	s-d	m	m	sf
Rivers	HP	1832	Laffay M	mr	dbl	l	vig	
Rivers, Climbing	HArv			lp	f	m		
Rivers' George IV	HCh	1830	Rivers	dr	dbl		vig	
Rivers' Musk Cluster	HMsk	Pre 1846	Rivers	mp	dbl	s		vf
Rivers' Queen	Misc	Pre 1846		dp				
Rivers' Single Crimson Moss	M	Pre 1838	Rivers	dr	s to s-d	l		
Rivers' Super Tuscan	G	Pre 1837	Rivers	m	s-d	l		
			syn Tuscany Superb					
Robert	HP	1856	Robert	pb	dbl	m		
Robert Bruce	T	Pre 1846		w	f	l		f
Robert Bruce	HP	1850	Paul A	mr		m	vig	
Robert Burns	HP			mr				
Robert de Brie	HP	1860	Granger	lp	dbl	l		
Robert Duncan	HP	1897	Dickson A	pb	vdbl	l	vig	m
Robert Fortune	M	1853	Robert	m	f	m		
Robert Fortune	HP	1861	Ducher	mp	f	m	m	
Robert Lebaudy	HP	1895	Lévêque	dr				
Robert le Diable	G/C	Pre 1837		m	f	m		m
Robert le Diable	T			lp	f	l	vig	
Robert Marnock	HP	1878	Paul G	r	f	l	vig	
Robert Perpétuel	P	1856	Robert	m	dbl	m		
Robert Pourtac	M			lp				
Robert Wace	HP	1849	Oger	mr	f	m	vvig	
Robin	B			mr	f	m		
Robin	C			mr				
Robin Hood	HP	Pre 1850		mr	f	l	vvig	vf
Robusta	B	1877	Soupert & Notting	mr	f	l	vvig	vf

Rochambeau	B	1862	Robert & Moreau	mp	vdbl	m	vvig	
Rochambeau	HP		Plantier	mr	f	l	wk	
Rochebrun (e)	HP	1863	Pradel	lp				
Roch-Fouchard (Roche Fouchard)	HP	1854	Robert	mp	f	m	vvig	
Roch Plantier	HP	Pre 1846		mr				
Roeser	HCh		Roeser	lp	f	l	vig	
Roeser	HSpn	Pre 1846		mr	f	m		
Roger Lambelin	HP	1890	Schwartz Vve	rb	dbl	m	vig	vf
Roi Blanc	P		syn Blanche du Roi	w	f	m		
Roi Couronné	G	Pre 1830	syn Couronne Royale	mp	f	m		
Roi d'Angleterre	G	Pre 1830	Prévost	m	vf	m		
			syn Duc de Berry					
Roi d'Angleterre	G	Pre 1830	Margat Jeune	mr	vf	s-m		
Roi d'Angleterre	Ch	Pre 1846		mr				
Roi David	HP	1861	Oger	dr	f	l		
Roi de Bavière	HP	1857		mr	f	m	m	
Roi de Hollande	G/Ch	Pre 1834		dr	f	m		
Roi de Hongrie	G	Pre 1830	Miellez	dp		m		
Roi de Naples	G	Pre 1830						
Roi de Perse	C	Pre 1820	Prévost	lp	f	s		
		syn	Petite Junon de Holla-	nde				
Roi de Perse	G		Prévost	mr	vdbl	m		
Roi de Rome	G	Pre 1820	Prévost	mp	f	m		
		syn	Nouveau Triomphe					
Roi de Rome	G	Pre 1824	Prévost	lp	f	s-m		
			syn Enfant de France					
Roi de Saxe	T			mp	s-d	m		
Roi de Saxe	Ch		Laffay	dp	vf	m		
Roi de Siam	T	1825	Laffay	lp	s-d	l		m
			syn Le Roi de Siam					
Roi des Aunes	S	1885	Geschwind	dp	f	l	vvig	
Roi des Belges	HT			lp	f	l		
Roi des Belges	G		syn Superbe en Brun	r				
Roi des Belges	Ch		syn Fragolette	lp	f	l		
Roi des Blanches	Bks			w	s-d	s		
Roi des Écarlates	G			mr	f	m		
Roi des Hybrides	HCh	1826	Lecomte	lp	vf	m		
Roi des Pays-Bas	D	Pre 1826		mp	vdbl	l		
Roi des Pourpres	P	Aft 1810	Descemet	dp	f	m		
			syn Magador					
Roi des Pourpres	G	Pre 1817	Descemet	dr	vdbl	s		
Roi des Quatre Saisons	D			lp				
Roi des Roses	G	Pre 1830	Vibert	mp	f	m-l		
Roi d'Espagne	HP	1854	Fontaine	mr	f	l	vig	
Roi d'Italie	T			w	f	m		
Roi d'Yvetot	Ch		Laffay	mp	dbl	l		
Roi Feu	G	Pre 1830	Prévost	mr	s-d	m		
Roi François d'Assise d'Espagne	HP	1887	Lévêque	mr	f	l	vig	
Roi Maximilian de Bavière	HP	1857	Touvais	m	f	m		
Roi Pourpre	HCh		syn Crimson Superbe	mr	f	m		
Roland Delattre	G		Parmentier	mp	f	m		
Romain	T	Pre 1846		w	f	l		f
Romain Desprez	B	Pre 1835	Desprez	mr	f	m	vig	
Romelia	Ch		Laffay	lp	f	s		
Romélie	Ch		Laffay	mr				
Romeo	Ch	Pre 1846		dr	f	m		
Romulus	G			mr		m-l		
Ronald's China	Ch	Pre 1846						
Ronald's White	Ch	Pre 1846		w				
Ronce d'Autriche	Sp	1542	Hermann syn r.foetida	my	s			m
Ronsart	HP	1847	Vibert	mr	f	m		
Rosa abyssinica	Sp	1814		w				m
Rosa acicularis	Sp	1805	Lindley	dp			vig	m
Rosa acicularis nipponensis	Sp	1894	Koehne	dp	s			
Rosa acicularis sayi	Sp	c 1834	Rehder	m		l		
Rosa agrestis	Sp	c 1878	Savi	lp	s			
Rosa alba	Sp	Pre 1600	see Alba and	w	s	m		m
			White Rose of York					
Rosa albertii	Sp	1877	Regel	w				
Rosa andreae	Sp	1874	Lange					
Rosa anemoneflora	Sp	1844	Fortune	w	vdbl			
Rosa arkansana	Sp	1880	Porter	mp				
Rosa arvensis	Sp	Pre 1762	Hudson	w	s			sf
Rosa asperrima	Sp	Pre 1885	Godet	mp	s			
Rosa banksiae banksiae	Sp	1807	Aiton	w	dbl	s		sf
Rosa banksiae lutea	Sp	c 1824	Rehder	ly	dbl	s	vig	sf
Rosa banksiae lutescens	Spn	c 1816	Voss	my	s	s		sf
Rosa banksiae normalis	Sp	c 1877	Regel	w	s	s		sf
Rosa barbierana	HWich	Pre 1900	Barbier	rb	s			
Rosa beggeriana	Sp	1881	Schrenk	w		s		f
Rosa beggeriana anserinifolia	Sp	Pre 1886	Regel	w				
Rosa blanda	Sp	1773	Aiton	mp	s			

Name	Type	Date	Authority / Synonym					
Rosa blanda glandulosa	Sp	1898	Schuette	mp				
Rosa Bonheur	M	1852	Laffay	mp	f	l	m	
Rosa Bonheur	HP	1871	Fontaine	mr				
Rosa bracteata	Sp	1793	Macartney	w	s	l		f
Rosa bridgesii	Sp	1896		mp				
Rosa brunonii	Sp	1822	Lindley	w	s		vvig	
Rosa californica	Sp	1878	Chamisso & Schlechtendahl	mp	s			
Rosa californica plena	S	1894	Rehder	mp	s-d			
Rosa canina	Sp	Pre 1737	Linnaeus	lp	s		vig	f
Rosa canina andegavensis	Sp	1809	Desportes	mp				f
Rosa canina blondaeana	Sp	1861	Rouy	w				
Rosa canina froebelii	Sp	1890	Christ	w		s		
Rosa Capreolata	Misc	Pre 1846			s			
Rosa carolina	Sp	1826	Linnaeus	mp				
Rosa carolina alba	Sp	1880	Rehder	w	s			
Rosa carolina villosa	Sp	1887	Rehder	mp				
Rosa caudata	Sp	c 1896	Baker	mr	s			sf
Rosa centifolia batavica	C	1583	Clusius	dp				
Rosa centifolia bipinnata	C	Pre 1802	Thory	lp	f	m		
Roas centifolia carnea	C	Pre 1820		lp		m		
Rosa centifolia muscosa	C	Pre 1596	syn Communis	mp	vdbl	vl	vig	f
Rosa centifolia muscosa alba	C	Pre 1820		w	dbl	l		
Rosa centifolia mousseux	C	1727	Miller					
Rosa centifolia simplex	C	Pre 1820		dp		l		
Rosa centifolia semi-plena	C	Pre 1820		dp	f	l		
Rosa chinensis	Sp	Pre 1759	Jacquin	mr	s to s-d			
Rosa chinensis longifolia	Sp	1820	Voss	dp	s			
Rosa chinensis minima	Sp	1815	Voss	w	s-d			
Rosa chinensis spontanea	Ch	1885	Rehder & Wilson	dr	s	m	m	
Rosa cinnamomea	Sp	Pre 1600	Linnaeus	lp	vdbl	s		m
Rosa clinophylla	Sp	Pre 1817	Thory	w		vl		
Rosa collina	Misc	Pre 1788	Jacquin	mp				
Rosa coriifolia	Sp	1878	Fries	lp				
Rosa corymbifera	Sp	1838	Berghausen	w				
Rosa corymbosa	Sp	Pre 1830	Lahaye	mp	s-d	m		
Rosa damascena	Sp	Pre50BC		lp	dbl	m		vf
Rosa damascena carnea	Sp	Pre 1821		lp		l		sf
Rosa dumalis	Sp	1872	Bechstein	lp	s			
Rosa ecae	Sp	1880	Aitchison	dy	s	s		
Rosa eglanteria	Sp	Pre 1551	Linnaeus syn r.rubiginosa	lp	s			f
Rosa elasmacantha	Sp	1858	Trautvetter	my				
Rosa elymaitica	Sp	1867	Boisser&Haussknecht	mp		s		
Rosa x engelmannii	Misc	1891	Watson	dp				
Rosa farreri persetosa	Sp	Pre 1900	Stapf	mp				
Rosa fedtschenkoana	Sp	1876	Regel	w	s			
Rosa foetida	Sp	Pre 1542	Hermann	my	s			m
Rosa foetida bicolor	Sp	c 1596	Jacquin	rb	s			
Rosa foetida persiana	Sp	1837	Rehder	my	dbl			
Rosa foliolosa	Sp	c 1880	Nuttall	mp				
Rosa x francofurtana	Sp	Pre 1583	Clusius	m	s-d			
Rosa gallica	Sp	Pre 1500	Linnaeus	dp			m	
Rosa gallica officinalis	Sp	c 1200		dp	s-d			m
Rosa gallica pumila	Sp	Pre 1824	Seringe	dp	s			
Rosa gallica versicolor	Sp	Pre 1581	Linnaeus	pb	s-d			m
Rosa gigantea	Sp	1889	Collett	w	s		vig	m
Rosa giraldii	Sp	1897	Crépin	pb	s			
Rosa glauca	Sp	1789	syn r.rubifolia	mp				
Rosa glutinosa	Sp	1821	Sibthorp & Smith	w		s		m
Rosa glutinosa dalmatica	Sp	1882	Kerner	mp				
Rosa gymnocarpa	Sp	1893	Nuttall	lp	s			
Rosa Hardy	HMac		Hardy	my	s	m		
Rosa hemisphaerica	Sp	c 1600	Herrmann	my	s			
Rosa horrida	Sp	1796	Fischer	w				
Rosa hugonis	Sp	Pre 1899	Hemsley	my	s	m		
Rosa Inermis Albo Sub-Viridis	A	Pre 1830	syn Pompon à Coeur Vert	w	f	s		
Rosa Inermis Morleti	N	1883	Morlet Père & Fils	lp	s-d		vvig	
Rosa inodora	Sp	1875	Fries	w				
Rosa x involuta	Misc	Pre 1800	Smith	lp	s		m	
Rosa x involuta wilsonii	Misc	Pre 1863	Baker				vig	
Rosa x kochiana	S	Pre 1869	Koehne	dp				
Rosa x koehneana	S	Pre 1893	Rehder	m				
Rosa kotschyana	Sp	Pre 1885	Boisser					
Rosa laevigata	Sp	1759	Michaux	w	s			m
Rosa laxa	Sp	1803	Retzius	w	s	s	vig	
Rosa leschenaultii	Sp	1830	Wight & Arnott	w				
Rosa luciae	Sp	1880	Franchet&Rochebrune	w				
Rosa macounii	Sp	1826	Greene	lp	s	s	sp	
Rosa macrocarpa	Sp	1882		ly				
Rosa macrophylla	Sp	1818	Lindley	dp	s		vig	
Rosa majalis	Sp	1596	Herrmann	m	dbl			m

Rosa marginata	Sp	1870	Wallroth	lp			vig	
Rosa maximowicziana	Sp	1880	Regel	w				
Rosa micrantha	Sp	Pre 1800	Borrer	lp		s	vvig	
Rosa microphylla	Sp	1820	syn r.roxburghii plena	lp		m		
Rosa minutifolia	Sp	1882	Engelmann	p or w				
Rosa mollis	Sp	1818	Smith	dp	s			
Rosa Monnet	HP	1885	Monnet	dp				m
		syn	Madame Rosa Monnet					
Rosa montana	Sp	1872	Chaix	lp			vig	
Rosa montezumae	Sp	1825	Humboldt&Bonpland	dp	s			
Rosa monticola	Sp	Pre 1794	Aiton	dp				
Rosa moschata	Sp	1540	Herrmann	w	s-d	m		m
Rosa moschata plena	Sp	Pre 1596		w	dbl			vf
Rosa moyesii	Sp	1896	Hemsley & Wilson	mr	s			
Rosa multiflora	Sp	1784	Thunberg	w				
Rosa multiflora alba	Sp	1844		w	vdbl	m		
Rosa multiflora calva	Sp	Pre 1900	Frachet & Savatier	w				
Rosa multiflora carnea	Sp	1804	Thory	lp	dbl			
Rosa multiflora nana	Pol	Aft 1875		w	s to s-d	vs		
Rosa Mundi	G	Pre 1581	syn r.gallica versicolor	pb	s-d	m	m	
Rosa Mundi	HP	1864	Ducher	lp	f	l		
Rosa Mundi	T	1898	Conard & Jones	dr		l		
Rosa nitida	Sp	1807	Willdenow	mp	s			
Rosa nivea	Misc	1822	Decandolle / Prévost	w	s	l		
Rosa Nivea	M		Dupont					
			syn Belle Henriette					
Rosa noisettiana	N	1814	Thory (Noisette)	w				
Rosa Nora	HCh	Pre 1830	Vibert	lp	vdbl	m		f
Rosa nutkana	Sp	1876	Presl	mp	s			
Rosa omeiensis	Sp	Pre 1900	Rolfe	w			vig	
Rosa palustris	Sp	1726	Marshall	mp				f
Rosa palustris scandens	Sp	1726		mp	dbl			f
Rosa Pedro Costae	HP	1889	Da Costa	or				
Rosa pendulina	Sp	1753	Linnaeus	dp	s			
Rosa pendulina laevis	Sp	c 1820	Thory	rb	s			
Rosa pendulina oxyodon	Sp	1896	Rehder	mp	s			
Rosa pendulina pyrenaica	Sp	1815	Keller	mp	s			
Rosa pennsylvanica plena	Sp	1803	Marshall	mp	dbl			
Rosa persetosa	Sp	1895	Rolfe	dp	s		vig	
Rosa phoenicia	Sp	c 1885	Boissier	w	s			
Rosa pisocarpa	Sp	1877	Grav	mp	s		wk	
Rosa Plena	Cl		Laffay	lp	f	l		
Rosa punicea	Sp	c 1597	Jacquin	rb	s			
			syn r.foetida bicolor					
Rosa x reversa	Misc	1820	Waldstein & Hitaibel	mr	s			
Rosa richardii	Sp	Pre 400	syn r.sancta	lp	s	m		
Rosa roxburghii	Sp	Pre 1814	Trattinnick	mp	dbl			
Rosa roxburghii hirtula	Sp	Pre 1862	Rehder & Wilson	mp				
Rosa roxburghii normalis	Sp	1864	Rehder & Wilson	lp	s			
Rosa roxburghii plena	Sp	1820	Rehder	lp		m		
Rosa rubiginosa	Sp	Pre 1551	Linnaeus	lp	s			
Rosa rubiginosa aculeatissima	Sp	Pre 1830	Thory	p	s			
Rosa rubiginosa duplex	Sp	Pre 1700		m				vf
Rosa rubrifolia	Sp	1789	Villars	mp				
Rosa rudicaulis	Misc	Pre 1830	Vibert	lp	f	m		
Rosa rugosa	Sp	1784	Thunberg	m				
Rosa rugosa alba	Sp	1784	Rehder	w	s	l		
Rosa rugosa plena	Sp	c 1880	Byhouwer	m	dbl			
Rosa sancta	Sp	Pre 400		lp	s	m		
Rosa sempervirens	Sp	1629	Linnaeus	w	s		vig	m
Rosa sempervirens latifolia	Sp	Pre 1824	Thory	w				
Rosa sempervirens scandens	Sp	Pre 1750	De Candolle	w				vf
Rosa sericea	Sp	1820	Lindley	w	s		vig	
Rosa sericea pteracantha	Sp	1890	Franchet	w	s		vig	m
Rosa setigera	Sp	1810	Michaux	dp	s			
Rosa setigera tomentosa	Sp	1811	Torrey & Gray	dp		s		
Rosa setipoda	Sp	1895	Hemsley & Wilson	lp	s			
Rosa sicula	Sp	Pre 1894	Trattinnick	lp		s		
Rosa soulieana	Sp	1896	Crépin	w	s			
Rosa spinosissima	Sp	Pre 1600	Linnaeus	w	s			
Rosa spinosissima altaica	Sp	c 1820	Bean	w	s			
Rosa spinosissima bicolor	Sp	Pre 1832	Andrews	pb	s-d			
Rosa spinosissima ciphana	Sp	1684	Siebold	pb				
Rosa spinosissima hispida	Sp	Pre 1781	Koehne	my			vig	
Rosa spinosissima myriacantha	Sp	Pre 1820	Koehne	w		s		
Rosa x spinulifolia	Sp	Pre 1805	Dematra	mp	s			
Rosa Sphamea	Sp	1885	Watson	mp	s	s		
Rosa stellata	Sp	1897	Wooton	m				
Rosa stylosa	Sp	1838	Desvaux	w				
Rosa tomentosa	Sp	1820	Smith	lp				
Rosa tomentosa subglobosa	Sp	1824	Smith	lp				
Rosa velutinaeflora	Sp	Pre 1872	Déséglise	pb		l		

Rosa villosa	Sp	1771	Linnaeus	mp	s			
Rosa virginiana	Sp	Pre 1724	Miller	mp	s			
Rosa virginiana lamprophylla	Sp	1881	Rehder	mp				
Rosa virginiana plena	Sp	Pre 1759		dp	dbl	s		m
Rosa watsoniana	Sp	c 1870	Crépin	lp	s-d	s		
Rosa webbiana	Sp	1879	Royle	lp		l		
Rosa wichurana	Sp	1886	Crépin	w	s			m
Rosa woodsii	Sp	1820	Lindley	mp	s			
Rosa woodsii fendleri	Sp	1888	Rehder	mp				
Rosa woodsii ultramontana	Sp	1888	Watson	mp				
Rosa xanthina	Sp	1820	Lindley	my	dbl			
Rosa yenoensis	HMult	1832	Siebold syn Iwara	w	s			
Rosalba	HCh			mp	f	s		
Rosalba	G	1829	Vibert	mp		l		
Rosalie	D		Hardy	mp				
Rosalie	M			mp	vdbl	l		
Rosalie	C	Pre 1811	Vilmorin syn Unique Carnée	lp	f	l		m
Rosalie	T	1884	Ellwanger & Barry	mp	vf	m		m
Rosalie de Wincop	HP	1881	Vigneron	mp	f	l	vig	
Rosamonde	G	Pre 1846	Robert	mp	f	m		
Rosaria Castel	T	1892	Pries	lp				
Rose	N		Nicolle	p				
Rose	P		Poilpré	p				
Rose	HMult			lp	s-d	m		
Rose	HSpn	Pre 1834		lp	s-d	s		
Rose	T	Pre 1834	Guérin	lp		m		
Rose à Bois Jaspé	S	1876	Brassac	mr	f	l		
Rose à Cent Feuilles	C	Pre 1596	syn Cabbage Rose	mp	vdbl	m-l		m
Rose à Feuilles de Laitue	C	1815	Duhamel syn Bullata	mp	vdbl	l		
Rose à Feuilles Luisantes	M	1843	Vibert see À Feuilles Luisantes	lp	f	m		f
Rose à Longs Pédoncules	N	1825		r	dbl	m		
Rose à Mille Fleurs	Misc	Pre 1846						
Rose à Parfum de Grasse	D	Pre 1867		mp	dbl	m		vf
Rose Angle	Ayr	Pre 1838	Martin	mp	s-d		vvig	fol vf
Rose Apples	HRg	1895	Paul	dp	s-d	l	vig	m
Rose Ayez	HSem	Pre 1832	Jacques (?) / Vibert syn Spectabilis	m	dbl	m	vig	vf
Rose Bleu	G	Pre 1790	syn Charles de Mills	dr	vdbl	m		sf
Rose Bleu	G	c 1810	Descemet / Vibert	m	f	m		
Rose Bordée de Blanc	C	c 1810	Descemet syn Comtesse de Chamois	mp				
Rose Bradwardine	HEg	1894	Penzance	mp	s	s	vig	fol vf
Rose Brillante	G	c 1810	Descemet syn Brillante	mp	f	l		
Rose Buffon	P	Pre 1821	syn Buffon	lp	vdbl	l		
Rose-Button	P	Pre 1830	syn La Gracieuse	lp	vf	m		f
Rose Capucine	Sp	c 1596	Jacquin syn r.foetida bicolor	rb	s	m		
Rose Capucine	HEg	Pre 1834		y		m		
Rose Cartier	D	1821	Vibert syn Cartier	mp	vdbl	m	vig	
Rose Cent-Feuilles	C			mp	vf	l	vig	f
Rose Cent-Feuilles Mousseuse	C			mp	vf	m		vf
Rose Charmeux	HP	1874	Gautreau	dr	f	m	m	
Rose Châtaigne	Sp	Pre 1814	Traittinnick syn r.roxburghii	mp	dbl			
Rose Chou de Hollande	C	Pre 1596	syn Cabbage Rose	mp	vdbl	l		m
Rose Cornet	HP	1845	Lacharme F syn Cornet	m	vdbl	vl	vig	m
Rose d'Amour	Misc	Pre 1759		dp	dbl	s		m
Rose d'Anjou	T	Pre 1830	Vibert	dp	dbl	l		sf
Rose d'Anjou	N	Pre 1834		lp		s		
Rose de Batavie	C	Pre 1596	syn Cabbage Rose	mp	vdbl	l		m
Rose de Bengale	Ch	Pre 1818	syn Sanguinea	dr	dbl		wk	
Rose de Brown	HCh	Pre 1834		lp		l		
Rose de Dijon	C	1789	Sweet syn Rose de Meaux	dp	vdbl	s		m
Rose de France	Sp	Pre 1500	syn r.gallica	dp		l	m	
Rose de France	HP	1893	Verdier E	mp	f	m-l		
Rose de Gréville	HMult		Laffay	w	s	s		
Rose de Jessaint	C		Girardon	mp	f	l	vig	f
Rose de Juno	C	Pre 1846		lp				
Rose de la Floride	Bslt	Pre 1824	Vibert syn Blush Boursault	lp	vdbl	vl	vvig	
Rose de la Maître d'École	G	1831	Coquerau	m	dbl	vl		
Rose de la Reine	G	1817	Vibert	lp	f	m		
Rose de la Reine	HP	1841	Laffay	mp	vdbl	vl		
Rose de l'Hymen	A	Pre 1770	syn Plena	w	s-d			
Rose de l'Ile-Bourbon	B	Pre 1834		dp		m		

Name	Class	Date	Breeder / syn				
Rose de l'Ile-Bourbon à FleursDoubles	B	Pre 1834		mp	dbl	m	
Rose de Mai	Sp	1596	Hermann syn r.majalis	mp	dbl	s		m
Rose de Meaux	C	1789	Sweet syn De Meaux	dp	vdbl	s		m
Rose de Meaux White	C	Pre 1799	Sweet	w			
Rose de Nancy	C	Pre 1834		dp		l	
Rose de Pâques	Sp	1596	Hermann syn r.majalis	m	dbl			m
Rose de Portugal	P						
Rose de Puebla	HP	1867	Fontaine syn François Fontaine	mr	f	m	
Rose de Rescht	P	c 1880		dp	vdbl		vig	vf
Rose de Schelfhout	G	1840	Parmentier	lp	f			m
Rose de Trianon	P	c 1830	Vibert	mp	dbl	m	vig
Rose de Trianon Double	P	1847	Vibert syn Adèle Mauzé	lp	f	m-l	
Rose de Van Huysum	D	Pre 1817	syn Celsiana	lp	s-d	l	vig	m
Rose de Virginie	Sp	Pre 1830	Lindley syn r.virginiana	mp	s		
Rose des Alpes	Sp	1753	Linnaeus syn r.pendulina	dp	s		
Rose des Alpes, sans Épines	G	Pre 1830	syn Rose Pavot	mp	dbl	m	
Rose des Parfumeurs	D	Pre 1826	Jamain syn Rose du Puteaux	mp	dbl	m		m
Rose des Peintres	C	Pre 1806		mp	f	vl	vig	f
Rose des Peintres, Blanche	A	Pre 1830		w			
Rose des Quatre Saisons	D	Pre 1849	syn Autumn Damask	mp	dbl	m	vvig	m
Rose d'Est	HCh	Pre 1830					
Rose d'Evian	T	1895	Bernaix A	pb	vdbl	vl	vig
Rose d'Herbeys	T	1897	Guillot syn Souvenir de J B Guillot	or	f	l	
Rose d'Italie	D	Pre 1812	Godefroy	lp	dbl	m		f
Rose d'Italie, Blanche	D	1812	Carlet / Coquerel syn D'Italie for both	w	dbl	m		f
Rose Double	N	1825	Vibert	lp		s	
Rose du Luxembourg	T	Pre 1846		mp			
Rose du Maître d'École	G	see	Rose de la Maître d'Éc ole				
Rose du Puteaux	D	Pre 1826	Jamain	mp	dbl	m		m
Rose du Roi	P	1815	Lelieur-Souchet syn Lelieur	mr	s-d	m	vig	vf
Rose du Roi	G	Pre 1830	(Holland)	lp	f	m	
Rose du Roi à Fleurs Blanches	D	1849	Dubois syn Celina Dubois	w				vf
Rose du Roi à Fleurs Pourpres	HP	1819		dr	f	m	
Rose du Roi Panachée	P	Pre 1848	syn Panachée de Lyon	pb	dbl	m	m	vf
Rose du Roi Strié	P	Pre 1843	syn Capitaine Rénard	pb	vf	l	
Rose du Saint Sacrament	Sp	1596	Hermann syn r.majalis	m	dbl	s	vig	f
Rose du Serail	G	Pre 1801	syn La Belle Sultane	dr	s-d	m	
Rose Dubreuil	B	1818	Perichon/Neumann syn Rose Edouard	mp	dbl	s	vig	f
Rose d'York	A	Pre 1818	Miellez syn Duc d'York	w	dbl	l	
Rose Edenberger	A						
Rose Edouard	B	1818	Perichon / Neumann	mp	dbl	s	vig	f
Rose Edward	B	1817	syn Bourbon Rose	dp	s-d		vig	m
Rose et Blanche	HP	1852	Oger	w	s-d	m	
Rose Feu	G		Trébucien	dp			
Rose Foncé	HMult		syn Coccinée	mp			
Rose Foncé	M	Pre 1777	syn Rubra	mr	dbl	m	
Rose Foncé Pleine	M		syn Des Peintres	mp			
Rose Fortuné	Bks			w	vf	m	
Rose Foucheaux	G	Pre 1846	syn Foucheaux	mr	f	m	
Rose Frisée	HSpn	1826	Toutain				
Rose Impératrice	HP	1871	Garçon				
Rose Jacques	B	1821	Breon/Jacques syn Rosier de Bourbon	dp	s-d	m	
Rose Jay	HEg	Pre 1824	Descemet syn Clémentine	pb	s-d	m	
Rose Lée	G	c 1825	Vetillart syn Léa	dp	f	l	
Rose Lelieur	P	c 1819	Souchet or Ecoffé syn Rose du Roi	mr	s-d	l	vig	vf
Rose Marguerite	G	Pre 1821	Steigerhoek syn Tricolore	rb	f	s	
Rose Mauve	G	Pre 1811	syn Bourbon	pb	s-d	m		m
Rose Mayet	Misc	1821					
Rose Menoux	B	Pre 1846		mr	vdbl		
Rose Mille	A	1826	Cartier	w	f	m	
Rose Mousseuse Ordinaire	M	Pre 1720	syn Communis	mp	dbl	l	
Rose Multiple	HSpn		Prévost	p			
Rose Nabonnand	T	1883	Nabonnand G	pb	f	l	vvig	vf
Rose Neumann	B	1818	Perichon/Neumann syn Rose Edouard	mp	dbl	s		m

Name	Type	Date	Raiser / syn					
Rose Oeillet de Saint Arquey (Vilfroy)	Ch	1831	Jacques	pb	f	m		sf
			syn Serratipetala					
Rose of Castile	D	Pre 1600	syn Summer Damask	lp	dbl	m		vf
Rose of Love	Sp	Pre 1824	Seringe	dp	s			
			syn r.gallica pumila					
Rose of Miletos	Sp	Pre 1500	Linnaeus syn r.gallica	dp		m		
Rose of Paestum	D	Pre 1600	syn Summer Damask	lp	dbl	m		vf
Rose of Provence	C	Pre 1596	syn Cabbage Rose	mp	vdbl	l		m
Rose of Provins	Sp	Pre 1500	Linnaeus syn r.gallica	dp		m		
Rose of Provins	Sp	Pre 1600	Thory	dp	s-d			m
			syn r.gallica officinalis					
Rose of Rhone	C	Pre 1596	syn Cabbage Rose	mp	vdbl	l		m
Rose of Rove	C	Pre 1596	syn Cabbage Rose	mp	vdbl	l		m
Rose of the Tombs	S	Pre 1867	syn Saint John's Rose	lp	s	m		
Rose Pavot	S	Pre 1799		dp	dbl	m-l		
		syn	Grosse Mohnkopfs Rose					
Rose Pavot	G	Pre 1830	Lahaye Père	mp	dbl	m		
Rose Pluton	G	1843	Vibert syn Pluton	m	f	m		
Rose Prolifère	C	Pre 1824		mp		l		vf
		syn	Prolifera de Redoute					
Rose Renoncule	G	1820	Godefroy	mr	vf	s-m		
			syn Renoncule Rouge					
Rose Romarin	T	1888	Nabonnand					
Rose Schelfhout	G	Pre 1847	Parmentier	lp	dbl	m		
			syn De Schelfhout					
Rose Simple	Ch			p				
Rose Tendre Incarnata	Misc	Pre 1846		lp				
Rose Tulipe	HFt	Pre 1817	Dupont / Noisette	yb				
Rose Unique	C	1775	Grimwood	w	dbl	l		m
			syn White Provence					
Rose van Sian	G	Pre1847	Parmentier	m	vdbl	s		
			Cardinal de Richelieu					
Rose Verreux	D	Pre 1848		dp	f	m		
Rose Verte	A	Pre 1830		w	f	s		
		syn	Pompon à Coeur Vert					
Rose Virginale	Misc	1846		lp				
Rosea	G	Pre 1811	syn Gallica Alba	w	dbl		m	m
Rosea	Bslt	1824	Boursault	lp				
Rosea	HBc	Pre 1840						
Rosea	Bks	Pre 1846		mp				
Rosea	HMcr	Pre 1846		mp	s			
Rosea Flora	HP	1877	Lemée	mp	vf	m	wk	
Rosea Grandiflora	HSpn	1861	Freundlich	p				
Rosea Major	HSem	Pre 1846		lp				
Rosea Plena	HSem	Pre 1888	Laffay	w	vdbl	l		
Rosea Pulchella	HSpn	1861	Freundlich	p				
Rosée du Matin	A	Pre 1810	syn Chloris & Elisa	lp				
Rosella	G	Pre 1830	Racine	lp	f	m-l		
Rosemary	G	1842	Vibert	m	f	l		
Rosemonde	Sp	Pre 1581	Linnaeus	pb	s-d			m
			syn r.gallica versicolor					
Rosemonde (?as above)	D	1825	Toutain	pb				
Rosenberg	A	Pre 1813	syn Beauté Tendre	lp	f	vl		
Rosette de la Légion d'Honneur	HT	1896	Bonnaire	op	s-d	m		
Rosier à Feuilles de Pimprenelle	Sp	Pre 1600	Linnaeus	w	s	s-m		
			syn r.spinosissima					
Rosier à Fruit	Sp	1771	Linnaeus syn r.villosa	mp	s	s-m		
Rosier-Corail sans Épines	Sp	Pre 1724	Miller syn r.virginiana	mp	s	s-m		
Rosier d'Amérique	Sp	1810	Michaux syn r.setigera	dp	s	s-m		
Rosier d'Amérique à Feuilles de Grand	Sp	Pre 1724	Miller	mp	s	s-m		
Pimprenelle			syn r.virginiana					
Rosier d'Amour	G	Pre 1806	Crantz (?)	m	s	l		m
Rosier d'Autriche	G	Pre 1806	Crantz (?)	m	s	l		m
			syn Rosier d'Amour					
Rosier de Bourgogne à Grandes Fleurs	C	Pre 1791	syn Petite de Hollande	mp	dbl	s		m
Rosier de Bourgon	B	1821	Breon / Jacques	dp	s-d	m		
Rosier de Crète	Sp	1821	Smith	lp	s	s		f
			syn r.glutinosa					
Rosier de Damas	D	1840		mp	dbl	m		m
Rosier de Grèce	Sp	Pre 1551	syn r.rubignosa	lp	s			
Rosier de la Carolina	Sp	Pre 1830	Lindley	lp	s			
Rosier de la Chine	Sp	1803	Michaux	w	s			m
			syn r.laevigata					
Rosier de la Malmaison	P	Pre 1815	Dupont	dp	s-d	m		m
		syn	Quatre Saisons d'Italie					
Rosier de Normandie	B	1853	Paul A syn Vivid	m	dbl	s-m	vig	m
Rosier de Philippe Noisette	N	1814	Noisette	w				
		syn	r x noisettiana(Thory)					
Rosier de Portland	P	c 1770		mr	s-d	l	m	m

Name	Class	Date	Raiser / synonym					
			syn Duchess of Portland					
Rosier de Thionville	M	1835	Laffay M	w	dbl	m	m	
			syn Quatre Saisons Blanc Mousseux					
Rosier des Dames	C	Pre 1791	syn Petite de Hollande	mp	dbl	s		m
Rosier des Marais	Sp	1726	Marshall syn r.palustris	mp	s			
Rosier des Pyrénées	Alp	Pre 1830		mp	s			
Rosier des Quatre Saisons	D	Pre 1849	syn Autumn Damask	mp	dbl			m
Rosier des Turcs	Sp	Pre 1503	Hermann	my	s	s		
			syn r.hemispherica					
Rosier du Bengale	Ch	1790	Slater	mr	dbl		m	
			syn Slater's Crimson China					
Rosier Glutineux	Sp	1821	Smith	lp	s	s		
			syn Rosier de Crète					
Rosier Jaune	Sp	Pre 1542	Hermann syn r.foetida	my	s			m
Rosier Jaune, Simple	HSpn	1823	Vibert	ly	s			
Rosier Lisse	Sp	1803	Michaux	w	s			m
			syn r.laevigata					
Rosier Mousseux	M	Pre 1720	syn Communis	mp	dbl	l		
Rosier Muscade d'Alexandria	Sp	1540	Hermann	w	s-d			m
			syn r.moschata					
Rosier Panaché d'Angleterre	D	Pre 1867	syn York & Lancaster	pb	dbl			m
Rosier Petit à Cent Feuilles	C	Pre 1791	syn Petite de Hollande	mp	dbl	s		m
Rosier Ponceau	Sp	c 1596	Jacquin	rb	s			
			syn r.foetida bicolor					
Rosier sans Épines des Alpes	Sp	1753	Linnaeus	dp	s	s		
			syn r.pendulina					
Rosière d'Enghein	B	1875	Dallemagne	lp		s	vvig	
Rosiériste Chauvry	HP	1885	Gonod	mr	f	l		
Rosiériste Harms	HP	1879	Verdier E	mr	f	l	vig	f
Rosiériste Jacobs	HP	1880	Ducher Vve	mr	f	l	vig	
			syn Duke of Wellington					
Rosiériste Max Singer	HMult	1885	Lacharme F	dr	dbl	m	vig	m
Rosine Barron	HP	1860	Fontaine	mr	f	m		
Rosine Dupont	HCh		Jacques	w	vf	m		
Rosine Margottin	HP	1849	Margottin	lp	f	m		m
Rosine Navaux	HP	1864	Fontaine	dp	f	l		
Rosine Parron	HP	Pre 1870		mr	f	l		
Rosinella	M	Pre 1846		mr	f	m	vvig	
Rosomane Alix Huguier	HT	1895	Bonnaire	w	f	vl	m	
Rosomane Gravereaux	HT	1899	Soupert & Notting	w	vf	vl		
Rosomane Hubert	T	1883	Bernède	dy			vvig	
Rossy	N							
Rosy Morn	HP	1878	Paul W	op	f	vl	vvig	sf
Rothanger	N	Pre 1846		mp	f	m	wk	
Rote Hermosa	Ch	1899	Geissler	mr	dbl	m		m
Rotkäppchen	Pol	1887	Geschwind R	mr	vdbl	m		sf
Rotrou	M	1848	Vibert	m	dbl	m		
Rouge	C	Pre 1629	syn Rubra (C)	mr	dbl	m		sf
Rouge	M	Pre 1777	syn Rubra (M)	mr	dbl	m		
Rouge	D	Pre 1789	syn Red Damask	mr	dbl	m		vf
Rouge	HSpn	c 1808	Descemet	mp	dbl	m		
Rouge	T	1822	Laffay					
Rouge	T	Pre 1830	Nicolle	mr	vf	m-l		f
Rouge	HMult	Pre 1830	Pronville	mp	vdbl	s		
			syn Multiflore Rose Foncé					
Rouge	HCh	Pre 1836	syn Jenny	dr				
Rouge	HBc			mp				
Rouge	Pom			mr				
Rouge	T	1875	Touvais	mr	f	m	vig	
Rouge Admirable	G	Pre 1811	syn Pourpre Charmant	mr	dbl	l		m
Rouge Admirable	G	Pre 1826	Vibert	m	f	l		
			syn Orphise					
Rouge Admirable de Bastien	G			mr	f	l		
Rouge Admirable Striée	G/C	Pre 1831	Vibert	m		l		
Rouge Agréable	G	Pre 1811	Dupont syn Junon	dp	f	l		sf
Rouge à Petites Feuilles	HMult		Laffay	mp				
Rouse Ardoisé	G	Pre 1830	Calvert	mr		l		
Rouge Brillant	G	Pre 1830	Vibert	mr	f	m		
			syn Soleil Naissant					
Rouge Captain Christy	HT	1898	Perrier	dp				
Rouge de Belgique	G	Pre 1791		mr	dbl	l		
Rouge Éblouissant	G	1823	Delaâge	dr	dbl	l		sf
			syn Assemblage de Beauté					
Rouge Éblouissant	G	Pre 1830	Vibert	mr	f	m		
Rouge Éclatant	G			rb	f	m		
Rouge Élégante	G			mr				
Rouge Favorite	G			mr				
Rouge Formidable	G	Pre 1811		mr	vdbl	m		
Rouge Gloriante	G			dr				
Rouge Marbrée	HP	Pre 1870		mr	vdbl	l		
Rouge Marbrée	B			ob				
Rouge Plein	Pom	1826	Laffay					

Name	Class	Date	Breeder / Syn					
Rouge Pleine	HRg	syn	Kaiserin des Norden	lp				
Rouge Pleine	Ayr		syn Miller's Climbing and Rubra Plena	dp				
Rouge Pourpre	HMult			mr				
Rouge Rayé	G	Pre 1810	Descemet syn Beauté Tendre	dp	vdbl	l		
Rouge Renommé Superbe	Pom			mr				
Rouge Striée	HMcr	Pre 1846		mr		l		
Rouge Superbe Actif	G	Pre 1811		dr	vdbl	s		m
Rouge Tendre	D			lp				
Rouge Transparente	Ch			mp	s-d	m		
Rouge Vermeille	G			mr				
Rouge Vif	C	Pre 1811	syn Capricornus	mr	vdbl			
Rouge Violacé	HBc	syn	Violette Cramoisie	mr				
Rougeatre	Misc	Pre 1830	Noisette	mr	s			
Rougeau Virginale	C	1818	Laffay syn Héloïse	lp	f	l		
Rouget de l'Isle	G	1843	Vibert	mp	f	m		
Rougier Chauvière	HP	1890	Liabaud	rb				
Rouillé	HEg			lp				
Rouillé à Fleurs d'Anémones	HEg							
Rouletii	Ch	1815		mp	dbl	s		
Rouletii, Climbing	Cl Ch	c 1839	syn Pompon de Paris,	Clg mp				
Rouppe	G		Parmentier	dp				
Routrou	M	1849	Vibert syn Rotrou	m	dbl	m		
Rovelli Charles	T	1876	Pernet Père	lp	f	l	vig	
Roxburghiana	HMult	Pre 1828	syn Grevilii	w	s			
Roxelana	HCh	c 1825	Prévost syn Roxelane	mp	vdbl	s		
Roxelane	G	1811		dp	s-d			
Roxelane	HCh	c 1825	Prévost	mp	vdbl	s		
Royal	HEg	Pre 1846		lp				
Royal	M			p				
Royal	Pom			p				
Royal Agate	G	Pre 1834		lp		m		
Royal Blush	Misc	Pre 1846		lp				
Royal Bouquet	Misc	Pre 1846						
Royal Cluster	HMult	1899	Dawson	lp	s	s		
Royal Crimson	Misc	Pre 1846		mr				
Royal Epoux	HP	1859	Damaizin	mp	f	l	m	
Royal Purple	Misc	Pre 1846		dr				
Royal Scarlet	HP	1898	Paul G	mr	s		vig	
Royal Standard	HP	1876	Turner	mp	f	l	vig	
Royal Virgin Rose	G	1819/20	Vibert syn Aimable Rouge	dp	vdbl	m		m
Royal Welsh	C	Pre 1846		lp		l		
Royale	G	Pre 1811	Godefroy	lp	dbl	m		
Royale	A	Pre 1834		lp		m		
Royale	HP		syn Esquermes	mp				
Royale Aurore	A	Pre 1810	Charpentier (?) syn Celestial	lp	dbl	l	vig	vf
Royale Marbrée	G	Pre 1837	Moreau-Robert	m	vdbl	m	vig	
Royale Rouge	A	Pre 1830	Prévost syn Belle Thérèse	lp	dbl	m-l		
Royale Veloutée	G	Pre 1815	Schwarzkopf syn Holoserica Regalis	m	dbl			m
Royer Collard	Misc	1827	Noisette	m				
Ruban Doré	G	Pre 1821	Steigerhoek syn Tricolore	rb	vdbl	s		
Rubens	Ch	Pre 1846		lp	f	l		
Rubens	G			lp				
Rubens	HP	1852	Laffay	mr	dbl	l		
Rubens	T	1859	Robert	w	dbl	l	vig	m
Rubens	HP	1864	Verdier C	yb	f	l	vvig	
Rubigens	A		Prévost syn Peti-te Cuisse de Nymphe	lp	f	m	vvig	
Rubigneux	Sp	Pre 1830		lp	s	s		
Rubigneux à Fleur Rose	HEg	Pre 1830		mp	dbl	m		
Rubigneux à Petites Folioles Étroites	Sp	Pre 1830		w	s	s		
Rubignosa	C	Pre 1629	syn Rubra (C)	mr	dbl	m		sf
Rubignosa	HEg	Pre 1846	Lee syn Hebe's Lip	w	s-d		vig	
Rubignosa Multiplex	HEg	1828	Vibert					
Rubin	HMult	1899	Kiese	mr	s-d	m		m
Rubis	Ch		Laffay	mr	s-d	s		
Rubra	C	Pre 1629		mr	dbl			sf
Rubra	M	Pre 1777		mr	dbl	m		
Rubra	HCh	Pre 1836	syn Jenny	dr				
Rubra	HMcr	Pre 1846		mp		l		
Rubra	S	Pre 1848		lp	f	l	m	
Rubra	T	1874	Touvais syn Rouge	mr	f	m	m	
Rubra	HWich	Pre 1900	Barbier	rb	s			

Name	Class	Date	Raiser / syn					
			syn r.barbierana					
Rubra	HRg		Thunberg	mr	s			
			syn Taïkoun					
Rubra à Fleurs Pleines	HRg		Regel	m	f	l		
Rubra Duplex	HBc	Pre 1836		dp				
Rubra Plena	HMcr			dr				
Rubra Plena	HSpn	c 1808	Descemet syn Rouge	mp	dbl	m		
Rubra Radiata	C			lp	f	m-l		
Rubra Simplex	HRg		Thunberg	mr	s			
Rubra Variegata	S	Pre 1817	syn Striata	rb	f	l		
Rubrifolia	Alp	Pre 1830		mr	s	m	vig	
Rubrifolia à Fleurs Pleines	Alp	1896	Schmidt J C	rb	dbl	m		
Rubro-Purpurea	D	Pre 1789	syn Red Damask	mr	dbl	m		vf
Rubrotincta	HEg	Pre 1846	Lee syn Hebe's Lip	w	s-d		vig	
Ruby Gold	T	1874	Ducher Vve	op	s-d to dbl			m
			syn Jean Ducher					
Rubygold	T	1891	O'Connor	y				
Ruby Queen	HWich	1899	Van Fleet	dp	dbl	s		sf
Rudicanlis	Misc	Pre 1846						
Rudolph Einhard	HP	1899	Welter	mr				
Rudolphus	Cl			w				
Ruga	Ayr	Pre 1820		w	s-d	l	vig	m
Rugosa	HRg	1879	Thunberg	m	dbl	l		f
		syn	Kaiserin des Nordens					
Rugosa Alba	HRg		Thunberg	w	s	l	m	f
Rugosa Rose	Sp	Pre 1846	Thunberg	m	s	l	m	
			syn r.rugosa					
Rugueuse	D	Pre 1846		lp	f			
Ruhm von Schwerin	T		Lobedanz	w				
Ruhm von Thalwitz	HP	1866	Peters	mr	f	m-l	vig	
Rushton-Radclyffe	HP	1864	Verdier E	mr	f	l	vvig	
Russelliana	HMult	Pre 1826	Cormack & Sinclair	m	dbl	m		m
Russell's Cottage	HMult	Pre 1826	Cormack & Sinclair	m	dbl	m		m
			syn Russelliana					

NAME	TYPE	YEAR	RAISER	COLOUR	BLOOM	SIZE	GROWTH	SCENT
S M Nicholas II	Misc		Gauthier					
S Reynolds Hole	HP	1873	Paul G	rb	f	l	vig	f
			syn Reynolds Hole					
Sabine	Misc	1824	Vibert	dp	s	m		
Sabine	Alp		Noisette	mr & w				
Sablée	G	1836	Vibert	dr				
Safrano	T	1839	Beauregard	ab	s-d	l	vig	m
Safrano à Fleurs Rouges	T	1867	Oger	rb	s-d	m	m	f
Saint Aldégonde	C	Pre 1834		pb		m		
Saint Barthélemy	HP	Pre 1846		lp	s-d	m		
Saint Cloud	T	Pre 1846		lp				f
Saint Fiacre	HP	Pre 1846		m	f	m	vig	
Saint Francis	C	Pre 1846		dp	dbl	s		
	syn	Pompon	de Saint François					
Saint François	Pom	c 1850	Robert syn above	dp	dbl	s		
Saint George	HP	1874	Paul W	mr	f	l	vig	
Saint John' Rose	S	Pre 400	Damann	lp	s	m		
			syn rosa sancta					
Saint Mark's Rose	Misc	Pre 1759	syn Rose d'Amour &	dp	dbl			m
			syn r.virginia plena					
Saint Max	B			lp	f	m	vig	
Saint Priest de Breuze	Ch	1838	Desprez	rb	dbl	m		
Saint Samson	Ch			mp	f	m		
Saint Victor	C			mp				
Saint Vincent	B			dr				
Sainte Hélène	G		Cartier	dp				
Sainte Radegonde	Pom			dp				
Sainte Suzanne	M		Foulard	lp	f	m		
Sakoura	HMult	1893	Turner syn Ibara	mr	s-d to dbl		vvig	
Salamander	HP	1891	Paul W	mr	dbl	l	vig	
Salomon	G		Calvert	lp				
Salet	M	1854	Lacharme	mp	f	vl	vig	m
Salicetti	Ch		Laffay	dr	dbl	m		
Salluste	G	1852	Robert	mp	f	l		
Salmacis	C	1841	Vibert	mr	f	m		
Salamon	G	c 1825	Calvert	pb	f	m-l		
Salomon	HP	1858	Guinoisseau	lp				
Salomon de Mowpoditz	M			dp	f	m		
Salvator Rosa	HP	1851	Laffay	mr	f	l	vig	
Samatigui	Sp	1830	Wight & Arnott	w				
			syn r.leschenaultii					
Samson	G		Miellez	dp	f	l		
San Rafael Rose	Misc	1845		yb	dbl	l		m
		syn	Fortune's Double Yello	w				
Sanchette	N	1830	Vibert	w		s		
Sanchette	G	1837	Vibert	dp	f	m		
Sancho Pança	G	1843	Vibert	mr	f	l		
Sancta	S	Pre 1867	Damann	lp	s	m		
			syn Saint John's Rose					
Sang	G	Pre 1819	syn Hector	m	dbl	s		
Sang de Boeuf	G	Pre 1820		dr	s	m		
		syn	Sanguineo-Purpurea	Simplex				
Sang de Vénus	P	1823	Bizard	mr				
Sanglant	Ch	1870	Cherpin / Liabaud	mp	vdbl	m	vig	f
Sanguin	Ch	Pre 1828	Laffay	m	vdbl	m	wk	
Sanguine	G	Pre 1819	syn Hector	m	dbl	s		
Sanguinea	Ch	Pre 1818		dr	vdbl	m	wk/sp	
Sanguinea	G	Pre 1830	Calvert	mp	vf	m		
Sanguinea	M	1824	Lemeunier	dr	dbl	m		
			syn De La Flèche					
Sanguinea	M	1840	Vibert	pb	f	m		
		syn	Anémone Sanguinea					
Sanguineo-Purpurea Atra	G	Pre 1811	syn Ombre Superbe	m	dbl	l		
Sanguineo-Purpurea Simplex	G	Pre 1820		dr	s	m		
Sanguisorbaefolia	Pom	Pre 1830	Noisette / Godefroy	w	s			f
Sans Épines	Alp	Pre 1830		lp	f	m	vvig	
Sans Épines	A	Pre 1846	syn Thornless	w				
Sans Épines	C							
Sans Épines	Ch			dr				
Sans Épines	T	1876	Joly	w				
Sans Épines	HSpn			rb				
Sans Épines à Fleurs Doubles	Alp		Prévost	mr				
Sans Pareille	G			m				
Sans Pareille	G			lp				
Sans Pareille de Hollande	D	Pre 1830	Vibert	lp	f	vs		
Sans Pareille Pourpre	G	Pre 1811		dr	f			m
Sans Pareille Rose	G	Pre 1811		dp	vdbl	l		m
Sans Rival	Misc	Pre 1846						
Sans Sépales	M	1839	Foulard	lp	dbl	s		

Name	Class	Date	Origin					
Santa Rosa	Ch	1899	Burbank	mp	dbl	l	m	m
Saphirine	HCh			mr	f	l		
Sapho	G	1818	Vibert	pb	f	m		
Sapho	C	1832	Vibert	lp		m		
Sapho	P	1847	Vibert	w	f	s		
Sappho	A	Pre 1817		w	s	m		
Sappho	HSet	Pre 1846			f			
Sappho	T	1888	Paul W	pb	f	l	vig	m
Sarah	A	1822	Calvert	lp	f	s		
Sarah	G		Calvert	lp				
Sarah Isabella Gill	T	1897	Gill	y				
Saris Sepals	M	1839		mp				
Sarmenteuse	N	Pre 1846	Vibert	lp				
Sarmenteux	N		Noisette L	lp				
Sarmenteux	Ch			w				
Saturnia	HSpn	1846						
Saturne	G		Miellez	dr				
Saudeur Panaché	HCh	Pre 1846		mr				
Scabriusculus	HBc	Pre 1822	Noisette	w	s			
Scaliger	G	1858	Robert & Moreau	mr				
Scandens	Ayr	Pre 1804		w	s-d		m	vf
Scandens	HSem	Pre 1830	Miller	w	s			
Scandens Rosea Alba	HSem			lp				
Scarlet	D			mp	s-d	m		
Scarlet Brabant	Misc	Pre 1846						
Scarlet Grevillea	HMult	Pre 1826	Cormack & Sinclair syn Russeliana	m	dbl	m		m
Scarlet Hip	Can	Pre 1830 syn Egl-	Lee antier à FleursÉcarlate	mr	dbl	m		
Scarlet Maria Leonida	HBc	Pre 1846	Rivers	mr	f	l		
Scarlet Moss	M	1824	Lemeunier syn De la Flèche	dr	dbl	m		
Scarlet Pompone	M	Pre 1846		mr		s		
Scarlet Provence	C	Pre 1867		mr				
Scarlet Sweet Brier	HEg	c 1820	 syn La Belle Distinguée	mr	dbl	s		f
Scharnkeana	S	Pre 1900		m				
Schiller	HP			mp	f	m		
Schismaker	G	Pre 1846	Parmentier	m	f	l		
Schloss Luegg	HMult	1886	Geschwind	mp	dbl	l		
Schneelicht	HRg	1894	Geschwind	w	s	l	vvig	sf
Schœne von Hohenburg	T	1890	Menges	w				
Schultheiss	HP	1882	Bennett syn Heinrich Schultheiss	lp	dbl	vl	vig	
Scipion	HP	1852	Avoux & Crozy	pb	f	l	m	
Scipion Cochet	B	1850	Cochet	dp	dbl	m	vvig	
Scipion Cochet	HP	1887	Verdier E	dr	f	l	vig	
Scotch Briar	Sp	Pre 1600	syn r.spinosissima	w	s	s		
Scotch Double White	HSpn	Pre 1818	 syn Double White Burnet	w	s-d		vig	vf
Scotch Perpetual	HSpn	1819	 syn Perpetual Scotch	lp	dbl	m-l	m	m
Scotch Rose	Sp	Pre 1600	syn r.spinosissima	w	s	s		
Scotica	HSpn	1888		p				
Scris Rose	G	Pre 1830	Calvert syn Couronne de Brabant	lp	f	l		
Sebastiani	HCh		Laffay	dr	dbl	l		
Sebille Noire	Misc	Pre 1846		dr				
Secrétaire Allard	HP	1869	David	mr	f	l		
Secrétaire Général Delaire	HP	1899	Corbœuf	dr	vf	vl		
Secrétaire Jean Nicolas	HP	1883	Schwartz J	m	dbl	l	vvig	f
Secrétaire Noe	T	1888	Nabonnand	mr	f	l	vig	f
Séguier	G	1853	Robert	m	dbl	m		
Seigneur d'Harzelhaard	G	Pre 1830	Calvert	m	f	m		
Seleron	C			dr				
Sélima Dubos	D	1849	Dubos syn Célina Dubos	w				vf
Sélina	D			lp				
Sélina	M	Pre 1843	Hardy syn Célina	m	dbl	l		
Sémelé	T	1841	Guérin	w	vdbl	m		
Semi-Double	G	1818	Godefroy/Descemet syn Aigle Noir	dr	dbl	m		
Semi-Double	M	Pre 1826	Vibert	dp	s-d	l		
Semi-Double	A			w	s-d			
Semi-Double	M			mp	s-d			
Semi-Double	Pom		Mademoiselle Leloup		s-d			
Semi-Double	HCan		Prévost		s-d			
Semi-Double Marbled Rose	G	Pre 1754	syn Marmorea	rb	s-d	m		
Semi-Double Striped Moss	M	c 1818	Shailer syn Panachée	w	s-d	m		
Semi-Double Ponctuée	M	Pre 1834	Robert	mp	s-d	m		
Semi-Double Purple (Pourpre)	M	Pre 1834		m	s-d	l		
Semi-Double Rose	HSem		Descemet		s-d			

Name	Class	Date	Origin / syn	Colour	Form	Size	Vigour	Fragrance
Semi-Double Velvet Rose	G	Pre 1629	syn Holoserica Duplex	dr	dbl			
Semi-Double White	A	Pre 1846		w	s-d	l		
Semi-Plena	A	Pre 1754	syn Alba Semi-Plena	w	s-d			vf
Semilasso	G			mp				
Semiramis	G							
Semiramis	D	1841	Vibert	pb	dbl	l	vvig	
Semiramis	HP	1864	Touvais	lp		l		
Sémonville	A	Pre 1815	Charpentier	w	dbl	m		
Sémonville à Fleurs Doubles	A	1823	Hardy	pb	dbl	l		
Semperflorens	Ch	1790		mr	dbl	m	m	
			syn Slater's Crimson China					
Sempervirens	Sp			mp	f	m		
Sempervirens à Petites Feuilles	HSem			w				
Sempervirens Carnea Multiplex	HSem	Pre 1830	Laffay	lp	vdbl			
Sempervirens Couché	HSem							
Sempervirens Double	HSem	1828	Vibert	w	s-d	s		
Sempervirens Major	HSem	Pre 1830	Vibert syn Plena	w	s	m		
Sempervirens Major Double	HSem	1825	Vibert	w	vdbl	m		f
Sempervirens Minor	HSem	Pre 1830	Vibert syn Scandens	w	s			
Sempervirens Pleine	HSem	1828	Vibert	w	s			
Sempervirens Pleno	HSem	Pre 1830	Laffay M syn Plena	lp	dbl			
Sempervirens Rosea Multiplex	HSem	Pre 1830	Laffay	mp	dbl	s		
Sénat Romain	G	1821	Prévost	lp	f	vl		m
			syn Duc de Guiche					
Sénateur Chevreau	HP	1869	Pernet Père	mr	f	l	vig	
Sénateur Favre	HP	1863	Rousseau	dr	f	l	vig	
			syn Puebla					
Sénateur Favre	HP	1867	Fontaine	mr	f	m-l		
			syn François Fontaine					
Sénateur Loubet	T	1891	Reboul	yb	vf	l	vig	
Sénateur Réveil	HP	1863	Damaizin	rb	f	m		
Sénateur Vaïsse	HP	1859	Guillot Père	rb	dbl	l	vig	vf
Senator McNaughton	T	Pre 1895	California Nursery Co	w	f	l		
Seneca	Ch	Pre 1846						
Séphora	Ch	1829	Vibert	m		s		
Séphora	C	1842	Robert	lp	f	l		
Séphora	HP	1852	Laffay	mr	f	l		
Séphora	D	1861	Robert & Moreau	w				
Sepintarus	B	1846	Guillot Père	lp				
Septhun	Misc	Pre 1846		mr				
Septime	G	Pre 1830	Calvert	m	f	m		
Septunie	G			w				
Seraphine	A	Pre 1834		lp		l		
Séraphine	G	Pre 1838		w		l		
Seraphine	HSet	1840	Prince Nursery	pb	vdbl			
Serena	HSet	Pre 1846						
Seringa	G			mr	f	m		
Serné	G	1825	Hardy	p		l		
Serratipetala	Misc	1828	Prévost	dp	dbl	s		
Serratipetala	Ch	1831	Jacques	pb	f	m		sf
Servilie (Serville)	M	1853	Robert	lp	f	l		
Setigera	Cl Set			dp	s-d	m		
Setina	Cl HCh	1879	Henderson P	lp	f	m	vvig	m
			syn Climbing Hermosa					
Setina	Cl B	1879	Schwartz, Bennett	dp				
Seven Sisters	HMult	1815		pb	s-d	m	vig	m
Sévigné	G	1819	Vibert	dp	f	l		
Sextus Pompilius	HP	Pre 1846	Vibert	mr				
Shailer's Provence	C	Pre 1799	Shailer	lp	dbl		vig	f
Shailer's White Moss	M	1788	Shailer	w	vdbl	m		
Shakespeare	G	Pre 1843	syn Kean	m	f	m-l	vig	
Shandon	HT	1899	Dickson A	dr	dbl	l		vf
Shantung Yellow	Ch	Pre 1867		my				
Sheila	HT	1895	Dickson A	mp				
Shi Tz-mei	HMult	1893	Turner	mr	s-d	s	vvig	
			syn Crimson Rambler					
Shigyoku	G	Pre 1883		m	f	m		
Shining Rose	Sp	1807	Willdenow	mp	s	s		
			syn r.nitida					
Shirley Hibberd	T	1874	Levet F	my	f	m	m	
Siberian Yellow	HEg	Pre 1846	syn Lutescens	ly	s	s		
Sibirica	HSpn							
Sicilian Rose	Sp	Pre 1894	Trattinnick syn r.sicula	dr		s		
Sidonie	G	1829	Vibert	mp	f	l		
Sidonie	HP	1847	Vibert	mp	f	l		m
Siegfried	T	1893	Drögemüller	op	f	l		
Sieguier	G	1853	Robert	m				
Silène	T	Pre 1846		op	f	l	vvig	m
Silver Queen	HP	1886	Paul W	pb	f	l		
Silvia	D	1819	Vibert	m	dbl	l	vig	
Silvia	HP	1871	Fontaine	dr	f	l	vig	
Similor	N	1840	Boyau	pb	vf	s		f

Simon de St Jean	HP	1861	Liabaud	m	vdbl	l		
Simon Lazard	HP	1885	Singer	mp	f	vl	vvig	
Simon Lebonk (Le Bouck)	G			mr	vdbl	m		
Simon Oppenheim	HP	Pre 1870		mr	f	m	vvig	
Simonneau	G		Parmentier	dr	f	m		
Simple	C			p				
Simple	M	1807	Wandes syn Single	lp	s	m		
Simple	Min		Noisette L	p				
Simple à Petites Feuilles	Pol			w				
Simple Carnée	G		Noisette					
Simple Jaunâtre	T	1825	Laffay					
Simple Jaune Pâle	HSpn		Prévost	ly				
Simple Nouvelle	M	Pre 1834		lp		m		
Simple Parviflora	A	1826	Bozérain					
Simplex	M		syn Single	w				
Simplice	HCh	1827	Noisette L	m	s-d			
Simplicifolia	HRg			p				
Simplicité	C			mp	f	m		
Single	M	1807	Wandes	lp	s	m		
Single Cherry	HSpn	Pre 1840		pb	s	m		
Single Chestnut Rose	Sp	1864	Rehder & Wilson	lp	s			
		syn	r.roxburghii normalis					
Single Crimson Bedder	HP	1896	Cooling	mr				
Single Crimson Moss Rose	M	Pre 1838	Rivers	dr	s-d			
		syn	Rivers' Single Crimson					
Single Lawrence	Min			p				
Single Lilac	M	Pre 1846						
Single Moss	M	Pre 1720	syn Communis	mp	dbl	l		
Single Red Thornless	Misc	Pre 1846		mr	s			
Single Rose	M	Pre 1846		mp				
Single Sweet Brier	HEg	Pre 1846			s			
Single Variegated	HSpn	Pre 1846			s			
Single White	HSpn	Pre 1846		w	s			
Single Yellow	E	1888	syn Aurantiaca	ob	s	m	m	
Sinica Anemone	S	1896	Geschwind/Schmidt	lp	s	l	vig	m
		syn	Anemone					
Sir Garnet Wolseley	HP	1875	Cranston	mr	f	vl	vvig	f
Sir John Franklin	HP	Pre 1860		mr				
Sir John Sebright	Ayr	Pre 1846		mp	dbl	s		
Sir Joseph Paxton	B	1852	Laffay M	dr	f	l	vig	m
Sir Robert Duff	Cl T	1893	Johnson	lp				
Sir Rowland Hill	HP	1887	Mack	m	vdbl	l		f
Sir Walter Scott	N	Pre 1846		mp	f	l		
Sirène	HP	1874	Touvais	dr				
Sisley	HP	1835	Sisley	mr	f	m	vig	
Six Juin	HP	Pre 1834		mp	f	m		
Skobelef	HP	1889	Verdier E	lp				
Slater's Crimson China	Ch	1790	Slater	mr	dbl		m	
Small-flowered Rose	Sp	Pre 1800	syn r.micrantha	lp		s	vvig	
Smithii	T	1834	Smith	dy	f	l	vig	
		syn	Smith's Yellow China					
Smith's Parish	T	1844	Fortune	w	vf	l	m	vf
		syn	Fortune's Free-coloure	d Rose				
Smith's Yellow China	T	1834	Smith	dy	f	l	vig	f
Snelgrave	Ch			mr	f	m		
Snow-Bush Rose	Misc	1817	syn Dupontii	w	s	m		sf
Snowball	B	1867	Lacharme F	w	dbl			
			syn Boule de Neige					
Snowflake	T	1886	Lambert E	w	dbl			
			syn Marie Lambert					
Snowflake	T	1890	Strauss & Co	w				
Sobiesky	M	1852	Robert	m	s-d	l		
Soc d'Hort de Melun & Fontainebleau	HP	1852	Cochet	w	f	m		
Société d'Agriculture de la Marne	T			mr				
Socrate	T	1858	Moreau-Robert	pb	dbl	l	vig	f
Socrates	HP		Vibert	lp				
Socrates	Ch		Péan	mp	vdbl	m	vig	
Soeur Agathe	B	1852	Lartay	lp	f	m		
Soeur Athanase	HP	1874	Fontaine	mp	f	l	vig	
Soeur Bernède de St-Vincent de Paul	HP	1879	Bernède	dp	vf	l	vvig	
Soeur des Anges	HP	1862	Oger	lp	f	vl	vig	
Soeur Hospitalière	G		Miellez	m	vdbl	m		
Soeur Josephe	D	1820	Vibert	lp	vdbl	s		
			syn Deiphille					
Soeur Marthe	M	1848	Vibert	dp	f	l		m
Soeur Séverin	T	1892	Reboul	w				
Soeur Thècle (las)	HP	1866	Fontaine	mp		l	vig	
Soeur Vincent	D	1820	Vibert	lp	f	m		
Soeur Vincent	M	1851	Robert	lp	f	m		
Soeur Vincent	C							

Name	Type	Year	Breeder					
Soleil Brillant	G	Pre 1790		dp		m		m
Soleil d'Austerlitz	HP	1847	Lacharme	mr	f	l		
Soleil d'Or	HFt	1897	Pernet-Ducher	yb	f	l	vig	m
Soleil Naissant	G	Pre 1830	Boutigny	mr	f	m		
Solfaterre	N	1843	Boyau / Lamarque	my	dbl	l	vig	vf
Soliman	T	Pre 1846		lp		l		f
Solitaire	N			lp	vf	m	vig	
Sombre	Ch			mr				
Sombre Agréable	Misc	Pre 1846						
Sombreuil	A	Pre 1830	Vibert	w	f	m		
Sombreuil	G/C	Pre 1838		mp				
Sombreuil	Cl T	1850	Robert	w	dbl	l	vig	f
Sombreuil	T	Pre 1870		lp		l		
Sommeson	G	Pre 1820	Pelletier	mp	f	s		
Somptueuse	G	Pre 1830	Racine	mp	f	l		
S A R La Princesse de	T	1886	Nabonnand	rb	dbl	vl		
Hohenzollern, Infante de Portugal		syn	PrincesseHohenzollern					
Sophie Cellier	G			lp		l		
Sophie Coquerel	HP	1842	Coquerel	mr	f	l	vig	
Sophie Cottin	M	1861	Robert & Moreau	pb	f	m		
Sophie Cottin	G	1832	Vibert	dp	f	l		
Sophie de Barrière	G							
Sophie de Bavière	A	Pre 1826	Cottin / Vibert	lp	f	m	vig	
Sophie de Marsilly	A	Pre 1846		pb	f	l	vig	
Sophie de Marsilly	M	1863	Robert & Moreau	pb	dbl	m	vig	
Sophie de Villeboinet	HP	1867	Trouillard	lp	f	l	vig	
Sophie d'Houdetot	HCh	1841	Vibert	mp	f	l		
Sophie Fouquier	G			dr	f	m		
Sophie Portal	T	1853	Pradel	dr	f	m		
Sophie Reine de Hollande	HP	1879		p				
Sophocle	C			lp				
Soris Rosa	G		Calvert	p				
Souchet	T			w	f	m		
Souchet	C	Pre 1806	syn Rose des Peintres	m	f	vl		
Souchet	B	1842	Souchet	m	dbl	l	m	vf
Soufflé de Zéphire	A	c 1815	Descemet	w				
Soufre	Ch		Péan	ly	dbl			
Soukara-Ibara	HMult	1893	Turner	mr	s-d	s	vvig	
			syn Crimson Rambler					
Soulès Pierre	B			lp				
Soupert & Notting, Frères	T	1871	Levet	yb	f	m		
Soupert & Notting	M	1874	Pernet Père	dp	f	s	vig	vf
South Orange Perfection	HWich	1899	Horvath	pb	dbl			m
Southern Beauty	HP	1888	Nanz & Neuner	mp				
Southern Beauty	HT	1897	Dingee & Conard					
Souvenir d'Abraham Lincoln	HP	1865	Verdier E	mr	f	m	vig	
Souvenir d'Adèle Launay	B	1872	Moreau-Robert	mr	f	l	vig	
Souvenir d'Adolphe Thiers	HP	1877	Moreau-Robert	mr	dbl	vl	vig	m
Souvenir d'Adrien (Ba)hivet	HP	1867	Cochet	dp	f	l	vig	
Souvenir d'Aimée Terrel des	Ch	1897	Schwartz Vve	op	dbl	s	m	
Chênes								
Souvenir d'Albert La Blottais	HP	1895	Pernet Père	mr				
Souvenir d'Alexandre Hardy	HP	1898	Lévêque	mr	dbl	l		
Souvenir d'Aline Fontaine	HP	1879	Fontaine	lp	vdbl	l	vvig	
Souvenir d'Alphonse Lavallée	HP	1884	Verdier C	dr	f	l	vig	m
Souvenir d'André Raffy	HP	1899	Vigneron	dr	dbl	l		vf
Souvenir d'Anna Lee	HP			mp				
Souvenir d'Anselme	HP	Pre 1846		dp	dbl	l		
Souvenir d'Arthur de Sansal	HP	1876	Guénoux	mp	dbl	l	vig	vf
Souvenir d'Auguste Legros	T	1890	Bonnaire	mr	dbl	l		
Souvenir d'Auguste Métral	HT	1895	Guillot P	dr	f	l	vig	m
Souvenir d'Auguste Rivière	HP	1877	Verdier E	rb	f	l	vvig	f
Souvenir de Bellanger	HP	1871	Eude	dr	f	m	vig	
Souvenir de Béranger	HP	1857	Bruant	lp	dbl	l	m	
Souvenir de Bernardin de St-Pierre	HP	1864	Guillot Fils	dr	f	l	m	
Souvenir de Bertrand Guinoisseau	HP	1895	Chédane-Guinoisseau	m	vdbl	l		m
Souvenir de Bordeaux	HP	1853	Laffay	dr	f	l	vig	
Souvenir de Brod	HSet	1886	Geschwind R	rb	dbl	l	vig	m
		syn	Erinnerung an Brod					
Souvenir de Caillat	HP	1867	Verdier E	rb	f	l	m	
Souvenir de Catherine Guillot	T	1895	Guillot P	rb	dbl	l	m	vf
Souvenir de Cécile Vilin	HP	1890	Verdier E	rb				
Souvenir de Charles Montau(l)t	HP	1862	Moreau-Robert	dr	f	m	vig	f
Souvenir de Charles Seymour	HP	1874	Lacharme F	m	dbl	l	vig	
		syn	Souvenir du Baron de	Sémur				
Souvenir de Charles Summer	HP	1874	Verdier E	mr	f	l	m	
Souvenir de Charles Verdier	HP	1894	Verdier E	m	f	m-l		
Souvenir de Christophe Cochet	HRg	1894	Cochet-Cochet	mp	s-d	l	vvig	m
Souvenir de Clairvaux	T	1890	Verdier E	pb	f	l	vig	m
Souvenir de Coulommiers	HP	1868	Desmazures	dr	f	l		
Souvenir de David d'Angers	T	1856	Robert	dr	dbl	vl	m	f
Souvenir de David d'Angers	HP	1875	Moreau-Robert	dr				

Name	Class	Year	Breeder					
Souvenir de Désirée	B	1846	Lacharme	mr	f	m	vvig	
Souvenir de Douai	T	1892	Soupert & Notting	y				
Souvenir de Ducher	HP	1874	Verdier E	m	f	m	vig	f
Souvenir de Dumont d'Urville	B	1842	Souchet	mr	f	m	wk	
Souvenir de François Gaulain	T	1889	Guillot	rb	dbl	l		m
Souvenir de François Ponsart	HP	1867	Touvais	mp	f	l	vig	
Souvenir de Franz Deak	T	1894	Perotti	w	f	l		
	syn		Souvenir de S A Prin-	ce				
Souvenir de Ferike d'Antunovics	T	1895	Soupert & Notting	w				
Souvenir de Gabrielle Drevet	T	1884	Guillot et Fils	op	f	l	vig	vf
Souvenir de Garnet Wolseley	HP	see	Sir Garnet Wolseley					
Souvenir de Général Gange	B	1855	De Fauw	dp	f	m		
Souvenir de Geneviève Godard	T	1893	Godard	mp				
Souvenir de George Sand	T	1876	Ducher Vve	yb	f	vl		
Souvenir de Germain de St-Pierre	T	1882	Nabonnand	dr	f	l	vvig	
Souvenir de Gonod	HP	1890	Gonod	mr	f	vl		
Souvenir de Grégoire Bordillon	HP	1889	Moreau-Robert	mr	f	vl		
Souvenir de Hennecourt	HP		Desmazures	mp	f	l	vig	
Souv de Henri Lévêque de Vilmorin	HP	1899	Lévêque	dr	f	l		
Souvenir de Henry Clay	HSpn	1854	Boll	lp		m		
Souvenir de J B Guillot	T	1897	Guillot P	or	f	l	vig	
Souvenir de Jean Sisley	HP	1891	Dubreuil	m	f	l		
Souvenir de Jeanne Balandreau	HP	1899	Vilin	mr	f	m	vvig	f
	see	Souv de	Mme Jeanne Balandre	-au				
Souvenir de Jeanne Cabaud	T	1896	Guillot P	yb	f	vl	m	m
Souvenir de Jenny Pernet	T	1863	Pernet Père	lp	f	m		
Souvenir de John Gould Veitch	HP	1872	Verdier E	dr	f	l	vig	
Souvenir de Joseph Pernet	HP	1888	Pernet Père	mr	vdbl	l	vig	
Souvenir de Jules Godard	T	1894	Godard	w	f	m		m
Souvenir de Julie Gonod	HP	1871	Gonod	mp	f	l		
Souvenir de Kaiser Wilhelm I	HP	1885	Schultz	dr	f	l	vig	
Souvenir de Katia Mertschersky	T	1884	Nabonnand	w	s-d	vl	vvig	
Souvenir de la Bataille de Marengo	HMult	Pre 1826	Cormack & Sinclair	m	dbl	m		m
			syn Russelliana					
Souvenir de la Malmaison	B	1842	Béluze	lp	vf	vl	vig	vf
Souvenir de la Malmaison, Climbing	Cl B	1893	Bennett	lp	vf		vvig	m
Souvenir de la Malmaison Jaune	B	1887	Volvert	w	vdbl	l	vig	vf
	syn		Kronprincessin Victor	-ia von Pr	eussen			
Souvenir de la Malmaison Rose	B	1845	Béluze	mp	f	l	vig	
			syn Leweson Gower					
Souvenir de la Malmaison Rouge	B	1882	Gonod	dr	f	m		
		see	Malmaison Rouge					
Souvenir de la Princesse Amélie des Pays-Bas	HP	1873	Liabaud	m	dbl	l	m	
Souvenir de la Princesse de Lamballe	B	1834	Mauget	pb	dbl	s	m	vf
			syn Queen of Bourbons					
Souvenir de la Reine d'Angleterre	HP	1855	Cochet Frères	mp	dbl	vl	vvig	
Souvenir de la Reine des Belges	HP	1850	De Fauw	pb	f	l	m	
Souvenir de la Reine des Pays-Bas	HP	1876	Schwartz	m				
Souvenir de Lady Ashburton	T	1890	Verdier C	rb	dbl	l	vig	f
Souvenir de Lady Cordlay	HP	1861	Guillot Père	mr	f	l	vig	
Souvenir de Laffay	HP	1878	Verdier E	mr	vf	l	vig	f
Souvenir de l'Ami Labruyère	HP	1884	Gonod	mp	f	l	vvig	
Souvenir de l'Ami Pancher	HP	1879	Verdier E	mr	f	m	vig	
Souvenir de l'Amiral Courbet	T	1885	Pernet Père	mr	dbl	m		
Souvenir de l'Arquebuse	B	1852	Vivian-Faivre	mr				
Souvenir de Laurent Guillot	T	1894	Bonnaire	pb	f	l		
Souvenir de l'Elysée (Elizé)	T	1854	Marrest	mp		m	m	
Souvenir de l'Empereur Maximilien	T	Pre 1870		mr	f	l		
Souvenir de l'Empire	HP	1852	Guillot Père	dr	f	m		
Souvenir de Léon Gambetta	HP	1883	Gonod	dr	dbl	vl	vvig	
Souvenir de Léon Lille	HP	1852	Lille	dr	f	l		
Souvenir de Leveson Gower	HP	1852	Guillot Père	mr	f	vl	vig	
Souvenir de l'Exposition de Brie	HP	1861	Granger	mr	dbl	l	vig	vf
	syn		Maurice Bernardin					
Souvenir de l'Exposition de Darmstadt	HP	1871	Soupert & Notting	m	vdbl	l	vig	
Souvenir de l'Exposition de Londres	B	1851	Guillot Père	mr		f	m	
Souvenir de Louis Gaudin	B	1864	Trouillard	dr	f	m	vvig	
Souvenir de Louis Moreau	HP	1891	Moreau-Robert	mr	f	l		
Souvenir de Louis Van Houtte	HP	1874	Cranston	mr	dbl	l	vig	f
			syn Crimson Bedder					
Souvenir de Louis Vilin	HP	1899	Vilin	mr				
Souvenir de Louis Xavier Granger	T	1888	Godard	pb				
Souvenir de Lucie	N	1893	Schwartz Vve	dp	dbl	m		
Souvenir de Ludovic de Talancé	T	1892	Pelletier	w				
Souvenir de Mme A Henneveu	T	1892	Bernaix	pb	dbl			

Name	Class	Year	Raiser					
Souvenir de Mme Alexis Michaut (x)	HP	1872	Vigneron	dp	f	l	vig	
Souvenir de Mme Alfred Vy	HP	1880	Jamain	dr	f	l	vig	
Souvenir de Mme Auguste Charles	B	1866	Moreau-Robert	mp	f	m	vig	sf
Souvenir de Mme Berthier	HP	1881	Liabaud	dr	vf	l	vvig	
Souvenir de Mme Boll	HP	1866	Boyau	rb	f	vl	vig	m
Souvenir de Mme Breuil	B	Pre 1889		dp	f	l	vig	vf
Souvenir de Mme Bruel	B	1889	Levet	mr	f	l	vvig	
Souvenir de Mme Camusat	HT	1896	Bonnaire	lp	f	l		
Souvenir de Mme de Corval	HP	1867	Gonod	dp	dbl	m		
Souvenir de Mme Dor	HP	1892	Liabaud	dr				
Souvenir de Mme Dussordet	HP	1860	Clément/Guillot Père	mp				
Souvenir de Mme Ernest Cauvin	HT	1898	Pernet-Ducher	pb	vf	l	m	
Souvenir de Mme Eugène Verdier	HT	1894	Pernet-Ducher	w	vf	l	vig	
Souvenir de Mme Eugène Verdier	HP	1894	Jobert	pb	f	vl	vig	
Souvenir de Mme Faure	HP	1887	Bernaix	dr	vf	vl	vig	
Souvenir de Mme Fontaine	B	1856	Cherpin syn Toujours Fleuri	m		l		
Souvenir de Mme Gaston Ménier	HT	1897	Schartz Vve	mr				
Souvenir de Mme Hélène Lambert	T	1885	Gonod	pb	f	l		f
Souvenir de Mme Hennecourt	HP	1869	Carré / Cochet S	mp	dbl	l	vig	
Souvenir de Mme Jeanne Balandreau	HP	1899	Vilin	mr	f	m	vvig	f
Souvenir de Mme Jennie (y) Pernet	T	1876	Pernet Père	lp	s-d	vl	m	f
Souvenir de Mme Joseph Métral	T	1887	Bernaix	mr	dbl	vl	vvig	f
Souvenir de Mme l'Advocat	N	1899	Veysset	op	dbl	m		
Souvenir de Mme Lambard	T	1890	California Nursery Co	yb		l		
Souvenir de Mme Léonie Viennot	Cl T	1897	Bernaix	yb	vdbl	vl	vig	vf
Souvenir de Mme Levet	T	1891	Levet F	ob	f	l		
Souvenir de Mme Lille	HP		Lille L	m				
Souvenir de Mme Ludmilla Schulz	T	1894	Soupert & Notting	w				
Souvenir de Mme Robert	HP	1879	Moreau-Robert	lp	dbl	l	vvig	
Souvenir de Mme Rousseau	HP	1861	Fargeton syn Souv de M Rousseau	mr	dbl	l		
Souvenir de Mme Rousseau d'Angers	HP	1861	Lévêque	mr	f	m		
Souvenir de Mme Sablayrolles	T	1890	Bonnaire	ab	f	l	vvig	
Souvenir de Mme Sadi Carnot	HP	1898	Lévêque	dr		vl		
Souvenir de Mme Victor Verdier	HP	1883	Verdier E	dp	f	l	vig	vf
Souvenir de Mme William Wood	HP	1865	Verdier E	m			vig	
Souvenir de Mlle Élise Chatelard	Pol	1890	Bernaix	mr				
Souvenir de Mademoiselle Gourdin	T	1879	Nabonnand	lp	vf	l	vig	
Souvenir de Mlle Marie Drivon	HT	1899	Schwartz Vve	w				
Souvenir de Mlle Terrel des Chênes	Ch	1897	Schwartz Vve	mp				
Souvenir de Mlle Victor Caillet	T	1892	Bernaix	w	f	m		
Souvenir de Marie Détrey	T	1877	Ducher Vve	mp		l	vig	
Souvenir de Mauget	B		Moreau-Robert	dp				
Souvenir de Maximilien	T	1867	Moreau-Robert	mr	f	l	vig	
Souvenir de Mère Fontaine	HP	1874	Fontaine	mr	f	vl	vig	
Souvenir de Monceaux	HP			mr	f	l	vig	
Souvenir de Monsieur Boll	HP	1866	Boyau	mr	f	vl	vig	
Souvenir de Monsieur Brédeaux	HP			mp	f	l		
Souvenir de Monsieur Bruel	B	1889	Levet syn Souv de Mme Bruel	mr	f	l		
Souvenir de Monsieur Claude Dupont	T	1893	Godard	dp	f	l		
Souvenir de Monsieur Dussordet	HP	1860 syn Souv	Clément/Guillot Père de Mme Dussordet	mp				
Souvenir de Monsieur Droche	HP	1881	Pernet Père	mp	vdbl	l	vig	
Souvenir de Monsieur Faivre	HP	1879	Levet	mr	f	vl	vvig	
Souvenir de Monsieur Gomot	HP	1890	Schwartz Vve	mr		m	vig	
Souvenir de Monsieur Poncet	P	1892	Pernet Père	lp	dbl	l		
Souvenir de Monsieur Rousseau	HP	1861	Fargeton	mr	dbl	l		
Souvenir de Némours	B	1859	Hervé	lp	f	l	vvig	m
Souvenir de Paul Neyron	T	1871	Levet A	yb	f	l	vvig	vf
Souvenir de Philémon Cochet	HRg	1899	Cochet-Cochet	w	vdbl	l	m	m
Souvenir de Pierre Clémençon	T	1894	Pelletier	mr				
Souvenir de Pierre Dupuy	B	1876	Levet	dr	f	vl	vig	m
Souvenir de Pierre Leperdrieux	HRg	1895	Cochet-Cochet	mr	s-d	l	vvig	
Souvenir de Pierre Magne	T	1896	Puyravaud	dp				
Souvenir de Pierre Oger	HP	1896	Mlle Oger	mp				
Souvenir de Pierre Vibert	M	1867	Moreau-Robert	rb	dbl	vl	m	sf
Souvenir de Poiteau	HP	1868	Margottin	op	f	l		
Souvenir de Ponsart	HP	1868	Liabaud	pb	f	l		
Souvenir de Redouté	HP	1867	Fontaine	dr	f	m	vig	
Souvenir de René Bahaud	T	1897	Bahaud	op	f	l		
Souvenir de René Lévêque	HP	1882	Verdier E	dr	f	m	vvig	f
Souvenir de Romain Desprez	HP	1871	De Sansal	lp	f	vl	m	
Souvenir de Rosalie Sichel	HP	1885	Singer	dr	f	l	vvig	
Souvenir de Rosalie Singer	HP	1885	Singer	dr	f	l	vig	
Souvenir de S A Prince	T	1889	Dingee & Conard	w	f	l	vig	f

Name	Class	Date	Raiser					
Souvenir de Simon de St-Jean	HP			mr				
Souvenir de Solférino	HP	1861	Margottin	dp	f	l		
Souvenir de Spa	HP	1872	Gautreau	dr	f	l	vig	f
Souvenir de Thérèse Levet	T	1882	Levet A	dr	f	l	vig	m
Souvenir de Toulouse	HP			m				
Souvenir de Trente Mai	T	Pre 1846		lp				
Souvenir de Victoire Landeau	HP	1884	Moreau-Robert	pb	f	l	vvig	
Souvenir de Victor Emmanuel	HP	1878	Pernet Père	lp	f	l	vig	
Souvenir de Victor Emmanuel	HP	1878	Moreau-Robert	dr	f	vl	vvig	
Souvenir de Victor Gautreau	HP	1888	Gautreau Fils	mr	f	m	vig	
Souvenir de Victor Hugo	HP	1885	Pernet Père	lp	vdbl	vl		
Souvenir de Victor Hugo	T	1883	Bonnaire	pb	dbl	l	vig	vf
Souvenir de Victor Landeau	B	1890	Moreau-Robert	mr	dbl	l		m
Souvenir de Victor Verdier	HP	1878	Verdier E	rb	f	l	vig	f
Souvenir de William Robinson	T	1899	Bernaix Fils	op	dbl	l	vig	
Souvenir de William Wood	HP	1863	Verdier E	dr	f	l	vig	m
Souvenir de Yeddo	HRg	1874	Morlet	mp	dbl	l		
Souvenir des Braves	HP	1852	Lartay	dr	f	l		
Souvenir des Français	G	Pre 1830		mr	f	m		
Souvenir des Françaises	G	Pre 1834	Hardy syn Napoléon	m	dbl	vl	vig	
Souvenir d'Elisa	T			mr				
Souvenir d'Elisa	T	Pre 1870		w	f	m		
Souvenir d'Elise Vardon	T	1854	Marest	w	dbl	vl	m	m
Souvenir d'Enghein	M	c 1830	Parmentier	mp	f	m		
Souvenir d'Espagne	T	1888	Pries / Ketten Bros	yb	dbl	m		
Souvenir d'Eugène Erèbe	HP	1885	Singer	dr	f	l	vig	
Souvenir d'Eugène Karr	HP	1885	Schwartz	mr		m	vig	
Souvenir d'Ingres	HP	1875	Pradel	dr	vdbl	m		
Souvenir du Baron de Rochetaillée	HP	1888	Liabaud	m	f	l	vig	
Souvenir du Baron de Rothschild	B	1868	Avoux & Crozy	mp	f	l		
Souvenir du Baron de Sémur	HP	1874	Lacharme	m	dbl	l	vig	
Souvenir du Capitaine des Mares	HP	1886	Moreau-Robert	mr	f	vl		
Souvenir du Capitaine Marc	HP	1874	Oger	mr	f	m	m	
Souv du Centenaire de Lord Brougham	Ch	1879	Nabonnand	mr	vdbl	vl	vvig	
Souvenir du Champs de Mars	HP	1867	Fontaine	dr	f	m		
Souvenir du Colonel Morhange	HP	1885	Singer	dr	f	l		
Souvenir du Comte de Cavour	HP	1861	Margottin	mr	f	l	vvig	
Souvenir du Comte de Cavour	HP	1861	Robert & Moreau	dr				
Souvenir du Docteur Davier(s)	HP	1871	Moreau-Robert	dr	f	m	vig	
Souvenir du Docteur Jamain	HP	1865	Lacharme F	dr	dbl	l	m	vf
Souvenir du Docteur Passot	T	1889	Godard	mr	f	l		
Souvenir du Docteur Payen	HP	1892	Vigneron	mr				
Souvenir du Gange	B		Fauw	lp	f	m		
Souvenir du Général Charreton	T	1887	Reboul	w	f	l	vig	f
Souvenir du Général Douai	HP	1871	Pernet Père	mp	vdbl	l	m	
Souvenir du Général Richard	HP	1889	Liabaud	dp				
Souvenir du Lieutenant Bujon	B	1891	Moreau-Robert	mr	dbl	vl		m
Souvenir du Maréchal Serrurier	HP	Pre 1870		mr	f	l	vig	
Souvenir du Père Lalanne	T	1895	Nabonnand	mr				
Souvenir du Petit Caporal	HP	1855	Guillot Père	dp	f	m		
Souvenir du Petit Roi de Rome	HP	1850	Béluze	lp	f	m		
Souvenir du Président Carnot	HT	1894	Pernet-Ducher	lp	f	l	m	m
Souvenir du Président Lincoln	B	1865	Moreau-Robert	mr	f	m	vvig	sf
Souvenir du Président Porcher	HP	1880	Granger	dp	f	l	vig	
Souvenir du Prince Charles d'Arenberg	HT	1896	Soupert & Notting	my	f	l		m
Souvenir du Prince Royal de Belgique	HP	1869	Gautreau	mr	f	l		
Souvenir du Quatre Mai	B			mr	f	m		
Souvenir du Rosiériste Gonod	HP	1889	Ducher	mr	dbl	vl	vig	vf
Souvenir du Rosiériste Rambaux	T	1883	Rambeaux	pb		m	vvig	vf
Souvenir du Sénateur Defly	T	1891	Perny					
Souvenir du Trente Mai	T			lp	f	l		
Souvenir d'un Ami	T	1846	Belot-Defougère	lp	dbl	vl	vig	vf
Souvenir d'un Brave Normand	Misc		Tessier					
Souvenir d'un Frère	B	1850	Oger	dr	dbl	m		
Souvenir d'un Mère	HP	1864	Touvais	lp	f	l		
Souvenir of Wootton	HT	1888	Cook J	mr	dbl	vl	vig	vf
Souvenir of Wootton, Climbing	Cl HT	1899	Butler	mr	f	l		
Spanish Musk Rose	HMsk	Pre 1629		w	s	m		
Spartacus	Ch	1851	Lartay	lp	f	l		
Speciosa	T			lp	f	m		
Speciosa	B			mr	f	s		
Spectabilis	HSem	Pre 1832	Vibert	dp	dbl	m	vig	vf
Spectabilis	G			m	f	vl		
Spectabilis	Alp		syn Boursault	mr				
Spectabilis	HArv			lp	f	m		
Spencer	HP	1892	Paul W	lp	dbl	l	vig	m
Splendens	G	Pre 1583		mr	f	m		vf
Splendens	Misc	Pre 1629	Muenchhausen	m	s-d			

Name	Class	Date	Raiser					
			syn r.x francofurtana					
Splendens	Ch	Pre 1830	Vibert	lp	s-d	m		
Splendens	Ayr	Pre 1835		w	s-d	m		vf
Splendens	M	Pre 1846		lp		l		
Splendens	B		Hennequin	lp	f	l	vig	vf
Splendeur	Ayr			lp				
Splendid	HEg	Pre 1846		dp				
Splendid Beauty	Misc	Pre 1846						
Splendid Garland	HMult	1835	Wood or Wells	w	s-d		m	m
			syn The Garland					
Splendid Garland	HSem	1835	Wells	lp	dbl	m		
Splendid Sweet Brier	Ayr	Pre 1835	syn Splendens	w	s-d			f
Splendide	HP	1888	Perny	mp				
Spong	C	1805	Spong	mp	vdbl	s		f
Spotted	C	Pre 1846		dp		l		
Spotted	HSet	Pre 1846			s			
Spotted Bengal	Ch			lp				
Stadtholder	HCh	Pre 1846						
Stadtkassier Wilhelm Liffa	HT	1899	Geschwind	mp	dbl	l		f
Staffa	HSpn	1832		w	s-d	l	m	vf
Standard of Marengo	HP	1851	Guillot Père	mr		l	vig	
		syn	Étendard de Marengo					
Stanislas Dubourg	B	c 1850	Pradel	dp	f	m		
Stanwell	HSpn	1838	Stanwell	mp	dbl	m	vvig	vf
Stanwell Perpetual	HSpn	Pre 1836	Lee	w	dbl	m	m/sp	m
Star of Waltham	HP	1875	Paul W	mr	dbl	m	vig	m
Starry	Ch			dp	f	s		
Statholder	G	Pre 1860						
Steban	Misc	Pre 1846						
Steeple Rose	C	Pre 1824		mp	f			vf
		syn	Prolifera de Redouté					
Stella	G	Pre 1846		p				
Stella Polaris	HRg	1890	Jensen	w	s	l	vig	
Sténie	A	1825	Toutain	lp				
Stéphanie	G	1819	Vibert syn Aspasie	lp				
Stéphanie Charreton	HP	1886	Gonod	w				
Stéphanie Chevrier	G		Hardy	lp	vdbl	l		
Stéphanie de Beauharnais	HP	Pre 1870	Trouillard	mp	f	m		
Stéphanie et Rodolphe	N	1880	Levet	ob	f	m	vvig	
		syn	Fiançaille s de la Stéph & de l'Ar	Chiduc Ro	dolphe			
Stéphanie et Rodolphe	T	1880	Levet A	op	dbl	l	vvig	f
		syn	Princesse Stéphanie					
Stéphanie Fouquier	G			mr	f	m		
Sterckmanns	G	1847	Vibert	dp	vf	l		
		syn	Triomphe de Sterckma	nns				
Stevens Rose	Sp	1596	(Hermann)	m	dbl			m
		syn	r.majalis					
Stradella	C	1844	Vibert	p	f	m		
Stratonice	G	Pre 1834				m		
Striata	S	Pre 1817		rb	f	l		
Strié	B	Pre 1846		dr	f			
Strié	T			lp	f	m		
Strié	HBc							
Striped Crimson	HP			mr	f			
Striped Crimson Perpetual	P	1895	Dubreuil	pb	dbl	m	m	m
		syn	Panachée de Lyon					
Striped La France	HT	1890	Veysset	pb	dbl	l		
		syn	Mme Angélique Veyss	et				
Striped Moss	M	c 1818	Shailer syn Panachée	w	s-d	m		
Striped Moss	M	Pre 1844	Robert (?)	w	f	m		
		syn	Panachée Pleine					
Striped Moss	M	1888	Verdier C	pb	f	s	wk	m
		syn	Œillet Panachée					
Striped Unique	C	1821	Chaussée, Mme	w	dbl	l	vig	
		syn	Unique Panachée					
Striped Velvet	Misc	Pre 1846						
Strombio	T	Pre 1830		w		m		f
Suaveolens	Ch		Laffay	lp	f	l		vf
Subalba	HPom		Noisette E	w	vdbl		vig	
Sublime en Beauté	G	Pre 1830						
Subnigra	G	Pre 1811		m	s-d	m		
Subnigra Marron	G		as above					
Subrotundifolia Crenata	G	Pre 1820	Descemet	pb	f	m		
		syn	Illustre					
Subrubra	HFt			rb	s	m		
		syn Bic-	olore Puniceo Subrubra					
Subviolacea	Ch	c 1830	Ternaux syn Ternaux	m	f	m		
Sully	Ch	Pre 1846		lp				f
Sulphur Rose	Sp	Pre 1503	(Hermann)	my	s			
		syn	r.hemispherica					
Sulphurea	Misc	Pre 1629	syn Multiplex	my	vdbl	vl		
Sulphurea	HSpn	Pre 1838	Hardy	ly	vf	m	vvig	

Name	Class	Date	Raiser / syn					
Sulphurea Nana	Misc	Pre 1806	syn Pompon Jaune	my	vdbl	s		
Sulphureux	T	1869	Ducher	dy	f	m	m	
Sulkowsky	C			mr	f	m		
Sully	B	1846	Vibert	mr	vf	m		
Sully	G	1847	Verdier V	mr	f	m		
Sultan of Zanzibar	HP	1875	Paul	m	f	m	m	
Sultana	N	Pre 1846						
Sultana	Ch	Pre 1885	syn Regina	mp	vdbl	m	vig	vf
Sultane Favorite	G	1820	Vibert syn Félicie	m	dbl	s	vig	f
Sultane Favorite	P	Pre 1830		lp	f	s	vvig	
Summer Damask	D	Pre50BC	syn r.damascena	lp	dbl	m		vf
Sunrise	T	1899	Piper	op	dbl	m		
Sunset	T	1883	Henderson P	dy	f	m	wk	m
Superb	HEg	Pre 1846		lp				
Superb-Striped Unique	C	1821	Chaussée, Mme syn Unique Panachée	w	dbl	l	vig	
Superb Tuscan	G	Pre 1837	Rivers syn Tuscany Superb	m	dbl	l		
Superba	HSet	1843	Feast	lp	vdbl	m		
Superba	N	Pre 1846						
Superbe	Ch		syn Grand Salomon	mp				
Superbe	G	c 1810	Descemet syn Couronne Impériale	m	f	l		
Superbe	G	Pre 1811	syn Cramoisi Triumphante	dp		s		m
Superbe	G	Pre 1821	Stegerhoek syn Tricolore	rb	f	s		
Superbe	D	1827	Noisette	mr				
Superbe	A	Pre 1846		w	f			
Superbe	HP			mp	f	l		
Superbe Brune	G	Pre 1810	Miellez syn Achille	dr	dbl			
Superbe Cramoisie	G	1832	Vibert	mr		l		
Superbe Cramoisie	G	c 1850	Robert	mr	f	vl		
Superbe du Bengale	Ch	1834	Guérin syn Louis-Philippe	rb	f	m		
Superbe en Brun	G	Pre 1810	Dupont	m	dbl	m		
Superbe Lilloise	G	1825	Vibert	mr				
Superbe Marbrée	G	Pre 1846		m				
Superbe Modeste	T			lp	f	l	vig	
Superbe Violette	G	1825	Vibert	m		m		
Superbissima	G	Pre 1787	syn Admirable (G)	mr	f			
Superior	Misc	Pre 1846						
Surabondant Boyron	T			p				
Surlet de Chokier	G			mr	f	m		
Surpasse Antionoüs (?)	HP							
Surpasse Comice de Seine et Marne	B	1852	Guillot père	mr	f	m		
Surpasse Singleton	G	Pre 1820	Descemet syn Illustre	pb	f	m		
Surpasse Tout	G	Pre 1811		mr	f	m	vig	m
Surpasse Triomphe du Luxembourg	T			mr				
Surpassing	Misc	Pre 1846						
Suscaniette	HCh			lp				
Suter's Pink	N	Pre 1846		lp				
Sutton F R C	HP	1883	Frettingham	dp	f	l	vig	vf
Suzanna(e) Schultheiss	T	1880	Nabonnand	y	f	l	vig	
Suzannah	N	Pre 1846	Suter	w				
Suzanne	G		Miellez	dp				
Suzanne Blanchet	T	1885	Nabonnand G	lp		l		vf
Suzanne Bouyer	HP	1879	Gonod	mr				
Suzanne-Marie Rodocanachi	HP	1883	Lévêque	mp	f	vl	vig	
Suzanne Rodocanachi	HP	1879	Verdier E	mp	dbl	l		
Suzanne Wood	HP	1869	Verdier E	mp	dbl	l		
Swamp Rose	Sp	1726	Marshall syn r.palustris	mp				
Swamp Rose	Sp	1726	syn r.palustris scandens	mp	dbl			
Sweet Anise Rose	T	1859	Avoux & Crozy syn Narcisse	my	dbl	l		
Sweet Brier Rose	Rbg	Pre 1551	syn r.rubignosa	lp	s			
Sweetbriar	Rbg		as above					
Sweetheart Rose	Pol	1880	Ducher, Vve syn Mme Cécile Brunner	lp	dbl	s		m
Sweetheart Rose, Climbing	Cl Pol	1894	Hosp syn Mme Cécile Brunner, Climbing	lp	dbl	s		vf
Sydney Linton	HP	Pre 1899		dp	f			
Sydonie	HP	1847	Vibert syn Sidonie	mp	f	m		m
Sydonie	G	Pre 1846	Miellez	mp				
Sydonie Dorizy	HP	1846	Dorisy	op	vf	m	vig	f
Sylph	T	1895	Paul W	w		l		
Sylphide	G			w	f	m		
Sylphide	T	Pre 1870	Laffay	mp	f	m		
Sylvain	C	Pre 1846		mp				
Sylvain	B	Pre 1846		mp				

Sylvain Caubert	B				mr			
Sylvain Péan	B	1827	Péan		mr			
Sylverie	G	Pre 1830	Vibert		mp	f	m-l	
Sylvia	D	1819	Vibert	syn Silvia	mp	vdbl	m-l	
Sylvia	HP	1871	Fontaine		dr			
Sylvia	HP	1895	Geschwind		mp	dbl	l	
Sylvie	G		Miellez		w			
Syren	Misc	Pre 1846						
Syrène	HP	1874	Touvais		dr	f	l	m
Syrius	G	Pre 1830	Coquerel		mp	vdbl	l	

NAME	TYPE	YEAR	RAISER	COLOUR	BLOOM	SIZE	GROWTH	SCENT
T B Haywood	HP	1895	Paul G	mr			vig	
T W Girdlestone	HP	1891	Dickson A	mr	f	vl		
Taffin	G		Miellez	dr				
Taglioni	T	Pre 1834		w	f	l	vig	f
Taïcoun	HRg	Pre 1872	Thunberg	mp				
Talbot	G			dr	f	m		
Talbot	HP			mr	f	m		
Talbot	Ch	Pre 1830	Prévost	w	vdbl	m-l		
Talleyrand	C	1826	Vetillard	m				
Talma	B	1854	Robert	dr	f	m		
Talma	G	Pre 1830	Prévost	m	vf	m		
Tamogled	HRg	1894	Kaufmann	mr	dbl	l	vig	
Tancrède	G		Miellez	dr				
Tancrède	Ch	Pre 1846		dr	f	l	vvig	
Tancrède	HP	1876	Oger	mr	f	m	m	
Tanger	HP	1851	Foulard	mr				
Tanger	HP	1876	Oger	mr	f	m		
Tantine	T	1874	Pradel	mr	f	m	vig	
Targélie	HCh			dr	f	m		
Tartarus	HP	1887	Geschwind	m	vdbl	l	m	vf
Tatiana Onéguine	HP	1881	Schwartz/Lévêque	mr	f	l-vl	vig	
Tatius	G			dr	f	m		
Tea Rose	T	1809	Hume/Banks/Colville	lp	dbl	l		vf
	syn	Hume's	Tea-Scented China					
Tea-Scented Ayrshire	Ayr	Pre 1820	synRuga	w	s-d			m
Tea-Scented Rose	T	1809	Hume/Banks/Colville	lp	dbl	l		vf
	syn	Hume's	Tea-Scented China					
Tearose of Cels	T	c 1840	Cels syn Coccinea	m	f	m		
Teint Doux	D	Pre 1834	Miellez	lp		m		
Télémaque	G	1830	Vibert	dp		s		
Télémaque	HP	1864	Moreau-Robert	dr	f	m		
Télésille	G	1820	Vibert	dr	f	s-m		
Telson	Ch	1825	Laffay	pm	dbl	m		f
Temple d'Apollon	G	1816	Prévost (?)	dr	dbl	l		
Ten Sisters	HMult	1893	Turner	mr	dbl	s	vvig	
			syn Crimson Rambler					
Tendresse Admirable	D	c 1811	Vibert	lp	vdbl	m		vf
			syn Marie-Louise					
Tendresse d'Apollon	G	Pre 1830	Prévost	lp	f	m		
Ténébreuse	G		Miellez	dr				
Teneriffe	Misc	Pre 1846						
Tennessee Belle	HSet	Pre 1898		mp	dbl	l	vig	m
Terminale	G	1819	Vibert	dr	vf	m		
Ternata	Sp	1803	(Michaux)	w	s			m
			syn r.laevigata					
Ternaux	Ch	Pre 1830	Vibert / Ternaux	mr	f	m		
Terror	HMult	1888	Geschwind	dr				
Tête de Mort	G			dp	f	m		
Tête de Nègres	G	Pre 1830						
Tête de Pavot	S	Pre 1799		dp	dbl	l		
	syn	Grosse	Mohnkopfs Rose					
Tewfik	HP			dr				
Thaïs	G		Noisette L	dp	vdbl	m		
Thalia	G	Pre 1811	Descemet(?)	dp	vf	s		m
			syn Thalie la Gentille					
Thalia	HMult	1895	Schmitt	w	dbl	s	vvig	m
Thalie	D	1819	Vibert	dp	f	s		
Thalie la Gentille	G	Pre 1811	Descemet (?)	dp	vf	s		m
Thargélie	HCh	1826	Vibert	m	f	m		
Thé à Fleur Gigantesque	T	1835	Hardy/Sylvain-Péan	lp	f	l	sp	
			syn Gigantesque					
The Abyssinian Rose	Sp	1814	syn r.abyssinica	w				m
The Apothecary's Rose of Provins	Sp	Pre 1600	syn r.gallica officinalis	dp	s-d			m
The Bishop	C	Pre 1790		m	vdbl	m		f
	syn	L'Évêqu	e & Le Rosier Évêque					
The Bourbon Jacques	B	1817	syn Bourbon Rose	dp	s-d		vig	m
The Bride	T	1885	May	w	dbl	l	m	f
The Crepe Rose	HP	1870	Levet	lp	vdbl	l		
			syn Paul Perras					
The Dawson Rose	HMult	1888	Dawson syn Dawson	mp	s-d	s	vig	m
The Gem	T	1871	Ducher	pb	vdbl	l	vig/sp	
			syn Marie van Houtte					
The Garland	M	1835	Wells	w	s-d	m	m	f
The Green Rose	Ch	Pre 1856	Bambridge & Harrison	w	dbl		m	
			syn Green Rose					
The Hughes	T	1892	Moore syn Bridesmaid	lp	dbl	l	vig	
The Jacobite Rose	A	Pre 1867	syn Alba Maxima	w	dbl	l		m
The Macartney Rose	HBc	c 1793	syn rosa bracteata	w	s	l		f
The Macartney Rose	HBc	Pre 1834		lp	dbl	m		f

The Maréchal	N	1830	Maréchal	w	dbl		vig	vf
			syn Lamarque					
The Meteor	HT	1887	Evans	dr	s-d	l		m
The Pompeii Rose	D	Pre 1600	syn Summer Damask	lp	dbl	m		vf
The Portland from Glendora	P	1846	Vibert	m	dbl			m
			syn Joasine Hanet					
The Portland Rose	P	c 1770		mr	s-d	l	m	m
		syn	Duchess of Portland					
The Prince	G	Pre 1846		mr				
The Puritan	HT	1886	Bennett	w	f	l		m
The Queen	T	1889	Dingee & Conard	w	f	l		
		syn	Souvenir de S A Prince					
The Rouge	Ch	Pre 1830	Godefroy	dp	vdbl	m		f
The Sapho	B	1832	Laffay M	lp	vdbl	l	vig	
		syn	Mistress Bosanquet					
The St Mark's Rose	Misc	Pre 1768	syn Rose d'Amour	dp	s-d			m
The Shah	HP	1874	Paul G	mr				
The Sweet Little Queen of Holland	T	1897	Soupert & Notting	yb	dbl	l		vf
Théagène	G	1820	Vibert syn La Pucelle	dp	f	m-l		
Théagène	G	Pre 1828	Miellez	pb	f	l		
			syn Pucelle de Lille					
Théano	HWich	1894	Geschwind	lp	s-d	s		
Thebe	T	Pre 1846						f
Thelaïre	N	1846		w				
Thélésille	N	1830	Vibert	mp		m		
Thémis	T			lp	f	m		vf
Thémis	B	c 1826	Bertin	lp	s-d	m		
Thémis	G/Ch	Pre 1834		lp				
Thémistocles	T	Pre 1846		w	s-d	s	vig	f
Théobaldine	T	Pre 1846		mp				
Théobaldine	N	Pre 1846		mr	f	m		
Théocrite	HP	1851	Laffay	mp	f	l		
Théodolinde	G		Vibert	mp				
Theodora	G/C	1819		lp				
Theodora	Misc	1832	Vibert	dp				
Théodore	G			p				
Théodore Buchetet	HP	1873	Verdier E	m	f	l	m	
Théodore Bullier	HP	1879	Verdier E	mr	f	l	vig	
Théodore Liberton	HP	1887	Soupert & Notting	mr	dbl	l		m
Théone	C	Pre 1820	Noisette L	mp	vf	m		
Theophanie	M	1818	Prévost	mp	dbl	m		
Theophanie	D	1818	Vibert	mp	vdbl	m		
Thera Hammerich	HP	Pre 1870		lp	f	l		
Thérèse (a)	HP	1871	Fontaine	lp	f	l		
Thérèse	G		Lixau	m				
Thérèse Barrois	T	1894	Nabonnand	mp	dbl	l	vig	
Thérèse de Saint-Remy	HP	1851	Oger	m	f	l	vig	
Thérèse Genevay	T	1874	Levet	pb	f	vl	vig	
Thérèse Lambert	T	1887	Soupert & Notting	pb	f	l	vig	
Thérèse Levet	HP			mp	f	l		
Thérèse Loth	T	1874	Liabaud	lp	f	l	vig	
Thérèse Margat	B	Pre 1846	see Augustine Margat	mp	vf	m		f
Thérèse Reynaud	HP	1852	Liabaud	lp	f	m	vig	
Thérèse Stravius	Ch	Pre 1846	see Belle Emilie	w	dbl	l	m	
Thérèse Welter	T	1888	Nabonnand	w	dbl			
		syn	Baronne Henriette de Loew					
Thérèsita	B	Pre 1846		lp	f	m	vvig	
Thétis	B		Robert	dp	f	m		
Thiaffait	B	Pre 1846		mp				
Thiars	HCh	Pre 1834		m		s		
Thibault	HP	Pre 1846		dp	f	m		
Thiers	HP			mp	f	l		
Thimoclée	B			p				
Thirion-Montauban	T	1892	Puyravaud	p				
Thisbé	HSem	c 1825	Vibert / Noisette	lp	f	m	vvig	m
Thisbé	B	Pre 1846	Robert	m		l		
Thomas Methven	HP	1869	Verdier E	dp	f	l	vig	
Thomas Mills	HP	1873	Verdier E	dp	dbl	l	vig	f
Thomas Morus	B			mr	f	m	vig	
Thomas Rivers	HP	1857	Margottin	mp	f	l	m	
Thomasine	Ch	Pre 1834		mr		s		
Thoresbyana	Ayr	1840	Bennett	w	s-d	m	vig	vf
		syn	Bennett's Seedling					
Thorin (Thouin)	HP	1866	Lacharme	mp	dbl	l	vvig	
Thornless	A	Pre 1846		w				
Thornless	Bslt	Pre 1846		mp		l		
Thornless Violet	N			dr	f	m	wk	
Thouin	T	Pre 1834		lp	f	m		f
Thouin	G	Pre 1830	Prévost	mr	f	l		
Thouliet	T	Pre 1834		lp				
Three-Leaf Rose	Sp	1844	syn r.anemoneflora	w	vdbl	s		
Threepenny Bit Rose	Sp	Pre 1900	syn r.farreri persetosa	mp				

Name	Type	Date	Raiser					
Thunberg	HP	1867	Verdier E	m	f	l	vig	
Thurette	HCh	Pre 1834	Noisette L	m	vdbl	m	vig	
Thusnelda	HRg	1886	Müller Dr F	mp	s-d	l	vig	m
Thyra Hammerich	HP	1868	Hugues Vilin	lp	vdbl	l	vvig	m
Tibulle	G	Pre 1846		lp	f	l		
Tige Rude	P	1822	Vibert					
Tigré	D	1825	Toutain	m				
Timarette	G	Pre 1846		lp				
Timocles	B	Pre 1846		mp	vdbl	l		
Tinwell Moss	M	Pre 1827	Tinwell / Lee	dp	dbl	l	vig	
Tipo Ideale	Ch	Pre 1894	syn Mutabilis	yb	s			
Tippoo Saib	B	Pre 1846		dp				
Tiresias	HP	1852		mp				
Tite Live (Titus Livius)	HP	1847	Vibert	lp	f	m		
Titus	HCh	Pre 1834	Laffay	dr	f	m		
Toison d'Or		1825	Hardy	y				
Tom Jones	HSpn	1888		lp				
Tom Wood	HP	1896	Dickson A	mr	dbl	vl		m
Tomato Rose	Sp	Pre 1846	(Thunberg) syn r.rugosa	m				
Tombeau de Napoléon	G	Pre 1846		dr	f	m		
Tomenteux	D	Pre 1820	Miellez	mp	dbl	m		
Tomentosa Alba	A	Pre 1830	Pronville syn Pompon Bazard Descemet	lp	f	s-m		
Toque Violette	G							
Torrida	HP	1839	Boyau	pb	dbl	m		
Toujours Fleuri	B	1856	Cherpin	m	s-d	l	vig	f
Toujours Vert	Cl		Laffay	lp		m		
Tour Bertrand	T	1869	Ducher	y	f	vl	vvig	
Tour d'Auvergne	G			mp	f	l		
Tour de Malakoff	C	1856	Pastoret	m	dbl	l		m
Tour Malakoff	G	1856	Robert	m	f	l		
Tournefort	M	1854	Robert	rb	f	m		
Tournefort	HP	1867	Liabaud	mr	f	vl		
Tourville	B/HCh	1846	Vibert	rb	f	l		
Tourville	HP	1879	Moreau-Robert	mr	f	vl	vvig	
Toussaint	G			mr	f	m		
Toussaint	HCh	1826	Margottin Fils	lp				
Toussaint l'Ouverture	B	1849	Miellez	m	f	m		
Tous Mois Blanc	D			w				
Tous Mois Gris	D			lp				
Tous Mois Rouge	D			mr				
Toutain	C	1823	Toutain	dp				
Toutain	G/C	Pre 1830	Vibert	lp	dbl	m		
Tout Aimable	G	Pre 1830	Pelletier	mr	f	s		
Tout Aimable	D	c 1811	Vibert syn Marie-Louise	lp	vdbl	m		
Toute Bizarre	HSpn	1819	Vibert	lp	s-d	l	vig	
Townsend	HSpn	Pre 1885		mp	dbl	s		
Trajan	HP	1849	Vibert	dr	f	m		
Transon-Gombault	G	Pre 1848		mr	f	l		
Transparens	HSpn	1888		pb				
Transparente	G		Miellez	lp				
Transparente	C		Prévost	lp	f	m		
Transparente	A		Hardy	yb				
Transparente	M	c 1805	Vilmorin syn Vilmorin	lp	f	m-l		
Trébutien	M							
Très-Petite Fleur	HMult	1866	Cochet	lp	dbl	s		
Très Sombre	G							
Trésarin	G	Pre 1830	Calvert	mr	vf	m		
Trianon	HP	Pre 1834		lp	s-d	m		
Trianon Double	P	1847	Vibert syn Adèle Mauzé	lp	f	m-l		
Tricolore	G	Pre 1821	Stegerhoek	rb	vdbl	s		
Tricolore	G	1827	Lahaye Père	pb	dbl	s		m
Tricolore	G	Pre 1834	Vibert syn Reine Marguerite	dp		m		
Tricolore	HMult	1863	Robert & Moreau	pb	f	m	vig	
Tricolore	Pol			lp				
Tricolore de Flandres	G	1846	Van Houtte	pb	f	m	m	m
Tricolore de Wazemmes (Vazemmes)	G	Pre 1846		m		m		
Tricolore d'Enghien	P	c 1830	Parmentier	pb	f	s		
Tricolore d'Orléans	G	Pre 1846		rb	f	m		
Tricolore Moyenne	G		Vibert	lp				
Tricolore Moyenne No 1	G		Vibert	w				
Tricolore Moyenne No 2	G	Pre 1846	Vibert	dr				
Tricolore Moyenne No 3	G	Pre 1846	Vibert	dr				
Tricolore Moyenne No 4	G		Vibert	mr				
Tricolore Moyenne No 5	G	Pre 1846	Robert	m				
Tricolore Superba	G	Pre 1846		m				
Trigintipetala	D	Pre 1689		mp	dbl	m		

Name	Type	Date	Raiser / Synonym					
Triomphant	Ch	Pre 1870		mr	f	vl	vvig	
Triomphante	Bks			w	s-d	s		
Triomphante	C	Pre 1830	syn La Triomphante	lp	vdbl	m		
Triomphante	Cl			mp				
Triomphante	Ch		syn La Superbe	m				
Triomphante	G	1880	Pierre	mp		s	vig	
Triomphante de Gand	Ch			mp	f	l		
Triomphe	C		Godefroy	dr	f	l		
Triomphe d'Abbeville	C			mp	f	vl		
Triomphe d'Alençon	HP	1858	Touvais	dp	dbl	vl	vvig	f
Triomphe d'Alger	T			mp	f	l	vvig	f
Triomphe d'Amiens	HP	1861	Mille-Mallet	rb	dbl	l	vig	vf
		see	Général Jacqueminot					
Triomphe d'Angers	HP	1862	Robert & Moreau	dr	f	m	vvig	vf
Triomphe d'Angers	HCh	Pre 1834	Laffay	dr	f	m		f
Triomphe d'Angers	Cl			mr	f	l	vvig	
Triomphe d'Arcole	N	Pre 1846		yb				
Triomphe d'Avranches	HP	1855	Baudry	mr	f	l	vig	
Triomphe de Bagatelle	HP	Pre 1870		mr	f	l		
Triomphe de Bayeux	HCh	1888		w				
Triomphe de Beauté	G	Pre 1834		dr	f	m		
Triomphe de Beauté	HP	1853	Oger	dp	f	vl		
Triomphe de Bellevue	HP			lp	f	l		
Triomphe de Bolwyller	HSem	Pre 1846	Baumann	w	f	l	vig	m
Triomphe de Bordeaux	B			mr				
Triomphe de Brabant	C	1821	Miellez	mp	f	m-l	m	
		syn	Duchesse d'Angloulê-	me				
Triomphe de Caen	HP	1861	Oger	dr	f	l		
Triomphe de Caen	HP	1875	Cant B R	mr	vf	m	vig	vf
			syn Prince Arthur					
Triomphe de Coster	G	Pre 1860						
Triomphe de Coulommiers	HP	1868	Desmazures	dr	f	l		
			syn Souv de Coulommi	ers				
Triomphe de Dusseldorf	G			lp				
Triomphe de Flore	G	Pre 1821	Prévost	lp	vf	m		
Triomphe de France	HP	1875	Garçon	mp	vdbl	vl		m
Triomphe de Gand	HP			lp	f	l		
Triomphe de Gand	T/Ch	Pre 1834		mr	f	l		
Triomphe de Guérin	HCh	Pre 1834	Guérin	mp	f	l	vig	
Triomphe de Guillot Fils	T	1861	Guillot Fils	pb	dbl	vl	vvig	vf
Triomphe de Guillotière	T	1861	Guillot Fils	w	dbl	m		
Triomphe de Guillotière	S	1863	Guillot Fils	w	f	l	vvig	
Triomphe de Jaussens	G	Pre 1850		dp				
Triomphe de la Duchère	B	1846	Béluze	lp	f	m		
Triomphe de la Guillotière	HMcr	1863	Guillot	lp	f	m		f
Triomphe de la Queue	HCh	Pre 1846		lp	f	l		f
Triomphe de la Terre des Roses	HP	1864	Guillot Père	mp	dbl	l	m	
Triomphe de Laffey	HCh	1830	Laffey	w	vdbl	m		
Triomphe de l'Exposition	HP	1855	Margottin	mr	vdbl	l	vig	f
Triomphe de Lille	D	Pre 1826	Vibert	lp	f	m		
Triomphe de Lille	T	Pre 1846		lp				f
Triomphe de Louvain	G			mr	vf	vl		
Triomphe de Lyon	HP	1859	Cordier	mr	dbl	l	m	
Triomphe de Macheteaux	HMcr	Pre 1846		lp	f	l		
Triomphe de Meaux	HP	1851	Quettier	lp	f	m		
Triomphe de Milan	T	1876	Ducher Vve	w	f	l	vig	
Triomphe de Montmorency	HP	Pre 1846	Duval	mp	f	l	vig	
Triomphe de Montrouge	HP	1858		mr	f	m		
Triomphe de Nancy	HP	1862	Crousse	dr	f	l	vig	
Triomphe de Navarin	T	Pre 1834		lp		m		
Triomphe de Paris	HP	1852	Margottin	dr	vf	vl	vvig	
Triomphe de Parmentier	G		Parmentier	m	f	m-l		
Triomphe de Pernet Père	HT	1890	Pernet Père	mr	vdbl	l	vvig	
Triomphe de Plantier	B	1837	Plantier	pb	vf	l		
Triomphe de Rennes	G	Pre 1846		dr	vf	vl		
Triomphe de Rennes	T	1857	Panaget / Lancezeur	my	f	l	vig	vf
Triomphe de Rouen	P	1826	Lecomte	mp	f	l		
Triomphe de Rouen	HP	Pre 1834		lp		l		
Triomphe de Rouen	HP	1864	Garçon	mr	f	l		
Triomphe de Saintes	HP	1885	Derouet	mr	vf	l		sf
		syn Le	Triomphe de Saintes					
Triomphe de Soissons	HP	1866	Fontaine	mp	f-d	l	vig	
Triomphe de Sterkmanns	G	1847	Vibert	dp	f	l		
Triomphe de Toulouse	HP	1873	Brassac	rb	f	l	vig	
Triomphe de Valenciennes	HP	1847	Schneider	lp	f	l		
Triomphe de Vannes	HP							
Triomphe de Vibert	G	c 1835	Vibert	mr	f	m		
Triomphe de Villecresne	HP	1861	Lédéchaux	mr	f	l		
Triomphe de Zehler	G			rb		m		
Triomphe des Beaux-Arts	HP	1857	Fontaine	m	f	l		
Triomphe des Dames	G	Pre 1830	Hardy	mr	vf	s-m		
Triomphe des Français	S	1834	Lartay	lp	f	l	vig	

Name	Type	Date	Raiser					
Triomphe des Français	HP	1864	Pernet Père	mr	f	l		
Triomphe des Noisettes	N	1887	Pernet Père	dp	f	vl	vvig	
Triomphe des Rosomanes	HP	1872	Gonod	mr	f	l	vig	
Triomphe d'Europe	G	Pre 1830	Prévost	mr	vf	m		
Triomphe d'Orléans	T	Pre 1870		w	f	l		
Triomphe d'Oudin	B	1850	Oudin	mr				
Triomphe du Luxembourg	T	1835	Hardy	pb	f	l	vig	vf
Triomphe du Luxembourg	HMcr	Pre 1870		mr		m		
Triomphe Royal	G	Pre 1830	Lahaye Père	mp	vf	m-l		
Triomphe Turgot	T			mp				
Triompheronde	Misc	Pre 1846		m		l		
Triptolème	HP	1865	Oger	mp	vf	m	vvig	
Triumphant	HSet	Pre 1846	Pierce	mp	vdbl	m		
Trompeter von Säckingen	HMult	1890	Geschwind R	m	f	m		m
Tuguriorum	HArv			mr				
Tulipe Paltot	C	1821	Chaussée, Mme syn Unique Panachée	w	dbl	l	vig	
Tullie	G			mr				
Tullie	HSpn	Pre 1830						
Turban Royal	G			mr	f	m		
Turcica	HFt			y				
Turenne	G	1846	Vibert	dp	f	l		
Turenne	M	1858	Robert & Moreau	m				
Turenne	HP	1861	Verdier V	dr	f	m	vig	
Turenne	Ch		Laffay	m	f	s		
Turenne	Pom							
Turgida	S	Pre 1770	syn Turneps	dp	dbl	m-l		
Turgot	T	1846	Robert	mr	f	l	vvig	
Turkische Rose	HFt			y				
Turneps	S	Pre 1770		lp	dbl	m-l		f
Turneps à Fleur Simple	Misc	1827	Prévost	lp	s	s		f
Turneps Bicolor	Misc	1827	Prévost	lp	dbl	s-m		
Turneps Macrocarpa	Misc	1825	Prévost	mp	dbl	m-l		
Turner's Crimson Rambler	HMult	1893	Turner syn Crimson Rambler	mr	vdbl	s	vvig	
Turnip Rose	S	Pre 1770	syn Turneps	dp	dbl	m-l		
Tuscany	G	Pre 1598		m	s-d	l	vig	m
Tuscany Superb	G	Pre 1837		m	dbl	l		

NAME	TYPE	YEAR	RAISER	COLOUR	BLOOM	SIZE	GROWTH	SCENT
Ulana	HMult	1890	Geschwind	r				
Ulmifolia	C			p				
Ulrich Brunner Fils	HP	1882	Levet A	dp	f	l	vig	vf
Ulster	HP	1899	Dickson A	mp	dbl	l	vig	
Ulyesse	G	Pre 1838	Cramwell	mr				
Una	Cl T	1898	Paul G	ly	s-d	l	vig	f
Undulata	Ch	Pre 1846						
Unguiculata	C	1789	Poilpré	lp	dbl	s	vig	m
			syn Oeillet					
Unguiculata Cariophyllata	G		Dupont	lp				
Unica	C	1778	Grimwood	w				
Unica Alba	C	1775	Grimwood	w	dbl	l		m
			syn White Provence					
Uniflore	G	Pre 1830	Vibert	lp	f	m		
			syn La Victoire					
			and La Glacée					
Uniflore Marbrée	G	Pre 1846	Moreau-Robert	mr		m		
Union	T	1871	Lartay	pb	f	vl		
Unique	C	1775	Grimwood	w	dbl	l	m	m
			see White Provence					
Unique	HSpn	c 1825	Cartier	w	f	m-l		
Unique	Ch	Pre 1834	Laffay	w	f	m		
Unique	M	1852	Robert	mr	f	m		
			syn Unique Nouvelle					
Unique	T	1869	Guillot Fils	w	f	l	m	
Unique	Ch			lp				
Unique	T	1872	Moreau-Robert	r & y		m	vig	
Unique Admirable	C	Pre 1820	Descemet	mr	f	m		
Unique Anglais	C	Pre 1629	syn Rubra	mr	dbl	m		sf
Unique Anglaise	C	Pre 1810	Cels syn Unique Rose	lp	dbl	m-l		m
Unique Blanche	C	1775	Grimwood	w	dbl	m	vig	m
			syn White Provence					
Unique Blanche	M	Pre 1870		w	f	m		
Unique Blanche Panachée	C	1821	Chaussée, Mme	w	dbl	l	vig	
			syn Unique Panachée					
Unique Carnée	C	Pre 1811	Vilmorin	lp	f	l		m
Unique de Bruxelles	G	1826		lp	vdbl	m		
Unique de Hollande	G	Pre 1830	Prévost	dr	vf	m		
Unique de Provence	C	1775	Grimwood	w	dbl	l		m
			syn White Provence					
Unique de Provence	M	1844	Robert	w	dbl	m		
			syn Unique Moss					
Unique Jaune	N	1872	Moreau-Robert	y	f	m	vig	f
Unique Moss	M	1844	Robert	w	dbl	l		
Unique Nouvelle	M			mr				
Unique Panachée	D	Pre 1810	Dupont syn La Félicité	pb	s-d	l		
Unique Panachée	C	1821	Madame Chaussée	w	dbl	m	vig	
Unique Rose	C	Pre 1629	syn Rubra	mr	dbl	m		sf
Unique Rose	C	Pre 1810	Cels	lp	dbl	m-l		m
Unique Rouge	C	Pre 1629	syn Rubra	mr	dbl	m		sf
Unique Rouge	C	Pre 1824		mp	dbl	m		
Unique Violet Tigré	C	1827	Laffay					
Universal Favorite	HWich	1898	Horvath	mp	dbl		vig	m
Uranie	N			mp	f	s	vvig	
Ursule Devaux	HCh			lp	f	l	vig	

NAME	TYPE	YEAR	RAISER	COLOUR	BLOOM	SIZE	GROWTH	SCENT
V Viviand-Morel	T	1887	Bernaix	dr	dbl	l		
V Vivos E Hyjos	T	1894	Bernaix	rb		m	vvig	vf
Vacquerie	HP	1850	Robert	dr	f	l		
Vaillante Bergère	HP	1846	Guillot	lp	f	m	vig	
Vainqueur de Goliath	HP	1862	Moreau F	mr	dbl	vl	vig	vf
Vainqueur de Solférino	HP	1857	Trouillard	dr	vf	l	vig	
			syn Cardinal Patrizzi					
Valdine	M			mp	f	m		
Valeda	B		Bertin Fils	mp	f	m		f
Valence Dubois	G	1880	Fontaine	mp	dbl	m		
Valentine	T	Pre 1846		lp	f	l	vvig	f
Valentine	G	Pre 1830	Vibert	dp	f	s-m		
Valentine Altermann	T	1896	Nabonnand	w	f	m	vig	
Valentine de Marcellus	G	1827	Noisette	m				
Valentine de Nerval	HP	Pre 1870		dp	f	m		
Valentine Gaunet	T	1894	Nabonnand	lp				
Valérie	T			lp				
Valérie	G	Pre 1834		lp	f	m		
Valérie	B			dr	f	m		
Valérie	C	Pre 1830	Prévost	lp	f	vs		
Valette	D	1823	Vibert syn Lavalette	dp	f	m		
Valida	B			mp	f	m	vig	vf
Validatum	G			dr	vf	l		
Validé	M	1857	Robert & Moreau	lp	f	m		
Vallée de Chamonix	T	1872	Ducher	yb	f	m	vig	
Vallière	M	1846	Vibert	lp	f	l		
Valmore Desbordes	G		Robert	lp	dbl	l		
Van Artevelde	G	Pre 1847	Parmentier	dp	vdbl	l		
Van-Dael	G	1820	Vibert	dp	f	l		
Van Dyck	G		Parmentier	mr	f	l		
Van Houtte	HP	1863	Granger	dp	f			
		syn	Louis Van Houtte					
Van Huysem	D	Pre 1841	Parmentier	dr	dbl	l		
Van Huysum	D	Pre 1817	syn Celsiana	lp	s-d	l	vig	m
Van Huysum	HP	1870	Lacharme	rb	f	vl	vvig	
Van Mons	HP			mp	f	vl	vvig	
Van Siebold	M	1855	Robert	lp	f	m		
Van Spaendonck	C	1821	Cartier	dp	f	m-l		
Vandael	M	1850	Laffay M	m	dbl	m	vig	
Vandael	T	Pre 1846		mr	f	l		f
Vandaels	HCh	Pre 1846		dr				
Vander Mersch-Mertens	T	1881	Nabonnand	w	f	l	m	
Vanhuisson	D	Pre 1841	Parmentier	dr	dbl	l		
			syn Van Huysem					
Vanilla	Ch	Pre 1846						
Vanneau	G	1830	Vibert	mr	f	l		
Vanneau	HP	1849	Vibert	lp	f	l		
Varacel	M	Pre 1846		mr	f	s		
Varrata	P	Pre 1830	Vibert syn Warrata	mr	vf	m-l		f
Variabilis	T			w				
Variegata	Alp			lp				
Variegata	M	c 1818	Shailer syn Panachée	(M) w	s-d	m		
Variegata	C	c 1845		pb	vdbl		vig	
Variegata Tea Rose	T			y				
Variété de Carmin Brillanté	G			mr				
Variegated Beauty	Misc	Pre 1846						
Variegated Crimson	Misc	Pre 1846		mr				
Variegated Damask	D	c 1820	Godefroy syn Panachée	(D) pb	dbl	m		
Variegated Leaved	Ayr	Pre 1846		lp	s			
Varin	C	1822	Calvert syn Sarah	mp				
Varin	C	1826	Prévost	lp	dbl	l		
			syn Belle de Cels etc					
Vase d'Election	HP	1864	Ducher	lp	f	m	vig	
Vauban	G		Miellez	lp	vdbl	m		
Vaucanson	HP	1871	Schwartz	mp	f	l	m	
Vaucresson	A	Pre 1885		lp	f	m		
Vauquelin	M	1847	Vibert	dr	dbl	m		
Veillard	M	Pre 1846		mp	vdbl			
Veiné Marbré	C	Pre 1830		lp	dbl	m-l		
Véléda	B	Pre 1834		mp		l		
Velours d'Enghein	G			m	vdbl	s		
Velours Épiscopal	HCh	Pre 1846		m	f	l	m	m
Velours Noir	G		Dupont	mr	dbl	l		
Velours Pourpre	G	Pre 1811		dr	vdbl	m		
Velours Pourpre	M	Pre 1846		mr	vdbl			
Velours Pourpre	HP	1866	Verdier E	m	f	l	vvig	
Velours Pourpre Nouveau	G	1828	Prévost	dr				
Velours Violet	HCh	1825	Vibert	m	s-d	m		
Velouté d'Orléans	HP	1852	Dauvesse	m	f	l		

Name	Type	Year	Breeder / syn	Col	Form	Season	Extra1	Extra2
Velutina	G	1810	Van Eeden	m				
Velvet Rose	G	Pre 1629	syn Holoserica	dr	dbl			
Ventoris	G	Pre 1830		dr				
Venus	B	1817		r				
Venus	G	1845	Vibert	w	f	m-l		
Venus	A	Pre 1846		w	f	m		
Venus	HSpn	Pre 1846		dp				
Venus	HP	1895	Kiese	dr	f	l		
Venus d'Italie	D			lp				
Venus Mère	G	Pre 1811	Noisette	mp	dbl	m-l		
		syn	Bouquet Charmant					
Venusta	A			w	s-d	m		
Venusta	P	Pre 1814	Descemet	lp	f	m		
Venusta	T	Pre 1834		w		m		
Venusta Pendula	Ayr			w	s-d		vig	
Venustus	G	Pre 1830	Calvert	dr	f	m		
Venustus Vigo	G	1846						
Verdier	Ch		Laffay	dr				
Vergrandus	Misc	Pre 1846						
Verhaux	D	Pre 1848	syn Rose Verreux	dp	f	m		
Vermont	T	c 1840	Béluze	mp	f	m		
Vernon	G			dr	f	m		
Versicolor	G	Pre 1659	syn Rosa Mundi	mp	dbl			
Versicolor	D	Pre 1629	syn York & Lancaster	lp	dbl			
Verte	HCh	1856	Bambridge & Harrison	g	s-d	m		
			syn Viridiflora					
Verte Blanche	G		Hardy	lp	dbl	l		
Vesta	G	1816	Prévost (?)	dr	s-d	l		
			syn Temple d'Apollon					
Vesta	G	Pre 1829	Coquerel	mr	dbl	l		
			syn Feu de Vesta					
Vestale	A		Vibert	w	dbl	m		
Vésuve	Ch	1825	Laffay M	pb	vdbl	l		
			syn Le Vésuve					
Vesuveus	Ch	1825	syn Le Vésuve	pb	vdbl	l		
Vesuvius	M	Pre 1846		mp				
Véturie	G	Pre 1830	Vibert	mp	f	l		
Véturine	D	1842	Vibert syn Véturie	mp	f	m		
Vibert	HCh	Pre 1830	Vibert	dr	f	m		
Vibert	Cl			w	vf	m		
Vick's Caprice	HP	1891	Vick	pb	dbl	l	m	m
Vicomte de Douglas	HP	1870	Gonod	mr	f	m		
Vicomte de Lauzières	HP	1889	Liabaud	m	f	vl		
Vicomte de Schrymacker	A	1898		mr		l		
Vicomte de Spoelberg	G			mr	vdbl	m		
Vicomte de Vezins	HP	1868	Gautreau	mp	f	l	vig	
Vicomte Fritz de Cussy	B	1845	Margottin	m	f	l	m	
Vicomte Imbert de Corneillan	T	Pre 1870	Pradel	w	f	l		
Vicomte Maison	HP	1868	Fontaine	mr	f	l	vvig	
Vicomte Vigier	HP	1861	Verdier V	dr	f	l	vig	
Vicomtesse d'Avesnes	N	1847	Roeser	mp	f	m	vig	
Vicomtesse de Belleval	HP	Pre 1870		mp	f	m		
Vicomtesse de Bernis	T	1884	Nabonnand G	op	dbl	l	vig	vf
Vicomtesse de Chaffaud	T	1891	Reboul	pb				
Vicomtesse de Grassin	T	1899	Levrard	pb				
Vicomtesse de Montesquieu	B/HP	1861	Quétier	op	vdbl	m		
Vicomtesse de Stratham Man	HSpn			p				
Vicomtesse de Terrail	B	1883	Vigneron	lp	f	l	vig	
Vicomtesse de Terves	HP	1886	Moreau-Robert	mp				
Vicomtesse de Vezins	HP	1867	Gautreau	mp	vdbl	l	vig	
Vicomtesse de Wauthier	T	1886	Bernaix	rb	f	l		
Vicomtesse d'Hautpoul	T	1881	Brassac	w	vf	l	vvig	
Vicomtesse Decazes	T	1844	Pradel	dy	f	l	m	f
Vicomtesse Douglas	HP	1863	Gonod	mp	f	l		
Vicomtesse Dulong de Rosnay	T	1886	Nabonnand	mp				
Vicomtesse Héricart de Thury	T			w				
Vicomtesse Laure de Gironde	HP	1851	Pradel	mp	f	m		
Vicomtesse Marie de Bourges	HP	1853	Cherpin	mp	f	l		
		syn	Comtesse Marie de Bourges					
Vicomtesse R de Sevigny	T	1899	Guillot	pb	f	l	vig	m
Victoire Argentée	B	Pre 1846		lp				
Victoire Bizarre	G	Pre 1846		mr				
Victoire Daumy	Ch	Pre 1846		dr				
Victoire Daumy	N	Pre 1846		dr				
Victoire d'Angers	Ch			dp	f	m		
Victoire d'Austerlitz	HP	1847	Pélisson	mp	f	m		
		syn	Comice de Marseille					
Victoire de Bragance	G	Pre 1830	Prévost	mr	f	m		
			syn Dorothée					
Victoire de Magenta	B	1864	Moreau-Robert	mr	f	l		
Victoire de Waterloo	G			mp	f	m		
Victoire Fontaine	B	1882	Fontaine	m	vf	m-l	vig	

Name	Class	Date	Raiser / synonym					
Victoire Helye	HP	1878	Verdier E	lp	f	l		m
Victoire Modeste	HBc	Pre 1835	Guérin	pb	f	l		
Victor de Tracy	HCh	Pre 1834	Laffay	dr	f	l		
Victor-Emmanuel	B	1859	Guillot Père	dr	dbl	l	m	vf
Victor Hugo	HCh	c 1840		m	f	vl		
Victor Hugo	HP	1884	Schwartz J	dr	dbl	l	vig	m
Victor le Bihan	HP	1868	Guillot Père	mp	f	vl		m
Victor Lemoine	HP	1888	Lévêque	dr	dbl	l		
Victor Olry	N		Pirolle	w	vf			
Victor Parmentier	G	Pre 1847	Parmentier	mp	dbl	m		m
Victor Pulliat	T	1870	Ducher	ly	f	m	m	
Victor Robin	HP	1853	Ohl	dp	f	l		
Victor Trouillard	HP	1855	Trouillard	dr	f	l		
Victor Trouillard Père	HP	1868	Trouillard	m	f	vl	vig	
Victor Varengot	B	Pre 1846		mp	vdbl			
Victor Verdier	B	1852	Frinck Dorisy	mr	f	m	vvig	
Victor Verdier	HP	1859	Lacharme F	dp	vf	l	vig	m
Victor Verdier, Climbing	Cl HP	1871	Paul G	mp	f	l	vvig	
Victor Verne	HP	1871	Damaizin	mr	f	l	vig	
Victoria	A	Pre 1826	Descemet	w	f			m
			syn Antoinette					
Victoria	HFt	Pre 1846	Guérin	yb	s-d	l		
Victoria	N	Pre 1846						
Victoria Kronprincessin von Deutschld	T	1874	Ducher, Vve	op	dbl	l		m
			syn Jean Ducher					
Victorien Sardou	HP	1869	Gayneux	mr	f	m		
Victorieuse	T	Pre 1860		w	f	l		f
Victorine Helfenbein	HP	1850	Guillot Père	mp	f	m		
Victorine la Couronnée	G	Pre 1811		pb	f	m		sf
Vidua	G	Pre 1846		mr				
Vierge	A	Pre 1754	syn Alba Semi-Plena	w	s-d			vf
Vierge	C	Pre 1806	syn Rose des Peintres	mp	f	vl		
Vierge	HSpn	1820	Prévost	w	vdbl	l	vvig	vf
Vierge de Cléry	HSpn	1820	Prévost syn Vierge	w	vdbl	l	vvig	vf
Vierge de Cléry	C	1888	Baron-Veillard	w	f	m	vig	
Vierge de Lemnos	B	1849	Morel	lp	f	l		
Vierge de Samos	T			lp	f	l		
Vihorlat	HMcr	1894	Kaufmann	mr				
Villa des Tybilles	HRg	1899	Gravereaux	mr	s	l		
Village Maid	G	Pre 1829	syn La Rubanée	pb	f	l		m
Villageoise Parée	G							
Villaret de Joyeuse	HP	1874	Damaizin	mp	f	vl	vig	m
Ville de Bruxelles	D	1836	Vibert	mp	vdbl	m		vf
		syn	La Ville de Bruxelles					
Ville de Clamart	HP	1879	Fontaine	mp	f	l	vig	
Ville de Laon	HP	1869	Fontaine	lp	f	l	vig	
Ville de Londres	G	1850	Robert	dp	f	vl		f
Ville de Lyon	HP	1866	Ducher	mp	f	vl	vig	
Ville de Saint Denis	HP	1853	Thomas	mp	f	l	m	
Ville de Toulouse	G	1876	Brassac	pb	f	m		sf
Villoresi	Ch		Vibert	dr	f	m		
			syn Belle Villoresi					
Villosa	Sp	Pre 1815		mp	dbl	m		sf
Villosa Duplex No 1	Sp	Pre 1830	Vibert	mp	dbl	m		sf
		syn	Wolley-Dod's Rose					
Villosa Fulgens	Sp	Pre 1830	Vibert	mp	dbl	m		
Vilmorin	M	1805	Vilmorin	lp	f	m	vig	
Vilmorin	C	Pre 1811	Vilmorin	lp	f	l		m
			syn Unique Carnée					
Vilmorin Purpurea	C							
Vimercati	G/Ch	Pre 1830		dr		s		
Vincent-Hippolyte Duval	HP	1879	Duval H	mp	f	l	vvig	
Vinck Noir	G			dr	f	m		
Vineta	B	1895	Geschwind	lp	dbl	m		
Vineuse	A			w				
Vineux	HCh		Cugnot	m	s-d	m		
Vingt-Neuf Juillet	HCh	Pre 1836		dr	f	l		
		syn	Le Vingt-Neuf Juillet and Coccinea Superba					
Vingt-Sept Mai	G			dr				
Violacea	G	Pre 1801	syn La Belle Sultane	dr	s-d	m	vig	
Violacée	A		Vibert	w				
Violacée	N			mp				
Violacée	M	1876	Soupert & Notting	m	dbl	l		
Violacitus	Misc	Pre 1846		dr				
Violet	D		(Trianon)	dr				
Violet	Ch	Pre 1830	syn L'Héritier	m	s-d	m		
Violet	P							
Violet	T		Buffon	mp	s-d	m		
Violet à Coeur Rouge	G	Pre 1846		mr				
Violet à Grandes Fleurs	G			m	vf			

Name	Class	Date	Raiser / Synonym						
Violet Agréable	Pom			dr					
Violet Bengal	Bslt	c 1810	Vilmorin syn Reversa	m	s-d	m			
Violet Bengal	Ch	1827	Vibert syn Purple Bengal	dr					
Violet Billard	HCh			m	f	m			
Violet Brillant	G	1817	Godefroy syn Rouge Formidable etc	dr	vdbl	m			
Violet Bronzé	G			dr					
Violet Cramoisi	HBc		syn Cramoisi	mr	s-d	m			
Violet Crème	G			m	f	l			
Violet de Belgiqie	HCh	Pre 1834		m	f				
Violet de Canterbury	G			m	f	m			
Violet de Crémer	G	1824	(Douai)	m					
Violet de Douai	G			dr	f	m			
Violet Incomparable	G			m	f	m			
Violet Magnifique	G								
Violet Marbled	G	Pre 1846		mr					
Violet Merveilleux	G		Miellez	m					
Violet Ombré	G								
Violet Queen	HP	1892	Paul G	m	dbl	m			
Violet sans Aiguillons	HCh	Pre 1834	syn Thornless Violet	dr	f	m		wk	
Violet Virginie	G	1825	Vibert						
Violette Agréable	G	Pre 1815	Descemet	m					
Violette Bouyer	HP	1881	Lacharme	w	dbl	l			f
Violette Bronzée	G	Pre 1790	syn Charles de Mills	dr	vdbl	m			sf
Violette Cramoisi	HBc								
Violette de Crémer	G	1824		m	vf	l			
Violette de Jacques	HCh	Pre 1830	Prévost syn Conquête de Jacques	m	f	m			
Violette de Verguy	Ch		Gossart syn Extra de Gossart	m					
Violette Double	HSpn		Prévost	m					
Violette et Rouge	G	Pre 1834		m					
Violette Ponctuée	G	Pre 1830	Vibert	m	dbl	m			
Violette Rouge	G			rb					
Violette sans Aiguillons	HCh	Pre 1830	Vibert syn Violette de Jacques	m	f	m			
Violette sans Pareille	G	1822	Vibert	dp		m			
Violiniste Emile Lévêque	HT	1897	Pernet-Ducher	lp	dbl	l			
Virago	HSet	1887	Geschwind R	lp	s-d	m		vvig	
Virago	B			dp					
Virgile	B	Pre 1846		mp	f	l			
Virgile	HP	1849	Robert						
Virgile	HP	1870	Guillot Père	mp	vdbl	vl	m		
Virgin Blush	Misc	Pre 1846							
Virginal	G	Pre 1787	syn Admirable	mr					
Virginal	M	1817	Slater syn White Bath	w	f	l			
Virginal	C	Pre 1830		lp	dbl	m			
Virginal	HP	1898		lp	dbl	l	m		
Virginale	C			w					
Virginale	D	Pre 1811	Descemet syn Beauté Virginale	w	f	m			
Virginale	HP	1858	Lacharme syn Mme Liabaud	w	dbl	m	m		
Virginale	Ch	Pre 1846		w		m			
Virginale	T	1888	syn Mme Lacharme	lp	f	m			
Virginia	T	1894	Dingee & Conard	dy					
Virginia R Coxe	HCh	1894	Geschwind R syn Gruss an Teplitz	mr	f	m		vig	vf
Virginia Rose	Sp	Pre 1724	(Miller) syn r.virginiana	mp	s				
Virginian Lass	HSet	c 1846	Pierce	w	f	m			
Virginian Rambler	Ayr	Pre 1855		lp	dbl	s		vvig	
Virginie	G	1825	Vibert	mp	f	l			
Virginie	Ch	Pre 1846		pb	vf	l			
Virgine Baltet	HP	1854	Baltet	dp					
Virgine Bréon	B	1847	Belet syn Mme Eugénie Bréon	my					
Virginie Lebon	Ch			w	f	l			
Viridiflora	Ch	Pre 1743	Harrison (1856) syn À Fleurs Vertes	g	dbl	m		vvig	
Viridis	A	Pre 1846		w					
Viscountess Falmouth	HT	1879	Bennett	pb	dbl	vl			m
Viscountess Folkestone	HT	1886	Bennett	pb	dbl	l		vig	vf
Visqueuse	G	Pre 1811	Vibert syn Bourbon	pb	dbl	m			m
Vitellina	N	Pre 1846		lp	f	m			f
Vitex Spinosa	G	1817	Godefroy syn Rouge de Belgique	mp	dbl	l			
Vitruvius	G			lp	f	m-l			
Vive l'Empereur	HP			mr	f	m			
Viviand-Morel	T	1887	Bernaix	mp					
Vivid	B	1853	Paul A	rb	f	s-m		vig	m

Vix Bifera	A	Pre 1846		mp				
Volcy	HP			mp				
Volème	G		Girardon	mr				
Volidatum	G	Pre 1830	Vibert	mr	vf	m		
		syn	Gloire des Pourpres					
Volney	HCh		Laffay	lp	f	m		
Volney	M	1849	Vibert	lp	f	m		
Volta	HP	1852	Laffay	mp	f	vl		
Volumineuse	G	Pre 1828		mp	f	l		
Volumnie	N		Laffay	w	f	m		
Volupté	G	Pre 1828	Bizard syn La Volupté	dp	f	l		
Vorace	B	1849	Lacharme	mr	f	m	m	
Vulcain	G	Pre 1830						
Vulcain	HP	1861	Verdier V	dr	dbl	l	m	f
Vulcanie	B	1840	Bizard	mp	f	m		
Vulgaria	A			m				

NAME	TYPE	YEAR	RAISER	COLOUR	BLOOM	SIZE	GROWTH	SCENT
W Wilson Saunders	HP	1874	Paul G	mr	f	m	vig	
Waban	T	1891	Wood	dp				
Waitziana	HMac	c 1823		dp	s			f
Walter Scott	T	Pre 1846	syn Sir Walter Scott	mp	f	l		f
Waltham Climber No 1	Cl HT	1885	Paul W	mr	dbl	l	vig	vf
Waltham Climber No 2	Cl HT	1885	Paul W	or	dbl	l	vig	vf
Waltham Climber No 3	Cl HT	1885	Paul W	mr	dbl	l	vig	vf
Waltham Standard	HP	1897	Paul W	dr		m	vig	vf
Wang-Jang Ye	Misc	1845		yb	dbl	m		m
		syn	Fortune's Double Yell	ow				
Wargny	G			mp	f	m		
Wariricus	G	c 1829	Calvert	dp	f	l		
Warrata	P	Pre 1830	Noisette L	m	vf	m-l		f
Warratah	D	Pre 1846		m				
Washington	G	Pre 1834		mr	vf	m		
Wassili Chludoff	N	1896	Nabonnand	pb	f	l	vig	f
Wassilissa	HSet	1886	Geschwind	br				
Watson's Blush	Misc	Pre 1846		lp				
Watsoniana	Sp	c 1870	(Crépin)	lp	s	vs		
			syn r.watsoniana					
Watsoniana	HRg	1893	Schmitt	w				
Watts' Celestial	Ch	Pre 1846		mp		l		
Waverley	G			dr	f	m		
Waverley	Pom							
Wazemme(s)	G			lp	f	m		
Weisse Seerose	HT	1887	Drœgemüller	w	dbl	m		
			syn Nymphaea Alba					
Weisser Herumstreicher	HMult	1899	Kiese	w	dbl	l	vig	
Weisser Maréchal Niel	N	1896	Deegan	w	f	l		m
Wellington	C	1832	Calvert	m	f	m		
Wellington	G	Pre 1834	Vibert	dp	f	m		
			syn Lord Wellington					
Wells' White Climber	HMult	c 1835	Wells	w	s-d	s		m
			syn Mme d'Arblay					
Wells' Garland	HMult	1835	Wells syn The Garland	w	s-d		m	m
Wez	G			lp	f	m		
White	HSpn	Pre 1846		w	dbl			
White	HCh	1888	syn Alba	w	dbl	m	m	
White	D			w	f	l		
White American	HEg	Pre 1846		w				
White Banksia	Sp	1807	(Aiton)	w	dbl	s		vf
			syn r.banksia banksia					
White Baroness	HP	1882	Paul G	w	f	l		
White Bath	M	1810	Salter	w	f	l	vig	f
White Bon Silène	T	1884	Morat	ly	f	m		
			syn Bon Silène Blanc					
White Bougère	T	1898	Dunlop	w				
White Boursault	Bslt	Pre 1824	syn Blush Boursault	pb	vdbl	vl		
White Burgundy	Pom	Pre 1848		w	vdbl	vs		
White Cabbage	C	Pre1860		w				
White Camelia	Ch			w	f	l		
White Catherine Mermet	T	1885	May	w				
			syn The Bride					
White Cochet	T	1896	Cook J W	w	dbl	l		
		syn	White Maman Cochet					
White Daily Rose	Ch	1802	syn Indica Alba	lp				
White De Meaux	C	Pre 1824		w				
		syn	Rose de Meaux White					
White Dog Rose	Sp	1762	(Hudson)	w		s		sf
			syn r.arvensis					
White Duchesse de Brabant	T	1880	Schwartz J	w	dbl	m	vig	
		syn	Mme Joseph Schwartz					
White European	HEg	Pre 1846		w				
White Four Seasons Rose	D	Pre 1785		w				
White French	M	Pre 1846		w				
White Hermosa	T	1886	Lambert E	w	dbl			
			syn Marie Lambert					
White La France	HT	1889	Guinoiseau Fils	lp	f	l		
		syn	Augustine Guinoiseau					
White Lady	HT	1888	Paul W	w	vdbl			
White Maman Cochet	T	1896	Cook J W	w	dbl	l	vig	f
White Maman Cochet	B	1898	Cooling	w				
White Maréchal Niel	T	Pre 1899	Deegen's	w	dbl	l	vvig	vf
		syn	Weisse Maréchal Niel					
White Moss	M	1843	Vibert	w	dbl	l		
		syn	Comtesse de Murinais					
White Moss Rose	M	1788	Shailer	w	dbl	l		
		syn	Shailer's White Moss					
White Pearl (Perle)	T	1890	Ritter/Nanz & Neuner	w			vig	

NAME	TYPE	YEAR	RAISER	COLOUR	BLOOM	SIZE	GROWTH	SCENT
White Pet	Pol	1879	Henderson P	w	dbl	s		sf
White Pet, Climbing	Cl Pol	1894	Corboeuf	w				
White Provence	C	1775	Grimwood	w	dbl	l	m	f
White Rambler	HMult	1895	Schmitt syn Thalia	w	dbl	s		m
White Rose de Meaux	C	c 1824		w				
		syn	Rose de Meaux White					
White Rose of York	A	Pre 1597		w	dbl	m		f
White Rose of York	A	Pre 1818	Miellez	w	dbl	l		
			syn Duc d'York					
Whitsuntide Rose	Sp	1596	(Hermann)	m	dbl			m
			syn r.majalis					
Wiener Rose	S	1633	syn Jaune Bicolor	yb	s	m	vig	
Wilberforce	C	1840		dr	dbl	l		
Wild Banks Rose	Sp	c 1877	(Regel)	w	s	s		
		syn	r.banksias normalis					
Wilhelm Koelle	HP	1878	Pernet	mr	vdbl	l	vig	
Wilhelm Liffa	HT	1889	Geschwind	mr				
Wilhelm Pfitzer	HP	1861	Verdier E	mr	f	l	vig	
		syn	Marechal Vaillant					
William Allen Richardson	N	1878	Ducher Vve	yb	dbl	m	vvig	f
William Bull	HP	1861	Verdier E	mr	f	l	vig	
William Francis Bennett	HT	1886	Bennett	mr	dbl	l		m
William Griffiths	HP	1850	Portemer	pb	vf	m	vig	
William Grow	M	1858	Laffay M	dr	dbl	m		
William Herbert	HP			mp	f	l	vvig	
William Hooker	M	1855	Robert	rb				
William IV	HSpn	Pre 1838		w		s-m		
William Jesse	HCh/B	1838	Laffay M	mr	dbl	l	vig	vf
William Lobb	M	1855	Laffay M	m	dbl	m	vig	m
William Paul	HP	1862	Guillot Père	mr	f	l	m	
William Rollison	HP	1865	Verdier E	mr	f	l	m	
William Tell	G	Pre 1846		mp	f	l		
William Wallace	T	Pre 1846		p	dbl	l	vig	
William Warden	HP	1878	Mitchell	op	f	vl	vig	sf
William Wood	HP			mr				
William's Double Yellow	HFt	Pre 1819	Williams, John	my	dbl	m	m	vf
William's Evergreen	HSem	1850	Williams	w			vig	
William's Sweetbriar	HEg	c 1800	Williams	lp	dbl			
Wingthorn Rose	Sp	1890	(Franchet)	w			vig	m
		syn	r.sericea pteracantha					
Winnie Davis	T	1892	Little	mp	s-d			m
Winter Gem	T	1898	Childs	lp	dbl	l		
Wodan	HMult	1890	Geschwind R	mr	s-d	l		sf
Wolley-Dod's Rose	Misc	Pre 1770	syn Duplex	mp	s-d	m		sf
Wood's Garland	HMult	1835	Wood or Wells	w	s-d		m	m
			syn The Garland					
Woods Rose	Sp	1820	(Lindley) syn r.woodsii	mp	s			
Woolfield	HP	1868	Guillot	mp	f	l		
		syn	Monsieur Woolfield					
Worthington	Sp	1840		lp	s-d			
Wu Se' Quaing Wei	Ch	Pre 1620		r, p, w				

NAME	TYPE	YEAR	RAISER	COLOUR	BLOOM	SIZE	GROWTH	SCENT
Xavier Olibo	HP	1865	Lacharme F	dr	f	l	m	vf
Xénophon	G	1846	Vibert	dr	f	m		
Xiang Fen Lian	T	1855	Marest	w	dbl	vl	m	m
		syn	Souvenir d'Elise Vard-	on				

NAME	TYPE	YEAR	RAISER	COLOUR	BLOOM	SIZE	GROWTH	SCENT
Ye Primrose Dame	T	1886	Bennett	yb	f	l		
Yèbles	C			p				
Yèbles	T			lp				
Yellow	T	1824	Parks	my	dbl	vl		f
		syn	Parks' Yellow Tea-Scented	China				
Yellow (a k a Banksian Yellow)	Sp	c 1824	(Rehder)	ly	dbl	s	vig	
			syn r.banksiae lutea					
Yellow	Misc	1845		yb	dbl	s		m
		syn	Fortune's Double Yell	ow				
Yellow	HSpn	Pre 1846		y	dbl			
Yellow	HSpn	Pre 1846		my	s			
Yellow	N	1876	Woodthorpe	ob	vf			
Yellow Banksia	Bks	Pre 1846		my				
Yellow Bordé Rose	T			y	f	m		
Yellow Cécile Brunner	Pol	1875	Rambeaux	yb	vdbl			vf
			syn Perle d'Or					
Yellow Lady Banks' Rose	Sp	c1824	(Rehder)	ly	dbl	s	vig	

NAME	TYPE	YEAR	RAISER	COLOUR	BLOOM	SIZE	GROWTH	SCENT
			syn r.banksiae lutea					
Yellow Maman Cochet	T	1897	Buatois	dy	dbl		vig	
		syn	Mme Derepas-Matrat					
Yellow Mermet	T	1898	Dickson A	yb	f	vl		
			syn Muriel Grahame					
Yellow Noisette	T	1834	Smith	dy	f	l	vig	f
		syn	Smith's Yellow China					
Yellow Pompon	Misc	Pre 1806	syn Pompon Jaune	my	vdbl	s		
Yellow Provence	Sp	Pre 1503	(Hermann)	my	s	s		
			syn r.hemispherica					
Yellow Rambler	HMult	1896	Schmitt syn Aglaia	ly	dbl	s	vig	m
Yellow Sweetbrier	Sp	Pre 1542	(Hermann)	my	s	m		m
			syn r.foetida					
Yolande d'Aragon	HP	1843	Vibert	mp	vdbl	vl	vig	vf
Yolande Fontaine	B	1840		m	f	m		
York and Lancaster	D	1551	Monardes	pb	dbl	m	vig	vf
York and Lancaster	C		Miellez	w	s-d	m		
York Élégant	G			lp	f	m		
York Minor	A	Pre 1830		w				
York Rouge	A	Pre 1830	Miellez	dp	f	m		
Yorkshire Provence	C	Pre 1821		mp				
Ypsilanti	G	1821	Vibert	mp	f	l	vig	
Yueh Yueh Hong	Ch	1790		mr	dbl		m	
		syn	Slater's Crimson China					

NAME	TYPE	YEAR	RAISER	COLOUR	BLOOM	SIZE	GROWTH	SCENT
Zabeth	HEg	Pre 1813	Vibert / Dupont	mp	dbl	m		m
Zacharula Rubrifolia	HCan	1895	Geschwind	lp	s-d	m		
Zaïre	G	1817	Vibert	dp	dbl	l		
Zaire	M	1849	Vibert	dp	vdbl	m		
Zébré	D		Godefroy	lp				
Zebrina	T	Pre 1846		w				
Zélia	Ch		Laffay	dp	dbl	m		
Zélia Pradel	N/T	1860	Pradel	w	f	l		m
Zélie	Ch	1827	Tireau	mp	f	l	vvig	
Zélinde	HCh			lp	f	l		
Zeller	HCh							
Zelpha	HP			lp	f	m	vig	
Zénaire	G	Pre 1828	Dubourg	m				
Zenobia	M	1892	Paul W	mp	f	l	vig	m
Zenobie	A	Pre 1844	Vibert	lp	f	m		
Zenobie	Ch		Laffay	lp	dbl	l		
Zéphir	HCh		Pirolle	pb	s-d/dbl		vig	
Zéphirine	HCh			mr	f	l		
Zéphirine Drouhin	Cl B	1868	Bizot	mp	dbl	l	vig	m
Zephora	Ch	Pre 1846		mr				
Zephyr	Ch	Pre 1846		ob				
Zephyr	T	1895	Paul W	yb	f	l	vig	
Zérah	C			lp	f	m		
Zerbine	HSpn	1822	Vibert	lp	dbl	l		
Zerbine	M	1847	Vibert	mr	f	m		
Zietrude	N	Pre 1846		mr	f	m	vig	
Zigeunerblut	Bslt	1890	Geschwind	dr	f	l		m
Zilia Pradel	T	1861	Pradel	w	f	l		m
			syn Zélia Pradel					
Zirko	Ch			mp	vf	m		
Zobeïde	N	Pre 1846		mp	f	m		
Zobeïde	M	1851	Robert	lp	f	l		
Zoé	Ch		Laffay	dp		l		f
Zoé	G	Pre 1826	Miellez	mp	vdbl	l		m
Zoé	M	1829	Barbet	mp	vdbl	m	vig	m
Zoé	M	1861	Pradel	mp				m
Zoé Barbet	M	Pre 1829	syn Zoé	mp	vdbl	m	vig	m
Zoé Meyrel	B		Pradel	lp				
Zostérie	Ch	1827		mp	dbl	m		
Zuccariniana	HRg	1879		m	dbl	l		
		syn	Kaiserin des Nordens					
Zuléma	G	1828	Vibert	mp				
Zuleima	B	1820	Vibert	mp	f	m	vig	
Zulmé	HCh	Pre 1830	Vibert syn Descemet	mr	vdbl	s-m		
Zulmalacarreguy	G			mp				

www.ingramcontent.com/pod-product-compliance
Lightning Source LLC
Chambersburg PA
CBHW081227250726
48654CB00012B/1240